# Learning DCOM

# Learning DCOM

Thuan L. Thai

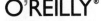

O'REILLY®

*Beijing · Cambridge · Köln · Paris · Sebastopol · Taipei · Tokyo*

*Learning DCOM*
by Thuan L. Thai

Copyright © 1999 O'Reilly & Associates, Inc. All rights reserved.
Printed in the United States of America.

Published by O'Reilly & Associates, Inc., 101 Morris Street, Sebastopol, CA 95472.

**Editor:** Andy Oram

**Production Editor:** Jeffrey Liggett

**Editorial and Production Services:** Electro-Publishing

**Printing History:**

April 1999:          First Edition.

ISBN: 1-56592-581-5

*To my grandfather,*

*whose benevolence sprinkles*

*comfort among his descendents,*

*and*

*to my parents,*

*without whom*

*I wouldn't be where I am today.*

# Table of Contents

# *Preface*

If you have written complex client/server communications protocols before, you would be thankful for a facility that allows you to call functions (procedures) remotely. If you had such a facility, you might wish that there would be an object-oriented means for objects in cyberspace to collaborate with one another. And if object-oriented remote procedure call is what you desire, you are reading the right book.

This book is a combination of my exposure to Distributed COM through research, teaching, and systems architecture, design, and development. It is about building distributed software using Distributed COM. Distributed COM is not solely about distributed computing though. It is also about building better software—software modules that can peacefully coexist and collaborate with one another regardless of who has developed them. But since distributed computing is the focus of this book, I will escort you through the distributed aspects of COM without neglecting the required fundamentals that you need to be a competent COM programmer.

## Scope of This Book

I've designed this book so that each chapter assumes knowledge from the previous one. This allows you to read the book from beginning to end, limiting the need for jumping here and there among chapters. To give you a heads up, here are brief summaries for the chapters and appendices covered in this book.

Chapter 1, *Distributed Computing*, takes a brief look at the progress of distributed computing. While it describes several popular distributed computing technologies, its real purpose is to point out that the communications layer becomes more advanced as time progresses. It is this advancement that gives birth to technologies such as RPC and Distributed COM.

Chapter 2, *Distributed COM Overview*, provides a high-level introduction to COM and the motivation of this ubiquitous technology. This chapter also provides a general examination of the important facilities and services that a typical distributed object technology should support. It uses the COM terminology that prepares you to take on the rest of the chapters in this book.

Chapter 3, *Objects*, gets down to the nuts and bolts of COM. This chapter teaches you the fundamental elements and requirements for building a distributed object using pure C++. Since COM enforces the separation of interface from implementation, I first take you on a tour of interface definition and then show you how to implement the specified interfaces. Along the way, you'll learn the Microsoft Interface Definition Language (MIDL), MIDL data types, error handling, the binary layout of a COM interface, and factories. By the time you finish reading this chapter, you will learn the fundamentals of writing a COM object using C++.

Chapter 4, *Components*, is a follow-up to Chapter 3. The COM objects developed using the techniques described in Chapter 3 cannot execute alone—they require a hosting binary module, such as a DLL or an EXE. In this book, we call these binary modules components. This chapter shows you how to wrap a number of COM classes (whose instances are called COM objects) into a server component. You'll also learn how to develop a client component that uses the services exposed by a server component.

Chapter 5, *Infrastructure*, expands your understanding of COM. The knowledge gained in Chapters 3 and 4 are enough to build and use distributed components, but they're not enough to build real distributed systems that take memory, threading, and security management into account. This chapter continues Chapter 4 by filling the memory, threading, and security management gaps. You'll learn what the COM infrastructure does and why it does what it does. By the time you finish this chapter, you will know the fundaments necessary to build distributed systems using COM.

Chapter 6, *Building Components with ATL*, examines the Active Template Library (ATL), which makes developing components much easier. After reading Chapters 3 through 5, you will realize that most of the code developed in Chapters 3 and 4 is boilerplate code. In fact, you can write template classes and macros to hide the boilerplate code, so that it will take less code to write a component. This is exactly what ATL does. It is a set of C++ template classes and macros that hides the boilerplate code. By using these classes and macros, you reduce the amount of code that you must write to build a distributed component.

Chapter 7, *Using COM Objects*, presents several ways to use a distributed COM object. In this chapter, you will learn four different techniques for using a COM object developed by someone else. Some of these techniques are easier to use than others, but you should know them all. This knowledge will allow you to choose an appropriate technique when using a COM object.

Chapter 8, *COM in Cyberspace*, shows you how to build ActiveX controls that can be embedded into a container application, such as Internet Explorer. You'll build an ActiveX control without a complex user interface and two other ones with a complex user interface. Since you can put these ActiveX controls into a web page, you will also develop the web pages that can host them. In addition, you'll learn how to expose your COM object's properties through the use of property pages.

Chapter 9, *Applying Security*, elevates your understanding of Chapter 5. You'll build a server component that takes advantage of the access token, server-side COM security, Windows NT security, auditing, and administrative alerts. You'll also build a client component that takes advantage of client-side COM security, which includes specifying the process-wide security, choosing an identity that is used for launching distributed components, and using call-level security.

Chapter 10, *Connecting Objects*, reminds you that the main importance of Distributed COM is that it allows a pointer to be passed from one machine to a second, from the second to a third, and so on. This notion is the key that opens the doors into the world of distributed objects computing. It also allows two objects to pass interface pointers between themselves to achieve bi-directional communications. To grasp this notion, you'll build a simple chat system that includes a chat broker, server, and client.

Appendix A, *Debugging Techniques*, describes three simple, but very powerful, techniques for debugging distributed components. Learn these techniques because they can be very valuable.

Appendix B, *Performance*, exhibits the performance data for in-process, local, and remote method invocations. This appendix also shows the drastic performance differences among different threading models for in-process COM objects.

Appendix C, *New COM Features and COM+*, introduces you to the new features of COM in Windows NT 4.0 Service Pack 4 and above. This appendix also includes a brief discussion of COM+, which will be released with Windows 2000.

Appendix D, *Hello, Universe!*, serves as a supplement to help you understand the source code located within the *Hello* directory. This appendix is for those who want to get a sneak preview at the kind of code that must be written in order to develop simple distributed components using COM. Again, I provide this appendix solely as a supplement, so you must read the whole book to really build distributed systems using COM.

# Some Assumptions About the Reader

In this book, I assume that you have a working knowledge of C++ and object-oriented programming. You should also have basic knowledge of the Visual C++ integrated development environment, but you don't have to know ATL or MFC. You will write some HTML scripting, but you don't really have to know HTML, because the source code will be provided in full. Other than these basic assumptions, you should be running Windows NT 4.0 and using Microsoft Visual C++ 6.0. In addition, it would be great if you have two or more computers on which to test and help you understand the distributed aspects of COM.

# Accompanying Source Code

You can download the accompanying source code from the O'Reilly ftp site. This section describes two methods for doing so, regular FTP and FTPMAIL.

## FTP

If you have an Internet connection (permanent or dialup), the easiest way to use FTP is via your web browser or favorite FTP client. To get the examples, simply point your browser to:

*ftp://ftp.oreilly.com/published/oreilly/nutshell/dcom/DCOMcode.zip*

If you don't have a web browser, you can use the command-line FTP client included with Windows NT (or Windows 95/98).

```
% ftp ftp.oreilly.com
Connected to ftp.oreilly.com.
220 ftp.oreilly.com FTP server (Version 6.34 Thu Oct 22 14:32:01 EDT 1992)
ready.
Name (ftp.oreilly.com:username): anonymous
331 Guest login ok, send e-mail address as password.
Password: username@hostname          Use your username and host here
230 Guest login ok, access restrictions apply.
ftp> cd /published/oreilly/nutshell/dcom
250 CWD command successful.
ftp> get README
200 PORT command successful.
150 Opening ASCII mode data connection for README (xxxx bytes).
226 Transfer complete.
local: README remote: README
xxxx bytes received in xxx seconds (xxx Kbytes/s)
ftp> binary
200 Type set to I.
ftp> get DCOMcode.zip
200 PORT command successful.
150 Opening BINARY mode data connection for DCOMcode.zip (xxxx bytes).
226 Transfer complete. local: DCOMcode.zip remote: DCOMcode.zip
```

```
xxxx bytes received in xxx seconds (xxx Kbytes/s)
ftp> quit
221 Goodbye.
%
```

You should unzip the DCOMCode.zip file into an empty working directory. Once you have done this, you will find a number of subdirectories, that contain the source code for all the examples discussed in this book. The following table summarizes the contents of these subdirectories:

| Chapter | Directory that contains the supporting source code |
|---|---|
| Chapter 1, *Distributed Computing* | N/A |
| Chapter 2, *Distributed COM Overview* | N/A |
| Chapter 3, *Objects* | Basics |
| Chapter 4, *Components* | Basics |
| Chapter 5, *Infrastructure* | Infrastructure |
| Chapter 6, *Building Components with ATL* | OCRServer |
| Chapter 7, *Using COM Objects* | OCRClient |
| Chapter 8, *COM in Cyberspace* | Cyber |
| Chapter 9, *Applying Security* | Security |
| Chapter 10, *Connecting Objects* | Chat |

Not shown in this table are the *include* directory, which contains several useful, helper classes that you can use, and the *Hello* directory, which contains a project for a simple distributed system with a client printing the "Hello, Universe!" message to the server. The example is provided primarily to show the typical code that's required to build a simple distributed system using COM. See Appendix D for more information. Besides these two directories, be sure to check each subdirectory for a *readme.txt* file, because it tells you what you need to do to get the source code to compile and run.

## *FTPMAIL*

FTPMAIL is a mail server available to anyone who can send electronic mail to and receive electronic mail from Internet sites. Any company or service provider that allows email connections to the Internet can access FTPMAIL, as described in the following paragraph.

You send mail to *ftpmail@online.oreilly.com*. In the message body, give the FTP commands you want to run. The server will run anonymous FTP for you and mail the files back to you. To get a complete help file, send a message with no subject and the single word "help" in the body. The following is an example mail message that gets the examples. This command sends you a listing of the files in the selected directory and the requested example files. The listing is useful if you are interested in a later version of the examples.

```
Subject:
reply-to username@hostname          (Message Body) Where you want files mailed
open
cd /published/oreilly/nutshell/dcom
dir
get README
mode binary
uuencode
get DCOMcode.zip
quit
.
```

A signature at the end of the message is acceptable as long as it appears after "quit."

## Conventions

The following typographical conventions are used in this book:

Plain text

> is used for computer output, such as what you would see on the screen or in a dialog box.

*Italic*

> is used for API function calls, class names, commands that should be typed on the command line, filenames, interface names, method names, and normal function calls.

Constant Width

> is used for code samples, phrases (each is a group of words) that you see on a dialog box, structure names, and variable names.

---

 The owl symbol is used to indicate a tip, suggestion, or general note.

---

 The turkey symbol is used to indicate a warning.

---

# *Related Sources of Information*

Contained in the following lists are some relevant and insightful sources that have definitely contributed to my understanding of COM and to the creation of this book. Some of these sources are fairly dated, but the concepts and insights given are invaluable. Almost all of these sources can be found in the most current Microsoft Developer's Network (MSDN) CDs. I've listed these sources in the order that I think you should read them. For up-to-date information on COM, visit *http://www.microsoft.com/com*.

## *Specifications and References*

*The Component Object Model Specification*, Draft Version 0.9, Microsoft Corporation, 24 October 1995.

Kindel, Charlie and Brown, Nat. *Distributed Component Object Model Protocol (DCOM/1.0)*. Microsoft Corporation, January 1998.

*MIDL Programmer's Guide and Reference*. Microsoft Platform SDK. Microsoft Corporation, 1992-1998.

*COM Programmer's Reference*. Microsoft Platform SDK. Microsoft Corporation, 1994-1998.

*Automation Programmer's Reference*. Microsoft Platform SDK. Microsoft Corporation, 1995-1997.

## *The Classics*

Williams, Tony. *Dealing with the Unknown*. *http://research.microsoft.com/comapps/unknown.doc*, Microsoft Corporation, December 1988.

Horstmann, Markus and Kirtland, Mary. *DCOM Architecture*. Microsoft Corporation, 23 July 1997.

Kindel, Charlie. *The Rules of the Component Object Model*. Microsoft Corporation, 20 October 1995.

Kindel, Charlie. *Designing COM Interfaces*. Microsoft Corporation, 20 October 1995.

Goswell, Cripin. *The COM Programmer's Cookbook*. Microsoft Corporation, 13 September 1995.

Horstman, Markus. *From CPP to COM*. Microsoft Corporation, 19 October 1995.

Brockschmidt, Kraig. *Inside OLE*. 2d ed. Microsoft Press, 1995.

## Knowledge Base Articles

*INFO: Descriptions and Workings of OLE Threading Models*, KB Article ID: Q150777, Microsoft Corporation, 28 July 1998.

*FAQ: COM Security Frequently Asked Questions*, KB article ID: Q158508, Microsoft Corporation, 10 December 1997.

*INFO: COM Servers Activation and NT Windows Stations*, KB Article ID: Q169321, Microsoft Corporation, 21 November 1997.

*How To Configure a Non-DCOM Server and Client to Use DCOM*, KB Article ID: Q158582, Microsoft Corporation, 6 November 1996.

*FAQ: DCOM95 Frequently Asked Questions*, KB Article ID: Q174024, Microsoft Corporation, 22 October 1997.

## Technical Articles

Box, Don. "Introducing Distributed COM and the New OLE Features in Windows NT 4.0." *Microsoft Systems Journal.* May 1996.

Box, Don. "ActiveX/COM Q&A." *Microsoft System Journal.* November 1996, January, March, May, July, September, November 1997.

Box, Don. "OLE Q&A." *Microsoft Systems Journal.* February, April, June 1996.

Platt, David. "Give ActiveX-based Web Pages a Boost with the Apartment Threading Model." *Microsoft Systems Journal.* February 1997.

Platt, David. "Fashionable App Designers Agree: The Free Threading Model is What's Hot This Fall." *Microsoft Systems Journal.* August 1997.

Nelson, Michael. "Using Distributed COM with Firewalls." http://www.microsoft.com/com/wpaper/dcomfw.asp, Microsoft Corporation. 20 June 1998.

Kirtland, Mary. "The COM+ Programming Model Makes it Easy to Write Components in Any Language." *Microsoft Systems Journal.* December 1997.

Kirtland, Mary. "Object-Oriented Software Development Made Simple with COM+ Runtime Services." *Microsoft Systems Journal.* November 1997.

Reed, Dave, Trewin, Tracey, and Tomsen, Mai-lan. "Microsoft Transaction Server Helps You Write Scalable, Distributed Internet Apps." *Microsoft Systems Journal.* August 1997.

Richter, Jeffrey. "Win32 Q&A." *Microsoft Systems Journal.* May 1996.

## Other Related Documentation

Williams, Sara and Kindel, Charlie. *The Component Object Model: A Technical Overview.* Microsoft Corporation, October 1994.

"Microsoft Windows NT Security Support Provider Interface." White Paper, Microsoft Corporation, 1996.

Microsoft Platform SDK. *Security Support Provider Interface for Microsoft Windows NT 4.0.* Microsoft Corporation, 1996.

*Windows NT 4.0 Access Control.* Microsoft Platform SDK. Microsoft Corporation, 1996.

*Window Stations and Desktops.* Microsoft Platform SDK. Microsoft Corporation, 1996.

*Microsoft Windows NT Distributed Security Services.* Microsoft Corporation, 1996.

*Taking Advantage of the OLE Automation Marshaller.* Microsoft Corporation, 18 October 1995.

*Microsoft Transaction Server Version 2.0.* Microsoft Platform SDK. Microsoft Corporation, 1997-1998.

*MS Windows NT Workstation 4.0 Resource Guide.* Microsoft Corporation, 1995.

# Acknowledgments

Creating a book is a challenging task that requires an effort from many people. I owe enormous thanks to Andy Oram, my acquisitions and technical editor, for noticing the value of my original manuscript and extending me a contract to write a real book. Andy has not only taught me a tremendous amount about writing, but he has so often impressed me with his remarkable understanding of COM and his extraordinary recommendations that made the book better. Without Andy, this book would not have landed in your hands right now.

Mary Kirtland deserves high praise and much appreciation for reviewing this book. Mary not only read the book very carefully and thoroughly, but also generously made key recommendations that made the book much more accurate and up-to-date. Of course, I must also thank Saji Abraham because, without Saji's help, this book would never have reached Mary.

Besides Andy Oram, the only other person who read every chapter of the book prior to technical review was Hoang Lam. Thanks to Hoang for reading the first draft of every chapter in this book and ensuring that the technical information given was accurate. Thanks to Shaun Flisakowski for using his valuable time to review the whole book during technical review. Other people who read partial drafts and returned feedback included Kevin Thai, Huy Thai, Tim Kroll, Janusz Wnek, Roger Bradford, Richard Bankhead, Steve Friedl, and Jay Chapman.

Without the production staff at O'Reilly, there would be no book. Thanks to Rob Romano for creating awesome looking figures, Edie Freedman for designing the cover, and Maureen Dempsey for coordinating the technical reviews.

Thanks to my instructor relations coordinators at Learning Tree, especially Michael Tapp, for their patience and understanding while I was writing this book. Now, I no longer have a reason for canceling and refusing to teach so many courses. Thanks to Kathy LaVigne for allowing me the opportunity to lead the architecture and development of the first Distributed COM-based system in the division. In addition, thanks to my colleagues in Division 278 and Division 1137 at SAIC for preserving a friendly working environment.

Finally, I would like to thank my family and friends for their support. Mom and Dad have sacrificed so much in order to provide their children with a better life. Other people who have supported me through this effort included my Canadian relatives and good friends, colleagues, or siblings shown in Figure 10-3.

Thuan L. Thai
Herndon, Virginia
November 1998

1

# Distributed Computing

Distributed computing is nothing new. From the birth of computer science, there has been a struggle for distributed computing, whether it be using terminals to gain access to massive computers, running bulky clients to interact with remote servers over a LAN, or executing applets to manipulate data over the Internet. In this chapter, we will briefly examine the progress of distributed computing since the dawn of computer science.

As you read this chapter, notice that the communication infrastructure between two endpoints (e.g., a client and server) gradually becomes more sophisticated. Because of this sophistication, new approaches are needed to minimize the development effort of a given system. As a result, the support for this intercommunication is pushed increasingly closer toward the operating system as time unfolds. Developers need this support in order to concentrate their valuable time on developing the functionality of their software—not developing communications protocols, as this is complicated, time consuming, and error prone. We'll start off talking about dumb terminals and eventually end up with what we desire to learn: distributed components.

## Dumb Terminals

Figure 1-1 shows a dumb terminal that displays output from a remote, monolithic process running on a gigantic mainframe or a powerful UNIX server. Note that the dumb terminal does no work, except to serve as remote eyeglasses into the process running on the mainframe through some type of direct link.

In the 1950s and 1960s, large enterprises normally leased a mainframe so many employees could share it to perform routine tasks. Since there were so few of these machines (and because they were so expensive), engineers came up with

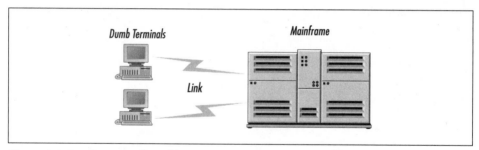

*Figure 1-1. Dumb terminals and large machines*

ways to use mainframes remotely. One of these ideas included a dumb terminal. The communication technique behind a dumb terminal was extremely simple. The engineers literally took a wire and connected it from a dumb terminal to the host mainframe. In this respect, a dumb terminal didn't have to determine where to send the data, because it communicated with the mainframe through a direct link.

People used dumb terminals to access the mainframe from a distance. In a sense, the mainframe moved a bit closer to the users, and since moving closer brought comfort, the users asked for more. Thus, dumb terminals quickly led to the birth of smarter terminals. These more intelligent terminals often contained specialized circuitry, firmware, and possibly a communications protocol to specifically collaborate with their mother computer. In essence, these intelligent terminals led to the first glimmerings of distributed processing. The only things these smart terminals lacked to be stand-alone, personal computers (PC) were a local disk and an operating system.

As PCs came into the picture, a new idea emerged: terminal emulation. Using a simple terminal emulation software, hundreds of users could remotely log on to a powerful mainframe or a UNIX server. Unlike dumb terminals, the communication between the terminal emulators and their hosts became more complex. Users were able to configure their terminal emulators to use a particular communications protocol. This flexibility came with the price of complexity. For example, any slightest communications protocol incompatibility would almost definitely inhibit emulator to host communications.

For some time, terminals were great, because they allowed users to remotely control their business processing. However, as PCs became increasingly powerful, cheaper, and popular, software developers realized that this method of remote computing was a waste, since this environment restricted the power of the PC. In other words, some of the work the server did for two thousand users could have been done on each of the two thousand separate PCs. This was one of the reasons for the birth of client/server computing.

# Client/Server Computing

This client/server technology seen in Figure 1-2 is what is now called the two-tier client/server environment. The client typically has a graphical user interface that talks to the server using various communications protocols, including netbios, named pipes, and sockets. Servers typically manage the back-end persistent data.

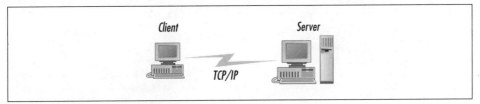

*Figure 1-2. Client/server technology*

Now the client had become even smarter; for example, it used the CPU productively to perform business logic and complex calculations. In fact, client applications became increasingly sophisticated. At the same time, the communication between the client and the server became more complex. With a client/server environment, the communications layer, or marshaling software, must be developed to handle client/server interaction. This kind of software was later called a *middleware*—a mediator for client/server interactions.

Here's an explanation of marshaling. A process understands intelligible data, but it doesn't understand a raw network stream. An example of intelligible data is a function argument, which has a size and a type. On the other hand, a raw network stream is broken into the bits that paddle across the network. Because there are different representations of data, network communication needs a translation mechanism called a marshaler. A *marshaler* is simply a piece of code that performs marshaling. *Marshaling* is the packaging of intelligible data into a raw stream. The client communications layer sends this raw stream to the server, via the network layer. Once the server communication layer receives the raw stream, it needs to unmarshal the raw stream into an intelligible format for the server, so that the server can correctly service the client request. Unmarshaling is thus the reverse of marshaling. For brevity, software developers use the term marshaling to describe both the packaging and unpackaging of communication data.

Figure 1-3 shows an example of the marshaling process, which can be divided into the following steps:

1. A client calls *SetPage,* passing in a document identifier, a page number, and page information.

2. The marshaler packages the data in a marshaled representation and sends the raw stream to the target server.

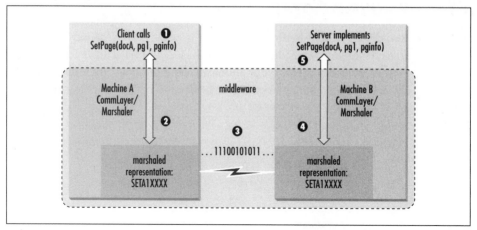

*Figure 1-3. Marshaling*

3. The raw stream turns into raw bits, and the bits swim across the network.

4. The marshaler on the server side unmarshals the data.

5. The server then invokes the target *SetPage* function. The process is practically the same upon return.

Back to the discussion of client/server architecture, the marshaling layer is usually written to take advantage of a single, specific protocol. To use another network protocol, a separate marshaling software has to be developed. Definitely not a pretty sight. This isn't the only problem with client/server computing though. Listed below are other apparent problems exhibited by the client/server technology:

- Business logic and complex calculations are too expensive on client computers.

- Clients suffer dramatically from performance impacts, since clients run on "puny" machines.

- Software developers spend too much time writing protocol specifications and code to handle client/server communication.

- Each client/server system must utilize some form of security to prevent potential attacks.

- Security software is usually home grown, conforming to no standard.

Taking these problems into account, a better method had to be found. The search for a better method started the notion of three-tier client/server computing, or more generally distributed computing.

# *Distributed Computing Using RPC*

In a three-tier environment such as the one shown in Figure 1-4, software developers distributed responsibility among each participant. They took away some intelligence from the clients, in a way that clients would act only as a front-end. In other words, clients were responsible for simply displaying, capturing, and validating user data. From this, a new terminology came into existence. The term "thin client" was used to represent the first tier in a three-tier system. PCs that ran these clients did not need to be high-end. These first-tier clients would communicate with the middle-tier servers via a remoting standard, remote procedure calls (RPC), to be discussed in a moment.

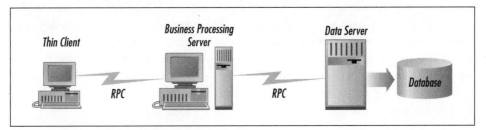

*Figure 1-4. Three-tier technology*

The middle tier was a server tier that supported complex business processing (e.g., calculate expense and calculate factorials) for its clients. Most of the performance problems found on the client end in the client/server scenario had now been relocated to this second tier. Therefore, the middle tier had to be powerful and smart. It had to be a high-end computer, running operating systems such as Windows NT or Solaris, with multiple CPUs to take advantage of symmetric multiprocessing. These middle-tier servers would communicate with the back-end third tier, again using the RPC standard.* The third-tier, back-end servers managed persistent business data, and usually exchanged information directly with a database. This tier was also placed on high-end computers.

As you can see, a three-tier architecture allows separation of responsibility, thereby permitting each participant to perform only what is suited to it. To assist in distributing responsibility, software developers use some form of RPC—either the version developed by Sun Microsystems (ONC RPC) or the Distributed Computing Environment (DCE RPC).

RPC is a well-known standard that supports the idea of calling functions remotely. For example, assume you have a function called *CalculateExpense*, which is

---

* Or some other form of communication might be used. For consistency, the example shown here uses RPC as the mechanism for second- to third-tier communications. Other three-tier systems may choose another mechanism for second- to third-tier communications.

implemented on a remote server. To invoke this function, a client would make a normal function call. However, the function is actually executed on the server machine that could be anywhere. This is what we call *location transparency*, since the called function can be implemented locally or remotely. In other words, the caller is oblivious to the location of the target function.

How is this possible? It is possible through the basic principle of separating interface from implementation. Before you can take advantage of RPC, you must specify an interface using the Interface Definition Language (IDL). Think of an interface as an application level communications protocol that includes a number of functions (intelligent verbs) that clients and servers can use to collaborate. The interface, which is identified by a Universally Unique Identifier (UUID), describes a group of function prototypes that can potentially be called remotely. Once you have specified your interface, you would then use an IDL compiler to automatically generate marshaling code called client and server stubs. After linking these stubs into your client and server applications, you can easily make remote function calls. It is the job of the client stub to marshal the data and send it to the server stub. The server stub executes the target function and returns data to the client stub, which then returns the data to the caller.

RPC brings dramatic value to the software world. Since the marshaling code is automatically generated, software developers can now totally eliminate the arduous hours they have previously wasted in developing customized marshaling software. Put differently, RPC allows developers to concentrate their efforts on the functionality of their application, not on communications and network protocols.

The obvious advantage that RPC brings is location transparency. Thanks to the seamless support for location transparency, developers can easily extend the idea of three-tier systems into multi-tier systems. In fact, this notion allows commercial vendors to introduce brokers into distributed systems to manage server location, naming, and load balancing. Besides the location transparency benefit, RPC comes with built-in support for security, thereby allowing software developers to remove themselves from building nonstandard security functionality into their systems. Moreover, RPC supports the notions of multithreading and network protocol independence. With the advent of RPC, it becomes easy to distribute functionality and services across the entire enterprise, and as a result this popularized the term distributed computing.

## *Distributed Objects*

Distributed computing did not stop with RPC. After recognizing the potential gains to be derived from object-oriented programming, software developers spread this success to distributed computing. Similar to C (a functional paradigm), which had slowly progressed into C++ (an object-oriented paradigm), the idea of metamorphizing RPC into an object-oriented cousin became popular. Thus, software vendors and developers came together to slowly migrate the RPC (a functional paradigm) idea into a more object-oriented notion.*

Distributed objects embody all the ideas from RPC; for example, marshaling and security are both integrated. However, instead of calling functions, you can now instantiate objects and send messages to them. These objects can be anywhere on the local network or in cyberspace. The client does not care where the objects reside or what platform they execute on. Figure 1-5 shows how distributed technology can tie platforms together.

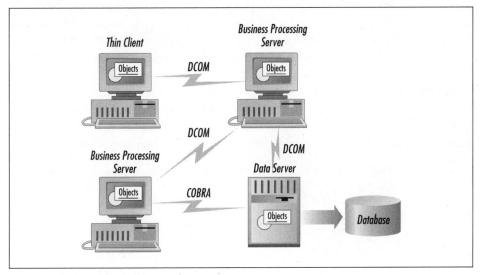

*Figure 1-5. Distributed objects*

In distributed objects technology, the Object Request Broker (commonly referred to as an ORB) is the "bus" or "channel" through which objects can discover and communicate with each other at runtime. It is a middleware that provides a common set of functionality for all objects, including concurrency, load balancing, fault tolerance, context management, and more.

## *Distributed Components*

Gigantic mainframes run monolithic software. With client/server and distributed computing technologies, you can distribute work and develop less monolithic

---

* In fact, before distributed objects hit the commercial market, one of the tasks in a project that I worked on was using RPC to build a marshaling layer for objects and functional programming conversion. We called this marshaling layer the "Dispatcher". Not only did the "Dispatcher" maintain security, session, context, and other communications management on top of RPC, it was the layer responsible for translating function calls into object messages and vice-versa.

applications. Before you learn about distributed components, let's first examine how to make software less monolithic.

One technique is simply to develop special purpose modules, or static libraries. Applications use these static libraries by linking with them. With static libraries, you gain reusability at the source level. Notice that you also gain maintainability with a static library, because it contains a lump of code with a well-defined purpose. You build applications by integrating a number of these static libraries, allowing your application to become less monolithic. That's fairly good—but not good enough.

Unlike static libraries, component technology supports the notion of pluggable components. Look at Figure 1-6 and consider this scenario. I have two mother boards that I want to sell. Board A has all the peripherals (CPU, RAM, video, sound, modem) built-in. Furthermore, there are no expansion slots. Board B is a Pentium 60, upgradable to Pentium 90. It has 16MB RAM, expandable to 128MB. And by the way, it has 3 ISA slots and 4 PCI slots. If you buy board B, I'll throw in a cheap video, modem, and sound card. Board A cost $40 and board B cost $50. Which mother board would you buy? Of course, you'd buy B. Why? Because A is hideously monolithic, and B supports the notion of component plug-ins.

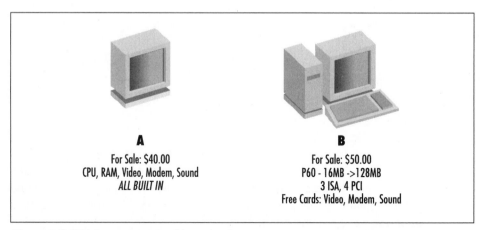

**A**
For Sale: $40.00
CPU, RAM, Video, Modem, Sound
*ALL BUILT IN*

**B**
For Sale: $50.00
P60 - 16MB ->128MB
3 ISA, 4 PCI
Free Cards: Video, Modem, Sound

*Figure 1-6. Which computer would you buy?*

This is exactly the goal of component technology. Unlike monolithic software, a component is a piece of software with a well-defined purpose. It is easily maintainable and reusable at the binary level. Note the drastic difference between a component and a static library; unlike a static library, a component can be reused at the binary level. This means you can buy a component and plug it into your application, without ever needing a header file or an import library! This plug-in aspect of software integration is truly black-box programming. You don't have to know anything about the code in a component to use it.

One of the advantages of a component technology is that it has no bias toward language, tools, operating systems, or network; that is, it can interoperate regardless of differences in these domains (or at least, this is the goal). As shown in Figure 1-7, software components, usually dynamic linked libraries (DLL files) or executables (EXE files), are built from COM classes whose runtime instances are referred to as COM objects (or more generally, distributed objects). COM objects are based on the rules of the Component Object Model (COM). A COM object exposes one or more COM interfaces to support the services that it provides.

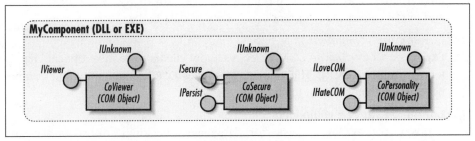

*Figure 1-7. A COM component can host many COM objects*

In Figure 1-7, a box represents a COM object and "lollipops" represent a COM object's exposed interfaces. Clients use a COM object via its contractual, published interfaces. The clients know only of interfaces; they must not care about implementation details. So, component technology takes the separation of interface and implementation to the fullest to achieve black-box programming.

Component is a nasty word because one person may use it to refer to an object and another may use it to refer to a binary module. To be consistent, this book uses the term *COM component* (or simply *component*) to refer to a binary module, such as a DLL or an EXE. It uses the term *COM object* to refer to a runtime instance of a COM class whose source code is linked into a COM component. In general, a *COM class* is an object definition in source code that implements at least the *IUnknown* interface. To translate this into C++, a COM class is simply an abstract data type (class definition) for an object that implements the *IUnknown* interface.

Let's look at a simple component imaging architecture that is based on Distributed COM. As shown in Figure 1-8, this architecture includes the following distributed components, which can interoperate seamlessly with one another regardless of their locality:

*Client components*

Can use the services exposed by server components without the need for the server component's source code or an import library. This is reuse at the binary level. Examples include Microsoft Internet Explorer or any other application.

*The* BlobViewer *component*

Exposes a *CoViewer* COM object that can display any data blob, such as a TIFF image or a Microsoft office document. This component is a DLL, so it can be dynamically loaded into any client component. A client component that embeds the BlobViewer component can take advantage of an already built and tested viewer that can render a variety of data blobs.

*The* OCRServer *component*

Exposes a *CoOcrEngine* COM object to allow clients to request optical character recognition (OCR). The BlobViewer uses OCRServer, a remote component, to perform OCR on images.

*The* LanguageServer *component*

Exposes two COM objects for language checking: *CoDictionary* and *CoThesaurus*. The BlobViewer and the OCRServer components can use the services exposed by the LanguageServer to check for spelling and lookup synonyms and antonyms.

Because these components can be distributed among many computers, a communications mechanism is needed. If you were to use TCP/IP to support the interaction among these components, you would be writing application-specific protocols until you were blue in the face. But if you use a component technology, such as Distributed COM, you will gain the important benefits of distributed and plug-in interoperability. This is because Distributed COM supports location transparency and binary interoperability.

Let's study these components in further detail. The OCRServer EXE shown in Figure 1-8 is a component. It is a well-defined piece of software that can be deployed and reused. Yet, it is simple to maintain because it is small and has a well-defined purpose: to perform optical character recognition for requesting clients. It houses a COM object, called *CoOcrEngine*, that exposes the *IOcr* interface. It is this interface that allows clients to perform OCR.

Similarly, the BlobViewer component is itself a stand-alone piece of software. It houses a COM object that exposes an *IViewer* interface, allowing clients to programmatically control the BlobViewer. A COM interface may support both properties and methods. Interface *properties* are accessors; in other words, they are getters and setters. For example, the *IViewer* interface can expose a property called ShowToolbar that allows a user to set or get the visibility of the BlobViewer's toolbar. A user can hide or show this toolbar by setting the ShowToolbar property to false or true, respectively. Aside from properties, an interface is largely

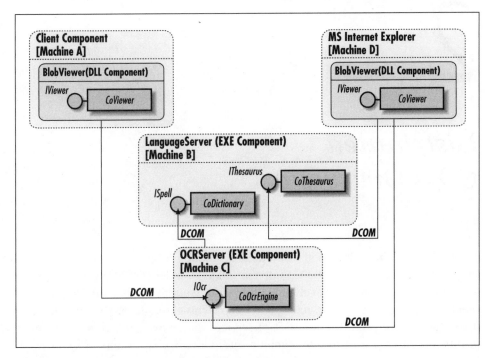

*Figure 1-8. A simple component-based imaging system*

made up of methods. An example of a *method* in the *IViewer* interface can be *ZoomIn*, which allows a client to tell the BlobViewer to enlarge an image.

COM also supports the notion of *events*, also called *notifications*. Assume that the *IOcr* interface supports a method that's called *ProcessImageForTwoHours* (who cares what it does). When this method is invoked, the user of the client component surely wouldn't want to stare at the frozen user interface for two long hours. To solve this problem, you use COM's support for events. By using this technique, a client asks the server to notify it when the image has been processed. Immediately after the image has been processed, the server notifies the client of such an event. In this particular case, the notion of events saves two valuable hours and liberates the user from staring at a frozen application.

As shown in Figure 1-8, components can be widely distributed. Since a component in cyberspace can be both a client and a server, the notion of clients and servers weakens. Thus, you tend to leave off the client/server buzzword and simply call the COM objects (within the software components) distributed objects.

# 2

*In this chapter:*
- *COM*
- *Distributed COM*
- *COM Facilities and Services*
- *Applying COM*

# Distributed COM Overview

The previous chapter discussed distributed computing in general. We now want to focus on one area: Distributed Component Object Model (DCOM). Before getting to the nuts and bolts of developing distributed systems based on DCOM, let's briefly examine COM and the motivation behind this technology. DCOM is nothing more than a wire protocol and a set of services that allow COM components in a distributed environment to intercommunicate. Once we've examined COM, we'll learn about the facilities and services that COM provides to make it a viable distributed objects technology.

## COM

As its name implies, the Component Object Model is a model that you can utilize to build software components. As stated in Chapter 1, a *component* is a package or a module, more often referred to as an executable (EXE) or a dynamic linked library (DLL). Being a model, COM is fully specified in a formal document called the "The Component Object Model Specification." This document specifies a binary standard that allows heterogeneous components to seamlessly interoperate with one another. COM is referred to as a binary standard, because it allows one component to reuse another component without the need of the second component's source code. In addition to being a binary standard, COM specifies a number of rules and requirements to build software components. However, being just a specification, it doesn't enforce the use a specific language, tool, or operating system to create component software.

As exhibited in Figure 2-1, the COM specification encompasses several previously successful technologies. One technology that COM takes advantage of is dynamic linking. Dynamic linked libraries (DLLs) have been successful, for the most part, because they save space, support upgrades, and allow a runtime selection of

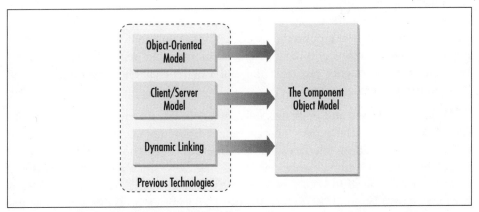

*Figure 2-1. Previous technologies used by COM*

functions needed by a client program. The other two important technologies, which deserve a more detailed discussion, include the object-oriented and client/server models.

## *The Object-Oriented Model*

Object-oriented programming is a successful technology because it supports encapsulation, inheritance, and polymorphism. We will briefly review these traditional concepts. As we do so, we'll briefly note how COM ratifies and promotes them.

### *Encapsulation*

*Encapsulation,* or the hiding of variables and possibly functions so that the calling program sees only what it needs to see, is an important principle of object-oriented programming. Hiding information from the calling program allows an object to control its internals and prevent faulty or illegal external access. This is important because it permits the calling program to reliably use the object, while minimizing maintenance in the event that the object changes or enhances its internals.

In addition to supporting the packaging of states and behaviors, encapsulation allows us to separate interface from implementation. Collectively, the set of an object's published behaviors is called an *interface.* The world interacts with an object through its published interface. For example, a car encapsulates its states (horsepower, maximum speed, etc.) and behaviors (turn left, accelerate). A car's driver should not directly change the states of the car. Even though the driver can make the car accelerate, he should do it by pressing a pedal and not care what the car does in order to accelerate. Modern automobile technology shows the value of separating the interface from the implementation in real life: makers of electric cars can provide the same controls gasoline cars offer so that the buyer can get behind the wheel and just drive away.

Separating interface from implementation means that the world should not care about the nasty implementations behind the published behaviors. These behaviors effectively form a barrier around the object, encapsulating and protecting the object's internal implementations and data. This reduces coupling between the object and its clients, as the clients see only the published behaviors, never the internal implementations or data.

COM not only praises and embraces encapsulation, but it firmly enforces this concept. COM demands the separation of interface from implementation. In COM, the world knows only about interfaces that an object supports. The world will never see the object's internal implementations. By being very strict about encapsulation, COM has earned itself the outstanding success that it's experiencing today. This is because encapsulation, if used correctly, can lead to black-box component integration. This concept allows components to robustly evolve over time without breaking a previously integrated system.

### Inheritance

*Inheritance* allows you to extend or inherit the states and behaviors of classes; the initially defined class is the *base class* and one created by extending it is called a *derived class*. Simple inheritance provides both interface and implementation reusability. Referring to the previous example, a car inherits its states and behaviors from a vehicle. For instance, a stick-shift car and an automatic car can further inherit states and behaviors from the plain car class.

This notion is powerful since you don't have to forever copy and paste code, the poor-man's technique for code reuse. By inheriting the base class, you gain all the states and behaviors that base class has established. Implementation inheritance, a technique for reusing previously-written code, is extremely appealing. But it has drawbacks too. For example, you must intimately understand your parent's implementation details, which inhibit the ideas of black-box programming. Consider the following *TurnLeft* method implemented by the *Car* class:

```
class Car {
public:
   virtual void TurnLeft()
   {
      // Derived class must call me first,
      // or else the engine will blow up!
   }
};
```

There is a potential side effect here that the derived class must know about. If a derived class overrides this method, it must call *Car::TurnLeft* first, as mandated by the comments in the earlier code snippet. Now consider what would happen with the following:

```
class SportsCar : public Car {
   void BurnRubber(int mph);
```

```
public:
    virtual void TurnLeft()
    {
        // I'll speed up to 1000MPH
        BurnRubber(1000);
        // Then I call my parent's TurnLeft
        Car::TurnLeft();
    }
};

SportsCar coolCar;
coolCar.TurnLeft();       // Hah!  The engine will blow up.
```

Clearly in this case, either the implementor of the *SportsCar* class wants to put its manufacturer to shame, or he doesn't know about the havoc that will arise. In the latter case, he's assuming that everything will work fine. Unfortunately, there is a strong and deadly cohesion between the two classes. Obviously, when the `coolCar` is told to *TurnLeft*, the engine will blow up in the driver's face. This is because the *Car* class requires its derived class to call its *Car::TurnLeft* method first, but implementation inheritance provides no simple way for the *Car* class to robustly enforce this requirement. To prevent the `coolCar` from blowing up, the *SportsCar::TurnLeft* method must intimately understand the implementation of *Car::TurnLeft*; that is, *SportsCar::TurnLeft* must call *Car::TurnLeft* before it can call *BurnRubber*. Fixing this problem requires that you either have the source code of the *Car* class in hand or some really good documentation for the *Car::TurnLeft* method.

Instead of supporting implementation inheritance and suffering from the problem just discussed, COM supports reuse. Traditionally, reuse can be achieved at the source code level, but in the component software world, reuse means much more than this. In COM, reuse can be achieved at the binary level. Binary reuse allows greater interoperability among heterogeneous components, which are developed by different vendors who are no longer restricted to use a particular programming language or tool.

### Polymorphism

*Polymorphism* is the use of a single name to refer to a set of different methods (functions). This notion allows the most appropriate method to be executed at runtime based on the object. In other words, it allows late binding, which is the ability to dynamically and selectively invoke a method based on the object's true type at runtime.

Consider a car, a plane, a boat, and a motorcycle. These are classes that derive from an abstraction called a vehicle. Take examples of these vehicles and throw them into a bag of vehicles. Then, while closing your eyes, pick up a vehicle from the bag and tell it to *TurnLeft*. What turns left (a car, a plane, a boat, etc.) depends on the true type of vehicle you have in your hands. The beauty here is you can later add a bicycle and the polymorphic *TurnLeft* behavior will still work.

COM not only warmly accepts polymorphism, but it strengthens and improves this concept. In traditional object-oriented programming, polymorphism works only with methods. You will learn in this book that COM adds a twist to polymorphism that makes it a very powerful environment. The "Object Orientation" section in Chapter 4 will reveal that COM supports interface-level polymorphism in addition to traditional method-level polymorphism.

## *The Client/Server Model*

There are many benefits to the client/server model, but one notable benefit that the client/server model conveys is systems robustness. In the client/server world, a server can support numerous clients simultaneously. If a single client crashes, it will not bring down the server and all the other clients. Likewise, if the server crashes, it will not bring down its clients, assuming those clients gracefully handle the disconnection. Robustness is the main reason why COM embraces the client/server model.

The client/server model is not perfect, however. For the purpose of this discussion, a *client* is an entity (any piece of code) that uses the services of another entity, and a *server* is an entity that serves a client's request. If you take these simplistic interpretations, you can derive a number of client/server analogies:

- A process (client) communicating with a dynamic linked library (server), by making simple function calls

- A process (client) communicating with the operating system (server), by making system calls

- A process (client) communicating with another process on the same machine (server), by using named pipes

- A process (client) communicating with another process on a remote machine (server), by using sockets

In all these scenarios, you witness the client/server concept. However, there is a problem. The communication between the client and the server is drastically different in each case. Specifically, you see four heterogeneous ways for a client to interoperate with a server.

To eliminate these differences, COM specifies a communication standard to which all components must conform. This communication standard is a *COM interface*, which can be regarded as a common approach for a client to interoperate with a server. With COM interfaces, you can agree on a single way to communicate—a universal language, so to speak. COM derives this standard from RPC, which supports client/server communications via an RPC interface. For brevity, refer to a COM interface simply as an interface.

# Distributed COM

COM supports interoperability within the confines of a single machine, but DCOM extends COM to support distributed objects. This extension adds support for location transparency, remote activation, connection management, concurrency management, and security. In fact, many presenters and writers speak of DCOM as "COM with a longer wire." If you come from a traditional distributed objects world and like to keep your terms straight, DCOM is broadly regarded as the "Microsoft ORB."

As seen in Figure 2-2, the DCOM wire protocol is built on top of Microsoft RPC, Microsoft's implementation of DCE RPC. This upper layer is termed ORPC, since it is a protocol that supports object-oriented remote procedure calls. You might have guessed that the "O" in ORPC stands for Object.

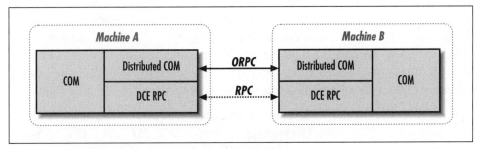

*Figure 2-2. Distributed COM is built on top of DCE RPC*

Simply put, DCOM allows developers to concentrate their efforts on developing the functionality of their applications, without the worries of data marshaling and network protocol management. DCOM provides this support for easy distribution of objects in the global cyberspace. Its accessibility is superb, because it is an integrated part of Windows NT, Windows 95, Windows 98, and future Windows platforms.* Soon, it will be supported on a variety of UNIX platforms; check out Software AG's "EntireX DCOM" product line at *http://www.sagus.com.*

This book tries to avoid making distinctions between COM and DCOM, because COM was designed from the beginning to support distributed objects. So at this point, the term DCOM refers specifically to the wire protocol that allows COM to break through the machine barriers. COM itself is a distributed technology. In fact, all legacy components can be widely distributed by adding a few configuration values. You may add these configuration values either by manually using the registry editor† or provided DCOM configuration tools.‡ So really, there shouldn't even

---

* You must install DCOM95 to use DCOM on Windows 95.

† There are two different registry editor tools on NT: *regedit.exe* and *regedt32.exe*. For NT, these tools are described in *Managing the Windows NT Registry* from O'Reilly & Associates.

‡ There are two COM tools that you must know: the DCOM configuration tool (*dcomcnfg.exe*) and the OLE Viewer tool (*oleview.exe*).

be a D in DCOM, but it's there for two possible reasons: stress the distributed notion or refer to the DCOM wire protocol.

# COM Facilities and Services

A distributed objects architecture needs to support a number of features that are commonly recognized as necessary. In this section, you'll learn some of the features that COM supports. We'll start off with the most obvious notion in distributed computing, location transparency. Then we'll connect one feature to the next, examining the importance of each. We'll finally end up with a brief introduction of applied COM. So buckle up and get started.

## Location Transparency

When a client invokes a method using COM, it thinks that the method is executed locally. But in fact, the method can be anywhere in cyberspace. It could live in the same process as the client, a different process on the same machine, or a process on a machine two hundred miles away. From the client's perspective, there's no difference. This is the idea behind location transparency.

Location transparency depends primarily upon marshaling. To support marshaling, COM uses a previous, proven technology known as DCE RPC.* DCE RPC supports location transparency in the functional world. COM, which is built on top of RPC, supports location transparency in the object-oriented world. Like RPC, COM uses an interface to define a set of related functions, which are used for client and server communications. Given an interface, we can use a tool, called the Microsoft Interface Definition Language (MIDL) compiler, to fully generate corresponding marshaling code. This marshaling code is also referred to as proxy/stub code.† In COM, each interface has an interface proxy and an interface stub. When a remote method invocation is made, possibly because the target object is two hundred miles away, these interface proxies and stubs will come to the rescue.

As the left side of Figure 2-3 shows, the client invokes a method as if the method exists in the current process. In reality, the interface proxy will intercept the call. Its job is to marshal the intelligent data into a raw buffer and send the raw buffer to the interface stub on whatever machine it may be, perhaps two hundred miles away. (The marshaled data sent over the network is shown as a dotted line in the figure.) When the interface stub receives the raw buffer, it unmarshals the buffer

---

* DCE RPC transfers data using Network Data Representation (NDR). NDR provides a common format for transferring data across heterogeneous machines that may represent data in different ways (e.g., 16-/32-bit, big/little endian, ASCII/EBCDIC).

† RPC uses the terms "client stubs" and "server stubs." The term "proxy" maps to "client stub" and "stub" maps to "server stub."

into a format that it can use to invoke the actual interface method in the target object. When the call returns to the interface stub, the interface stub marshals the return values into a raw buffer, and sends the buffer back to the interface proxy. After the interface proxy receives the raw buffer, it unmarshals the return data for the client.

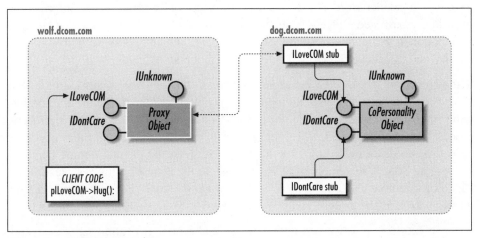

*Figure 2-3. Location transparency*

Location transparency conveys a number of benefits. It permits you to write the code that talks to a target object without worrying about where the object actually exists. The fact that objects can be located anywhere allows for greater flexibility and distribution. Location transparency also allows greater scalability and fault tolerance. For example, if an OCRServer is overloaded, you can easily and gradually add new ones, eventually forming a cluster of OCRServers. Then, you can build a simple broker or referral component to route clients to appropriate OCRServers. If a particular OCRServer fails, the world won't end. All you need to do, in this case, is refer the client to a different OCRServer.

## *Dynamic and Remote Object Activation*

In an RPC environment, a server must be started manually or during computer start up. It must also listen for requests on a specific port. With COM, servers don't have to be started manually, because the COM infrastructure supports dynamic object activation. In other words, COM will dynamically activate servers upon client requests. With COM, a server doesn't have to listen for client requests the way legacy servers do in a client/server environment.* COM handles this transparently.

---

\* What I've just described is true on Windows NT 4.0 and Windows 2000 but not on Windows 95 and Windows 98. On these platforms, servers must be started before its objects can handle remote client requests. Why? Because these platforms are ignorant when it comes to security. Thus, remote activation is prevented on Windows 95 and Windows 98 as a precaution.

The object worries only about the services it provides, and this is a clear separation of responsibility.

The COM Service Control Manager (SCM)*, which is not the same as the NT SCM, supports remote activation. It lives on every machine that supports COM. One of its missions is to locate and activate distributed objects dynamically upon client requests. It works in conjunction with the system registry, since information regarding distributed objects is recorded in the registry. In Windows 2000, this information is maintained by the COM+ catalog, which works with the system registry and the active directory to locate components.

If an object lives in a DLL on the same machine, COM will dynamically load the DLL for the client process that uses the object. If an object lives in a separate EXE on the same machine, COM requests its local SCM to activate the EXE, so that the client process can use the object. If an object lives in a remote machine, there needs to be some coordination. In this case, the local SCM on the client machine contacts the remote SCM. The remote SCM is responsible for activating the remote EXE or DLL. For a remote EXE, the remote SCM simply spawns it. For a remote DLL, the remote SCM activates a registered surrogate process† to dynamically load the DLL.

So there you have it. COM supports dynamic and remote activation seamlessly and transparently. This is a significant feature that allows you to command objects to come to life when you need them.

## *Security*

One of the most important attributes of a distributed system is security. COM supports *launch*, *access*, and *call-level* security. Launch security, which is also called activation security, determines who can launch or activate the server component, and thus protects the server machine. With this support, the server component can be launched only by users or groups that are given the rights to do so. Remember that any client anywhere in cyberspace can potentially activate COM servers, so it would be disastrous if COM lacked support for launch security.

At this point, assume that a client has launch permissions and has successfully launched a remote server. It's fine if a client meets the launch security requirement, but does the client have access to the component in question? Controlling access to a component, called access controls or access security, is the answer to this question, because it raises authorization to another level. Access controls allow the server component to limit user access to its objects, thereby protecting its objects from offenders.

---

* Pronounced: "scum."

† A user or setup program stores this information in the registry, like all other COM information.

Now assume that a client has met both the launch and access security requirements. In other words, you have successfully established a connection and conversation with your remote object. What do you do about sniffers in the wild cyberspace who are tailgating, analyzing, and possibly modifying your packets? Call-level security shown in Figure 2-4 goes a step further to put these offenders to rest. For each method call, you can adjust the degree of data protection by changing the authentication level of the method invocation. The are several authentication levels supported by COM, but for now focus on data integrity and data privacy.

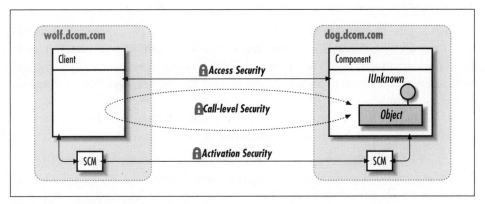

*Figure 2-4. COM security*

As data moves across the network, it can be potentially modified by attackers. To prevent this, COM offers data integrity in which every data packet floating through the net is required to hold authentication information. If the data has been modified during transmission, the call will fail. Note that data integrity only protects modification of data.

In addition to protecting data modification, COM offers data privacy to prevent attackers from spying on our data. This technique requires that every data packet be encrypted before it floats through the net, thus achieving the maximum data protection. However, it does much, much more than other data protection alternatives (authentication levels), so performance will drop significantly.

COM also supports impersonation. This feature allows the server to run under the security context of the user who activated or executed the client process—in other words, the server can do things that the rest of the system allows the client to do. All accesses that the object makes, after impersonating the client, will be restricted by the security context of the client user. After performing tasks in place of the client for the client, the object then reverts to its own security context.

For example, you have an NT service that runs in the system security context and contains a COM object. Although this service runs in the system security context, you don't want to use the system security context to perform work for your clients, because the system security context has enormous power. To solve this problem, you make use of COM's impersonation feature. Of course, your clients must first allow you, the server component, impersonation rights before this can happen.

On Windows NT 4.0, there's a drawback with impersonation, since COM uses Windows NT Lan Manager Authentication Protocol (NTLM). NTLM uses challenge/response authentication that prevents the server object from knowing the password of the client. This is great (because not knowing the password means good security), but if the server object uses some services from another remote object, that other object cannot impersonate the original client. Why?

To answer this question, look at what happens in challenge/response authentication. First, a client contacts a server object. The server object sends back a challenge packet to the client. The client uses its password to encrypt the packet and then sends the encrypted packet to the server. The server encrypts the original packet with the password of the user identifier that is recorded in its Security Accounts Manager (SAM) database. Once this is done, it compares the two packets. If the comparison test passes, then authentication is successful.*

Knowing how challenge/response works, we can answer why the second server component cannot impersonate the original client. The reason is that the original client didn't send a password to the first server component, via challenge/response authentication. Therefore, when the first server component communicates with another totally different server, impersonation will not work. Since the server doesn't have the password of the original client, it can't encrypt the challenge packet it receives from the second server component. And since challenge/response authentication will not work, impersonation chaining doesn't work with NTLM. See Figure 2-5. This type of impersonation chaining is called *delegation* and is supported by Kerberos† in Windows 2000. Multiple hops delegation is carried out through cloaking, which is discussed in the Chapter 5 section "Programmable Security." And if you are really adventurous, you can write your own SSP to support customized security.

## Interfaces

You always hear people say that it's best to separate interface from implementation. They're right, because doing this allows easier integration among different components. For instance, if I use a service that you provide, all I want to do is

---

* I made it sound like the client and server are doing all the work, but really it's the client NTLM Security Support Provider (SSP) and server NTLMSSP that are doing this work.

† Kerberos is a shared secret, ticketing-based authentication protocol. Kerberos tickets include expiration timestamps, so they will become invalid when expired.

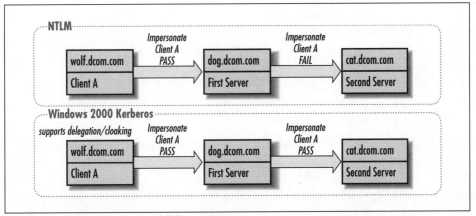

*Figure 2-5. Impersonation and delegation*

simply use your services via published interfaces. I don't care what you do underneath those interfaces, because I don't care about your implementation, so long as I get the services I need. Same idea applies to COM.

You can think of the COM interface as a contract you sign with the world regarding a provided service that you promise never will change. Each interface is unique in time and space, because it is assigned an interface identifier (IID), a 128-bit globally unique identifier (GUID).* This also means that version support is practically automatic, because each interface contains an identifier that is universally unique.

Interfaces are defined using MIDL, which is based on DCE IDL. MIDL is critical to COM because it defines the classes your library supports, the interfaces these classes support, and the methods offered by these interfaces. Typically, a COM object includes a number of well-defined and unalterable interfaces.

In COM, all interfaces must be derived from a special interface called *IUnknown*. This interface is required to support the fundamentals of a robust and changing component, and it includes three extremely important methods: *QueryInterface*, *AddRef*, and *Release*. Clients call *QueryInterface* to dynamically discover other interfaces supported by an object, while *AddRef* and *Release* are used for management of an object's life cycle.

## Lifetime Support and Dynamic Discovery

One of the most important aspects of an object is its life cycle, because objects must be correctly created and destroyed. This can get nasty in a distributed environment,

---

* This is the Microsoft alias for DCE RPC's Universally Unique Identifier (UUID).

as a distributed object may be used by many remote clients at any time. If the object is not currently in use, it should be deactivated to release resources. You've seen earlier that COM helps activate a remote object, but does it help deactivate it? Unfortunately, it doesn't, because it doesn't know about our object's internal details, specifically how many clients are currently using your object. No client can deactivate the object either, because no client knows the object's internal implementation. That leaves you with the object itself. Assuming that the object would commit suicide, when would be the right time?

COM supports object lifetime management via the use of a reference count. Typically, an object keeps a count of all its clients. Each time a client asks to use an object's interface, the object's reference count is incremented (via *IUnknown::AddRef*). When a client releases the interface, the reference count is decremented (via *IUnknown::Release*). As soon as the reference count becomes zero, the object automatically cleans up and destroys itself.

In the effort to support lifetime management, clients and objects can exchange millions of calls to *AddRef* and *Release*. This can seriously jam the network. COM optimizes this by using a special version of the *IUnknown* interface, known as *IRemUnknown.** A client can call *IUnknown::Release* as many times as it wants, and the calls will not be transmitted to the remote object. The last call to *IUnknown::Release* will force the one and only *IRemUnknown::RemRelease* call to the remote machine, therein minimizing network traffic.

Recall that *IUnknown* also supports the *QueryInterface* method. *QueryInterface* allows a client to dynamically discover other services a particular object provides. Assuming that a client has an interface pointer to an object, it can dynamically and robustly query for another interface from the object. If the object supports such service, the client can proceed to use the requested interface. If not, the client can recover gracefully when object rejects the query.

This facility is great for version support. For example, a client can ask a *SportsCar* object for an *IAccelerate2* interface. If the object supports it, the client can use the *IAccelerate2* interface for quicker acceleration. However, if the object replies it doesn't support the *IAccelerate2* interface, the client can revert to using the original *IAccelerate* interface, knowing that *IAccelerate2* is not supported. As shown by the left side of Figure 2-6, since version 2 of *SportsCar* is not supported on Machine A, client B can gracefully use version 1. On the other hand, since version 2 of *SportsCar* is supported on Machine B, Client B can take advantage of the newer version.

---

* The *IRemUnknown* interface is exposed by a special object called an "OXID object," discussed in Chapter 5.

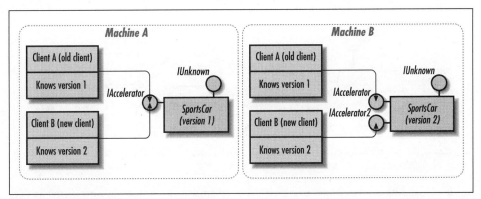

*Figure 2-6. COM solves version problems*

Like *RemRelease*, there is also an *IRemUnknown::RemQueryInterface*. *RemQueryInterface* provides performance improvement in a distributed environment, as it can retrieve an array of interfaces with a single network round-trip.

## Binary Interoperability

Binary interoperability is an important aspect of software reuse. As stated earlier in the text, in the old days when you deployed a development library, you had to ship header and library files. Your customers had to link your library into their system in order for the system to work. With the advent of component technology, you need to ship only your binary. Your customers no longer see header files or need to link with your libraries. Not only does binary interoperability make software integration easier, it allows the development and integration of plug-in components.

In COM, binary interoperability is achieved, believe it or not, by the use of interfaces. Each interface has a binary signature, via the use of a `vtbl` (table of function pointers) and `vptr` (pointer to a vtbl), as shown in Figure 2-7. To use an object, we must first acquire an interface pointer. The interface pointer points to the `vptr`, which points to the `vtbl`. Each instantiated object has a `vptr`, but there's a single `vtbl` per class. Once we get to the `vtbl`, we can find the resulting function. This `vptr/vtbl` technique is commonly used by C++ compilers to provide support for dynamic binding or polymorphism, and it is used here for binary interoperability.

The extra levels of indirection has a powerful benefit for flexibility in languages. Any language or tool with a facility to support a notion of a pointer/reference can interoperate with COM objects.

## Connection Management

Connection management is important in a distributed environment. Normally, a client doesn't have to worry about connection management. For example, assume

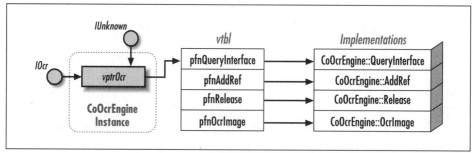

*Figure 2-7. COM binary specification*

that a client has successfully established a connection with an object in a server component. If a client invokes a method and it doesn't get a response, it can assume that the server component is dead. It is easy for a client to detect the liveliness of its server component, but the reverse (i.e., a server component detecting the liveliness of its clients) is much more difficult.

Simple connection management relies on the object lifetime management discussed earlier. An object keeps virtual connections to its client as long as there is at least one reference to it. In other words, if the reference count is greater than zero, the object can assume that its clients are alive. Unfortunately, this assumption does not always work. For example, if a client has crashed and failed to release a reference to an interface in the object, the object will never release its resources. To fix this problem, COM supports connection management via a simple paranoia check. It requires a client to send a small packet to the server indicating that it's alive, a technique that we call a *ping*.

A client constantly pings its objects. If an object has not heard a ping within a given time-out, the object can assume that its client has died. This method works fine in theory; however, a distributed environment can potentially consist of millions of objects—and the more objects, the more pings. You can easily see that it doesn't take long to hog the network. Therefore, COM actually uses something called *delta pings* in order to reduce network traffic. Basically, instead of pinging the object, COM intelligently pings the machine.

Every COM machine runs a special coordinator/manager called an OXID Resolver. Pings are coordinated by the OXID Resolvers on every machine. The server-side OXID Resolver listens for pings from a client-side OXID Resolver. The client-side OXID Resolver groups together all pings for a particular machine. This grouping is called a ping set and is represented by a dynamically generated ping set identifier (SETID). With this grouping, the client-side OXID Resolver can send the server-side OXID Resolver one ping message, which may represent hundreds of simple client-to-object pings, thereby reducing network traffic jams. To further improve performance, COM periodically sends only the changes (deltas) in these groupings. If the server-side OXID Resolver has not received a ping for a particular object after three ping periods (2 minutes each), COM will assume that the client has died and will perform g:arbage collection to clean off dangling references.

## Concurrency Management

The concept of distributed computing is great, because everyone can develop objects and share them with the world. A typical distributed system nicely separates interface from implementation. As long as the world can agree on published contracts (interfaces), everyone is happy. This implies that you are at liberty to do whatever you wish under those contracts; for example, you may develop very sophisticated software by taking advantage of multithreading and by making your objects thread-safe. Other developers may not want to bother with the complexity of thread synchronization and management, as they have more important things to do. Their software will then be thread-ignorant. When you consider the seamless binary interoperability aspect of COM, you'd definitely want to make use of a software component that's already been developed and fully tested. You don't know whether that specific software is thread-safe or ignorant. The good thing is you don't have to, as those are implementation details. Every software component should work together, because they agree on published contracts.

Since no one cares about others' implementations, the distributed infrastructure itself has to support these differences. So it's crucial for COM to provide a facility for concurrency management. COM separates objects with different concurrency semantics into distinct execution contexts, called *apartments*. An object comes into life, lives, and dies within its apartment, and to use this object in a different apartment, you must marshal it across.* Marshaling implies that the importing apartment will deal with a proxy object, not the original object. This proxy object lives inside the importing apartment and shares the same concurrency semantics as its client code.

COM provides a number of different threading and concurrency models to support heterogeneous component software development. Two notable threading models, which will be discussed in Chapter 5, include the single-threaded apartment (STA) and multi-threaded apartment (MTA) models.

## Reuse

Reuse is a goal in every software shop. In a typical object-oriented environment, reuse is supported via implementation inheritance, but COM doesn't currently provide this type of reuse. Recall that implementation inheritance can be

---

* Technically, you *marshal an interface* across apartments (i.e., execution contexts). At this point, we use the word "object" to keep the discussion simple.

dangerous, because the derived method has to know about the base method's implementation.

What COM currently supports is containment and aggregation as shown in Figure 2-8. As a traditional and simple technique for reuse, containment allows you to hide the reused object behind the object you are developing. You then publish a number of pass-through or proxy methods to allow your clients to use the services of the hidden object. When your clients call these pass-through methods, you simply delegate the calls to the contained object that you are reusing.

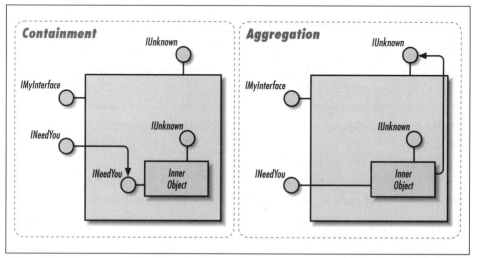

*Figure 2-8. Containment vs. Aggregation*

A second way to implement reuse is aggregation. Aggregation allows you to expose the interfaces of the reused object as if they were your own. To aggregate, your object must pass its *IUnknown* pointer to the reused object, so that lifetime management will work correctly. Because of this requirement, not all objects can be aggregated.

## Interface Repository

To make reuse and integration easier, a distributed object's environment must provide a way for clients to discover objects and their supported interfaces. In COM, an object's type information is stored in detail within interface repositories, called *type libraries*. A type library stores everything about its objects and their supported services. Traditionally, a type library is a separate binary file with a *.tlb* extension. However, it is so useful that some components merge this type information right into the shipped binary (i.e., DLL, OCX, etc.). This is a convenience in terms of administration since managing one file is easier than managing two or more.

An application can dynamically use services of any COM object that exposes its type information in a type library. Furthermore, type libraries allow development environments such as the Visual Studio to generate C++ wrapper classes for COM interfaces. A development environment can do this, because all information regarding a particular component is explicitly recorded in the type library. Here's one very appealing reason to provide a type library: if you deploy a type library instead of a C++ header file when you sell your component, every developer (C++, Visual J++, Visual Basic, etc.) can use your component—not just C++ developers.

## Implementation Repository

We now know how to get information regarding a component, but we have yet to find out where the component resides. In a distributed object's environment, an implementation repository stores the location of an object's implementation. COM supports this notion via the registry. The COM SCM uses the location of a particular implementation recorded in the registry to dynamically activate objects.

On the client side, the SCM looks into the registry to determine where the remote component resides. It then contacts the remote SCM on the server computer. The remote SCM looks into its local registry to obtain the exact location of the component, so that it can activate the component. Of course, if you are not using remote activation, the local SCM is responsible for locating and activating the component locally; that is, it doesn't contact a remote SCM.

COM provides better support for implementation repositories in Windows 2000. On this platform, an implementation repository can support a whole group of users, technically called an *organizational unit*. This repository is called the *active directory*. A registry serves as a local implementation repository and an active directory serves as an enterprise implementation repository.

There are advantages to the active directory. If a component is not registered in the local implementation repository, COM will automatically reference the active directory and dynamically pull down the target component. The active directory allows an administrator to push new components up to the active directory once, but COM will automatically pull a component down to the local workstation as many times as necessary. Say bye-bye to version problems.

## Static Invocation

Static invocation is a fancy term for a simple function call. A static invocation requires the method and its signature to be known at compile time, so that a compiler can enforce some restrictions on the way you call the method.

There are several techniques for static invocations in COM. The first and simplest is directly calling a method via an interface pointer. This is called *vtbl binding* and it allows interface methods to be called via a `vtbl`. This type of invocation indirectly refers to the actual method, because you can follow the interface pointer to the `vptr` to the `vtbl`, which contains pointers to actual methods. This technique is also called *very early binding* and gives the most performance gain. However, here's the drawback: in order to perform static invocation, you must know the specification of the interface during compile time, and compile the header file into your application.

Another method of static invocation is via the use of type libraries and a special interface called a *dispatch interface* (*IDispatch*). The type library contains a magic number called a *dispatch identifier* (`dispid`) that aliases an actual method in the dispatch interface. So, to call the method, use the `dispid`. This method is called *early binding* or *ID binding*. The advantage: tools can reverse engineer the type information stored in a type library to generate compatible language bindings. For example, Visual Studio can generate corresponding C++ wrapper classes from this information. The disadvantage: it's slower than `vtbl` binding, and you are forced to use Automation compatible types (discussed in Chapter 3).

COM also supports dual interfaces that permit both *IDispatch* and `vtbl` invocations. A dual interface is the best of both worlds, as it allows you to use *IDispatch* for better integration (e.g., VBScript likes *IDispatch*) and use `vtbl` binding for performance.

## Dynamic Invocation

This method of invocation is more frequently called *late binding*. In COM, dynamic invocation is called Automation and is supported by *IDispatch*. COM objects can be dynamically invoked and discovered through the *IDispatch* interface, but dynamic invocation is expensive since it requires a lookup operation. In this expensive operation, a method or property name is given in exchange for an associated `dispid`. After the lookup, the desired method can be invoked using this magic `dispid`.

This technique allows for dynamic method invocation and is the most flexible type of binding, but imposes a performance impact through the lookup operation. However, dynamic method invocation means a client can use a component even without access to a component's type library. That means remarkably easy component integration and reuse, because applications don't have to know about a particular COM object at compile time. Assuming that the object supports late binding, client applications can dynamically use the object at runtime time. For example, if you write a client application that uses late binding to manipulate COM objects, your application will be able to manipulate COM objects written two years from now. In fact, late binding allows scripting languages, like VBScript, JScript, and your client application to easily use COM objects that expose the *IDispatch* interface.

## Events

One extremely important aspect of a distributed computing environment is the ability for objects to notify one another when a specific event has occurred. This type of event notification helps other objects decide what actions they need to take.

For example, in a workflow environment, after an object processes a specific document and returns it to the workflow manager, the workflow manager decides where to route the document next. When it has determined the next destination, it *fires* an event to a number of potential target workflow clients. The first client that responds to this event gets a crack at the document.

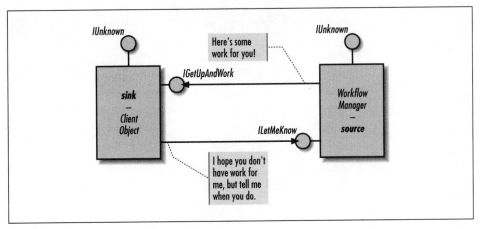

*Figure 2-9. Event notification in COM*

Events are of paramount importance in a distributed architecture. COM supports events via a concept called connection points, which requires two collaborators: *sources* and *sinks*. Clients (sinks) interested in capturing specific events must advise their objects (sources) of such intentions. Sources throw, or fire, events to their registered sinks. See Figure 2-9.

# Applying COM

This chapter lists only the services that are important for a distributed system. Your job is to apply and extend COM, by adding new interfaces, which are essentially immutable contracts. Make the contracts public, and the whole world can share them. In a sense, these interfaces are immortal. Everyone can communicate with them, like universal languages.

Let's quickly run through a few of the important standard interfaces that Microsoft has provided. Dynamic invocation is supported by the *IDispatch* interface, and event notification is supported by the *IConnectionPoint* family of interfaces. If you look further, there is the *IPersist* family of interfaces, which supports distributed object persistence. There is also the *IMoniker* family of interfaces that supports a smart aliasing, that allow a client to dynamically connect to the object to which the moniker refers. For uniform data transfer, use the *IDataObject* interface. And if you're looking for transaction support, check out Microsoft Transaction Server (MTS).

An interface is just a specification, because there's no implementation attached to it. Any COM object can implement these published interfaces to actually provide the corresponding services. In Chapter 3, you'll learn how to specify interfaces and implement them in our COM objects.

In this chapter:
• Interfaces
• Objects
• Class Factories

# 3

# Objects

Having gone through a general overview of COM in the last chapter, you now will get intimate with it. First, let's get one thing straight. COM is nothing new because it builds purely on top of proven successful software technologies, including object-oriented and distributed computing technologies. These technologies thoroughly separate interface from implementation. Everyone who has any exposure to encapsulation and software layering can more or less relate to COM.

 The interface definitions and C++ code that you see in this chapter can be automated by Visual C++ and the ATL wizards with a few mouse clicks. Even so, it's important for you to see what's going on in the code and not just rely on clicking a few buttons. You can't understand what choices to make from the wizards until you know how to create a COM object from scratch. Moreover, performance is heavily affected by the choices that you make. Consider the information in this chapter (and in Chapters 4 and 5), the internals of the wizard-generated code that is presented in Chapter 6, and onwards. In short, you'll be empowered with the knowledge gained from Chapters 3 through 6.

Similar to other programming disciplines, the basics of COM include three things: COM interfaces, COM objects, and COM class factories.* For brevity, we usually leave off the word COM and simply say interfaces, objects, and class factories. In COM programming, an interface contains a number of related methods, an object implements a number of interfaces, and a class factory is a special COM object that creates or instantiates other COM objects.

---

* Apartments are also a fundamental of COM and are discussed further in Chapter 5.

We'll take the bottom-up approach to learning the basics of COM. This means that you should read this chapter in order, because each section builds on top of the previous. Each section is crucial in the process of learning COM. As you read, you may feel that there are missing elements in each section, but your questions will be answered in subsequent sections. You will gain the basics of creating COM objects by the time you finish this chapter. Let the knowledge sink in and review the relevant sections in this chapter as needed when you're actually developing your distributed components. Here's an outline of what you'll learn in this chapter.

1. Interfaces—Real world distributed computing starts with the interface definition process. You'll learn how to specify interfaces according to the rules of COM. Once an interface has been specified, you'll learn how to build its associated marshaling code, so that you can later distribute your objects. You'll also examine the binary interface layout required by COM and learn several colloquial interface terminologies.

2. Objects—You'll learn how to assemble an object from a number of interface implementations. An object can implement one or more previously-specified interfaces, but it must implement at least the *IUnknown* interface. The *IUnknown* interface is the bedrock of a COM object, and it's the soul of COM's sacred rules for object identity, interface negotiation, and lifetime management.

3. Factories—In C++, you create an instance of a C++ class that is also referred to as a C++ object. This metaphor is similar in COM. In COM, you create an instance of a COM class that is referred to as a COM object. To push encapsulation to its limits, COM doesn't offer a client component a direct way to instantiate instances of a COM class whose implementation is maintained by a remote server component. So the client component must ask the COM infrastructure for help. The COM infrastructure works with special COM objects called *class factories*, which are exposed by the server component, in order to carry out distributed object instantiation. A class factory is so named because it manufactures objects. You'll learn two different types of factories: standard and custom.

Interfaces, objects, and factories are three fundamental elements that you must understand in order to develop distributed COM objects. Notations shown in Figure 3-1 illustrate these three elements throughout this book.

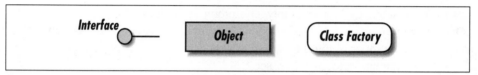

*Figure 3-1. Interface, object, and factory notations used in this book*

This chapter discusses the theory involved in developing COM objects. You need to put the code for these objects into a dynamic linked library (DLL) or an executable (EXE) before others can use them. We call these DLLs or EXEs *COM components*. Components will be discussed in Chapter 4, so logically, you must read Chapter 4 after this chapter if you want to build a complete distributed application.

---

## Checklist for Creating a COM Object

Creating Interfaces and Objects (required)

- Define custom interfaces using MIDL scripts.
- Generate C++ header files and marshaling code using the MIDL compiler.
- When implementing your COM object, choose either the nesting or inheritance technique.
- Implement (code) the interfaces.
- Follow the identity rules to write the *IUnknown::QueryInterface* method.
- Follow the lifetime rules to write the *IUnknown::AddRef* and *IUnknown::Release* methods.
- Implement your own interface methods.

Creating a Class Factory (required)

- Decide whether you want to expose a custom or standard factory interface.
- For a standard factory interface, implement the *CreateInstance* and *LockServer* methods.

Optional

- If you need to support dynamic invocation, implement the *IDispatch* interface.
- If you wish to support any other custom or standard interfaces, implement them.

Once you have checked all items on this list, you are ready to put your COM object into a component. You'll learn how to do this in Chapter 4.

---

There is a lot to learn in this chapter. Some of the fundamentals that you will learn in this chapter are optional in creating a COM object. However, they are important to understand when you run across these optional items when you develop your own or use other's COM objects. See the "Checklist for Creating a COM Object" sidebar for a checklist that lists the required and optional steps involved in creating a COM object. This checklist serves as a roadmap in case you feel lost anywhere in this chapter.

# Interfaces

COM strictly separates interface from implementation. An interface that you specify says nothing about its implementation details. Once published, developers can implement your interface however they want, using whatever language or platform they desire. In other words, an interface specification is implementation, language, and platform independent. It is, therefore, the basic unit that supports universal interoperability and location transparency in COM. As such, interfaces are the first requirement for distributed objects.

Distributed objects can live anywhere in cyberspace. In order to send messages to one another, they must know, at a contractual level, the kinds of messages they can send. In COM, you can specify the details of these messages using interfaces. An interface is a group of related functions that forms a logical set of functionality.

For example, say you have an extremely powerful optical character recognition (OCR) engine, which can read characters at a rate of 100 pages per minute and with a 99.9 percent accuracy. In order to allow the world to use this precious power in a distributed environment, you need to provide your service by exposing an interface, which I'll call *IOcr*. *IOcr* supports a number of related functions, including *OcrImage* to obtain text for a given image and *OcrZone* to obtain text for a selected rectangle of an image. These two functions are related, which is why they're grouped together under a single interface, *IOcr*. By convention, interfaces are prefixed with an uppercase I, and it is pictorially represented by a "lollipop," as shown in Figure 3-2. For brevity, interface methods are never shown in COM object diagrams.

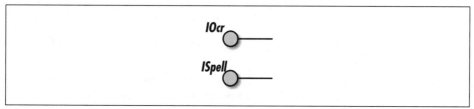

*Figure 3-2. Two COM interfaces, each pictorially represented by a "lollipop"*

Each interface that you specify is a contract, and you sign this contract with the world and with COM. To help you through this process, Microsoft provides a special language (MIDL) and a compiler specifically designed to create such contracts, MIDL and the MIDL compiler. The contract creation or interface specification process is simple. By using MIDL, you specify all your interfaces, classes, and type information in an interface definition language (IDL) file. Once this is done, you use the MIDL compiler to generate a number of files, which are necessary for distributing objects across the global cyberspace.

In this section, you'll learn all about interfaces. You'll start off with the ubiquitous *IUnknown*, and then you'll learn how to specify custom interfaces. You'll also use the MIDL and C/C++ compilers to generate interface marshalers, which will allow a wide distribution of your objects. This section concludes with the *IDispatch* interface, which is an optional, but important, interface in COM.

## IUnknown

*IUnknown* is the root of all interfaces in COM. The COM Specification requires that all COM compatible interfaces be derivatives of *IUnknown* for two extremely important reasons. The first is dynamic discoverability.* Recall that one of the goals of COM is black-box interoperability. A client can use only an object's published interfaces, as the object's implementation is totally hidden. Therefore, there needs to be a facility to allow dynamic discovery of interfaces.

A COM object can support a number of interfaces, each of which supports a special service the object provides. If you have a pointer to one of the interfaces exposed by the object, you should be able to query for other services provided by the object. For example, let's assume that you know only of the *IOcr* interface supported by the OCR engine. Then say further that you have a pointer to such an interface. Using this interface pointer, you can query for other services the OCR engine object furnishes. In other words, COM provides a robust way to guess or discover other supplied services within a COM object.

Here's the code snippet that demonstrates dynamic discovery of interfaces using the *QueryInterface* method of *IUnknown*. As shown later, you ask, using the *QueryInterface* method, whether the OCR engine COM object supports an *ICasino* interface, which is represented by `IID_ICasino`. Remember, to you, the OCR engine is just a black box. You don't know if this object supports the *ICasino* interface, but it doesn't hurt much to ask. (Who knows? Luck may strike and you'll hit the jackpot.) If the *ICasino* interface is not supported, then you didn't lose anything but some CPU cycles and possibly some network packets. This technique is robust because it allows the client to healthily recover after a failure; that is, if the requested interface is not supported, the client doesn't use it.

```
extern IOcr *p; ICasino *pCasino=NULL;

// Dynamically discover the ICasino interface.
// We may be dealing with an OCR engine, but maybe
// it's got an ICasino interface.  Maybe not,
```

---

\* Another important reason deals with an object identity, which will be discussed in the "Objects" section of this chapter.

```
// but it doesn't hurt much to ask.
// Let's take a gamble and hope we'll hit the jackpot.
HRESULT hr = p->QueryInterface(IID_ICasino,
                               reinterpret_cast<void**>(&pCasino));
if (SUCCEEDED(hr)) {
    // Yes! The object supports the ICasino interface.
    // Of course, we now know what to do.
    hr = pCasino->HitTheJackpotAndRun();
    ...
}
```

By the same token, you can use this *QueryInterface* technique to robustly query different versions of supported interfaces. As you can see in the following code snippet, dynamic discovery allows you to safely select the version you want. Specifically, you ask the object for a newer interface before calling the *Oui* method, which is only supported by the new interface. If the object doesn't support the new interface, then you know you cannot call the *Oui* method; you can only call methods supported by the old interface.

```
extern IOldVersion *p; INewVersion *pNewVersion=NULL;

// Ask whether object supports the INewVersion interface
HRESULT hr = p->QueryInterface(IID_INewVersion,
                               reinterpret_cast<void**>(&pNewVersion));
if (SUCCEEDED(hr)) {
    // Use the new version, which supports the Oui method
    hr = pNewVersion->Oui();
    ...
} else {
    // Use the old version, which doesn't support the Oui method
    hr = p->Non();
}
```

Traditional software doesn't provide a standard way to perform this type of interface negotiation. In traditional software development, if you call the *Oui* method and don't have the new version of the DLL, your code will crash. However, in COM, your code will not crash because you must ask before you use it.

The second reason for the *IUnknown* requirement is lifetime management. In a distributed system, there needs to be a reliable way to manage an object's life cycle. In traditional programming techniques, we typically allocate an object, use it, and delete it. We commonly do this by using *static (global) objects*, *stack-based objects*, and *heap-based objects*. Static objects are typically constructed upon program execution and automatically destructed when execution ends. Stack-based objects are automatic objects, constructed in a local scope and destructed when the scope ends. Heap-based objects are allocated and de-allocated explicitly using operator new and operator delete. These are simple rules that must be kept in mind when using C++.

# C++ Casting Operators

We all know the power or evilness of the C-style cast, which allows us to cast a given type to practically any other type that we want. For example, we can cast a human into an ant. This can be extremely dangerous, because it can create uncontrollable and error-prone software. To mitigate casting problems, C++ allows us to specifically indicate the kind of cast that we want to apply. Check with compiler documentation for the details of these C++ casting operators. In a nutshell, here they are and their short meanings.

`dynamic_cast`
> Used to convert polymorphic types. Runtime checks will be made to ensure the validity of the cast. If the cast is not safe, a `bad_cast` exception will be thrown.

`static_cast`
> Used to convert nonpolymorphic types. No runtime check is involved.

`const_cast`
> Used to cast away const-ness and volatile-ness of an object.

`reinterpret_cast`
> Used to cast any pointer or integral type into another pointer or integral type. This is the most flexible and the most dangerous of the C++ casting operators, second only to the traditional C casting operator.

In the old days, we would do the following to cast a double pointer into a `void**`:

```
(void**)(&pSome)
```

If we wanted to use the C++ casting operators, we would write the above code as follows:

```
reinterpret_cast<void**>(&pSome)
```

The syntax of the other C++ casting operators follows the same pattern as `reinterpret_cast`.

---

However, things aren't that straightforward in a distributed environment. For example, assuming that 100 clients can use a COM object, would you rather let one object service the 100 clients or create 100 objects, each servicing a client? One compelling reason for rejecting the latter is that creating 100 objects can be a resource hog on any machine. On the other hand, if you rather let one object service all 100 clients, when should the object be destroyed?

COM solves this problem using a simple lifetime management technique, by maintaining reference counts.* An object increments its reference count as it hands off interfaces to clients. To complement that, a client must notify the object that it has finished using an interface, so that the object can decrement its reference count. This implies that the client indirectly participates in the management of an object's lifetime.†

## *Microsoft Interface Definition Language*

Now that you're familiar with *IUnknown*, we can take a closer look at the scripting language MIDL.‡ MIDL allows you to specify in detail all user-defined types, interfaces, and methods that you intend to use remotely. In addition, it allows you to specify exactly the interfaces your COM object exposes. And for diverse interoperability, it permits you to define a type library, which is an interface repository that contains detailed type information (or metadata) of your distributed objects and their interfaces. MIDL is the language we use to publish our contracts (interfaces) to the world.

### *MIDL basics*

MIDL provides a C-like syntax, so if you know C, you will definitely feel at home with MIDL. The only thing that would be new to you is the notion of *attributes*. The characteristics of all data, methods, interfaces, classes, and libraries are described by attributes. Attributes are enclosed within brackets (e.g., [attr1, attr2...]), and they prefix the data they describe.

For example, the following MIDL snippet says that **age** is an input to the *SetAge* method, because it is being described by the [in] attribute:

```
HRESULT SetAge([in] short age);
```

As you can see, the syntax of the *SetAge* function prototype is equivalent to a function prototype in the C language. The only thing that is different is the [in] attribute. This attribute is important because it tells the MIDL compiler to generate the code to marshal the data only from the client to the object. There is no need to marshal the same data back to the client since the data is an input.

Because you're able to specify that **age** is an input, you've just saved a few bytes that don't need to travel from the object back to the client. In this regard, attributes

---

* Components, objects, and interfaces can all maintain their own reference counts. However, these are implementation details that clients should not care about.

† There are special rules to *QueryInterface*, *AddRef*, and *Release*, but these will be discussed later in this chapter.

‡ MIDL is based on OSF DCE IDL, which allows specifications for remote procedure calls. MIDL extends IDL to support COM. COM doesn't require that you use MIDL to specify interfaces, because you can specify interfaces by hand using C/C++. However, MIDL makes life simpler for you, because it generates the necessary files for distributing objects (i.e., type library, C/C++ header files, and interface marshalers).

specify the semantics of your parameters, methods, and interfaces so they will be tuned in a distributed environment.

Here's another example: you can specify that you want a piece of data to flow from the object back to the client by using the [out] attribute:

```
HRESULT GetAge([out] short *age);
```

As you can see, there is no need to waste network bandwidth when you call this function. The requested **age** should only be sent back to the client upon the return of this function.

When the data needs to flow in both directions, you use the [in, out] attribute, as follows:

```
HRESULT ChangeAge([in, out] short *age);
```

Notice that **age** is being described by two attributes to obtain the precise semantics. You can apply many attributes to parameters, methods, and interfaces in MIDL to get the meanings you want.

There are a large number of attributes in MIDL. However, this book discusses only the necessary elements of MIDL that allow you to define your custom interfaces, so it won't delve deeply into the details of MIDL. Refer to the MIDL Language Reference, part of the SDK documentation, for the details of MIDL.

### Defining a custom interface using MIDL

Now dive in and create your *IOcr* interface specification using this scripting language. You may use a simple text editor to create the following script for your *IOcr* interface:

```
// Include the specification of the IUnknown interface
import "unknwn.idl";

[ object, uuid(D9F23D61-A647-11d1-ABCD-00207810D5FE) ]
interface IOcr : IUnknown
{
    . . .
}
```

Notice that the *IOcr* interface has two attributes that describe it. The first is [object], which specifies that the *IOcr* interface is a COM interface. If you leave this attribute off, the *IOcr* interface will be a simple Microsoft RPC (MS RPC) interface. The [object] attribute is extremely important because without it, the marshaling code that is generated will not be compatible to that of standard marshaling provided by the COM library (runtime).

The second attribute you see is the declaration of the universally unique identifier (UUID) of this interface. This is the static and unique interface identifier (IID) of the *IOcr* interface. It is a machine-generated number that is unique across time and space. Since there is a potential for millions of interfaces to be generated at the same time, there is a potential for two developers to name their interfaces *IOcr*, resulting is a name clash. For example, *IOcr* represents "optical character recognition" to us, but someone else can use *IOcr* to represent "online credit report." A UUID helps solve this problem, since it's a huge 128-bit number, generated using mainly a machine unique identifier, NIC address, and the current time. Specifically, our *IOcr* interface's UUID is [D9F23D61-A647-11d1-ABCD-00207810D5FE]. As you see, an interface has two names: a logical name (*IOcr*), which does not have to be unique, and a physical name [D9F23D61-A647-11d1-ABCD-00207810D5FE], which has to be unique.

There are two common ways to generate a UUID. You generate a UUID by using the GUID generator (*guidgen.exe*). Simply execute this tool and copy the generated UUID to your source code. In the rare case that you need to dynamically generate a UUID in your programs, you use the following COM API function:

```
HRESULT CoCreateGuid(GUID *pguid);  // Returns a GUID
```

Clearly from the previous discussion, every COM interface must include, at least, the `[object]` and `[uuid]` attributes. The former tells the MIDL compiler to generate the correct interface proxy/stub code and the latter uniquely identifies an interface.

### Examining the attributes of IUnknown

You might have noticed that *IOcr* is derived from *IUnknown*, an interface that all COM compliant interfaces must extend. The *IOcr* interface definition complies with this requirement. Before delving further into the *IOcr* interface, study the specification of the ubiquitous *IUnknown* interface so you really get to know *IUnknown*, and take advantage of this opportunity to learn a little more about MIDL. Shown here is the interface specification for *IUnknown*:

```
[ local, object,
  uuid(00000000-0000-0000-C000-000000000046),  // UUID of IUnknown
  pointer_default(unique) ]
interface IUnknown
{
   typedef [unique] IUnknown *LPUNKNOWN;

   cpp_quote("//////////////////////////////////////////////////////////////")
   cpp_quote("// IID_IUnknown and all other system IIDs are provided in UUID. LIB")
   cpp_quote("// Link that library in with your proxies, clients and servers")
   cpp_quote("//////////////////////////////////////////////////////////////")

   HRESULT QueryInterface([in] REFIID riid,
                             [out, iid_is(riid)] void **ppvObject);
      ULONG AddRef();
      ULONG Release();
   }
```

As you can see, the *IUnknown* interface is a root interface, because it doesn't derive from anything. It is a COM compliant interface, since it's described with the `[object]` and `[uuid]` attributes. The `[local]` attribute, which can modify a function or interface, tells the MIDL compiler to prevent the generation of an interface proxy and stub, the code to marshal the interface across the network. Since there's no proxy or stub, the methods in the *IUnknown* interface cannot be called remotely.[*]

The *IUnknown* interface also has the `[pointer_default()]` attribute, which sets the default pointer attribute for all embedded pointers that have not been explicitly qualified. *Embedded pointers* include member pointers of structures, unions, and arrays. In contrast, the term *top-level pointer* is used to refer to pointers that appear in parameter lists. For example, a pointer to a structure is a top-level pointer whereas a member pointer within the structure is called an embedded pointer, as shown in the following MIDL snippet:

```
[ object, uuid(...), pointer_default(unique) ]
interface IWantYouToShowMeEmbeddedAndTopLevelPointers
{
    struct TopLevel {
        // An embedded pointer, affected by pointer_default(unique),
        // and thus, implicitly a unique pointer.
        short *m_pEmbeddedPointer;

        // An embedded pointer, which is explicitly qualified,
        // and thus, unaffected by pointer_default(unique).
        [ref] short *m_pExplicitlyQualifiedPointer;
    };

    // pTopLevelPointer is a top-level pointer, and therefore,
    // unaffected by pointer_default(unique).
    // Note: Even though unaffected,
    // the default mode is [unique], unless explicitly qualified.
    // Therefore, pTopLevelPointer is implicitly a [unique] pointer.
    HRESULT TopLevelPointer([out] TopLevel *pTopLevelPointer);
}
```

The default pointer attribute for all pointers within an interface specification is whatever appears between the parentheses within the expression: `[pointer_default(unique)]`. In this case, `[unique]` is the default pointer attribute for all embedded pointers within the interface. This means that all embedded pointers will be implicitly regarded as `[unique]` pointers. But what is a `[unique]` pointer? Let's answer this question by examining the three types of pointers supported by MS RPC:

- `[ref]` pointers are reference pointers and can never be NULL.

- `[unique]` pointers are simple pointers that can be NULL. However, the proxy doesn't provide any support for duplicate pointer detection. For example, if

---

[*] The remote version of this interface is called *IRemUnknown*, which will be discussed in Chapter 5.

ptr1 and ptr2 both point to the same data, two copies of that data is sent to the remote object. This is the default pointer type for all pointers that are not explicitly qualified.

- [ptr] pointers are full pointers. These pointers provide the closest semantic equivalence to pointers in the C language. In this case, the proxy supports duplicate pointer detection. For example, if ptr1 and ptr2 both point to the same data, only one copy of that data is sent to the remote object. With full pointers, you send less data, but the duplicate checking can be very expensive.

Now if you refer back to the interface definition of *IUnknown*, you'll see a simple C-style typedef (also shown below for convenience). This essentially needs no discussion, except for acknowledging the fact that the pointer is explicitly qualified as a [unique] pointer.

```
typedef [unique] IUnknown *LPUNKNOWN;
```

Next, see the four lines starting with the cpp_quote keyword. This keyword directs the MIDL compiler to spit out the qualified string into the generated header file. Specifically, these four lines will produce C++ comments in the header file that the MIDL compiler will generate:

```
cpp_quote("////////////////////////////////////////////////////////////////")
cpp_quote("// IID_IUnknown and all other system IIDs are provided in UUID. LIB")
cpp_quote("// Link that library in with your proxies, clients and servers")
cpp_quote("////////////////////////////////////////////////////////////////")
```

Following the comments is a method named *QueryInterface*. *QueryInterface* is the method used for dynamic discovery. This method allows a client to dynamically query for a specific interface, passing in an IID, and getting back a pointer to such an interface. The HRESULT return type is a 32-bit value. The first parameter of *QueryInterface* is REFIID, which stands for a reference to an interface identifier. You can see that it's described by the [in] attribute. The [in] attribute tells the world that the IID is an input parameter; that is, it is being passed into the method call.

```
HRESULT QueryInterface([in] REFIID riid, [out, iid_is(riid)] void **ppvObject);
```

The second parameter is a void **, which returns the requested interface pointer to the caller. Since ppvObject is an output parameter, the [out] attribute is specified. Notice that there's another attribute, [iid_is()]. This is a pointer attribute (i.e., it's similar to [ptr], [ref], and [unique], which refer only to pointers). Notice also that it contains an argument, riid, which is passed in as the first parameter of *QueryInterface*. Effectively, the second parameter in *QueryInterface* says the following:

- ppvObject is of type void **

- ppvObject is an output parameter ([out])

- `ppvObject` is interface pointer (`[iid_is()]`)

- `ppvObject` is specifically an `riid` (e.g., `IID_ICasino`) interface pointer (`[iid_is(riid)]`)

Clearly, you can see that MIDL attributes are very rich in semantics, but why do you need the pointer attribute `[iid_is(riid)]`? You might not care about this information, but a marshaler will. Specifically, the stub needs to know the exact interface pointer (`riid`, which is some IID) it is marshaling, so that it can correctly marshal it across execution contexts (e.g., two different processes). So, in this case, you're not making yourself or your interface users happy, but you're making COM happy. COM needs to know the exact type and size of the data it's marshaling across the wire; therefore, you have to explicitly give it these details in the interface specification.

---

### MIDL Attributes

MIDL attributes are important because they tell the world the specifics of your interface specification. In addition, they explicitly tell the MIDL compiler to generate the correct marshaling code. You can impose strict semantics on all your methods, interfaces, and so forth, by using attributes. Since interfaces must never change once they are deployed, you should think very hard about your interface specification. Add the correct attributes to types, methods, interfaces, etc., because once an interface goes out the door, you do not ever change it. Period! An interface that you write is a contract to the world and to COM. The contract keeps the world happy, and it allows COM to generate the correct, seamless marshaling code in order to achieve the benefits of location transparency and much more.

---

Having seen *QueryInterface*, quickly examine the *AddRef* and *Release* methods, which are used for object lifetime management. They're simple in that they take nothing and return a `ULONG`. *AddRef* is called by any piece of code that makes a copy of this interface. On the other hand, *Release* is called when a piece of code no long needs this interface. The return value, of type `ULONG`, indicates the current number of outstanding references to a particular interface and should be used only for diagnostic purposes. There are specific rules for *AddRef* and *Release*, and they'll be discussed later in the section named "IUnknown Rules."

### *Arrays and strings as interface method parameters*

Enough about *IUnknown* for now, let's get back to defining the *IOcr* interface. One of the methods that's supported by *IOcr* is *OcrImage:*

```
[ object, uuid(D9F23D61-A647-11d1-ABCD-00207810D5FE) ]
interface IOcr : IUnknown
{
    HRESULT OcrImage([in] long lImageSize,
                     [in, size_is(lImageSize)] byte * pbImage,
                     [out, string] wchar_t **pwszOcrText);
    ...
}
```

The *IOcr* interface defines this method, *OcrImage*, to allow clients to perform OCR for a given image. *OcrImage* takes a block of bytes, along with the size of the block, and returns a wide-character string. This string represents the textual representation of the given image after OCR processing. The first parameter indicates the size of the image we are sending. It is an input parameter, so it has the [in] attribute.

The second parameter represents a pointer to a chunk of image data, and it's also an input parameter, which is why it has the [in] attribute. How large is this binary data? It's lImageSize large. You use a MIDL attribute to tell COM that pbImage is a pointer to a block of data that is lImageSize large. In particular, you use the [size_is()]* attribute for this. By adding [size_is(lImageSize)], you can explicitly tell the marshaler that your pointer is actually pointing to a chunk that is lImageSize bytes long. If you don't tell the marshaler that the image is lImageSize long, how will the marshaler know how much memory to allocate? It won't know.

The pbImage argument, described using the [size_is()] attribute, is called a *conformant array*, since its size can be dynamically set at runtime. In other words, the size of the chunk pointed to by pbImage will be unknown until a client calls *OcrImage*, at which time the client gets to specify this size. Conformant arrays are great for passing dynamic data into a remote method invocation.

The third parameter to *OcrImage* is a Unicode string.† This is an output parameter, since you want to get the text representation for a given image. The [string] attribute indicates to the marshaler that *pwszOcrText, which is of type wchar_t *, is a string—meaning it's null-terminated.

This brings up a different discussion. If you pass a string into a method, you don't have to use a conformant array, because the marshaler will know the size of your

---

* The [size_is()] attribute is very versatile; for example, it allows you to specify the dimensions of multiple dimensional arrays, including the ability to deal with multiple levels of pointers. I'll leave these topics to the MIDL Language Reference, in keeping with our promise not to delve deeply into MIDL in this book.

† On Windows NT 4.0 and above, all strings are manipulated as Unicode strings; likewise in COM, all strings are marshaled as Unicode strings. This means if you use a char *, it will be converted to a wchar_t * by both NT and COM. So you might as well use Unicode on NT to save those extra CPU cycles. If you don't like this reasoning, then what about supporting OCR for Chinese characters? Besides, the COM Specification says the strings should be Unicode.

string based on the NULL terminator. However, you must remember to add the magic [string] attribute to your parameter as follows:

```
HRESULT MyNameIs([in, string] wchar_t *pwszName);
```

### *Custom types as interface method parameters*

So far, you have specified a method in the *IOcr* interface to OCR a whole image. However, there are times when you would just want to get OCR text for a specific rectangular area of an image. To support this functionality, you'll add a method to OCR a specific zone. Before doing that, you need to specify a C struct to represent a zone. The zone structure is composed of an x, a y, a width, and a height, as shown in the following MIDL snippet:

```
struct Zone {
    short m_sX;
    short m_sY;
    short m_sWidth;
    short m_sHeight;
};

[ object, uuid(D9F23D61-A647-11d1-ABCD-00207810D5FE) ]
interface IOcr : IUnknown
{
    HRESULT OcrImage([in] long lImageSize,
                     [in, size_is(lImageSize)] byte * pbImage,
                     [out, string] wchar_t **pwszOcrText);

    HRESULT OcrZone([in] long lImageSize,
                    [in, size_is(lImageSize)] byte * pbImage,
                    [in] struct Zone zone,
                    [out, string] wchar_t **pwszOcrText);

}
```

The *OcrZone* method is almost a replica of *OcrImage*, with the exception of the added parameter, Zone. As you can see, it is an [in] parameter. You don't need to specify the size, because it's implicit based on the definition of Zone.

Now, what if you also want to return the overall dimension of the image, in addition to the OCR text? If you wanted to do this, you would write the following MIDL script:

```
HRESULT OcrZoneAndGetImageDimension([in] long lImageSize,
                  [in, size_is(lImageSize)] byte * pbImage,
                  [in, out] struct Zone *pZoneInputDimensionOutput,
                  [out, string] wchar_t **pwszOcrText);
```

Notice that pZoneInputDimensionOutput is both an input and output parameter. Here again, you're only dealing with one single zone, so the marshaler will know the size of Zone. However, if you have an array of zones, you would use a conformant array. For example, you may want a method to convert an array of zones from pixels into inches, based on a given resolution:

```
HRESULT Pixels2Inches([in] struct Resolution res,
                      [in] long lArraySize,
                      [in, out, size_is(lArraySize)] struct Zone **pZone);
```

pZone is a conformant array of lArraySize elements. On input, it represents an array of zones in pixels; on output, it represents an array of zones in inches. In all cases, the marshaler will know the size of each parameter, because you have fully specified this information by using MIDL attributes.

### Adding more custom interfaces

A COM object can expose more than one interface, so now try adding another simple interface to your OCR engine that allows clients to perform spell checking. A client can use the *ISpell* interface to check the spelling of a word, via the *Check* method. After calling the *Check* method with a word, the OCR engine will return two possible choices to the client. You've learned enough MIDL by now to be able to read the following MIDL script without any problems:

```
// Possible Words
struct PossibleWords
{
        wchar_t wszOne[16];
        wchar_t wszTwo[16];
};

//  Interface for spell checking
[ object, uuid(D9F23D63-A647-11d1-ABCD-00207810D5FE) ]
interface ISpell : IUnknown
{
    HRESULT Check([in, string] wchar_t * pwszWord,
                  [out] struct PossibleWords *pWords);
}
```

At this point, you can use the MIDL compiler to generate interface marshalers for these two interfaces. However, you're not going to do that just yet, as there are a number of important things left to learn.

### Defining a type library

It's now a good time to learn how to specify an interface repository using MIDL. In COM, an interface repository is called a *type library*, which includes all the type information regarding a component.

To specify a type library, you use the library keyword that tells the MIDL compiler to create a type library for a given component. This library includes all the type information specified in the library block. The type library has a UUID, so that, like interfaces, it is unique in time and space. Since you have only one kind of COM objects (namely the *CoOcrEngine* COM class), your type library will expose type information for that single COM class (`coclass`). However, you may add as many supported COM classes within the library block as you desire. Like interfaces and libraries, a COM class is associated with a UUID, specifically called a CLSID, as shown in the following MIDL snippet:

```
[ uuid(36EFD0B1-B326-11d1-ABDE-00207810D5FE), version(1.0) ]
library OCREngineLib
{
    [ uuid(DF22A6B2-A58A-11D1-ABCC-00207810d5fe) ]
    coclass CoOcrEngine
    {
        [default] interface IOcr;
        interface ISpell;
    }
}
```

A COM object that is an instance of the *CoOcrEngine* COM class supports two interfaces: *IOcr* and *ISpell.* Use the `coclass` keyword to specify that *CoOcrEngine* exposes these interfaces. A `coclass` should specify all interfaces that its COM objects implement. It has a UUID, called a class ID (CLSID), so it will also be unique. Notice that a `library` and a `coclass` are not described using the `[object]` attribute, as this attribute is only used to describe COM interfaces. In addition, *IOcr* is specified to be the `[default]` interface, allowing a language like Visual Basic to use the names *CoOcrEngine* and *IOcr* interchangeably. If `[default]` is not specified, the first interface in the `coclass` will implicitly become the `[default]`.*

### Published interfaces must never change

A stated earlier, COM specifies that once you have deployed your component, you must never, ever modify the specification of its interfaces. In the event that you must enhance one of the interfaces supported by the component, you must create a brand new interface, typically derived from the old one. For example, if you wanted to add new functionality to the *IOcr* interface, you would not modify the *IOcr* interface. What you must do is create an *IOcr2* interface derived from *IOcr*, as follows:

```
[ object, uuid(9372A220-B4BD-11d1-ABE1-00207810D5FE) ]
interface IOcr2 : IOcr
{
    HRESULT MyNewMethod();
}
```

The *IOcr2* interface must have a new UUID. Even though implementation has not been introduced yet, you are free to reuse your implementation in anyway you

---

* A coclass can have only one incoming (sink) `[default]` interface and one outgoing (source) `[default]` interface.

want, since this is of no concern to your clients. In other words, your clients see your COM objects as follows:

- A client sees a COM object as black box.

- A client doesn't know and doesn't care about your COM object's implementation.

- A client can query for new interfaces supported by a COM object.

- A client can rest assured that a COM object's interfaces never change.

## Return Values

MIDL and COM support a finite number of legal return values and data types. Since there's only one return type to discuss, now will be a good time to explain it.

### HRESULT

Every COM interface method returns an HRESULT. The MIDL compiler will crumple up and toss your code back at you if you fail to comply. There are several reasons for this requirement. Here are two with which to begin. The first reason is simplicity and uniformity of error handling. The second is that there are always at least three parties involved in a method invocation in COM: your object, your object's client, and COM. Assume a client uses the following methods:

```
void CoOcrEngine::BeBad() {}

HRESULT CoOcrEngine::BeGood() { return S_OK; }
```

Neither method returns an error, but this doesn't necessary mean that the invocation will be successful, because there are other parties that are involved in a remote method invocation. That is, COM is doing other things underneath, and one of these things includes marshaling the data back to the client. During this process, an error could occur. Say that the RPC layer, upon which the COM remoting architecture is built, detects a network error and needs to relay the error back to the client. In the case of the *BeBad* call, there's no place within the method to report this error. However, with the *BeGood* call, the RPC layer can place the error inside the returned HRESULT, overriding the previous S_OK status code.

As shown in Figure 3-3, an HRESULT is a 32-bit value that is composed of four different parts:

*Severity*
    Was the call successful? A 1-bit answer meaning success (0) or failure (1).

*Reserved*
    Two bits that must always be zero, so don't mess with it.

*Facility*

> Who generated the error? A 13-bit facility code (indicating for example, RPC, WIN32, DISPATCH, etc.).

*Code*

> What actually happened? A 16-bit return code specific to a facility.

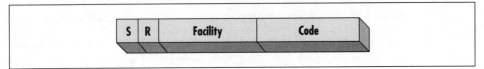

*Figure 3-3. An HRESULT is a 32-bit value that has four parts*

COM provides a number of macros to easily extract and assemble an HRESULT from its smaller parts. In programming, you can assemble an HRESULT using the following macro:

```
MAKE_HRESULT(sev,fac,code)
```

A severity code can be either SEVERITY_SUCCESS or SEVERITY_ERROR. A facility code can be any one of the following predefined values: FACILITY_NULL, FACILITY_RPC, FACILITY_DISPATCH, FACILITY_STORAGE, FACILITY_ITF, FACILITY_WINDOWS, FACLITY_WIN32, FACILITY_SSPI, FACILITY_CONTROL, FACILITY_CERT, and FACILITY_INTERNET. Of these, FACILITY_NULL includes a number of generic and convenient status codes that we will often use in the implementation of our interface methods. Some of these status codes include:

```
S_OK            // Success
S_FALSE         // False
E_UNEXPECTED    // Unexpected, can be a catastrophic failure
E_NOTIMPL       // Method not implemented
E_OUTOFMEMORY   // Errors dealing with memory allocations
E_NOINTERFACE   // Interface not supported, used in QueryInterface
E_POINTER       // Invalid pointer
E_FAIL          // Generic error, no details available
```

### Custom HRESULTs

In addition to generic status codes supported by FACILITY_NULL, you can also construct your own, customized status codes. In essence, these customized status codes are private return messages that clients should be programmed to understand. You, as COM programmers, define customized status codes for the COM interface facility, FACILITY_ITF. You can create whatever status codes you want for FACILITY_ITF, and because of this flexibility, your status codes may collide with the status codes invented by others. More crucially, if you're not careful, they may collide with other status codes you have previously invented. For example, a client may use two different objects that return the same status codes; however, they bear different meanings, because they came from different sources. Be careful!

To compose a custom HRESULT and return it to the caller, you would do the following:

```
#define RC_MY_CUSTOM_ERROR 0x201
return (MAKE_HRESULT(SEVERITY_ERROR, FACILITY_ITF, RC_MY_CUSTOM_ERROR));
```

Notice that the code returned is 0x201. The COM specification recommends that all interface method status codes be in the range 0x200 to 0xFFFF. This is to decrease the possibility of collisions with predefined COM status codes.

There are a number of other macros similar to MAKE_HRESULT that could make your life simpler when you deal with HRESULTs, especially for client-side programming. Given an HRESULT, you can use the following macros to retrieve its specific parts and status:

```
ULONG sev = HRESULT_SEVERITY(hr)   // Gets the severity portion of an HRESULT
ULONG fac = HRESULT_FACILITY(hr)   // Gets the facility portion of an HRESULT
ULONG code = HRESULT_CODE(hr)      // Gets the code portion of an HRESULT


SUCCEEDED(hr)   // Tests for success
FAILED(hr)      // Tests for failure
IS_ERROR(hr)    // Tests for SEVERITY_ERROR
```

For example:

```
HRESULT hr = p->OcrImage();
if (SUCCEEDED(hr)) { /* successful calling OcrImage */ }
```

## Data Types

Just as return values must be HRESULTs, COM supports a finite list of data types for arguments. This is important for the COM marshaling layer, since it must know the size of all data in order to marshal the data across the wire.

### Base data types

COM provides a number of base data types, exhibited in Table 3-1. The wchar_t data type is a standard for wide-characters used internationally.

*Table 3-1. Data types for method arguments*

| MIDL Data Type | COM's Perspective | C++ Mapping |
| --- | --- | --- |
| boolean | 8-bit | unsigned char |
| byte | 8-bit | unsigned char |
| char | 8-bit | unsigned char |
| wchar_t | 16-bit | wchar_t |
| float | 32-bit | float |
| double | 64-bit | double |
| small | 8-bit | char |
| short | 16-bit | short |

*Table 3-1. Data types for method arguments (continued)*

| MIDL Data Type | COM's Perspective | C++ Mapping |
|---|---|---|
| long | 32-bit | long |
| hyper | 64-bit | _ _int64 |
| IUnknown * (or derivative) | Object Reference (a magical thing discussed in Chapter 5) | IUnknown * (or derivative) |

You must use these listed data types in all your interface specifications. You may specify your own user data type, by creating a **struct** that includes one or more of these data types or another **struct**. Unfortunately, you are constrained to this list, because the COM marshaling layer must know the size of all data that is to be marshaled. Without knowing the exact data size, the marshaling architecture will not be able to send the data across the wire. Therefore, in the effort of achieving location transparency, COM requires us to work with these limited base types.

These base types[*] are straightforward to use in COM programming. In addition, you're free to always modify each of these base types with a pointer; that is, you're free to specify **char \***, **char \*\***, and so forth. But this ability permits you to specify very complicated semantics, leading to the need for complex memory management.[†]

All strings are Unicode in COM, so if you need to pass strings back and forth, use **wchar_t \*** (or **OLECHAR**, which is an alias of **wchar_t**). If you use a **char \***, the string will be converted into a **wchar_t \*** by COM, which needlessly wastes CPU cycles.

### Automation compatible types

MIDL also supports a number of extended data types, which helps tremendously in dynamic invocation. Some of these important data types include **VARIANT**, **BSTR**, and **SAFEARRAY**. In the world of COM, dynamic invocation is supported by a technology called *Automation*. These three mentioned data types are called Automation compatible data types. Here's a brief discussion of a **VARIANT**. **BSTR** and **SAFEARRAY** will be discussed in Chapter 5.

A **VARIANT** is a universal data type that lets your code be called from programming languages such as Visual Basic, Visual J++, VBScript, and so forth. It can be thought of as a value holder. In other words, it can hold or represent different types of data at different times. For example, you can use one **VARIANT** to hold an interface pointer, another **VARIANT** to hold a float, and yet another different

---

[*] The **boolean**, **byte**, **hyper**, **small**, and **wchar_t** data types are not Automation compatible types. As discussed shortly, Automation types are data types that can be used in dynamic invocation.

[†] Memory management is discussed in Chapter 5.

VARIANT to hold a date. Technically, a VARIANT is just a union of a bunch of special data types, called Automation data types. For brevity, I will not show the full
variant structure, as it is enormous (refer to *oaidl.h*, provided by Visual C++, for
more information). This structure is fairly simple and is summarized here:

```
typedef struct tagVARIANT {
  VARTYPE vt; // vt tells us the type of data we're holding
  WORD wReserved1; WORD wReserved2; WORD wReserved3;
  union {      // contains over 40 members, refer to "oaidl.h"
    . . .
    ULONG ulVal;
    . . .
  };
};
```

Notice that you're not seeing anything within the union except ulVal, which will
be used to demonstrate using a VARIANT in a moment. The important part of this
structure is the variant type (vt), which can be one of the values defined in an
enum called VARENUM (look for this enum in *wtypes.h* for more information, as it is
also quite large).

```
enum VARENUM {
  . . .
  VT_UI4 = 19,    // represents a ULONG
  . . .
};
```

Given what you know so far, here's how you would create a value holder that
holds a ULONG. As the boldfaced statements indicate, you must correctly set the
VARIANT's type and its holding value:

```
VARIANT vMyLong;         // Create value holder
VariantInit(&vMyLong);   // Initialize
vMyLong.vt = VT_UI4;     // Set value holder type.  (VT_UI4 shown earlier)
vMyLong.ulVal = 1000;    // Hold a ULONG.  (ulVal also shown earlier)
CallFunc(vMyLong);       // Use the variant
VariantClear(&vMyLong);  // Clean up
```

One nice—or nasty, depending on your perspective—aspect of a VARIANT is that
it supports type coercion; that is, you can change its type dynamically. You can
initialize, clear, and coerce a variant using the following simple API functions:

```
void VariantInit(VARIANTARG * pvarg);

HRESULT VariantClear(VARIANTARG * pvarg);

HRESULT VariantChangeType(
  VARIANTARG FAR* pvargDest,  // ptr to the destined variant, can == src
  VARIANTARG FAR* pvarSrc,    // ptr to src variant to be coerced
  unsigned short  wFlags,     // coercion control flags
  VARTYPE  vt                 // destined type
);
```

A VARIANT is fairly straightforward to use, and from a distance, a variant sounds nifty because it can act as any type. Looking at it closer, a VARIANT can be a complex beast for complicated VARIANT composites. For example, a VARIANT can contain an array of VARIANTs, and each VARIANT within the array can contain an array of VARIANTs—and recursively so on. In addition, the BSTR and SAFEARRAY types, which are Automation compatible types, have their own memory allocation and deallocation API functions and will be discussed in Chapter 5.

## *Interface Marshalers: Proxy and Stub*

After you have specified your interfaces, classes, and type library, you would use the MIDL compiler to generate a number of files that permit the easy distribution of objects. The files created by MIDL and other compiler tools are shown in Figure 3-4. Given a single IDL file, the MIDL compiler can generate a type library and all definition and implementation files needed to build a proxy/stub DLL. In standard marshaling, the proxy/stub DLL is dynamically loaded by COM to correctly marshal data across apartments.

For example, assuming that you've saved your interface specifications in a file called *ocr.idl*, you would compile this file by invoking the following command:

*midl /Oicf ocr.idl*

The /Oicf switch should be used in Windows NT 4.0, or above, as it generates fully interpretive marshaling code, which can improve performance.

One of the files generated is a header file (*xxxx.h*) that includes C and C++ definitions of your interfaces and is based on the specifications you have created in the IDL file. This header file is important, because it includes the binary layout of all specified interfaces. An object implementor uses this header file to implement one or more interfaces for a COM object. A client developer uses this header file to obtain services from any object that exposes any interface defined within this header file.

The MIDL compiler also generates an implementation file (*xxxx_i.c*) that contains definitions for all the GUIDs specified in the IDL file. Recall that interfaces, classes, and libraries all have unique 128-bit identifiers, called GUIDs. These GUIDs are globally defined in this generated implementation file. The MIDL compiler uses the following naming convention to name these GUIDs:

*Interface*

> The MIDL compiler prefixes the interface name with IID_

*Coclass*

> The MIDL compiler prefixes the class name with CLSID_

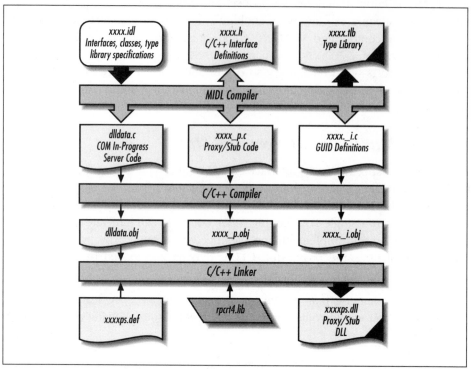

*Figure 3-4. The proxy/stub DLL generation process*

*Library*

The MIDL compiler prefixes the library name with `LIBID_`

Here's typical content for a *xxxx_i.c* file.

```
const IID IID_IOcr =
    {0xD9F23D61,0xA647,0x11d1,{0xAB,0xCD,0x00,0x20,0x78,0x10,0xD5,0xFE}};
const IID IID_ISpell =
    {0xD9F23D63,0xA647,0x11d1,{0xAB,0xCD,0x00,0x20,0x78,0x10,0xD5,0xFE}};
const CLSID CLSID_CoOCREngine =
    {0xDF22A6B2,0xA58A,0x11D1,{0xAB,0xCC,0x00,0x20,0x78,0x10,0xd5,0xfe}};
const IID LIBID_OCREngineLib =
    {0x36EFD0B1,0xB326,0x11d1,{0xAB,0xDE,0x00,0x20,0x78,0x10,0xD5,0xFE}};
```

There are usually three names for an interface: a GUID (e.g., `IID_IOcr`), a class or structure name used in programming (e.g., *IOcr*), and possibly a human readable name (e.g., "OcrEngine.1"). Of these, only the GUID uniquely identifies an interface.

In addition, the MIDL compiler generates an implementation file (*xxxx_p.c*) that includes marshaling code for all defined interfaces. The marshaling code for each interface is called an interface marshaler. As the masterminds behind location transparency, these interface marshalers collaborate with COM's standard marshaler* to transfer data across the network.

If you had specified a library in the IDL file, the MIDL compiler will also spit out a binary file that includes detailed type information for all user-defined types, methods, and interfaces. This is the type library, which tools and external clients can utilize to get detailed information regarding a component.†

The generated files can be combined to form a dynamic linked library that hosts the marshaling code for the interfaces we've developed. This DLL is automatically loaded when COM detects that marshaling is needed for remote method invocation. Figure 3-4 (shown earlier) reveals the inputs and outputs for building this DLL.

You can build this DLL using the following sample **makefile** script, by running it through *nmake.exe*:

```
ocrps.dll: dlldata.obj ocr_p.obj ocr_i.obj
    link /dll /out:ocrps.dll /def:ocrps.def \
    /entry:DllMain dlldata.obj ocr_p.obj ocr_i.obj kernel32.lib rpcrt4.lib

.c.obj:
    cl /c /DWIN32 /D_WIN32_WINNT=0x0400 /DREGISTER_PROXY_DLL $<
```

For example, if you save the earlier script into a file called *ocrps.mk*, you can build the DLL by invoking the following command:

*nmake –f ocrps.mk*

Look back to the script where *rpcrt4.lib* is the RPC library that you must link your proxy/stub code with. The *.def* file specifies four exports for all COM DLLs, including *DllGetClassObject, DllCanUnloadNow, DllRegisterServer,* and *DllUnregisterServer.* These functions support dynamic activation, component lifetime management, and component registration. They will be discussed in Chapter 4. MIDL doesn't generate a *.def* file, so you'll have to create this file by yourself. Shown below is a typical *.def* file for the proxy/stub DLL:

```
LIBRARY        "ocrps"

DESCRIPTION    'Proxy/Stub DLL'

EXPORTS
    DllGetClassObject      @1    PRIVATE
    DllCanUnloadNow        @2    PRIVATE
    DllRegisterServer      @4    PRIVATE
    DllUnregisterServer    @5    PRIVATE
```

---

* The *standard marshaler* is built by Microsoft, and it is an intimate part of COM. In order to use standard marshaling, we must provide interface marshalers (generated by the MIDL compiler).

† Type libraries are binary files that typically have extensions such as *.tlb* and *.olb*. Tools like Visual Basic, Visual J++, and Visual C++ can generate corresponding language mappings from the metadata stored in the type libraries.

You must mark these exports as PRIVATE, or you will receive nasty linkage errors if the exports ever show up in a static library (*.lib*).

## *The Binary Layout*

As mentioned above, the header file that the MIDL compiler generates includes C++ definitions for all COM interfaces defined in the IDL file. Each of these definitions has a binary layout that conforms to the COM binary specification, which allows for binary interoperability. This binary layout uses the vptr (virtual pointer) and vtbl (virtual table of function pointers) technique, as used in C++ to support polymorphism.

Before you look at the binary layout of a COM interface, refresh your memory regarding the way C++ uses vptr and vtbl. Think of a vtbl as a static member of a class; that is, there's only one vtbl per class. The C++ compiler generates a vtbl when a C++ class has at least one virtual function. The *IUnknown* class shown below fits this basis, as all of its functions are virtual:

```
class IUnknown  {
public:
   virtual HRESULT QueryInterface(REFIID riid, void **ppvObject) = 0 ;
   virtual ULONG AddRef(void) = 0 ;
   virtual ULONG Release(void) = 0 ;
};
```

A vtbl is a table of pointers to each defined virtual function. So, in this case, if the compiler generates a vtbl,[*] it will look something like Figure 3-5.

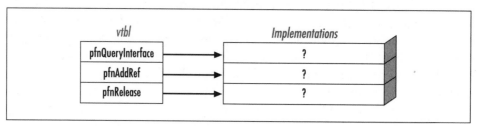

*Figure 3-5. Theoretical vtbl for an ABC*

All entries in *IUnknown*'s vtbl point to nothing because they're all pure virtual functions (indicated by =0). In C++, if you declare a function to be a pure virtual function, you're mandating an interface that derived classes must comply with. Also, you are asserting that you don't provide any implementation for the pure virtual function; a derived class must implement that function according to the function prototype you have put forth. In other words, you're saying to derived classes that they must implement the pure virtual function. In C++, a class that declares at

---

[*] I said "if," because ABCs cannot be instantiated, so vtbls for ABCs are unnecessary.

least one pure virtual function is called an *abstract base class* (ABC). This means the class is only an abstraction. Because this class is only an abstraction, no instances of this class can be instantiated. Given the *IUnknown* definition shown earlier, the following is illegal:

```
IUnknown Unk;     // Error: cannot instantiate an ABC
```

ABCs are the C++ technique that COM uses to support the binary layout of COM interfaces. Since all functions within the class are declared to be pure virtual, a derived class must implement all specified functions. Since ABCs carry no implementations, derived classes inherit only the interface. Because a COM interface carries no implementation and requires a binary layout, it naturally maps to an ABC in C++.

To get a **vtbl** with valid function pointers, you would implement the *IUnknown* interface, as follows:

```
class CoMyObject : public IUnknown {
public:f
    virtual HRESULT QueryInterface(REFIID riid, void **ppvObject) { ... }
    virtual ULONG AddRef(void) { ... }
    virtual ULONG Release(void) { ... }
};
```

*CoMyObject* implements the *IUnknown* interface by overriding and implementing all pure virtual functions from *IUnknown*. With this implementation, we have a *CoMyObject* **vtbl** that contains valid pointers to implemented virtual functions, as exhibited in Figure 3-6.

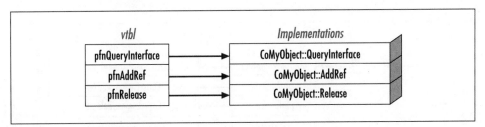

*Figure 3-6. CoMyObject's vtbl*

So how does the **vptr** fit into this picture? Unlike a **vtbl**, which is statically attached to a class, a **vptr** belongs with each instantiated object. So to get a **vptr**, you simply instantiate the *CoMyObject* class, as shown in the following:

```
// (*pUnk) will now contain a hidden vptr to the vtbl
CoMyObject *pUnk = new CoMyObject;
```

Given the code above, Figure 3-7 shows you have a new **vptr**/**vtbl** layout. This is the layout of a simple COM object. A client always holds onto an interface pointer. From the interface pointer, it can get to the **vptr**, to the **vtbl**, and to the destined method.

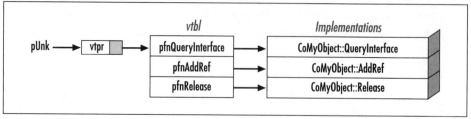

*Figure 3-7. The binary layout of an implemented COM interface*

With what you know so far, examine the *IOcr* interface generated by the MIDL compiler. As shown, *IOcr* is derived from *IUnknown*, inheriting all the pure virtual functions of *IUnknown*. *IOcr* is also an ABC, because it contains pure virtual functions.*

```
// interface is typedef'ed to a struct
interface IOcr : public IUnknown {
    virtual HRESULT OcrImage(long lImageSize,
                             byte *pbImage,
                             wchar_t **pwszOcrText) = 0;

    virtual HRESULT OcrZone(long lImageSize,
                            byte *pbImage,
                            struct Zone zone,
                            wchar_t **pwszOcrText) = 0;
};
```

Assuming that your *CoOcrEngine* COM object is a simple COM object, and it implements this interface, the binary layout of the implemented *IOcr* interface may resemble Figure 3-8.

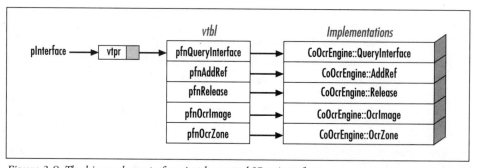

*Figure 3-8. The binary layout of an implemented IOcr interface*

Summing up, every COM interface has a binary layout that conveniently maps to C++'s support for virtual functions. Notice that you can construct this binary layout using any language or tool that understands the notion of a pointer or reference.

---

* It would still be an ABC even if it didn't have any pure virtual functions, since it inherits pure virtual functions from *IUnknown* (assuming *IOcr* didn't implement the three inherited functions).

# Dispatch and Dual Interfaces

Thus far, you have learned only about custom interfaces, which are interfaces that you create or specify. Microsoft provides a large number of standard interfaces that anyone can use, and *IDispatch* is one of these standard interfaces. You can't leave the interface topic without a brief discussion of the *IDispatch* interface, because it supports dynamic invocation. As implied by the tone of the previous sentence, this section is purely optional for building your own distributed systems, so you may skip this section and move on the next section, "Objects." If you skip this section, you should revisit it to understand how dynamic invocation is supported in COM, because many languages support only dynamic invocation. Remember that dynamic invocation is also colloquially called Automation by the COM community.

Dynamic invocation allows a third-party software to dynamically inquire an object at runtime to see whether it supports a particular interface method. All this software has to know is the name of the method. If the object supports such a method name, the software will then be given a magic cookie, which it can use to dynamically call the target method. This is different from static invocation, where the code for the software and the compiler that compiles said code must know the complete method signature at compile time.

To specify that your interface supports dynamic invocation, you'd either derive your interface from *IDispatch* or use the `dispinterface` keyword. The latter technique is shown below. Notice that each property or method supported is assigned a `dispid` using the `[id()]` attribute. The keywords `properties:` and `methods:` are valid only within the specification of a `dispinterface`.

```
[ uuid(87C828DE-B609-11D1-ABE6-00207810D5FE)]
dispinterface IOcrPanel {
properties:   // dispinterface's supported properties
    // this is a shorthand for the [propget] [propput] attributes
    [id(1)] short Status;
methods:      // dispinterface's supported methods
    [id(2)] short Initialize();
};
```

The `properties:` section allows you to create properties. Alternatively, you can achieve the same effect by creating two methods using the `[propget]` and `[propput]` attributes as follows:

```
[propget, id(3)] short Status();
[propput, id(3)] HRESULT Status([in] short status);
```

MIDL supports the `[propget]` and `[propput]` attributes that permit the specification of two different methods with the same name to represent a single property. Notice in the MIDL script above that the two methods share the same `dispid` (3), because they both represent one property. One of these methods is a getter and the other is a setter.

An object that correctly implements the *IOcrPanel* interface (shown above) will support dynamic invocation, because the *IOcrPanel* interface is a `dispinterface`. Such an object must implement the following seven methods:

- *IUnknown::QueryInterface*

- *IUnknown::AddRef*

- *IUnknown::Release*

- *IDispatch::GetTypeInfoCount*—This method gets the number of type information interfaces. This function should always return 1.

- *IDispatch::GetTypeInfo*—This method gets the type information for an object.

- *IDispatch::GetIDsOfNames*—This method gets a list of `dispids`, given a list of method names.

- *IDispatch::Invoke*—This method invokes the target method or property using a `dispid`.

A client can ask whether the object supports dynamic invocation by querying for the *IDispatch* interface. It will then use the dispatch interface pointer to get `dispids` from the object by calling *IDispatch::GetIDsOfNames* and passing in human-readable method names. Once the `dispids` are obtained, the client can then call *IDispatch::Invoke* using a `dispid` to dynamically invoke the method. Following is a code snippet that illustrates this process. This code assumes that Microsoft Word is installed on your system, since it will dynamically invoke a method to show Microsoft Word. Refer to the SDK documentation for the details on the DISPPARAMS structure and the parameters of *IDispatch::GetIDsOfNames* and *IDispatch::Invoke*. Ignore these details here because dynamic invocation is not the focus of this book.

```
CoInitialize(0);

// Get the CLSID that maps to the program ID named Word.Basic.
GUID clsid;
CLSIDFromProgID(L"Word.Basic", &clsid);

// Activate the object and request for as IDispatch interface.
IDispatch *pDisp = 0;
CoCreateInstance(clsid, NULL, CLSCTX_LOCAL_SERVER,
                 IID_IDispatch, (void**)&pDisp);

// We need to know the name of the method we want to invoke.
OLECHAR *method = L"AppShow";

// The AppShow method expects no parameter.
DISPPARAMS parms = {NULL, NULL, 0, 0};

// Given a method name, get back the corresponding dispid.
DISPID dispid;
pDisp->GetIDsOfNames(IID_NULL, &method, 1, LOCALE_USER_DEFAULT, &dispid);
```

```
// Dynamically invoke the the AppShow method using a dispid.
pDisp->Invoke(dispid, IID_NULL, LOCALE_USER_DEFAULT,
            DISPATCH_METHOD, &parms, NULL, NULL, NULL);

//  Do whatever....

pDisp->Release();
CoUninitialize();
```

There are performance problems with a dispatch interface, because it involves an extensive lookup to resolve dispids from given method names. *IDispatch* is great for clients who definitely need dynamic invocation, because they don't have prior knowledge of a particular interface's methods. An example of this type of clients is a scripting language like VBScript.

If a client doesn't want to follow the crowd by using *IDispatch* and suffering the performance impact, it can take advantage of prior interface specification knowledge. In other words, if there is a header file, the client can be compiled with that header file. If there is a type library, the programmer can use tools to generate wrapper classes to represent the required interfaces.

To make these clients happy, Microsoft also provides dual interfaces. A *dual interface* supports the following types of invocation in addition to the *IDispatch* technique just discussed:

*Very Early Binding (vtbl binding)*

This technique requires the client to compile with a given header file generated by MIDL. Clients can attain maximum performance, because the calls are made directly via pointers. Another advantage is that it is easy to use in C++.

*Early Binding*

This technique requires prior knowledge of dispids. Development tools can obtain these dispids from a type library. For example, Visual Studio can reverse engineer type information, contained within the type library, to create a C++ wrapper class. Even better, the generated wrapper class contains resolved dispids. Since the dispids are already resolved, clients don't have to call *GetIDsOfNames*, which means you no longer have the performance hit of looking up dispids.

To specify that you want your interface to be a dual interface, you must add the [dual] attribute. In addition, your interface must be derived from *IDispatch*.

```
[ dual,
  object, uuid(87C838F1-B609-11D1-ABE6-00207810D5FE) ]
interface IOcrPanel : IDispatch
{
        [id(1)] HRESULT Initialize([out, retval] short *pShort);
};
```

All dual interface methods must return an HRESULT. Return values should be the right-most function parameter and be marked as [out, retval], so that scripting environments can easily capture the return data. This allows scripting clients simply to execute.

```
// In VBScript or Visual Basic,
// More natural; the return value is captured in rc.
rc = ocr.Initialize()

// In C++,
// You'd have to do the following:
short s;
HRESULT hr = pOcr->Initialize(&s);
```

There is another requirement for a dual interface: all types used in your IDL file must be Automation compatible types. Specifically, this means only types listed in the VARIANT union may be used in dual interfaces.*

## An Interface Recap

It is a good time at this point to recap what you have learned about defining a COM interface. You have learned a lot, but defining an interface boils down to conforming to the following rules:

- An interface must inherit from *IUnknown.*

- An interface must have an IID.

- An interface must never change once published.

- Return values for interface methods must be HRESULTs.

- Strings should be Unicode.

These are the basic rules that the COM Specification enumerates for being a COM compliant interface. Once your interface definition meets these basic requirements, you can use the MIDL compiler to generate the necessary code for distributed computing, including the code to marshal our custom interface across the wire.

In this section, you also examined COM's supported base data types and Automation compatible types. Moreover, COM's binary standard was discussed in detail. And finally, you learned about dispatch and dual interfaces, which are optional features in distributed component development. In the next section, you'll learn how to package COM interfaces together to form a COM object.

---

* This implies that structs aren't allowed as arguments in methods of a dual or dispatch interface at the time of this writing. However, Windows NT 4.0 Service Pack 4 (and above) will support this.

## *Interface Terminology*

*Standard interface*

This term is used to describe the collection of interfaces that Microsoft developed and deployed. They are the de facto standard and are implemented and used for better interoperability. For example, if you develop an object that supports a standard interface, someone else will be able to use your object because standard interfaces are publicly documented. Standard interfaces are also often referred to as OLE interfaces. Some of these interfaces include *IMoniker, IPersist, IConnectionPoint, IDispatch*, and so forth.

*Custom interface*

A custom interface is a user-defined interface, that uses `vtbl` binding. Custom interfaces are the ones that really do the work you created your components for in the first place. This type of interface allows you the freedom to express yourself in specifying interface methods. However, there are drawbacks depending on which camp you come from. In order for a client to communicate with a remote object, you must provide a proxy/stub DLL. The proxy/stub DLL contains the marshaling code for your custom interface, and it works in conjunction with COM's standard marshaler. The interface identifier (IID) of your custom interface must be registered before a client can communicate with your COM object. Another drawback is that custom interfaces don't support dynamic invocation. Thus, everything must be known at compile time.

*Automation interface*

An Automation interface is a user-defined interface that supports dynamic invocation and late binding via the *IDispatch* interface. The advantage of an Automation interface is that it can be used in a wide range of environments and tools, because it supports dynamic invocation. In addition, you don't have to create proxy/stub DLLs because Microsoft provides generic marshaling code in the Automation marshaler (*oleaut32.dll*). Instead of using proxy/stub DLLs, the Automation marshaler uses a type library, which stores detailed type information regarding objects and their supported interfaces. The drawback is that it only supports Automation compatible types. When you hear Automation, think *IDispatch*.

*—Continued—*

*Dual interface*

A dual interface is required to support both the *IDispatch* and `vtbl` binding. This is really a compromise between flexibility and speed: *IDispatch* supports dynamic invocation and `vtbl` supports speed. One drawback of this technique is that you must use Automation compatible types, such as the ubiquitous `VARIANT`. In addition, all interface methods must return `HRESULT`. In the case of an accessor (i.e., a getter) method that typically returns a value, you must specify the return parameter with an [`out, retval`] attribute; this must be the right-most parameter.

*Tear-off interface*

A tear-off interface is used to describe "just-in-time" or "on-the-fly" interfaces. In other words, these interfaces don't exist until a client specifically queries for them. When a tear-off interface is requested (of course, the client doesn't know that it's requesting a tear-off interface), the COM object's *QueryInterface* method dynamically allocates it. This is an optimization technique, valuable when the object implements a large number of interfaces. Since each implemented interface has a `vptr`, you save four bytes for each interface. If, for some weird reason, you have an object that implements 1005 interfaces and only five specific interfaces are commonly used, you can potentially save 4k bytes if you use the tear-off optimization technique. Basically, this is a technique that says, "If you don't need an interface, don't waste four bytes."

# *Objects*

In this section, you'll learn how to implement published interfaces—that is, to write the code that carries out what our interface promises to do. You'll also learn the sacred elements of COM, which include identity and lifetime rules. Finally, you'll assemble a COM object from several interface implementations. As you march along, you'll create a COM object that exposes the *IOcr* and *ISpell* interfaces, which were specified in the previous section. Recall that these interfaces can be implemented and used in a distributed environment, because the MIDL compiler has fully generated the code to marshal data across the network. In essence, you are putting together a distributed object in this section.

You have just signed a few contracts in the previous section; or to use the correct wording, you've just specified a few interfaces. These interfaces have now become everlasting protocols. To the world, a COM object is a bunch of interfaces. To a COM object's implementor, it can be anything, as long as the internal implementation meets a few basic elements, including binary interface layout, identity, and lifetime rules.

A COM object is represented pictorially using a rectangular box, with its interfaces, which look like lollipops, protruding outward, as shown in Figure 3-9. The top vertical lollipop represents the required *IUnknown* interface that all COM objects must implement.

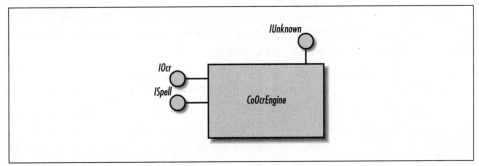

*Figure 3-9. A simple COM object diagram*

## Implementing Interfaces

Which language you choose to implement a typical COM interface is not important; we can choose Visual Basic, Visual J++, C, C++, and many other languages and environments that understand COM. Since this book is more C++ oriented, you will choose C++ to implement a typical interface. Even after choosing a language, you still have several ways to implement a COM interface. Remember that the world knows nothing about your internal implementations, as long as the COM object provides the needed services to the world.

One way to implement a typical interface in C++ is by inheriting from the C++ interface definition generated by the MIDL compiler. For example, the MIDL compiler generates the following C++ mappings for the *IOcr* interface:

```
interface IOcr : public IUnknown {
    virtual HRESULT OcrImage(long lImageSize,
                             byte *pbImage,
                             wchar_t **pwszOcrText) = 0;

    virtual HRESULT OcrZone(long lImageSize,
                            byte *pbImage,
                            struct Zone zone,
                            wchar_t **pwszOcrText) = 0;
};
```

The **interface** keyword is an alias for a **struct**. The *IOcr* interface definition contains two pure virtual functions, *OcrImage* and *OcrZone*, which you must implement according to the rules of C++. To implement this interface, derive a class from it.

```
class CoOcrEngine : public IOcr {
public:
```

```
    // IOcr Methods
    STDMETHODIMP OcrImage(long lImageSize, byte *pbImage,
                    wchar_t **pwszOcrText) { }
    STDMETHODIMP OcrZone(long lImageSize, byte *pbImage,
                    Zone zone, wchar_t **pwszOcrText) { }
};
```

*CoOcrEngine* is a C++ class that implements the *IOcr* interface. You may be wondering what the `STDMETHODIMP` type is, so here's the answer right now. COM provides two macros for `STDMETHODIMP` as follows:

| | | |
|---|---|---|
| **STDMETHODIMP_(ULONG)** | ⇒ **expands to** ⇒ | **ULONG __stdcall** |
| **STDMETHODIMP** | ⇒ **expands to** ⇒ | **HRESULT __stdcall** |

At this point, the *CoOcrEngine* class will not compile. You are supposed to return a status code in the body of both methods, which are currently empty. However, that's not the important point. The real problem is that you haven't taken care of the *IUnknown* interface, so to make the C++ compiler happy, you must override all pure virtual functions, including the ones in *IUnknown*. Remember that the *IOcr* interface is derived from *IUnknown*, and that *IUnknown* is the one interface that must be implemented by all COM objects. To obey the C++ compiler and this COM rule, you'll add the implementations for the *IUnknown* methods.

```
class CoOcrEngine : public IOcr {
public:
    // IUnknown Methods
    STDMETHODIMP QueryInterface(REFIID iid, void **ppv) { return S_OK; }
    STDMETHODIMP_(ULONG) AddRef(void) { return 0; }
    STDMETHODIMP_(ULONG) Release(void) { return 0; }

    // IOcr Methods
    STDMETHODIMP OcrImage(long lImageSize, byte *pbImage,
                    wchar_t **pwszOcrText) { return S_OK; }
    STDMETHODIMP OcrZone(long lImageSize, byte *pbImage,
                    Zone zone, wchar_t **pwszOcrText) { return S_OK; }
};
```

That looks better, but you have no code in the implementations yet. What's notable is that you have met two fundamental rules of COM. First, you have implemented the methods for *IUnknown*. Second, you have the binary interface layout that COM requires. You meet this second rule because the C++ compiler generates the correct `vtbl` for the *CoOcrEngine* C++ class. As you can see, it is simple to implement a COM interface in C++ because the COM binary interface standard maps directly to that of C++'s virtual functions.

There are more rules that you must satisfy before calling *CoOcrEngine* a COM class whose runtime instances are called COM objects. Almost all of these rules surround the ubiquitous *IUnknown*. These rules are the reasons why all COM interfaces must derive from *IUnknown*.

# IUnknown Rules*

As just mentioned, the *IUnknown* interface has a number of rules that you must follow. These can be functionally separated into two categories: identity and existence rules. To be a good citizen in the world of component development, you must abide by them. There are specific rules for clients and specific rules for objects. The first set of rules you will learn are those concerning an object's identity.

### Identity rules

Identity rules reside solely in *IUnknown*'s *QueryInterface* method. Recall that a client is free to query for any interface it needs from a COM object. Earlier, it was said that a programmer can implement an interface in any desired way. COM specifies a policy for implementing *QueryInterface*, so that the freedom to express these implementations will not get out of hand. This policy includes five rules that maintain an object's identity and integrity, shown in the sidebar entitled "Identity Rules."

As you progress through these rules, the discussion assumes that the COM object won't die unexpectedly. To help you build a mental image of these rules, you'll have Mr. RoboCOM helping you. The left side of Figure 3-10 shows him flaunting his five limbs, each of which represents an interface. The right side shows him in the standard representation of a COM object with five interfaces. Mr. RoboCOM is a single entity, and you must follow COM's identity rules to support his integrity.

The first rule states the *QueryInterface* method must be consistent when giving out an interface pointer. This means that if a client has successfully obtained a pointer to a given interface, it must be able to obtain that interface pointer upon subsequent calls to *QueryInterface*. On the flip side, if a client has failed to obtain an interface pointer to a given interface, it must never succeed in subsequent calls to *QueryInterface*. In other words, the way *QueryInterface* gives out *interfaces must be static*. *QueryInterface* must be consistent; it can't have an attitude. COM forbids a COM object like Mr. RoboCOM to say, "Yes, here's my left arm for you to hold," one day and say, "No, I've got no left arm," on the next. Once he gives out his left arm, he must always give it out until his death. This rule is exhibited below:

```
HRESULT hr = pUnk->QueryInterface(IID_ILeftArm,
                                  reinterpret_cast<void**>(&pLeftArm));
if (SUCCEEDED(hr)) {
    ILeftArm *pLeftArm2=NULL;
    // If we have successfully obtained a pointer to IID_ILeftArm,
    // we must be able to obtain a pointer to IID_ILeftArm upon
    // subsequent calls to QueryInterface.
    hr = pUnk->QueryInterface(IID_ILeftArm, reinterpret_cast<void**>
      (&pLeftArm2));
    // Must evaluate to true, else violation of static rule.
```

---

* You're at liberty to read this as the "Rules of IUnknown" or "IUnknown Rules".

# *Identity Rules (for QueryInterface)*

For all interfaces, *a*, *b*, and *c*, exposed by a COM object, the following must always be true:

*Static*

> If you can query for *a* once, you can always query for *a*. If you can't query for *a*, you can never query for *a*.

*Reflexive*

> If you have *a*, then you can query for *a* from itself.

*Symmetric*

> If you can query for *b* using *a*, then you can query for *a* using *b*.

if  then

*Transitive*

> If you can query for *b* using *a* and if you can query for *c* using *b*, then you can query for *c* using *a*.

if  and then

*Identity*

> If you use any interface exposed by an object to query for `IID_IUnknown` multiple times, you will get the same physical pointer value each time.

```
    assert(SUCCEEDED(hr));
    pLeftArm2->Release(); pLeftArm->Release();
} else {
    // If we have unsuccessfully obtained a pointer to IID_ILeftArm
    // we must never be able to obtain a pointer to IID_ILeftArm upon
    // subsequent calls to QueryInterface.
    hr = pUnk->QueryInterface(IID_ILeftArm, reinterpret_cast<void**>
      (&pLeftArm));
    // Must evaluate to true, else violation of static rule.
    assert(FAILED(hr));
}
pUnk->Release();
```

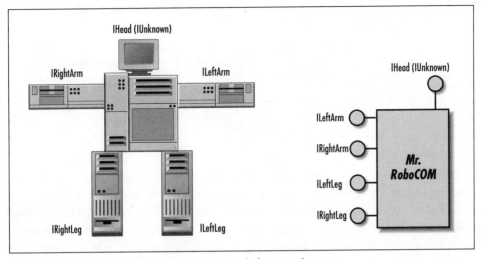

*Figure 3-10. Mr. RoboCOM is a COM object with five interfaces*

The second rule says that *QueryInterface* must be *reflexive.*\* That is, if you use a valid interface pointer to query for the same interface, *QueryInterface* must succeed. In this sense, if you're holding onto Mr. RoboCOM's left leg, Mr. RoboCOM had better give you his left leg in subsequent queries. If this is an invalid assertion, the left leg that you're holding onto definitely didn't belong to Mr. RoboCOM; it could perhaps belong to Mrs. RoboCOM. This rule is illustrated in the following snippet:

```
HRESULT hr = pUnk->QueryInterface(IID_ILeftLeg,
                            reinterpret_cast<void**>(&pLeftLeg));
if (SUCCEEDED(hr)) {
    ILeftLeg *pAgain=NULL;
    // If we have a valid interface pointer to IID_ILeftLeg,
    // we must be able to use the pointer to query for IID_ILeftLeg again!
    hr = pLeftLeg->QueryInterface(IID_ILeftLeg,
                            reinterpret_cast<void**>(&pAgain));
    // Must evaluate to true, else violation of reflexive rule.
    assert(SUCCEEDED(hr));
    pAgain->Release(); pLeftLeg->Release();
}
pUnk->Release();
```

*QueryInterface* must also be *symmetric*. Suppose you're holding onto Mr. RoboCOM's left arm. If you can reach over and grab Mr. RoboCOM's right arm and let go of his left arm, you better be able to grab his left arm at a later time. If you can't do this, you may be dealing with a ghost, not Mr. RoboCOM. Here's a snippet to demonstrate this rule:

---

\* I believe that there is a typo in the COM Specification, version 0.9. It uses the term symmetric to describe the reflexive rule, and it uses the term reflexive to describe the symmetric rule.

```
HRESULT hr = pLeftArm->QueryInterface(IID_IRightArm,
                                reinterpret_cast<void**>(&pRightArm));
if (SUCCEEDED(hr)) {
    ILeftArm *pLeftArm2=NULL;
    // If we can get IID_IRightArm from IID_ILeftArm,
    // then we must be able to get IID_ILeftArm from IID_IRightArm.
    hr = pRightArm->QueryInterface(IID_ILeftArm,
                                reinterpret_cast<void**>(&pLeftArm2));
    // Must evaluate to true, else violation of symmetric rule.
    assert(SUCCEEDED(hr));
    pLeftArm2->Release(); pRightArm->Release();
}
pLeftArm->Release();
```

Fourth, since you're on a roll with the reflexive and symmetric rules, here's the discussion of the *transitive* rule of *QueryInterface*. You're holding onto Mr. RoboCOM's left arm again. Holding his left arm, you can grab his right arm (and then let go of his left arm). Furthermore, if you can use his right arm to grab his right leg, then you must also be able to grab his right leg when you have a hold of his left arm. And if this isn't the case, someone may have broken and thrown away Mr. RoboCOM's arms or legs, so that they no longer belong to a single entity. Here's a snippet showing the transitive rule:

```
HRESULT hr = pLeftArm->QueryInterface(IID_IRightArm,
                                reinterpret_cast<void**>(&pRightArm));
if (SUCCEEDED(hr)) {
    IRightLeg *pRightLeg=NULL;
    // If we can get IID_IRightArm from IID_ILeftArm
    // and we can get IID_IRightLeg from IID_IRightArm,
    hr = pRightArm->QueryInterface(IID_IRightLeg,
                                reinterpret_cast<void**>(&pRightLeg));
    if (SUCCEEDED(hr)) {
        IRightLeg *pRightLeg2=NULL;
        // then, we can get IID_IRightLeg from IID_ILeftArm.
        hr = pLeftArm->QueryInterface(IID_IRightLeg,
                                reinterpret_cast<void**>(&pRightLeg2));
        // Must evaluate to true, else violation of transitive rule.
        assert(SUCCEEDED(hr));
        pRightLeg2->Release(); pRightLeg->Release();
    }
    pRightArm->Release();
}
pLeftArm->Release();
```

You've used both of Mr. RoboCOM's arms and legs, but you've haven't dealt with his head, which is the most important thing on his body. He can lose his arms and legs and still survive, but this is impossible without a head. Mr. RoboCOM's head represents the *IUnknown* interface. A COM identity rests solely upon *IUnknown*; hence rule five. The COM Specification mandates that requests for the *IUnknown* interface must always return the exact physical pointer value each time, regardless of the fact that different interfaces are used to get to *IUnknown*. This means that if you're holding Mr. RoboCOM's left arm, you can get to Mr. RoboCOM's head (i.e., the *IUnknown*). Also, if you're holding Mr. RoboCOM's right arm, left leg, or right leg, you can get to Mr. RoboCOM's head. In any of these cases, the head you obtain must be exactly equivalent (i.e., the physical pointer values returned are exactly the same)—no replica accepted. This enables you to simply compare the returned interface pointer values to determine whether you're dealing with one single entity. This is the notion of a COM identity.* Given this rule, you can determine whether you're dealing with the same identity using the following code:

```
// Use IID_ILeftArm to get IID_IUnknown.
HRESULT h  = pLeftArm->QueryInterface(IID_IUnknown,    // Mr. RoboCOM's head
                                  reinterpret_cast<void**>(&pHead));
// Use IID_IRightArm to get IID_IUnknown.
HRESULT hr = pRightArm->QueryInterface(IID_IUnknown,    // Mr. RoboCOM's head
                             reinterpret_cast<void**> (&pBetterBeHead));
if (SUCCEEDED(h) && SUCCEEDED(hr)) {
    // According to the identity rule of COM,
    // if the following test failed, pLeftArm and pRightArm did
    // not belong to one single entity (Mr. RoboCOM).
    assert(pHead==pBetterBeHead);
    pHead->Release(); pBetterBeHead->Release();
}
pLeftArm->Release(); pRightArm->Release();
```

Having learned these identity rules, you should notice that COM allows you a lot of freedom in implementing *QueryInterface*. You're restricted only to maintaining object identity under *IUnknown*. You can be very creative in developing all other interfaces within your COM object, as long as you meet the static, reflexive, symmetric, transitive, and identity rules. These rules allow a client to freely use any interface it wants, in any order that it wants. It can move from one interface to another by dynamically discovering these interfaces.

### Existence rules

Recall that *IUnknown*'s *AddRef* and *Release* methods manage an object's lifetime. Recall also that maintaining a reference count of 100 is better than spawning 100 objects to support 100 requests. The simple reason for this is to prevent wasted system resources. In addition, only the object knows when it should commit suicide, because all implementation details must be totally hidden from the outside world.

However, I have not discussed exactly when a reference count must be incremented and decremented. The COM Specification stipulates a number of lifetime management rules that both the client and object must adhere to. These rules provide a consistent management of reference counts.

---

* This is the COM identity within a single execution context.

Notice that clients take part in determining an object's existence. Since a client is an outside entity, it should only see an interface pointer. With this interface pointer, a client can call *AddRef* and *Release* to increment and decrement an interface reference count, respectively. An object can implement reference counting anyway it chooses, but a client shouldn't care about this implementation detail. Having said that, when do you call *AddRef* and when do you call *Release?* See the sidebar entitled "Existence Rules," because it answers this question by showing the foundation for managing an object's reference count.

---

### *Existence Rules (for AddRef and Release)*

A. Each time you make a copy of an interface pointer, you must *AddRef* the interface pointer.

B. When you no longer need an interface pointer, you must *Release* it.

C. If you have special knowledge of a particular interface pointer's lifetime, you may cheat.

---

Since the sidebar talks about "making a copy," you need to know what is meant by making a copy of an interface pointer. If you assign or initialize a pointer with a valid interface pointer, you are effectively making a copy of the interface pointer. The following code snippet illustrates this:

```
extern IOcr *pOcr;      //A valid interface pointer

IOcr *pOcrInit1 = pOcr; //Initialization - making a copy of an interface
                        //pointer
IOcr *pOcrInit2(pOcr);  //Initialization - making a copy of an interface
                        //pointer

IOcr *pOcrAssign=NULL;
pOcrAssign = pOcr ;     //Assignment - making a copy of an interface pointer
```

Since you know the foundation of lifetime management, here are specific rules called out by the COM Specification.

1. If you make a copy of a global variable, you must *AddRef.* Call *Release* on the duplicated pointer when done using it.

2. For [in, out] interface pointer parameters, the caller and called function must follow these steps for consistency and predictability:

   a.   The caller calls *AddRef* before invoking the method.

   b.   The called function calls *Release* before overwriting the pointer.

    c.   After overwriting, the called function calls *AddRef* for the pointer.

    d.   The client is responsible for calling *Release* on the received pointer.

3. A function such as *QueryInterface*, which magically brings a new interface pointer to life, must *AddRef* the synthesized pointer. This means that the caller must *Release* the returned interface pointer when the pointer is no longer needed.

4. When a called function returns a copy of an internal interface pointer, it must *AddRef* the interface pointer. The caller is responsible for calling *Release*.

You must always follow these four rules, in addition to rules A and B, shown in the "Existence Rules" sidebar. But you can cheat on rules A and B if you have definite knowledge regarding the birth and death of two or more copies of a given interface pointer. With this special intelligence, you can exclude certain *AddRef* and *Release* calls. Specifically, there are two fairly safe cases in which you can cheat.

1. For [in] interface pointer parameters to subroutines, you don't need calls to *AddRef* and *Release*, because the lifetime of the duplicated pointer is nested within a larger scope.

2. For duplicated interface pointers that are local variables, you may exclude the *AddRef* and *Release* calls. This is possible because the original interface pointer will survive until the end of the code block.

Other than these two cases, you'd better be very sure about the lifetime of the duplicated interface pointer before cheating. In other words, you can save a lot of headaches if you stick with just rules A and B.

## Implementing COM Objects

You've learned how to implement an interface, but you haven't actually put the meat on the bones. Specifically, you've just stubbed the interface methods. No rush was made into implementation, because you had to learn the identity and existence rules of COM. Now that you have all this knowledge, you'll learn how to put together a COM object. In this section, you'll assemble your *CoOcrEngine* COM object.

The *CoOcrEngine* COM object exposes two interfaces: one that supports optical character recognition (*IOcr*) and one that supports spell checking (*ISpell*). Thus far, you have only partially implemented the *IOcr* interface, which also includes *IUnknown*. A typical COM object supports more than one interface just like the *CoOcrEngine* object does, so it is important to learn the prevalent techniques for implementing a COM object that exposes multiple interfaces.

*COM object definition using the nested classes technique*

There are several ways to implement multiple COM interfaces in C++; however, two techniques are commonly used. The first is by using nested classes, as shown in the following code snippet:

```
class CoOcrEngine : public IUnknown {
public:
    // IUnknown methods - master vtbl for CoOcrEngine
    STDMETHODIMP QueryInterface(REFIID iid, void**);
    STDMETHODIMP_(ULONG) AddRef();
    STDMETHODIMP_(ULONG) Release();

    // Implementation of the IOcr Interface - vtbl for CIOcr
    class CIOcr : public IOcr {
    public:
        CoOcrEngine * m_pHost;          // Points back to host object

        // Easy to keep interface-level reference count.
        // How many references to this interface?
        LONG m_lInterfaceLevelRefCount;

        // IUnknown methods - delegate outward to the hosting object's
        // (CoOcrEngine) IUnknown methods.
        STDMETHODIMP QueryInterface(REFIID iid, void** ppvObj);
        STDMETHODIMP_(ULONG) AddRef();
        STDMETHODIMP_(ULONG) Release();

        // IOcr Methods
        STDMETHODIMP OcrImage(long lImageSize, byte *pbImage,
                        wchar_t **pwszOcrText);
        STDMETHODIMP OcrZone(long lImageSize, byte *pbImage, Zone zone,
                        wchar_t **pwszOcrText);
    } m_IOcr ;

    // Implementation of the ISpell Interface - vtbl for CISpell
    class CISpell : public ISpell {
    public:
        CoOcrEngine * m_pHost;          // Points back to host object

        // Easy to keep interface-level reference count.
        // How many references to this interface?
        LONG m_lInterfaceLevelRefCount;

        // IUnknown methods - delegate outward to the hosting object's
        // (CoOcrEngine) IUnknown methods.
        STDMETHODIMP QueryInterface(REFIID iid, void** ppvObj);
        STDMETHODIMP_(ULONG) AddRef();
        STDMETHODIMP_(ULONG) Release();

        // ISpell Methods
        STDMETHODIMP Check(wchar_t *pwszWord, PossibleWords *pWords);

    } m_ISpell;
```

```
public:
    // Object-level reference count.  How many references to this object?
    LONG m_lRefCount;
};
```

As you can see, you have to implement a separate C++ class for each interface. The outer class implements the *IUnknown* interface, and the two nested classes implement the *IOcr* and *ISpell* interfaces. Furthermore, each interface must also provide implementations for *IUnknown*, since each interface is derived from *IUnknown*. In addition, you need to point back to the hosting object. The embedded or nested C++ objects delegate all their *IUnknown* calls outward to the hosting object, because a query for an *IUnknown* interface on this COM object must always return the exact physical pointer value. In other words, if a client queries this COM object for the *IUnknown* interface, the object will return a pointer to the instantiated *CoOcrEngine* object every single time, obeying the identity law of COM. Put differently, even though you have three implementations for *IUnknown* using this nested classes technique, only the outer *IUnknown* implementation can represent the identity of the *CoOcrEngine* object. This is why the *IUnknown* implementations in *CIOcr* and *CISpell* delegate outward to the implementation of *IUnknown* in *CoOcrEngine*.

This nested classes technique allows an easy way to keep interface-level reference counts, but requires more coding. You may want to keep track of an interface-level reference count for debugging or for other purposes, such as a customized or unique implementation of a particular interface. Having seen this approach, look at a more concise technique.

### COM object definition using the multiple inheritance technique

You can use C++ multiple inheritance to implement our *CoOcrEngine* COM object. This technique saves many keystrokes and allows you to share the same *IUnknown* implementation for all your exposed interfaces. In other words, you write the code for *IUnknown's* methods only once. Contrast this to previous technique in which you have to implement three sets of *IUnknown* methods. As a result, this approach is more efficient than the previous one, since there are no outward delegations. However, this approach doesn't allow you to easily keep an interface-level reference count. That doesn't really matter, because it's not needed in many implementations. The real drawback with multiple inheritance is that method names that support different functionality may collide. For example, let's assume that *IOcr* and *ISpell* contain a method with an identical signature, such as:

```
HRESULT Initialize();
```

Judging by the name of the method, a COM object that supports these two interfaces will want to implement two functionally different methods with the same signature—one method for *IOcr* and the other for *ISpell*. You should have two different implementations of *Initialize*, because initializing an *IOcr* interface should be different than initializing an *ISpell* interface. However, C++ multiple inheritance only allows you to implement exactly one function of a given signature, inhibiting you from providing two different implementations of this particular method.* The good thing is that this problem doesn't normally exist. Just be careful when you design or specify your COM interfaces.

Since multiple inheritance makes your life simpler, you'll use it to implement your *CoOcrEngine* COM object. Using this technique, here's a C++ class definition (COM class) for *CoOcrEngine* that supports two different interfaces:

```
class CoOcrEngine : public IOcr, public ISpell {
private:
    // Object-level reference count.  How many references to this object?
    LONG m_lRefCount;

public:
    // Constructors/destructors
    COcrEngine() : m_lRefCount(0) { ComponentAddRef(); }
    ~COcrEngine() { ComponentRelease(); }

    // The factory will call this method to actually create this object.
    static HRESULT CreateObject(LPUNKNOWN pUnkOuter, REFIID riid, void** ppv);

public:
    // IUnknown Methods
    STDMETHODIMP QueryInterface(REFIID riid, void **ppv);
    STDMETHODIMP_(ULONG) AddRef(void);
    STDMETHODIMP_(ULONG) Release(void);

    // IOcr Methods
    STDMETHODIMP OcrImage(long lImageSize,
                          byte *pbImage,
                          wchar_t **pwszOcrText);
    STDMETHODIMP OcrZone(long lImageSize,
                         byte *pbImage,
                         Zone zone,
                         wchar_t **pwszOcrText);

    // ISpell Methods
    STDMETHODIMP Check(wchar_t *pwszWord,
                       PossibleWords *pWords);
};
```

Notice that an object-level reference count is kept. Initialize it in the constructor's initializor list. This reference count will allow you to control the lifetime of your COM object. The constructor and destructor call the special helper functions,

---

* You can solve this name clashing problem with a few simple C++ tricks though. Simply write a *CIOcr* class that inherits from *IOcr* and implement the *Initialize* method to call *InitializeIOcr*, which is a pure virtual function defined in the *CIOcr* class. By the same token, write a *CISpell* class that inherits from *ISpell* and implement the *Initialize* method to call *InitializeISpell*, which again is a pure virtual function defined in the *CISpell* class. Then, let the *CoOcrEngine* class inherit from *CIOcr* and *CISpell* and implement the *InitializeIOcr* and *InitializeISpell* methods.

*ComponentAddRef* and *ComponentRelease*, to coordinate the lifetime of the whole COM component (i.e., an EXE or DLL). The *CreateObject* function is a static function that allows a simple and controlled way to create instances (COM objects) of this COM class. The purpose of these functions will be clearer when you actually implement them.

If you compare this technique against the nested classes technique, you'll see that this approach is much simpler, if not more concise. This class supports the three *IUnknown* methods, which are shared among all supported interfaces. It also supports the two methods from *IOcr* and the only method from *ISpell*, as clearly marked by the emphasized comments. Now that you've seen the class definition, examine the implementation of the three *IUnknown* methods, starting with *QueryInterface*.

### Implementing IUnknown methods

As mentioned, you need to implement only one *QueryInterface* function when using the multiple inheritance technique. *QueryInterface* tells the world whether a COM object supports a particular interface. The first parameter indicates the interface (represented by the riid, which is a reference to an IID) requested by a caller. The second parameter returns the interface pointer requested.

```
STDMETHODIMP CoOcrEngine::QueryInterface(REFIID riid, void **ppv)
{
    if (ppv==NULL) return E_INVALIDARG;

    if (riid==IID_IUnknown) {
       *ppv = static_cast<IOcr *>(this);
    } else if (riid==IID_IOcr) {
       *ppv = static_cast<IOcr *>(this);
    } else if (riid==IID_ISpell) {
       *ppv = static_cast<ISpell *>(this);
    } else {
       *ppv = NULL; return E_NOINTERFACE ;
    }

    reinterpret_cast<IUnknown *>(*ppv)->AddRef();
    return S_OK;
}
```

As in almost all implementations of *QueryInterface*, this implementation returns a this pointer for every requested interface. To be more precise, you cast the this pointer into the correct vptr pointing to the appropriate vtbl (i.e., the vtbl of either *IOcr* or *ISpell*). See Figure 3-11 for the binary layout and the effect of casting the this pointer into a specific interface pointer type. If *QueryInterface* supports a requested interface, it will first increment the object's reference count and return S_OK as an affirmative response. If it doesn't support a requested interface, it simply nulls out the returned pointer and returns E_NOINTERFACE. As discussed earlier, these constants are predefined and commonly used HRESULTs.

Refer to the *QueryInterface* method to see the relationship between the code and Figure 3-11. The numbered sets of boxes, shown in Figure 3-11, represent the following:

1. An instance of the *CoOcrEngine* COM class at runtime (or a *CoOcrEngine* COM object). Note that it has two hidden `vptrs`, one for the *IOcr* interface and the other for the *ISpell* interface.

2. The `vtbl` for the *IOcr* interface. Casting the `this` pointer into an *IOcr* or an *IUnknown* pointer type produces a pointer that refers to the `vtbl` for *IOcr*.

3. The `vtbl` for *ISpell*. Casting the `this` pointer into an *ISpell* pointer type produces a pointer that refers to the `vtbl` for *ISpell*.

4. The actual code for all the implemented methods. Note that the implementation of the *IUnknown* methods are shared by *IUnknown*, *IOcr*, and *ISpell*.

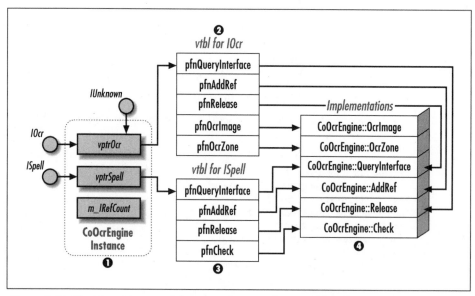

*Figure 3-11. The binary layout of three interfaces implemented by CoOcrEngine*

Remember the identity and integrity rules? They are all fulfilled by *QueryInterface*. *QueryInterface* must meet COM's static, reflexive, symmetric, transitive, and identity rules. Ask Mr. RoboCOM to validate the implementation of this particular *QueryInterface* method, and he will give thumbs up. If you don't believe him, inspect the *QueryInterface* method (shown previously) really hard and you'll realize that it fulfills these five rules. You can be as ingenious as you want in implementing this function, as long as you meet these specified rules. If you fail to comply, your object is not a COM object.

Now look at the implementation for *AddRef* and *Release*. The *AddRef* method simply increments the object's reference count.

```
STDMETHODIMP_(ULONG) CoOcrEngine::AddRef(void)
{
    return InterlockedIncrement(&m_lRefCount);  // Increment m_lRefCount
}
```

The implementation for *Release* is also straightforward. The only thing to note is that you decrement the object's reference count before deleting the object. You must code this method like this, because an object's member variables are invalid after the object is destroyed. Therefore, it would be bad if you had deleted the object first and then returned the value received from *InterlockedDecrement* to the caller.

```
STDMETHODIMP_(ULONG) CoOcrEngine::Release(void)
{
// Decrement m_lRefCount
    ULONG ulCount = InterlockedDecrement(&m_lRefCount);
    if (ulCount == 0) { delete this; }
    return ulCount;
}
```

In both of these methods, notice that you use the *InterlockedIncrement* and *InterlockedDecrement* Win32 functions to atomically increment and decrement the reference count, respectively. This is definitely needed in a multithreaded environment where this object may be concurrently used by many threads.

### Implementing other interface methods

The *IUnknown* methods mandate a set of rules that objects must obey. For all other methods, do whatever you like. These are methods that really do the work in a COM object. They contain the guts and the glory details that make a distributed object tick. There are a number of memory management rules that must be followed for [out] and [in, out] parameters, but these rules will be discussed in Chapter 5.

# Class Factories

So far, you've learned how to specify your interfaces and learned how to implement a COM object that supports a couple of interfaces. You've got an object, but how do you bring it to life? Technically, you can create and use your COM object as a normal C++ object. However, the goal is to expose this object to the world so that everyone, who has the correct permissions, can use the services exposed by our object.

As is, your COM object cannot be used in a distributed environment. For example, how will a remote client create a new object, using C++'s operator new, on a machine that is 200 miles away? They can't, so remote clients can't use your COM object just yet. You need a class factory: a COM object whose sole purpose in life is to manufacture COM objects of a specific COM class. Like interfaces, a

COM class has an associated class identifier (CLSID). The CLSID is in fact a GUID, and therefore, it is a globally unique name of a class, which universally prevents name collisions. Figure 3-12 shows a class factory and its manufactured COM objects, which are instances of a COM class known to the class factory (this will be clear in Chapter 4).

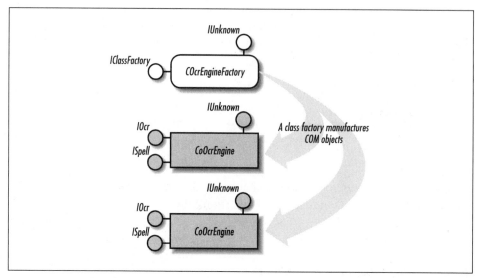

*Figure 3-12. A class factory and its manufactured COM objects*

A class factory is a vital element in a distributed environment, because it adds another level of indirection that allows COM to arbitrate and coordinate dynamic and remote activation.* There are two different factory models in COM, including standard and custom factories. Standard factories support a generic interface that is specified by COM and used for object creation. On the other hand, you can provide your own private interface to create objects. You'll learn both strategies in this section.

## *Standard Factories*

As mentioned, factories manufacture objects. Standard factories support the generic *IClassFactory* interface to allow a common way to bring COM objects to life. Implementing a standard factory is straightforward in C++, because all you have to do is implement the standard *IClassFactory* interface. This interface specifies

---

* You don't necessarily need a class factory if you don't require dynamic and remote activation support. For example, some sink objects do not require the support for dynamic or remote activation because they are privately instantiated by a client to capture events fired off by servers. Consequently, these sink objects need not expose a class factory.

two methods: *CreateInstance* and *LockServer*. Before you examine these methods in more detail, look at a typical implementation of a standard factory:

```
class COcrEngineFactory : public IClassFactory {
public:
    // IUnknown Methods
    STDMETHODIMP QueryInterface (REFIID riid, void** ppv);
    STDMETHODIMP_(ULONG) AddRef(void)  { return 1; }
    STDMETHODIMP_(ULONG) Release(void) { return 1; }

    // IClassFactory Methods
    STDMETHODIMP CreateInstance(LPUNKNOWN punkOuter,
                                REFIID iid,
                                void **ppv);
    STDMETHODIMP LockServer(BOOL fLock);
};
```

*IClassFactory* is a COM interface, which means that it derives from *IUnknown,* and therefore must implement the *QueryInterface, AddRef,* and *Release* methods. Notice that *AddRef* and *Release* are both stubbed up to return a magic number—anything you choose. The reason for this simplistic implementation results from the fact that factories are typically singletons. That is, they are typically created once as a global variable and live for the lifetime of the component that hosts them. Therefore, they don't need to determine when to delete themselves, as they will die along with their associated components. Aside from this, you may choose to implement *AddRef* and *Release* to deal with a real reference count for debugging purposes. Having said that, look at a de facto *QueryInterface* implementation of a standard factory:

```
STDMETHODIMP COcrEngineFactory::QueryInterface(REFIID riid, void** ppv)
{
    if (ppv==NULL) return E_INVALIDARG;

    if (riid==IID_IUnknown) {
        *ppv = static_cast<IClassFactory *>(this);
    } else if (riid==IID_IClassFactory) {
        *ppv = static_cast<IClassFactory *>(this);
    } else {
        *ppv = NULL; return E_NOINTERFACE ;
    }

    reinterpret_cast<IUnknown *>(*ppv)->AddRef();
    return S_OK;
}
```

As shown, the code for a factory's *QueryInterface* method looks similar to *CoOcrEngine's QueryInterface* method, with the exception of casting the `this` pointer into an *IClassFactory* pointer. Aside from this, this method needs no further discussion.

Turn your attention to the guts of a class factory: *CreateInstance.* This method is the purpose of a factory's existence: to create an uninitialized COM object. The first parameter points to a controlling unknown, which is used for aggregation (a method of component reuse discussed in Chapter 4). The second parameter indicates the target interface that is requested by a client. The third parameter returns the requested interface pointer to the client.

```
STDMETHODIMP
COcrEngineFactory::CreateInstance(LPUNKNOWN pUnkOuter, REFIID riid,
                                  void **ppv)
{
    // Call CoOcrEngine's static function to create
    // a CoOcrEngine COM object.
    return CoOcrEngine::CreateObject(pUnkOuter, riid, ppv);
}
```

The above implementation delegates the responsibility of actually instantiating the COM object to the static *CoOcrEngine::CreateObject* function. Recall that this was declared a static function earlier in the *CoOcrEngine* class definition, but you haven't implemented it. Here's its implementation:

```
HRESULT CoOcrEngine::CreateObject(LPUNKNOWN pUnkOuter, REFIID riid,
                                  void** ppv)
{
    *ppv = NULL;

    // CoOcrEngine doesn't support aggregation
    if (pUnkOuter != NULL) { return CLASS_E_NOAGGREGATION; }

    // Create a CoOcrEngine COM object
    CoOcrEngine * pEngine = new CoOcrEngine;
    if (pEngine == NULL) { return E_OUTOFMEMORY; }

    HRESULT hr = pEngine->QueryInterface(riid, ppv);
    if (FAILED(hr)) { delete pEngine; }

    return hr;
}
```

The first line of this method nulls out the return interface pointer in case of a failure. In the next line, if an outer unknown is passed in, it means the caller requests to aggregate your COM object (*CoOcrEngine* instance). Aggregation is a technique for object reuse in COM. If aggregation is requested, you return CLASS_E_NOAGGREGATION to inform the caller that this COM object doesn't support aggregation. After the check for an outer unknown, you dynamically instantiate your object on the heap. If this heap-based allocation fails, you return E_OUTOFMEMORY indicating the problem. Otherwise, you use the instantiated object to query for the requested interface, indicated in the second parameter as riid. If the query succeeds, ppv is set. If the query fails, you delete the previously created object. Recall that *QueryInterface* internally increments its object's reference count upon success. In any case, you propagate the status code back to the caller.

The *LockServer* method allows a caller to lock the server in memory, allowing for faster creation of COM objects. You can use *LockServer* as a way to manage a component's (i.e., EXE or DLL) lifetime. The COM runtime, specifically the SCM, calls this method to prevent a possible race condition dealing with the premature death of a server during remote activation requests.

```
STDMETHODIMP LockServer(BOOL fLock)
{
    if (fLock) {
        ComponentAddRef();
    } else {
        ComponentRelease();
    }
    return S_OK;
}
```

In this implementation, if a TRUE is passed into the method, the component-level reference count would be incremented. Otherwise, the component-level reference count would be decremented. *ComponentAddRef* and *ComponentRelease* are two helper functions that we write to support the management of a component-level reference count. We will discuss these helper functions in Chapter 4, as their implementations depend on the server type.

It is worth it to at least mention after going over *IClassFactory* that there is an *IClassFactory2* interface, which specifies three additional methods for licensing support. *IClassFactory2* is derived from *IClassFactory*. This is a perfect example of the immutable interface rule: "Once an interface is published, you should never change it." Since you shouldn't change it, you derive from the original interface and specify additional methods. The new interface gets a new name and IID.

## Custom Factories

You don't have to implement standard factories to support dynamic and remote activation. If you want to provide a non-standard factory to get some privacy of object creation, you may do so. But doing this will limit the creation of your COM object, as several popular tools (like the OLE/COM Object Viewer) dynamically create objects using specifically the standard *IClassFactory* interface. Therefore, typical factories don't support custom factory interfaces. However, if you implement a custom factory, you can be as creative as you want when dealing with object creation.

With that said, you can implement a custom factory by:

- Specifying your custom factory interface using MIDL and compiling it using the MIDL compiler
- Implementing your custom object creation interface

---

### *Standard or Custom?*

Throughout this chapter, the words standard and custom described interfaces, factories, and marshaling. The following officially clarifies these terms.

- Interfaces that Microsoft develops are referred to as *standard interfaces*. Popular standard interfaces include dispatch and dual interfaces (see the "Interfaces" section).

- Interfaces that anyone else develops are referred to as *custom interfaces*.

- Factories that implement the *IClassFactory* interface are referred to as *standard factories*.

- Factories that implement a custom interface for object creation are referred to as *custom factories*.

- The COM runtime provides *standard marshaling* so that you don't have to write any marshaling code, as standard marshaling uses the proxy/ stub code automatically generated by the MIDL compiler. In this category, there's also *Automation marshaling*, which requires no proxy/stub code. However, Automation marshaling requires the creation and registration of a type library.

- COM allows you the freedom to implement your own *custom marshaling*. If you implement custom marshaling, you have full control of the remote transfer of information between the client and the object. See Chapter 5 for more information.

---

The following MIDL snippet shows a simple example of a custom factory interface that supports one method for object creation. This is the *GiveMeOcrEngine* method that returns an *IOcr* interface pointer to the caller. As implied by the name of this method, the purpose of this custom class factory interface is to create *CoOcrEngine* COM objects, which expose the *IOcr* interface.

```
[object, uuid(A85BFC90-BBFB-11d1-ABF1-00207810D5FE)]
interface IOcrEngineFactory : IUnknown
{
    HRESULT GiveMeOcrEngine([out] IOcr **ppOcr);
};
```

An implementation of this would go something like this:

```
class COcrEngineFactory : public IOcrEngineFactory {
public:
    // IUnknown Methods
    STDMETHODIMP QueryInterface (REFIID riid, void** ppv) { ... }
    STDMETHODIMP_(ULONG) AddRef(void)  { return 1; }
    STDMETHODIMP_(ULONG) Release(void) { return 1; }
```

```
// IOcrEngineFactory Methods
STDMETHODIMP GiveMeOcrEngine(IOcr **ppOcr)
{
    *ppOcr = NULL;

    CoOcrEngine * pEngine = new CoOcrEngine;
    if (pEngine == NULL) return E_OUTOFMEMORY;

    *ppOcr = pEngine ;
    pEngine->AddRef();

    return S_OK;
}
};
```

As you can see, implementing a custom factory is reasonably straightforward. The *GiveMeOcrEngine* method simply returns to the caller a pointer to an instantiated *CoOcrEngine* instance.

4

*In this chapter:*
• *Servers*
• *Clients*
• *Object Orientation*

# Components

In the last chapter, you learned how to package a COM object from a number of interfaces. You also learned how to build a class factory that can dynamically create your COM objects in a distributed environment. You wrote the code, but you couldn't test the COM object just yet, because you haven't put the code for the COM object and its class factory inside a binary module, such as a DLL or an EXE, that can be executed.

In this chapter, you will learn how to build these binary modules, which can both use and expose COM objects. We call these binary modules *COM components*. As shown in Figure 4-1, a client component can be any COM application that uses a COM object's interfaces. Server components, on the other hand, are the ones that host COM objects and their associated class factories.

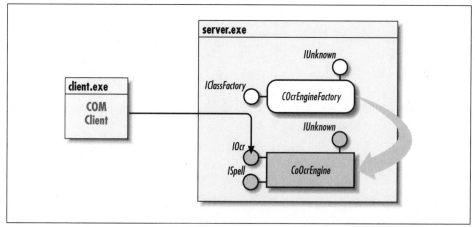

*Figure 4-1. Client and server components*

The C++ code that you see in this chapter can be automated by Visual C++ and the ATL wizards with a few mouse clicks. However, knowing what's needed to create a component from scratch will empower you. There's no magic in the wizard-generated code, shown in Chapter 6 and onwards.

By the time you finish this chapter, you will know how to package COM objects into a COM application suitable for a distributed environment. You will also know how to write client applications that make use of remote COM objects. Furthermore, you'll know how to dynamically reuse COM objects that are already developed and deployed.

Here's a list of what's covered in this chapter.

1. Servers—Class factories and objects cannot execute alone. They need either a house (EXE) or a shed (DLL) to host them. Like an EXE, a house stands alone, whereas, a shed—like a DLL—is useful only next to a structure. Recall that components are DLLs, OCXs, and EXEs. You'll learn the necessary code for developing a component in this section. Specifically, we'll examine the required code for component initialization, termination, dynamic activation, lifetime, and registration.

2. Clients—Clients are components that use a different component's objects. You'll learn the necessary code for developing a COM compatible client in this section. These clients must abide by the initialization, termination, object creation, interface usage, and lifetime management rules of COM.

3. Object Orientation—Having learned the basics of COM, we can judiciously discuss the object orientation aspects of COM. In this section, you'll also learn COM's component reuse mechanisms: containment and aggregation.

This chapter is a sequel to the previous one. The previous chapter and this chapter capture all the basic elements for building distributed components. Like the last chapter, you should read this chapter from beginning to end for understanding. Then, review the relevant sections in this chapter, as well as the last chapter, when you build your own distributed components.

## Servers

In the last chapter, you developed a class factory that could create COM objects upon request. However, the class factory and the objects themselves could not execute alone. They need to be packaged together into a component, such as an EXE or a DLL. With the hospitality of a component, class factories can register themselves to the SCM so that clients anywhere in the universe can access them,

# *Creating a Server Component*

Initialization and Termination

> *Out-of-process server*
>> All threads using COM must initialize COM by calling *CoInitialize[Ex]*. All threads must call *CoUninitialize* after using COM.

> *In-process server*
>> No need to call *CoInitialize[Ex]* or *CoUninitialize*. because the hosting application does this.

Dynamic Activation

> *Out-of-process server*
>> Register all class objects (synonym for class factories) with the SCM, using *CoRegisterClassObject*.

> *In-process server*
>> Write *DllGetClassObject* to expose all class objects within a DLL.

Lifetime Management

> *Both types*
>> Manage component-level reference counts using helper functions, such as *ComponentAddRef* and *ComponentRelease*. These are your own functions, which can be named anything you prefer. They are called by constructors and destructors of all COM objects and by *IClassFactory::LockServer*.

> *Out-of-process server*
>> Support server shutdown signals, which can be a Win32 event object in an MTA or a window message in an STA.

> *In-process server*
>> Write *DllCanUnloadNow* to support automatic DLL unloading.

Registration

> *Out-of-process server*
>> Support `-RegServer` and `-UnRegServer` command-line options and write the code to register and unregister all supported class objects.

> *In-process server*
>> Implement *DllRegisterServer* and *DllUnregisterServer* for registration and unregistration. Use *regsvr32.exe* to register an in-process server.

> *Interface marshalers*
>> Use *regsvr32.exe* to register proxy/stub DLL for remote interfaces.

barring security constraints of course. A typical component, more often referred to as a server, may package together multiple factories that can create different object types. Recall that a class factory can create instances of a particular COM class, which has an associated class identifier (CLSID). Clients use the CLSID to find the correct factory that can create the associated COM object.

In this section, you'll learn how to share your factories and their associated objects with the world. You'll assemble the code for your factories and their associated objects into a COM compatible server.* First, you'll learn the preliminary terms related to server types, including *out-of-process (outofproc)* and *in-process (inproc)* servers, because server requirements differ slightly for each server type. Then you'll learn the necessary server initialization and termination requirements. Next, we'll look at managing a server's lifetime, as this is important in terms of system resources and types of execution contexts. Finally, you'll learn how to add support for dynamic activation, in addition to registering your classes against the implementation repository (the Windows Registry).

## Server Types

There are two general categories of servers in the world of COM: out-of-process and in-process servers. They differ in many aspects, including initialization, dynamic activation, implementation registration, and component lifetime management. First there will be a brief discussion of the types. Second, we will focus on the specific differences.

### Out-of-process servers

Before out-of-process servers are discussed, two important terms need to be defined. This book uses the term *execution context* to refer to an encapsulated execution scope, which can be a single thread, a group of threads, a process, or the whole machine. COM formally calls an execution context an *apartment*.

Out-of-process servers are standalone executables. As such, they run in a different execution context from the client executable. These servers can reside on a client's local machine or on a remote machine. Servers with the EXE extension are out-of-process servers. See Figure 4-2. To be specific, there are two different types of out-of-process servers. Executables that reside and execute on a client's machine are called *local servers*, whereas ones that reside and execute on a remote machine are called *remote servers*.

When a client invokes a method in an out-of-process server, the method invocation will cross apartment, process, and possibly machine boundaries, which means

---

* This section deals only with the basics of a COM server. Chapter 5, *Infrastructure*, deals with concurrency management, which requires changes to the COM server in order to correctly function with the COM runtime.

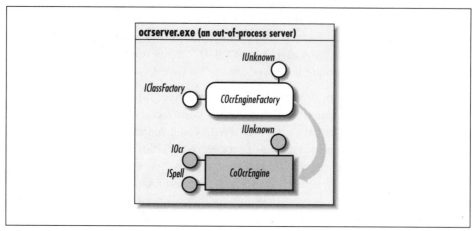

*Figure 4-2. An out-of-process server*

that marshaling is involved. In standard marshaling, COM sets up a proxy on the client side and a stub on the object side. The proxy lives locally in the client's address space. The client talks directly to this proxy, the proxy talks to the stub, and the stub talks to the target object. The out-of-process server is a separate process that runs in a totally different execution context from the client. All method invocations are dispatched using ORPC across different execution contexts. For this reason, out-of-process servers offer poorer performance than in-process ones, since interprocess communication is involved, on top of security, network bandwidth, protocol activation, and so forth. The impact is far more brutal for remote servers than for local servers.* However, out-of-process servers provide scalability and fault tolerance, because they can be isolated or distributed on many different physical hosts. If you're interested in seeing representative data regarding in-process and out-of-process performance, see Appendix B.

### In-process servers

As shown in Figure 4-3, in-process servers need a hosting executable in order to be active. The hosting executable is the client that uses the in-process server. In other words, in-process servers run in the same process as a client executable. They are dynamic link libraries with extensions such as DLL and OCX. Because they execute within your client's process, you experience the best possible performance. All method invocations are directly made using `vptrs` and `vtbls`. This is an efficient way to invoke an interface method, as it is equivalent to a C++ virtual function call. Be forewarned that this is true only when both the client and the server component share the same execution context, as discussed in Chapter 5.

---

* COM can optimize marshaling for local servers using lightweight RPC (LRPC). LRPC is based on window messages.

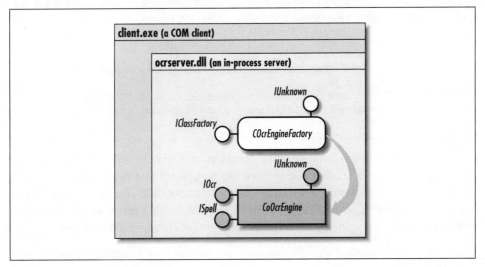

*Figure 4-3. An in-process server*

If you need to use in-process servers remotely, you need a surrogate EXE and its required registry settings on the server side. This surrogate hosts the in-process server. On the client side, you need the required registry settings to point to the remote host.

There are also other variants of in-process servers. These are called *in-process* handlers, which are DLLs that represent custom marshalers. These DLLs contain code to perform custom marshaling for an object's supported interfaces.

## Initialization and Termination

As you've just seen, a component is either an EXE or a DLL. Before you can publish your components, you must follow a number of rules, one of which deals with initialization and termination. COM initialization and termination are required at the thread level. That is, every thread in a process that uses COM must initialize the COM library. Before a COM thread vanishes, it must uninitialize the COM library to correctly release COM related resources.

In 32-bit Windows, every process starts off with one thread—the process is the first thread, which is commonly referred to as the *main thread*. Therefore, the lifetime of the first thread is the lifetime of the process. For simplicity, you'll be thread illiterate in this chapter, since Chapter 5 exploits the threading models of COM.

### Out-of-process servers

Every process must initialize COM before it can call any other COM API functions or do COM related work. There's only one exception: you may call COM memory allocation routines (*CoGetMalloc, CoTaskMemAlloc, CoTaskMemFree,* etc.) before initializing COM. Other than this exception, every thread that uses COM must initialize COM by calling one of the following COM API functions:

```
// To use CoInitializeEx, you must define _WIN32_DCOM
// pvReserved - Reserved and must be NULL
// dwCoInit   - Indicates the concurrency model of the current execution
//              context
//            - Either COINIT_APARTMENTTHREADED or COINIT_MULTITHREADED
HRESULT CoInitializeEx(LPVOID pvReserved, DWORD dwCoInit);

HRESULT CoInitialize(LPVOID pvReserved);
```

*CoInitialize* is the original initialization function, replaced by its more flexible successor, *CoInitializeEx*. *CoInitialize* is essentially a shorthand for *CoInitializeEx*, as it calls *CoInitializeEx* with the COINIT_APARMENTTHREADED flag. Your COM applications should use *CoInitializeEx* to initialize COM, as this function allows you to explicitly specify the concurrency model of your current execution context.

Once you have specified the concurrency model for your execution context, you may not change it. In other words, you cannot do the following:

```
// Thread A first calls
CoInitializeEx(NULL, COINIT_APARTMENTTHREADED);
// Thread A later tries to change the concurrency model
CoInitializeEx(NULL, COINIT_MULTITHREADED);  // ERROR:  RPC_E_CHANGED_MODE
```

Just leave these models alone for now; you'll use them later in Chapter 5.

You should call *CoUninitialize* when you finish using COM in order to free up COM related resources used by the corresponding execution context. You must do this for each successful call to *CoInitialize* or *CoInitializeEx*. This API function is trivial, because it takes no argument.

Having seen these API functions, you can now add COM initialization and cleanup to your server. The following shows a shell of a simple COM server:

```
void main(int argc, char **argv)
{
    // Initialize COM
    HRESULT hr = CoInitializeEx(NULL, COINIT_MULTITHREADED);

    // ...

    // Uninitialize COM
    if (SUCCEEDED(hr))
        CoUninitialize();
}
```

As you can see, a simple COM server must initialize and clean up COM. You have called *CoInitializeEx* with COINIT_MULTITHREADED to simplify your server code—you'll see why in Chapter 5. Other important things, such as server lifetime management and factory registration, are also necessary and will be discussed in a moment.

### In-process servers

In-process servers are hosted by a client executable, since they can't execute by themselves. For this reason, in-process servers do not call *CoInitialize[Ex]* or *CoUninitialize*, since the hosting client should make these calls. However, an in-process server can still specify the concurrency model of its COM objects using a registry key, but you'll learn how to do to this in Chapter 5.

## Dynamic Activation Support

Once you have initialized COM, you may publish your factories to the world dynamically at runtime. The way you do this depends on the type of server you're dealing with (out-of-process or in-process). Each class factory is mapped to a particular COM class's CLSID, and the CLSID is what clients use to get to a particular class factory. So when you publish your factories dynamically at runtime, you associate the factories with their related CLSIDs. By the same token, when your server shuts down, you must revoke this announcement. Examine in the next two sections how to do this for both out-of-process and in-process servers.

### Out-of-process servers

For an out-of-process server, you publish your factories dynamically by registering them with the Service Control Manager (SCM). Recall that the SCM is part of the COM runtime that plays a vital role in dynamic and remote activation. In order to help the SCM do its job, you must notify the SCM that your class factories are ready to manufacture COM objects. Typically you do this upon server startup by calling the *CoRegisterClassObject* COM API function:

```
HRESULT CoRegisterClassObject(
    REFCLSID rclsid,         // CLSID to be registered
    IUnknown * pUnk,         // Pointer to the factory's IUnknown
    DWORD dwClsContext,      // One of the values from the CLSCTX enumeration
    DWORD flags,             // Type of connections to the factory
    LPDWORD lpdwRegister     // Pointer to returned cookie
);
```

This API function basically enters the class factory associated with a given CLSID into a global class table maintained by COM. The first parameter lets you specify the CLSID associated with the class factory that you are registering, and the second parameter lets you pass in a pointer to the class factory's *IUnknown*. In essence, these two parameters let you assign or map a CLSID to a class factory, thus saying that the class factory can create instances of a COM class identified by said CLSID. This allows a client anywhere in cyberspace to ask COM for this class factory using the associated CLSID. For example, when a client makes an activation request using this CLSID, the SCM can return to the client a pointer to this class factory's *IUnknown*.

In the third parameter of *CoRegisterClassObject*, you may pass any combination of the following values:

```
CLSCTX_INPROC_SERVER
CLSCTX_INPROC_HANDLER
CLSCTX_LOCAL_SERVER
CLSCTX_REMOTE_SERVER
```

This parameter allows you to specify how clients can use the registered class factory. For example, if you specify CLSCTX_INPROC_SERVER, the class factory will be registered to support in-process activation requests. This means that COM will return the registered *IUnknown* pointer to the client that requests in-process (in-process server) activation of this class factory. Likewise, if you specify CLSCTX_LOCAL_SERVER, the class factory will be registered to support local out-of-process (local server) activation requests. This means that COM will return the registered *IUnknown* pointer to the client that requests for local out-of-process activation. And so on.

Because it is possible to combine these values, COM defines three shortcuts as shown:

```
#define CLSCTX_SERVER (CLSCTX_INPROC_SERVER| \
                       CLSCTX_LOCAL_SERVER|  \
                       CLSCTX_REMOTE_SERVER)
#define CLSCTX_INPROC (CLSCTX_INPROC_SERVER| \
                       CLSCTX_INPROC_HANDLER)
#define CLSCTX_ALL    (CLSCTX_INPROC_SERVER| \
                       CLSCTX_INPROC_HANDLER|\
                       CLSCTX_LOCAL_SERVER|  \
                       CLSCTX_REMOTE_SERVER)
```

Given these shortcuts, if you specify CLSCTX_SERVER, the class factory will be registered to support in-process, local out-of-process (local server), and remote out-of-process (remote server) activation requests. This means that COM will return the registered *IUnknown* pointer to the client that requests for in-process, local, or remote activation. For simplicity, you normally pass CLSCTX_SERVER into the third parameter (more on this later in the discussion of "Clients").

It's important to note the fourth parameter, since it indicates how the class factory is to behave. A server may pass any one of the following registration flags into the fourth parameter of *CoRegisterClassObject*:

```
REGCLS_SINGLEUSE
REGCLS_MULTIPLEUSE
REGCLS_MULTI_SEPARATE
REGCLS_SURROGATE
REGCLS_SUSPENDED
```

When you register a class factory with the REGCLS_SINGLEUSE registration flag, you are specifying that the factory can be used only once. Since factories are singletons, this implies that a new client request for the factory will cause the SCM to launch a new out-of-process server to handle the new request. This can be a nice functionality for some applications, but it can be a resource hog for others, because every single client request means spawning a new server process. For these other implementations, we can use the REGCLS_MULTIPLEUSE or REGCLS_MULTI_SEPARATE flag to indicate that our registered class factory can be used multiple times. For simplicity, use REGCLS_MULTIPLEUSE since there are subtle differences between these two flags.

The subtlety appears when you pass CLSCTX_LOCAL_SERVER as the third parameter. If you specify CLSCTX_LOCAL_SERVER and REGCLS_MULTIPLEUSE, the class factory will be automatically registered to support in-process activation requests. In this case, when *client code within the same server* requests for in-process activation of the registered class factory, COM will return a pointer to the registered *IUnknown* pointer.

However, if you specify CLSCTX_LOCAL_SERVER and REGCLS_MULTI_SEPARATE, the class factory will *not* be automatically registered to support in-process activation requests. In this case, when *client code within the same server* requests for in-process activation of the registered class factory, COM will not return the registered *IUnknown* pointer. Instead, COM will load an in-process server that supports the requested class factory into the client process. It will then return the *IUnknown* pointer obtained from the loaded in-process server to the client code, which happens to exist in the same process as the loaded in-process server. So, the REGCLS_MULTI_SEPARATE registration flag allows finer control over a class factory's behavior.

The REGCLS_SURROGATE registration flag is used for custom surrogate processes, in case you don't want to use the default system surrogate (*dllhost.exe*). Remember from Chapter 2 that a surrogate server is used to host a remote in-process server, as an in-process server cannot run alone. When you use the REGCLS_SURROGATE registration flag to register a class factory, you are telling COM that the factory is a generic factory for the surrogate process. As such, this class factory is a shell that delegates all factory calls to the actual class factory within the hosted in-process server.

The REGCLS_SUSPENDED registration flag is important in out-of-process servers. It allows you to register all factories exposed by the server without making them active. This is important to prevent certain race conditions that may occur in a multithreaded environment. For example, assume you have two factories to register, and you have registered only the first one. If you don't suspend the first factory, COM will immediately allow incoming activation requests to be serviced. Before you can register the second factory, an event might have signaled a request to shut down the server, causing possible access violations in future calls to use the second class factory. To prevent race conditions, COM allows you to register all your factories using the REGCLS_SUSPENDED flag. Once you have registered all supported factories, you tell COM to reveal all your factories to the world at once by calling the following simple COM API function:

```
HRESULT CoResumeClassObjects();
```

A successful call to *CoRegisterClassObject* returns a registration cookie that you must hold onto. When you want to shut down the factory (normally right before your application exits), you would use this cookie to withdraw or revoke the class factory from public view. Failing to properly revoke your class factories prior to application shutdown can be a fatal mistake, as the registered *IUnknown* pointers for these class factories are no longer valid. To revoke a class factory, you would call the following API function, passing in the cookie:

```
HRESULT CoRevokeClassObject(DWORD dwRegister);
```

Here's an example of an out-of-process server that registers and revokes class factories to help COM support dynamic activation. Notice that you globally instantiate two factories, *COcrEngineFactory* and *CRoboCOMFactory*. Since they are globally instantiated, they are singletons that live for the lifetime of your server. Each of these factories can dynamically manufacture their associated COM objects upon client request.

```
COcrEngineFactory g_OcrEngineFactory;
CRoboCOMFactory g_RoboCOMFactory;

void main(int argc, char **argv)
{
    // Initialize COM
    HRESULT hr = CoInitializeEx(NULL, COINIT_MULTITHREADED);


    // Call CoRegisterClassObject for each exposed factory and save
    // the associated returned cookie for unregistration.
    DWORD dwRoboCOMCookie = 0;
    DWORD dwOcrCookie = 0;
    // Register COcrEngineFactory with COM, but don't make it active.
    // This can be done using the REGCLS_SUSPENDED flag.
    hr = CoRegisterClassObject(CLSID_OcrEngine,
                        &g_OcrEngineFactory,
                        CLSCTX_SERVER,
                        REGCLS_MULTIPLEUSE | REGCLS_SUSPENDED,
                        &dwOcrCookie);
    // Register CRoboCOMFactory with COM, but don't make it active.
    // This can be done using the REGCLS_SUSPENDED flag.
    hr = CoRegisterClassObject(CLSID_RoboCOM,
                        &g_RoboCOMFactory,
                        CLSCTX_SERVER,
                        REGCLS_MULTIPLEUSE | REGCLS_SUSPENDED,
                        &dwRoboCOMCookie);

    // Register other supported factories.
```

```
      // Let all the factories loose.
      hr = CoResumeClassObjects();

         // ...

      // Revoke our factories.
      // Call CoRevokeClassObject for each factory,
      // passing in the associated cookie, to
      // revoke the class factory from public view.
      hr = CoRevokeClassObject(dwOcrCookie);
      hr = CoRevokeClassObject(dwRoboCOMCookie);

      // Uninitialize COM
      CoUninitialize();
   }
```

After initializing the COM library, call *CoRegisterClassObject* to register each factory that you want to make public, in order to support dynamic activation. Since you have two factories, you call this function twice passing in the appropriate information and getting back two different cookies. You need to save these cookies so that you can later revoke the factories. Note that you pass REGCLS_MULTIPLEUSE|REGCLS_SUSPENDED in the fourth parameter. This indicates that the g_OcrEngineFactory can be used multiple times. In addition, it must not be active until you call the *CoResumeClassObjects* API function to prevent activation-related race conditions. After you let the factories loose, they're ready to service activation and object creation requests. Before you close down your server, you must revoke all the registered class factories using the associated cookies that you have previously saved.

### In-process servers

Unlike out-of-process servers, in-process servers are loaded by a client process. Therefore, in-process servers typically do not register their supported factories with the SCM. The COM runtime requires in-process servers to expose a DLL entry point called *DllGetClassObject*, which will be called by COM. This entry point returns a requested class factory interface pointer to a client, if the in-process server exposes the requested factory. Here's an example of *DllGetClassObject* that must be supported by an in-process COM server:

```
COcrEngineFactory g_OcrEngineFactory;
CRoboCOMFactory g_RoboCOMFactory;

STDAPI DllGetClassObject(REFCLSID rclsid, REFIID riid, void** ppv)
{
   HRESULT hr = S_OK;

   if (rclsid == CLSID_OcrEngine) {
      hr = g_OcrEngineFactory.QueryInterface(riid, ppv);
   } else if (rclsid == CLSID_RoboCOM) {
      hr = g_RoboCOMFactory.QueryInterface(riid, ppv);
   } else {
```

```
        hr = CLASS_E_CLASSNOTAVAILABLE; *ppv = NULL ;
    }

    return hr;
}
```

Again, notice that your factories are global variables, because they're singleton objects. The *DllGetClassObject* function takes a reference to a CLSID that identifies the factory. It also takes an IID that represents the interface that a caller is requesting. Typically, this IID will be `IID_IClassFactory`, which is the standard interface for object creation. The resulting interface pointer will be returned to the caller via the third parameter. The code for this function is straightforward. For each CLSID that you support, you simply delegate the interface pointer request to the corresponding class factory's *QueryInterface* function. As you have learned earlier, the target factory's *QueryInterface* function will return the resulting interface pointer via `*ppv` upon success or return an `E_NOINTERFACE` status code upon failure. If you don't support a requested CLSID, you simply return the `CLASS_E_CLASSNOTAVAILABLE` status code. In addition, you must also set the resulting pointer to `NULL`.

Typically, you don't call *CoRegisterClassObject* within in-process servers. However, no one's stopping you from doing so. You can call *CoRegisterClassObject* (and company) after the in-process server is loaded into memory. For example, you may do this by spawning a thread, which enters into an execution context. Within this execution context, you may register and unregister factories as you've seen earlier.

## Component Lifetime

Now that you know how to support dynamic activation, turn your attention to server management. Initialization and termination were talked about earlier, but they are only half the story to server management. Before you can uninitialize COM, you must make sure that no external sources are holding references to your server. Simply put, you must make sure that it's safe to shut down your server before attempting the shutdown. As a general rule, you must keep a component alive if any of the following holds true:

- There are living COM objects.
- There are locks on the server.
- There is user interaction.
- There are references to any class factory.

Of these, you must take into account the first two cases. You need to worry about the third rule only when your component is in fact a user interface application (for instance, a spreadsheet application). In this case, even if all conditions are met for server shutdown, your server may not initiate shutdown if a user is interactively working with it. In simple implementations, you normally don't worry about the fourth rule, since a factory is a usually a singleton object. This means that typically only one instance of a factory exists during the lifetime of a given server. In this sense, managing reference counts for factories is unnecessary.

Knowing these kinks, here is a general rule for component lifetime management: keep the server alive if there are living COM objects or outstanding locks on the server. To manage living COM objects, call a special function named *ComponentAddRef* in the constructors of all your COM objects, except the factory's constructor. Likewise, call *ComponentRelease* in all destructors of your COM objects. For example, here are the constructor and destructor of the *CoOcrEngine* COM object, which you have seen earlier in Chapter 3:

```
CoOcrEngine::CoOcrEngine() : m_lRefCount(0) { ComponentAddRef(); }
CoOcrEngine::~CoOcrEngine() { ComponentRelease(); }
```

*ComponentAddRef* and *ComponentRelease* are global helper functions that you write. They increment and decrement a global component-level reference count. A component-level reference count includes the counts of both living COM objects and server locks.

To manage server locks, you will need to add the following code, which you've also seen earlier, to your factory's *LockServer* method:

```
STDMETHODIMP LockServer(BOOL fLock)
{
    if (fLock) {
       ComponentAddRef();
    } else {
       ComponentRelease();
    }
    return S_OK;
}
```

When this method is called with a **TRUE** argument, meaning someone asks you to lock your server in place so that it won't die unexpectedly, you increment the component-level reference count. When it is called with a **FALSE** argument, meaning someone releases a server lock, you decrement the component-level reference count.

You will implement *ComponentAddRef* and *ComponentRelease* next, since their implementations depend on server types.

### Out-of-process servers

For a multithreaded COM server, managing server lifetime can be simply done using a Win32 event object. For instance, here's the newly added code to manage the lifetime of your server component:

```
HANDLE g_hExitEvent = NULL;
COcrEngineFactory g_OcrEngineFactory;

void main(int argc, char **argv)
{
    // Server lifetime management.
    g_hExitEvent = CreateEvent(NULL, FALSE, FALSE, NULL);
    if (g_hExitEvent == NULL) assert(false);

    // Initialize COM
    HRESULT hr = CoInitializeEx(NULL, COINIT_MULTITHREADED);


    // Register COcrEngineFactory with COM, but don't make it active.
    // Call CoRegisterClassObject for each exposed factory and save
    // the associated returned cookie for unregistration.
    DWORD dwOcrCookie = 0;
    hr = CoRegisterClassObject(CLSID_OcrEngine,
                               &g_OcrEngineFactory,
                               CLSCTX_SERVER,
                               REGCLS_MULTIPLEUSE | REGCLS_SUSPENDED,
                               &dwOcrCookie);

    // Register other supported factories.

    // Let the all the factories loose.
    hr = CoResumeClassObjects();

    // Server lifetime management: sit and wait until exit event is signaled.
    WaitForSingleObject(g_hExitEvent, INFINITE);

    // Revoke our factories.
    // Call CoRevokeClassObject for each factory,
    // passing in the associated cookie, to
    // revoke the class factory from public view.
    hr = CoRevokeClassObject(dwOcrCookie);

    // Uninitialize COM
    CoUninitialize();
    CloseHandle(g_hExitEvent);
}
```

As you can see, server management using a global event is flairy simple. In *main*, you create a Win32 event object, which represents an exit event. After you have registered and resumed all the supported factories, you sit and wait until this event is signaled. Once you have received this signal, you revoke your factories and uninitialize COM. This is all fine so far, but who does the signaling? *ComponentRelease* will do the signaling at the right time.

COM supports a global per-process reference count, which is maintained internally by the COM library for each out-of-process server. An out-of-process server needs to increment and decrement this per-process reference count to correctly manage server lifetime in a multithreaded environment. To atomically increment or decrement this process-wide reference count, you must use the following COM API functions:

```
ULONG CoAddRefServerProcess();
ULONG CoReleaseServerProcess();
```

*CoAddRefServerProcess* atomically increments the per-process reference count, which is managed internally by COM. *CoReleaseServerProcess* atomically decrements this reference count. The real reason for using these API functions is to prevent race conditions dealing with untimely activation requests.

Assume for the moment that you're not using these atomic operations. In a multi-threaded environment, it is possible for a component-level reference count to become zero, and for a thread switch to occur before a server revokes a given class factory. During this minute window, a new activation request may arrive targeting the still valid factory. This can potentially cause an access violation, since the server is about to die off. Aware of this problem, COM provides the *CoReleaseServerProcess* API function to suspend all factories in the server, preventing these new activation requests from coming in. COM does this when it detects that the per-process reference count becomes zero. If a request comes at this moment, the SCM will launch a new server to support the new activation request, since it sees a disabled factory, which is suspended by COM. COM knows when the per-process reference count becomes zero, because it is responsible for maintaining this count. Your job is just to correctly call these atomic operations at the appropriate time (i.e., in a COM object's constructor and destructor and in a factory's *LockServer* method).

Knowing these API functions, you can implement the *ComponentAddRef* and *ComponentRelease* helper functions, which respectively increment and decrement the component-level reference count. The *ComponentAddRef* helper function is straightforward; it just increments the per-process reference count managed by COM. Recall that *ComponentAddRef* is called by `LockServer(TRUE)` and by the constructors of all COM objects.

```
// Return value use only for debugging purposes
inline ULONG ComponentAddRef()
{
    return (CoAddRefServerProcess());
}
```

The *ComponentRelease* method is the reverse of *ComponentAddRef*, as it decrements the per-process reference count that's maintained by COM. Recall that *ComponentRelease* is called by `LockServer(FALSE)` and by COM objects' destructors. In other words, your server decrements the per-process reference count when a COM object dies off or when a lock is being released. *ComponentRelease* will also signal server shutdown at the appropriate time. In particular, it sets the exit event when the per-process reference count falls to zero; that is, when there are no longer any locks or living COM objects. Thus, you can tell the server to shut down by signaling an exit event.

```
inline ULONG ComponentRelease()
{
    ULONG ul = CoReleaseServerProcess();
    if (ul==0) { SetEvent(g_hExitEvent);   }
    return ul ;
}
```

That, in a nutshell, is all there is to lifetime management of a multithreaded out-of-process server. There are subtle differences between single-threaded apartment (STA) and multithreaded apartment (MTA) servers, but these topics will be discussed in Chapter 5.

### In-process servers

Component lifetime management for in-process servers is managed differently than for out-of-process servers. You don't use the *CoAddRefServerProcess* and *CoReleaseServerProcess* API functions, because an in-process server is usually hosted by its client, the EXE that's loading and using it.

In order to implement lifetime management of in-process servers, you typically keep a global variable that represents the component-level reference count. This component-level reference count keeps a count of both the living objects and outstanding locks, as shown here:

```
// Counts the number of living objects and outstanding locks.
LONG g_lComponentRefCounts = 0;
```

You can then replace the *ComponentAddRef* and *ComponentRelease* helper functions as follows:

```
// Return values for debugging purpose only
inline ULONG ComponentAddRef()
{
    return (InterlockedIncrement(&g_lComponentRefCounts));
}

inline ULONG ComponentRelease()
{
    return (InterlockedDecrement(&g_lComponentRefCounts));
}
```

*ComponentAddRef* atomically increments the component-level reference count, since it's using the thread-safe *InterlockedIncrement* Win32 API function. Likewise, *ComponentRelease* atomically decrements the component-level reference count. Unlike the earlier implementation, which is geared toward out-of-process servers, *ComponentRelease* doesn't set an event to end the server; it just decrements the component-level reference count. So how can the hosting process unload this in-process server when the component-level reference count falls to zero?

COM requires that all in-process servers implement a special DLL entry point called *DllCanUnloadNow* for this specific purpose. A hosting process may call this function at arbitrary intervals to ask whether it can unload the in-process server. When this function returns S_OK, indicating that there is no longer any living object or server lock, the hosting process unloads the in-process server. This function is simple:

```
STDAPI DllCanUnloadNow(void)
{
    if (g_lComponentRefCounts==0) {
        return S_OK;
    } else {
        return S_FALSE;
    }
}
```

## Implementation Registration

You know how to dynamically publish the availability of your factories. You also know how to correctly manage the lifetime of your server. In order for COM to find a COM object requested by clients, COM must know about the location and configuration information of the COM object's associated COM class. On a local workstation, all the configuration information regarding a COM class is stored in an implementation repository called a registry.* All COM related configuration information on the local workstation is stored in the following registry keys:

```
// Windows NT 4.0
[HKEY_LOCAL_MACHINE\Software\Classes]

// HKEY_CLASS_ROOT is a short cut for the above.
// HKEY_CLASS_ROOT is also retained for backwards compatibility.
[HKEY_CLASSES_ROOT]

// Windows 2000
[HKEY_CURRENT_USER\Software\Classes]
```

Although Windows NT 4.0 supports COM configuration only at the machine level, Windows 2000 supports COM configuration at the user level. This finer support allows easier COM-related security configurations.

COM looks for a component's configuration information to correctly load it. Configuration information mainly deals with a particular COM class, identified by a specific CLSID. In addition, COM also looks for interface and security-related configuration information in the registry to manage marshaling and distributed access.

---

* In Windows 2000, there is a global implementation repository that is called the *active directory.*

There is quite a bit of configuration information regarding a component. One way to configure a component is to create a registry script file and merge it with the system registry. You may also use the registry editor to enter all the configuration data into the registry by hand, but this is extremely tedious and error prone. Therefore, COM servers should support self registration in order to minimize installation complexity.

In the next section, you'll learn how to support self registration. As you do this, you'll also pick up the necessary registry entries that COM looks for. Like everything else, self registration and registry entries are different for out-of-process and in-process servers.

### Out-of-process servers

To support self registration, an out-of-process server should support the following command-line options:

```
-RegServer
-UnRegServer
```

The `-RegServer` switch indicates that the server must enter all supported COM-related configuration information (specific to the server of course) into the registry. The `-UnRegServer` switch indicates that the server must remove all COM-related configuration information from the registry. Here's example code in *main* to support these options:

```
void main(int argc, char **argv)
{
    // Implementation repository registration.
    if (argc > 1)
    {
        if (_stricmp(argv[1], "-RegServer")==0 ||
            _stricmp(argv[1], "/RegServer")==0) {
          RegisterComponent();
          return ;
        }
        if (_stricmp(argv[1], "-UnRegServer")==0 ||
            _stricmp(argv[1], "/UnRegServer")==0) {
          UnregisterComponent();
          return ;
        }
    }

    // Initialize COM
    // ...
    // Uninitialize COM
}
```

Before you implement the *RegisterComponent* and *UnregisterComponent* helper functions, study the minimum registry entries needed for an out-of-process server.

An out-of-process server must provide configuration information for each supported COM class. If you were to register the `OcrEngine` COM class into the registry, you would need at least the following registry entries. Each entry in brackets is a *registry key*. Each entry without brackets is called a *named value*. The @ sign indicates the *default value* of a given key.

```
[HKEY_CLASSES_ROOT\CLSID\{DF22A6B2-A58A-11d1-ABCC-00207810D5FE}]
@="OcrEngine"
[HKEY_CLASSES_ROOT\CLSID\{DF22A6B2-A58A-11d1-ABCC-00207810D5FE}\
    LocalServer32]
@="c:\dcom\ocrsvr.exe"
```

You may be wondering about `OcrEngine`. This is simply a human-readable description for the given CLSID; as such, you can give it any string value you like. These two registry entries say that *ocrsvr.exe* is an out-of-process server, which exposes a COM class, identified by the [DF22A6B2-A58A-11d1-ABCC-00207810D5FE] CLSID. You must register the path to your out-of-process server under `LocalServer32`, so that COM can find your server during a client activation request. Basically, this is all you need to register a COM class for an out-of-process server.

However, in order to support distribution, you should provide an application identifier (AppID). AppIDs are saved under the following key:

```
[HKEY_CLASSES_ROOT\AppID]
```

An AppID is a GUID, which can be generated using the *guidgen.exe* utility. This GUID groups together a bunch of COM classes that belong to the same COM server. In this sense, this grouping virtually represents a COM application (therein lies the name AppID). COM uses this grouping in order to simplify the administration of common security and remote server settings. If you don't specify an AppID, the DCOM Configuration (*dcomcnfg.exe*) tool will automatically add an AppID entry for an out-of-process server to support distributed computing. All CLSIDs that point to the same AppID will share the same remote configuration settings. As shown below, our `OcrEngine` COM class points to the AppID [EF20ACA0-C12A-11d1-ABF6-00207810D5FE], and therefore uses the remote configuration settings specified under such AppID:

```
[HKEY_CLASSES_ROOT\CLSID\{DF22A6B2-A58A-11d1-ABCC-00207810D5FE}]
@="OcrEngine"
"AppID"="{EF20ACA0-C12A-11d1-ABF6-00207810D5FE}"

[HKEY_CLASSES_ROOT\AppID\{EF20ACA0-C12A-11d1-ABF6-00207810D5FE}]
@="OcrEngine"

[HKEY_CLASSES_ROOT\AppID\ocrsvr.exe]
"AppID"="{EF20ACA0-C12A-11d1-ABF6-00207810D5FE}"
```

The last entry shown above identifies an EXE that maps to a specific AppID. This specific entry is not totally necessary, but good to maintain as a cross-reference.

For example, COM looks at this entry to get the AppID for a given executable file name, as discussed in Chapter 5.

Now that you know the basic registry entries required by COM, you may write your *RegisterComponent* helper function.

```
void RegisterComponent()
{
    wchar_t wszKey[MAX_PATH];
    wchar_t wszValue[MAX_PATH];
    HKEY hKey = 0;

    // Create the key to hold our CLSID.
    // HKCR is a common shorthand used in written text for HKEY_CLASSES_ROOT.
    // HKCR\CLSID\{DF22A6B2-A58A-11d1-ABCC-00207810D5FE}
    wcscpy(wszKey, TEXT("CLSID\\{DF22A6B2-A58A-11d1-ABCC-00207810D5FE}"));
    RegCreateKey(HKEY_CLASSES_ROOT, wszKey, &hKey);

    // Add the following default value to represent the name of our COM class.
    // @="OcrEngine"
    wcscpy(wszValue, TEXT("OcrEngine"));
    RegSetValueEx(hKey, 0, 0, REG_SZ, (BYTE*)wszValue, ByteLen(wszValue));

    // Associate this COM class with an AppID.
    // "AppID"="{EF20ACA0-C12A-11d1-ABF6-00207810D5FE}"
    wcscpy(wszValue, TEXT("{EF20ACA0-C12A-11d1-ABF6-00207810D5FE}"));
    RegSetValueEx(hKey, TEXT("AppID"), 0, REG_SZ,
                  (BYTE*)wszValue, ByteLen(wszValue));
    RegCloseKey(hKey);

    // Create a key under the CLSID entry to store the local server path.
    // HKCR\CLSID\{DF22A6B2-A58A-11d1-ABCC-00207810D5FE}\LocalServer32
    wcscpy(wszKey, TEXT("CLSID\\{DF22A6B2-A58A-11d1-ABCC-00207810D5FE}\\")
           TEXT("LocalServer32"));
    RegCreateKey(HKEY_CLASSES_ROOT, wszKey, &hKey);

    // Dynamically determine and add the server path.
    // @="...path...\ocrsvr.exe"
    GetModuleFileName(0, wszValue, MAX_PATH);
    RegSetValueEx(hKey, 0, 0, REG_SZ, (BYTE*)wszValue, ByteLen(wszValue));
    RegCloseKey(hKey);

    // Create key to store AppID information for
    // security and remote configuration.
    // HKCR\AppID\{EF20ACA0-C12A-11d1-ABF6-00207810D5FE}
    wcscpy(wszKey, TEXT("AppID\\{EF20ACA0-C12A-11d1-ABF6-00207810D5FE}"));
    RegCreateKey(HKEY_CLASSES_ROOT, wszKey, &hKey);
    // Default value
    // @="OcrEngine"
    wcscpy(wszValue, TEXT("OcrEngine"));
    RegSetValueEx(hKey, 0, 0, REG_SZ,
                  (BYTE*)wszValue, ByteLen(wszValue));
    RegCloseKey(hKey);
```

```
    // Not necessary but nice to have as a cross-reference.
    // Add a cross-reference mapping of an executable to its associated AppID.
    // HKCR\AppID\ocrsvr.exe
    wcscpy(wszKey, TEXT("AppID\\ocrsvr.exe"));
    RegCreateKey(HKEY_CLASSES_ROOT, wszKey, &hKey);
    // "AppID"="{EF20ACA0-C12A-11d1-ABF6-00207810D5FE}"
    wcscpy(wszValue, TEXT("{EF20ACA0-C12A-11d1-ABF6-00207810D5FE}"));
    RegSetValueEx(hKey, TEXT("AppID"), 0, REG_SZ,
                    (BYTE*)wszValue, ByteLen(wszValue));
    RegCloseKey(hKey);
}
```

This function is fairly straightforward. Simply use the Win32 registry API functions to create keys and add the necessary named values into the registry. To create a registry key, use the *RegCreateKey* API function, which returns a handle to the created registry key (**HKEY**). You can use this handle to further create other keys or named values under this registry key. To create a named value, call the *RegSetValueEx* API function. The *RegCloseKey* API function is used to close the opened registry handle. The *wcscpy* function is the wide-character version of the ANSI *strcpy* function.

Now, let's breeze through the *UnregisterComponent* helper function. This function is extremely simple, because it deletes all the keys created in the *RegisterComponent* function.

```
void UnregisterComponent()
{
    RegDeleteKey(HKEY_CLASSES_ROOT, TEXT("CLSID\\")
            TEXT("{DF22A6B2-A58A-11d1-ABCC-00207810D5FE}\\")
            TEXT("LocalServer32"));
    RegDeleteKey(HKEY_CLASSES_ROOT, TEXT("CLSID\\")
            TEXT("{DF22A6B2-A58A-11d1-ABCC-00207810D5FE}"));
    RegDeleteKey(HKEY_CLASSES_ROOT, TEXT("AppID\\")
            TEXT("{EF20ACA0-C12A-11d1-ABF6-00207810D5FE}"));
    RegDeleteKey(HKEY_CLASSES_ROOT, TEXT("AppID\\ocrsvr.exe"));
}
```

You should note one subtlety with this function though. You must delete all child registry keys before you can delete a parent registry key. That's why we delete **LocalServer32** before we actually delete the CLSID key [DF22A6B2-A58A-11d1-ABCC-00207810D5FE] itself.

Once you have implemented all this for your out-of-process server, you may simply register and unregister all COM-related configuration information by executing the following at the command prompt, assuming the executable name of our server is *ocrsvr.exe*.

*ocrsvr.exe -RegServer*     (To register the ocrsvr.exe out-of-process component)

*ocrsvr.exe -UnRegServer* (To unregister the ocrsvr.exe out-of-process component)

## In-process servers

You now will learn how to add registration and unregistration support for in-process servers. Unlike out-of-process servers, which use command switches, in-process servers expose two DLL entry points for server registration and unregistration. These functions are *DllRegisterServer* and *DllUnregisterServer*.

*DllRegisterServer* adds configuration information into the registry. An in-process server may host a number of COM classes. You must register all COM classes into the registry if you want COM to find and dynamically load your in-process server. As seen in the following code, this function simply calls the *RegisterComponent* helper function to register all the COM classes supported by the in-process server:

```
// Adds entries to the system registry.
STDAPI DllRegisterServer(void)
{
    RegisterComponent();
    return S_OK;
}
```

The *DllUnregisterServer* function will undo what has been done by *DllRegisterServer*. Particularly, it will clean up registry entries no longer needed. This function calls the helper function, *UnregisterComponent*, to accomplish this.

```
// Removes entries from the system registry.
STDAPI DllUnregisterServer(void)
{
    UnregisterComponent();
    return S_OK;
}
```

For an in-process server, you need to add a CLSID entry into the registry for all COM classes your DLL supports. In addition, each one of these entries must point to the location of the in-process server. The location of the in-process server must be registered under the **InprocServer32** subkey, as follows:

```
[HKEY_CLASSES_ROOT\CLSID\{DF22A6B2-A58A-11d1-ABCC-00207810D5FE}]
@="OcrEngine"
[HKEY_CLASSES_ROOT\CLSID\{DF22A6B2-A58A-11d1-ABCC-00207810D5FE}\
    InprocServer32]
@="c:\dcom\inproc.dll"
```

Here's a simple implementation of the *RegisterComponent* helper function for an in-process server:

```
void RegisterComponent()
{
    wchar_t wszKey[MAX_PATH];
    wchar_t wszValue[MAX_PATH];
    HKEY hKey = 0;

    // Create the key to hold our CLSID.
    // HKCR\CLSID\{DF22A6B2-A58A-11d1-ABCC-00207810D5FE}
```

```
wcscpy(wszKey, TEXT("CLSID\\{DF22A6B2-A58A-11d1-ABCC-00207810D5FE}"));
RegCreateKey(HKEY_CLASSES_ROOT, wszKey, &hKey);

// Add the following default value to represent the name of our COM class.
// @="OcrEngine"
wcscpy(wszValue, TEXT("OcrEngine"));
RegSetValueEx(hKey, 0, 0, REG_SZ, (BYTE*)wszValue, ByteLen(wszValue));
RegCloseKey(hKey);

// Create a key under the CLSID entry to store the local server path
// HKCR\CLSID\{DF22A6B2-A58A-11d1-ABCC-00207810D5FE}\InprocServer32
wcscpy(wszKey, TEXT("CLSID\\{DF22A6B2-A58A-11d1-ABCC-00207810D5FE}\\")
       TEXT("InprocServer32"));
RegCreateKey(HKEY_CLASSES_ROOT, wszKey, &hKey);

// Add the in-process server path.
// @="...path...\inproc.dll"
// We can obtain the module name of the DLL by calling
// GetModuleName in DllMain,
// save it in a global variable, and use it here.
wcscpy(wszValue, g_wszModuleName);
RegSetValueEx(hKey, 0, 0, REG_SZ, (BYTE*)wszValue, ByteLen(wszValue));
RegCloseKey(hKey);
}
```

This function is straightforward and really deserves no further discussion. The implementation for *UnregisterComponent* is also straightforward, as shown here:

```
void UnregisterComponent()
{
    RegDeleteKey(HKEY_CLASSES_ROOT,
               TEXT("CLSID\\{DF22A6B2-A58A-11d1-ABCC-00207810D5FE}")
               TEXT("\\InprocServer32"));
    RegDeleteKey(HKEY_CLASSES_ROOT,
               TEXT("CLSID\\{DF22A6B2-A58A-11d1-ABCC-00207810D5FE}"));
}
```

You have exposed the two entry points required for in-process server self-registration support, but when will these entry points be called? You can either write a small utility to load the in-process server and invoke these functions, or you can use an SDK utility that does it for you. This utility is called *regsvr32.exe*. To register and unregister an in-process server using this utility, you would invoke the following commands at the command prompt:

*regsvr32 inproc.dll*        (To register the inproc.dll in-process server)

*regsvr32 -u inproc.dll*        (To unregister the inproc.dll in-process server)

### Registering interface marshalers

The last thing that you need to register is the proxy/stub DLL, so that COM can marshal your supported custom interfaces (*IOcr* and *ISpell*). Recall that you used MIDL and its compiler to specify and compile the interfaces that make up the DLL. Since these are custom interfaces, you have to use interface marshalers for out-of-process requests. Because the MIDL compiler generates registration and unregistration code for the proxy/stub in-process server, all you would have to do to register this in-process server is use the *regsvr32.exe* utility. For example, to register your proxy/stub DLL, you would execute the following command:

*regsvr32 ocrps.dll*

When you do this, the in-process server adds the following registry entries for each interface under [HKEY_CLASSES_ROOT\Interface]:

```
[HKCR\Interface\{D9F23D61-A647-11D1-ABCD-00207810D5FE}]
@="IOcr"
[HKCR\Interface\{D9F23D61-A647-11D1-ABCD-00207810D5FE}\NumMethods]
@="5"
[HKCR\Interface\{D9F23D61-A647-11D1-ABCD-00207810D5FE}\ProxyStubClsid32]
@="{D9F23D61-A647-11D1-ABCD-00207810D5FE}"
```

These entries are added for the *IOcr* interface. The first two lines say that the [D9F23D61-A647-11D1-ABCD-00207810D5FE] interface is named *IOcr*. The second two lines say that it has five methods. The last two lines say that the CLSID for the proxy and stub implementation for the *IOcr* interface is [D9F23D61-A647-11D1-ABCD-00207810D5FE]. That is, the lines tell COM to go look at that CLSID for the in-process server that implements the proxy and stub for *IOcr*. Now that you know how to read the earlier six lines, you should be able to read the following six lines without difficulty:

```
[HKCR\Interface\{D9F23D63-A647-11D1-ABCD-00207810D5FE}]
@="ISpell"
[HKCR\Interface\{D9F23D63-A647-11D1-ABCD-00207810D5FE}\NumMethods]
@="4"
[HKCR\Interface\{D9F23D63-A647-11D1-ABCD-00207810D5FE}\ProxyStubClsid32]
@="{D9F23D61-A647-11D1-ABCD-00207810D5FE}"
```

The following is registered information regarding the CLSID to which both the *IOcr* and *ISpell* interface refer. As expected, there is an **InprocServer32** entry that holds the destination of the resulting in-process server that implements the proxy and stub code for both interfaces. This is the DLL that is loaded by COM each time a proxy or stub is needed for marshaling:

```
[HKCR\CLSID\{D9F23D61-A647-11D1-ABCD-00207810D5FE}]
@="PSFactoryBuffer"
[HKCR\CLSID\{D9F23D61-A647-11D1-ABCD-00207810D5FE}\InProcServer32]
@="c:\dcom\ocrps.dll"
"ThreadingModel"="Both"
```

(You will examine the named value **ThreadingModel** in Chapter 5.)

---

### *Creating a Client Component*

Initialization and Termination

- All threads using COM must call *CoInitialize* [*Ex*] and *CoUninitialize.*

Creating and Initializing an Object

- Use *CoCreateInstance* [*Ex*] or *CoGetClassObject* to request a server component to dynamically create a COM object for you.

- Use *CoGetInstanceFromFile* if the object supports file persistence.

- For a custom factory, you must use the *CoGetClassObject* function.

Using and Releasing an Object

- You must successfully query (*QueryInterface*) for an interface prior to
  using it.

- Use *IMultiQI* to query for multiple interfaces in one network round-trip.

- *Release* the appropriate interface when you're done using it.

---

# *Clients*

Now that you have a distributed component in place, you can make use of its
exposed COM objects. For simplicity, the term *client* refers to any piece of code
that makes use of a COM object's interface pointer. This implies that a COM object
may be a client to another COM object. In other words, any COM object can be
both a client and a server at the same time. It is this ability that allows maximum
distributed capabilities.

In this section, we'll examine the basics for using services of a distributed COM
object. You'll learn how to instantiate a distributed object, use it, and release the
acquired resources.

## *Initialization and Termination*

Recall that before a piece of code can use COM, it must first initialize the COM
library. A client can call *CoInitialize* or *CoInitializeEx* to initialize the library. To
be precise, any thread that uses COM must do this. This means that if your application spawns ten threads that use COM, all must call *CoInitialize* or
*CoInitializeEx.* After you initialize COM, you may create, use, and release COM
objects. When you're all done, you should call *CoUninitialize.*

## *Creating an Object*

To use a distributed COM object, you must first instantiate it. There are several ways to instantiate COM objects in COM, and we will discuss four common ones. Each of these techniques has advantages and disadvantages.

### *CoCreateInstance*

The easiest way to create a COM object is by using the *CoCreateInstance* COM API function:

```
HRESULT CoCreateInstance(
  REFCLSID rclsid,      // CLSID of the COM class
  LPUNKNOWN pUnkOuter,  // Pointer to an outer unknown, used for aggregation
  DWORD dwClsContext,   // Preferred server context(s)
  REFIID riid,          // IID
  LPVOID * ppv          // Resulting interface pointer requested
);
```

This API function asks the class factory associated with the specified COM class, identified by the given CLSID (`rclsid`, the first parameter), to create a new COM object.

We'll ignore the second parameter because it is used for aggregation, a topic that is discussed in the "Object Orientation" section of this chapter.

The third parameter indicates the type of server that you prefer to use. This parameter allows you to indicate virtually how far the target COM class is from the client (the caller). Specifically, you can indicate to COM that the COM object you need lives in an in-process server, in-process handler, out-of-process server, remote server, or any combination of these. These different choices are defined in the **CLSCTX** enumeration, shown earlier in the discussion of the *CoRegisterClassObject*, but redisplayed here for quick reference:

```
typedef enum tagCLSCTX  {
  CLSCTX_INPROC_SERVER,
  CLSCTX_INPROC_HANDLER,
  CLSCTX_LOCAL_SERVER,
  CLSCTX_REMOTE_SERVER
} CLSCTX;

#define CLSCTX_SERVER (CLSCTX_INPROC_SERVER| \
                       CLSCTX_LOCAL_SERVER| \
                       CLSCTX_REMOTE_SERVER)
#define CLSCTX_INPROC (CLSCTX_INPROC_SERVER| \
                       CLSCTX_INPROC_HANDLER)
#define CLSCTX_ALL    (CLSCTX_INPROC_SERVER| \
                       CLSCTX_INPROC_HANDLER|\
                       CLSCTX_LOCAL_SERVER| \
                       CLSCTX_REMOTE_SERVER)
```

The four flags have the following meanings:

### CLSCTX_INPROC_SERVER

The COM class, along with the code that manages the instances of this class, lives within an in-process server. This implies that the COM class and all the code that manages its instances will be loaded within the same process as the client code.

### CLSCTX_INPROC_HANDLER

The COM class, along with the code that manages the instances of this class, lives within an in-process handler. A handler is a special in-process server that virtually implements customized proxies for remote method invocations.

### CLSCTX_LOCAL_SERVER

The COM class lives within an out-of-process server. Furthermore, the out-of-process server is a local server, meaning it lives on the same machine as your client code.

### CLSCTX_REMOTE_SERVER

The COM class lives within a remote out-of-process server, meaning that the server executes on a totally different machine.

If you don't really care which type of server creates instances of the requested COM class, you would just use the CLSCTX_SERVER context. This context includes all server contexts except CLSCTX_INPROC_HANDLER. When you use CLSCTX_SERVER, you tell COM to choose the best (nearest) server to create an instance of the requested COM class. COM will first look for an in-process server that supports such COM class. If there's none, COM will look for a local out-of-process server. If this fails, it will look for a remote out-of-process server that can serve up the requested instance. COM refers to the registry to get this information. This means that all COM configuration information for each server type must be correctly configured first. You may also specify CLSCTX_ALL to encompass all server contexts, including CLSCTX_INPROC_HANDLER.

The fourth parameter is an interface identifier (IID) of the interface that you are requesting. The fifth and last parameter is an output parameter that returns a pointer to the requested interface specified by the IID. Here's how you can create and instance of a COM class:

```
IOcr *pOcr = NULL ;
HRESULT hr = CoCreateInstance(CLSID_OcrEngine, NULL, CLSCTX_SERVER,
            IID_IOcr, reinterpret_cast<void**>(&pOcr));
```

The code asks the class factory associated with CLSID_OcrEngine to create a COM object that is an instance of the COM class whose GUID is CLSID_OcrEngine. When this happens, it returns a pointer to an *IOcr* interface of the instantiated COM object.

An advantage of this API function is simplicity. It won't allow you to specify a target remote server. In order to create an instance on a remote machine using this API function, you must configure the `RemoteServerName` named value in the registry (on the client machine) under the `AppID` key that refers to the target server. This can be regarded as an advantage or a disadvantage. From the advantage viewpoint, this allows pre-DCOM servers to support location transparency, without changing a single line of code. In addition, this allows an administrator to configure the target server. The registry entry required for this configuration is:

```
[HKEY_CLASSES_ROOT\AppID\{EF20ACA0-C12A-11d1-ABF6-00207810D5FE}]
@="OcrEngine"
"RemoteServerName"="dog.dcom.com"
```

The easiest way to add this entry is to either use *dcomcnfg.exe* or *oleview.exe*. You can also manually add this entry into the registry yourself.

Configuring a remote server is an inappropriate choice if you want dynamic selection of target remote servers. In other words, there are situations in which you would want to allow a user to pick a target server at runtime. In these cases, static configuration of a remote server name is a disadvantage. There's also another disadvantage with this API function, which deals with performance. You can request only one interface pointer per call (network round-trip).

### CoCreateInstanceEx

In a distributed environment, the *CoCreateInstance* API function would be slow to the groaning point if you wanted to query for 100 interfaces on a remote server. Making a 100 network round-trips is more expensive than making a single one. *CoCreateInstanceEx* is an API function that's optimized for this sort of thing. As an extension to *CoCreateInstance*, *CoCreateInstanceEx* solves the two problems of a configured-only server destination and poor performance.

```
HRESULT CoCreateInstanceEx(
    REFCLSID rclsid,            // CLSID of the COM class
    IUnknown *pUnkOuter,        // Pointer to an outer unknown, used for
                                // aggregation
    DWORD dwClsCtx,             // Preferred server context(s)
    COSERVERINFO *pServerInfo,  // Target machine
    ULONG cmq,                  // Size of MULTI_QI array
    MULTI_QI *pResults          // MULTI_QI array containing resulting QI
                                // requests
);
```

The first three parameters of this API function correspond exactly to the ones in *CoCreateInstance*. The fourth parameter, `COSERVERINFO`, allows you to indicate information regarding a target server. You may specify the name of the target host via the `pwszName` member. This can be a netbios name (e.g., "dog"), a DNS name (e.g., "dog.dcom.com"), or an actual IP address ("192.0.0.1").[*]

```
typedef struct _COSERVERINFO {
    DWORD dwReserved1;         // Must be 0
    LPWSTR pwszName;           // Server name
    COAUTHINFO *pAuthInfo;     // Security information, discussed in Chapter 5
    DWORD dwReserved2;         // Must be 0
} COSERVERINFO;
```

With the `COSERVERINFO` structure, you can dynamically select a server to create a COM object. This allows greater flexibility than the static `RemoteServerName` named value registry configuration. For example, this allows you to dynamically ask the user for a target server name.

To avoid network traffic, the *CoCreateInstanceEx* also supports the request for multiple interface pointers in one network round-trip. Each interface request can be specified using a `MULTI_QI` structure. The sixth parameter of *CoCreateInstanceEx* can be an array of these structures. The size of this array is indicated by the fifth parameter of this function.

```
typedef struct _MULTI_QI {
    const IID*   pIID;
    IUnknown *   pItf;
    HRESULT      hr;
} MULTI_QI;
```

You may create an array of these structures, each of which includes a requested IID, the resulting interface pointer, and the resulting status code. Simply set the first member to the requested IID, the second member to `NULL`, and the third member to `S_OK`. Given what you know so far, here's how you can create a COM object on a selected server and retrieve back an array of interface pointers of interest:

```
// Request for IOcr and ISpell
MULTI_QI mqi[] ={ {&IID_IOcr, NULL, S_OK}, {&IID_ISpell, NULL, S_OK} };

// Target hostname
COSERVERINFO csi = { 0, TEXT("dog.dcom.com"), NULL, 0 } ;

// Create a COM object and get back two interfaces
HRESULT hr = CoCreateInstanceEx(CLSID_OcrEngine, NULL, CLSCTX_SERVER,
                &csi, sizeof(mqi)/sizeof(mqi[0]), mqi);
```

### CoGetClassObject

*CoCreateInstance* and *CoCreateInstanceEx* both use standard factories to create COM objects. Recall that standard factories implement the standard *IClassFactory*

---

[*] At the time of this writing, there is a bug regarding the use of a DNS name or an IP address that refers to the same machine as your client. This problem is fixed in Windows NT 4.0 Service Pack 4, Windows 2000, and DCOM 95 1.2.

interface. This implies that you can create COM objects using these API functions only if the target class factory implements *IClassFactory*.

Briefly put on your object implementor's hat. If you want the general public to instantiate your objects, the factories you create must implement the standard *IClassFactory* interface. However, if you want to prevent generic instantiation, perhaps because you need customized or private object creation that's not supported by the standard *IClassFactory* interface, you would implement your own custom factory interface to support object creation. This implies that clients may not use *CoCreateInstance* or *CoCreateInstanceEx* to create your objects.

To create an object whose factory is a custom factory, you use the *CoGetClassObject* API function. This API function allows you to obtain an interface pointer to a custom interface for object instantiation. The drawback of this method is you must know the IID of the object creation interface. However, this drawback can be regarded as an advantage, since it offers more programming flexibility.

```
HRESULT CoGetClassObject(
    REFCLSID rclsid,              // CLSID of the COM class
    DWORD dwClsContext,           // Preferred server context(s)
    COSERVERINFO * pServerInfo,   // Target machine
    REFIID riid,                  // Custom factory interface identifier
    LPVOID * ppv                  // Resulting pointer to custom factory
                                  // interface
);
```

You are already familiar with the first three parameters of this function. However, the last two parameters deserve some discussions. The fourth parameter allows you to specify the custom factory interface that supports custom creation of COM objects. You must know the custom creation interface before you can call *CoGetClassObject*. The requested interface pointer is returned in the last parameter. Note that the last parameter returns a pointer to the custom factory interface that can create objects.

Here's an example. Assume there's a factory associated with the CLSID `CLSID_MyCustomFactory`. In addition, assume that this factory implements the *IMyCustomFactory* interface, as opposed to the standard *IClassFactory* interface. In order to create a COM object that this custom factory manufactures, you must first acquire the *IMyCustomFactory* interface by using its identifier, `IID_IMyCustomFactory`. You use all this information to make the call to *CoGetClassObject*, as follows:

```
// Get a custom interface pointer for object instantiation
IMyCustomFactory *pCustomFactory = NULL;
HRESULT hr = CoGetClassObject(CLSID_MyCustomFactory, CLSCTX_SERVER, NULL,
        IID_IMyCustomFactory,
        reinterpret_cast<void**> (&pCustomFactory));
```

Notice that you pass NULL in the third parameter, neglecting to programmatically specify a server destination. This tells COM to look into the registry for target host information in the RemoteServerName named value of the correct AppID key (which is referred to by CLSID_MyCustomFactory).

Upon successfully calling *CoGetClassObject*, you get back a pointer to the *IMyCustomFactory* interface, which supports object creation. You then use this interface to actually create the COM objects that you need. Assume that this custom interface supports the *MakeMeAnObject* method that does the actual object creation. Further, once this method creates a COM object, it returns an *IMyInterfaceOnTheCreatedObject* pointer. Given these assumptions, you can create a COM object and get back a pointer to it, as shown here:

```
if (SUCCEEDED(hr)) {
    // Now create a COM object using
    // the custom interface for object creation.
    IMyInterfaceOnTheCreatedObject *pMyInterfaceOnTheCreatedObject = NULL;
    hr = pCustomFactory->MakeMeAnObject(&pMyInterfaceOnTheCreatedObject);
}
```

The pMyInterfaceOnTheCreatedObject pointer points to an interface supported by the COM object that is instantiated by the custom factory. Once you have this interface pointer, you may use the services exposed by the instantiated object. For example, assuming that the *IMyInterfaceOnTheCreatedObject* interface supports a *ShowMeSomeMagic* method, you can do the following:

```
pMyInterfaceOnTheCreatedObject->ShowMeSomeMagic();
```

Other than the ability to create objects using a custom factory, *CoGetClassObject* possesses another key advantage over *CoCreateInstance[Ex]* when you create multiple objects of a specific type or COM class. This advantage deals with performance, because each call to *CoGetClassObject* or *CoCreateInstance[Ex]* requires the COM infrastructure to locate the component implementation. Thus, given the following code, you create two COM objects of a specific type, CLSID_OcrEngine, but pay only a one-time component implementation lookup, since you call the *CoGetClassObject* API function only once.

```
// Overhead:  locate the component implementation.
IClassFactory *pFactory = NULL ;
CoGetClassObject(CLSID_OcrEngine, CLSCTX_SERVER, NULL,
                 IID_IOcr, reinterpret_cast<void**>(&pFactory));

// Create the first object.
IOcr *pOne = NULL;  pFactory->MakeMeAnObject(&pOne);

// Create the second object.
IOcr *pTwo = NULL; pFactory->MakeMeAnObject(&pTwo);
```

However, if you use *CoCreateInstance[Ex]* to create these two COM objects, you will pay for this lookup overhead each time you call *CoCreateInstance[Ex]*, as shown here:

```
// Overhead:  locate the component implementation.
// Create the first object.
IOcr *pOne=NULL ;
HRESULT hr = CoCreateInstance(CLSID_OcrEngine, NULL, CLSCTX_SERVER,
                IID_IOcr, reinterpret_cast<void**>(&pOne));

// Overhead:  locate the component implementation.
// Create the second object.
IOcr *pTwo=NULL ;
HRESULT hr = CoCreateInstance(CLSID_OcrEngine, NULL, CLSCTX_SERVER,
                IID_IOcr, reinterpret_cast<void**>(&pTwo));
```

We can't leave this topic without noting that *CoCreateInstance* and *CoCreateInstanceEx* are really just convenient functions, which internally call *CoGetClassObject* to request the *IClassFactory* interface, and then invoke the *IClassFactory::CreateInstance* method to create the actual COM object. Consider the following code, which uses the convenient *CoCreateInstance* function:

```
IOcr *pOcr=NULL ;
HRESULT hr = CoCreateInstance(CLSID_OcrEngine, NULL, CLSCTX_SERVER,
                IID_IOcr, reinterpret_cast<void**>(&pOcr));
```

The earlier code is essentially equivalent to the following:

```
IClassFactory *pFactory = NULL ;

// Get a custom interface pointer for object instantiation
HRESULT hr = CoGetClassObject(CLSID_OcrEngine, CLSCTX_SERVER, NULL,
                IID_IClassFactory, reinterpret_cast<void**>(&pFactory));

if (SUCCEEDED(hr)) {
    IOcr *pOcr = NULL;
    // CreateInstance internally creates the object
    // and returns the requested interface pointer.
    hr = pFactory->CreateInstance(NULL, IID_IOcr,
                            reinterpret_cast<void**>(&pOcr));
    pFactory->Release();
}
```

The advantage of using *CoGetClassObject* is flexibility. If a factory exposes a private or custom interface for object creation, you must use *CoGetClassObject*. The more convenient *CoCreateInstance* and *CoCreateInstanceEx* API functions won't do, because they both internally request for the *IClassFactory* interface when calling *CoGetClassObject*, as shown in the earlier code.

### Class monikers

Another way to create an object is by using a *class moniker*, a naming object that refers to another COM object. In this sense, a moniker can hide information regarding an object to which it refers. If a client uses a moniker, it is liberated from having to know which object it needs to deal with, because the object that's needed can be embedded inside a moniker. In order to be a moniker, an object must implement the standard *IMoniker* interface.

There are different types of monikers, but the one that deals with object instantiation is the class moniker. A class moniker portrays a class factory. If you have a class moniker, you can use it to bind to the factory that it represents. Once you've bound to the factory, you can request for an *IClassFactory* or a custom object creation interface. Through this interface, you can request the factory to manufacture objects for you.

There are several ways to do this, but this discussion will focus on one flexible technique. Before you can bind to a moniker, you must first create a bind context and obtain the *IBindCtx* pointer. You can easily do this by calling the *CreateBindCtx* API function.

```
HRESULT CreateBindCtx(
    DWORD reserved,    // Reserved
    LPBC * ppbc        // Return IBindCtx interface pointer
);
```

Once you have obtained a bind context, you can use it to call a special COM API function (*MkParseDisplayName*) to convert a textual name into a moniker, which refers to an object represented by the textual name. This API function takes a bind context and a textual name that represents the object to be bound to. It returns the number of characters successfully parsed and the resulting *IMoniker* pointer on the created moniker object.*

```
HRESULT MkParseDisplayName(
    LPBC pbc,               // Bind context
    LPCOLESTR szUserName,   // Textual name
    ULONG FAR *pchEaten,    // Characters successfully parsed
    LPMONIKER FAR *ppmk     // Resulting IMoniker pointer
);
```

After you call *MkParseDisplayName*, you can then bind to the target object. To do this, you simply invoke the *BindToObject* method of the *IMoniker* interface, which is obtained from calling *MkParseDisplayName*. This *BindToObject* interface method has the following signature:

```
HRESULT IMoniker::BindToObject(
    IBindCtx *pbc,          // Bind context
    IMoniker *pmkToLeft,    // In composites, points to preceding moniker
    REFIID riidResult,      // IID
```

---

* Instead of calling *CreateBindCtx* and *MkParseDisplayName*, you can simply call *CreateClassMoniker*. If you take this alternative, you can use *CLSIDFromString* to convert the textual representation of a CLSID into a real CLSID, which is input for the first parameter of *CreateClassMoniker*.

```
    void **ppvResult        // Resulting interface pointer of type IID
);
```

Monikers are very powerful and can refer to practically anything. If an object implements the *IMoniker* interface, it can be used as a moniker. In the context of object creation, here's a demonstration of the use of a class moniker:

```
// Dynamically get the newest OCR Factory
wchar_t *pwszFactory = GetNewestOcrFactory();
```

The given code obtains a textual representation of a CLSID from some arbitrary function, called *GetNewestOcrFactory*. This function simply returns a human-readable representation of a CLSID, which corresponds to the class moniker syntax specified by COM. If you take a larger viewpoint, this function can be seen as something magical that miraculously gives out a textual representation of the newest OCR factory.

```
wchar_t *GetNewestOcrFactory()
{
    static wchar_t *pwszChangeableFactory =
        TEXT("CLSID:DF22A6B2-A58A-11d1-ABCC-00207810D5FE:");
    return pwszChangeableFactory;
}
```

This function, or magical thing, shields a client from having to know a specific CLSID of the latest and greatest OCR factory, which is especially beneficial, because this CLSID, representing the latest OCR factory, can vary over time. For example, the current OCR engine supports optical character recognition for only the English alphabet, but two years later, a totally different OCR engine may support optical character recognition for the Chinese alphabet. Therefore, a moniker provides an additional level of indirection that frees the client from a particular implementation.

A client would simply call *GetNewestOcrFactory* to get the textual representation of the newest OCR factory. It then would create a bind context object using the *CreateBindCtx* API function. Once it has a bind context pointer, it simply converts the textual representation into a moniker object, using the *MkParseDisplayName* API function. With the received *IMoniker* pointer, it may call the *BindToObject* method to officially bind to the target object to which the moniker refers.

```
HRESULT hr = S_OK;

// Create a bind context.
IBindCtx *pBind=NULL;
hr = CreateBindCtx(0, &pBind);

// Create a class moniker based on the textual name.
// A class moniker represents a factory.
ULONG ulEaten = 0; IMoniker *pMon=NULL;
hr = MkParseDisplayName(pBind, pwszFactory, &ulEaten, &pMon);
```

```
// Bind to the factory and get the IID_IClassFactory interface.
IClassFactory *pClassFactory=NULL;
hr = pMon->BindToObject(pBind, 0, IID_IClassFactory, (void**)&pClassFactory);

// Tell the factory to manufacture an object
// and get back a pointer to its IOcr interface.
IOcr *pOcr=NULL;
hr = pClassFactory->CreateInstance(0, IID_IOcr, (void**)&pOcr);

// We can now call IOcr's methods.
```

As seen in the earlier code fragment, you obtain an *IClassFactory* interface during the moniker binding process. Once you get this pointer, you can call its *CreateInstance* method to create the object you want. You may think that this is a complex and long process to create objects, but this technique shields a client from having to know a specific CLSID, which can be very beneficial.*

## *Initializing an Object*

Creating an object is one thing, but initializing it is another. So far, you've only heard about creating uninitialized objects. If you want to support object initialization after objects are created, you must either implement your own code to support initialization or use one of the provided standard interfaces.

One simple way to support object initialization is by providing your own interface method, such as *InitializeThySelf,* which a client can call to initiate object initialization. When a client calls this interface method, you would then initialize your object however you choose. The problem with this approach is that you're expecting your clients to know about this specific *InitializeThySelf* interface method. This is an extremely bad expectation in a distributed and component-based environment, because *InitializeThySelf* is just an ad hoc method that's hacked up to support initialization.

To avoid such arbitrary implementations, COM provides a number of standard interfaces that support object initialization, and one of these interfaces is *IPersistFile.* A COM object that implements this interface supports object persistence using a persistent file—in other words, an object can save its states to a file for later retrieval. Saving an object's states to persistent storage is important, because this allows you to bring the same object back to life years from now.

---

* This book does not cover standard interfaces in any great detail, as it only deals with distributed computing. Monikers are objects that implement the *IMoniker* interface, which deserves your attention if you plan to use naming objects in your distributed architectures. Refer to the SDK documentation for further details. From this short description, you should find a solid grounding from which to peruse other moniker-related topics, because the binding process is almost exactly the same. On a totally different note, you may want to look up other ways to create (and possibly initialize) a component object, including *CoGetClassObjectFromURL* and *CoGetInstanceFromIStorage.*

We'll examine an API function that both creates and initializes a COM object from a persistent file: *CoGetInstanceFromFile*. After manufacturing an object, it calls *IPersistFile::Load* to initialize the object from a given file (see *objidl.h* for the definition of *IPersistFile*). The COM object must implement the *IPersistFile* interface, before you can successfully utilize this technique.

```
HRESULT CoGetInstanceFromFile(
    COSERVERINFO *pServerInfo,    // Target host
    CLSID *rclsid,                // CLSID pointer
    IUnknown *pUnkOuter,          // Outer unknown used for aggregation
    DWORD dwClsCtx,               // Server context
    DWORD grfMode,                // Open mode
    OLECHAR *pwszName,            // Persistent file name
    DWORD dwCount,                // Size of MULTI_QI array
    MULTI_QI *pResults            // Array of requested interfaces
);
```

You've seen practically all of these parameters. The second parameter takes a pointer to a CLSID. If you don't pass a CLSID pointer into this call, the API function will derive the CLSID from the persistent file name, passed in via **pwszName**. *CoGetInstanceFromFile* internally determines the CLSID by calling a COM API function named *GetClassFile*.

The fifth parameter indicates the persistent file's open mode, which includes values such as **STGM_READ**, **STGM_WRITE**, and so forth. As their names imply, **STGM_READ** is used when reading from the opened file and **STGM_WRITE** is used when writing to the file.

Here's how we would use this function to create an object and initialize it from a file. The following code passes in the name of the persistent file, *c:\test.doc*, which you want a COM object hosted by Microsoft Word to load. Since you don't pass in the CLSID, this API function will automatically figure out the correct CLSID based on the name of the persistent file by calling *GetClassFile*. You also query the *IDataObject* interface, which is a standard interface that supports uniform data transfer.

```
wchar_t *pwszPersist = TEXT("c:\\test.doc");
MULTI_QI mqi[] = { {&IID_IDataObject, NULL, S_OK} };
HRESULT hr = CoGetInstanceFromFile(NULL, NULL, NULL, CLSCTX_SERVER,
                   STGM_READ, pwszPersist, sizeof(mqi)/sizeof(mqi[0]),
                   mqi);
IDataObject *pData=NULL;

if (SUCCEEDED(hr)) {
    pData = static_cast<IDataObject*>(mqi[0].pItf);
    // use the IDataObject interface . . .
    . . .
}
```

Instead of using *CoGetInstanceFromFile*, you can also use the following short-hand version, which does the same thing:

```
hr = CoGetObject(pwszPersist, 0, IID_IDataObject, (void**) &pData);
```

Upon successfully calling *CoGetInstanceFromFile*, you may use the *IDataObject* interface pointer for operations, such as to display all the text within this Microsoft Word document.\*

## *Using an Object*

After object creation, you may use the services exposed by the COM object. Recall that you use an object by calling methods supported by exposed interfaces. In COM programming, a client should never have access to a COM object in any way other than through interface pointers.

Typically, you receive a requested interface pointer to the instantiated object after calling one of the object creation API functions. Use the received interface pointer by invoking its supported methods. If you want to use a different service exposed by the object (i.e., if you want to use a different interface), use the *QueryInterface* method to query for another interface. Recall that every COM object implements *QueryInterface* because every interface derives from *IUnknown*.

When you use a COM object, you also have another important responsibility: you should always check the returned status code. Recall that even if the object returns a success status code, the RPC layer can potentially override this success status, so it's extremely important to check all status codes. Consider the following simple code:

```
// Request for the IOcr (mqi[0]) and IPersist (mqi[1]) interfaces
MULTI_QI mqi[] = { {&IID_IOcr, NULL, S_OK},
{&IID_IPersistFile, NULL, S_OK}
    };
COSERVERINFO csi = {0, TEXT("dog.dcom.com"), NULL, 0} ;
HRESULT hr = CoCreateInstanceEx(CLSID_OcrEngine, NULL, CLSCTX_SERVER,
                       &csi, sizeof(mqi)/sizeof(mqi[0]), mqi);
if (SUCCEEDED(hr)) {              // Did the call succeed?
   if (SUCCEEDED(mqi[0].hr)) {     // Verify status code of IOcr.
      IOcr *pOcr = static_cast<IOcr *>(mqi[0].pItf);
      // Use the IOcr interface.

      ISpell *pSpell=NULL;
      // Query for ISpell.
      hr = pOcr->QueryInterface(IID_ISpell, reinterpret_cast<void**>
        (&pSpell));
      if (SUCCEEDED(hr)) {    // Make sure success before using pSpell.
         // Use the spell interface.
```

---

\* Refer to the provided sample program, called Persist, to see how this is done, as this is not relevant to the current discussion.

```
        . . .
    }
        . . .
}

if (SUCCEEDED(mqi[1].hr)) {      // Verify the status code of IPersistFile.
    IPersistFile *pPersist = static_cast< IPersistFile *>(mqi[1].pItf);
        . . .
    }
}
```

Upon object instantiation, you query for both the *IOcr* and the *IPersistFile* interfaces. After calling *CoCreateInstanceEx* to create the object, you must check the returned status code of this call. Even when this call succeeds, it's possible that not all requested interfaces were returned. Therefore, before you can use one of the two requested interfaces, you must specifically check for its status code. For example, check for *IOcr's* status code before using it.

Use pOcr in the previous code to query for an *ISpell* interface. Recall that the *CoOcrEngine* object implements both of these interfaces. Again, you check for the status code of this query before you actually use the *ISpell* interface pointer. If you have an interface pointer, you can get to other interface pointers within the COM object through *QueryInterface*.

You also request for an *IPersistFile* interface in the earlier code snippet (mqi[1]). Recall that if an object supports the *IPersistFile* interface, you may load its states from a persistent file. So here's another way to initialize an object after creation. Notice that we check for *IPersistFile's* status code before using it. This check will fail, since we haven't implemented *IPersistFile* for the *CoOcrEngine* COM object.

You might have noticed that *QueryInterface* is inefficient if you want to query for 10 interfaces at one time, but there is a way to do this without compromising network efficiency. COM provides the *IMultiQI* interface, which is implemented by the local proxy object. To use this interface, you first query for it and then use it to query for a number of interfaces in a single network round-trip. Be aware that the *IMultiQI* interface exists only after you have successfully created a remote object, and therefore, its local proxy. Indeed, this happens only if the client and object live in different apartments (execution contexts). In the following snippet, you'll assume that you have a valid *IUnknown* interface and that we're using a remote object. Here's how we would use the *IMultiQI* interface:

```
IMultiQI *pMulti=NULL;
// Query for the IMultiQI interface, which is implemented by the local proxy.
hr = pUnk->QueryInterface(IID_IMultiQI, reinterpret_cast<void**>(&pMulti));
assert(SUCCEEDED(hr));

MULTI_QI mqi[] = { {&IID_IOcr, NULL, S_OK}, {&IID_ISpell, NULL, S_OK} };
hr = pMulti->QueryMultipleInterfaces(sizeof(mqi)/sizeof(mqi[0]), mqi);
assert(SUCCEEDED(mqi[0].hr)&&SUCCEEDED(mqi[1].hr));
    . . .
```

You can query for the *IMultiQI* interface only if a local proxy for a remote object exists. This simple interface has a single method, *QueryMultipleInterfaces*, which queries for an array of interfaces in one single network round-trip.

To recap, using a COM object is straightforward. Just remember these rules:

- In general, always check returned status codes.

- Use *QueryInterface* to discover other services provided by the object.

- If using a remote object, use *IMultiQI* for efficiency.

Other things you need to understand include memory management, which will be discussed in Chapter 5, and object lifetime management, which will be discussed next.

## Deleting an Object

A client is obligated to partly assist objects in their lifetime management. The COM lifetime rules mandate that a client must release a requested interface after it is done using it. You need to obey the lifetime rules in order to allow your object's existence to be correctly managed. This means that when you are done using an interface pointer, you must invoke *Release* upon the interface pointer to notify the target object of your intentions. If you fail to do this correctly, a distributed object will either live forever or die too soon, leading to possible resource leaks or access violations. In short, you need to obey the COM lifetime rules, discussed in the "Objects" section of Chapter 3.

You have seen the following code before without the calls to *Release*. Notice that after you've finished using an interface, it's released. Notice also that you use and release an interface only when the status code is a success.

```
if (SUCCEEDED(mqi[0].hr)) {
    IOcr *pOcr = static_cast<IOcr *>(mqi[0].pItf);
    // Use the IOcr interface
    . . .
    ISpell *pSpell=NULL;
    hr = pOcr->QueryInterface(IID_ISpell, reinterpret_cast<void**>(&pSpell));
    if (SUCCEEDED(hr)) {
        // Use the ISpell interface
        . . .
        pSpell->Release();
    }
    // Use the IOcr interface some more
    . . .
    pOcr->Release();
}

if (SUCCEEDED(mqi[1].hr)) {
    IPersistFile *pPersist = static_cast<IPersistFile *>(mqi[1].pItf);
    // Use the persist interface
    . . .
```

```
        pPersist->Release();
    }
```

In addition, it is important to invoke *Release* upon the correct interface pointer. For example, after you use the *ISpell* interface, you release the *ISpell* interface (not some other interfaces, such as *IOcr* or *IPersist*). Since you have the internal knowledge that the *CoOcrEngine* object keeps an object-level reference count (because you developed it), you could have invoked *Release* three times upon the *ISpell* interface pointer. That is, you could have used `pSpell` everywhere you see the *Release* method invocation in the earlier code. This would work for the *CoOcrEngine* object, because you know the internals of its implementation. However, this can be deadly because it may not work for other objects. Never assume that an object keeps an object-level reference count, but act as if all interfaces keep personal interface-level reference counts. This is a COM mandate—and you should discipline yourself to follow the rules of COM, in this case for uniformity. We shouldn't assume the internals of any COM object. Invoke *Release* only upon the interface pointer returned to you, nothing else.

Following is more code you've seen. Notice that you release the *IMultiQI* interface after you've finished using it, and you cast each of the interfaces in the `MULTI_QI` array to the correct interface pointer type before calling *Release*. As we've just noted, this is extremely important because you should not call *Release* upon any other interfaces exposed by the object, except the interface that's given to you.

```
IMultiQI *pMulti=NULL;
// Query for the IMultiQI interface, which is implemented by the local proxy
hr = pUnk->QueryInterface(IID_IMultiQI, (void**)&pMulti);
assert(SUCCEEDED(hr));

MULTI_QI mqi[] = { {&IID_IOcr, NULL, S_OK}, {&IID_ISpell, NULL, S_OK} };
hr = pMulti->QueryMultipleInterfaces(sizeof(mqi)/sizeof(mqi[0]), mqi);
pMulti->Release();
assert(SUCCEEDED(mqi[0].hr)&&SUCCEEDED(mqi[1].hr));

// Release the correct interface.
static_cast<IOcr *>(mqi[0].pItf)->Release();
// Release the correct interface.
static_cast<ISpell *>(mqi[1].pItf)->Release();
```

## In- and Out-of-Process Issues

There's one last issue regarding developing COM clients. Clients should call the *CoFreeUnusedLibrary* API function periodically or during idle processing* to unload in-process servers that are no longer in use. Recall that all in-process servers

---

* In Windows programming, an empty message queue means that the application has no work to do (therefore, idle). The application is not busy handling window messages, so you can do whatever you want during this short period. This short period is intended for idle processing, and it should be kept short or else arriving window messages will not be handled in a timely manner.

implement the *DllCanUnloadNow* entry point to support the component's unloading. The *CoFreeUnusedLibrary* API function calls *DllCanUnloadNow* on each in-process server, and unloads the ones that are no longer needed. An in-process server can be unloaded when its component-level reference count falls to zero.

Don't do this for out-of-process servers, since these servers are totally different processes. They commit suicide when their component-level reference count falls to zero.

---

 At this point, you have enough knowledge to build server and client components using COM. Refer to the "Creating a Server Component" sidebar for a checklist of creating server components, and refer to the "Creating a Client Component" sidebar for a checklist of creating client components.

---

# Object Orientation

The object orientation topic hasn't been touched yet because you must first know COM before we can really speak about COM object orientation. Thus far, you have gained all the basics of COM. You've learned how to wrap up a component from a number of classes, objects, and interfaces. You've also learned how to use the services exposed by these COM objects, and you've worked very hard to get to here. Everything you've learned so far involves classic notions of traditional systems programming: interfaces, objects, and classes. In this section, we will examine the object-oriented aspect of COM. Remember that COM is a model. The model supports the traditional object-oriented notions which include encapsulation, polymorphism, and reuse (or inheritance). In all these cases, COM surpasses the traditional notions, because it ratifies and strengthens them. We'll first briefly examine these notions in the following sections, and then you'll learn to write code that allows you to dynamically reuse binary components.

## Encapsulation

COM not only supports the notion of encapsulation, but it strongly enforces it. The basis of COM is the distinct separation of interface from implementation. All COM objects are built from interfaces and all interfaces must be specified. Interfaces contain specification of methods, but don't contain specification of states or implementations. In other words, an interface groups together a number of methods that a COM object supports, but it doesn't specify the states of the object, which are totally implementation details. In addition to the fact that interfaces carry no implementation details, they must never be changed once they are published. With this support, any object may implement a published interface, but how the object implements the interface is its own business. In this respect, an object's implementation details are all hidden or encapsulated behind exposed interfaces.

A COM object is a black box with a bunch of lollipops. In order to eat a particular lollipop, you have to ask the object whether it's got that lollipop. A COM object is so well encapsulated that you can't use it until you actually query for a particular interface that it supports. This support raises encapsulation to a higher level, allowing clients to dynamically and robustly discover an object's exposed services. If a client asks for a particular interface that an object doesn't support, the sky won't fall, since the object returns a negative response, indicating to the client that it should take appropriate action to gracefully recover.

## Polymorphism

Compared to traditional object-oriented paradigm, polymorphism is better supported in COM. Traditional support for polymorphism allows only methods to be polymorphic, but COM extends polymorphism to a COM interface. For example, the *IUnknown* interface is polymorphic across all COM objects. Any COM client can talk to any other COM object in cyberspace, since every COM object must implement *IUnknown*. At the method level, *QueryInterface* (and company) is polymorphic across all interfaces. This allows anyone to get from one COM interface to another. It is the polymorphic aspects of *IUnknown* that uphold the COM philosophy.

*IUnknown* is not the only interface that is polymorphic in COM, though; every interface in COM is polymorphic across all COM objects that implement it. Since an interface is like an application-level communications protocol, you are essentially creating a colloquial dialect that can be potentially turned into standard speech. And once it turns into a well-known interface, such a standard interfaces provided by Microsoft, everyone will be able to speak your colloquial dialect. This is an extremely powerful idea.

Knowing a particular interface specification, a client can use the services exposed by any COM object that implements and supports that interface. This is true regardless of how the interface is implemented. As shown in Figure 4-4, if three different objects correctly implement an *ISpell* interface, everyone who knows how to talk the *ISpell* protocol can use all three objects, despite drastic implementation differences among them. Therefore, specified interfaces are polymorphic across all COM objects.

## Reuse

Traditional object-oriented techniques support reuse via the notion of implementation inheritance, which can be potentially risky, as presented in Chapter 2, *Distributed COM Overview*. Even though COM doesn't support implementation inheritance, it doesn't mean that you can't use traditional

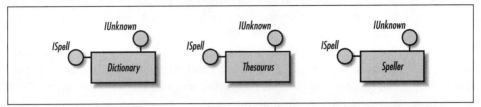

*Figure 4-4. The IUnknown and ISpell interfaces are polymorphic across all of these objects*

implementation inheritance for the internal implementations of your COM objects. Remember that COM is language independent, so theoretically, you can use any language you want to develop component software. If you happen to use C++ to develop COM objects, by all means, be as skillful as you want in exploiting C++ inheritance. Whatever you do inside the object will not affect the outside world, because everything you do internally is implementation detail that clients need not care about.

However, reuse in COM doesn't mean reusing source code because it means much more than that. In COM, you reuse a binary COM object. For example, consider a *CoOuter* COM object that reuses the binary *CoInner* COM object. With binary reusability, when the implementation of the *CoInner* object changes, no implementation changes to the *CoOuter* are required. Hence, binary reusability removes the coupling between the *CoOuter* and *CoInner* objects. There are two ways to implement binary reuse in COM: containment and aggregation.

## *Containment*

*Containment* is the traditional technique for reuse, which C++ developers have grown to know and trust. In classical object-oriented programming, you use containment to build a larger object that is composed of many smaller ones. For example, a car (the outer object) contains an engine (the inner object) and delegates engine-related functionality to its engine. A car cannot accelerate without an engine; therefore, it has to delegate this responsibility to its contained engine. For this reason, containment is also called *delegation*. This is a simple idea that's been in use for years.

We can apply the same technique in reusing binary COM objects. Recall that you've developed a COM object, called *CoOcrEngine*, which exposes two interfaces (*IOcr* and *ISpell*). If you were to develop a *CoDictionary* COM object, you might want to support an *IDictionary* and an *ISpell* interface, but since you've already written the code for *ISpell* in the *CoOcrEngine* object, it'd be nice to reuse that particular implementation. You can easily do this using COM containment.

You've seen a simple picture of COM containment in Chapter 2, but Figure 4-5 more accurately depicts COM containment. This simple reuse mechanism allows the outer object (*CoDictionary*) to delegate method invocations to the inner object (*CoOcrEngine*), effectively reusing the inner object's implementation. The *CoDictionary* object will pass all *ISpell* calls to its contained object's *ISpell* interface. In this sense, all *ISpell* methods in the *CoDictionary* (outer object) object are stubs that automatically forward their calls to the corresponding methods implemented by *CoOcrEngine* (inner object). For this reason, the *CoDictionary's ISpell* interface is often called a pass-through interface, because it doesn't do anything. It simply forwards the calls to the target destination.

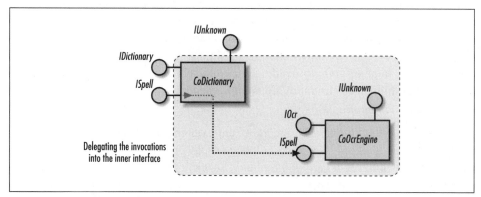

*Figure 4-5. COM containment*

The dotted rectangle represents the *CoDictionary* object as seen by a client. You may have realized that *CoDictionary* may be a server to other clients, but it is simply a client to *CoOcrEngine*. Thus, the *CoOcrEngine* that is reused could live on a totally different machine, proving that you're getting both binary and distributed component reuse.

Here's how you would use containment to gain binary reusability. As shown in the code following, *CoDictionary* implements *IDictionary* and *ISpell*. *CoDictionary* is implemented exactly like any other COM object; however, it is also a client to the *CoOcrEngine* COM object. Therefore, it keeps a reference to *CoOcrEngine's ISpell* interface as a member variable. It creates the *CoOcrEngine* object in the constructor, by calling a private helper function, *CreateInnerObject*, which will be discussed in a moment. The destructor simply releases the interface.

```
class CoDictionary : public IDictionary, public ISpell {
    LONG m_lRefCount;
    // We specifically want to reuse the ISpell interface that belongs to
    // the inner object -- using the containment technique
    // we're keeping a reference to the inner,
    // reused object (CoOcrEngine).
    ISpell *m_pISpell ;
public:
    CoDictionary() : m_lRefCount(0), m_pISpell(0)
    {
        ComponentAddRef();
```

```
        // Create the inner object.
        CreateInnerObject();
    }

    ~CoDictionary()
    {
        // Release the interface of the inner object
        // that we've been keeping for inner method delegation.
        if (m_pISpell) { m_pISpell->Release(); }
        ComponentRelease();
    }

    // The factory will call this method to actually
    // create this object.
    static HRESULT CreateObject(LPUNKNOWN pUnkOuter, REFIID riid, void** ppv);

public:
    // IUnknown Methods
    STDMETHODIMP QueryInterface(REFIID riid, void **ppv);
    STDMETHODIMP_(ULONG) AddRef(void);
    STDMETHODIMP_(ULONG) Release(void);

    // IDictionary
    STDMETHODIMP LookUp()
    { wprintf(TEXT("Lookup success...\n")); return S_OK; }

    // ISpell methods
    // We're reusing the implementation of an inner
    // binary object.  Simply forward the calls...
    STDMETHODIMP Check(wchar_t *pszWord, PossibleWords *pWords)
    { return m_pISpell->Check(pszWord, pWords); }

private:
    // Helper member function to create the inner object for reuse.
    void CreateInnerObject();
};
```

As just shown, you provide a simple implementation of *LookUp* (*IDictionary*'s method). In the simple implementation of *Check* (*ISpell*'s method), you simply pass the buck to m_pISpell, which is a pointer to *CoOcrEngine*'s *ISpell* interface. This interface pointer is obtained in the private helper function, *CreateInnerObject*:

```
void CoDictionary::CreateInnerObject()
{
    MULTI_QI mqi[] = { {&IID_ISpell, NULL, S_OK} };
    // Create the inner object for reuse by containment
    HRESULT hr = CoCreateInstanceEx(CLSID_OcrEngine, NULL, CLSCTX_SERVER,
                                    NULL, sizeof(mqi)/sizeof(mqi[0]), mqi);
    if (SUCCEEDED(hr) && SUCCEEDED(mqi[0].hr)) {
        // Save the interface pointer as a member variable
        m_pISpell = static_cast<ISpell *>(mqi[0].pItf);
    } else {
        assert(false);
    }
}
```

You shouldn't be surprised that *CoCreateInstanceEx* is used to create the inner COM object, because after all, the *CoDictionary* COM object is simply a client to *CoOcrEngine*. Notice that you request the *ISpell* interface, because that's the interface you want to save, and to which you'll later forward method invocations. *CoCreateInstanceEx* also allows you to get an array of interfaces at one time, so if needed, you can take advantage of this feature.

Here's one place that you shouldn't specify a server destination (the fourth parameter of *CoCreateInstanceEx*), but instead allow the server name to be derived from the RemoteServerName named value registry entry, which can be easily configured using *dcomcnfg.exe* or *oleview.exe*. Remember that the outer and inner objects can be located anywhere after you've deployed your components. If you hard code the inner object's server name, there's no way to configure the destination of the inner object. Put differently, you wouldn't want to change the code of your outer object each time you relocate the inner object to a different machine. Thus, don't specify a hard-coded server destination when you are writing a COM object that internally uses another object. If you don't heed this advice, you may encounter the infamous RPC_S_SERVER_UNAVAILABLE return code.

The advantage of COM containment is simplicity, because the outer object simply acts as a client to the inner object. This implies that the inner object can exist anywhere in cyberspace, and reuse is still possible. Another advantage is that any COM object can be reused by virtue of containment. These are the reasons why containment is preferred over aggregation.

## *Aggregation*

Aggregation is another technique for binary reuse in COM, which allows a number of COM objects to be aggregated together into one single entity. When you use this technique, your outer object can expose an inner object's interfaces as if the outer object implemented them. Furthermore, you can selectively choose the inner interfaces that you want to expose. A client that uses the your outer object will not know that you have indeed reused one or more binary components. A client sees only one single entity, the outer object.

For instance, if you were to develop a *CoThesaurus* (outer) COM object, you might like to support an *ISpell* interface, in addition to possibly supporting an *IThesaurus* interface. Since *CoOcrEngine* (inner object) has already implemented the *ISpell*, it would be wise to reuse the implementation. If you were to use aggregation, we would aggregate the *ISpell* (and maybe even the *IOcr*) interface of the *CoOcrEngine* object into your *CoThesaurus* object. Aggregation allows you to hallucinate clients into thinking that the *CoThesaurus* COM object implements the *ISpell* interface, when in fact the *ISpell* interface is actually implemented by the inner object. As seen in Figure 4-6, the *ISpell* and *IOcr* interface have been extended to clients of the *CoThesaurus* object. Note that you can selectively expose the inner interfaces to your clients. For example, the *CoThesaurus* object shown in Figure 4-6 supports the *IOcr* interface, but it doesn't have to support this functionality.

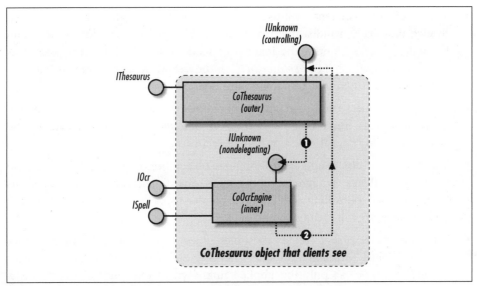

*Figure 4-6. COM aggregation*

Though you've seen a simple picture of COM aggregation in Chapter 2, Figure 4-6 more accurately depicts COM aggregation. COM Aggregation allows the outer object (*CoThesaurus*) to aggregate the inner object's (*CoOcrEngine*) interfaces, so that clients see all inner interfaces as part of the outer object. There are two requirements needed to preserve the outer object's identity.

- The outer object keeps a reference to the inner object's *implicit* (or *nondelegating*) unknown.

- The inner object knows (holds onto) the outer object's unknown, so that it can delegate all delegating *IUnknown* methods out to the outer object's unknown (called the *controlling unknown*). The dotted rectangle in Figure 4-6 represents the *CoThesaurus* object as seen by a client.

Figure 4-6 looks fairly straightforward, but you need to provide special support in both the inner and outer objects to successfully take advantage of aggregation. A COM object can be aggregated only if it supports the aggregation guidelines set forth by the COM Specification, so naturally not every COM object can be aggregated. The good thing is COM doesn't mandate that objects support aggregation, but if you want to use aggregation, here are five requirements for both the outer and inner objects.

- When being aggregated, the inner object must provide special support for the outer object's identity and lifetime management. This requires the inner object to provide two sets of implementations for *IUnknown* (one called the *delegating unknown* and the other called the *nondelegating* or *implicit unknown*).

- The outer object's clients will use the inner object's delegating unknown, even though they have no idea that they're actually doing this. In order to maintain the outer object's identity, the inner object's delegating unknown routes all its method invocations (*QueryInterface, AddRef,* and *Release*) outward to the outer object's *IUnknown*, the controlling unknown.

- The outer object will use the inner object's nondelegating or implicit *IUnknown*. This inner object's implicit *IUnknown* must not delegate to the outer object, in order to prevent infinite recursion.

- When an outer object aggregates an inner object, the outer object must tell the inner object that it is aggregating the inner object. The outer object does this by passing its controlling unknown (a pointer to its own *IUnknown*) into the inner object when it creates the inner object.

- When the outer object creates the inner object, it can ask only for the inner object's implicit *IUnknown* interface, nothing else. This is required to prevent infinite recursion, as only the implicit unknown of the inner object prevents outward delegation.

That's quite a bit of work. So before you go on to the code that's required to fulfill these requirements, first examine some advantages and disadvantages of aggregation. After the explanation of these advantages and disadvantages, you can decide whether you would want your COM objects to support aggregation.

If your COM objects support aggregation, here are two benefits:

- Other objects can reuse your object by aggregation or containment.

- If your object supports an interface with 100 methods, other objects can use aggregation so that they don't have to implement 100 passthrough methods when reusing this particular interface.

However, here are two notable drawbacks of aggregation:

- COM objects that support aggregation are harder to implement than simple COM objects. For example, you must write special code for your object to support aggregation.*

---

* There are other subtle and complex problems with aggregation, which are beyond the scope of this book.

- Aggregation doesn't work across apartments (execution contexts), which is a drawback that prevents distributed reuse. This also means that in order for an object to be aggregated, it must be packaged into an in-process server.[*]

### Using objects that support aggregation

Now that you've examined the obvious advantages and disadvantages of aggregation, look at what's needed to aggregate an inner object that supports aggregation. Consider a *CoThesaurus* COM object that implements the *IThesaurus* interface. It also aggregates the *CoOcrEngine* object to expose the *IOcr* and *ISpell* interfaces to its clients as if these interfaces were its own. To do this, it needs to keep a pointer to an implicit *IUnknown* interface of the inner object, shown in the following code as m_pUnkAggregate. Like containment, you create the inner object in the constructor by calling the helper function *CreateInnerObject*, and you release m_pUnkAggregate in the destructor. Unlike containment, you don't implement any pass-through interface methods for *ISpell* and *IOcr*.

```
class CoThesaurus : public IThesaurus {
    LONG m_lRefCount;
    // To support aggregation, keep a pointer to the
    // implicit (nondelegating) unknown
    // of the object we're aggregating (the inner object)
    IUnknown *m_pUnkAggregate;

public:
    CoThesaurus() : m_lRefCount(0), m_pUnkAggregate(0)
    {
        ComponentAddRef();
        // Create the inner, reused object
        CreateInnerObject();
    }

    ~CoThesaurus()
    {
        if (m_pUnkAggregate) { m_pUnkAggregate->Release(); }
        ComponentRelease();
    }

    // The factory will call this method to actually
    // create this object.
    static HRESULT CreateObject(LPUNKNOWN pUnkOuter, REFIID riid,
                                void** ppv);
public:
    // IUnknown Methods
    STDMETHODIMP QueryInterface(REFIID riid, void **ppv);
    STDMETHODIMP_(ULONG) AddRef(void);
    STDMETHODIMP_(ULONG) Release(void);

    // IThesaurus
```

---

[*] Furthermore, the in-process server must have the same concurrency semantics as the thread that loads it.

```
STDMETHODIMP LookUp()
{ wprintf(TEXT("Lookup success...\n")); return S_OK; }

private:
    // Helper member function to create the inner object for reuse.
    void CreateInnerObject();
};
```

So far, everything's fairly simple. Now look at the private *CreateInnerObject* function, which creates and aggregates the inner object. As seen in the following code, you query only for the inner *IUnknown* when creating the inner COM object, as this is a requirement stipulated by COM. If you request for any other interface at this moment, you won't be able to create the inner object for aggregation. Also, notice that when you create the inner object (*CoOcrEngine* represented by CLSID_OcrEngine) using the *CoCreateInstanceEx* API function, you pass the this pointer as the second parameter, which represents the outer (controlling) *IUnknown*. As another requirement mandated by COM, this allows the inner object to detect that it is being aggregated, so that it will provide the correct support for the COM identity of the outer object.

```
void CoThesaurus::CreateInnerObject()
{
    // Only request for inner IUnknown when aggregating.
    MULTI_QI mqi[] = { {&IID_IUnknown, NULL, S_OK} };

    // Prevent possible premature self-destruction.
    InterlockedIncrement(&m_lRefCount);

    // Create the inner object, notifying it that we're aggregating it.
    HRESULT hr = CoCreateInstanceEx(CLSID_OcrEngine,
        this, // Outer unknown, tells the inner object it's being aggregated.
        CLSCTX_SERVER, NULL, sizeof(mqi)/sizeof(mqi[0]), mqi);

    InterlockedDecrement(&m_lRefCount);

    if (SUCCEEDED(hr) && SUCCEEDED(mqi[0].hr)) {
        // Save the inner unknown as a member variable.
        m_pUnkAggregate = reinterpret_cast<IUnknown *>(mqi[0].pItf);
    } else {
        assert(false);
    }
}
```

Notice that a pair of *InterlockedIncrement*/*InterlockedDecrement* calls wraps the *CoCreateInstanceEx* invocation. This is a technique that protects the outer object from premature self-destruction. Recall that the constructor of *CoThresaurus* calls this function, which means that, at this moment, the reference count (m_lRefCount) of this object is zero.

Assume in the earlier code that you don't have the pair of *InterlockedIncrement*/*InterlockedDecrement* wrapping the *CoCreateInstanceEx* call. When you call

*CoCreateInstanceEx*, the inner object will be created. During its creation, assume for some weird reason that the inner object queries the outer object for an *IThesaurus* interface, which increments the outer object's m_lRefCount to one. Assume also that it then releases the interface, sending the outer object's m_lRefCount back to zero. Then recall that in the *Release* method, an object deletes itself when it detects that its reference count has fallen to zero, which means that the call to *Release* will trigger the untimely destruction of the outer object. To prevent this problem, you can temporarily bump up the outer object's reference count before creating the inner object. Now, if the inner object queries for an outer interface (outer m_lRefCount=2) and immediately releases (outer m_lRefCount=1) it, the reference count of your object will be one, which fixes the premature self-destruction problem. Be advised that you're calling *InterlockedDecrement* instead of calling your own *Release* method. If you had called *Release*, you would face the same problem of premature self-destruction. Since we use *InterlockedDecrement*, you'll need to be consistent and also use *InterlockedIncrement*.

Finally, you need to add simple code to the outer object's *QueryInterface* method. As seen in the following, you forward all the *QueryInterface* calls for *IOcr* and *ISpell* to the inner object, using the implicit *IUnknown* pointer (m_pUnkAggregate) that you've saved earlier.

```
STDMETHODIMP
CoThesaurus::QueryInterface(REFIID riid, void** ppv)
{
    if (ppv==NULL) { return E_INVALIDARG; }

    if (riid==IID_IUnknown) {
        *ppv= static_cast<IThesaurus *>(this);
    } else if (riid==IID_IThesaurus) {
        *ppv= static_cast<IThesaurus *>(this);
    } else if (riid==IID_IOcr||riid==IID_ISpell) {
        // Support Aggregation...
        // Let the inner object handle this request,
        // since both interfaces belong to the inner object.
        return m_pUnkAggregate->QueryInterface(riid, ppv) ;
    } else {
        *ppv=NULL; return E_NOINTERFACE ;
    }

    reinterpret_cast<IUnknown *>(*ppv)->AddRef();

    return S_OK;
}
```

As you can see, it's easy to reuse a COM object that supports aggregation. However, developing COM objects that support aggregation requires much more effort.

## Developing objects that support aggregation

So far, we've gone over the code that's necessary for an outer object to aggregate an inner object, but you haven't learned about what's needed for an inner object to support aggregation. This is what you're about to embark upon. First, an inner object that supports aggregation must be packaged in an in-process server, since aggregation doesn't work across apartment boundaries. An in-process server will likely meet this criteria, since it runs in the same process as the outer object.*

Besides this requirement, you need to provide two different implementations of *IUnknown*, as mandated by the COM Specification. Figure 4-7 shows two instances of the *CoOcrEngine* object that can be aggregated. The instance on the left is a normal *CoOcrEngine* object, and the one on the right is a *CoOcrEngine* object that is being aggregated by an outer entity. Each of these objects has a group of finely dotted lines along with an arrow.

To provide two different implementations of *IUnknown*, you need to perform a few C++ tricks. The tricks you perform must point this arrow to the correct unknown that manages the resulting object's identity. Depending on whether this object is being aggregated, this can be either the inner object's implicit unknown or the outer object's controlling unknown. Specifically, when the inner object is not being aggregated, you must point this arrow to the implicit unknown. In this case, no outward delegation happens. However, if the inner object is being aggregated, you must point this arrow to the controlling unknown, which is owned by the outer object. This allows the inner object to delegate outward. Imagine Figure 4-7 as you implement the two unknowns.

The first *IUnknown* is the implicit unknown, which is clearly labeled in Figure 4-7. This is the unknown that is normally used when the inner object is not being aggregated. Shown below is a generic and templatized implementation of the implicit unknown (See the "C++ Templates" sidebar found later if you're not familiar with C++ templates). The implicit unknown simply implements the *IUnknown* interface. The *Bkptr* function is used to set the back pointer to the object (*CoOcrEngine*) that implements the nondelegating methods of the implicit unknown, which include *InternalQueryInterface, InternalAddRef,* and *InternalRelease* (to be discussed in a moment).

```
// IMPLITCIT UNKNOWN
// Works with three special, private methods to implement
// the nondelegating unknown.
template<class T> class CImplicitUnknown : public IUnknown {
public:
    // m_pbkptr points to the object implementing the
    // nondelegating IUnknown methods.
```

---

* We say "likely" because the outer and inner objects can possibly live in separate apartments. This is true when the outer and inner objects have different concurrency semantics, as discussed in Chapter 5.

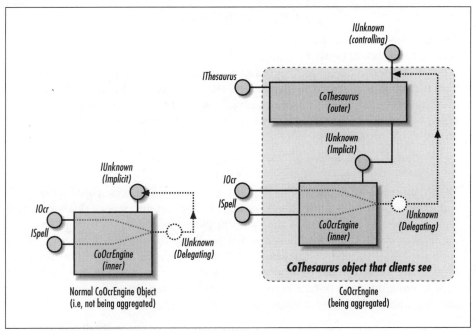

*Figure 4-7. CoOcrEngine is a COM object that supports aggregation*

```
    void Bkptr(T *p) { m_pbkptr=p; }

    STDMETHODIMP QueryInterface(REFIID iid, void **ppv)
    { return m_pbkptr->InternalQueryInterface(iid, ppv); }
    STDMETHODIMP_(ULONG) AddRef(void)
    { return m_pbkptr->InternalAddRef(); }
    STDMETHODIMP_(ULONG) Release(void)
    { return m_pbkptr->InternalAddRef(); }

private:
    T *m_pbkptr;
};
```

Since *CImplicitUnknown* is a template class, T represents the class that implements these internal methods. Even though *CImplicitUnknown* is generic, it assumes that the nondelegation *IUnknown* methods are named *InternalQueryInterface*, *InternalAddRef*, and *InternalRelease*. As shown in the earlier code snippet, the *QueryInterface*, *AddRef*, and *Release* methods simply forward to m_pbkptr's *InternalQueryInterface*, *InternalAddRef*, and *InternalRelease* respectively. This will be clear in a moment when you implement *CoOcrEngine*, but here's a hint: m_pbkptr will be pointing to a *CoOcrEngine* object. Thus, *CoOcrEngine* must implement the nondelegating *InternalQueryInterface*, *InternalAddRef*, and *InternalRelease* methods.

# C++ Templates

The fundamental idea motivating all C++ template classes is that functionally related code should be written once and be reused forever with many different types. Put in technical terms, C++ template classes allow type parameterization. This is the notion that a particular generic class can be specifically further qualified by a type or many types. For example, if we have a C++ template *Array* class, we can make specific and widely different instantiations for this generic *Array* class as follows:

```
Array<int> anIntegerArray;   // An array of integers.
Array<Dog> aDogArray;        // An array of dogs.
```

Before the days of templates, to support an array of integers, you'd have to write the code for this array. If you wanted to support an array of dogs, you'd simply copy and paste most of the code for the array of integers to implement an array of dogs. The only difference that you have to take into account is the type (i.e., **dog** instead of **integer**). Put differently, the functionality of the array is the same, but the type supported by the array is different. It would be nice to write the code once and reuse it forever without doing the error-prone copying and pasting. C++ template allows this.

Here's a partial example of a generic array class that works with all types:

```
template<class T> class Array { public: T & operator[](int i); }
```

**T** is a placeholder for the resulting type. Thus, if you instantiate an array of cars as follows:

```
Array<Car> aCarArray;        // An array of cars.
```

The resulting class is an array of cars, as each appearance of **T** is replaced with *Car*. The resulting index operator (**operator[]**) is declared to return a reference to a *Car* in the i^th element of the array.

From a programmer's perspective, templates are sort of like C macros on steroids. Templates are like macros because they can save lots of typing. Template classes are on steroids, because they behave just like any normal C++ class; that is, you can instantiate them, derive from them, and do whatever you like with them as you can with normal C++ classes.

---

The second *IUnknown* is the delegating unknown, which delegates all *IUnknown* methods outward to the controlling unknown of the outer object. The reason for this is to maintain the outer object's COM identity and lifetime management, since the outer object is the only object of this aggregate that a client sees. Put differently, an outer object's client will never know that an inner object exists. However, if a client calls *QueryInterface* on an interface (not including *IUnknown*) pointer that really belongs to the inner object, the inner object must notify the outer object of the *QueryInterface* call to allow the outer object to correctly manage its identity. Likewise calls to *AddRef* and *Release* must also be delegated to the outer object to allow the outer object to correctly manage its lifetime.

Remember, these outward delegations are shown by the group of dotted lines in Figure 4-7. The lollipop for the delegating unknown is dotted to show that it delegates outward to the controlling unknown only when the inner object is being aggregated. When the inner object is not being aggregated, it delegates to its own implicit unknown.

Following is a rewrite of the *CoOcrEngine* COM object to support aggregation. Notice that you have a member variable that represents the implicit unknown, m_InnerUnk. Also, you keep a member variable called m_pOuterUnk, which points either to the outer object's controlling unknown when being aggregated or to this object's implicit unknown when not being aggregated.

```
class CoOcrEngine : public IOcr, public ISpell {
    LONG m_lRefCount;
    friend CImplicitUnknown<CoOcrEngine>;

    // Represents the implicit IUnknown of this object.
    CImplicitUnknown<CoOcrEngine> m_InnerUnk;

    // Points either to the outer object's IUnknown
    // or to this object's implicit IUnknown.
    IUnknown *m_pOuterUnk;
```

Correctly setting the m_pOuterUnk pointer is the trick to developing objects that support aggregation. Specifically, m_pOuterUnk must point to the unknown that manages the resulting object's identity. Set this pointer in the constructor of *CoOcrEngine*.

As shown in the later code snippet, the constructor has a parameter that represents the outer *IUnknown* pointer. If this pointer is non-NULL, this object is being aggregated. In this case, you make a copy of the outer unknown's interface pointer (m_pOuterUnk(pOuterUnk)). However, don't call *AddRef* on this pointer because the inner object's lifetime is a subset of the outer object's lifetime. In other words, the outer object determines the creation and destruction of the inner object.

On the other hand, if the pointer passed into the constructor is NULL, this object is not being aggregated; and therefore, you've got no outer object. In other words, you are either being contained or being used as a normal object. In this case, you need to set m_pOuterUnk to point to m_InnerUnk (the implicit unknown). Since there's no outer object, you delegate to your own implicit unknown to preserve the object's identity.

```
public:
    CoOcrEngine(IUnknown *pOuterUnk)
        : m_lRefCount(0), m_InnerUnk(), m_pOuterUnk(pOuterUnk)
    {
```

```
ComponentAddRef();
// Set the inner unknown back pointer to point to this object,
// so that we can later call special internal functions,
// which supports the implementation of the implicit unknown.
m_InnerUnk.Bkptr(this);

if (pOuterUnk==NULL) {
  // We're not being aggregated; therefore, we've got no outer object.
  // Set the outer unknown to be the non-delegating or implicit unknown,
  // since we're either being contained or used as a normal object.
  m_pOuterUnk = &m_InnerUnk;
  }
}

~CoOcrEngine()
{ ComponentRelease(); }

static HRESULT CreateObject(LPUNKNOWN pOuterUnk,
                            REFIID riid, void **ppv);
```

As shown in the earlier code snippet (m_InnerUnk.Bkptr(this)), you set the back pointer of the implicit unknown to point to this object regardless of the argument passed into the constructor. You do this so that you can later call the nondelegating *InternalQueryInterface*, *InternalAddRef*, and *InternalRelease* methods. You will write the code for these methods shortly.

For now, examine the code for the delegating *IUnknown* methods, which are shown in the following code snippet. Remember, the delegating *IUnknown* methods delegate to the unknown that manages the object's identity. When this object is being aggregated, these methods (*QueryInterface*, *AddRef*, and *Release*) simply delegate outward to the controlling unknown of the outer object. When this object is not being aggregated, these methods simply forward calls to the implicit unknown, which reroutes the calls to the nondelegating *InternalQueryInterface*, *InternalAddRef*, and *InternalRelease* methods. The resulting behavior depends upon where m_pOuterUnk points. Recall that you make m_pOuterUnk point to either the implicit or the controlling unknown in the constructor of *CoOcrEngine*.

```
public:
    STDMETHODIMP QueryInterface(REFIID iid, void **ppv)
    { return m_pOuterUnk->QueryInterface(iid, ppv); }
    STDMETHODIMP_(ULONG) AddRef(void)
    { return m_pOuterUnk->AddRef(); }
    STDMETHODIMP_(ULONG) Release(void)
    { return m_pOuterUnk->Release(); }

    // IOcr Methods
    STDMETHODIMP OcrImage(long lImageSize,
                          byte *pbImage,
                          wchar_t **pwszOcrText);
    STDMETHODIMP OcrZone(long lImageSize,
                         byte *pbImage,
                         Zone zone,
```

```
                    wchar_t **pwszOcrText);

    // ISpell Methods
    STDMETHODIMP Check(wchar_t *pwszWord, PossibleWords *pWords);
```

Now for the nondelegating *IUnknown* methods. These methods are an exact replica of the normal implementation of *IUnknown* for a simple COM object, except for the following code shown in boldface. Really, only the names have been changed, because you can't overload functions with the same signature in C++. The bold-faced code within the *InternalQueryInterface* method is needed, because COM mandates that when anyone queries for the *IUnknown* interface of your inner object, you always return the implicit unknown pointer. Recall that the implementation of the *CImplicitUnknown* methods simply forwards to these internal methods.

```
    private:
      HRESULT InternalQueryInterface(REFIID iid, void **ppv)
      {
          if (ppv==NULL) { return E_INVALIDARG; }

          if (riid==IID_IUnknown) {
              // Always return the implicit unknown,
              // when anyone requests for IUnknown.
              *ppv= static_cast<IUnknown *>(&m_InnerUnk);
          } else if (riid==IID_IOcr) {
              *ppv= static_cast<IOcr *>(this);
          } else if (riid==IID_ISpell) {
              *ppv= static_cast<ISpell *>(this);
          } else {
              *ppv=NULL; return E_NOINTERFACE ;
          }

          reinterpret_cast<IUnknown *>(*ppv)->AddRef();
          return S_OK;
      }

      ULONG InternalAddRef(void)
      { return InterlockedIncrement(&m_lRefCount); }
      ULONG InternalRelease(void)
      {
          long lCount = InterlockedDecrement(&m_lRefCount);
          if (lCount == 0) { delete this; }
          return lCount;
      }
    };
```

There are a few remaining important points before you can complete the support for aggregation. Recall that *CreateObject* is a static method that is called by a class factory's *CreateInstance* method to actually create the COM object. COM mandates that in order for an outer object to aggregate the inner object, it must only request for the inner object's *IUnknown* when it creates the inner object. Check this requirement in the first few lines of the following code snippet:

```
HRESULT CoOcrEngine::CreateObject(LPUNKNOWN pOuterUnk, REFIID riid, void**
    ppv)
{
    *ppv = NULL;

    // If aggregating, must initially request for IID_IUnknown.
    if (pOuterUnk != NULL && riid != IID_IUnknown)
        return CLASS_E_NOAGGREGATION;
```

You then dynamically allocate the inner object, passing along the outer unknown. If the argument is NULL, this inner object is either being contained or being used normally by a client.

```
    // Create the new object with a possibly valid outer unknown.
    CoOcrEngine * pEngine = new CoOcrEngine(pOuterUnk);
    if (pEngine == NULL) { return E_OUTOFMEMORY; }
```

Finally, you query for the requested interface using *InternalQueryInterface*, which is a nondelegating method of the inner object's implicit unknown. We must use the nondelegating *InternalQueryInterface* method when the object is created. Do not call *QueryInterface*. If you do, it will delegate outward to the outer object's *QueryInterface* method, which will delegate back into the inner *QueryInterface* method, and so on recursively.

```
    // If aggregating, the first query MUST be sent to the implicit
    // IUnknown requesting for IUnknown.
    HRESULT hr = pEngine->InternalQueryInterface(riid, ppv);
    if (FAILED(hr)) {   delete pEngine;   }

    return hr;
}
```

As you have seen, it takes some work on both the outer and inner objects to provide support for aggregation. You know a few major advantages and disadvantages associated with COM aggregation. Be aware that aggregation will not work across apartment boundaries, including processes and machines. Since this is very important for distributed computing, many developers choose containment over aggregation as the binary reuse mechanism.

# 5

# *Infrastructure*

While you can actually write complete, functioning server and client components from the material given in the previous chapters, you'll find them very limited. In order to give you the bare bones, the following considerations have been ignored:

*Memory management*

Some programs contain complicated, many-layered pointers as function arguments. These require special handling to send their data across a connection.

*Location transparency*

Objects can locate anywhere in cyberspace. Location transparency allows a single programming model that allows clients anywhere to refer to distributed objects. In COM programming, you know this object reference as an interface pointer, which can be passed to any component in cyberspace.

*Multithreading*

Multithreaded programming in COM is different from traditional multithreaded programming. To take advantage of multithreading, you need to learn an important concept called apartments.

*Security*

You haven't been shown how to restrict access to a service. Security can be configured by an administrator and can also be finely controlled through programming.

These are the sorts of supporting infrastructure that will be discussed in this chapter.

Before we delve in to these discussions, we must introduce an important Distributed COM concept called apartments. You've already seen the little boxes with protruding lollipops in Figure 5-1, which are COM objects. You also know that the components marked HOUSE or SHED are COM components and that the wavy lines

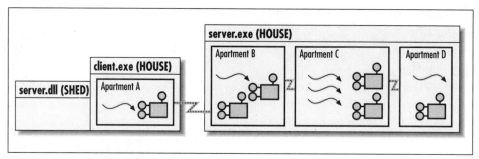

*Figure 5-1. COM applications and apartments*

are threads. However, the boxes marked `Apartment` A, B, C, or D are new. These boxes are execution contexts and are specifically called apartments in COM. As illustrated in Figure 5-1, an apartment is not a process, since a process can have an arbitrary number of apartments. It is not a thread, because a single apartment can have many threads. However, an apartment can be thought of as a logical grouping of COM objects that share the same concurrency semantics. In other words, objects that are thread-safe should be put in an apartment that supports multithreading. Objects that are thread-ignorant should only be put in a apartment that prevents multiple access.

Each of the boxes marked as an apartment is an implementation scope that helps COM manage distributed issues regarding location transparency and concurrency. Every process, whether a COM server or a COM client, that uses COM has at least one apartment. If cross apartment calls are made between two apartments with different concurrency models, COM can detect the discrepancies and can interpose to guarantee that remote method invocations are successfully carried out. Even though COM automatically does this underneath, there are times when we have to help COM out by telling COM our intentions regarding memory, location transparency, concurrency, and security. For the things that COM does automatically in support of these issues, you must understand what is going on in order to build real distributed systems.

We'll take apartments as the theme for this chapter and you'll learn the how to manage dynamic memory across remote apartments. You'll also learn the transparency or remoting architecture in enough depth that allows you to understand the actual wire protocol used by COM. In addition, you'll learn the COM concurrency infrastructure, which leverages the remoting architecture. Finally, you'll learn how to configure and program security in COM.

# *Memory*

Recall that COM must know the exact size of all data that is sent back and forth between a client and its objects. For simple data types (e.g., `short`, `long`, or our `Zone` structure), COM knows their sizes. However, you can modify these data types with pointers (e.g., `Zone *`, and so forth). When you're calling a function on a different system (or even a different address space on the same system), COM can't get away passing the four-byte address in the pointer; COM has to pass all the data being pointed to.

We know the importance of dynamic memory management in C and C++. Good programming requires allocated memory to be correctly destroyed. If your code lies in one single process, you know when to deallocate heap-based memory, which you have previously allocated. However, in a distributed architecture, which likely contains multiple execution contexts, you have a client and an object, including the object's associated proxy and stub. Remember that after you've deployed your components, ten thousand clients may use your objects. How should the clients, objects, and proxies/stubs deal with dynamic memory management?

COM, which relies on RPC, provides a number of rules that you must follow to correctly manage dynamic memory. When you specify a COM interface, you designate memory management assumptions by using the `[in]`, `[out]`, and `[in, out]` MIDL attributes. These attributes are hints that allow COM to correctly manage memory at the proxies and stubs level in standard marshaling. These attributes also tell an interface implementor and a client developer how memory should be managed at the application level.

In general, the rules for memory management are fairly simple and straightforward. These rules are succinctly exhibited in the Figure 5-2, which shows a caller (client) and a callee (object) living in two different apartments.* Figure 5-2(A) applies to all simple data types, *top-level pointers* (e.g., `short *p`), *secondary pointers* (e.g., `short **pp`), and *embedded pointers* (e.g., pointers embedded within a structure). Figure 5-2(B) and 5-2(C) apply only to secondary and embedded pointers and require you to use the COM memory allocator, a special memory manager that you should use when allocating memory in one component but deallocating it in a different one.

In this section, we will use these general rules to discuss the memory management for simple data types, top-level pointer types, secondary pointer types, embedded pointer types, and character pointer types. We will also discuss the memory management of two important Automation data types, including `BSTR` and `SAFEARRAY`.

---

* These rules don't apply to an interface pointer, which is an ORPC marshaled interface reference (object reference). An object reference is so important that it deserves its own moment of fame in the next section, "Transparency."

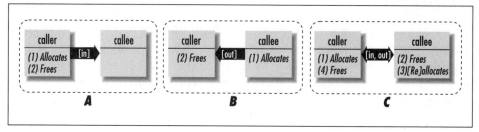

*Figure 5-2. Memory management rules*

## Simple Data Types and Top-Level Pointers

Let's first examine the simple case where a parameter is not even a pointer. Consider that we have a method *SetAge* that has a simple [in] parameter of type short, as shown below. COM knows the size of a short and thus can exchange the short between two different apartments without difficulty.

```
HRESULT SetAge([in] short sAge);
```

The object-side implementation of this method is simple, as shown below. It doesn't have to do any fancy memory management.

```
STDMETHODIMP CoPerson::SetAge(short sAge)
{
    // Use sAge
    return S_OK;
}
```

On the client side, you can allocate an [in] parameter anyway you want. This means that you can allocate the [in] parameter globally, on the stack, or even on the heap. COM can always find the memory and send the data across the connection. In this respect client code for an [in] parameter is also simple:

```
short age=1; // Allocate a short on the stack
p->SetAge(age);
```

If every parameter were just simple MIDL base types, then we wouldn't need to do anything regarding memory management. However, the world is not so perfect. There are many situations when we must pass parameters by reference. In C, we simulate this by modifying the parameter with a pointer. A pointer itself has a size that is specific to the operating system platform. It is the size of the data being pointed to that is important, so we need to coordinate with COM to make sure we're reading the same sheet of music.*

Let's take a look at an interface method with a pointer parameter. The *GetAge* method returns a short, which has an [out] attribute. Just as in any C or C++

---

\* MIDL does not support reference (&) parameters as C++ does.

program, an [out] parameter must be modified by a pointer to signify A pass-by-reference. Recall from Chapter 3, *Objects*, that a parameter such as psAge, in the following method signature, is an example of a top-level pointer:

```
HRESULT GetAge([out] short *psAge);
```

The object-side implementation of this method shows that you simply dereference the pointer and set 100 as the age. For top-level pointers, don't worry about memory management,* because the type (short) signifies the size of the data being pointed to:

```
STDMETHODIMP CoPerson::GetAge(short *psAge)
{ *psAge = 100; return S_OK; }
```

On the client side, you can allocate age however you want and pass its address into the *GetAge* function so that you can capture the returned data. This is simple and no different from C/C++:

```
short age=0; p->GetAge(&age);
```

Let's look at [in, out] top-level pointers. *ChangeAge* is a method that changes a given age and thus its parameter is modified using the [in, out] attribute. Again, psAge must be a pointer since you are effectively passing by reference:

```
HRESULT ChangeAge([in, out] short *psAge);
```

The object-side implementation of this method looks like the following simple and self-explanatory code. The implementation is similar to the previous cases, but notice that you can use psAge in this method, because it's both an input and an output. In addition, since this method's functionality is to change the age, you'll be positive and rejuvenate everyone that's older than thirty.

```
STDMETHODIMP CoPerson::ChangeAge(short *psAge)
{
    // Use (*psAge).  Valid because it's an input and an output.
    if (*psAge>30) { *psAge -= 10; }
    return S_OK;
}
```

On the client side, we pass the address of a **short** into the *ChangeAge* method. The **short** is allocated on the stack in the following code, but it could have been allocated globally or on the heap because the pointer passed to *ChangeAge* is a top-level pointer. Upon return of this method invocation, we will obtain the modified age.

```
short age=10; // Allocate on the stack
p->ChangeAge(&age);
```

---

* Unless we're dealing with an embedded pointer or a secondary (i.e., int **ppNum) pointer representing an array of things. Embedded pointers are discussed next.

These examples demonstrate that managing simple MIDL data types and top-level pointers is simple. There's not much to it since the size of a base type is known. As you can see, the management of top-level pointers maps directly to what you know in C/C++.

## Secondary and Embedded Pointers

Unlike top-level pointers, secondary and embedded pointers are much more complicated to manage. Luckily, the rules for managing secondary and embedded pointers are the same, so let's just concentrate on embedded pointers. Recall from Chapter 3 that embedded pointers are pointers that are embedded within an array or a structure. Embedded pointers can be reached using a top-level pointer or another embedded pointer. The pointer member, m_pBuffer, shown in the following structure, is considered to be an embedded pointer:

```
struct BinaryData {
    long m_lSize;  // Data size
    [ptr, size_is(m_lSize)] byte *m_pBuffer;  // Binary data
};
```

This structure encapsulates a buffer along with its size. Notice that m_pBuffer is also a conformant array. Embedded pointers must follow the memory management rules of COM and in general, they must be allocated and deallocated using COM memory allocation API functions.

### COM API functions for distributed memory management

*CoTaskMemAlloc* is the COM allocation API function that returns a chunk of memory when given a size, and it's similar to *malloc* in the C library. It is obvious that you cannot use *malloc* to allocate memory that is to be managed by the COM remoting infrastructure, because *malloc* lacks the knowledge for managing memory in a distributed environment. However, *CoTaskMemAlloc* has this knowledge, because it is provided by the COM library.

On the caller end, you'd use this API function to allocate memory for all secondary and embedded [in, out] pointers. On the callee end, you'd use this API function to allocate memory for all secondary and embedded [out] and [in, out] pointers. These are general rules that will be clear in the next section where concrete examples are illustrated.

```
LPVOID CoTaskMemAlloc(ULONG cb);
```

*CoTaskMemRealloc* is the COM reallocation API function that changes the size of a previously allocated memory chunk, and it's similar to *realloc* in the C library.

Typically, a callee calls this API function for [in, out] parameters to reallocate a chunk of memory that's been previously allocated by the caller.

```
LPVOID CoTaskMemRealloc(LPVOID pv, ULONG cb);
```

*CoTaskMemFree* is similar to *free* in the C library. You must use this COM API function on the caller end to free [out] or [in, out] secondary and embedded pointers. On the callee end, you must use *CoTaskMemFree* to deallocate secondary and embedded [in, out] pointers if deallocation is needed.

```
void CoTaskMemFree(LPVOID pv);
```

The *CoTaskMemAlloc*, *CoTaskMemRealloc*, and *CoTaskMemFree* COM API functions are shorthand functions for the methods of the *IMalloc* interface, which is not shown here for brevity. But I'll describe the use of *IMalloc* so that you can witness the internals of these shorthand functions. In order to use *IMalloc*, you must first get the COM task memory allocator by calling the *CoGetMalloc* COM API function, which returns a pointer to *IMalloc*. Once you get the *IMalloc* pointer, you may use it to allocate, reallocate, and deallocate memory that COM internally manages. For example, the following snippet illustrates the allocation of 1000 bytes using the *IMalloc* interface and its *Alloc* method:

```
IMalloc * pIMalloc = NULL;
CoGetMalloc(MEMCTX_TASK, &pIMalloc);
void *p=pIMalloc->Alloc(1000);  // Alloc is a method of IMalloc
pIMalloc->Release();
```

This earlier code is semantically equivalent to the following code, which uses the more convenient *CoTaskMemAlloc* function. In fact, *CoTaskMemAlloc* essentially encapsulates the code fragment shown before:

```
void *p=CoTaskMemAlloc(1000);
```

This idiom can also be applied to *CoTaskMemRealloc* and *CoTaskMemFree*. These shorthand memory allocators are a tiny bit less efficient than using *IMalloc* because they call *CoGetMalloc* and *Release* each time. However, they help keep the code clean and reduce programming errors.

### Managing embedded pointers

Now that we know about the COM memory allocators, let's see how we can use them to manage embedded pointers. Recall that we have four different entities that deal with memory management. As shown in Figure 5-3, these entities are the client (caller) code, the object (callee), and the object's proxy and stub. For [in] embedded pointer parameters, the client code (1) allocates the embedded pointer buffer, which the proxy passes to the stub. Since the stub is in a different address space (and perhaps a different machine), it has to dynamically (2) allocate the memory to hold the buffer pointed to by the embedded pointer. It then passes the buffer to the target callee. Like the proxy, the callee doesn't do anything special regarding memory management. Upon the return from the callee, the stub (3) frees the memory it's allocated after passing control back to the proxy, which then passes control back to the caller. The caller then (4) frees the memory that it has previously allocated.

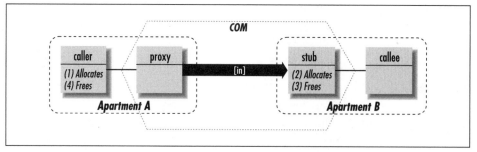

*Figure 5-3. A close-up view of Figure 5-2(A)*

Knowing the responsibility of each of the four participants, let's look at an example of an [in] parameter with an embedded pointer to reinforce the illustration in Figure 5-3. In the MIDL method signature shown below, notice that there's no top-level pointer in the *SetBinaryData* method, but there is an embedded pointer that's hidden inside the **BinaryData** structure, which we've seen earlier:

```
HRESULT SetBinaryData([in] struct BinaryData Data);
```

The object-side implementation of this method doesn't have to do anything special regarding memory management, as indicated by Figure 5-3 and the following code snippet:

```
STDMETHODIMP CoBlob::SetBinaryData(BinaryData data)
{
    if (data.m_pBuffer) {
        // data.m_pBuffer holds a binary buffer
        // data.m_lSize holds the size of the binary buffer
    }
    return S_OK;
}
```

On the client side, you may allocate the memory pointed to by the embedded pointer anyway you like (i.e., globally, on the stack, or on the heap) for all types of [in] pointers, including embedded ones. This example uses the *operator new* and *delete* to allocate and deallocate the embedded pointer. The size of this memory chunk is identified by **m_lSize**, which must be correctly set or else COM will not know the size of the memory chunk. Instead of using *new*, you may also use *CoTaskMemAlloc* to allocate this memory. If you use *CoTaskMemAlloc* to allocate this buffer, you must use *CoTaskMemFree* to free it.

```
BinaryData data;
char *pBuffer = "JackAndJill";
data.m_lSize = strlen(pBuffer);
```

```
data.m_pBuffer = new BYTE [data.m_lSize]; // allocate [in] embedded pointer
memcpy(data.m_pBuffer, pBuffer, data.m_lSize);
hr = p->SetBinaryData(data);   // call the target function
delete [] data.m_pBuffer ;     // deallocate [in] embedded pointer
```

Again, it is important to note that the client may allocate the embedded or secondary pointer in anyway it likes as long as the corresponding deallocation is done appropriately. The task memory allocators need not be used for [in] parameters. However, this isn't true for [out] embedded pointers.

Figure 5-4 shows a caller invoking a remote method with an [out] parameter containing an embedded pointer. Upon this invocation, the proxy will pass control to the stub, which invokes the target method. The callee, or the target method, uses *CoTaskMemAlloc* to (1) allocate a chunk large enough to hold the embedded data (the data pointed to by the embedded pointer), which is to be returned to the caller. The stub is responsible for (2) freeing this embedded data, using *CoTaskMemFree*, after sending the data back to the proxy. The proxy uses *CoTaskMemAlloc* to (3) allocate a chunk to hold the returned embedded data, which the caller must (4) deallocate using *CoTaskMemFree*. Since the proxy uses *CoTaskMemAlloc* to allocate the embedded data, you must use *CoTaskMemFree* to free the data on the caller end. Likewise, since the stub uses *CoTaskMemFree* to free the embedded data, you must use *CoTaskMemAlloc* to allocate the embedded data on the callee end.

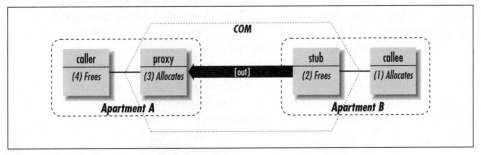

*Figure 5-4. A close-up view of Figure 5-2(B)*

Here's an example to reinforce Figure 5-4. The *GetBinaryData* method specification, shown below, has an [out] top-level pointer (of type BinaryData *). Recall that BinaryData contains an embedded pointer.

```
HRESULT GetBinaryData([out] struct BinaryData *pData);
```

The object-side implementation of this method may look as shown in the following code snippet. Notice that the callee must use *CoTaskMemAlloc* to allocate a chunk pointed to by the embedded pointer to hold the returned data. The callee must not use *operator new* to allocate this chunk. It must use *CoTaskMemAlloc* because the stub will use *CoTaskMemFree* after sending the data back to the proxy. The size of the data must also be set because m_pBuffer is a conformant array.

```
STDMETHODIMP CoBlob::GetBinaryData(BinaryData *pData)
{
    char *pBuffer = "HumptyDumpty";
    pData->m_lSize = strlen(pBuffer);
    // Callee allocates embedded pointer to return to client
    pData->m_pBuffer = static_cast<BYTE*>(CoTaskMemAlloc(pData->m_lSize));
    memcpy(pData->m_pBuffer, pBuffer, pData->m_lSize);
    return S_OK;
}
```

On the client side, the caller must use *CoTaskMemFree* to deallocate the embedded data as shown below. The caller must do this to prevent memory leakage, since the proxy allocates this buffer using *CoTaskMemAlloc* when it receives the data from the stub.

```
BinaryData data;
hr = pMem->GetBinaryData(&data);
// HERE: Caller can now use data.m_lSize and data.m_pBuffer
CoTaskMemFree(data.m_pBuffer); // deallocate embedded pointer
```

Thus, for [out] embedded or secondary pointers, you must use the COM task memory allocators.

For [in, out] parameters, as shown in Figure 5-5, a caller uses *CoTaskMemAlloc* to (1) allocate embedded data before invoking the method. The proxy sends the data to the stub and then possibly (2) frees the embedded data using *CoTaskMemFree*. The stub will (3) allocate a chunk to hold the embedded pointer, using *CoTaskMemAlloc*, before it invokes the target callee. The callee, if it needs to change the size of the data, can (4) free, and (5) reallocate the embedded data. It must use *CoTaskMemAlloc*, *CoTaskMemRealloc*, and *CoTaskMemFree* for all embedded pointer manipulation. After the callee returns control to the stub, the stub sends the data back to the proxy and then (6) frees the embedded data. The proxy uses *CoTaskMemAlloc* to (7) allocate the embedded data, which the caller is responsible for (8) freeing, using *CoTaskMemFree*.

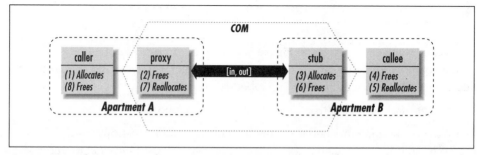

*Figure 5-5. A close-up view of Figure 5-2(C)*

Here's an example that demonstrates manipulating [in, out] parameters with embedded pointers. Assume the following method signature:

```
HRESULT ChangeBinaryData([in, out] struct BinaryData *pData);
```

The object-side implementation of this method can use the embedded data, free the embedded data, and then reallocate a new chunk of embedded data to be passed back to the caller. In the following code snippet, we first free the embedded data using *CoTaskMemFree* and then reallocate a new chunk for the embedded data using *CoTaskMemAlloc*. Recall that we must use *CoTaskMemAlloc* because the stub frees this chunk using *CoTaskMemFree*.

```
STDMETHODIMP CoBlob::ChangeBinaryData(BinaryData *pData)
{
    if (pData->m_pBuffer) {
      // HERE: Callee uses pData->m_lSize and pData->m_pBuffer anyway it likes
        CoTaskMemFree(pData->m_pBuffer);  // Delete old embedded pointer
    }
    char *pBuffer = "HumptyHasBeenChanged";
    pData->m_lSize = strlen(pBuffer);
    // Allocate new embedded pointer for return to caller
    pData->m_pBuffer = static_cast<BYTE*>(CoTaskMemAlloc(pData->m_lSize));
    memcpy(pData->m_pBuffer, pBuffer, pData->m_lSize);

    return S_OK;
}
```

On the client side, the caller must use *CoTaskMemAlloc* to allocate the chunk for the embedded data. After invoking the *ChangeBinaryData* method, the caller frees the embedded data using *CoTaskMemFree* because the proxy has allocated the embedded data using *CoTaskMemAlloc* when it receives the data chunk from the stub. In addition, the caller calls *CoTaskMemFree* to prevent memory leakage.

```
BinaryData data;
char *pBuffer = "Humpty";
data.m_lSize = strlen(pBuffer);
// Allocate embedded ptr
data.m_pBuffer = (BYTE*)CoTaskMemAlloc(data.m_lSize);
memcpy(data.m_pBuffer, pBuffer, data.m_lSize);
pMem->ChangeBinaryData(&data);
// HERE: data.m_lSize and data.m_pBuffer have been changed
CoTaskMemFree(data.m_pBuffer);  // Deallocate embedded pointer
```

As shown in these few earlier examples, [out] and [in, out] embedded (and secondary) pointers are the real reason why COM has to provide its own memory allocators. Thus, do not forget to use these allocators for [out] and [in, out] embedded and secondary pointers.

## Character Pointers

Strings are represented by a null-terminated character pointer and they follow the same memory management rules we've specified previously. Since they appear

often, we'll go over a simple example here. Recall that MIDL allows you to indicate a string parameter by using the [string] attribute. Recall also that you've
specified a method, *OcrImage*, in the *IOcr* interface in Chapter 3, but you haven't
implemented it. Here's the definition of this method, which takes a binary image
buffer, along with its size, and returns the corresponding OCR text. Notice that the
[string] attribute is used to indicate that **pwszOcrText** is a null-terminated character array. Therefore, you technically don't need to worry about its size, since the
size of this string is implied by its null terminator.

```
HRESULT OcrImage([in] long lImageSize,
                 [in, size_is(lImageSize)] byte * pbImage,
                 [out, string] wchar_t **pwszOcrText);
```

Given the above method signature, you can implement it as shown in the following code. This implementation simply returns a hard-coded string representing the
binary image buffer's corresponding OCR text. Notice that you use
*CoTaskMemAlloc* to allocate a chunk of bytes pointed to by the secondary pointer
(*pswzOcrText*) to hold the returned OCR text.

```
STDMETHODIMP CoOcrEngine::OcrImage(long lImageSize,
                                    byte *pbImage, wchar_t **pwszOcrText)
{
    // HERE: OCR the image buffer (pbImage)
    // Allocate memory pointed to by the secondary pointer
    // and return fake OCR data.
    wchar_t wszOcrText[MAX_PATH];
    wcscpy(wszOcrText, TEXT("This is fake OCR text"));
    long lAllocSize = (wcslen(wszOcrText)+1) * sizeof(wchar_t);
    *pwszOcrText = static_cast<wchar_t *>(CoTaskMemAlloc(lAllocSize));
    wcscpy(*pwszOcrText, wszOcrText);
    return S_OK ;
}
```

On the client side, allocate a chunk to hold the image buffer pointed to by the
top-level pointer (**pbImage**). Notice that since **pbImage** is a conformant array,
COM will know the size (**lImageSize**) of this array for correct data marshaling.
Besides, recall that for an all [in] pointers, you may allocate the chunk however
you like. The important thing to note is that you must use *CoTaskMemFree* to deallocate the secondary pointer (**pOut**), which is passed into the *OcrImage* method
with an extra level of indirection (&pOut).

```
// Allocate top-level [in] pointer on the heap
BYTE *pbImage = new BYTE[dwFileSize];
// Bring in an image from a file.
ReadFile(hFile, (void *)pbImage, dwFileSize, &dwRead, NULL);
// Allocate top-level [out] pointer on the stack
wchar_t *pOut=0;
hr = pOcr->OcrImage(dwFileSize, (byte*)pbImage, &pOut);
delete [] pbImage ;  // Free image data because you don't need it anymore
wprintf(TEXT("OCR Text returned: (%s)\n"), pOut);
CoTaskMemFree(pOut);
```

As you can see, strings follow the same memory management rules laid out previously in this section. Since strings are null-terminated, you must use the [string] attribute so that COM can figure out their sizes for marshaling.

## Automation Data Types

Recall that Automation is a COM-based technology that supports a wider spectrum of interoperability. Remember also that a COM object is Automation compatible when it implements the *IDispatch* interface and uses Automation compatible data types. Two important Automation data types must be discussed in terms of memory management, because they have their own memory allocation API functions. These are the BSTR and SAFEARRAY.

### Memory management for a BSTR

A BSTR, which stands for basic string, represents an Automation compatible string. It is a pointer to an array of null-terminated Unicode characters, and it's special in that the character buffer is prefixed with a character count. There are two simple API functions for manipulating a BSTR. Instead of *CoTaskMemAlloc*, we use the *SysAllocString* API function to allocate memory for a BSTR. Likewise, we use *SysFreeString* in order to free the memory allocated for a BSTR. The signatures of these API functions are as follows:

```
BSTR SysAllocString(const OLECHAR *); // Allocate a BSTR from a character
                                      //array
void SysFreeString(BSTR); // Free the BSTR
```

We will show an example of using a BSTR in a moment, but before we do that, let's briefly check out the memory management API functions for a SAFEARRAY.

### Memory management for a SAFEARRAY

You've seen that a custom interface allows you to define an array of anything using normal C-language syntax. Unlike a custom interface, a dispatch interface, which is always used for dynamic invocation (a.k.a. Automation), requires that you use a SAFEARRAY for an array of elements. In other words, the only way to use an array in a dispatch interface is by using a SAFEARRAY. As a corollary, a SAFEARRAY is useful for interpreted languages, such as Visual Basic, and scripting languages, such as VBScript.

A SAFEARRAY is used to represent a single or multiple dimensional array, and it can be made up of any one of the Automation data types; that is, any one type that belongs to the VARIANT's union can be store within the cells of the

SAFEARRAY. Shown below are the API functions that can be used to manage a SAFEARRAY:

```
// Create a single- or multi-dimensional array.
SAFEARRAY * SafeArrayCreate(VARTYPE vt, UINT cDims, SAFEARRAYBOUND *
    rgsabound);
// Create a single dimensional array.
SAFEARRAY * SafeArrayCreateVector(VARTYPE vt, LONG lLbound, ULONG cElements);
// Get the upperbound (size) of a given dimension of an array.
HRESULT SafeArrayGetUBound(SAFEARRAY * psa, UINT nDim, LONG * plUbound);
// Access/unaccess the data within the array.
HRESULT SafeArrayAccessData(SAFEARRAY * psa, void HUGEP** ppvData);
HRESULT SafeArrayUnaccessData(SAFEARRAY * psa);
// Clean up the data.
HRESULT SafeArrayDestroyData(SAFEARRAY * psa);
// Destroy the array.
HRESULT SafeArrayDestroy(SAFEARRAY * psa);
```

Here are the general steps for creating a SAFEARRAY:

1. Create a SAFEARRAY using one of the SAFEARRAY creation API functions, shown above.

2. Access the SAFEARRAY data using *SafeArrayAccessData* and store your data into the SAFEARRAY. This will increment the lock count on the array.

3. After storing your data, call *SafeArrayUnaccessData* to decrement the array's lock count.

4. Use the SAFEARRAY. For example, pass the SAFEARRAY to a server component.

5. When you no longer need the SAFEARRAY, you need to call *SafeArrayDestroy* to destroy it.

To obtain the data within a SAFEARRAY that is passed to you, simply follow steps 2 and 3.

Given the general steps, let's examine how we can use a SAFEARRAY, along with several other Automation compatible types. We'll work through an example that takes into consideration the use of a VARIANT, BSTR, and SAFEARRAY in one shot. To do this, we'll create another variation of the *OcrImage* method that we've been working with. In this variation, we'll pass the image data into the object as a VARIANT (not a byte *). To be more precise, this VARIANT holds a SAFEARRAY of bytes, representing the image that we'd like to OCR.* The output from calling this function is a BSTR (not a wchar_t *), which represents the textual representation of our image data. Here's the signature for this new method:

```
HRESULT OcrImage([in] VARIANT binaryImageArray, [out] BSTR *pOcrText);
```

---

* As discussed in Chapter 3, a VARIANT can hold any Automation compatible type. Since a SAFEARRAY is an Automation compatible type, it can be embedded within a VARIANT.

You'll need to write some code now to demonstrate the use of these Automation types. As seen in the following implementation, first check that binaryImageArray is indeed a SAFEARRAY of bytes. If this check fails, you would return with the generic error E_INVALIDARG. Otherwise, extract the actual SAFEARRAY from the VARIANT. Then, access the image data within the SAFEARRAY in the proper way by calling the *SafeArrayAccessData* API function. Once you've done using the data, you notify the Automation marshaler of this fact by calling the *SafeArrayUnaccessData* API function. Finally, you return the OCR text via *pOcrText, which is of type BSTR. Notice that you have to use the special *SysAllocString* API function to correctly communicate the size of this BSTR with the Automation marshaler.

```
HRESULT CoOcrEngine::OcrImage(VARIANT binaryImageArray, BSTR * pOcrText)
{
    // The VARIANT (value holder) must be a SAFEARRAY of BYTEs
    if (binaryImageArray.vt == (VT_ARRAY|VT_UI1)) {
        // Reference the array.
        SAFEARRAY *pArray = binaryImageArray.parray ;
        // Access the data.
        unsigned char *pRawData;
        HRESULT hr = SafeArrayAccessData(pArray, (void HUGEP**)&pRawData);
        // Get the data size.
        unsigned long arraySize = pArray->rgsabound[0].cElements ;
        // Do our stuff with the binary buffer; e.g., perform OCR ...
        // Release the data.
        SafeArrayUnaccessData(pArray);
        // Let the Automation marshaler know about the return value, by
        // calling SysAllocString.  The Automation marshaler will call
        // SysFreeString after marshaling the string back to the client.
        *pOcrText = SysAllocString(TEXT("This is fake OCR text"));
    } else {
        // Invalid argument
        return E_INVALIDARG ;
        }
    return S_OK;
}
```

So, in this method implementation alone, we have all three Automation types at work: a VARIANT, BSTR, and SAFEARRAY. Let's examine how a client will invoke this method. Notice that we use *SysFreeString* to free the returned BSTR to prevent memory leakage.

```
void CallOcrImage(IOcr *pIOcr, BYTE *pImage, ULONG len)
{
    // Create a one-dimensional SAFEARRAY of BYTEs (VT_UI)
    // The size of this array is len, which represents our image length.
    SAFEARRAY *psa = SafeArrayCreateVector(VT_UI1, 0, len);
    // Access the data pointer
    unsigned char *pc = NULL;
    SafeArrayAccessData(psa, reinterpret_cast<void HUGEP**>(&pc));
    // Copy our binary image data into array
    memcpy(pc, pImage, len);
```

```
      // Done accessing, so unaccess now.
      SafeArrayUnaccessData(psa);
      // Now we've got the array, we need to store it in
      // a VARIANT (the value holder).
      VARIANT vImage;          // So, let's create a variant
      VariantInit(&vImage); // Initialize the variant
      // Tell the value holder it's holding a SAFEARRAY of bytes
      binaryImageArray.vt = (VT_ARRAY|VT_UI1) ;
      binaryImageArray.parray = psa;   // Let the variant hold the array
      // Yes!  That much set up work before we can invoke a method!
      // Now for the method invocation...
      BSTR pOcrText ;  // Where the OCR text will be stored
      HRESULT hr = pIOcr->OcrImage(vImage, &pOcrText);
      if (SUCCEEDED(hr)) {
         m_strOCRResults = pOcrText ;
         SysFreeString(pOcrText) ;
      }
      SafeArrayDestroyData(psa);   // Destroy the data within the SAFEARRAY
      SafeArrayDestroy(psa);       // Destroy the SAFEARRAY
      // Clear the data
      VariantClear(&binaryImageArray);
   }
```

We just used the *SafeArrayCreateVector* API function to quickly create a one-dimensional array. If we wanted to create a multi-dimensional array, we'd need to use the standard *SafeArrayCreate* API function, which takes an array of SAFEARRAYBOUNDs. Each SAFEARARYBOUND represents the bounds of a given dimension within the multidimensional SAFEARRAY. A SAFEARRAYBOUND is defined as follows:

```
   typedef struct tagSAFEARRAYBOUND {
         unsigned long cElements;     // Size of array; i.e., how many elements?
         long lLbound;                // Lower bound, typically 0.
   } SAFEARRAYBOUND;
```

With this structure defined, we could simply substitute the following lines for *SafeArrayCreateVector* in the previous *CallOcrImage* function, and the functionality for *CallOcrImage* would be an exact equivalence:

```
   // Create the SAFEARRAY.  Notice we have only one SAFEARRAYBOUND,
   // meaning we're defining only one dimension.  Here is where you get to
   // specify the dimension of the array.
   SAFEARRAYBOUND sabound[1];  // The 1 means a one-dimensional array.
   sabound[0].cElements = len;
   sabound[0].lLbound = 0;
   // Create safearray of unsigned char.
   SAFEARRAY *psa = SafeArrayCreate(VT_UI1, 1, sabound);
```

If you think that this is too much work, no one would disagree with you. It is too much in C++, but a SAFEARRAY offers an environment like Visual Basic the simplicity its developers need, because all this dirty plumbing can be internally handled by the Visual Basic runtime.

# *Transparency*

When a client invokes a method on a remote object's interface, it doesn't know, and doesn't have to know, where the target object exists. Yet the method invocation will find its way to the target object. This is the idea of location transparency, and it is one of the beauties of COM. As you have seen, the marshaling provided automatically by RPC is usually sufficient to pass arguments from a client to a server component. COM needs a little help, however, in one situation: where you try to pass an *interface pointer as an argument* so that the same object can be used by both a client and a server.

When you pass data between two different execution contexts (e.g., two processes) in COM, it is said to go from one apartment to another. In this section, assume that a client and a server occupy separate apartments and you have to get the interface pointer between them.

COM marshals an interface pointer in one apartment (the exporting apartment) and unmarshals it in another (the importing apartment). If a client invokes an interface method implemented by a particular object to obtain an interface pointer, as indicated by the [out] attribute in the following method signature, COM, on the object side, will marshal the interface pointer into a chunk (series of bytes) using the *CoMarshalInterface* API function.

On the client side, COM will unmarshal the chunk into a valid interface pointer, using the *CoUnmarshalInterface* API function.

```
HRESULT TakeOcr([out] IOcr **ppOcr);
```

The same can also be done in reverse. If the client invokes an interface method and passes in an interface pointer, as indicated by the [in] attribute in the following method signature, COM will marshal the interface pointer on the client side and it will unmarshal the chunk on the object side.

```
HRESULT GiveOcr([in] IOcr *ppOcr);
```

The magic that makes this chunk valid in a remote apartment is specified in the DCOM wire protocol, which is documented in an Internet-draft called "Distributed Component Object Model Protocol (DCOM/1.0)," by Nat Brown and Charlie Kindel. This is the protocol that COM uses to uphold the remoting architecture, and it is called Object RPC. ORPC is purely based on DCE RPC, which uses NDR to transmit packages independent of system-specific formats such as byte ordering. One data type that ORPC adds on top of NDR is something called an object reference.[*] In this section, we will examine the object reference and its role in support of remote activation, remote invocation, and remote connection management.

---

[*] By the way, this is the only extension to NDR that DCOM makes. An object reference is transferred only in little endian format.

We'll will also examine the various types of marshaling that COM supports such as standard, custom, handler, and Automation marshaling.

## *Structure of a Marshaled Interface Reference*

When we deal with a single apartment, an interface pointer is just an address in memory that references something meaningful, but this address is meaningless in a remote apartment. To be valid in a different apartment, this pointer must be bolstered with additional information that uniquely identifies the pointer on all system everywhere in the universe and shipped across to the resulting apartment. This is where the DCOM wire protocol enters. It specifies an object reference (OBJREF), which makes an interface pointer meaningful in a remote apartment. An OBJREF uniquely represents a particular interface pointer in the intergalactic cyberspace. It is the OBJREF that allows COM to transparently handle all the grunt work of distributed computing.

As shown in Figure 5-6, an OBJREF has (1) a special signature that happens to correspond to the word MEOW in little endian byte order, (2) a flag indicating the type of object reference, (3) a physical IID identifying the interface to be marshaled, and (4) an object reference whose type is based upon the flag just mentioned. An OBJREF can at any time represent one of three different types: OBJREF_STANDARD for standard marshaling, OBJREF_CUSTOM for custom marshaling, or OBJREF_HANDLER for handler marshaling.

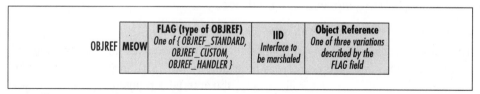

*Figure 5-6. Structure of an OBJREF*

A marshaled interface reference is simply a chunk that represents an OBJREF and can be sent over the network to a remote client. Once the remote client acquires this chunk, it can unmarshal it to get a local interface pointer. This interface pointer can be used to indirectly invoke methods in a remote object, since it contains all the information necessary to get back to the target object.

## *Activation*

COM seamlessly supports dynamic activation (loading/executing) of COM servers. No matter where the COM class exists in cyberspace, COM can find and activate its server (assuming the COM class is registered on both the client and server machine). Recall that there are several ways to cause dynamic activation of COM servers, such as *CoGetClassObject*, *CoCreateInstance*, *CoCreateInstanceEx*,

*CoGetInstanceFromFile*, and so forth. You can activate the server that implements the COM class identified by `CLSID_OcrEngine`, using the *CoCreateInstanceEx* API function, as shown in the following code. This API function also asks the class factory associated with the COM class to instantiate a COM object and return the *IOcr* interface pointer in one network round-trip.

```
MULTI_QI mqi[] ={ {&IID_IOcr, NULL, S_OK} };
HRESULT hr = CoCreateInstanceEx(CLSID_OcrEngine, NULL, CLSCTX_SERVER,
                                NULL, sizeof(mqi)/sizeof(mqi[0]), mqi);
```

In the earlier code snippet, we passed in `CLSCTX_SERVER` to say that COM may activate any server that implements the COM class whose CLSID equals `CLSID_OcrEngine`. Recall from Chapter 4, *Components*, that `CSLCTX_SERVER` is defined to encompass all server types, which means that we are not picky in terms of which server (in-process, out-of-process, or remote) should be activated. In your own systems, you should be picky about this, because it affects performance and security.* In addition, since we set no server destination in the fourth parameter, COM will look for a `RemoteServerName` entry in the registry under the server's associated `AppID` key. It will do this only if there isn't an in-process or local out-of-process server that implements such COM class. Given the earlier code snippet, let's briefly examine what happens when *CoCreateInstanceEx* is invoked.

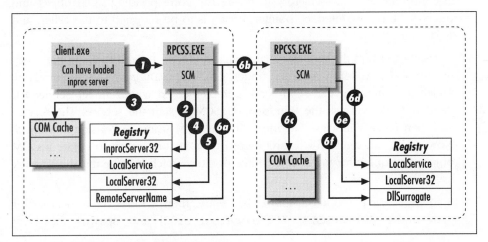

*Figure 5-7. The steps to dynamic activation*

---

* Using a remote object is extremely more expensive than an in-process object, because of security, marshaling, and inter-process communication overhead. However, using an in-process server may potentially be a security risk because an in-process server runs in the same security context as the client. Can we, as a client, trust an in-process server developed by someone else? Therefore, security is a big issue when we're using an in-process server.

Figure 5-7 illustrates the steps discussed in the following list. Notice that in all steps (except step 1), COM returns the requested interface pointer to the client if activation is successful, otherwise, the next step in the chain will be taken.

1. Client calls *CoCreateInstanceEx* causing COM* to delegate the activation request to its local SCM.

2. The local SCM looks into the local registry† under [HKCR\CLSID\*CLSID*\ InprocServer32] for an in-process server that implements this COM class. If it finds an in-process server, it returns the path to the in-process server to COM. COM then loads the in-process server, calling *DllGetClassObject* to get the *IClassFactory* interface pointer. It uses this pointer to create the COM object and queries for the *IOcr* interface pointer, which is to be returned to the caller. If the concurrency models of the client and object's apartments match, the client will get a direct pointer to the requested interface; and we're done. But if the concurrency models are different, the client will get a pointer to a proxy—a subject fully examined in the "Concurrency section.

3. If the SCM can't find an in-process server that implements the requested COM class, it looks into its cache to see whether the requested COM class's class factory has been registered by an already running local server.‡ If so, COM can ask the registered class factory to create the corresponding COM object and query for the *IOcr* interface pointer, which is to be returned to the caller; and we're done.

4. If it still can't find the requested class factory in its cache, it looks in the registry for a LocalService entry under [HKCR\AppID\*AppID*\LocalService], which indicates that the COM class is implemented within an NT service.§ If needed, COM will ask the Windows NT SCM to start the service. The service will then register its class factories with the SCM using *CoRegisterClassObject*. Now, COM can query for the requested class factory, ask it to create a COM object, and query for the *IOcr* interface pointer, which is to be marshaled back to the caller.

5. If the SCM can't find a LocalService entry, then it looks for a local server path under [HKCR\CLSID\*CLSID*\LocalServer32] and spawns the local

---

* In support of component categories, COM first calls *CoTreatAsClass* to get the resulting CLSID, but we ignore this fact for brevity. You can configure a particular COM class to be treated as another COM class.

† For brevity, I have simplified the activation process a lot here. For one thing, I'm not taking security into consideration. In addition, note that I just say local registry, when in fact COM looks for activation information in the following order in Windows 2000: 1) [HKCU\Classes], 2) [HKCR], and 3) active directory. The abbreviation [HKCU] indicates HKEY_CURRENT_USER and [HKCR] indicates HKEY_CLASSES_ROOT.

‡ If you wonder why do 2 before 3, the answer is that 3 will definitely return a pointer to an interface proxy whereas 2 may return a direct pointer, depending on the object's apartment model (a subject discussed in "Concurrency"). The alternative answer is that 2 is always before 3.

§ An NT service is simply a special executable that is similar to a Unix daemon in that it can be configured to execute by itself upon system startup. In addition, it can run in any specified security context.

server, which registers its supported class factories. Again, COM can query for the requested class factory, ask it to create a COM object, and query for the *IOcr* interface pointer, which is to be marshaled back to the caller.

6. If the SCM can't find a local server, it will look for the `RemoteServerName` entry under [`HKCR\AppID\`*AppID*`\RemoteServerName`]. It then contacts the remote SCM and asks the remote SCM to handle the activation request. The remote SCM will, following steps 3 through 5, try to spawn a remote process that supports the requested factory, create a COM object, and query for the *IOcr* interface pointer, which is to be marshaled back to COM on the client machine. If no local server on the remote machine supports such class factory, then the remote SCM checks for a `DllSurrogate` entry under [`HKCR\`AppID\*AppID*`\DllSurrogate`] and spawns the surrogate process, which hosts a particular in-process server that implements the requested class factory. If the `DllSurrogate` named value exists but is empty, then a system default surrogate process, called *dllhost.exe*, will be started.

As you can see from the above six steps, the responsibility of locating and activating COM servers lies in the hands of the local SCM and possibly a remote SCM. For steps 3 through 6, the *IOcr* interface pointer is marshaled from the exporting (target) apartment into the importing (client) apartment. You might have already guessed that this interface pointer is represented by an `OBJREF`, since you are crossing apartment boundaries.

To see how the `OBJREF` fits in, let's assume that the target COM class is implemented in a component on a remote machine. The COM library loaded into the client process works with the local SCM to activate the component that supports the class. Note that there's only one SCM per machine and it locates COM servers by looking up such information for the requested COM class from the registry. If remote activation is required, the local SCM contacts the remote SCM by calling the *RemoteActivation* method of an RPC interface called *IRemoteActivation*. This RPC interface is implemented by the SCM on each machine. Calling *RemoteActivation* essentially delegates the activation responsibility to the remote SCM.

Let's assume we have an out-of-process server on the remote machine that implements the target class, so that the remote SCM will activate or start this COM server. Upon start up, the COM server calls *CoInitializeEx* causing COM to create the first apartment in the process. This apartment registers its supported class factories with the remote SCM using *CoRegisterClassObject*. COM then uses the class factory to create an associated COM object (*CoOcrEngine* in our case), and queries for the *IOcr* interface that is to be sent back to the calling machine. It is here that COM makes the decision on which type of `OBJREF` to create, or to put differently, it determines what type of marshaling to use. To make this determination, it queries the target object for *IMarshal* and *IStdMarshalInfo.** If the object implements *IMarshal*, COM will use custom marshaling. If the object implements *IStdMarshalInfo*, COM will use handler marshaling. If the object implements neither of these interfaces, COM will use standard marshaling. We will examine these three types of marshaling next.

## Standard Marshaling

By default (when an object doesn't implement the *IMarshal* or *IStdMarshalInfo* interface), standard marshaling will be used. In standard marshaling, the type of OBJREF is OBJREF_STANDARD. OBJREF_STANDARD indicates that the OBJREF contains a standard object reference (STDOBJREF) and a buffer holding an OXID Resolver endpoint and security bindings. The STDOBJREF is the most important element in the COM standard marshaling architecture. As shown in Figure 5-8, it is made up of three important elements: OXID, OID, and IPID. These three things allow COM to accurately find a particular apartment, object, and interface throughout cyberspace.

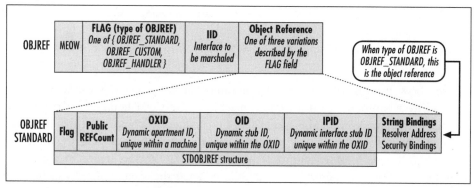

*Figure 5-8. Structure of a STDOBJREF*

*OXID*

COM dynamically assigns a 64-bit object exporter identifier (OXID) to an apartment that exports an interface (or marshals an interface for a remote client). The OXID is unique within a given machine and is managed by a special COM service called an OXID Resolver, which resolves OXIDs and returns their network connection information.

---

* If you wonder what COM queries from your object during the marshaling of an interface pointer, you should put printf statements in the *QueryInterface* method to observe this. When you do this, you will see that COM queries for the following interfaces from your object: (1) *IUnknown*, (2) *IMarshal*, (3) *IdentityUnmarshal*, (4) *IUnknown*, (5) *IStdMarshalInfo*, (6) *IExternalConnection*, and finally (7) the target requested interface. The *IdentityUnmarshal* interface is undocumented. The *IExternalConnection* allows an object to decide the death of a stub manager by explicitly calling *CoDisconnectObject*. An object that implements *IExternalConnection* will be notified when there are additions or deletions of external references.

*OID*

> COM dynamically assigns a 64-bit object identifier (OID) to a stub manager, which can be thought of as a fake client on the object side, when it's created. The OID is unique within a particular apartment and it's mainly used by COM for connection management.

*IPID*

> COM dynamically assigns a 128-bit apartment-unique interface pointer identifier (IPID) to an interface stub when it's created. An IPID represents a unique interface pointer throughout cyberspace.

The STDOBJREF structure also contains two less important fields. One is a flag that you can use to indicate whether pinging for connection management is needed on a particular OID. The other is the number of public reference counts that have been requested for the marshaling of this interface pointer (IPID). This reference count is used to reduce round-trips in case additional references to this IPID are needed. For example, at the time of this writing, the standard marshaler acquires five references to this IPID by default. This means that the client can call *AddRef* four additional times, and no round-trip to the server will take place (since these calls can be supported locally by the client side marshaling layer).

We've mentioned earlier that OBJREF_STANDARD includes end point and security bindings that are used by COM on the client side to get back to the apartment identified by the assigned OXID. The end point includes protocol sequences and network addresses to reach an OXID Resolver on the machine where the interface pointer was originally exported. The OXID Resolver is a special COM service that can resolve a given OXID and return the connection information associated with that apartment. The security binding information includes a principle name and the authentication/authorization services or packages used by this standard object reference.

Normally, all you need in support of distributed computing is COM's standard marshaling. You need to add no special code to your objects in order to take advantage of this mechanism. All you need is a proxy/stub DLL that implements the interface proxies and stubs for all custom interfaces implemented by your objects. This requires no additional work since the MIDL compiler generates the code for the proxy/stub DLL. The code for this DLL lives in a MIDL generated implementation file called *dlldata.c*. Actually, this file includes a bunch of magic macros that the C/C++ compiler can preprocess into code for an in-process server, specifically code that supports registration, activation, and deactivation entry points for a COM in-process server.

Using *regsvr32.exe*, you simply register this proxy/stub DLL on both the client and server machines. This is required since the interface stubs are dynamically loaded on the server side and interface proxies are dynamically loaded on the client side. The registration of this DLL will insert the correct configuration information into the registry under [HKCR\Interface\*IID*], where COM will look as it needs to dynamically load interface proxies or stubs.

A proxy/stub DLL is nice, since COM can dynamically load it when required. Alternatively, you may omit the registration of a proxy/stub DLL if you build your client or server with the generated proxy/stub code. When you do this, you will have to use the *CoRegisterPSClsid* API function in both the client and server code to dynamically register your custom interface. This feature reduces COM application setup and administration efforts (several variations of this technique are explained in Chapters 8 through 10).

In this section, we will reveal how and when these interface proxies and stubs are loaded by examining the architecture of standard marshaling. Let's now continue the discussion that we began in an earlier section, "Activation."

### More on activation

Since we are activating a server, this is the first time COM marshals an interface pointer of the target object on the server side; this object is shown as O on the right side of Figure 5-9. At this time, COM conceptually creates an associated stub manager, shown as S in Figure 5-9. When COM creates the associated stub manager for the target object, it passes along the object's (*CoOcrEngine's*) *IUnknown* pointer and assigns the stub manager an apartment-unique OID. The stub manager holds a pointer to the target object's *IUnknown* and thus keeps a reference to the target object for lifetime management. Since we asked for an *IOcr* interface pointer in the *CoCreateInstanceEx* call during activation, the stub manager queries its target object for the *IOcr* pointer. If the object supports this interface, COM dynamically loads the *IOcr* interface stub, which is shown as I in Figure 5-9, and assigns it an IPID. Recall that COM can find the in-process server that implements the corresponding interface proxy/stub by looking in the registry under [HKCR\Interface\*IID*\ProxyStubClsid32]. The *IOcr* interface stub (shown as I) holds on to the real or target *IOcr* interface (implemented by the object labeled as O) so that it can later invoke the real *IOcr* methods. The arrow from S to O illustrates this relationship.

When the first interface pointer is exported from the server apartment, COM creates (on the server side) the OXID object that supports the *IRemUnknown* interface, which is used internally by COM on the client side. Only one OXID object exists in each server apartment. This OXID object is marked XO in Figure 5-9. The *IRemUnknown* interface minimizes network round-trips associated with dynamic discovery and lifetime management of multiple interfaces on multiple objects. It supports *RemQueryInterface* to allow a proxy to query for multiple interface pointers on multiple objects in a single network round-trip. *RemUnknown* also supports *RemAddRef* and *RemRelease* to increment or decrement an arbitrary number of reference counts on multiple IPIDs in a single call.

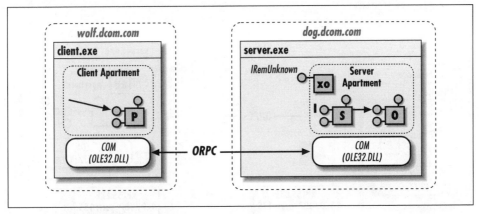

*Figure 5-9. The remoting infrastructure*

In addition, because this is the first time an interface is exported, COM also assigns the exporting apartment an OXID. This means that the box marked as Server Apartment in Figure 5-10 (which is a more detailed view of Figure 5-9) is identified by a unique OXID. COM registers this OXID with the remote machine's OXID Resolver. This is done so that the OXID Resolver on this machine can return network connection information for a given OXID upon request. As seen in Figure 5-10, there's only one OXID Resolver per machine and it communicates with other OXID Resolvers on other machines using the *IOXIDResolver* interface, which is a raw RPC interface. COM registers all apartments that export interfaces with their machine's OXID Resolver. Thus, the OXID Resolver knows the connection information for all registered OXIDs on its system and can resolve OXIDs into connection information upon request.

COM takes all this information (OXID, OID, IPID) and creates an OBJREF that can be represented in a serialized format called a marshaled interface reference. This marshaled interface reference, the IPID of the *IRemUnknown* interface, the OXID Resolver's address, and some other less important information are marshaled back to the client SCM.*

After successfully calling *IRemoteActivation::RemoteActivation*, the client SCM returns control to the client COM library. COM unmarshals the network packet and dynamically creates a proxy manager, which is marked as P in Figure 5-10, as a result of the activation request. COM unmarshals the associated OBJREF, and the proxy manager loads and aggregates the resulting interface proxy into the proxy manager.† Recall

---

* If you are interested, check out the specification of the *IRemoteActivation* interface in "Distribute Component Object Model Protocol–DCOM/1.0" for more details.

† COM creates interface stubs using *IPSFactoryBuffer::CreateStub* and creates interface proxies using *IPSFactoryBuffer::CreateProxy*. The *IPSFactoryBuffer* interface is a custom factory interface (i.e., not the standard *IClassFactory*) that all proxy/stub DLLs implement. Since *RemoteActivation* can deal with multiple interface requests in one single network round trip, many interface proxies can be loaded and aggregated.

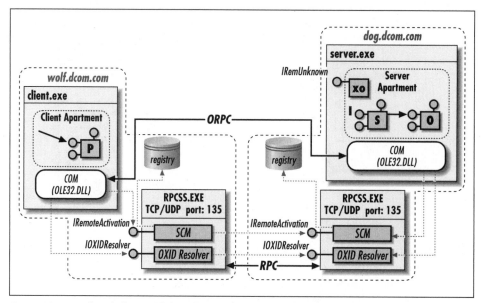

*Figure 5-10. A detailed view of the remoting infrastructure*

that aggregation allows an outer object (in this case, the proxy object) to expose interfaces implemented by inner objects (in this case, the interface proxies) as if these interfaces were its own. Aggregation is a simple technique that allows a collection of interface proxies to appear as a single proxy object—or more precisely, a single COM identity. Earlier in Figure 5-10, the interface proxy is being pointed to by the slanted arrow, which illustrates that some client code has a pointer to the interface proxy.

The interface proxy must now obtain the connection information so that it can talk to its interface stub in the future. To get this information, COM asks the local OXID Resolver, shown on the left side of Figure 5-10, to resolve the OXID by calling the *ResolveOxid* method of the *IOXIDResolver* interface, passing along the OXID and the protocol sequences it wants to use. At this point, the OXID Resolver looks into its cache to see whether such OXID exists. If not, the local OXID Resolver goes to the remote OXID Resolver, which is the one on the right in Figure 5-10, to obtain the connection information. As shown by the double-headed arrow marked as RPC in Figure 5-10, the local OXID Resolver communicates with the remote OXID Resolver using raw RPC—not ORPC. This means that if you want to write your own COM remoting infrastructure, you can do so by using raw RPC and the DCOM wire protocol.

If the remote apartment's process, shown as `server.exe` in Figure 5-10, has not loaded the requested protocol, the remote OXID Resolver tells the process to load the needed protocol. This allows COM to load protocols for a process only when needed. In any case, the connection information for the OXID is returned to the client OXID Resolver who caches and returns the connection information to the proxy manager. COM uses the connection information to establish an RPC connection (colloquially called an RPC channel) from the local interface proxy to the remote interface stub. This relationship is shown by the double-headed arrow marked as ORPC in Figure 5-10 (See Figure 5-11 for a more detailed illustration of this relationship). The proxy manager connects the interface proxy to its associated RPC channel. Once this is done, COM returns to the client the *IOcr* interface pointer, which points to the interface proxy.

Since we now have all the pieces that make up a marshaled interface reference, let's do a quick recap. The proxy manager creates and aggregates all its supported interface proxies so that it can fool its client into thinking that it's the real object. To the client, the proxy manager looks exactly like the real object with the exception that it implements a few extra interfaces, such as *IMultiQI* and *IClientSecurity*. The interface proxy connects to its associated channel object, which is a piece of code (implemented within the COM library) that manages the RPC connection for a particular interface proxy and knows how to get to the associated interface stub in the remote apartment. The interface stub knows how to invoke the target method, since it holds on to the real interface implemented by the target object. The stub manager, which virtually acts as a client on the server side, creates all its supported interface stubs that support the interconnections for associated remote interface proxies. Unlike the proxy manager, the stub manager doesn't aggregate all its associated interface stubs. Aggregation is not necessary since the stub manager doesn't have to be seen as a whole object by any normal client. The only client is COM who communicates privately and intimately* with the stub manager. Notice that interface stubs and proxies are themselves COM objects in order to allow COM to seamlessly load them.

As you can see, remote activation involves the creation of possibly a number of OBJREFs and the assistance of two special interfaces implemented by the SCM and OXID Resolver. These are the raw RPC interfaces known as *IRemoteActivation* and *IOXIDResolver*. Note that COM also sets up an environment that is specified by the DCOM wire protocol; in particular, we see that COM dynamically creates an OXID object for the exporting apartment and an OBJREF, which includes the OXID, OID, and IPID, for each interface that is to be exported out of an apartment.

### Remote invocation

Now that we've seen remote activation, remote invocation works pretty much the same way. If we zoom into the two apartments and the ORPC connection as shown in Figure 5-10 (in "More on activation"), we would have a picture that looks

---

* We say "intimately" because COM knows the inner-workings of the stub manager and the OXID object, which exposes the *IRemUnknown* interface needed for remote interface discoveries and lifetime management.

something like Figure 5-11, without the unshaded pieces. The shaded pieces are created during activation. The shaded pieces are the pieces that we'll now examine.

To get the unshaded pieces, we'll use the *IOcr* interface pointer to query for the *ISpell* interface from the remote object as follows:

```
pIOcr->QueryInterface(IID_ISpell, reinterpret_cast<void**>(&pSpell));
```

As the *IOcr* interface proxy receives this invocation, it delegates the query to its proxy manager's *IUnknown*, since it is being aggregated. The proxy manager will call *IRemUnknown::RemQueryInterface* implemented by the remote OXID object. It does this by marshaling the data and calling *IRpcChannelBuffer::SendReceive*, a method implemented by the RPC channel object, which provides the gateway to the OXID object. Note that COM can find the OXID object because its IPID is returned during remote activation. In addition, note that *RemQueryInterface* can query for multiple IPIDs in a remote apartment in a single network round-trip.

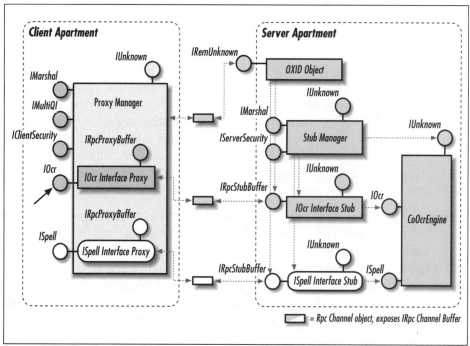

*Figure 5-11. Standard marshaling architecture created by the MIDL compiler*

Upon receiving the invocation, the OXID object will delegate the *QueryInterface* call to the *IOcr* interface stub by calling *IRpcStubBuffer::Invoke*, which is implemented by the interface stub. The interface stub invokes the target *QueryInterface* method on the real *IOcr* interface. After successfully calling the real *QueryInterface* method, COM knows that it must marshal the *ISpell* interface pointer back to the client because the second parameter of *QueryInterface* has an [out] attribute.

COM dynamically loads the *ISpell* interface stub, assigns it an IPID, and calls *IRpcStubBuffer::Connect* to connect it to the real *ISpell* interface for future method invocations. After this, COM creates an OBJREF and marshals it back to the client.

On the client side, the proxy manager unmarshals the OBJREF and loads the interface proxy for *ISpell*. The proxy manager also connects this interface proxy to its associated RPC channel. It does this by calling the *IRpcProxyBuffer::Connect* method implemented by the interface proxy, and passing along a pointer to the *IRpcChannelBuffer*, which points to an interface implemented by the RPC channel object.

The process of marshaling and unmarshaling is in general the same for all interface pointers. If the client happens to pass an interface pointer from the client apartment to a remote apartment, then the stub manager and corresponding interface stub will be created on the client side (the reverse of what we've seen earlier). The client apartment will then be the exporting apartment with a unique OXID. The remote apartment receiving the OBJREF will be the importing apartment. COM will create a proxy manager and associated interface proxy for the interface in the remote apartment. As object implementors, we don't do anything extra to take advantage of this standard marshaling architecture. COM does all the work to transmit the data between the client and the server for us—and this is the beauty of component-based distributed computing.

## Custom Marshaling

Standard marshaling does a lot for you. Unless you have a darn good reason otherwise, you should always use standard marshaling. One reason for excluding standard marshaling is that you want to totally replace the transport layer. Another reason is for caching an object that, once instantiated, never changes states. For this type of object, you'd just want to bring all its states back to the local apartment so that you don't have to make further network round-trips. This technique, which significantly reduces unnecessary network traffic, is colloquially called *marshal-by-value*. To implement these techniques, you would use custom marshaling.

Unlike standard marshaling, custom marshaling allows you to do anything you want in terms of marshaling. As seen in Figure 5-12, you simply implement the *IMarshal* interface on the object side (Server Apartment). On the client side, you provide a custom proxy that breaks you loose from COM's standard marshaling architecture. Within the custom proxy, you can do anything you want, but what you do internally is your business—contact a legacy OCR server using a proprietary network protocol for instance. This means that the custom proxy can be as simple as just caching data or can be much more complicated than ORPC itself.

Recall that when an interface is marshaled, COM asks the object that implements the marshaled interface whether it supports custom marshaling. COM does this by

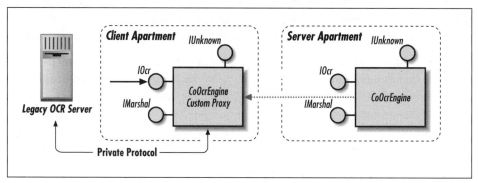

*Figure 5-12. An example of custom marshaling*

virtue of a simple *QueryInterface* for *IMarshal* from the target object. If the object affirmatively replies, COM will call methods of the *IMarshal* interface to get the required information for creating a custom object reference, shown in Figure 5-13. Notice that the custom object reference is much simpler than the standard object reference. In Figure 5-13, the plus sign (+) stands for the word "and" or "plus." The `CLSID` indicates the custom proxy to be created on the client side upon unmarshaling. The `Data` portion stores all the data that the object will send back to the client, and its size is indicated by `Size`. The object on the server side fills in all these fields for the custom object reference when it custom marshals an interface pointer.

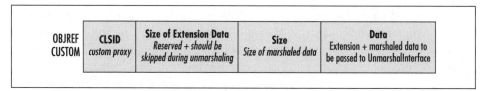

*Figure 5-13. Custom object reference is used in custom marshaling*

Again, to create the custom object reference shown in Figure 5-13, your object must implement the *IMarshal* interface. For easy reference, here's the specification of the *IMarshal* interface:

```
[local, object, uuid(00000003-0000-0000-C000-000000000046)]
interface IMarshal : IUnknown {
    // Implemented by object: returns a custom proxy CLSID
    HRESULT GetUnmarshalClass([in] REFIID riid, [in, unique] void *pv,
        [in] DWORD dwDestContext, [in, unique] void *pvDestContext,
        [in] DWORD mshlflags, [out] CLSID *pCid);
    // Implemented by object: returns size of private marshaling data
    HRESULT GetMarshalSizeMax([in] REFIID riid, [in, unique] void *pv,
        [in] DWORD dwDestContext, [in, unique] void *pvDestContext,
        [in] DWORD mshlflags, [out] DWORD *pSize);
    // Implemented by object: write private marshaling data
    HRESULT MarshalInterface([in, unique] IStream *pStm, [in] REFIID riid,
```

```
    [in, unique] void *pv, [in] DWORD dwDestContext,
    [in, unique] void *pvDestContext, [in] DWORD mshlflags);
// Implemented by custom proxy: read private marshaling data
HRESULT UnmarshalInterface([in, unique] IStream *pStm,
    [in] REFIID riid, [out] void **ppv);
// Implemented by custom proxy: free marshal data packet
HRESULT ReleaseMarshalData ([in, unique] IStream *pStm);
// Implemented by object: destroys the stub (called by CoDisconnectObject)
HRESULT DisconnectObject ([in] DWORD dwReserved);
}
```

On the object side, COM asks the object for the CLSID of the custom proxy, by calling *IMarshal::GetUnmarshalClass*. COM also expects the object to write its own marshaling data as a stream into this custom object reference in the object's *IMarshal::MarshalInterface* implementation. This data can be anything, such as private connection information, object states, or hints to the custom proxy for malleable client-side management. You specify the size of this data in the implementation of *IMarshal::GetMarshalSizeMax*. Once the custom object reference is created on the server side, it is marshaled back to the client.

On the client side, COM unmarshals the custom object reference, reads the CLSID, and creates a custom proxy. Like the object, a custom proxy must implement *IMarshal*, because COM assumes the custom proxy knows the private custom marshaling data passed back from the object. COM calls *IMarshal::UnmarshalInterface* to give the custom proxy the custom marshaling data, which could represent private connection information, for special custom proxy initialization. Once this is done, COM's remoting support is out of the picture, and the custom proxy is on its own.

Now that we know how custom marshaling works, let's see the responsibilities of the object and custom proxy in more detail.

### The object's responsibility

The object must implement at least three methods of the *IMarshal* interface in order to support custom marshaling: *GetUnmarshalClass*, *GetMarshalSizeMax*, and *MarshalInterface*. To demonstrate a simple implementation of custom marshaling, we'll add an implementation of *IMarshal* to the *CoOcrEngine* object. When an object reference is marshaled, the *CoOcrEngine* object will return a custom proxy CLSID and an IP address for the Legacy OCR Server. The custom proxy can then use the IP address to connect to the Legacy OCR Server. Let's examine how we do this.

In the implementation of *GetUnmarshalClass* we simply return the CLSID of the client-side custom proxy, as shown below:

```
STDMETHODIMP CoOcrEngine::GetUnmarshalClass(REFIID, void*,
    DWORD dwDestinationContext, void*, DWORD, CLSID* pCustomProxyCLSID)
{
```

```
    // The CLSID of custom proxy is globally defined
    *pCustomProxyCLSID = CLSID_OcrEngineCustomProxy;
    return S_OK;
}
```

The destination context (**dwDestinationContext**) specifies where or how far away will the interface pointer be unmarshaled, and it could be any one of the following values:

```
typedef enum tagMSHCTX {
    MSHCTX_LOCAL=0,                // A different process, with share memory access
    MSHCTX_NOSHAREDMEM=1,          // No share memory with the marshaling process
    MSHCTX_DIFFERENTMACHINE=2,     // Different machine
    MSHCTX_INPROC=3                // Different apartment in the same process
} MSHCTX;
```

If you were to implement custom marshaling only for a specific destination context, you may delegate the unsupported contexts to the standard marshaler. You can get a pointer to COM's standard marshaler by calling the COM *CoGetStandardMarshal* API function. For example, the following code is a rewritten version of the previous code to support custom marshaling only when the interface pointer is to be unmarshaled in a local server.

```
STDMETHODIMP CoOcrEngine::GetUnmarshalClass(REFIID riidToBeMarshaled,
    void* pIntToBeMarshaled, DWORD dwDestinationContext, void* pReserved,
    DWORD dwMarshalFlags, CLSID* pCustomProxyCLSID)
{
    HRESULT hr=S_OK;
    if (dwDestinationContext==MSHCTX_LOCAL) {
        // Support only local destination context
        *pCustomProxyCLSID = CLSID_OcrEngineCustomProxy;
    } else {
        // Delegate to the standard marshaler
        IMarshal *pMarshal=NULL;
        hr = CoGetStandardMarshal(riidToBeMarshaled,
            reinterpret_cast<IUnknown*>(pIntToBeMarshaled),
            dwDestinationContext, pReserved, dwMarshalFlags, &pMarshal);
        if (SUCCEEDED(hr)) {
            hr = pMarshal->GetUnmarshalClass(riidToBeMarshaled,
                pIntToBeMarshaled, dwDestinationContext, pReserved,
                dwMarshalFlags, pCustomProxyCLSID);
            pMarshal->Release();
        }
    }
    return S_OK;
}
```

In the earlier code snippet, note that the marshaler is an object that occupies space like any other and therefore must be released.

Besides *GetUnmarshalClass*, the object must also implement *GetMarshalSizeMax* to return the size of the private marshaling data, as shown below:

```
char g_szLegacyOcrServer[] = "monster.dcom.com";
```

```
STDMETHODIMP CoOcrEngine::GetMarshalSizeMax(REFIID, void*, DWORD, void*,
                                       DWORD, DWORD* pSize)
{
    *pSize = strlen(g_szLegacyOcrServer)+1;
    return S_OK;
}
```

In addition, the object must implement *MarshalInterface* to write the private mar-shaling data into the provided stream, which the custom proxy will use to possi-bly initialize itself:

```
STDMETHODIMP CoOcrEngine::MarshalInterface(IStream* pStream, REFIID, void*,
                                      DWORD, void*, DWORD)
{
    return pStream->Write(g_szLegacyOcrServer, strlen(g_szLegacyOcrServer)+1,
        0);
}
```

For a simple implementation of custom marshaling, this is all an object has to do.

### The custom proxy's responsibility

The custom proxy is dynamically loaded by COM upon receiving the custom object reference from the remote object. It must implement the *UnmarshalInterface* method of the *IMarshal* interface. COM will call *UnmarshalInterface* to pass the stream containing private marshaling data, which the custom proxy can use as hints or connection information provided by the object. In this regard, this data is the private communication handshake between the object and the custom proxy. This implies that the custom proxy must understand this message. After reading the marshaling data, this method should call the custom proxy's *QueryInterface* to return the requested interface to the client.

```
STDMETHODIMP CoOcrEngineCustomProxy::UnmarshalInterface(
    IStream* pStream, REFIID riid, void** ppv)
{
    pStream->Read((void *)m_szLegacyOcrServer, MAX_PATH, 0);
    // Maybe connect to the legacy server
    . . .
    return QueryInterface(riid, ppv);
}
```

Besides the *IMarshal* interface, the custom proxy should implement all interfaces that the original object supports. Remember that the client is not aware that it is dealing with a custom proxy. If fact, it thinks that the custom proxy is the real object. Even though the example shown here is very simple (and pretty useless), custom marshaling can be very complex. The complexity of writing custom prox-ies increases as you take into consideration mismatching concurrency models and issues relating to maintaining COM identity. In addition, you'd have to write your own custom proxy, which adds additional work. Therefore, unless you really have a good reason, don't use custom marshaling.

## *Handler Marshaling*

There are times when you want to take full advantage of standard marshaling, but cannot afford the performance impact of constant exchanging of network packets between a client and a remote server. Handler marshaling allows you to keep the standard marshaling architecture intact while allowing you to also take advantage of custom marshaling. In other words, whereas custom marshaling breaks you loose from the COM remoting infrastructure, handler marshaling allows you to reconnect back to the COM remoting infrastructure. This technique is used in some of the more bulky, GUI-oriented interfaces to cache large chunks of data locally, making network round-trips only when necessary.

The important point to note is that handler marshaling allows the custom proxy to do whatever it wants and still be able to selectively take advantage of standard marshaling. As shown in Figure 5-14, this is possible because the handler object, in the client apartment, sits between the *system identity object*, which is created internally and dynamically by COM, and the standard proxy manager. This implies that all client calls to *IOcr* and *ISpell* will be captured first by the handler object. The handler object can do whatever it wishes. When it needs to make a remote invocation, perhaps because its cached data is no longer valid, it delegates the call to the corresponding interface proxy aggregated by the proxy manager. And voilà, standard marshaling.

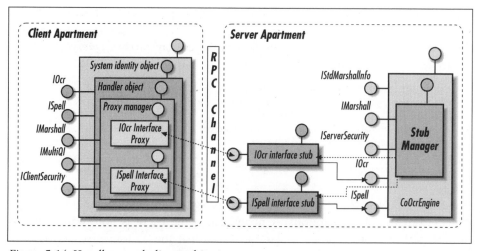

*Figure 5-14. Handler marshaling architecture*

Note that the client sees one single entity, the system identity object. The system identity object aggregates the handler object, which implements all the supported interfaces (i.e., *IOcr* and *ISpell*). The handler object in turn aggregates the proxy manager, which is standard marshaling's main client-side element that aggregates all interface proxies. You may say that this is aggregation abuse, but it allows a hook that makes it easy to keep the standard marshaling architecture intact.

As seen in Figure 5-14, in order to support handler marshaling, the object (in the Server Apartment) must implement *IStdMarshalInfo* and aggregate the standard stub manager upon object creation. To do this, the object's constructor calls the *CoGetStdMarshalEx* COM API function, passing along the `this` pointer into the first parameter, passing `SMEXF_SERVER` into the second parameter, and getting back a pointer to the standard stub manager. Here's *CoGetStdMarshalEx* for easy reference; be aware that this API function is supported only in Windows 2000 and above:

```
HRESULT CoGetStdMarshalEx(
    IUnknown * pUnkOuter,        // controlling unknown
    DWORD dwSMEXFlags,           // proxy (SMEXF_HANDLER) or stub (SMEXF_SERVER)
                                 // manager
    IUnknown ** ppUnkInner,      // returned pointer to aggregated marshaler
);
```

Recall that when an interface pointer is marshaled, COM will ask the object whether it supports handler marshaling by querying for the *IStdMarshalInfo* interface. If the object supports this interface, COM will call the *IStdMarshalInfo::GetClassForHandler* method to obtain the CLSID for the handler object to be created on the client side. As shown here, the *IStdMarshalInfo* interface has only one method:

```
[local, object, uuid(00000018-0000-0000-C000-000000000046)]
interface IStdMarshalInfo : IUnknown {
  HRESULT GetClassForHandler([in] DWORD dwDestContext,
          [unique][in] void *pvDestContext, [out] CLSID *pClsid);
}
```

When COM receives this CLSID, it will place it into the handler object reference (`OBJREF_HANDLER`) along with the information (i.e., `IPID`, `OID`, and `OXID`) that makes up a standard object reference. The resulting handler object reference is shown in Figure 5-15; this is the third type of object reference supported by ORPC.

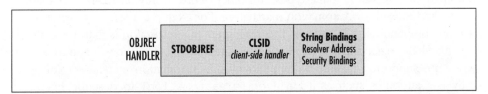

*Figure 5-15. Handler object reference*

On the client side, you must develop and provide a handler object similar to a custom proxy object previously studied in "Custom Marshaling". The handler must also be registered under [HKCR\ *CLSID*\ `InprocHandler32`], because that's where COM will look for the location of the in-process handler that it will load.

During unmarshaling of a handler object reference, COM will create a special system identity object on the client side and aggregate your handler into it. When COM creates your handler, it will pass along a special unknown pointer that represents the system identity object. In the factory's *CreateInstance* method exposed by your handler object, you need to call *CoGetStdMarshalEx*, passing along this special unknown pointer into the first parameter, passing SMEXF_HANDLER into the second parameter, and getting back the pointer to the aggregated proxy manager's unknown, which you must keep around for later method delegation. The end result is an object with a single identity that client code can use. Again, since your handler object sits between the system identity and proxy manager object, you may choose to handle method invocations for *IOcr* and *ISpell* anyway you like.

Let's close off this discussion with a few points. You can use custom marshaling to implement all that handler marshaling offers, but it requires grunt work to keep the standard marshaling architecture around. One other point to note is that handler marshaling is rarely used in real distributed systems, perhaps because you'd have to write the extra code to support the custom handler object. However, you may find handler marshaling to be useful once in a blue moon.

## *Automation Marshaling*

Automation is a technology that Microsoft developed to allow the maximum component interoperability. One benefit of Automation is dynamic method invocation, via *IDispatch*. Another benefit of Automation is the seamless support for 16- and 32-bit interoperability made possible by the support of the Automation marshaler, which is sometimes colloquially called the universal marshaler or type library marshaler. With Automation marshaling, you don't need MIDL generated interface marshalers (proxy/stub DLLs), but you need a type library in order to successfully use the Automation marshaler.

In order to take advantage of automation marshaling, your interface must use only Automation compatible data types. In other words, only VARIANT compatible types can be used for Automation marshaling. For example, a char * is not Automation compatible but a BSTR is. The reason for this restriction is that the Automation marshaler has built-in code that understands all the data types it supports. Any types not supported cannot be handled by the Automation marshaler. You typically use attributes such as [dual] or [oleautomation] to describe interfaces that are Automation compatible. Alternatively, you may also use the dispinterface keyword to signify an Automation compatible interface, as oppose to using the normal interface keyword.

If your interface meets the above requirements, all you need to do is register your type library using *RegisterTypeLib* and the correct registry entries will be inserted into the registry. For reference, here are typical registry entries that support Automation marshaling:

```
[HKCR\Interface\{D9F23D61-A647-11D1-ABCD-00207810D5FE}]
@="IOcr"
[HKCR\Interface\{D9F23D61-A647-11D1-ABCD-00207810D5FE}\ProxyStubClsid32]
@="{00020424-0000-0000-C000-000000000046}"
[HKCR\Interface\{D9F23D61-A647-11D1-ABCD-00207810D5FE}\TypeLib]
@="{36EFD0B1-B326-11d1-ABDE-00207810D5FE}"
```

The first two lines indicate the *IOcr* interface, and the second two lines say that the code to marshal the *IOcr* interface lives within the server that exposes the [00020424-0000-0000-C000-000000000046] CLSID. This CLSID happens to correspond to the Automation marshaler, which means that the *IOcr* interface is marshaled using the Automation marshaler. The last three lines say that the type information for the *IOcr* interface lives in the type library with the [36EFD0B1-B326-11d1-ABDE-00207810D5FE] type library identifier. Below are additional entries that show more of this information:

```
[HKCR\CLSID\{00020424-0000-0000-C000-000000000046}]
@="PSOAInterface"
// 32-bit Automation marshaler is oleaut32.dll
[HKCR\CLSID\{00020424-0000-0000-C000-000000000046}\InprocServer32]
@="oleaut32.dll"
[HKCR\CLSID\{00020424-0000-0000-C000-000000000046}\InprocServer]
@="ole2disp.dll"
// ocr.tlb is the type library that contains type information for IOcr
[HKCR\TypeLib\{36EFD0B1-B326-11d1-ABDE-00207810D5FE}\1.0\0\win32]
@="ocr.tlb"
```

If you look up the [00020424-0000-0000-C000-000000000046] CLSID, you will see that the 32-bit Automation marshaler is implemented in *oleaut32.dll* and the 16-bit version is implemented in *ole2disp.dll*. Again, the primary advantage of using automation marshaling is that 16- and 32-bit interoperability is supported by the Automation marshaler. If you look up the [36EFD0B1-B326-11d1-ABDE-00207810D5FE] type library identifier, you will find that the type library is named *ocr.tlb*.

Automation marshaling doesn't require that you register the proxy/stub DLL, but you do need to register the type library.

## *Remote Connection Management*

To leave the topic of transparency without discussing connection management doesn't do justice for DCOM. After all, DCOM goes to great length in supporting connection management. The basic idea of connection management is that, since there is no way for an object to know that its client has abnormally terminated, clients must ping the object. But simple, periodic pinging is too expensive for a distributed architecture, so DCOM introduces delta pings.

When a stub manager is created and assigned an OID, COM registers the OID with the machine's one and only OXID Resolver. Besides resolving bindings for OXIDs as we have learned earlier, an OXID Resolver on each machine coordinates with those on other machines to manage client connections to a particular OID. The OXID Resolver can group together pings for all OIDs of a particular machine into a ping set. To create a ping set, the local OXID Resolver calls *IOXIDResolver::ComplexPing* on the remote OXID Resolver, passing NULL for the ping set identifier (SETID) and an array of OIDs. The return of this call will pass back a SETID, which can be used to subsequently add or delete OIDs from the set. This means that COM pings only the changed OIDs, which is why this pinging mechanism is called *delta pinging*.

The OXID Resolver can delete OIDs from a set, because it will eventually notice that a process, which is a client of a particular OID, has died. The local OXID Resolver also uses this SETID to ping the remote OXID Resolver by calling *IOXIDResolver::SimplePing*. This single ping packet can represent thousands of ping messages targeting thousands of different OIDs. Recall (from Chapter 2) that if the server OXID Resolver has not received a ping for a particular object after three ping periods (2 minutes each), the OID will assume that the client has died and will take appropriate action to release held interfaces and reclaim resources. This process is referred to as distributed garbage collection.

## *Concurrency*

In most earlier discussions, we assume that the server process contains only one apartment and the client process contains only one apartment. However, a process can have many apartments in COM.

Apartments are a concept added by COM to older RPC and distributed computing technologies. While it may seem like just another headache at first—another layer of complexity for you to worry about—rest assured that apartments are actually there to simplify programming and make your life easier. Briefly put, having many apartments (each running a single thread*) relieves you of the need to make your COM objects thread-safe.

Since you have no control over who invokes a COM object (or when), the object normally has to be executed safely by multiple threads simultaneously. But you may not want to take the effort to make your object thread-safe, particularly if you're adopting legacy code. Instead, you can run this object in an apartment that is occupied by a single thread, and by doing so, you have just put the thread-safe problem to bed. However, you must do a few things to support multiple apartments, and that's what we'll discuss in this section. We will study two apartment models that COM provides: the single-threaded apartment (STA) and multithreaded

---

* You'll learn in a moment that this kind of apartment is called a single-threaded apartment (STA).

apartment (MTA) models. Each process can have many STAs, but at most one MTA (see Figure 5-16).

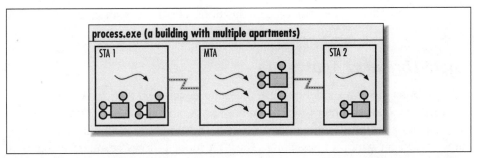

*Figure 5-16. A process can have an arbitrary number of STAs but it can have only one MTA*

Normally, COM assumes the responsibility of marshaling an interface pointer from one apartment to another. For example, when you pass an interface pointer as a parameter to a method implemented by a remote apartment, COM will automatically marshal the interface pointer for you. But if the remote apartment doesn't support such a method, how would you pass an interface pointer from one apartment to another? A pointer in a single process has valid meanings, but it is illegal to directly use a single, raw interface pointer in two apartments within a single process. Only the apartment that owns the interface pointer can directly use it. The key point to note is that when you want to access an interface pointer in another apartment, you'd have to *manually marshal the interface pointer to the target apartment*. You must marshal the pointer because it is crossing apartment boundaries. This is a basic rule imposed by the COM remoting architecture to support location transparency and to allow one apartment to be totally oblivious of another apartment's concurrency semantics.

COM takes advantage of its remoting architecture to support management of heterogeneous concurrency semantics imposed by different COM objects. COM allows each apartment to specify its own concurrency and reentrancy constraints. An apartment will receive all incoming method invocations for its contained COM objects. COM objects belonging to a particular apartment are assumed to support the concurrency and reentrancy constraints set forth by the apartment. These objects (including proxies) are created inside a particular apartment, lives, and eventually dies within it. In other words, a particular object (instance) belongs to one, and only one, apartment. These objects, along with their apartments, relate to the thread that executes them. A thread that uses COM must enter a particular apartment, execute inside that apartment, and exit the apartment when it has finished using COM. Furthermore, a particular thread can only execute in one apartment at a time.

We will learn how to manually pass an interface pointer from one apartment to another within in the same process. In addition, we'll examine important concurrency issues relating to out-of-process and in-process servers. We'll finally end with an examination of performance implications associated with concurrency and transparency.

## *Single-Threaded Apartment*

COM supports the STA model because there are developers that don't want to deal with the complexity of inter-thread communication and synchronization. There are also tons of older, thread-ignorant components and Windows programs that operate purely based on window messaging. The STA model allows seamless integration with components that have a user interface, and thus simplifies programming. Implementors don't have to provide the code to make their objects thread-safe, since COM provides the synchronization for method invocations using a standard window message queue.

For each STA, COM creates a hidden window, and on Win32, every thread that creates a window has an associated message queue. Since the Win32 operating system posts messages on the appropriate message queue and since the thread retrieves and handles the messages in order, messages are automatically serialized. So COM just submits its method invocations to the STA through the message queue. When a thread associated with the STA picks a message from the message queue and invokes an interface method within an object (through an interface stub), all subsequent method invocations* to that object's apartment will be queued. This is because only the thread associated with an STA can process the method invocation.

### *Basic requirements*

A single process can have any number of STAs, each of which contains one thread. The first STA created is called the *main STA*, and it is special when dealing with in-process servers. For a process that supports one and only one STA (the main STA), you don't have to provide any synchronization code to protect global, static, or instance data from concurrent access for the objects that are instantiated within this one STA. Besides this main STA, all other STAs are referred to simply as STAs. For these STAs, you will have do some work to support concurrent access but luckily not much at all. To take advantage of the simplicity of the STA model, you must consider the following basic requirements:

- A thread enters an STA by calling either *CoInitialize*, passing in NULL, or *CoInitializeEx*, passing NULL in the first parameter and COINIT_ APARTMENTTHREADED in the second parameter.

---

* Except for callbacks, as discussed in a moment.

- The STA thread must implement a message pump to get and dispatch messages (ORPC requests) to the window procedure of the thread's hidden window created by COM. A message pump is a term for the standard `GetMessage` and `DispatchMessage` calls that you find in every Windows program ever written. The thread that creates the hidden window has an associated message queue that is used to serialize incoming method invocations. The thread must provide a message pump or else no ORPC requests will ever be handled.

- A thread exits an apartment by calling *CoUninitialize*. After it does this, it can enter a different apartment if it wishes.

- Only one thread can ever execute within a particular STA.

The code snippet below creates the first and therefore the main STA. Notice that this first thread executes *CoInitializeEx*, passing in `COINIT_APARTMENTTHREADED`, to specify that it wants to enter into an STA. In order to support the STA model, this thread also provides a message pump that allows the thread to get and dispatch all window messages. These messages can represent ORPC requests that, once dispatched to the window procedure of the hidden window created by COM, will eventually invoke an interface stub method, which will in turn call the target method that's implemented by a particular object created within this STA. When this thread receives a `WM_QUIT` message, the message pump will end, and the thread can exit the apartment by calling *CoUninitialize*.

```
void main(int argc, char **argv)
{
    // This is the main STA, because it is the first thread that calls
    // the following function with COINIT_APARTMENTTHREADED
    CoInitializeEx(NULL, COINIT_APARTMENTTHREADED);
    // Spawn another thread, which then creates its own STA
    DWORD dwTid = 0;
    HANDLE m_hSTAThread = CreateThread(0, 0, STAThread, 0, 0, &dwTid);
    // Register factories here . . .
    // STAs must have a message pump that gets and dispatches messages
    MSG msg;
    while (GetMessage(&msg, NULL, 0, 0)) { DispatchMessage(&msg); }
    // Revoke factories here . . .
    CoUninitialize();
}
```

Recall that only one thread can enter and thus reside in an STA. If we have another thread that enters an STA, a brand new STA is created for it. This new STA has its own identity or OXID. Recall that an apartment is identified by an OXID as we've learn in the last section. Therefore, if the main STA spawns a thread and that thread requests to enter an STA, it will enter into a brand new STA as shown in the code below. Notice that we have all the requirements in place to take advantage of the STA model; in particular, we call *CoInitializeEx* to enter into an apartment and provide a message pump.

```
DWORD WINAPI STAThread(LPVOID)
{
    CoInitializeEx(NULL, COINIT_APARTMENTTHREADED);
    // Register factories here . . .
    MSG msg;
    while (GetMessage(&msg, NULL, 0, 0)) { DispatchMessage(&msg); }
    // Revoke factories here . . .
    CoUninitialize();
    return 0;
}
```

The above STA shows that it registers its factories with COM. Since factories are what make it possible to create COM objects, this apartment exposes COM objects and thus it is a server STA. In this case, you must provide a message pump for this thread because this STA will likely receive incoming method invocations. However, if you have a client STA thread that uses an object in a different apartment and never expect any incoming calls, you may omit the message pump.

### Synchronization

As previously mentioned, COM will serialize method invocations to objects within an STA. For example, let's say that you have an instance of *CoOcrEngine* and an instance of *CoDictionary* within the same STA. If several clients make a number of different method invocations targeting either of these objects, all these requests will be enqueued in the message queue. These requests will be serially delivered by the thread that is associated with the STA. Furthermore, each one of these requests will be handled by the single thread associated with the STA. This makes implementing the object much easier since the object instance will never, ever be accessed by more than one thread at a time. For this reason, you don't have to synchronize instance states (member variables). However, there is no concurrency (because there's only one thread).

Don't be discouraged because a process may have many STAs. To add some concurrency, each of the aforementioned instances can be created in its own STA. Each STA has an associated thread and its own message queue, so this time two requests may be processed concurrently. This means that all global or shared data must be protected using a system synchronization object such as a critical section or a mutex. Furthermore, if two STAs can host instances of a particular object, that object's static data must by protected, because the static data can be concurrently accessed by multiple threads. Therefore, to be sure that your objects can live within any STA (not just the main STA), you must protect shared and static data or resources from multiple, concurrent accesses. Protecting data against multi-threaded access is not specifically a COM requirement, but it is a requirement for building multithread software.

Here's a code snippet that protects shared and static data using a critical section:

```
CRITICAL_SECTION g_cs;    // Critical section object
long g_lShared=0;         // Global data

class CoOcrEngine : public IOcr {
public:
    CoOcrEngine() { InitializeCriticalSection(&g_cs); }
    ~CoOcrEngine() { DeleteCriticalSection(&g_cs); }

    void ModifyStaticAndSharedData();

    static long s_lStatic;    // Static data
    // Instance data need not be protected for STA compatibility
};

long CoOcrEngine::s_lStatic=0;   // Initialize static data

void CoOcrEngine::ModifyStaticAndSharedData()
{
    EnterCriticalSection(&g_cs);   // Lock
    // Static and shared being modified using protection
    g_lShared++;
    s_lStatic--;
    LeaveCriticalSection(&g_cs);   // Unlock
}
```

As you can see, you need to write a few lines of code to protect shared and static data to support the STA model. If you don't have any global or static data, your objects are automatically STA compatible and need no further refinements.

### Other issues

You must note that although COM prohibits concurrent executions on the same STA, it doesn't prevent reentrancy. COM supports reentrancy in STAs by processing certain window messages while the call is block-waiting for the return of a method invocation. For example, paint messages should be handled by a user interface thread even when waiting for a remote method invocation to return, so that the user interface appears responsive.

Another reason for the support of reentrancy is simply to prevent deadlocks. For example, if a thread in an STA makes an outgoing method invocation to another apartment, passing an interface pointer of its own for the second apartment to possibly make a callback (calls back into the STA), the outgoing call will be blocked. However, if the second apartment calls back into the STA using the interface pointer obtained, this call must be processed by the STA to prevent a deadlock.

From the RPC perspective, every COM method invocation contains an ORPCTHIS structure. This structure contains a *causality identifier*, which is an automatically generated GUID. If the causality identifier of an incoming method invocation matches that of the current outgoing method invocation, then the incoming method invocation is a callback. This callback must be processed to prevent a deadlock, but all other incoming method invocations will be queued up and handled normally.

You may provide code to hook into COM's internal messaging mechanism to selectively manage outgoing and incoming method invocations during the block-wait of an out-of-apartment method invocation. To do this, you must implement the *IMessageFilter* interface. Since only STAs provide message pumps, *IMessageFilter* is only valid for STAs. This interface has three methods that will be called by COM at the right moment to allow you to appropriately handle the each of these events:

*HandleIncomingCall*

> This function hook is automatically invoked by COM upon receiving a new ORPC request. Before actually invoking the target interface stub, COM allows you to selectively handle or reject the incoming request. If you reject the incoming request, the target method will never be invoked. This function is good for controlling incoming calls.

*RetryRejectedCall*

> This function hook is automatically invoked by COM upon detecting that an outgoing request has been rejected. This notification allows you to appropriately handle the problem such as by asking the user whether you should retry or cancel the outgoing method invocation. This function is good for managing outgoing calls that are rejected.

*MessagePending*

> This function hook is automatically invoked by COM to tell you that a window message has been received while your thread is making an outgoing call. This allows you to handle particular window messages as appropriate. This function is good for handling window messages during an outgoing method invocation.

After you've implemented this interface, you must register it with COM by calling the *CoRegisterMessageFilter* API function, as shown later. You typically do this right after your thread has entered an STA (i.e., right after calling *CoInitialize* or *CoInitializeEx* using `COINIT_APARTMENTTHREADED`). You'd pass a pointer to your message filter interface in the first parameter. The second parameter returns a pointer to the original (or previously installed) message filter, which you may use later in case you want to restore the original message filter.

```
HRESULT CoRegisterMessageFilter(IMessageFilter *lpMessageFilter,
                                IMessageFilter **lplpMessageFilter);
```

Reentrancy is automatically managed by COM unless you want to customize it yourself using a message filter, but you seldom have to deal with these issues in COM programming. What you must frequently deal with is sharing interface pointers between apartments within the same process, a topic that is discussed next. But before we move on to that topic, let's note a few things that we must be conscious of in regards to STAs.

The STA model allows you to easily develop multithreaded COM applications with minimum development efforts, since it seamlessly supports serialization via the message queue. In this regard, the STA model is simple and thus ideal, but this model doesn't scale extremely well. For example, if you have a large number of objects and dump them all into a single STA, then access to all these objects will be serialized through the message queue within the STA. Again, this means that only one method invocation can be handled at any single instance. On the other hand, if you create an STA to hold each object, you'd end up with a bunch of apartments, each of which contains a thread that executes all method invocations. Creating 1000 threads to support 1000 objects is not quite a feasible consideration. Apartments and threads do consume system resources.

## Sharing Interface Pointers Among Apartments

Within the same process, a global pointer may usually be used by any piece of code or any thread, but there is an exception in the case of an interface pointer. It cannot be used by two apartments within the same process. Only the apartment that owns the interface pointer can use the pointer (whether it be a direct pointer to the target object or a pointer to an interface proxy). If you want a different apartment to use that interface pointer, you must marshal it across. This is a golden rule of COM.

COM provides two API functions that allow marshaling and unmarshaling an interface pointer. To marshal a raw interface pointer, COM provides a simple API function called *CoMarshalInterThreadInterfaceInStream*, which is a shorthand for *CoMarshalInterface*. However, unlike *CoMarshalInterface*, which allows you to marshal an interface pointer from one process to another, *CoMarshalInterThreadInterfaceInStream* allows you only to marshal an interface pointer from one apartment to another apartment within the same process. The job of this API function is to simply create a marshaling packet and marshal the given interface. As you can see in the following code, this API function takes an IID, a pointer to the interface to be marshaled, and returns a pointer to an *IStream* interface that contains all the necessary information for the marshaling and unmarshaling:

```
HRESULT CoMarshalInterThreadInterfaceInStream(
    REFIID riid,      // IID of interface to be marshaled
    IUnknown *pUnk,   // Interface to be marshaled
    IStream **ppStm   // Resulting buffer ptr representing a marshaled interface
);
```

The returned *IStream* pointer can be legally used by any thread within the same process to unmarshal the interface pointer. To reverse what has been done by marshaling, you'd use the *CoGetInterfaceAndReleaseStream* API function, which internally calls *CoUnmarshalInterface*. The job of this API function is to unmarshal the interface pointer. This API function takes a pointer to an *IStream* containing the buffer that can be turned into a legal interface pointer within the target or importing apartment. It also takes an IID and returns to the caller the resulting interface pointer, which points to a local interface proxy.

```
HRESULT CoGetInterfaceAndReleaseStream(
   IStream *pStm,   // Pointer to the stream containing the interface reference
   REFIID riid,     // IID of interface to be unmarshaled
   LPVOID * ppv     // Resulting interface pointer unmarshaled
);
```

Given these two API functions, the following pseudo-code shows how they can be used to manually share an interface pointer between apartments within the same process. *STA1* marshals an interface pointer that *STA2* will unmarshal. The *IOcr* interface pointer cannot be passed in raw form from the thread in *STA1* to the thread in *STA2*. Only the *IStream* pointer holding the buffer for the marshaled interface reference can be accessed by multiple apartments. As indicated, g_pOcr is only valid within *STA1* and cannot be directly used by *STA2* or any other apartments, even though g_pOcr is visible to *STA2* from a C/C++ standpoint. *STA2* must unmarshal the stream (g_pStm) to get a pointer to an *IOcr* interface proxy before it can use the interface pointer.

```
IStream *g_pStm=NULL;
IOcr *g_pOcr;   // g_pOcr is valid only in STA1

int STA1()
{
   . . .
   CoMarshalInterThreadInterfaceInStream(IID_IOcr, g_pOcr, &g_pStm);
   //  Create STA2 to unmarshal this interface
   . . .
}

int STA2()
{
   . . .
   IOcr *pOcr=NULL;
   CoGetInterfaceAndReleaseStream(g_pStm, IID_IOcr, (void**) &pOcr);
   g_pStm=NULL;   // unmarshal only once
   . . .
}
```

One drawback with these two API functions is that you may unmarshal the interface pointer only once. If you need to unmarshal the interface pointer many times, you'd have to perform a few tricks in inter-thread communications or store these *IStream* pointers in many global variables, but these tricks can get to be really hairy. A better technique is to use the *global interface table* (GIT), which allows you to write the interface pointer once and read it many times. There is one such table per process and you may get a pointer to it by calling *CoCreateInstance* using the CLSID `CLSID_StdGlobalInterfaceTable`, as follows:

```
IGlobalInterfaceTable *g_pGIT=0;
CoCreateInstance(CLSID_StdGlobalInterfaceTable, NULL, CLSCTX_INPROC_SERVER,
                 IID_IGlobalInterfaceTable, (void **)&g_pGIT)
```

The *IGlobalInterfaceTable* interface contains three methods, which are very straightforward to use. As shown below, *RegisterInterfaceInGlobal* takes an interface pointer, along with the corresponding IID, and returns a cookie. This method is similar to *CoMarshalInterThreadInterfaceInStream* in that it marshals the interface pointer for use by another apartment within the same process. It is different from *CoMarshalInterThreadInterfaceInStream* in that the marshaled interface reference can be unmarshaled multiple times by multiple apartments. In this sense, you use *RegisterInterfaceInGlobal* to share a particular interface pointer with all apartments in the same process. The *RevokeInterfaceFromGlobal* method undoes what's been done by *RegisterInterfaceInGlobal* and removes the registration of the interface indicated by the given cookie. The *GetInterfaceFromGlobal* method returns an interface pointer, which points to a proxy, of course, that can be legally used by the calling apartment. You indicate which interface pointer you'd like to unmarshal by using the cookie and IID.

```
[local, object, uuid(00000146-0000-0000-C000-000000000046)]
interface IGlobalInterfaceTable : IUnknown {
    HRESULT RegisterInterfaceInGlobal(
        [in] IUnknown *pUnk,           // Interface to be registered and shared
        [in,iid_is(riid)] REFIID riid, // IID to be registered
        [out] DWORD *pdwCookie         // Resulting cookie for accessing
            interface
    );
    HRESULT RevokeInterfaceFromGlobal(DWORD dwCookie);
    HRESULT GetInterfaceFromGlobal(
        DWORD  dwCookie,   // Cookie
        REFIID riid,       // IID of registered interface
        void **ppv         // Resulting unmarshaled interface pointer
    );
}
```

Given the *IGlobalInterfaceTable* interface, sharing an interface pointer among many apartments is simple, as shown in the following pseudocode. *STA1* registers an interface pointer with the per-process GIT and gets back a corresponding cookie, which can be regarded as an apartment-neutral representation of an interface pointer. To actually use an interface pointer registered with the GIT, *STA2* must get it from the GIT using the apartment-neutral cookie.

```
DWORD g_dwCookie=0;
IGlobalInterfaceTable *g_pGIT; // Valid in all apartments
IOcr *g_pOcr; // Valid only in STA1

int STA1()
```

```
    {
        . . .
        CoCreateInstance(CLSID_StdGlobalInterfaceTable,
                        0, CLSCTX_INPROC_SERVER,
                        IID_IGlobalInterfaceTable,
                        (void**)&g_pGIT);
        g_pGIT->RegisterInterfaceInGlobal(IID_IOcr, g_pOcr, &g_dwCookie);
        // Create STA2 to unmarshal this interface
        . . .
    }

    int STA2()
    {
        . . .
        IOcr *pOcr=NULL;
        g_pGIT->GetInterfaceFromGlobal(g_dwCookie, IID_IOcr, (void**) &pOcr);
        // Other apartments can unmarshal this interface too
        . . .
    }
```

Even though not shown in the earlier pseudocode, you should note that by using the GIT, every thread within the same process can call *GetInterfaceFromGlobal* to unmarshal a registered interface pointer for its own use. Another thing that is not shown is that you can simply call *RevokeInterfaceFromGlobal* and pass in a cookie associated with the interface pointer to remove the interface pointer from the GIT.

Similar to the *IStream* pointer seen earlier, the interface pointer to the GIT (`g_pGIT`) can be used directly by multiple apartments without the need for marshaling and unmarshaling. This is not true for all other interface pointers, which must be marshaled from one apartment to another.

The global interface table is notorious for solving a complex problem dealing with objects that use the free-threaded marshaler, a subject examined in the "Free-Threaded Marshaler" subsection of this chapter. In particular, some objects that hold references to other interface pointers must keep an apartment-neutral interface pointer as member variables, meaning that these objects must keep cookies instead of keeping raw interface pointers as member variables. Because of these reasons, you should seriously consider the GIT over the *CoMarshalInterThreadInterfaceInStream/CoGetInterfaceAndReleaseStream* technique.

## Multithreaded Apartment

Unlike the STA model, the MTA model is geared toward high performance components without a user interface. These are server components that are very I/O intensive, such as database applications, or highly computational oriented, making them hungry for the last drop of component performance. From a COM perspective, the MTA model is very simple because it piggybacks from the thread pool mechanism implemented at the RPC layer. When an ORPC request arrives, the RPC runtime will pick one of the threads from the thread pool to service the request.

Since there is a pool of threads, ORPC requests can be serviced concurrently by the threads in the thread pool. Thus, the MTA model expects that all MTA compatible objects can be safely accessed by multiple threads simultaneously. This puts the burden on the object implementor, because not only must global and static data be protected, but instance data must also be protected as well.

### Basic requirements

A process can have at most one MTA, which allows many threads to enter and execute within it. Unlike the STA model in which only one thread can ever execute and deliver method invocations, many threads can enter the MTA and deliver incoming ORPC requests. As soon as an incoming invocation arrives, the RPC channel picks a thread from the RPC thread pool and hands the thread the marshaled interface reference, asking it to carry out the method invocation. The thread then enters the MTA and invokes the method on the interface stub, which calls the target method in the real object. In this sense, any thread from the RPC thread pool can enter the MTA and deliver a method invocation. After invoking the method, the thread returns to the pool waiting to be picked again. This means any thread entering the MTA can use any COM object that lives in the MTA. This is totally different from the STA model, where the one and only thread associated with the STA can deliver a method invocation. Here are the basic requirements of an MTA:

- A thread enters the only MTA in the process by calling *CoInitializeEx*, passing NULL in the first parameter and COINIT_MULTITHREADED in the second parameter.

- A thread exits an apartment by calling *CoUninitialize*.

- Many threads can execute concurrently within the one and only MTA in the process.

- No hidden window is created and no message pump is required.

- Message filters don't apply in the MTA, since the MTA model doesn't use window messaging.

Note that a process can have only one MTA but it can have any number of STAs. This means that a given process can have:

- No STA and no MTA, meaning that this process is not using COM.

- One STA, which is called the *main STA*. Recall that the first created STA in a process is the main STA of that given process. This process has only one thread using COM since only one thread can occupy an STA. From a programming perspective, this is the easiest situation to manage because there's only one thread of execution in the whole process.

- One or more STAs, with the first STA being the main STA. This process has multiple threads using COM and each thread is associated with one and only one apartment. In addition, each thread runs a message pump.

- One MTA, which may host any number of threads. This process has multiple threads using COM and all threads belong to the same MTA. The number of threads executing in this apartment can constantly fluctuate. This is good if you want to support concurrency. All threads within an MTA can use interface pointers directly without marshaling; this will improve performance.

- One MTA and one or more STAs. This is often referred to as the mixed model. This process has multiple threads: the MTA can host many threads, but each STA can host at most one thread. There are situations when a process contains both an MTA and STAs. For example, some objects are safe only within STAs, but not within an MTA, so if the process uses both MTA and STA objects, it will have both an MTA and one or possibly more STAs.

## Synchronization

Since method invocations to objects in an MTA are not synchronized by COM, the object must support concurrency. If you support the MTA model, you are essentially telling COM that all objects created within the MTA are totally thread-safe. Multiple threads can concurrently invoke methods on these objects, so all global, shared, and static data must be protected against concurrent access. Furthermore, all instance data and resources must be protected as well. This means that all class factory and object members must be synchronized using system primitives. For example, recall that we protected the reference count of our *CoOcrEngine* object from concurrent access in Chapter 3 as follows:

```
STDMETHODIMP_(ULONG) AddRef(void)
{
    return InterlockedIncrement(&m_lRefCount);
}

STDMETHODIMP_(ULONG) Release(void)
{
    long lCount = InterlockedDecrement(&m_lRefCount);
    if (lCount == 0) { delete this; }
    return lCount;
}
```

We noted that *InterlockedIncrement* and *InterlockedDecrement* are atomic operations provided by Win32, so only one thread may ever execute these operations at any given instance. Win32 also provides mutexes, semaphores, and critical sections for concurrency protection. It also provides events for inter-thread coordination and communications, but these topics are beyond the scope of this book.[*]

---

[*] O'Reilly publishes a book entitled "Win32 Multithreaded Programming."

### Other issues

Similar to STAs, reentrancy is supported in the MTA model. When a thread in an MTA makes a remote method invocation, it calls the proxy, which then calls the RPC channel. The thread will then be blocked inside the RPC channel until the method invocation returns. During this time, if an incoming ORPC request arrives, COM will pick a thread from the thread pool to handle the incoming request. This thread then enters the MTA and delivers the method invocation, whether it be a callback or a normal invocation. This means that objects that live in an MTA must support both concurrency and reentrancy.

Since incoming calls are handled by an arbitrary thread from the RPC thread pool, there is no correlation between objects and threads. In other words, each call to a given object can be handled by a different thread. This is different from the STA model in which objects have a strong attachment with the only thread that can ever execute their methods. Because there is no relationship between objects and threads in the MTA model, you must not save any kind of state in thread-local storage (TLS).

Even though the programming complexity increases because all resources and data must be protected, the MTA model offers two notable advantages. Generally speaking, the MTA model provides better performance, since objects in the MTA use protection measures to surround only small sections of code. This is untrue for the STA model, where the whole method invocation is synchronized. Protecting smaller sections of code is much more efficient than synchronizing the whole method invocation. Another advantage is that the threads that execute within an MTA can all access a raw interface pointer belonging to the MTA. As exhibited in the following pseudocode, both *MTAThread1* and *MTAThread2*, which live within the one and only MTA in the process, can access the interface pointer without marshaling because marshaling is never required within a single apartment. And since marshaling is expensive, this is an automatic performance gain if you use an MTA.

```
// g_pOcr is valid in the one and only MTA in the process
// and can be used by all threads within the MTA
IOcr *g_pOcr;

int MTAThread1()
{
    g_pOcr->OcrImage();  // Use pointer directly
}

int MTAThread2()
{
    g_pOcr->OcrImage();  // Use pointer directly
}
```

## Out-of-Process Server Considerations

Out-of-process servers can suffer from two notable race conditions. We've already talked about these race conditions dealing with activation and shutdown in Chapter 4, but let's briefly review them here since they relate to concurrency. Recall from Chapter 4 that during server startup, you would register your factories with the SCM using the *CoRegisterClassObject* API function. If you have multiple factories to register during server startup in a MTA, you must use the REGCLS_ SUSPENDED flag in those calls to *CoRegisterClassObject* to suspend the registration to the SCM. This is to prevent the factories from being immediately active. Once all factories have been registered, you would call *CoResumeClassObjects* to notify the SCM of all registered factories in one shot. An example of this follows. You saw this code in Chapter 4; it is abbreviated here for your convenience.

```
// Register COcrEngineFactory with COM, but don't make it active.
CoRegisterClassObject(CLSID_OcrEngine,
                      &g_OcrEngineFactory,
                      CLSCTX_SERVER,
                      REGCLS_MULTIPLEUSE | REGCLS_SUSPENDED,
                      &dwOcrCookie);
CoRegisterClassObject(CLSID_RoboCOM,
                      &g_RoboCOMFactory,
                      CLSCTX_SERVER,
                      REGCLS_MULTIPLEUSE | REGCLS_SUSPENDED,
                      &dwRoboCOMCookie);
// Let the all the factories loose.
CoResumeClassObjects();
```

If you don't use the REGCLS_SUSPENDED flag in an MTA, the first factory would be active immediately upon registration, so there is a slight chance that the server is signaled to shutdown before all factories are registered. This can happen immediately after the first call to *CoRegisterClassObject* when an object can be created and immediately destroyed, causing server shutdown. This race condition would not occur if all class factories are registered prior to allowing an object to be created. So just to be safe and to prevent this problem, you should use the REGCLS_ SUSPENDED flag when calling *CoRegisterClassObject* in an MTA.

There's also a possible race condition dealing with server shutdown, which was also discussed in Chapter 4. This race condition deals with the small window of opportunity for a new activation request to arrive while the server is about to die off. To prevent this potential race condition, which may likely cause an access violation, you should use the *CoAddRefServerProcess* and *CoReleaseServerProcess* API functions. These API functions allow you to increment and decrement the global per-process reference count, which is maintained internally by the COM library for all out-of-process servers. When this per-process reference count falls to zero, COM will suspend all registered class objects to prevent this shutdown race condition. Recall that we implemented the following helper functions in Chapter 4:

```
inline ULONG ComponentAddRef()
{
    return (CoAddRefServerProcess());
}

inline ULONG ComponentRelease()
{
    ULONG ul = CoReleaseServerProcess();
    if (ul==0) { SetEvent(g_hExitEvent);  }
    return ul ;
}
```

We mentioned that a COM object's constructor and LockServer(TRUE) should call *ComponentAddRef*. We also said that a COM object's destructor and LockServer(FALSE) should call *ComponentRelease*. Fulfilling these two requirements will save you unnecessary debugging time.

Before moving on, let's discuss one important issue regarding the *ComponentRelease* helper function. The *ComponentRelease* function shown previously supports component shutdown when the main thread is executing in an MTA. In the case that the main thread executes in an STA, there will be a message pump that waits for the WM_QUIT window message. In this case, *ComponentRelease* should post the WM_QUIT window message to the main thread to shut down the component. To do this, you will need to capture the main thread's thread ID and save it as a global variable. In order to capture the thread ID, use the *GetCurrentThreadID* API function, as demonstrated in the following code snippet:

```
DWORD g_dwMainThreadID = ::GetCurrentThreadID();
```

With this thread ID, the *ComponentRelease* helper function can shut down a component with the main thread executing in an STA as follows:

```
inline ULONG ComponentRelease()
{
    ULONG ul = CoReleaseServerProcess();
    if (ul==0) { ::PostThreadMessage(g_dwMainThreadID, WM_QUIT, 0, 0);  }
    return ul ;
}
```

As shown in the code snippet, instead of setting an exit event (as we have seen earlier), we post the WM_QUIT message to the thread that is identified by g_dwMainThreadID. We do this using the *PostThreadMessage* API function.

## In-Process Server Considerations

So far, you've only learned about the STA and MTA models for out-of-process servers. COM also supports in-process components that are loaded into the client process. Method invocations to objects within an in-process server are more efficient because the in-process server is loaded directly into the client process. This is true when the concurrency models of the client and the in-process server indeed match. If they don't match, performance will decline because COM will use the remoting infrastructure to arbitrate the differences. However, the client has to do to almost nothing special in using objects that have a different concurrency model.

When the concurrency models of the client and object fail to match, COM interposes to setup the necessary remoting environment for inter-apartment method invocations. For example, if a thread in the client apartment calls *CoCreateInstance* or *CoGetClassObject* to activate an object that has an incompatible concurrency model, COM will load the object into an apartment compatible to the object's concurrency model and marshal the requested pointer back to the client apartment to give the client a pointer to an interface proxy. This means that performance will degrade because of marshaling, but interoperation will be seamless. If the threading models match, then COM will instantiate the object inside the client apartment and give the client a direct pointer to the object, which means that method invocations will be extremely efficient, as no proxies and stubs are involved.

---

 For custom interfaces, you must provide and register a proxy/stub DLL, since it will be needed when the threading models of a client and its in-process objects are incompatible. Recall that you may alternatively compile and link the proxy/stub code into your in-process server to avoid registration. If you do this, you must internally register all supported interface marshalers. Chapters 8 through 10 provide several techniques for doing this.

---

Unlike out-of-process servers, in-process servers don't call *CoInitialize[Ex]* or *CoUninitialize* since these operations are already done by their loading process.* However, COM needs to know the concurrency model of objects within the in-process servers so that it can intervene when necessary. In-process objects tell COM their concurrency constraints by using registry entries. There are four different variations of concurrency, also called threading models, for in-process servers. Each COM class can specify the **ThreadingModel** that it supports by registering the appropriate named value under the associated CLSID entry. For example, the four variations can be specified using the following registry entries. If the class doesn't specify a **ThreadingModel**, it defaults to (empty).

```
[HKCR\CLSID\CLSID\InprocServer32]
@="c:\dcom\inproc.dll"
"ThreadingModel"=""
```

```
[HKCR\CLSID\CLSID\InprocServer32]
```

---

* Of course, if the DLL spawns a thread, the thread can enter whatever apartment it likes by calling *CoInitialize[Ex]*.

```
@="c:\dcom\inproc.dll"
"ThreadingModel"="Apartment"

[HKCR\CLSID\CLSID\InprocServer32]
@="c:\dcom\inproc.dll"
"ThreadingModel"="Free"

[HKCR\CLSID\CLSID\InprocServer32]
@="c:\dcom\inproc.dll"
"ThreadingModel"="Both"
```

Notice that `ThreadingModel` is associated with a CLSID, not with a DLL, which means that one DLL can have multiple objects that support a variety of `ThreadingModels`. Specifically, inside one DLL, there could be objects that are totally thread-ignorant, objects that support multithreading using the STA model, and objects that support real multithreading using the MTA model. Let's examine each of these variations in more detail.

### ThreadingModel="" (default)

For an in-process COM class (i.e., one that is implemented in a DLL) that has no configured `ThreadingModel`, the COM class and its instantiated objects can live and execute only in the client's main STA (MainSTA). It doesn't matter which client apartment activates this COM class, COM will place the instantiated object inside the client's MainSTA. This means that all calls to *DllGetClassObject*, *DllCanUnloadNow*, *IClassFactory* methods, and all other interface methods can only be directly invoked by the single thread that executes in the client's MainSTA. Since there's only one thread in the MainSTA, only that thread has a direct pointer to the activated object. Other than the MainSTA, all other apartments can gain access to the object only through proxies. This means that all method invocations to the object registered without a `ThreadingModel` will be marshaled between the calling apartment, be it another STA or the MTA, and the MainSTA, since only the MainSTA can directly invoke the target method. In other words, a method invocation will travel from the client apartment to the MainSTA to the target method of a particular object.

Table 5-1 shows the interaction between an in-process object with `ThreadingModel=""` and the client apartment that activates the object. The `Client Apt` column shows the client apartment that activates the object. The `Object Apt` column shows the resulting apartment in which the object will be instantiated. The `Access` column shows the resulting client access to the target object, whether it be a direct pointer or a pointer to an interface proxy.

As you read Table 5-1 through Table 5-4, keep two things in mind: (1) The content of the `Client Apt` column remains the same throughout; (2) The content of the `Object Apt` column changes depending upon the `ThreadingModel` of the COM class.

*Table 5-1. In-Process Objects with a Default (Null) ThreadingModel*

| Client Apt | Object Apt | Access | Performance | Remarks |
|---|---|---|---|---|
| MainSTA | MainSTA | Direct pointer | Good | There's one thread of execution in the client process. Direct access is very fast, but only one thread to handle all invocations. |
| STA | MainSTA | Through proxy | Moderate | Object will be created in the MainSTA, thus inefficient because of marshaling. Marshaling between the calling STA and the MainSTA. |
| MTA | MainSTA | Through proxy | Moderate | Object will be created in the MainSTA, which COM will create if necessary. Inefficient, because marshaling between calling MTA and the MainSTA. |

For in-process objects that don't support any `ThreadingModel`, COM assumes that the DLL, the class factory, and its associated objects are totally thread-ignorant. Therefore, object implementors need not protect any global, shared, or static states and resources. In addition, they don't need to protect instance states. This is possible, because all invocations will be made by the MainSTA thread, so there can be no multiple concurrent access to the object. Therefore, in-process objects that support no `ThreadingModel` are the easiest to implement, but since there's only one thread of execution doing all the work, you cannot take advantage of multithreading. Thus, this type of in-process object doesn't scale at all.

From a performance perspective, in-process objects that support no `ThreadingModel` are really only good for single-threaded clients with only one STA, like a single-threaded GUI application that uses COM. This is the only case in which the client will get a direct pointer, providing extremely efficient method invocations.* If the client application has an MTA or another STA, which activates the object, these apartments will acquire pointers to interface proxies, not direct

---

* A direct method invocation basically means a virtual function call, which means find the `vptr`, find the `vtbl`, and execute the target function. This is just a tiny bit more expensive than a normal function call.

interface pointers. Invoking a method that requires marshaling is many scores more expensive than invoking a method using a direct pointer.

### *ThreadingModel="Apartment"*

For an in-process COM class that has a configured `ThreadingModel= "Apartment"`, the COM class and its instantiated objects can live and execute in any client STA. Unlike in-process objects that support no `ThreadingModel`, this kind of object can be created in the MainSTA or any other STA in the client process. However, once the object is created, only the thread associated with the object's STA can actually access the object. All method invocations to this object are serialized by COM using a message queue. Table 5-2 shows the interaction between an in-process object with `ThreadingModel="Apartment"` and the client apartment that activates the object. Notice that if the client thread activating the target object lives in an MTA, the object will be instantiated in a COM created STA and the resulting interface pointer will be marshaled back to the client MTA.

*Table 5-2. In-Process Objects with ThreadingModel="Apartment"*

| Client Apt | Object Apt | Access | Performance | Remarks |
| --- | --- | --- | --- | --- |
| MainSTA | MainSTA | Direct pointer | Good | Typically, only one thread of execution in the client process. However, direct access is efficient. |
| STA | STA | Direct pointer | Good | Direct access is efficient. The resulting object will live in the client STA that activates the object. |
| MTA | STA | Through proxy | Moderate | Marshaling between the MTA and the MainSTA is inefficient. COM will create an STA to host the target object during object activation, and the created object will live in this newly created apartment. |

For `ThreadingModel="Apartment"`, COM assumes that the DLL is thread-safe but the object isn't. Since multiple STAs can potentially instantiate a particular object concurrently, you need to protect all global and static states against concurrent access. In addition, *DllGetClassObject* and *DllCanUnloadNow* must be thread-safe. If the DLL provides a singleton factory, the factory must itself be thread-safe, because it can be accessed by multiple threads associated with multiple STAs within the client process. This is not a big burden at all considering that you can take advantage of multithreading. Thus, your in-process objects should at least support the apartment threading model, so that clients with multiple STAs can take advantage of multithreading.

From a performance perspective, in-process objects that support `ThreadingModel="Apartment"` are great for multithreaded clients with multiple STAs. Here are two reasons why. First, multithreading is definitely an advantage in multiprocessor machines, because it allows true concurrent executions. Secondly, all STAs will obtain a direct pointer to the target object, since the object will be instantiated within the same STA. However, the client MTA will still obtain a pointer to an interface proxy because the target object must be instantiated within an STA.*

### *ThreadingModel="Free"*

For an in-process COM class that has a configured `ThreadingModel="Free"`, the COM class and its instantiated objects live and execute in the client's one and only MTA. COM will ensure that this kind of objects will be instantiated inside the MTA.† If any STA wants access to this kind of objects, it must go through a proxy. Table 5-3 shows the interaction between an in-process object with `ThreadingModel="Free"` and the client apartment that activates the object. Notice that only an MTA client gets a direct access to the interface pointer.

*Table 5-3. In-Process Objects with ThreadingModel="Free"*

| Client Apt | Object Apt | Access | Performance | Remarks |
|---|---|---|---|---|
| MainSTA | MTA | Through proxy | Moderate | Typically, only one thread of execution is in the client process. COM will create an MTA in the client process (if needed) and instantiate the object inside it. Marshaling occurs between the MainSTA and the MTA. This is inefficient; it does not take advantage of the thread-safe object at all. |
| STA | MTA | Through proxy | Moderate | COM will create an MTA in the client process (if needed) and instantiate the object inside it. Marshaling occurs between the client STA and the MTA. This is inefficient; it does not take advantage of the thread-safe object at all. |

---

\* Regarding performance, Microsoft Transaction Server, which supports multithreading using the STA model, works most efficient with in-process servers that implement objects that support `ThreadingModel="Apartment"`. Even though it works fine and seamlessly with in-process objects that support `ThreadingModel="Free"`, it will not be efficient since interface pointers must be marshaled.

† Since this kind of object is only safe in an MTA and never an STA, it must not aggregate with the free-threaded marshaler (FTM). The FTM will be discussed shortly.

*Table 5-3. In-Process Objects with ThreadingModel="Free" (continued)*

| Client Apt | Object Apt | Access | Performance | Remarks |
|---|---|---|---|---|
| MTA | MTA | Direct pointer | Good/ Excellent | Object will be instantiated into the client MTA, allowing direct access to the returned interface pointer by any thread within the MTA. This offers the best performance because you have both direct access and multiple threading support, taking full advantage of the thread-safe object. |

COM provides no synchronization at all for this kind of object as it assumes that the DLL and its implemented objects are all thread-safe. Since any thread within the MTA can concurrently use this object, all global, static, and instance states must be protected against concurrent access.

From a performance perspective, in-process objects that support `ThreadingModel="Free"` are good only for clients that have an MTA and have many worker threads spinning and constantly doing work. Recall that an MTA can support many threads, and these threads can share and pass interface pointers among themselves without marshaling. Thus, for an MTA client with many worker-bee threads, this kind of object provides excellent performance. However, if any STA activates the object, it will be instantiated into the MTA and the requested interface will be marshaled back to the STA. As a result, for clients with only STAs (e.g., user interface oriented clients), this kind of object will degrade performance since all accesses to the object is via a proxy.

### ThreadingModel="Both"

For an in-process COM class that has a configured `ThreadingModel="Both"`, the COM class and its instantiated objects may live and execute in any apartment (any STA or MTA). If an STA thread activates this object, the object will be created in that STA. If any thread in the MTA activates this object, the object will be created in the MTA. Neither of these threads has to go through a proxy. Table 5-4 shows the interaction between an in-process object with `ThreadingModel="Both"` and the client apartment that activates the object.

*Table 5-4. In-Process Objects with ThreadingModel="Both"*

| Client Apt | Object Apt | Access | Performance | Remarks |
|---|---|---|---|---|
| MainSTA | MainSTA | Direct pointer | Good | The object will be created in the MainSTA, thus allowing efficiency since the client apartment uses a direct pointer. |

*Table 5-4. In-Process Objects with ThreadingModel="Both" (continued)*

| Client Apt | Object Apt | Access | Performance | Remarks |
|---|---|---|---|---|
| STA | STA | Direct pointer | Good | The object will be created in the STA that causes the activation, thus allowing efficiency since the client apartment uses a direct pointer. |
| MTA | MTA | Direct pointer | Good/Excellent | The object will be created in the client's only MTA. Since all threads in this MTA gets a direct pointer access to the object and since the object supports multiple threading, efficiency is excellent. |

This kind of object, including its hosting DLL, must be totally thread-safe. Since the object's interface methods can be invoked by any thread concurrently, all global, static, and instance states must be protected against concurrent accesses.

There are two special requirements for an object that supports `ThreadingModel="Both"`. The first requirement deals with callbacks made from the object back into the client. The object can be safely called from any thread because it is thread-safe; however, it can make callbacks only using the thread that passes the callback interface pointer to it. This is a requirement because this kind of object can be created inside an STA or an MTA.

Let's say that the object is created inside an MTA. If a thread within the MTA passes a callback interface pointer to this object, the object can technically use any thread to make the callback, since an MTA can be entered by many threads. However, if the one and only thread inside an STA calls this object passing a callback interface pointer, the object can only use the thread associated with the STA to make the callback, since that's the only thread that can ever deliver method invocations inside an STA. For this reason, COM picks the lowest common denominator and requires that callbacks be made by the same thread that originally passes the callback interface pointer into the object. This is precisely the rule that allows this kind of object to be executed inside an STA.

The second special requirement is that interface pointers must always be marshaled between threads. Similar to the previous special requirement, this one also considers the lowest common denominator. Notice that this kind of object can live and execute inside an STA; however, you've learned that an STA has only one associated thread. If this STA thread wants to share an interface pointer with another thread, it must marshal the interface pointer since the second thread definitely belongs to a different apartment. Since this kind of object can be created inside an STA, COM requires that it always marshal interface pointers between threads. It is true that all threads in the MTA can share direct interface pointers without marshaling, but if this kind of object fails to marshal interface pointers between threads, it will not be able to support the STA model.

From a performance perspective, in-process objects that support `ThreadingModel="Both"` are great for any client. Threads in any apartment can directly use the object without interface pointer marshaling since the object can be instantiated directly in an STA or an MTA. In terms of performance, this kind of in-process object is the best that money can buy because its offers great performance regardless of the type of client apartment that activates the object. Performance is boosted even further if the object aggregates the free-threaded marshaler described in the next section.

### Free-Threaded Marshaler

Recall that if an object supports `ThreadingModel="Both"`, it must always marshal interface pointers between threads. Since marshaling is slow, COM provides the FTM that can be aggregated by objects with `ThreadingModel="Both"` and that can improve performance drastically. The FTM is a COM object that implements custom marshaling to marshal 32 bits, a `DWORD` representing a raw interface pointer, from one apartment to another within the same process. The importing apartment can unmarshal the `DWORD` and convert the 32 bits into a direct interface pointer, which it can use without the cost of any further marshaling. This is a direct pointer and it should pose no problems since this kind of object promises to be totally thread-safe. With the help of the FTM, interface pointers can be used directly by any thread, including all STA and MTA threads. You pay for the performance impact the first time the FTM custom marshals the 32 bits, but for subsequent method invocations on the interface pointer, you pay no further performance hit since you're using a raw interface pointer instead of a pointer to an interface proxy.

COM provides the *CoCreateFreeThreadedMarshaler* API function to allow objects that support `ThreadingModel="Both"` to aggregate the FTM.

```
HRESULT CoCreateFreeThreadedMarshaler(
  IUnknown *pOuter,        // Unknown of object supporting
                           // ThreadingModel="Both"
  IUnknown **ppMarshaler   // Returned unknown of the FTM
);
```

If the *CoThesaurus* object were to support `ThreadingModel="Both"` and wanted to provide efficiency to all types of client apartments, it would call this function in its constructor. Notice that it must keep the second argument, the inner unknown of the FTM, around for later release in the object's destructor, as shown in the following code snippet:

```
CoThesaurus::CoThesaurus() : m_lRefCount(0), m_pUnkAggregate(0)
{
  ComponentAddRef();
```

```
    // Aggregate the FTM
    CoCreateFreeThreadedMarshaler(this, &m_pUnkAggregate);
}
CoThesaurus::~CoThesaurus()
{
    if (m_pUnkAggregate) { m_pUnkAggregate->Release(); }
    ComponentRelease();
}
```

Within the *QueryInterface* method, the object simply delegates all requests to IID_ IMarshal into the aggregated object, as shown here:

```
STDMETHODIMP CoThesaurus::QueryInterface(REFIID riid, void** ppv)
{
    if (ppv==NULL) { return E_INVALIDARG; }
    if (riid==IID_IUnknown) {
        *ppv= static_cast<IThesaurus *>(this);
    } else if (riid==IID_IThesaurus) {
        *ppv= static_cast<IThesaurus *>(this);
    } else if (riid==IID_IMarshal) {
        return m_pUnkAggregate->QueryInterface(riid, ppv) ;
    } else {
        *ppv=NULL; return E_NOINTERFACE ;
    }
    reinterpret_cast<IUnknown *>(*ppv)->AddRef();
    return S_OK;
}
```

Even though it is trivial to aggregate the FTM, you must be very careful in implementing this kind of object if the object caches interface pointers as member variables. For example, if *CoThesaurus* supports ThreadingModel="Both" and aggregates the FTM, it can be instantiated in either a STA or an MTA. Let's say that it keeps an interface pointer to an *IOcr* interface whose object (*CoOcrEngine*) supports ThreadingModel="Apartment", as shown in Figure 5-17. Let's further assume that an instance of *CoThesaurus* is instantiated and executes inside STA1, as shown in Figure 5-17. This means that STA1 has a direct *IThesaurus* pointer to the *CoThesaurus* object and a direct interface pointer to the *IOcr* interface. If the object, which lives inside STA1 where it was instantiated, uses the cached *IOcr* interface pointer to invoke the *IOcr::OcrImage* method, it would work. In other words, everything inside STA1 in Figure 5-17 works. However, if STA1 passes the *IThesaurus* pointer to any another STA in the process, the second STA (which we have named STA2 in Figure 5-17) gets a direct pointer to *IThesaurus* since *CoThesaurus* aggregates the FTM. Now, let's say that the thread in STA2 calls an *IThesaurus* method that will in turn call *IOcr::OcrImage* using the cached *IOcr* interface pointer. We have a problem. The second STA is using an *IOcr* pointer directly, but this is illegal since the *CoOcrEngine* supports ThreadingModel="Apartment" and lives inside STA1. To obey the laws of COM, the *IOcr* pointer must be marshaled from the first STA (STA1) to the second STA (STA2). However, no one's doing the marshaling and hence the meltdown.

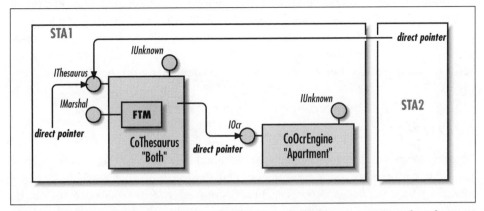

*Figure 5-17. Objects that aggregate the FTM should not hold direct pointers to other objects*

To solve this problem, instead of keeping a raw interface pointer to *IOcr* as a member variable, the *CoThesaurus* object must keep an apartment-neutral representation of the interface pointer. For example, you may keep an apartment-neutral stream pointer in place of the apartment-biased *IOcr* interface pointer. Every time you want to use the *IOcr* interface pointer, you simply unmarshal the stream. Calls such as *CoMarshalInterThreadInterfaceInStream* (et. al.) must be used to do the marshaling and unmarshaling of this stream pointer.

However, since the *CoMarshalInterThreadInterfaceInStream* (et. al.) technique allows you to unmarshal only once (and since it requires too many keystrokes), you should use the GIT. This means that instead of keeping a stream pointer, you keep the cookie that is associated with the registered *IOcr* interface pointer. See "Sharing Interface Pointers Among Apartments for more information regarding the GIT and *CoMarshalInterThreadInterfaceInStream*. In short, an object that aggregates the FTM must not hold direct pointers to other objects.* Always keep an apartment-neutral interface pointer representation such as a cookie or a stream pointer when aggregating the FTM.

## Performance

We've been saying that performance is moderate, good, or excellent, but we didn't have any data to back it up. Appendix B documents actual performance results illustrating that inter-apartment access is very expensive. It's essentially as expensive as inter-process access. The basic reason is that marshaling is obviously slow. Thus, if you don't want the headache of supporting `ThreadingModel="Both"` compatible objects in an in-process server, then you might as well put the objects in

---

* Actually, it would theoretically work if the objects, which are being pointed to by raw interface pointers, also aggregate the FTM. But if you didn't develop these particular objects, you'd be hallucinating if you bet that they aggregate the FTM.

an out-of-process server. Doing this, at least, allows fault tolerance. For example, if an object in an in-process server causes a crash, it will bring down the whole client application. On the other hand, if an object in an out-of-process server causes a crash, the client will most likely remain alive. So far, we have not considered security, which can further worsen performance depending on the degree of security used.

# Security

Security allows you to protect private or classified data from getting into the wrong hands. If you execute only components that live on the same machine, security might not be a big issue.* However, in a distributed system where objects can be potentially accessed by anyone in cyberspace, security is a must. COM provides a powerful security infrastructure that leverages RPC security. This security infrastructure uses the standard Security Support Provider Interface (SSPI), which is a specification that allows vendors to write their own private authentication packages called Security Service Providers (SSP) to which you were introduced earlier. Windows NT provides the NT Lan Manager (NTLM) authentication package, which is the only authentication protocol that COM supports in NT 4.0. Recall from Chapter 2, *Distributed COM Overview*, that NTLM utilizes challenge/response authentication and thus does not support delegation. Windows 2000 will support a more flexible and widely accepted authentication protocol called Kerberos, which supports both cloaking and delegation.

Whatever authentication package is used, security is seamlessly supported even for components that do not provide a single line of code to manage security. If this happens to be the case, the application silently accepts COM's default security, most of which is totally configurable by an administrator. For systems that must provide a high degree of protection from attackers, COM allows you to programmatically control security as needed by your applications. This brings us to the topics we'll discuss in this section: Configurable and Programmable Security.

## Configurable Security

As we have mentioned, you don't have to write a single line of code to take advantage of COM's powerful security infrastructure. This, like location transparency, is another goal of a distributed architecture—to liberate developers from writing customized communications and security protocols. After all, developers should be focusing on the functionality of their applications, not these—once you have done one, you've pretty much done them all—kinds of protocols.

---

* Note that using an in-process component—developed by someone you don't know—can be a potentially deadly security breach, because the component loaded into the process has full access to all resources as its host.

One tool that allows a programmer to view literally all aspects of COM, including configuring COM components and security, is the COM/OLE Object Viewer (*oleview.exe*). For administrators, Windows NT 4.0 provides the DCOM Configuration (*dcomcnfg.exe*) tool to allow easy configuration of COM security. The security options that can be configured include:

- Machine-wide security
- Application-wide security
- Application identity

Machine-wide security includes default security settings that will be used if an application neglects to specify them. Application-wide security includes launch and access settings, which, if not configured, will fallback to the machine-wide security settings. Application identity allows you to specify exactly which user account should be used for launching the COM server.

### *Machine-wide security*

Figure 5-18 shows the DCOM Configuration tool's `Default Properties` tab that allows an administrator to turn-on or turn-off Distributed COM for the whole machine and configure default authentication and impersonation properties. The `Enable Distributed COM on this computer` check-box allows an administrator to enable or disable Distributed COM for the entire machine. This check-box maps to the registry entry shown below. This means that, instead of configuring the `Enable Distributed COM on this computer` option using *dcomcnfg.exe*, you may directly manipulate it using the registry editor or through your own utility, assuming that you have administrator access. For this change to take effect, you must reboot the machine.

```
[HKEY_LOCAL_MACHINE\SOFTWARE\Microsoft\Ole]
"EnableDCOM"="Y"
```

Note that this registry entry doesn't apply to COM on the local machine, only distributed access and activation. Disabling Distributed COM for the machine prevents remote clients to activate components on the machine. However, be aware that users with access to the machine can still activate components on this machine. To prevent this, you must also disallow these users launch permissions, which can be found on the `Default Security` tab, to be discussed soon.

The last check-box, `Provide additional security for reference tracking`, allows an administrator to configure whether reference counts will be authenticated. Checking this prevents a vicious client from illegally ending the life of a particular COM object, as all *AddRef* and *Release* invocations will be authenticated. This check-box maps to the following registry entry.

```
[HKEY_LOCAL_MACHINE\SOFTWARE\Microsoft\Ole]
"LegacySecureReferences"="N"
```

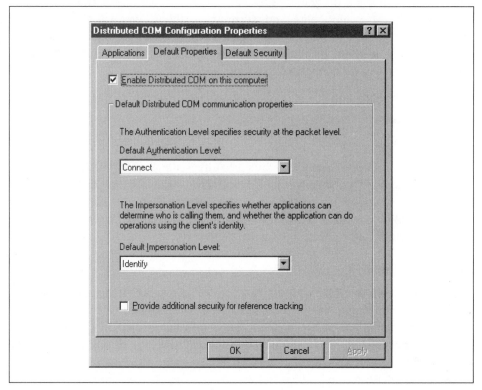

*Figure 5-18. Machine-wide security configuration*

The `Default Authentication Level`, shown in Figure 5-18, allows an administrator to configure the authentication level that is used by all COM applications on this system in the event that they don't provide their own authentication level, either through configuration or programming. When a remote client activates or communicates with such an application, it must have at least the authentication level configured in this list-box or else COM will deny the client access. On the other hand, when a local client—which has not specified its own authentication level by configuration or through programming—on this machine activates or communicates with a remote COM application on another machine, it will use the default authentication level configured here. If a local client ends up using this entry, it must be equal to or higher than the remote application's authentication level, or else access will be denied. This list-box maps to the following registry entry:

```
[HKEY_LOCAL_MACHINE\SOFTWARE\Microsoft\Ole]
    "LegacyAuthenticationLevel"=dword:00000002
```

Authentication levels are important in COM security because it allows gradations in the security that a client or a server is willing to negotiate. Authentication deals with two issues: validating that data comes from the expected client and validating the integrity of the data. COM supports a number of authentication levels, allowing users to appropriately configure the authentication level necessary for their components.

*None*

(RPC_C_AUTH_LEVEL_NONE) Indicates no authentication is used.

*Connect*

(RPC_C_AUTH_LEVEL_CONNECT) Indicates that the client will be authenticated upon initial connection only. The authentication protocol is entirely dependent upon the security package (authentication service) used. For example, NTLM uses the challenge/respond protocol discussed in Chapter 2. If authenticated, the client's identity will be cached on the server side and will be reused for subsequent method invocations. Be aware that subsequent calls will not be authenticated, which means that offenders can potentially do a significant amount of damage. If a connectionless transport protocol (i.e., UDP instead of TCP) is used, this level is the same as packet authentication level, discussed later.

*Default*

(RPC_C_AUTH_LEVEL_DEFAULT) Indicates that the default authentication level will be used for authentication. The default authentication level is dependent upon the security package installed on the system. For NTLM, it maps directly to the connect authentication level, discussed earlier.

*Call*

(RPC_C_AUTH_LEVEL_CALL) Indicates that every call will be authenticated, giving this authentication level a little more protection than the connect level. If a connectionless transport protocol is used, this is the same as packet authentication level, discussed later.

*Packet*

(RPC_C_AUTH_LEVEL_PKT) Indicates that every packet will be authenticated since a single call can be broken into many network packets. This authentication level gives more protection over the previous, because it ensures by encrypting the client's identity that all received data comes from the expected client.

*Integrity*

(RPC_C_AUTH_LEVEL_PKT_INTEGRITY) Indicates that every packet will be authenticated and validated to make sure that the data has not been modified during transmission. To do this, the security layer encrypts the client's identity and a checksum before transmission. This allows the security layer to validate the client and the data transferred, making sure it's from the expected client and has not been modified. However, the data is not encrypted at all and can be seen by potential attackers. Moreover, this is getting to be expensive because not only encryption but data validation is involved. Unless you really have to, don't configure this as a machine-wide default because of the performance hit.

*Privacy*

(RPC_C_AUTH_LEVEL_PKT_PRIVACY) indicates that it includes everything integrity does. It differs from integrity in that everything is encrypted, and it's the highest level of authentication in COM. It allows privacy but carries a significant performance impact. If you were to use this, use it judiciously; that is, use it selectively for a specific interface or a method call. We'll see how to do this programmatically soon.

Again, the default authentication level configured here is used only for an application that has not configured its own security. You may also dynamically increase or decrease the level of security potency within the program. As you can see, an authentication level allows a client and a server to set the authentication baseline that they can live by. The server says, "I support this authentication level and if you call me, then you must have an equal or higher authentication level." On the other hand, the client says, "I'm willing to use this authentication level and if you, server, can take it, then we're game." In this sense, the server is more assertive because it must protect itself from malicious clients.

Besides allowing a server to protect itself, COM also allows a client to protect itself from malicious servers. Clients can specify how much they trust servers using impersonation levels. An administrator can configure the default impersonation level that all clients on this machine will use, if they don't specify their own impersonation level through configuration or programming. This is done using the `Default Impersonation Level` drop-down list control, shown in Figure 5-18, and this configuration maps directly to the following registry entry:

```
[HKEY_LOCAL_MACHINE\SOFTWARE\Microsoft\Ole]
"LegacyImpersonationLevel"=dword:00000002
```

When a client grants an impersonation privilege to a server, it effectively says that the server can act for and in place of the client on the server machine. The client can specifically assert the degree of this privilege it allows the server to possess. This degree is expressed in impersonation levels as shown here:

*Anonymous*

(RPC_C_IMP_LEVEL_ANONYMOUS) Indicates that the client is anonymous and the server cannot obtain a client's identity and cannot impersonate the client. Be aware that this level is not currently supported in Windows NT 4.0 or Windows 2000.[*]

*Identify*

(`RPC_C_IMP_LEVEL_IDENTIFY`) Indicates that the server is allowed to impersonate the client for the sole purpose of obtain the client's identity. The server cannot impersonate (act in place of) the client in accessing local or remote resources. This is the default option and it allows the client to protect itself by saying, "I want to use your services so you may know who I am, but I don't really trust you enough to let you act as me." In other words, this impersonation level allows the server to identify the client, but not to act in place of it. True impersonation is discussed next.

*Impersonate*

(`RPC_C_IMP_LEVEL_IMPERSONATE`) Indicates that the server can impersonate the client to gain its identity and also to act in place of the client. When the client specifies this, it means that the client really trusts the server. That is, the server can do everything that a client can do. For example, when impersonating a client, the server can delete files owned by the client on the server machine. Impersonation is a powerful notion in the design and implementation of a software system. However, this impersonation level doesn't allow the server to access resources on any other machines on the network except the server machine itself. In other words, the server can act as the client but cannot tell another server down the chain to act as the client. Delegation supports this.

*Delegate*

(`RPC_C_IMP_LEVEL_DELEGATE`) Indicates that the server can fully impersonate the client and that the server can also access network resources accessible to the impersonated client. In addition, it can make a remote method invocation on an object that resides in a totally different machine. In other words, delegation goes further than impersonation: one server can pass the privilege to another server, and on to another, indefinitely. Delegation is supported only by Kerberos in Windows 2000. You should note that COM supports delegation on the local machine only using NTLM and it supports remote delegation only using Kerberos—kind of twitchy but that's how it is.

Once again, the `Default Impersonation Level` is used by all COM client applications on the machine that have not specified their own impersonation levels. Specifically, these impersonation levels can be configured on an application-by-application basis. For even finer control, they can be specified programmatically.

You should note that Windows NT 4.0 supports only the identify and impersonate impersonation levels. Only Windows 2000 supports delegation and a capability that

---

* If you want to support "anonymous" access, allow everyone to have launch and access permissions at the application level and also set the authentication level to `RPC_C_AUTH_LEVEL_NONE`. Read further to learn how to do this. See also the "Security Impact of the OBJREF" section in Chapter 10, *Connecting Objects.*

is called cloaking, which changes the rules for impersonation just a little. Since we can manipulate cloaking only in programming, we will deal with it in "Programmable Security."

So far, we have covered the `Default Properties`, but haven't discussed the `Default Security` tab. Under this tab, you'll find the following configurable items:

### Default Launch Permissions

This allows you to assign the users and groups that can launch COM applications, which have not specified their own launch permissions on this machine (You'll learn how to do this in the next subsection, "Application-wide security). The users and groups selected will be stored in an access control list (ACL) and COM will check for access as needed using this ACL. This ACL is stored in the registry in hex. Normally, a client calls an activation API function, such as *CoGetClassObject*, to cause the launch or activation of a particular COM application. The SCMs on the client and server cooperate to carry out activation requests. Before launching the requested application, the remote SCM must successfully verify that the client has launch permissions. Because launch permissions are checked by the server-side SCM, it can be configured only. It cannot be programmatically controlled, because the server is not active until it is launched by the SCM.

### Default Access Permissions

This item is like the previous one, but controls access permissions instead of launch. This default configuration value prevents all COM applications on the machine from unauthorized access, assuming that the applications don't override this assertion. Similar to launch permissions, access permissions are stored in an ACL. Launch permissions protect the machine in a sense, but default access permission protects the application and its objects. This allows finer control of security because after launching, the application is in control. Launch permissions is controlled by the SCM on each machine, but access permissions is controlled by the application.

### Default Configuration Permissions

This allows you to assign the users and groups that can install and administer DCOM applications. These permissions are also stored in an ACL.

The configuration for default access permissions and launch permissions are stored in hex under the following registry entries:

```
[HKEY_LOCAL_MACHINE\SOFTWARE\Microsoft\Ole]
"DefaultLaunchPermission"=hex:01. . .
"DefaultAccessPermission"=hex:AB. . .
```

Remember that all these configurations are machine-wide and will be used only if a particular application has neglected to specify them either through application-wide configuration of through programming.

### Application-wide security

Application-wide security can be easily configured using the DCOM Configuration tool. You simply pick the application you want to configure in the `Applications` tab shown earlier in Figure 5-18 and edit its properties. When you do this, you will see a different property sheet, as shown below in Figure 5-19.

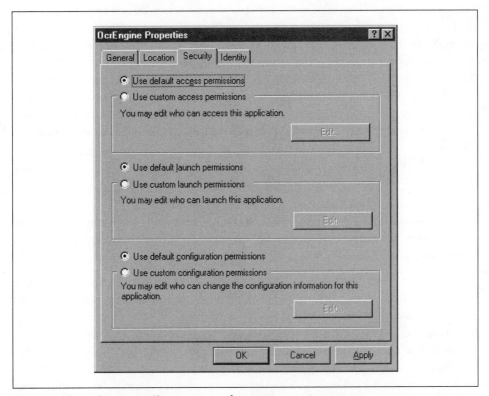

*Figure 5-19. Application-wide security configuration*

The `General` tab shows you the general properties currently configured for the application. The `Location` tab allows you to configure the location where COM will activate the application; you use this tab to configure the `RemoteServerName`, which can be an IP address, a DNS name, or a netbios name. Recall that this server name is not used if you programmatically specify the server name. The `Security` tab, shown in Figure 5-19, deals with application-wide security. We have already discussed the default access, launch, and configuration permissions at a machine-wide level, but COM allows you to get finer than that. You can specify custom access, launch, and configuration permissions for an application, thus overriding the machine-wide defaults.* The physical configuration values for custom access and launch permissions are stored in the registry under the following entries:

```
[HKEY_CLASSES_ROOT\AppID\AppID]
"AccessPermission"= hex:01. . .
"LaunchPermission"= hex:AB. . .
```

Application-wide security settings are configured under a specific application's AppID. Recall that an AppID groups together a number of COM classes that the application supports, which means that all COM classes that are mapped to a given AppID share the same application-wide security that's configured in the registry.

To quickly review, launch permissions specifies who can launch or activate a particular COM application, while access permissions determine who can access (for example, invoke methods in) an application after it is being launched. Both of these types of security protect the server, the application, and the objects within the application from unauthorized access. Launch permissions cannot be programmatically manipulated, but access permissions can be further programmatically refined. COM will look at these entries to determine whether launch or access is allowed. If these entries are missing, then it will use the machine-wide configured defaults.

### Application identity

There are four configurable variations of identity that can be used to execute the server application: the interactive user, the launching user, this user, and the system account. There are inherent implications with each of them and we'll briefly explore them below.

As you have seen, you can configure access and launch permissions at the machine-wide or application-wide scope. The SCM will launch applications for users with launch permissions. However, during the launch, should the SCM use the launching user's credentials (user identity and password) or should the application be run under a specific identity? You decide—as COM allows you to configure these options. These options can be configured using the `Identity` tab shown in Figure 5-19. Like launch permissions, identity cannot be programmatically controlled since the application doesn't exist until the SCM creates it.

*The interactive user* specifies that the associated server application will run under the identity of the user who is logged onto the server machine when the activation request is made. This means that application can access resources or do anything the currently logged-on user can. Furthermore, the application will run inside the

---

* Windows NT 4.0 Service Pack 4, allows you to configure authentication levels for a specific AppID.

logged-on user's window station.* Because this option requires a logged on user, no clients can use the target application if no one is interactively logged onto the server machine. For this reason, this option is used often for distributed applications that have an interactive graphical user interface. It is also nice for debugging purposes, but other than these reasons, it is not a viable option for real distributed servers. This configuration is saved under the associated AppID's **RunAs** named value in the registry.

```
[HKEY_CLASSES_ROOT\AppID\AppID]
"RunAs"="InteractiveUser"
```

*The launching user* specifies that the application will run under the identity of the user who activated or launched the application. Activating an application using the identity of the launching user means that a separate window station is created for the specific user. If you have many users using the same distributed application (and even worse, when you have many applications configured to run using the launching user), you can potentially have numerous window stations on the server machine. Since windows stations have a configurable limit and are a resource hog—and thus also a performance impact—running an application using the identity of the launching user will not scale well. One other thing to note that may be important in your design decisions is that the application, running under this identity, cannot make outgoing remote calls or use network resources under the launching identity. Finally, since this is the default, remember to manually change it when appropriate. A missing or empty **RunAs** named value under the associated AppID entry tells you that the default, the launching user, is used for activation.

*This user* specifies that the application will run under a specific and pre-configured user identity. When you choose this option, you must also type in the password, which will be kept in a private location in the registry and accessed only by NT's security subsystem. In addition, this user must have the **Log on as a batch job** advanced user right. To help you in case that you forget, *dcomcnfg.exe* grants this right to the configured user account. Since the application is launched using a single configured identity, only one window station is needed even if multiple instances of this application is launched. This can be an enormous advantage over the previously discussed options. However, the user account you choose must have access to any resources you expect the component to need. To further improve performance, the application should register class objects using the **REGCLS_MULTIPLEUSE** flag when appropriate, as this will allow multiple clients to

---

* Put in simple terms, a *window station* is a secure object that can be thought of as a virtual window environment since each window station has a desktop. You can have multiple window stations on a single NT machine at one time. There are two kinds of window stations: (1) The interactive window station is used by the logged-on user and is always visible; (2) all other window stations are call noninteractive because they are never visible. For the latter class, if a process pops up a dialog box, no one will be able to click on the OK button (if you want this message to appear in the interactive desktop so that the logged-on user can press the OK button, use *MessageBox* with the MB_SERVICE_NOTIFICATION flag). Window stations consume a significant amount of memory and thus only a finite number can be created.

use the same server, which further saves system resources. This configuration ("This user") is mapped to the following registry entry:

```
[HKEY_CLASSES_ROOT\AppID\AppID]
"RunAs"="dog\thuan"
```

*The System Account* specifies that the application will run under the identity of the system account. This option is used only by NT services and it is enabled only if the associated AppID contains a `LocalService` named value, as shown:

```
[HKEY_CLASSES_ROOT\AppID\AppID]
"LocalService"="OCRServer"
```

The COM SCM does not activate NT services but delegates this responsibility to the NT SCM. If you select `The System Account`, any pre-configured `RunAs` named value will be removed from the corresponding AppID registry key. If you select `This user`, COM will add a `RunAs` named valued under the associated AppID key. However, these identities are used by COM only to prevent malicious clients from launching the application. COM doesn't launch NT services! Since the NT SCM does this, you can actually configure the NT service to run under a totally different user account; Windows NT 4.0 allows you to do this using the `Services` applet found in the `Control Panel`. COM will never know about this configured information, and thus, it will never know exactly which user account is actually used to launch the service.

NT services are nice in that they can be configured to start by themselves during system startup and thus they can be active even without anyone logging on.

## *Programmable Security*

Certain COM security features, such as launch and identity, cannot be programmatically controlled. However, access and authentication can be dynamically fine-tuned by adding a small amount of security code to a program. For example, a COM server application can override preconfigured access permissions by specifically providing its own access permissions. Likewise, a COM client application can dynamically boost or lower the level of authentication to change the protection of specific method invocations. In addition, a COM client can say how much it trusts its COM servers. In this section, we'll discuss programmatic management of the following security features:

*   General application-wide security on both the client and server side
*   Access security on the server side
*   Activation security on the client side
*   Call-level security on the client side
*   Using the security context on the server side

Application-wide security is used by both the client and server and it applies to the whole process. To get finer security management, we'll discuss activation and call security from the client perspective, because these topics aren't applicable to a server (from the programming viewpoint). Specifically, activation (launch) permissions can be configured only on the server side. Call-level security will not be used by a server unless it is a client to some other server. We'll also discuss access security and using the client's security token from the server perspective, since the server must determine who can access its objects and when to impersonate a particular client to carry out method invocations.

### General application-wide security on both the client and server side

To manipulate security programmatically, COM applications, both servers and clients, call the *CoInitializeSecurity* API function upon application startup to set the default application-wide security. This application-wide security can override all preconfigured security information in the registry under the associated AppID key, depending on the arguments passed into the call. It is important to note that COM will call this function for all COM applications that provide no security code. COM will use the call to establish the default configuration on the host machine. Some features, like authentication and impersonation levels, set during this call apply to all proxies in the process by default but can be further dynamically managed and fine-tuned. *CoInitializeSecurity* is a complex API function because it takes into consideration many COM security aspects. Its signature is shown here:

```
HRESULT CoInitializeSecurity(
    PSECURITY_DESCRIPTOR pVoid,      // See "Access Security" below
    DWORD cAuthSvc,                  // How many SSPs
    SOLE_AUTHENTICATION_SERVICE * asAuthSvc,  // Array of SSPs
    void * pReserved1,               // Reserved; must be NULL
    DWORD dwAuthnLevel,              // Default auth. level for all proxies
    DWORD dwImpLevel,                // Default imp. level for all proxies
    RPC_AUTH_IDENTITY_HANDLE pAuthInfo,  // Reserved; must be NULL
    DWORD dwCapabilities,            // Additional capabilities
    void * pvReserved2               // Reserved; must be NULL
);
```

The second parameter (`cAuthSvc`) is the count of authentication services or packages, which are also called SSPs, to be registered during this call. An argument of `-1` should be passed in to tell COM to use the default authentication package. These packages are specified in an array referenced by the third parameter (`asAuthSvc`). COM will dynamically choose the authentication services, even if they are not specified in this call, to allow an interface proxy and stub to successfully communicate with one another. Recall that Windows NT 4.0 supports only NTLM SSP, but Windows 2000 supports both NTLM and Kerberos. And if you want to get fancy, this is where you can register your own private SSP, assuming that you have one.

The fifth parameter (`dwAuthnLevel`) allows you to set the default authentication level for the whole process. On the server side, this means that all incoming calls must have at least this authentication level. On the client side, all outgoing method invocations that are not further refined security-wise will use this authentication level. This basically means that all proxies get this default application-wide authentication level, unless the client changes this default prior to making a method invocation.

The sixth parameter (`dwImpLevel`) allows you to set the default impersonation level for all proxies in the whole process. This parameter is used only on the client side, because only a client should specify to what level it trusts a server. It shouldn't be astonishing that some servers set impersonation levels, because— remember—servers can be clients to other servers as well.

Authentication and impersonation levels are important during the call to *CoInitializeSecurity*, because all *AddRef* and *Release* calls will be made using the authentication and impersonation levels specified in this API function. Since *CoInitializeSecurity* is called only once for the whole process, you should be conscious of this fact in order to make good design decisions. Even if you refine these security levels for the *IUnknown* interface (you'll see how to do this in "Call-level security on the client side), only *QueryInterface* will assimilate the change, but *AddRef* and *Release* won't in Windows NT 4.0 Service Pack 3 and earlier versions.*

The eighth (`dwCapabilities`) parameter describes all the additional security capabilities supported by either the client or server. You can bitwise-or any value from the following enum to indicate the overall additional capabilities supported:

```
typedef enum tagEOLE_AUTHENTICATION_CAPABILITIES  {
    EOAC_NONE                     = 0x0,
    EOAC_MUTUAL_AUTH              = 0x1,
    EOAC_CLOAKING                 = 0x10,
    EOAC_SECURE_REFS              = 0x2,
    EOAC_ACCESS_CONTROL           = 0x4,
    EOAC_APPID                    = 0x8
} EOLE_AUTHENTICATION_CAPABILITIES
```

**EOAC_MUTUAL_AUTH** allows both the client and the server to know the identity of one another; that is, they can mutually authenticate one another. COM automatically determines mutual authentication in Windows 2000, since Kerberos supports mutual authentication. NTLM doesn't support this capability.

**EOAC_CLOAKING** indicates cloaking capabilities. If a client specifies this capability, then the client's security token will be cached by the local proxy and passed to the remote process. This capability allows a client to pass its security token to another process, and from that process to another process, and so forth, assuming that the

---

* In Windows NT 4.0 Service Pack 4, Windows 2000 and newer versions, *AddRef* and *Release* will assimilate this change.

server process impersonates the previous client and uses cloaking capability. In effect, you get a chain of processes that can all obtain a particular client security token through cloaking. The RPC_C_IMP_LEVEL_IMPERSONATE level along with cloaking capability will produce this chaining effect.

Every process in a chain that impersonates a client who specifies cloaking capability will get the security token of the original client. However, this chaining works for only one machine hop. To get this chaining to work over multiple machine hops, you need to combine the cloaking capability with the delegation (RPC_C_IMP_LEVEL_DELEGATE) impersonation level. This means that a client security token can be passed from one process to another process on another machine, and then to another process on yet another machine, and so on. This is a really powerful capability that is supported only in Windows 2000 locally using NTLM and remotely using Kerberos.

EOAC_SECURE_REFS specifies that all reference counts will be authenticated to prevent illegal server shutdown. Recall that this can also be configured using *dcomcnfg.exe*. We will discuss EOAC_ACCESS_CONTROL and EOAC_APPID in the next section. The last three capabilities (EOAC_SECURE_REFS, EOAC_ACCESS_CONTROL, and EOAC_APPID) in the enum shown above can only be manipulated through the call to *CoInitializeSecurity*. This means that you can set these capabilities only once and they last for the life of the process.

Knowing all these parameters (with the exception of the first parameter, which will be discussed in the next topic), here's how a typical server would call *CoInitializeSecurity*. Notice that this call passes –1 into the second parameter, telling COM to use the default SSP. In addition, the server will accept authentication levels that are equal or higher than RPC_C_AUTH_LEVEL_CONNECT. Furthermore, if the server makes an outgoing call, it will allow other servers to impersonate it. Lastly, because the next-to-last argument is EOAC_NONE, it specifies no additional capability.

```
CoInitializeSecurity (NULL, -1, NULL, NULL, RPC_C_AUTH_LEVEL_CONNECT,
                RPC_C_IMP_LEVEL_IMPERSONATE, NULL, EOAC_NONE, NULL);
```

*CoInitializeSecurity* should be called immediately following the call to *CoInitialize* or *CoInitializeEx*. If you don't follow this advice strictly, then make sure you call *CoInitializeSecurity* before any interface pointer is exported from or imported into your apartment. In other words, you must call this API function before the creation of any proxies or stubs.

### Access security on the server side

Although launch security cannot be controlled programmatically, access security can be. It is important to note that access security applies only on the server side. Recall that access security allows a server to prevent unauthorized access after the server has been launched. If the access permissions information configured in the registry under the corresponding `AppID` key is inappropriate for the systems that you build, you may add customized access control mechanisms into your server code. The advantage of this technique is that it gives you full control in determining access to your server application, which means that you can store access permissions in a flat file and then dynamically load the information each time upon application start up, making this approach portable across platforms. However, this is also a disadvantage because an administrator cannot configure access permissions for this kind of server using *dcomcnfg.exe.*

You need to learn a little about Windows NT to understand access controls. In general, Windows NT security supports secure resources using access tokens and security descriptors. An access token can be compared to a facility's access card. You know these cards—they're the things that get you into your office every morning. Security descriptors are like access sliders through which you can slide your access cards. Each facility has one of these access sliders and only the people with access cards associated with a specific facility's slider can gain access to that facility. Let's look at these elements from the Windows NT's perspective.

An *access token* is assigned to each user that logs onto a Windows NT machine. This access token contains all security information regarding the user, including the user's security identifier (SID), groups (group SIDs), and user rights or privileges. All processes that this user starts will, by default, use this access token.

All Windows NT objects or resources, such as a file or a window station, have associated with it an access slider called a *security descriptor.* One of the things that a security descriptor holds is a discretionary access control list (DACL). A DACL is composed of a list of access control entries (ACE). Putting this into a simple perspective, each ACE represents an NT user or an NT group along with an access indicator, which indicates that the user or group is granted or denied access.

Given an access token and a security descriptor associated with a resource, granting or denying access is simple. If a user, identified by the SID within the access token, cannot be found in the security descriptor, access to the resource is denied for that user. However, if the user can be found in the security descriptor, access to the resource is granted to the user if the ACL so indicates. If the ACL indicates no access, the user will be denied access.

With a basic understanding of Windows NT security, let's turn our attention to access security in COM. You might have noticed that we haven't discuss the first parameter of *CoInitializeSecurity* and the `EOAC_APPID` and `EOAC_ACCESS_CONTROL` capabilities. These things apply only to COM servers, not clients. During the call to *CoInitializeSecurity*, a COM server can tell COM its decision regarding the handling of access security. The first parameter of *CoInitializeSecurity* controls the users who can access the server and can indicate one of the following:

*NULL*

> This tells COM to perform no access checking and it means that anyone can access or communicate with the server. If the server is not yet launched, the user must still have launch access before the launch can take place. The authentication level can only be RPC_C_AUTHN_LEVEL_NONE when a NULL is passed as the first parameter to *CoInitializeSecurity*. If this parameter is not NULL, you may not specify RPC_C_AUTHN_LEVEL_NONE. All this applies when the EOAC_APPID capability in the eighth parameter of *CoInitializeSecurity* is not set.

*A pointer to a security descriptor*

> To use this feature, you must set neither the EOAC_ACCESS_CONTROL nor the EOAC_APPID capabilities in the eight parameter of *CoInitializeSecurity*. In order to pass in a valid security descriptor, you must create it using the Win32 security API functions. COM will use this security descriptor to make access check and grant or deny client access as appropriate.

*A pointer to a GUID representing the AppID*

> For this, you must set the EOAC_APPID capability in the eighth parameter of *CoInitializeSecurity*. You must set all other parameters of *CoInitializeSecurity* to NULL, as they will be ignored. COM will obtain all security information from the registry under the associated AppID key. If EOAC_APPID is set but the first parameter is NULL (i.e., no AppID is passed in), COM gets the AppID by looking for the key [HKCR\AppID\*server.exe*], where *server.exe* is the name of the current executable. If it finds this key, it will look for an AppID named value that points COM to the associated AppID key. If it can't find the key [HKCR\AppID\*server.exe*], it assumes that no security is configure for the application and uses the machine-wide defaults. Recall that we learned how to configured this key, [HKCR\AppID\*server.exe*], in Chapter 4. Here's one place where it's needed. It is important to note that the process described here is exactly what COM does automatically if the application has never called *CoInitializeSecurity*.

*A pointer to an IAccessControl interface*

> You must set the EOAC_ACCESS_CONTROL capability in the eighth parameter of *CoInitializeSecurity*. COM will use the given *IAccessControl* interface to check and grant or deny client access to the server.

Let's focus on the last possibility. You can get a pointer to an *IAccessControl* interface two ways. The first way to get it is by creating an instance of a system-provided object using CLSID_DCOMAccessControl, as shown below. By the way, other than *CoCreateInstance* on CLSID_DCOMAccessControl, you should almost never make any other COM related calls prior to calling *CoInitializeSecurity*. You must perform a *CoCreateInstance* on CLSID_DCOMAccessControl because you need the *IAccessControl* interface pointer prior to calling *CoInitializeSecurity*.

```
IAccessControl *pAccess=NULL
CoCreateInstance(CLSID_DCOMAccessControl, NULL, CLSCTX_INPROC_SERVER,
    IID_IAccessControl, reinterpret_cast<void**>(&pAccess));
CoInitializeSecurity (pAccess, -1, NULL, NULL, RPC_C_AUTH_LEVEL_CONNECT,
    RPC_C_IMP_LEVEL_IMPERSONATE, NULL, EOAC_ACCESS_CONTROL, NULL);
```

Once you get the *IAccessControl* interface pointer, you may set the appropriate access rights by calling the *SetAccessRights* method of the *IAccessControl* interface. Alternatively, you can also load access rights from a persistent store because this object supports the *IPersist* interface. Once you have the access rights set, you may then call *CoInitializeSecurity* passing in a pointer to *IAccessControl* (pAccess, in this case) as the first parameter. Also, remember to pass in EOAC_ACCESS_ CONTROL as the eighth parameter, or COM will think that pAccess is a pointer to a Win32 security descriptor.

Another way to get this interface is to implement your own object that supports the *IAccessControl* interface. After calling *CoInitialize*, instantiate this object on the stack and pass its address as the first parameter to *CoInitializeSecurity.** This object must be totally thread-safe because COM can call it on any thread at any time. When you implement this interface, you must write at least the *IsAccessAllowed* method, since that's the one used by COM when it does access checks. All other methods in the *IAccessControl* interface can return E_NOTIMPL.

### Activation security on the client side

On the server side, activation (launch) security can be configured only. It cannot be programmatically controlled because the application will not be active until it is launched. However, activation security can be programmatically controlled on the client side because of the mere fact that the client is active before it makes an activation call using *CoGetClassObject*, and others. Many COM activation API functions take a COSERVERINFO structure, which you've examined in Chapter 4. Recall that the COSERVERINFO structure allows you to store a target server and a pointer to a COAUTHINFO structure. You learned how to set target server information in Chapter 4, but you've totally ignored the COAUTHINFO structure, which allows a client to specify the activation security that the local SCM should use to make activation requests to the remote SCM. In Chapter 4, you created a distributed object using the following code, causing the remote SCM to activate the appropriate application:

```
MULTI_QI mqi[] ={ {&IID_IOcr, NULL, S_OK}, {&IID_ISpell, NULL, S_OK} };
COSERVERINFO csi = { 0, TEXT("dog.dcom.com"), NULL, 0 } ; // Target host
HRESULT hr = CoCreateInstanceEx(CLSID_OcrEngine, NULL, CLSCTX_SERVER,
                        &csi, sizeof(mqi)/sizeof(mqi[0]), mqi);
```

---

* I have intentionally made this discussion very brief because a full illustration would require a lengthy coverage of many complex Win32 security structures. However, this is enough insight to get you started in this path if you ever need to provide your own programmatic access control. Remember that access permissions can be configured easily, so you'd have to come up with some very good reasons (e.g., platform portability) for implementing your own access control mechanisms.

Notice that we set the third member of the COSERVERINFO structure to NULL, telling COM to use default activation security. This means that COM will take the
default authentication and impersonation levels into account. If you want to boost
up the authentication level during an activation request, then you need to fill out the
COAUTHINFO structure before calling an activation API function. The COAUTHINFO
structure is defined by COM as follows:

```
typedef struct _COAUTHINFO {
    DWORD               dwAuthnSvc;           // authentication service
    DWORD               dwAuthzSvc;           // authorization service
    LPWSTR              pwszServerPrincName;  // server principal name
    DWORD               dwAuthnLevel;         // authentication level
    DWORD               dwImpersonationLevel; // impersonation level
    COAUTHIDENTITY *    pAuthIdentityData;    // client identity
    DWORD               dwCapabilities;       // additional capabilities
} COAUTHINFO;
```

We have seen most of these security settings before in *CoInitializeSecurity*, but
here are a few points to note. If you don't require authentication during an activation call, set dwAuthnSvc to RPC_C_AUTHN_NONE. If you are using NTLM, you
must set dwAuthzSvc to RPC_C_AUTHZ_NONE. The pwszServerPrincName member is a pointer to a Unicode character array that sets the server principal name to
use for the authentication package. This member must be NULL if dwAuthnSvc is
set to RPC_C_AUTHN_WINNT. The pAuthIdentityData is specific to a particular
security package and it represents a set of client credentials. For NTLM, the following MIDL structure is used:

```
typedef struct _COAUTHIDENTITY
{
    [size_is(UserLength+1)] USHORT * User;      // user name
    ULONG UserLength;
    [size_is(DomainLength+1)] USHORT * Domain; // domain or machine name
    ULONG DomainLength;
    [size_is(PasswordLength+1)] USHORT * Password;  // password
    ULONG PasswordLength;
    ULONG Flags;
} COAUTHIDENTITY;
```

This structure allows you to dynamically create an object using a totally different
set of security credentials from the credentials of the current executing thread
(Chapter 9, *Applying Security*, shows you how to do this). If you don't care about
doing this, you may set pAuthIdentityData to NULL, telling COM to use the
security credentials of the current thread, which may most likely be the credentials of the logged-on user.

With an understanding of the COAUTHINFO structure, here's how we can boost the
authentication level of an activation call. In essence, the following activation call
will be completely encrypted as the packets travel from the client SCM to the
server SCM.

```
MULTI_QI mqi[] ={ {&IID_IOcr, NULL, S_OK}, {&IID_ISpell, NULL, S_OK} };
COAUTHINFO auth = {
  RPC_C_AUTH_WINNT, RPC_C_AUTHZ_NONE, NULL,
  RPC_C_AUTH_LEVEL_PKT_PRIVACY, RPC_C_IMP_LEVEL_IDENTIFY, NULL, EOAC_NONE
};
COSERVERINFO csi = { 0, TEXT("dog.dcom.com"), &auth, 0 };
HRESULT hr = CoCreateInstanceEx(CLSID_OcrEngine, NULL, CLSCTX_SERVER,
                             &csi, sizeof(mqi)/sizeof(mqi[0]), mqi);
```

Again, it is important to note that this only applies to the activation call, so adding these security settings to activation doesn't affect any other method invocations. To raise or lower security for method invocations, you'd need to use call-level security, as discussed next.

### Call-level security on the client side

Like activation security, call-level security can be managed by programs on the client side. The security settings specified in the *CoInitializeSecurity* call apply to every single interface proxy created on the client application, thus ensuring that all outgoing method invocations will use these application-wide security settings by default. However, there are times when a client needs to boost or lower the security of a particular method invocation or a particular interface, especially when protection or performance is important. For example, if the client is sending some highly classified data to the server, the data must be encrypted to prevent offenders from seeing it. On the other hand, the client may want to lower the authentication level because it can drastically improve performance. A well-designed client will likely consider both of the above examples.

As shown in Figure 5-20, COM makes it possible to programmatically specify many security features at the interface proxy level. You can also easily and selectively specify security features for every single method invocation.

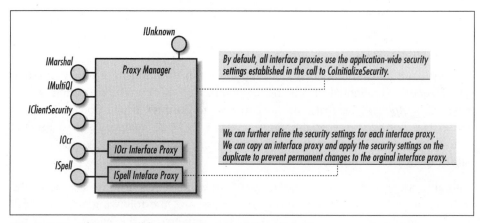

*Figure 5-20. Adjusting call-level security using IClientSecurity*

Recall that when an **OBJREF** is unmarshaled in standard marshaling, COM creates a local proxy object. One of the most powerful interfaces that this proxy object exposes is the *IClientSecurity* interface, which allows a client to dynamically control security features. The involvement of a proxy object means that *IClientSecurity* exists only when we're dealing with remote method invocations.

On a different note, recall that custom marshaling uses a custom proxy, which may or may not implement the *IClientSecurity* interface, so don't expect that you can always query for it. Put differently, you must not assume that *IClientSecurity* always exists, but you must query and check for the returned **HRESULT**—always. Having said that, here's the specification of the *IClientSecurity* interface:

```
[local, object, uuid(0000013D-0000-0000-C000-000000000046)]
interface IClientSecurity : IUnknown {
    // Get security settings for interface proxy.
    HRESULT QueryBlanket ([in] IUnknown *pProxy, [out] DWORD *pAuthnSvc,
            [out] DWORD *pAuthzSvc, [out] OLECHAR **pServerPrincName,
            [out] DWORD *pAuthnLevel, [out] DWORD *pImpLevel,
            [out] void **pAuthInfo, [out] DWORD *pCapabilites);
    // Change security settings for interface proxy.
    HRESULT SetBlanket([in] IUnknown *pProxy, [in] DWORD AuthnSvc,
            [in] DWORD AuthzSvc, [in] OLECHAR *pServerPrincName,
            [in] DWORD AuthnLevel, [in] DWORD ImpLevel,
            [in] void *pAuthInfo, [in] DWORD Capabilities);
    // Copy the interface proxy.
    HRESULT CopyProxy([in]  IUnknown *pProxy, [out] IUnknown **ppCopy);
}
```

Since we've indirectly covered most of the parameters to these methods, we will not discuss them here. However, the *IUnknown* pointers shown in these methods represent pointers to a particular interface proxy. The **pAuthInfo** parameter is specific to a security package; for NTLM, it's a pointer to the **COAUTHIDENTITY** structure that we learned previously in the "Activation security on the client side section. Like activation, you can dynamically specify that a particular interface proxy is to operate under a specific set of security credentials that can be entirely different from that of the logged-on user.

The *QueryBlanket* method of the *IClientSecurity* interface lets a client query for the current supported security features. If you call this function, you may pass **NULLs** for the things that you don't want the query to return. *SetBlanket* is the method that actually allows you to programmatically change the security settings for a particular interface proxy. *CopyProxy* allows you to copy a particular interface proxy so that the original interface proxy will not be modified. Normally, you should make security settings changes only to a copy of an interface proxy. This allows many different threads to specify their own security constraints on the same interface proxy without stepping on each other's toes. Unless you want permanent changes to the original interface proxy, you should never modify the original interface proxy. One important thing to note is that you may not duplicate the proxy object's *IUnknown* interface, because this would violate the identity laws of COM.

Here's an example of boosting an authentication level for a particular interface proxy. First, the code queries for the *IClientSecurity* interface, which will fail unless we have a proxy object. After getting the *IClientSecurity* interface pointer, we make a copy of the *IOcr* interface proxy using *CopyProxy*, so that we won't loose all the previous security settings for *IOcr*. Then, use *SetBlanket* to specify new security settings on the duplicated *IOcr* interface proxy (pSecureOcr). In effect, we're saying, "Don't use the application-wide security settings, but use the settings specified in the *SetBlanket* call." Note that we require encryption (RPC_C_AUTHN_LEVEL_PKT_PRIVACY) and allow the server to impersonate us (RPC_C_IMP_LVEL_IMPERSONATE).

```
IClientSecurity *pSec = NULL;
// Query for IID_IClientSecurity.
pOcr->QueryInteface(IID_IClientSecurity, reinterpret_cast<void**>(&pSec));
// Make a copy of the interface proxy.
IOcr *pSecureOcr=NULL;
pSec->CopyProxy(pOcr, static_cast<IUnknown**>(&pSecureOcr));
// Set the security features on the copied interface proxy.
pSec->SetBlanket(pSecureOcr, RPC_C_AUTH_WINNT, RPC_C_AUTHNZ_NONE, 0,
        RPC_C_AUTHN_LEVEL_PKT_PRIVACY,
        RPC_C_IMP_LVEL_IMPERSONATE, 0, EOAC_NONE);
```

The code is straightforward and you may use the same kind of code to dynamically modify security settings each time you make a method call. However, this requires a number of lines of code, so COM provides a few shortcuts. The *CoQueryProxyBlanket* encapsulates the query for the *IClientSecurity* interface, the call to the corresponding *IClientSecurity* interface method (*QueryBlanket*), and the release of the *IClientSecurity* interface. The *CoSetProxyBlanket* and *CoCopyProxy* API functions essentially do the same thing, with the exception that each calls its corresponding *IClientSecurity* interface methods. These shortcuts are listed below:

```
HRESULT CoQueryProxyBlanket(IUnknown *pProxy, DWORD *pwAuthnSvc,
    DWORD *pAuthzSvc, OLECHAR **pServerPrincName, DWORD *pAuthnLevel,
    DWORD *pImpLevel, RPC_AUTH_IDENTITY_HANDLE  *pAuthInfo,
    DWORD *pCapabilites);
HRESULT CoSetProxyBlanket(IUnknown *pProxy, DWORD dwAuthnSvc,
    DWORD dwAuthzSvc, OLECHAR *pServerPrincName, DWORD dwAuthnLevel,
    DWORD dwImpLevel, RPC_AUTH_IDENTITY_HANDLE  pAuthInfo,
    DWORD dwCapabilities);
HRESULT CoCopyProxy(IUnknown *pProxy, IUnknown **ppCopy);
```

With these shortcuts, the previous code could be rewritten more compactly as follows:

```
IOcr *pSecureOcr=NULL;
CoCopyProxy(pOcr, static_cast<IUnknown**>(&pSecureOcr));
```

```
CoSetProxyBlanket(pSecureOcr, RPC_C_AUTH_WINNT, RPC_C_AUTHNZ_NONE, 0,
    RPC_C_AUTHN_LEVEL_PKT_PRIVACY, RPC_C_IMP_LVEL_IMPERSONATE, 0, EOAC_
    NONE);
```

The one disadvantage with this code snippet is that it is less efficient than the previous, because each shortcut does a query and release on the *IClientSecurity* interface. However, these shortcuts are less error-prone and thus should be seen as an advantage.

### Using the security context on the server side

You've just seen how to change security settings dynamically at a method invocation level. Let's turn our attention to the server side and see how to manage calls based on a client's security context. The term *security context* means the security data associated with a communication link between a client and a server. This security data is negotiated by the client and server security layers for a given connection. Depending on the impersonation level and the additional capabilities that the client sets, the server can identify, impersonate (with or without cloaking), and delegate (with or without cloaking). When a server impersonates and acts in place of a client, you say that it is running under the client's security context.

One thing that most servers do is to obtain the client's security context before they will agree to service the client. When COM receives an incoming method invocation on the server side, it creates a call context based on the client's security context and associates it with the thread that carries out the method invocation. When the target method is invoked, the method can get the *IServerSecurity* interface implemented by the stub manager. To get this interface, the target method simply calls the following COM API function:

```
HRESULT CoGetCallContext(
    REFIID riid,        // only IID_IServerSecurity for standard marshaling
    void **ppInterface // Resulting IServerSecurity pointer.
);
```

In standard marshaling, the only supported interface on the server side is *IServerSecurity*. Even though the stub manager implements this interface, the call context lasts only for the duration of a each call, because the call context is associated with the thread executing the method. That means that after the method is invoked, that specific call context will no longer be valid, implying that calling the *IServerSecurity* interface methods upon different ORPC calls will return different results and behave differently. Here's the specification of the *IServerSecurity* interface:

```
[local, object, uuid(0000013E-0000-0000-C000-000000000046)]
interface IServerSecurity : IUnknown {
  // Get client security information.
  HRESULT QueryBlanket([out] DWORD *pAuthnSvc, [out] DWORD *pAuthzSvc,
```

```
    [out] OLECHAR **pServerPrincName, [out] DWORD *pAuthnLevel,
      [out] DWORD *pImpLevel, [out] void **pPrivs, [out] DWORD *pCapabilities);
  HRESULT ImpersonateClient(); // Impersonate client.
  HRESULT RevertToSelf();       // Stop impersonating.
  BOOL IsImpersonating();       // Currently impersonating?
}
```

The *QueryBlanket* method is the same as the *IClientSecurity* method of that name. This method allows the server to obtain the security information for the current call context. In particular, the server uses this method to mainly get the security information associated with the client that makes the method invocation. If you don't need certain information, you may pass NULLs into this method call. The pImpLevel parameter must be set to NULL. The pPrivs parameter is a string (i.e., domain\user for NTLM) that represents a readable name of the client who makes the method invocation. Do not free this string, as it is referencing memory that is internal to COM. This string is also only valid for the duration of the method invocation. In order for the server to obtain this string, the client must set the impersonation level to RPC_C_IMP_LEVEL_IDENTIFY, or higher, and the authentication level to RPC_C_AUTH_LEVEL_CONNECT, or higher.

Assuming that the client gives the server impersonation privilege, the *ImpersonateClient* method allows the server to impersonate and execute under the client's security context until the *RevertToSelf* method is called. The *IsImpersonating* method allows a server to detect whether it is currently impersonating. Depending on the settings of impersonation level and the additional capability, there can be a few different scenarios. These scenarios are shown in Table 5-5, which assumes that a nameless client invokes a method on server A that is located on a different machine from the client. Server B is a different server and executes on the same machine as server A. Server C is yet another server and executes on a third machine that's different from both the machine that hosts the client and the machine that hosts server A. Impersonation levels other than RPC_C_IMP_LEVEL_ IMPERSONATE and RPC_C_IMP_LEVEL_DELEGATE are trivial and don't apply to the cloaking capability available in Windows 2000, so they're not shown in this table.

*Table 5-5. The Implications of the Cloaking Capability*

| | RPC_C_IMP_LEVEL_IMPERSONATE (One Hop) | RPC_C_IMP_LEVEL_DELEGATE (Multiple Hops) |
|---|---|---|
| **No Cloak- ing** (Servers can- not pass cli- ent's token) | Using the client's security token, server A can make outgoing calls to server B, but server A cannot make outgoing calls to server C. Server A cannot access network resources using the client's security token. | Server A can make outgoing calls to server B and server C using the client's security token. Server A can access network resources using the client's security token. |

*Table 5-5. The Implications of the Cloaking Capability (continued)*

| | RPC_C_IMP_LEVEL_IMPERSONATE (One Hop) | RPC_C_IMP_LEVEL_DELEGATE (Multiple Hops) |
|---|---|---|
| **Cloaking** (Servers can pass client's token) | Everything above is true, plus... Server A can pass the client's security token to server B, but cannot pass the client's security token to server C. With impersonate impersonation level, cloaking works for only one hop—at most two physical machines can be involved. | Everything earlier is true, plus... Server A can pass the client's security token to server B and server C. Assuming that there is a server D on a different machine, server C can pass the client's token to server D—extremely powerful. With delegate impersonation level, cloaking works across multiple hops—the client token can be passed among many processes executing on different physical machines. |

Recall that cloaking (EOAC_CLOAKING) is an additional capability that is set once per application using *CoInitializeSecurity*. The impersonation level can be machine-wide configured using *dcomcnfg.exe*, set once per application, or dynamically controlled using *IClientSecurity* as a client makes an outgoing remote method invocation.

With an understanding of *IServerSecurity*, here's a simple example that takes advantage of the *IServerSecurity* methods. In the following code, notice that you use *QueryBlanket* to verify the authentication level set by the client. If this call is not encrypted, refuse to service the client; otherwise, impersonate the client and do whatever you want. Exactly what you can do here depends upon the client's impersonation level and the cloaking capability specified by both the client and server during the call to *CoInitializeSecurity*. After impersonating to do whatever is needed using the client's security token, you revert back to the thread's original security token. Take care to release the interface pointer obtained from *CoGetCallContext*.

```
HRESULT CoOcrEngine::OcrImage()
{
    IServerSecurity *pSec=NULL;
    CoGetCallContext(IID_IServerSecurity, (void**) &pSec);
    DWORD dwAuthnLevel;
    pSec->QueryBlanket(0,0,0,&dwAuthnLevel, 0,0,0);
    if (dwAuthnLevel!=RPC_C_AUTHN_LEVEL_PKT_PRIVACY) {
        // Don't handle calls that are unencrypted.
        pSec->Release();
        return E_ACCESSDENIED;
    }
    pSec->ImpersonateClient();
    // Do work using the client's security token.
    // Exactly what we can do here depends upon Table 5-5.
```

```
  pSec->RevertToSelf();
  pSec->Release();
  return S_OK;
}
```

Like *IClientSecurity*, the *IServerSecurity* interface also has a number of shortcuts that should be self-explanatory based on their names. *CoQueryClientBlanket* is a shorthand that calls *CoGetCallContext*, obtains client security information through calling the corresponding method in the *IServerSecurity* interface, and releases the *IServerSecurity* interface pointer. *CoImpersonateClient* and *CoRevertToSelf* do the same thing, with the exception that each calls the corresponding method in the *IServerSecurity* interface.

```
HRESULT CoQueryClientBlanket(DWORD *pAuthnSvc, DWORD *pAuthzSvc,
    OLECHAR **pServerPrincName, DWORD *pAuthnLevel, DWORD *pImpLevel,
    RPC_AUTHZ_HANDLE *pPrivs, DWORD *pCapabilities);
WINOLEAPI CoImpersonateClient();
WINOLEAPI CoRevertToSelf();
```

Here's an example that gets the client's user name and authentication level using *CoQueryClientBlanket*. Don't deallocate **pUserName**, because the SDK documentation explicitly says that you must not modify or deallocate it as it directly points to memory that is private to COM.

```
HRESULT CoOcrEngine::OcrImage()
{
  wchar_t *pUserName=NULL;
  CoQueryClientBlanket(0,0,0,&dwAuthnLevel, 0,(void**) &pUserName,0);
  if (dwAuthnLevel!=RPC_C_AUTHN_LEVEL_PKT_PRIVACY) {
    // Don't handle calls that are unencrypted.
    return E_ACCESSDENIED;
  }
  // Do work here . . .

  // For example, check pUserName against a list of valid users.

  // Do not modify or free pUserName as it simply points
  // to memory that is private to COM.
  return S_OK;
}
```

The *CoQueryClientBlanket* shorthand frees you from remembering to release the *IServerSecurity* interface pointer and thus makes the code a little bit less error-prone. However, it is less efficient than the previous technique.

One important thing to reiterate is that *IClientSecurity* and *IServerSecurity* are implemented by the proxy and stub in standard marshaling. If you use custom marshaling, you are on your own. This means that if you use custom marshaling and still want to keep a consistent programming model, then your custom proxy must implement the *IClientSecurity* interface and your custom stub must implement the *IServerSecurity* interface.

# 6

# *Building Components with ATL*

You've learned practically all the fundamentals of COM in the last few chapters. You wrote the code from scratch using C++, with the help of a number of important COM API functions and standard interfaces. However, you might have noticed that most of the code that you wrote is boilerplate code. In other words, most of the code that you have to write is the same across all components. For example:

- COM is purely based on COM interfaces. A COM object can implement a number of interfaces, but it must implement at least the *IUnknown* interface. Most of the code for *IUnknown* is boilerplate and to be blunt, the code for *QueryInterface, AddRef,* and *Release* is almost a replica from one implementation to another.

- A COM object is created by its corresponding class factory, which usually implements the *IClassFactory* interface. As we've seen in Chapter 3, almost all of the code for *IClassFactory* is boilerplate.

- A COM component hosts its supported COM classes. Its job is to expose the class objects or class factories associated with these COM classes to the world. If the COM component is an out-of-process server, then it registers its supported class objects with the SCM using *CoRegisterClassObject.* If it is an in-process server, then it exposes the *DllGetClassObject* and *DllCanUnloadNow* entry points, which will be called automatically by COM. Most of this code is also boilerplate.

- A COM component has at least one thread that must enter an apartment, may it be an STA or an MTA. An STA requires a message pump and an MTA requires a shutdown signal. Most of this code is also boilerplate.

The previous list includes everything you've learned so far, which means that about the only thing that is not boilerplate is the code for your own supported interfaces, may they be standard, custom, dispatch, or dual interfaces. Boilerplate code can be extremely error-prone because you tend to simply copy it from one file and paste in into another. At times, you forget to make the necessary—although tiny—changes, which may be bugs that can take hours to track down.

Microsoft has realized this fact and thus provided us with a wealth of tools and libraries to make life in the COM world simple. For example, Visual Basic and Visual J++ both provide immense support for building and using components. For C++ programmers, Microsoft provides the Microsoft Foundation Classes (MFC), which has enormous support for building and using components. The one draw-back with MFC is that it's really bulky. Put bluntly, when you develop a COM object using MFC, you end up linking in the extraneous richness of MFC, causing the final executable to become unnecessarily larger than it has to be. The main reason for this is that you cannot selectively delete the functionality that has already been built into MFC, unless you're willing to rebuild the MFC source code yourself.

Components are meant to be widely distributed. Because components and their users can be anywhere, you must be aware that your components can be down-loaded over a slow Internet link. A component built using MFC may be extremely powerful, but it takes time to download because it's so bulky. To eliminate this unnecessary bulkiness, Microsoft deploys the Active Template Library (ATL), a set of C++ template classes that implements much of the COM boilerplate code. How-ever, because ATL is a set of template classes, you're actually reusing only the source code that is needed within the component that you're developing. You don't pull in or link in anything that's not needed, making ATL components very lean. In fact, components built using ATL can be at least six times smaller than components built using MFC. As an added advantage, Microsoft Visual Studio also provides a number of wizards, like the `ATL COM AppWizard` and the `ATL Object Wizard`, to make life much, much simpler for COM development.

In this chapter, we'll develop a component using ATL so you can see how simple COM development is using this library. All the knowledge that you've learned in earlier chapters is not lost, since you must understand COM from the ground up in order to make good decisions in developing components. Moreover, this knowl-edge allows you to more easily read ATL or MFC COM source code.

In general, use the following steps to develop a basic but complete component using ATL:

1. Create a project to represent the component that you're building. The name of the component will be the same as the name of the project.

2. Add COM objects into your component. These are the objects that can be used by external clients.

3. Add the necessary interfaces to a COM object and implement them.

4. Build and register the component.

## Creating a Component

Since you've already learned how to create dynamic linked library and normal executable components, we're going to do something different in this chapter. You'll create an NT service that acts as an OCR server. Recall that an NT service can start up by itself when the machine is powered up. This can be an advantage after a power outage, at which time the machine powers itself back up, allowing your service to automatically come back to life. This is nice since it can happen without the need of an administrator.

However, this problem doesn't apply to COM components, because components can be dynamically activated. In other words, the SCM will launch the correct component upon client request even if the component was not an NT service. From the COM perspective, there is really no reason why we're creating an NT service other than the fact that the `ATL COM AppWizard` allows us to create this kind of component by simply checking a box. By checking this option, all the necessary code for an NT service is generated for you. Knowing this, even if you don't want to use COM, you can take advantage of this option to generate the underlining code for a regular NT service executable.

Before you build this component, you should take note that the screen shots shown throughout this book may differ slightly from the ones that you see on your computer monitors. This is because new features will continue to be added as ATL and MFC evolve.

To generate the shell of this component, you need to do the following:

1. Select `New` from the `File` menu and name this project `OCRServer`.

2. To create an ATL COM project, select the `ATL COM AppWizard` and click `OK`.

3. The `ATL COM AppWizard`, as shown in Figure 6-1, will appear. This wizard allows you to create a DLL or a normal EXE, which are familiar to us because we've seen these component types in Chapter 4. What we haven't seen is a component that is an NT service. By selecting `Service(EXE)` as the `Server Type`, the `ATL COM AppWizard` will generate the necessary code to make the out-of-process component an NT service. Since the `OCRServer` component is a service, it starts automatically each time the computer is booted.

4. Click `Finish` on the `ATL COM AppWizard` dialog to generate the necessary source files for the component.

Figure 6-1 also shows three check-boxes that are grayed out, as they are available only for a DLL component. The `Support MFC` check-box allows you to include

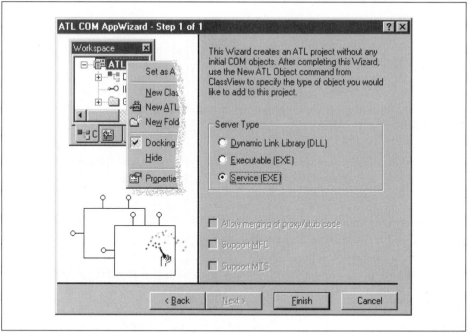

*Figure 6-1. The ATL COM AppWizard dialog box*

support for MFC, which simply means that you can use the MFC classes, such as *CString* or *CMap*. This option provides experienced MFC developers more productivity because they've been exposed to these common MFC classes. However, be aware that checking this option means that you agree to link in the MFC libraries, an act that can defeat the purpose of being a lean component. Instead of checking this option, you should think about learning the C++ Standard Template Library (STL), which provides corresponding classes, such as *string* or *map*.

The `Allow merging of proxy/stub code` check-box allows you to merge the proxy/stub code into your component. This simply means that you want to compile and link the proxy/stub code into your component. Doing this removes the need for registering a separate proxy/stub DLL, which is used in marshaling your custom interfaces. Using this technique, when the component starts up, the marshaling code is internally registered, and thus eliminating the need for a look up to the registry for the proxy/stub configuration information.

This technique is valuable if you're building an in-process server. Again, the advantage with this technique is that a client only needs to register the in-process server, not the corresponding proxy/stub DLL because the proxy/stub code is an integrated apart of the in-process server. Remember, COM needs the proxy/stub code to marshal your custom interfaces when the apartment models of the in-process server differs from the client executable that dynamically loads the in-process server. Without the proxy/stub code, this kind of client-server scenario would not work. The downside to this technique is that the size of the component enlarges.

When you click Finish on the ATL COM AppWizard, the wizard will generate the shell for your NT service component. At this time, if you look in ClassView, you will see one class that is generated by the ATL COM AppWizard: *CServiceModule*. This class, which is derived from *CComModule*, represents the component that you're building. There's one global instantiation of this object that lives for the lifetime of the application,

```
CServiceModule _Module;
```

The notable member functions of the *CServiceModule* class include *RegisterServer*, *UnregisterServer*, and *Run*. *RegisterServer* and *UnregisterServer* implement the code for server registration and unregistration. This is the boilerplate code for component registration and unregistration covered in Chapter 4, *Components*. The *Run* member function runs the service, and it looks similar to the main function written in Chapter 4. If you examine this function, you'll see that the thread that invokes this function enters into an apartment by calling *CoInitialize* and leaves the apartment by calling *CoUninitialize*. The relevant part of this function is shown here:

```
void CServiceModule::Run()
{
    CoInitialize(NULL);
    // This provides a NULL DACL which will allow access to everyone.
    CSecurityDescriptor sd; sd.InitializeFromThreadToken();
    CoInitializeSecurity(sd, -1, NULL, NULL,
            RPC_C_AUTHN_LEVEL_PKT, RPC_C_IMP_LEVEL_IMPERSONATE,
            NULL, EOAC_NONE, NULL);
    _Module.RegisterClassObjects(CLSCTX_LOCAL_SERVER|CLSCTX_REMOTE_SERVER,
                            REGCLS_MULTIPLEUSE);
    MSG msg;
    while (GetMessage(&msg, 0, 0, 0)) DispatchMessage(&msg);
    _Module.RevokeClassObjects();
    CoUninitialize();
}
```

As exhibited above, this function also calls *CoInitializeSecurity* to set the default application-wide security that all proxies will use. Notice that for access security, the generated code allows everyone access by default. If this isn't good, you can customize the security descriptor object, *CSecurityDescriptor*, to limit access. For example, you can use the *Allow* and *Deny* member functions of *CSecurityDescriptor* to change the access permissions for a given user.

This *Run* method also registers all the class objects that the component supports by calling the *RegisterClassObjects* method of *CComModule*, which is implemented by ATL. After doing this, this method runs the message pump to handle ORPC and window messages. When the message pump ends, the function revokes all the previously registered class objects by calling the *RevokeClassObjects* method of *CComModule*. We've arduously done all this by hand in Chapter 4, but the ATL COM AppWizard generates all this code for us. Almost all of the boilerplate code has already been implemented by the base ATL template classes.

The `ATL COM AppWizard` also generates a default IDL file and a registry script (RGS) file. This RGS file records the registration information for this component's `AppID`. It is linked into the component as a resource and is used at runtime to enter/remove the `AppID` key from the registry during server registration/ unregistration.

## *Adding an Object*

As you can see in the last section, by simply running the `ATL COM AppWizard`, the boilerplate code for a COM component is generated for you. You're now ready to add COM objects into this component. You can add as many COM objects to this component as you wish.

To add a COM object, select `New ATL Object` from the `Insert` menu to launch the `ATL Object Wizard`, which is shown in Figure 6-2. The `ATL Object Wizard` has a list-box on the left showing a number of options. The first selection, `Objects`, allows you to create a variety of simple COM objects, including MTS compatible objects, Internet Explorer compatible objects, etc. The similarity between these object types is that they are all COM objects, as they all implement at least the *IUnknown* interface. The difference between these different object types is that they implement different COM interfaces that are specific to a technology domain. The second list-box item, `Controls`, allows you to create a variety of ActiveX controls that are essentially COM objects that implement over a dozen COM interfaces and are usually graphical user interface oriented.

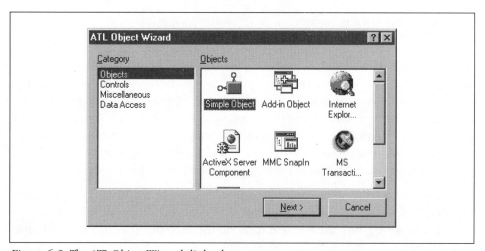

*Figure 6-2. The ATL Object Wizard dialog box*

For our purposes, we want to create a simple COM object that supports an interface for optical character recognition. For this, select `Objects` in the list-box on the left, select `Simple Object` in the list-view on the right, and click `Next` to proceed.

Once you've done this, you will then see the `ATL Object Wizard Properties` sheet, as shown in Figure 6-3. In the `Short Name` edit-box, type `OcrProcessor`; notice as you type this word, the rest of the edit-boxes fill themselves automatically. The `ATL Object Wizard` automatically names the default interface *IOcrProcessor* and names the C++ class that implements the *IOcrProcessor* interface *COcrProcessor*. *COcrProcessor* will be our first COM object for this component. *IOcrProcessor* will be defined in the generated IDL file and *COcrProcessor* is a C++ class that will be defined in the generated header file.

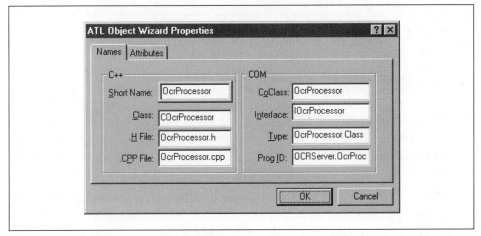

*Figure 6-3. The Names tab of the ATL Object Wizard Properties dialog box*

The `ProgID` edit-box shows the human-readable name that is associated with a COM class. The ProgID makes it easier for you to refer to a particular COM class by name. Remembering a name is definitely easier than remembering a 128-bit CLSID, but be aware that only the CLSID is unique in time and space. To convert a CLSID from a ProgID in programming, you'd use the *CLSIDFromProgID* API function, shown here:

```
HRESULT CLSIDFromProgID(LPCOLESTR lpszProgID, LPCLSID pclsid);
```

The `Attributes` page of the `ATL Object Wizard Properties` sheet, shown in Figure 6-4, is important because you get to tell the `ATL Object Wizard` the code you want it to generate for the resulting COM object.

In particular, you can specify the following information for the COM object:

- *The threading model that the resulting COM object will support.* As explained in Chapter 5, *Infrastructure*, there are special implications for each threading

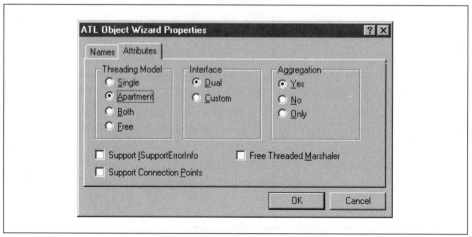

*Figure 6-4. The Attributes tab of the ATL Object Wizard Properties dialog box*

model, so you must understand each of the options found in `Threading Model` group. The radio button labeled `Single`, shown in Figure 6-4, is a special case of the STA model, and as such, `Single` is not technically a threading model. `Single` here simply means an STA model with only one thread, the main STA thread. If you select this option, your COM object can be created and executed only within the main STA. See Chapter 5 if you need to refresh your memory on the other threading models.

- *Whether your object supports a custom or dual interface.* A custom interface is any user-defined interface that we develop and, unlike other types of interfaces, it can be a direct derivative of *IUnknown.* A dual interface is one that supports both a dispatch (dynamic) and custom interface (static) method invocations. See Chapter 3, *Objects,* if you need more information regarding types of interfaces.

- *If the object can, cannot, or can only be aggregated.* Chapter 4, *Components,* delves into the topic of aggregation and states that objects must support aggregation before another object can aggregate them. Making an object aggregatable requires some boilerplate code, but with ATL, you simply click on the correct radio button to get this support.

- *Whether your object supports COM exception handling.* Microsoft supports COM distributed exception handling in a standard way using standard interfaces, such as *ISupportErrorInfo* and *IErrorInfo.* If you wish your COM object to support exception handling, check the `Support ISupportErrorInfo` checkbox. When you do this, the `ATL Object Wizard` will generate the code to implement the *ISupportErrorInfo* interface. To actually create an exception, you use the *CreateErrorInfo* COM API function, and to throw this exception, you must call the *SetErrorInfo* COM API function. To catch this exception on the client side, you must call the *GetErrorInfo* COM API function. Chapter 9, *Applying Security*, and 10, *Connecting Objects*, will teach you COM exception handling.

- *Whether your object supports connection points*. Connection points is a technique for supporting notification of events. For example, a client asks the object to tell it when a special event occurs; the object calls back to the client notifying such event at the correct moment. If you check the **Support Connection Points** option, the **ATL Object Wizard** will generate the code to implement the *IConnectionPointContainer* interface. This means that the object supports outgoing interfaces. In other words, this object will call back to the client using these outgoing interfaces. Of course, making this choice implies that the client will implement these interfaces. Chapter 10 will teach you how to use connection points.

- *Whether your object should aggregate the FTM*. We covered this topic in Chapter 5 pretty thoroughly. Aggregating the FTM simply means that interface pointers are custom-marshaled between two different apartments within the same process. FTM is a technique to marshal 32 bits that represent a raw pointer in memory from one apartment to another within the same process. When you look at it from another angle, it's a way to maximize performance by using a raw interface pointer in any apartment within the same process. Obviously, you need to be very cautious when using this feature. If you're still not sure about this feature, refer back to Chapter 5 for a complete discussion, including its implications.

This is a lot of functionality that can be totally generated by the **ATL Object Wizard** with the click of a button. To make it simple, we will just take the default selections in this dialog box and choose OK to allow the **ATL Object Wizard** to generate the necessary code in support of our simple object.

You may add many COM objects to a given component using the **ATL Object Wizard**. Each time you do this, the **ATL Object Wizard** adds the corresponding COM class to the object map, which starts with the **BEGIN_OBJECT_MAP** macro and ends with **END_OBJECT_MAP**. An ATL object map specifies all the classes that are supported by this component, and all these classes are captured between the **BEGIN_OBJECT_MAP** and **END_OBJECT_MAP** macros.

Do you remember the *Run* method implemented by the *CServiceModule* class? It calls *RegisterClassObjects* to register all the supported class objects belonging to this component. In turn, *RegisterClassObjects* refers to this object map to register all the supported class objects associated with the COM classes that are members of the object map. Additional configuration information for each of these COM classes is recorded in its associated RGS file. Put simply, COM classes that are not added to this object map will not get registered. For your application, the following object map includes only one COM class, which is identified by **CLSID_OcrProcessor** and represented by the *COcrProcessor* C++ class.

```
BEGIN_OBJECT_MAP(ObjectMap)
    OBJECT_ENTRY(CLSID_OcrProcessor, COcrProcessor)
END_OBJECT_MAP()
```

The **ATL Object Wizard** also generates associated *.h* and *.cpp* files for the COM class. Furthermore, it automatically adds the supported interface (*IOcrProcessor* in this case) into the IDL file and generates a separate RGS file for the COM class. This RGS file records the registration information for this particular COM class, including the COM class' CLSID, threading model, etc. This file is linked into the component as a resource and is used at runtime to register and unregister this COM class. *CComModule::RegisterClassObjects* and *CComModule::RevokeClassObjects* end up using the configuration information stored in the RGS file to carry out registration and unregistration of a COM class built using ATL. This is a lot of code and scripts generated with a few mouse clicks.

Now, if you look carefully in **ClassView**, you will find an icon for the *IOcrProcessor* interface and an icon for the *COcrProcessor* C++ class, as shown in Figure 6-5. Since you now have an interface, let's add a method to support OCR processing of an image buffer. To do this, right-click on the *IOcrProcessor* icon, as shown in Figure 6-5.

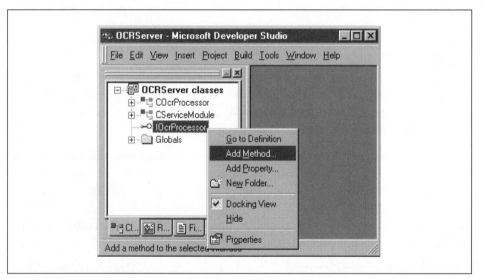

*Figure 6-5. Adding an interface method*

In the pop-up menu, select **Add Method**. This will take you to the **Add Method to Interface** dialog box, shown in Figure 6-6, where you can specifically enter the details of the method you are adding.

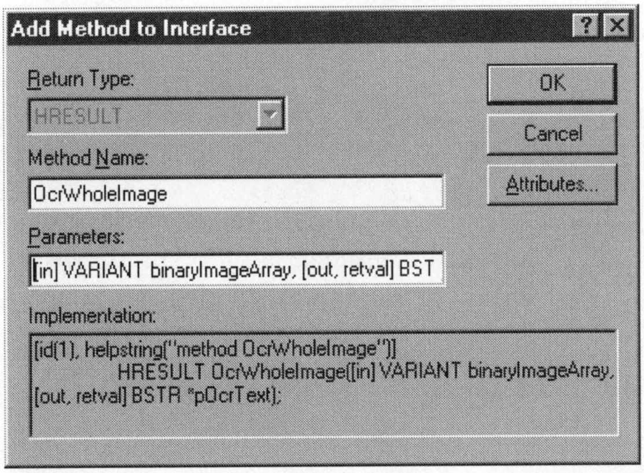

*Figure 6-6. The Add Method to Interface dialog box*

In the **Method Name** edit-box shown in Figure 6-6, type *OcrWholeImage*, and in the **Parameters** edit-box, type the following:

```
[in] VARIANT binaryImageArray, [out, retval] BSTR *pOcrText
```

You have to use Automation compatible types because your interface is a dual interface, the default option that you've never changed. So the first parameter is an input of type **VARIANT**. Recall that a **VARIANT** type can represent practically any data type. In a sense, it is a value holder and thus can be viewed as "typeless." You use it here to allow a client to pass a binary buffer (e.g., a TIFF image) to the *COcrProcessor* object. The second parameter is output and is also specified as a return value to pass back the ASCII text of the corresponding image buffer.

Notice that the second parameter has a [**retval**] attribute, which is nice for an environment such as Visual Basic, where you can do something like this:

```
strText= obj.OcrWholeImage(vImage)
```

instead of having to do the following in C++:

```
hr = pOcrProcessor->OcrWholeImage(vImage, &strText)
```

The [**retval**] attribute allows you to capture the return value on the left side of the method invocation in an environment such as Visual Basic. Clearly from the example, the [**retval**] attribute does not help out C++ programmers.

Once you have entered all parameters for the method, click OK in the **Add Method to Interface** dialog box to allow the wizard to generate this method in the IDL file and an empty implementation in the *OcrProcessor.cpp* file. For your information, the **Attributes** button in the **Add Method to Interface** dialog box allows you to add attributes, such as [**source**] or [**local**], to your interface method.

# *The Generated Code*

Now that we've generated a COM object that supports OCR processing, we should take this moment to examine the generated code in support of this COM object. In particular, we will examine the interface generated for our *IOcrProcessor* interface and the implementation of our COM object, including its interface implementations.

As we move along this discussion, you should reflect back to what you've learned in Chapters 3, 4, and 5. From this examination, you should realize that the generated code is exactly what you've learned in those previous chapters.

## *Generated Interface*

Let's start off by examining the interface that the ATL Object Wizard has just generated. If you extend the *IOcrProcessor* icon in ClassView (e.g., click on the plus sign), you will see the *OcrWholeImage* method. Double-clicking on this method will jump you to the target method in the IDL file, which should look similar to the IDL script shown here:

```
[object, uuid(00000001-AAAA-11D1-8753-006008CDD9AE), dual,
 helpstring("IOcrProcessor Interface"), pointer_default(unique)]
interface IOcrProcessor : IDispatch {
    [id(1), helpstring("method OcrWholeImage")]
        HRESULT OcrWholeImage([in] VARIANT binaryImageArray,
                            [out, retval] BSTR *pOcrText);
};


[uuid(00000001-CCCC-11D1-8753-006008CDD9AE), version(1.0),
 helpstring("OCRServer 1.0 Type Library")]
library OCRSERVERLib {
    importlib("stdole32.tlb");
    importlib("stdole2.tlb");

    [uuid(00000001-BBBB-11D1-8753-006008CDD9AE),
     helpstring("OcrProcessor Class")]
    coclass OcrProcessor {
        [default] interface IOcrProcessor;
    };
};
```

We've gone over MIDL fairly extensively in Chapter 3, so we will not go into a long discussion of IDL here. The only thing we haven't seen is the [helpstring()] attribute, which simply allows you to insert help strings for methods, interfaces, coclasses, etc. These strings serve as help documentation and they are stored within the type library.

In a nutshell, the IDL file generated, shown earlier, says that the library, OCRSERVERLib, supports a COM class, OcrProcessor, whose instances expose an interface named *IOcrProcessor*. The *IOcrProcessor* interface has one method called *OcrWholeImage*. In addition, this interface is a dual interface, meaning that it supports both late and very early bindings. Recall that dual interface is a default option in the **Attributes** page of the **ATL Object Wizard Properties** sheet. Recall also that an interface must implement *IDispatch* in order to support late binding; this is why the *IOcrProcessor* interface is derived from *IDispatch*.

The idea is simple. Looking at it from a general perspective, a library can contain one or more classes, and a class can contain one or more interfaces. Furthermore, these libraries, classes, and interfaces are unique in time and space when represented by their corresponding GUIDs.

As you can see, the *IOcrProcessor* interface supports the *OcrWholeImage* method, which you have added previously. The input of this method is **binaryImageArray**, which is of type **VARIANT**. This **VARIANT** is used to allow clients to pass a **SAFEARRAY** of unsigned characters, which holds the TIFF image buffer for optical character recognition. The output is **pOcrText** and is of type **BSTR \***, which will hold the returned OCR text for the corresponding image.

## Generated Implementation

Before we delve into the implementation of our object, you should be aware that the source code for ATL is located in the **atl\include** directory. This code is great for gaining insights on C++ techniques and strategies in COM programming, and it's a great resource for exploration, debugging, and generally finding out exactly what's done under the cover.

ATL provides a number of generic template classes to make it very simple to implement COM objects. If you are not familiar with C++ templates, see the "C++ Templates" sidebar in Chapter 4 for a short introduction. These template classes hide the boilerplate code and allow you to concentrate specifically on the implementation of your supported interfaces. This is great because no one wants to forever copy and paste boilerplate code.

Unlike MFC, which uses the nested-classes technique for implementing COM objects, ATL uses the multiple inheritance technique along with C++ templates. As you witnessed in Chapter 3, the multiple inheritance technique is much cleaner, because method implementations can be shared by multiple interfaces. For example, using the multiple inheritance approach, you would have to write only one implementation of *QueryInterface*, regardless of the number of interfaces that your object exposes. However, if you were to use the nested-classes technique, you would have to write many implementations of *QueryInterface*—one for each supported interface.

It would take a book to explain all the classes of ATL, so I won't do that. However, you must understand at least what's going on and how certain notable template classes are tied together to form a COM object. So let's examine the generated class, *COcrProcessor*, that models our OCR processor COM object. As you can see in the following code snippet, the *COcrProcessor* class multiply inherits from *CComObjectRootEx*, *CComCoClass*, and *IDispatchImpl*, giving this object basic COM behaviors along with a dual interface, *IOcrProcessor*, implementation.

```
class COcrProcessor :
  public CComObjectRootEx<CComSingleThreadModel>,
  public CComCoClass<COcrProcessor, &CLSID_OcrProcessor>,
  public IDispatchImpl<IOcrProcessor, &IID_IOcrProcessor, &LIBID_OCRSERVERLib>
{
public:
  COcrProcessor() {}

DECLARE_REGISTRY_RESOURCEID(IDR_OCRPROCESSOR)

BEGIN_COM_MAP(COcrProcessor)
  COM_INTERFACE_ENTRY(IOcrProcessor)
  COM_INTERFACE_ENTRY(IDispatch)
END_COM_MAP()

// IOcrProcessor
public:
  STDMETHOD(OcrWholeImage)(/*[in]*/ VARIANT binaryImageArray,
                           /*[out, retval]*/ BSTR *pOcrText);
};
```

Let's briefly study the template base classes, the classes from which *COcrProcessor* inherits in the code shown earlier. All COM server objects must directly or indirectly derive from the *CComObjectRoot* class. Derived from *CComObjectRoot*, *CComObjectRootEx* manages the reference count for your COM object. It also implements the boilerplate code for supporting aggregation, which is only used when the object is being aggregated. *CComObjectRootEx* takes a threading model type (e.g., *CComSingleThreadModel*) to tell COM that the object is intending to support a particular apartment model. If this parameter is *CComSingleThreadModel*, the *AddRef* and *Release* methods will not be protected with critical sections; but if this parameter is *CComMultiThreadModel*, the *AddRef* and *Release* methods will be made thread-safe.

The *CComObjectRootEx* class works closely with the COM map that is shown between the BEGIN_COM_MAP and END_COM_MAP macros. This map is used by the implementation of the *QueryInterface* method, and thus implying that all interfaces supported by the *COcrProcessor* object must be included between this map. As currently shown, our *COcrProcessor* COM object supports two interfaces, the *IOcrProcessor* interface and the *IDispatch* interface. Recall that the *IDispatch* interface is included because, by default, the ATL Object Wizard selects the dual interface option. The default implementation of *IDispatch* for the dual part of our *IOcrProcessor* interface comes for free with the *IDispatchImpl* template class. The first parameter of *IDispatchImpl* signifies the C++ type of the dual interface, the second parameter is a pointer to the IID of the dual interface, and the third parameter is a pointer to the type library identifier.

Notice that *COcrProcessor* also implements the *IOcrProcessor* interface. The ATL Object Wizard generates wrapper method declarations and definitions for all methods specified within the supported interface. This means that you're left with the job of filling in the actual functionality of your supported interface methods. You should realize by now that almost everything is done by the ATL template class and the ATL wizards—making COM development much easier and less error-prone. Since you've only defined a single method, *OcrWholeImage*, for this interface, that's the only wrapper method that you'll get.

The ATL Object Wizard also generates a registry resource that is used to register and unregister the necessary registry information for your *COcrProcessor* COM class. The DECLARE_REGISTRY_RESOURCEID macro takes this resource ID and expands to a function that updates the registry information associated with this class. This means that you don't have to write any specific registration and unregistration code for your class, since ATL completely generates all of this code for you. If you didn't use ATL, you would have to write this code by yourself, as discussed in Chapter 4. Even though the code to do this is brainless, it is very error-prone if you have to deal with the registration of many COM classes.

The last thing of significance in the class definition of *COcrProcessor* is *CComCoClass*. This class implements the default *IClassFactory* interface, which allows external clients to dynamically activate or create COM objects of this COM class. In essence, *CComCoClass* is the implementation for the class factory of this COM object, meaning that any object that needs to be externally and dynamically created must inherit from this template class (*CComCoClass*). The first parameter of *CComCoClass* is the name of the C++ class (COM class) you're implementing (i.e., *COcrProcessor*) and the second parameter is a pointer to the CLSID of the COM class, which is automatically generated by the ATL Object Wizard.

Looking at it from a general perspective, ATL implements all the default boilerplate code so that you don't have to—and this is the beauty of ATL. If you look at the generated and empty implementation of *OcrWholeImage*, you'll see that it looks like the following:

```
STDMETHODIMP
COcrProcessor::OcrWholeImage(VARIANT binaryImageArray, BSTR * pOcrText)
{
    // TODO:  Add your implementation code here
    return S_OK;
}
```

How much simpler could raw C++ COM implementation get? Just think how much code you have written so far. Then think how much free generated functionality has been provided. This is pretty much the ATL lifestyle. You concentrate on writing the code to support a system's business logic, not its underlying infrastructure.

# Common Responsibilities

The code that the `ATL Object Wizard` generates includes empty method implementations for our supported interface, *IOcrProcessor*. It is our responsibility to fill
in the functionality for the generated, empty methods. Also, there are often times
when we want to add a new interface to our COM object. We will show these
common responsibilities in this section.

## Implementing Interface Methods

Your *IOcrProcessor* interface specifies a method called *OcrWholeImage*, which
we'll now implement. A client will pass in a `SAFEARRAY` of unsigned characters in
the first parameter of *OcrWholeImage*. This is a `VARIANT` that represents an image
buffer passed into this function for OCR processing. Your job is to pull out this
binary buffer from the `SAFEARRAY` and perform the OCR processing. You then will
pass the OCR text back to the client via `pOcrText`, the second parameter of
*OcrWholeImage*. The implementation of *OcrWholeImage* is shown here:

```
STDMETHODIMP
COcrProcessor::OcrWholeImage(VARIANT binaryImageArray, BSTR * pOcrText)
{
    CComBSTR bstrOcrText;
    // Make sure that the variant contains a SAFEARRAY of bytes
    if (binaryImageArray.vt == (VT_ARRAY|VT_UI1)) {
        SAFEARRAY *pArray = binaryImageArray.parray ;
        unsigned char *pRawData;
        HRESULT hr = SafeArrayAccessData(pArray, (void HUGEP**)&pRawData);
        unsigned long arraySize = pArray->rgsabound[0].cElements ;
        // Pull out the image buffer from the SAFEARRAY
        unsigned char *pImageData = new unsigned char[arraySize] ;
        memcpy(pImageData, pRawData, arraySize);
        SafeArrayUnaccessData(pArray);
        // Perform OCR Processing
        string strOcrText = ProcessImage(pImageData, arraySize);
        bstrOcrText.Append(strOcrText.data()) ;
        delete [] pImageData ;
    } else {
        // Invalid SAFEARRAY type. Return dummy text and an error message.
        // Assume that g_szFakeOcrText is global holding dummy text.
        bstrOcrText.Append(g_szFakeOcrText) ;
        bstrOcrText.Append("***Received VARIANT is not valid***") ;
    }

    *pOcrText = bstrOcrText.Copy();

    return S_OK;
}
```

You've learned how to use a `VARIANT` and a `SAFEARRAY` in Chapter 5, so we will
not repeat the discussion here. One thing you we have not seen is *CComBSTR*,
which is an ATL class that encapsulates a `BSTR` for easier `BSTR` management. If

you're not familiar with the C++ Standard Template Library (STL), then the *string* class is another thing that looks unfamiliar to you. Use this *string* class for easy string manipulation. In order to use STL, you need to include the correct header files and use the `std` namespace, as shown in the following lines:

```
#pragma warning(disable:4786)   // Disable long name warnings
#include <string>
using namespace std;
```

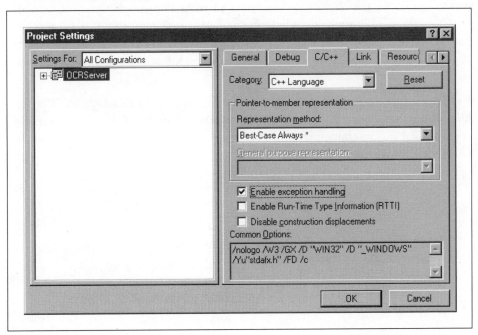

*Figure 6-7. The Project Settings dialog box*

Notice that STL uses C++ exceptions, so you should also turn on exception handling using the `Project Settings` dialog box, shown in Figure 6-7. You can get to this dialog box by selecting `Settings` from the `Project` menu or by simply pressing the `ALT-F7` accelerator. Check the `Enable exception handling` (GX option) when using STL.

In the *OcrWholeImage* method, you could use TCP/IP to communicate with a legacy OCR server for the OCR processing. If you wish, you could write your own OCR processor in this component, but since you're here to learn COM, we're not going to have you write a real OCR processor. Thus, you simply call a helper function, *ProcessImage*, to obtain some hard-coded text and pass this text back to the caller. You pass this OCR text back to the caller by allocating memory for the return `BSTR` because it's an [out] parameter. Since you're using *CComBSTR*, you can take advantage of its *Copy* method, which essentially performs the require allocation for us.

## Adding a Custom Interface

Even though it sounds like ATL saves the world, you would have to get used to ATL and its wizards. The wizards get you started, but you're on your own at times. For example, to add another interface definition into the generated IDL file at the time of this writing, you must do this by hand. This means that if you want your object to implement this new custom interface, you must add a COM_INTERFACE_ENTRY entry into the COM map and also provide implementations for all supported methods of the newly added interface. This isn't hard to do, but it requires that you have a basic understanding of the major ATL classes and macros, which were described earlier. Like everything else, this knowledge is gained through practice.

For learning purposes, let's add another interface into your COM object. The first thing you must do is modify the IDL file to add the new interface. For example, let's add an *ISpell* interface into the *COcrProcessor* object. The relevant part of the IDL file is shown here:

```
struct PossibleWords {
    wchar_t wszOne[16];
    wchar_t wszTwo[16];
};


[object, uuid(00000002-AAAA-11D1-8753-006008CDD9AE)]
interface ISpell : IUnknown
{
    HRESULT Check([in, string] wchar_t * pwszWord,
                  [out] struct PossibleWords *pWords);
}

[uuid(00000001-BBBB-11D1-8753-006008CDD9AE)]
coclass OcrProcessor {
    [default] interface IOcrProcessor;
    interface ISpell;
};
```

By now, the MIDL script shown is fairly obvious. PossibleWords is a structure that is used as a parameter of the *Check* method, which is declared within the *ISpell* interface. *ISpell* is a custom interface, because it derives directly from *IUnknown*. Since you want to expose type information for this interface, you add the *ISpell* interface inside the coclass definition, which is enclosed within the library block that causes the generation of a type library. One thing you should note is that the *ISpell* interface, being a custom interface, does not support *IDispatch* method invocations, which means that an environment like VBScript will not be able to use the *ISpell* interface.

To actually implement this interface, *COcrProcessor* must inherit the *ISpell* interface, as shown in the following class definition:

```
class COcrProcessor :
  public CComObjectRootEx<CComSingleThreadModel>,
  public CComCoClass<COcrProcessor, &CLSID_OcrProcessor>,
  public IDispatchImpl<IOcrProcessor, &IID_IOcrProcessor, &LIBID_ OCRSERVERLib>,
  public ISpell
{
public:
  COcrProcessor() {}

DECLARE_REGISTRY_RESOURCEID(IDR_OCRPROCESSOR)

BEGIN_COM_MAP(COcrProcessor)
  COM_INTERFACE_ENTRY(IOcrProcessor)
  COM_INTERFACE_ENTRY(IDispatch)
  COM_INTERFACE_ENTRY(ISpell)
END_COM_MAP()

// IOcrProcessor
public:
  STDMETHOD(OcrWholeImage)(/*[in]*/ VARIANT binaryImageArray,
                           /*[out, retval]*/ BSTR *pOcrText);

// ISpell
public:
  STDMETHOD(Check)(/*[in, string]*/ wchar_t * pwszWord,
                   /*[out]*/ struct PossibleWords *pWords);
};
```

In addition, you need to add a COM_INTERFACE_ENTRY entry that represents the *ISpell* interface into the COM map of the *COcrProcessor* C++ class. You must do this to support the *QueryInterface* method for the *IUnknown* implementation of *COcrProcessor*. Declare all interface methods of the newly added interface in the class definition of your COM object and implement them, as shown here:

```
STDMETHODIMP
COcrProcessor::Check(wchar_t * pwszWord, struct PossibleWords *pWords)
{
  wcscpy(reinterpret_cast<wchar_t *>(pWords->wszOne), OLESTR("ChoiceOne"));
  wcscpy(reinterpret_cast<wchar_t *>(pWords->wszTwo), OLESTR("ChoiceTwo"));

  return S_OK;
}
```

To sum up, adding a custom interface is simple. Just follow these steps:

1. Specify or include the custom interface into the IDL file.

2. Add the interface to the body of the associated coclass in the IDL file.

3. Inherit from the custom interface.

4. Add a COM_INTERFACE_ENTRY entry for the custom interface into the COM map.

5. Declare all methods specified by the custom interface.

6. Implement all methods specified by the custom interface.

## Adding Another Dual Interface

Adding a second dual interface is a bit trickier, so let's look at an example of adding a second dual interface to the *COcrProcessor* C++ class. First, you need to add
the dual interface definition to the IDL file. You'll add a very simple dual interface, *IDispSpell*, into the IDL file for this illustration. Following are the relevant
changes to the IDL file that defines this second dual interface. Notice that
*IDispSpell* is a dual interface as indicated by the [dual] attribute and the
*IDispatch* derivation. Also, place *IDispSpell* inside the OcrProcessor coclass to
indicate that instances of this COM class supports the *IDispSpell* interface.

```
[object, dual, uuid(00000003-AAAA-11D1-8753-006008CDD9AE)]
interface IDispSpell : IDispatch
{
    [id(1)] HRESULT Check();
}


[uuid(00000001-BBBB-11D1-8753-006008CDD9AE)]
coclass OcrProcessor {
    [default] interface IOcrProcessor;
    interface IDispSpell;
    interface ISpell;
};
```

We need to do a number of things in order to add the *IDispSpell* interface to our
*COcrProcessor* C++ class. To implement a dual interface, we must use the
*IDispatchImpl* class that provides the default *IDispatch* implementation. To get this
free *IDispatch* implementation, we simply inherit from *IDispatchImpl*, passing in
the dual interface type, its IID, and the LIBID that holds its type information. This
code is shown in the following modified *COcrProcessor* C++ class definition.

```
class COcrProcessor :
  public CComObjectRootEx<CComSingleThreadModel>,
  public CComCoClass<COcrProcessor, &CLSID_OcrProcessor>,
  public IDispatchImpl<IOcrProcessor, &IID_IOcrProcessor, &LIBID_ OCRSERVERLib>,
  public IDispatchImpl<IDispSpell, &IID_IDispSpell, &LIBID_OCRSERVERLib>,
  public ISpell
{
public:
            COcrProcessor() {}

DECLARE_REGISTRY_RESOURCEID(IDR_OCRPROCESSOR)
```

Notice from the earlier code that *COcrProcessor* is derived from the *IOcrProcessor*
interface and the *IDispSpell* interface. However, both *IOcrProcessor* and *IDispSpell*
are derived from *IDispatch*, meaning that there are two implementations of
*IDispatch*. This is also obvious because *COcrProcessor* inherits from *IDispatchImpl*

twice. We have one implementation that lives on the *IOcrProcessor* inheritance branch and one that lives on the *IDispSpell* inheritance branch. Looking at it from a different angle, we have two implementations of *IDispatch*, because we have two different dual interfaces, each of which derives from *IDispatch*. Since there are two implementations of *IDispatch*, which one should the compiler use? It would be ambiguous if we don't further qualify specifically the inheritance branch to take.

To disambiguate two branches of inheritance, ATL provides the COM_INTERFACE_ ENTRY2 macro, as oppose to the normal COM_INTERFACE_ENTRY macro. The COM_INTERFACE_ENTRY2 macro allows you to qualify specifically the name of the interface that is ambiguous as the first parameter. In the second parameter, you can specify the inheritance branch, using an interface name, to signify the implementation that you want to use.

For example, the COM_INTERFACE_ENTRY2(IDispatch, IOcrProcessor) entry, shown in the following code snippet, says that the *IDispatch* interface is ambiguous because it derives from at least two different inheritance branches. To resolve the ambiguity, we should use the *IDispatch* interface that is a base class of the *IOcrProcessor* interface. In other words, use the *IDispatch* that is associated with the *IOcrProcessor* inheritance branch. Once we have added the COM_INTERFACE_ ENTRY2 macro to resolve ambiguity, all *IDispatch* invocations will use the *IDispatch* implementation on the *IOcrProcessor* inheritance branch.

Other than this ambiguity, everything else is the same. Just add the corresponding COM map entry for the newly added dual interface and implement all the methods of that interface, as shown in the snippet here:

```
BEGIN_COM_MAP(COcrProcessor)
  COM_INTERFACE_ENTRY(IOcrProcessor)
  COM_INTERFACE_ENTRY2(IDispatch, IOcrProcessor)
  COM_INTERFACE_ENTRY(IDispSpell)
  COM_INTERFACE_ENTRY(ISpell)
END_COM_MAP()

// IOcrProcessor
public:
  STDMETHOD(OcrWholeImage)(/*[in]*/ VARIANT binaryImageArray,
                           /*[out, retval]*/ BSTR *pOcrText);
// ISpell
public:
  STDMETHOD(Check)(/*[in, string]*/ wchar_t * pwszWord,
                   /*[out]*/ struct PossibleWords *pWords);
// IDispSpell
public:
  STDMETHOD(Check)() { return S_OK; }
};
```

In essence, the COM_INTERFACE_ENTRY2 macro allows you to resolve ambiguity. We learn this method because there are often times when we must resolve this kind of ambiguity. This problem is not specific to dual interfaces or dispatch interfaces, but it also applies to other types of interfaces. In fact, it is a classic problem dealing with multiple inheritance in C++, thus implying that we can run into the same problem with a custom interface. For example, interface *A* and *B* are both custom interfaces that are derived from *BASE*. Further, *MyComObject* multiply inherits from interface *A* and *B*. In this case, *MyComObject* can use the implementation of *BASE* on either the *A* or *B* inheritance branch. In pure C++, we use casting operators to signify the inheritance branch that we want to take. When we develop COM objects using ATL, we simply signal this fact by using the `COM_INTERFACE_ENTRY2` macro.

## *Finishing Up*

We are now ready to wrap up our `OCRServer` component, but here are the last few steps required before a client can use this NT service:

1. Build the component.

2. Build the proxy/stub DLL using the *nmake.exe* utility.

3. Register the proxy/stub DLL using *regsvr32.exe*.

4. Register the service using the `-service` option.

5. Optionally configure security as needed using the *dcomcnfg.exe* utility.

6. Start the service using the *net.exe* utility or using the `Services` applet in the `Control Panel`.

Recall that the proxy/stub `makefile` is generated by the `ATL COM AppWizard`. This `makefile` is named *ProjectName*ps.mk. In our case, our file is particularly named *OCRServerps.mk*. You can run this make file through the *nmake.exe* utility to create this DLL, as follows:

*nmake -f OCRServerps.mk*

Alternatively, you can add this as a custom build step under your project settings. The `Project Settings` dialog, which can be launched by selecting `Settings` under the `Project` menu, has a `Post-build step` property page that allows you to add this custom build step.

Whichever way you choose to build this DLL, its purpose is to marshal custom interfaces between the component and its remote clients. This DLL contains all the marshaling intelligence between the object and its clients. Notice that you have not written (and you'll never have to write) a single line of marshaling code when using standard marshaling, since the interface proxy and stub are automatically generated based on the IDL file.

Technically, if we support only dual interfaces in our object, we will not need this proxy/stub DLL. This is possible because dual interfaces must use Automation compatible types—and marshaling Automation compatible types is an expertise of the Automation marshaler. Thus, we don't need our own proxy/stub DLL because the operating system-provided Automation marshaler will handle the marshaling for us. Of course, we have to add the appropriate registry entries for this to happen. Refer back to Chapter 5 if you need more information on Automation marshaling.

However, if we have a custom interface, we must provide this proxy/stub DLL because it provides the marshaling code needed to marshal the custom interface. In this case, both the client and server machine will need to register this proxy/stub DLL using the *regsvr32.exe* utility. If you want to eliminate this administrative task, you can merge the proxy/stub code into the client component—and maybe even the server component. You will learn several techniques for doing this in Chapters 8, 9, and 10.

Since our component is an NT service, we need to register/install it in a special way. At the command prompt, you should type the following:

*OCRServer -service*

The `ATL COM AppWizard` has generated code that will detect the `-service` command-line option. NT services support the `-service` command-line option to allow an administrator to install and configure them. When you execute `OCRServer` using this option, it will install and register itself as an NT service and as a COM component.

Having done this, you may start the service using the `Services` applet found in the `Control Panel`. Alternatively, you can start the service using the following command:

*net start OCRServer*

Similarly, you can stop the service using the `Services` applet or with the following command:

*net stop OCRServer*

To make debugging easier, you may prevent a component from running as an NT service. If this is what you want, don't install the component as an NT service. This means that you should not execute `OCRServer` using the `-service` command-line option, but simply register the component as a normal COM component using the `-RegServer` command-line option:

*OCRServer -RegServer*

In short, creating components using ATL is simple as most of the boilerplate code is either generated or previously implemented in the base ATL template classes. If you create components in C++, it is wise to use ATL because of the many freebies that are being offered.

This chapter hit the highlights of COM programming using ATL. In the next chapter, you'll build a client to talk to this distributed component. In particular, you'll make use of the *IOcrProcessor* and *ISpell* interfaces exposed by the *COcrProcessor* COM object hosted by the OCRServer component. You'll learn several different ways to make use of the services exposed by a distributed component.

# 7

# *Using COM Objects*

You built an **OCRServer** component in the last chapter, but you have not built a client to use the *IOcrProcessor* and *ISpell* interfaces exposed by **OCRServer**'s COM object. In this chapter, we'll discuss several techniques for using the services exposed by a distributed component. Specifically, we will discuss four different communication techniques to use with distributed components using C++. These techniques, for lack of better terms, include:

- The *COleDispatchDriver* technique

- The **#import** technique

- The manual technique

- The reusable technique

These techniques can be used to take advantage of the functionality exposed by typical distributed components. There are advantages and disadvantages in each of these methods, and we'll explore them along the way.

In this chapter, we will build a simple MFC client that will use the published services of the **OCRServer** component developed in the previous chapter. Before you begin, you must register **OCRServer** either as a service or as a local server on your machine, which requires that you have administrator privileges to the machine that houses **OCRServer**. You must perform this registration because COM looks in the registry for information regarding this component; see the end of the previous chapter for details on registering this component.

## *Simple Client*

Before we can discuss the different techniques for using distributed components, we need to create a simple client application, which will be a new project that

259

we'll name OCRClient. To keep things simple, we'll use MFC to create a simple dialog application. Follow these directions:

1. To create a new project, launch the New dialog box by selecting New from the File menu.

2. Choose the preferred location for the project and type OCRClient in the project edit-box.

3. Select MFC AppWizard(exe) and click OK to proceed, and you'll see the MFC AppWizard - Step 1 dialog box.

4. Choose Dialog based as the type of application, so that the MFC AppWizard will generate the code necessary for a dialog application for you.

5. Click Finish and the MFC AppWizard will generate the skeleton of a dialog application.

The code generated for this application is straightforward and won't be explained in this book. In brief, the generated *COCRClientApp* class models our simple application. When the application starts, it creates a dialog box and displays it until a user dismisses it, at which time the application ends. This dialog is represented by the *COCRClientDlg* class, which is generated by the MFC AppWizard when you create a dialog application. A dialog application is driven by the single *InitInstance* function of the generated *COCRClientApp* class.

```
BOOL COCRClientApp::InitInstance()
{
    . . .
    COCRClientDlg dlg;
    m_pMainWnd = &dlg;
    int nResponse = dlg.DoModal();
    . . .
}
```

As you can see from the generated code snippet, the *InitInstance* function first creates an instance of the dialog, sets the dialog as the main application window, and then shows the dialog by calling *DoModal*. When a user closes the dialog box, the *DoModal* call returns and thus ends the execution of our application.

## Initializing and Uninitializing COM

Once the MFC AppWizard has generated the code for your application, you need to fill in the functionality for being a COM client. Since you intend to use COM in this application, you first need to initialize the COM library, which can be done in several ways. You can initialize COM using *AfxOleInit*, *OleInitialize*, or *CoInitialize[Ex]* functions, and you can uninitialize COM using *AfxOleTerm*, *OleUninitialize*, or *CoUninitialize*. For your information, the *Afx-* versions call the *Ole-* versions and the *Ole-* versions call the *Co-* versions. You would only need to call the *Ole-* versions if you are using object linking and embedding (OLE) functionality such as the clipboard, drag and drop, and in-place activation. If you only need simple COM support, the *Co-* versions, as you have been using in the previous chapters, will suffice. However, you must use the *Afx-* versions when building MFC applications that make use of OLE functionality.

Since we're using MFC, we will use the *Afx-* versions, just in case we want to use other object linking and embedding functionality later on. Because everything happens in the *InitInstance* function of *COCRClientApp*, we'll call *AfxOleInit* in the beginning of the *InitInstance* function, and we'll call *AfxOleTerm* at the end of the *InitInstance* function, as exhibited by following the code snippet:

```
BOOL COCRClientApp::InitInstance()
{
    AfxOleInit();
    . . .
    COCRClientDlg dlg;
    m_pMainWnd = &dlg;
    int nResponse = dlg.DoModal();
    . . .
    AfxOleTerm();
    . . .
}
```

You must initialize the COM library or the `OCRClient` application will not be able to talk to `OCRServer`. The thread that calls *AfxOleInit* will eventually call *CoInitialize* to initialize COM and enter an STA, which indicates that this client application uses the STA model.

## Creating the User Interface

Having handled the preliminary requirement to be a COM client, let's now create the user interface for our client. If you look in `ResourceView`, you will see that the `MFC AppWizard` has generated a dialog template resource named `IDD_OCRCLIENT_DIALOG`. You would want to add controls to this dialog box to create a simple user interface. The resulting dialog box that you create should look something like the one shown in Figure 7-1.

As you can see from Figure 7-1, we need to add a few user interface elements to this dialog. We need an edit control for a `ServerName`, which will allow a user to type in the host destination of the machine on which `OCRServer` executes. Likewise, we need an edit control for an `ImageFileLocation`, which will allow a user to enter a file name of the TIFF image that is to be OCR processed by `OCRServer`. We also need a multiline edit control to store the OCR text after OCR processing. In addition, we need four buttons, each representing a technique to use the `OCRServer`'s services. Finally, we need a button to exit the application.

After painting the user interface for our client application, we need to add three *CString* member variables and bind them to the `ServerName`,

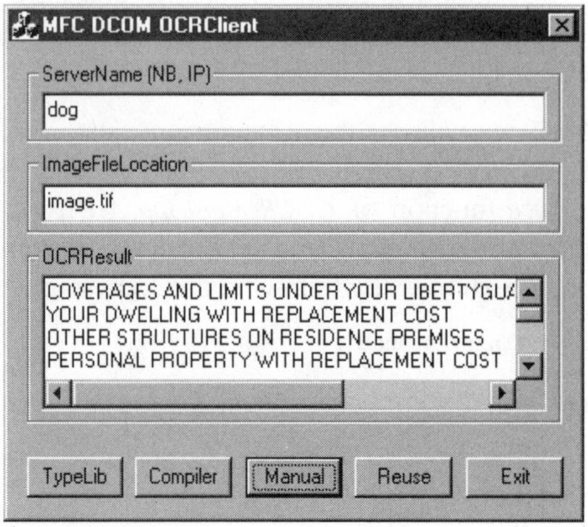

*Figure 7-1. The OCRClient application's user interface*

**ImageFileLocation**, and **OCRResult** edit controls. One way to bind controls to member variables is to simultaneously press the **CTRL** key while double-clicking the control. For example, if you do this on the **ServerName** edit control, you will see the **Add Member Variable** dialog box, which is shown in Figure 7-2.

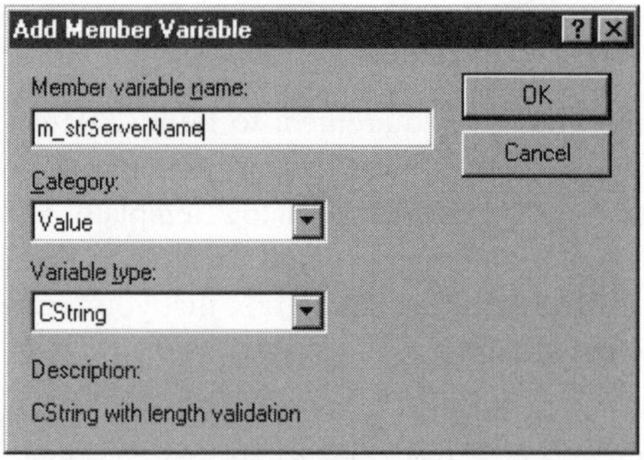

*Figure 7-2. Binding member variables to controls*

Since we want to keep a *CString* member variable for each control, take the defaults shown in **Category** and **Variable type**. Type in a member variable that corresponds to the selected control and click **OK** to proceed. Do this for all the edit controls on the dialog. You should name these variables **m_strServerName**, **m_strImageFileLocation**, and **m_strOCRResults**, respectively.

At this point, you should have painted the user interface for this application and bounded each edit control to an associated member variable of *COCRClientDlg*. Now is a good time to compile and run the application to make sure everything works.

The next thing to do is to fill in the functionality for each of the pushbuttons that appears on the dialog template (the buttons at the bottom of Figure 7-1). In particular, implement handler functions for all buttons, except the trivial **Exit** button. Each of the first four buttons represents a technique that we can use to talk to typical distributed components in cyberspace. For illustration purposes, we will talk to the **OCRServer** component, developed in the previous chapter, using these four techniques.

Table 7-1 captures the similarities and differences between the four techniques that we're about to discuss. You can see that the advantages and disadvantages of each technique really depend upon your needs and preferences. As Table 7-1 shows, some techniques are easier to use than others because C++ wrapper classes for COM interfaces can be generated from a type library. However, the flexibility of these techniques are minimized because the functionality has been encapsulated and usually cannot be further modified. On the other hand, the more flexible techniques are harder to use.

*Table 7-1. Similarities and Differences Among the Four Techniques for Using COM Objects*

| Technique | Easy to Use? | Flexibility | Code Generation? |
|---|---|---|---|
| COle-Dispatch-Driver | Yes. Generated C++ class to represent an *IDispatch*-based interface. However, you must perform initialization and clean up. | Low. For example, the remote server name is statically configured. Also, it works only with *IDispatch*-based interfaces. | Yes. C++ wrapper classes for interfaces can be generated from a type library. A type library must be available. |
| #import | Yes. Generated C++ class represents any COM interface. | Low. For example, the remote server name is statically configured. | Yes. Wrapper classes for interfaces can be generated from a type library. A type library must be available. Smart pointers are also generated. |
| Manual | No. Straight API. Must remember to balance *AddRef* and *Release* calls. | High. For example, the remote server name can be dynamically specified. Query is possible for multiple interfaces upon object activation. | No. A header file that defines the binary layout of the required interface is needed. This file is typically generated by the MIDL compiler. |

*Table 7-1. Similarities and Differences Among*
*the Four Techniques for Using COM Objects (continued)*

| Technique | Easy to Use? | Flexibility | Code Generation? |
|---|---|---|---|
| Reusable | Yes. C++ template class can be used to create different smart interface pointers. | Moderate. For example, the remote server name can be dynamically specified, but query is possible for only one interface upon object activation. | No. A header file that defines the binary layout of the required interface is needed. This is a hybrid between the #import and manual techniques. Although no code is generated, a C++ template class can be easily reused. |

Having seen Table 7-1, let's learn how to use each of these four techniques.

# The COleDispatchDriver Technique

Now that we have the user interface for the OCRClient application, let's learn the first technique to communicate with a distributed component: the *COleDispatchDriver* technique. This technique maps to the **TypeLib** button of the OCRClient dialog application.

Before we start, let's first say a few things to recap what we know about type libraries. A type library is a binary file that contains detailed type information of COM classes that are supported by a piece of deployable code called a component. A type library is not a component; it simply contains metadata for interfaces and objects within a component. Although not a component, a type library can be bounded into a component similar to the way a resource can be bounded, so don't be surprised to see type information in a DLL, an OCX, or an EXE.

Type libraries are built from IDL files by using the **library** keyword. A type library typically contains, in a nutshell, a library that includes a number of COM classes, each of which may support a number of COM interfaces. In turn, each of these interfaces may have a number of properties and methods. The library, classes, and interfaces are all unique, because they are all tagged with a GUID.

Since type libraries store detailed type information for COM components, a simple tool can easily use type libraries to dynamically discover the definitions for all supported objects and interfaces. The **MFC ClassWizard**, which is an integrated part of Visual C++, is capable of reading a type library and reverse engineering type information. This type information is used to generate C++ wrapper classes that can be used by client applications to communicate with a remote COM object's exposed services. We'll learn how to take advantage of this technique in the next section.

## Creating an Interface Wrapper Class

Our immediate goal is to create a C++ wrapper class for the OCRServer's *IOcrProcessor* interface. Using the MFC ClassWizard, you can select a type library and ask the MFC ClassWizard to generate the appropriate interface wrapper classes. You can launch the MFC ClassWizard by pressing the CTRL-W accelerator key. To the MFC ClassWizard's top right corner, there is a button that is labeled Add Class. Click this button and choose From a type library. Once you do this, browse and choose the OCRServer type library in the Import from Type Library dialog. Recall from the last chapter that the generated OCRServer type library has the name *OCRServer.tlb*. Click the Open button on the Import from Type Library dialog box to select the *OCRServer.tlb* file.

A type library allows tools to easily obtain type information for the associated component, an ability that allows for broader interoperability among components. Usually, a component is shipped with an associated type library, normally a file with a TLB extension. However, it is important to note that sometimes type information is linked directly into an executable or a dynamically linked file, so files with extensions such as OCX, DLL, OLB, TLB, and EXE are all candidates that can carry with them the type information of their supported objects. This is very valuable because you can obtain type information from EXEs or DLLs that have linked in COM type information. A facility like this makes it a cinch to integrate your application with a third party component. So, if you sell EXEs and DLLs that support COM interfaces, you should ship along your type libraries to improve the lives of your integrators (customers).

After you've selected the type library file, the Confirm Classes dialog box appears, as shown in Figure 7-3. Here, you may choose an interface or a number of interfaces exposed by OCRServer. Recall that the OCRServer component, developed in the last chapter, supports two dispatch interfaces: *IOcrProcessor* and *IDispSpell*. Only the interfaces that support *IDispatch* will be shown here. The reason for this limitation is that the generated wrapper class is derived from *COleDispatchDriver* and the *COleDispatchDriver* class, which is a part of MFC, works only with *IDispatch* interfaces (i.e., interfaces that are directly or indirectly derived from *IDispatch*).

In the Confirm Classes dialog box, choose the *IOcrProcessor* interface since that's the interface you want to use. Change the class name to *IOcrProcessorWrapper*. You're doing this to prevent a future name clash, as you'll use the actual *IOcrProcessor* definition in the manual technique discussed later on in this chapter. For now, take the rest of the values as defaults and click OK on the Confirm Classes dialog box to proceed.

As soon as you do this, a new C++ interface wrapper class is generated to support communication with the *IOcrProcessor* interface. This interface is exposed by the

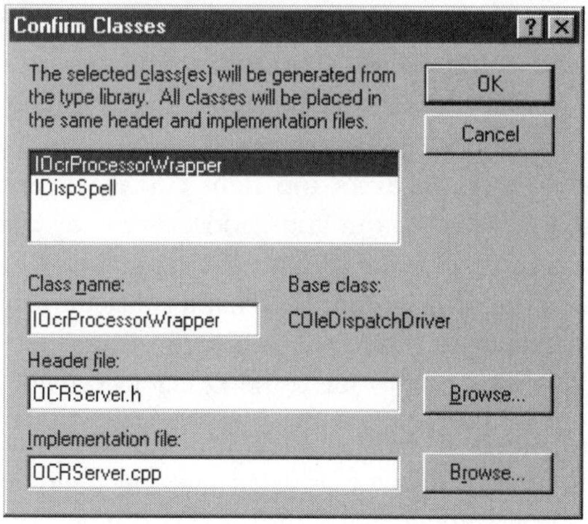

*Figure 7-3. A C++ wrapper class will be generated for each selected interface*

OcrProcessor COM objects that are active inside an OCRServer component at runtime. If you look in ClassView, you will see the newly added C++ class, *IOcrProcessorWrapper*, which is a local wrapper class that allows you to communicate with your remote OCRServer via its *IOcrProcessor* interface. To prevent confusion, let's emphasize that this is just a wrapper class that allows a simple way to use a remote *IDispatch* interface; it is not a proxy or an interface proxy. The code for the interface proxy lives in the proxy/stub DLL.

## *The COleDispatchDriver Class*

Since our generated wrapper class is derived from *COleDispatchDriver*, let's briefly examine the *COleDispatchDriver* class. *COleDispatchDriver* is an MFC class that encapsulates an *IDispatch* interface and internally performs method invocations using *IDispatch::Invoke*. This is great because calling *IDispatch::Invoke* is very tedious in C++. You won't have to deal with this tedium because the generated wrapper class includes implementation for all methods of the associated COM interface. For example, the following method is generated by the MFC ClassWizard for the *OcrWholeImage* method of OCRServer's *IOcrProcessor* interface:

```
CString IOcrProcessorWrapper::OcrWholeImage(const VARIANT& binaryImageArray)
{
  CString result;
  static BYTE parms[] = VTS_VARIANT;
  InvokeHelper(0x1, DISPATCH_METHOD, VT_BSTR,
               (void*)&result, parms, &binaryImageArray);
  return result;
}
```

This method is just a simple client-side wrapper that delegates the method invocation to the target *OcrWholeImage* method implemented by OCRServer's *IOcrProcessor* interface. Recall that the original *OcrWholeImage* method in the *IOcrProcessor* interface has two parameters: an [in] VARIANT and an [out, retval] BSTR. In the generated wrapper method shown earlier, note that the MFC ClassWizard converts the [out, retval] BSTR parameter into a comparable return type, which is shown in this method as an MFC *CString*.

In addition, this wrapper method simply calls the *InvokeHelper* member function implemented by the base class, *COleDispatchDriver*. As noted, *InvokeHelper* in turn gathers the necessary information and calls *IDispatch::Invoke* to use the correct dispid. The dispid for each method or property of a dispatch interface is obtained from the type library during the code generation of the wrapper class. The MFC ClassWizard automatically adds the appropriate dispid into each generated *InvokeHelper* invocation, so you don't have to manually use a dispid to invoke each of these generated methods.

Also in the earlier generated code, the *OcrWholeImage* wrapper method corresponds to dispid 0x1. This value is obtained from the type library and is added to the generated *OcrWholeImage* wrapper method during code generation. This dispid value is shown as the first parameter in the call to *InvokeHelper*. Given all that is generated, all that you would have to do is call the wrapper methods and COM will ensure that the real method, which can be miles away, will be invoked. Beside *InvokeHelper*, other methods of *COleDispatchDriver* that are important to a developer are shown in the shortened class definition for *COleDispatchDriver*, as exhibited here:

```
class COleDispatchDriver {
public:
  LPDISPATCH m_lpDispatch;
  BOOL CreateDispatch(REFCLSID clsid, COleException* pError = NULL);
  BOOL CreateDispatch(LPCTSTR lpszProgID, COleException* pError = NULL);
  void AttachDispatch(LPDISPATCH lpDispatch, BOOL bAutoRelease = TRUE);
  LPDISPATCH DetachDispatch();
  void ReleaseDispatch();
  . . .
};
```

As you can see, a *COleDispatchDriver* object keeps a pointer to its associated dispatch interface, m_lpDispatch. There are two overloaded member functions (both named *CreateDispatch*) that allow us to connect to a dispatch interface. One of these functions lets us do this using an associated CLSID and the other lets us do this using the associated ProgID. The *AttachDispatch* function let's us attach to a valid dispatch interface, and the *DetachDispatch* let's us detach from an attached dispatch interface. The *ReleaseDispatch* function allows us to detach from the attached dispatch interface and also release it. We will use these member functions shortly.

## Using COM Interfaces with Generated Wrappers

Knowing enough about the *COleDispatchDriver* class, let's use the generated *IOcrProcessorWrapper* class to communicate with OCRServer. First, you must add a handler for the TypeLib button. One way to do this is to use the MFC ClassWizard, shown in Figure 7-4. In the MFC ClassWizard dialog box, high-light the ID_TYPE_LIB object ID. Double-click on BN_CLICK in the Messages list-box and click OK on the Add Member Function dialog box. You can then choose Edit Code to edit the empty *OnTypeLib* handler just generated by the MFC ClassWizard.

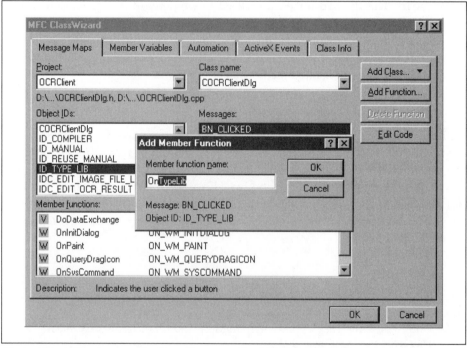

*Figure 7-4. Adding a command handler using the MFC ClassWizard*

In this handler, you will add the code needed to use OCRServer's *IOcrProcessor* interface. You need to do the following for the *OnTypeLib* function:

1. Create an instance of this interface wrapper class.

2. Initialize the dispatch interface by calling *CreateDispatch*, passing in a program or class identifier.

3. Use OCRServer's services by calling methods via this interface wrapper.

4. Clean up the dispatch interface by calling *ReleaseDispatch*.

The code for these four steps is shown in the following snippet. Of course, remember to include the header file for the wrapper class or the code will fail compilation.

```
//*********************************************************************
//*********************************************************************
//**   The COleDispatchDriver Technique
//*********************************************************************
//*********************************************************************
#include "ocrserver.h"  // Contains IOcrProcessorWrapper definition.
void COCRClientDlg::OnTypeLib()
{
    CWaitCursor wait ;
    // Update the member variables
    UpdateData(TRUE) ;
    // Create the safe array to transfer the binary data
    BinaryData binaryImageArray(m_strImageFileLocation) ;
    // Use the IOcrProcessor interface
    IOcrProcessorWrapper OcrInterface;
    COleException except;
    if (!OcrInterface.CreateDispatch("OCRServer.OcrProcessor.1", &except)) {
        except.ReportError() ;
        return ;
    }
    // Call interface methods through this wrapper object
    CString strResult =
        OcrInterface.OcrWholeImage(binaryImageArray.SafeArrayVariant());
    // Done using the interface, so release it
    OcrInterface.ReleaseDispatch();
    // Update the GUI
    m_strOCRResults = strResult ;
    UpdateData(FALSE) ;
}
```

The *OnTypeLib* function shown is fairly straightforward. You instantiate an *IOcrProcessorWrapper* C++ class (which encapsulates the *IDispatch* portion of the *IOcrProcessor* dual interface), call *CreateDispatch* to connect to the *IDispatch* interface implemented by a COM object within the **OCRServer** component, call *OcrWholeImage* for OCR processing, and finally call *ReleaseDispatch* to release the interface.

In the call to *CreateDispatch*, pass along a pointer to a *COleException* so that you can capture an exception when the call fails. The *COleException* class is an MFC class that converts an **HRESULT** into a readable error string, which you can display using the *ReportError* method of *COleException*.

Also, notice that you pass a human readable name, or a programmatic identifier (ProgID), in as the first parameter of *CreateDispatch*. A typical COM server that supports the use of a ProgID would save the ProgID under [HKCR\\*ProgID*]. The ProgID value has a standard format as shown:

```
<Vendor>.<Component>.<Version>
```

For the `OcrProcessor` COM class that you developed in the previous chapter, the server automatically registers the following ProgID entries:

```
[HKEY_CLASSES_ROOT\OCRServer.OcrProcessor]
@="OcrProcessor Class"
[HKEY_CLASSES_ROOT\OCRServer.OcrProcessor\CurVer]
@="OCRServer.OcrProcessor.1"
```

The four lines of registry entries indicate the version independent programmatic identifier, `OCRServer.OcrProcessor`. The first two lines record the general vendor/component information and the second two lines say that the current version of this COM class is `OCRServer.OcrProcessor.1`. The component built in the last chapter also registers another key, as shown here:

```
[HKEY_CLASSES_ROOT\OCRServer.OcrProcessor.1]
@="OcrProcessor Class"
```

This key contains a subkey that points to the target CLSID associated with this ProgID, as shown in the following two lines:

```
[HKEY_CLASSES_ROOT\OCRServer.OcrProcessor.1\CLSID]
@="{59BC2F74-EE1A-11D1-8753-006008CDD9AE}"
```

So given a particular ProgID, by following these registry entries, COM can get the CLSID for the COM class that you want to use. Of course, this is possible only if the registry entries shown earlier are correctly configured. It seems tedious to configure these required registry entries prior to using ProgIDs, but ProgIDs are easy to use programmatically, because remembering a name is easier than remembering a 128-bit number. On the flip side, you have to keep in mind that ProgIDs are not guaranteed to be unique like CLSIDs.

Having gone over this topic, we should note that there is an overloaded *CreateDispatch* member function of the *COleDispatchDriver* class that takes a CLSID as the first parameter. Thus, instead of passing a ProgID into the first parameter to *CreateDispatch*, we could have used the CLSID of the `OcrProcessor` COM class.

One thing that seems like magic in our *OnTypeLib* function is the *BinaryData* stuff, which needs some further discussion. *BinaryData* is a class that we implement to reduce the pain of managing a `VARIANT` containing a `SAFEARRAY`. We know how to manipulate such a `VARIANT`, so we will encapsulate that dirty code inside a C++ class, which will remove many lines of code, making the code in our handler easier to read.

Since we are using a `SAFEARRAY` to pass binary data to `OCRServer`, we need to manipulate this array correctly. We store it in the `VARIANT` that is passed to `OCRServer`. The code to manipulate the `SAFEARRAY` is located in several private member functions of the *BinaryData* class, which encapsulates a `VARIANT` containing a `SAFEARRAY`. This class allows clients to easily obtain a `VARIANT` containing a

SAFEARRAY of binary data (TIFF image, in this case). We will not delve into this topic, but we need to say enough so that we understand how the *BinaryData* object is used. The following is the class definition of this object:

```
class BinaryData {
public:
    BinaryData(const CString & strFileName);
    ~BinaryData();
    VARIANT & SafeArrayVariant() ;
private:
    BinaryData();
    BinaryData(const BinaryData & rhs);
    BinaryData &operator=(const BinaryData & rhs) ;
protected:
    unsigned char * LoadBinaryData(unsigned long & lSize);
    void ClearBinaryData(unsigned char *pData);
    SAFEARRAY *CreateBinaryDataArray(const unsigned char *pBinaryData,
        const unsigned long & lSize);
    void DestroyBinaryDataArray(SAFEARRAY *psa) ;
private:
    SAFEARRAY *m_pSafeArrayBuffer;
    VARIANT m_binaryImageArray ;
    CString m_strImageFileLocation ;
};
```

Client code (i.e., code that uses this C++ object) would instantiate *BinaryData* passing in a TIFF file name. To get a VARIANT containing a SAFEARRAY, the client would call the *SafeArrayVariant* member function, which returns a reference to such a VARIANT. Simple as that. The client needs to perform no clean up, since the destructor of this object handles that. It is up to you to implement this object, but, as an alternative, you may want to copy the code for this class since the source code is provided on the O'Reilly ftp site. However, if you have the urge to implement this object, here are short descriptions of the private utility functions to get you started:

*LoadBinaryData*
> Loads an image from a file into memory

*ClearBinaryData*
> Cleans up after *LoadBinaryData*

*CreateBinaryDataArray*
> Creates a SAFEARRAY of binary data for transmission to the server

*DestroyBinaryDataArray*
> Cleans up after *CreateBinaryDataArray*

Now that you understand the code in the OnTypeLib handler, let's build and execute the application. When the OCRClient application appears, enter a server destination and full path name of a TIFF image in the corresponding edit controls. Click the TypeLib button, and it will bring back some dummy OCR text for you. Notice that this will work only if you have registered the OCRServer component.

In addition, if `OCRServer` is located on a remote machine, you must use either *dcomcnfg.exe* or *oleview.exe* to configure COM security on the server machine to allow for appropriate launch and access permissions. You must also set the appropriate authentication levels on both the client and server machines. If you need more information regarding setting up COM security, see the last section of Chapter 5, *Infrastructure*.

You should notice that no matter what you type in the `ServerName` edit control field, `OCRClient` doesn't seem to obey; that is, it doesn't seem to contact the indicated machine. This can be regarded as a drawback of using the *COleDispatchDriver* technique. The server address, which can be configured using *dcomcnfg.exe* or *oleview.exe*, is statically obtained from the registry under the `RemoteServerName` named value of the application's associated `AppID` registry key.[*] Another disadvantage with this technique is that it works only with *IDispatch* interfaces, so you cannot use this technique for interfaces that are not based on *IDispatch*. However, the notable advantage of this technique is simplicity. All you have to do is pick an interface, ask the `MFC ClassWizard` to generate a C++ wrapper class for the target interface, and then simply use it.

# The #import Technique

In this section, we'll look at a different technique to communicate with `OCRServer`. In particular, we will use the `#import` technique to talk to distributed components. Visual C++ comes with a compiler directive, called `#import`, that works nicely with COM. Like the `MFC ClassWizard`, this directive reverse engineers the contents of a type library to create C++ representations of COM interfaces. You know how to add a handler for the `Compiler` button, so do that first and name the handler *OnCompiler*. In this handler, you will add code to use the *IOcrProcessor* interface with the `#import` technique.

## The #import Statement

To use this technique, simply import the appropriate type library into your header or implementation file. For example, to get C++ representations of all interfaces stored within the `OCRServer` type library, simply add the following lines to *OCRClientDlg.cpp* :

```
#import "..\OCRServer\OCRServer.tlb"
```

The `#import` directive tells the compiler to generate C++ wrapper code from the type information stored in the indicated type library. Since type information can

---

[*] Actually, with your knowledge of the activation API functions discussed in Chapter 4, *Components*, you can use *CoInitializeEx* and *COleDispatchDriver::AttachDispatch* to dynamically connect to a remote component, but we'll discuss *CoInitializeEx* separately in a moment, so let's ignore this workaround here.

reside in files with extensions such as TLB, EXE, OCX, and DLL, you can use the `#import` directive on all these file types, as long as they have COM type information built in. This directive is pretty nifty because it comes with a number of useful attributes. By default, the reverse engineered code is wrapped within a C++ namespace* whose name is derived from that of the selected type library; in our case, the namespace is `OCRSERVERLib`. If you don't like this name, you can use the `rename_namespace` attribute to modify it. For example, you can change the name of the default namespace to `OCRServerNS` as follows:

```
#import "..\OCRServer\OCRServer.tlb" rename_namespace("OCRServerNS")
```

However, if you totally want to do away with the generation of a namespace, you would use the `no_namespace` attribute, as shown here:

```
#import "..\OCRServer\OCRServer.tlb" no_namespace
```

The `no_namespace` attribute instructs the compiler to inhibit the generation of a namespace during reverse engineering.

Another attribute that is often used is the `rename` attribute, which allows you to basically do a global replace of a particular name. For example, the name for an interface method within the type library may be *OcrWholeImage*, but you may want to change it to *OcrImage*, perhaps because you want to type fewer characters. You can specify this as follows:

```
#import "..\OCRServer\OCRServer.tlb" rename("OcrWholeImage", "OcrImage")
```

A more common use of the `rename` attribute is to prevent a name collision with some other currently used name. The `rename` attribute is notably valuable in this regard.

## Using COM Interfaces with Smart Pointers

Adding the `#import` directive to your source file is the first step. In order to actually get C++ representations of type information stored in the type library, you must compile the source file that contains the `#import` directive. In your case, you must compile the *OCRClientDlg.cpp* file, since this file imports *OCRServer.tlb*. Assuming that you are working with a debug build, look into the `..\Debug` directory,† where you should find two files. One is named *OCRServer.tlh*, which is a header file that contains C++ type definition of the *IOcrProcessor* interface and its

---

* Namespace is a C++ feature that simply provides a standard way to reduce or prevent name collisions. For example, company A can name a function *Func* and company B can also name a different function *Func*. When you use the two libraries from the two companies within the same project, the names collide. In cases like this, company A can wrap their code with a namespace A and company B can wrap their code with a namespace B. If this is done, we can explicitly refer to the *Func* function in the appropriate namespace and the name collision is eliminated.

† It goes without saying that you should look in the `.\Release` directory if you're working with a release build.

methods. The other file is *OCRServer.tli*, which contains inline functions that serve as wrappers to the remote interface methods of *IOcrProcessor* implemented by the **OCRServer** component. If you view the *OCRServer.tlb* file, you will see the following line, which defines a smart pointer for the *IOcrProcessor* interface:

```
_COM_SMARTPTR_TYPEDEF(IOcrProcessor, _ _uuidof(IOcrProcessor));
```

The generated header file (*.tlb*) contains definitions that attach GUIDs to coclasses and interfaces. The `_ _uuidof` keyword, shown in the earlier code snippet, returns a GUID associated with the indicated interface or class symbolic name. In the earlier code snippet, this happens to be the *IOcrProcessor* interface. This `_ _uuidof` keyword is nice since it can obtain a GUID from many different inputs. For example, you can pass an interface type, a pointer to an interface type, or a reference to an interface type as an argument to `_ _uuidof`. In all three cases, you will get back the correct IID associated with the argument passed to `_ _uuidof`.

A smart pointer is a term used for a C++ object that encapsulates a pointer and handles all the resource management dirty work. Typically, a smart pointer object allocates resources during creation and automatically deallocates resources during destruction. The smart pointer that we are dealing with manages the release of an interface pointer when it goes out of scope, meaning that we don't have to remember to call *Release* to release a reference of a particular interface when we're done using it.

To create a smart pointer, take *IOcrProcessor* from the `_COM_SMARTPTR_TYPEDEF` definition and append a *Ptr*, resulting in *IOcrProcessorPtr*. This is the smart pointer representing the *IOcrProcessor* interface. Knowing this, you are ready to implement the handler for the **Compiler** button. As you can see in the following code snippet, using this smart pointer is simple. Instantiate the smart pointer, give it the ProgID (or class identifier) of your COM class, and call methods and properties via the smart pointer directly. You don't have to explicitly do any extra initialization and clean up, as you did with the previous technique.

```
//********************************************************************
//********************************************************************
//**  The #import Technique
//********************************************************************
//********************************************************************
#import "..\OCRServer\OCRServer.tlb"
void COCRClientDlg::OnCompiler()
{
    CWaitCursor wait ;
    UpdateData(TRUE) ;

    try {
        using namespace OCRSERVERLib ;
        IOcrProcessorPtr pInterface ;
        pInterface = IOcrProcessorPtr("OCRServer.OcrProcessor.1") ;
        BinaryData binaryImageArray(m_strImageFileLocation) ;
```

```
            _variant_t binArray(binaryImageArray.SafeArrayVariant());
            _bstr_t bstrResult = pInterface->OcrWholeImage(binArray);
            m_strOCRResults = (char*)bstrResult ;
        } catch (_com_error & error) {
            m_strOCRResults.Format(TEXT("%s[%x]"), error.ErrorMessage(),
            error. Error());
        }

        UpdateData(FALSE) ;
    }
```

You need the statement using namespace OCRSERVERLib, because the smart pointer and wrapper object are defined within the OCRSERVERLib namespace; you can verify this by looking at the generated *OCRServer.tlb* file. Recall that you can rename or totally remove this namespace using #import attributes, such as rename_namespace or no_namespace. Like the previous technique for using a remote interface, the generated *OcrWholeImage* wrapper function is mutated; specifically, the [out, retval] parameter has been made a return type.

As seen from the earlier code snippet, since you're using a smart pointer, you don't have to explicitly release the interface pointer when you're done using it. This is automatically done when the smart pointer object destroys itself.

Like the previous (*COleDispatchDriver*) technique, there is no way for you to specify the destination server programmatically with this technique. For instance, if you run OCRClient and specify a remote server name in the ServerName edit control, you'll realize that OCRClient doesn't contact your specified remote server. Instead, COM looks for the destination specified in the registry using the RemoteServerName named value of the application's associated AppID registry key. This is the exact drawback seen earlier in the *COleDispatchDriver* technique. However, this technique is in some respect superior to the previous one, because it allows you to generate C++ wrapper classes for not just *IDispatch*-based interfaces, but all COM interfaces described within a type library. It is actually even easier to use than the previous technique in that the smart pointer requires you to perform no clean up.

Refer back to the earlier code snippet and you'll realize that the error handling is very straightforward. Notice that you use standard C++ exception handling feature and the *_com_error* object that allows you to display the specific error message associated with an exception when you catch, or handle, the exception. Since you're using a smart pointer, you don't have to release the interface pointer, as this is automatically done for you by the smart pointer as soon as you fall off the try block. Because these features make exception handling much cleaner, we will delve a bit deeper into these topics.

# Native C++ Compiler Features

COM is so important that Microsoft provides several native compiler-level features especially for it, including a number of macros, global functions, and classes. Some of these classes include *_bstr_t* (which encapsulate a BSTR), *_variant_t* (which encapsulates a VARIANT), and *_com_ptr_t* (a smart pointer that encapsulates an interface pointer), which make their corresponding types much easier to use. The main reason for their ease of use is that these classes encapsulate the management of resource allocation and deallocation. In this section, we will focus on two features that makes client-side COM programming easier. We will talk first about smart pointers, and then we'll lead our ways into the realm of exception handling.

## More on smart pointers

We've touched the surface regarding smart pointers, but we've not described the hidden magic of the _COM_SMARTPTR_TYPEDEF macro. Recall that the #import directive generates statements such as the following:

```
COM_SMARTPTR_TYPEDEF(IOcrProcessor, _ _uuidof(IOcrProcessor));
```

We've said earlier that this statement defines a smart pointer for the *IOcrProcessor* interface, but we haven't justified this fact. So here's the magic. The _COM_ SMARTPTR_TYPEDEF macro actually expands into the following type definition:

```
typedef _com_ptr_t< _com_IIID<IOcrProcessor,
                    &(_ _uuidof(IOcrProcessor))> > IOcrProcessorPtr ;
```

The compiler supported type, *_com_ptr_t*, is a C++ class that represents a smart interface pointer. One of the basic features that this class takes into consideration is the management and automatic release of its associated interface pointer. To create a smart pointer for a particular interface type, you simply pass the interface type and its interface identifier into a special *_com_IIID* template class, which becomes an argument to *_com_ptr_t*. Given the above smart pointer, using the associated interface pointer is simple. We simply do the following to instantiate, activate, and use the smart pointer:

```
IOcrProcessorPtr pOcr;
pOcr = IOcrProcessorPtr(CLSID_OcrProcessor);
pOcr->OcrWholeImage(. . .);
```

In the code snippet, the first line simply instantiates a C++ object, which happens to be a smart pointer. The second line actually calls *CoCreateInstance* using the given CLSID and queries for the interface (*IOcrProcessor* in this case) pointer associated with the smart pointer; this association is established during smart pointer type definition. Notice that you don't have to release the interface pointer after you're done using it.

Because smart pointers are very useful, ATL provides several similar classes, such as *CComPtr* and *CComQIPtr*, that purport to solve the same problem. Let's briefly examine how to use these classes, as they're less cumbersome to define and instantiate than *_com_ptr_t*.

The *CComPtr* class is one of the base classes defined by the ATL class library. You can find this class in the base definitions of ATL (*atlbase.h*). *CComPtr* is a smart pointer class that automatically releases the interface pointer to which it refers. Here's how you would use this smart pointer. Simply instantiate the class by passing in the interface type as the template parameter, as shown in the bolded statement in the following snippet. When you do this, you're associating the smart pointer instance with the indicated interface type.

```
CCompPtr<IOcrProcessor> pOcr;
CoCreateInstance(CLSID_OcrProcessor, 0, CLSCTX_ALL,
                 IID_IOcrProcessor, (void**)&pOcr);
pOcr->OcrWholeImage(. . .);
```

In the code, notice that you don't have to release the interface pointer, since the smart pointer is responsible for this when it goes out of scope.

ATL also provides a another version of a smart pointer similar to *CComPtr*. This is the *CComQIPtr* template class, and as its name suggests, this smart pointer class differs from *CComPtr* in that it automatically does a *QueryInterface*. This implies that you need to pass along an existing and valid interface pointer during instantiation of this smart pointer class. During instantiation, you can tell it to query for another interface using the pointer. For example, you can give it an *IOcrProcessor* interface pointer and ask it to automatically query for an *ISpell* interface pointer for you. This is illustrated here:

```
CCompQIPtr<ISpell, &IID_ISpell> pSpell(pOcr);
pSpell->Check(. . .);
```

This code assumes that you have a valid pointer to an *IOcrProcessor* interface (shown here as pOcr). This valid pointer is passed to a constructor of *CComQIPtr*. The instantiated smart pointer object will then automatically query for the *ISpell* interface for you. Again, notice that you don't have to release the associated interface pointer, as the smart pointer object does this for you.

### Exception handling

Smart printers are nice because they automatically release their associated interface pointers. The automatic release of an interface pointer is important when you take exception handling into account. For example, if you don't use a smart pointer and an exception is thrown, you need to handle the exception and also release any held interface pointers. This means that you would have to declare the interface pointers so that they can be seen by the code that releases them. You can do this as follows:

```
extern IOcrProcessor *pOcr ; // Assume valid
ISpell *pSpell = NULL;
```

```
try {
    // Assume exception can be thrown anywhere within this block.
    // If you declare pSpell here, it may never be released.
    pOcr->QueryInterface(IID_ISpell, (void**)&pSpell);
    // Do whatever else we want.
} catch (...) {
    // Handle exception.
}
if (pSpell) pSpell->Release();
```

In the preceding code, you cannot declare the *ISpell* interface pointer within the **try** block, because there may be a possibility that it will never be released. This will be the case if an exception is thrown prior to releasing the *ISpell* interface within the **try** block. So to prevent such problems, you have to declare the *ISpell* interface at a scope where you can clean it up. The earlier code snippet is fine, but it makes programming a bit tedious, and it gets even worse if you have tons of conditional statements or iterative loops.

An arguably better and cleaner approach is to use a smart pointer. For example, you can rewrite the earlier code using a smart pointer as follows:

```
extern IOcrProcessor *pOcr ; // Assume valid
try {
    // Assume exception can be thrown anywhere within this block.
    CComQIPtr<ISpell, &IID_ISpell> pSpell(pOcr);
    // Do whatever else we want.
} catch (...) {
    // Handle exception.
}
```

Notice that we don't worry about releasing **pSpell**, as this will be automatically done for us when we exit the **try** block—no matter where the exception is raised within the **try** block. This is because the destructor of a C++ object is called automatically when the C++ object dies off. The destructor of a smart pointer class takes advantage of this default feature to clean up after itself.

Having somewhat justified the use of smart pointers, let's move forward with the native compiler support for COM exceptions. The awesome thing about the **#import** technique is that you can easily take advantage of C++ exception handling. This is made possible because the code generated by the **#import** directive converts an **HRESULT** into an exception for each method invocation, making our lives much simpler.

A notable class that makes error handling simpler is the *_com_error* class, which encapsulates a COM error (bad **HRESULT**) or an *IErrorInfo* interface. A single valuable member function that can save hours of debugging and tracking down problems associated with COM interface method invocations is *_com_ error::ErrorMessage*. This function returns a string telling you the exact error associated with the return status code of a COM method invocation. The *Error* method of *_com_error* returns the HRESULT associated with the error object. An abbreviated version of the *_com_error* class is shown here:

```
// Defined in comdef.h
class _com_error {
    . . .
    HRESULT Error() const throw();
    const TCHAR * ErrorMessage() const throw();
    . . .
};
```

To create a *_com_error* object, the code generated by the #import directive calls either of the following two special methods. These methods are supported by the Visual C++ compiler in support of COM development.

```
void _com_issue_error(HRESULT) throw(_com_error);
void _com_issue_errorex(HRESULT, IUnknown *, REFIID) throw(_com_error);
```

The *_com_issue_error* method allows the caller to construct a *_com_error* exception object associated with the given HRESULT and throw the exception back to the previous calling scope. For example, the code generated by the #import directive typically does the following in regards to generic error handling:

```
if (FAILED(_hr)) _com_issue_errorex(_hr, this, _ _uuidof(this));
```

This earlier code indicates that when we have a bad HRESULT, an exception object will be created from the HRESULT, the interface pointer, and the associated GUID. Once this exception is created, it will be thrown to the nearest exception handler. This means that we can use C++ try/catch clauses to easily handle COM errors. The code shown in the *OnCompiler* handler has a try block and a catch block as follows:

```
try {
    . . .
} catch (_com_error & error) {
    m_strOCRResults.Format("%s[%x]", error.ErrorMessage(), error.Error());
}
```

Within the try block, we can call as many methods as we want. And we don't even have to check the returned HRESULT after each and every single method invocation, which can end up with many nested if-else statements. If an invocation fails, an exception will be thrown by the #import generated wrappers and we can catch and handle the exception in a normal C++ catch block. This makes the code much cleaner and less error-prone.

# The Manual Technique

With the two previous techniques, your program has no way to control which machine OCRClient should talk to. Because there's no way to programmatically specify a server destination, COM looks into the registry to pull out a pre-configured server destination. The technique that we're about to discuss allows us to control which machine the `OCRClient` application should communicate with. To do this, we need to use one of the COM activation API functions discussed in Chapter 4. The first thing that you should do is to add a handler for the **Manual** button, because you will need to add code to this handler. We'll do that now, naming the handler *OnManual*.

## Remote Activation API Functions

COM publishes a number of activation API functions. The lowest API function is *CoGetClassObject*, which returns a requested class factory interface pointer for object creation. There are also the *CoGetInstanceFromFile* and *CoGetInstanceFromIStorage* API functions that activate an object and initialize it with persistent data.

However, the one that we often use is *CoCreateInstanceEx*, which allows us to pass along two important pieces of information. The first is the **COSERVERINFO** structure, which allows us to set security options and server destination. In this section, we will be simple and just set the server destination, as the security member of the **COSERVERINFO** structure is discussed in detail in Chapters 5 and 9. The second structure that you need to know is **MULTI_QI**, which allows you to pass in an interface identifier and get back a pointer to such interface, including a status code. The *CoCreateInstanceEx* API function accepts an array of **MULTI_QI** structures, allowing you to easily get 20 different interface pointers back at once and thus saving network round-trips as discussed in the Chapter 4.

## Using COM Interfaces Manually

You've have grown to know and love the *CoCreateInstanceEx* API function in Chapter 4. But since this chapter captures a variety of C++ techniques for using a distributed component, let's

capture a step-by-step usage of this technique. You'll also learn how to handle errors in a simpler manner than what you've been used to in Chapter 4.

In order to implement the *OnManual* handler, we must include the header file that contains the interface definition of *IOcrProcessor*, which we will utilize to perform OCR processing. Therefore, we should include the following header file:

```
#include "..\OCRServer\OCRServer.h"
```

The *OCRServer.h* file includes, among other things, definitions of the *IOcrProcessor* interface and its methods that we need.* The second thing that we need to do is change the **Project Settings** to include the **_WIN32_DCOM** preprocessor definition. To add this preprocessor definition, follow these directions:

---

\* Recall that this header file (*OCRServer.h*) is generated by the MIDL compiler using an associated IDL file as input.

1. From the `Project` menu, select `Settings` to launch the `Project Settings` dialog box.

2. Select the option to change settings for `All Configurations`.

3. Click the C/C++ Tab.

4. Select `Preprocessor` in the `Category` list-box.

5. Append `_WIN32_DCOM` to the `Preprocessor Definitions`.

6. Click `OK` to save the changes.

Alternatively, if you don't want to follow the above lengthy steps, you could place the following `#define` statement in the main header file (*stdafx.h*) so that every compilation unit within the project will see it:

```
#define _WIN32_DCOM
```

You must be wondering why you have to do this. The reason is simple—this macro allows you to use the API functions that support Distributed COM. For example, the *CoCreateInstanceEx* API function requires the definition of *_WIN32_DCOM*. If you use *CoCreateInstanceEx* without defining this macro, your source code will fail compilation.

Also, be sure to include the *OCRServer_i.c* file in the project by either inserting the source file into the project or simply including it by using the `#include` directive. Recall that the `OCRServer_i.c` file is generated by the MIDL compiler and it includes all the necessary GUIDs used by the MIDL generated header file.

Once you have all the preliminary requirements, you're ready to add the code to the *OnManual* handler. In the *OnManual* handler, you need to fill in the `COSERVERINFO` structure. For simplicity, ignore every member in the `COSERVERINFO` structure, except the server name (`pwszName`) member. If you want to deal with security, see Chapter 5. The code for the *OnManual* handler is shown in absorbable chunks.

Notice that we first set the members of the `COSERVERINFO` structure to zeros. If there is a server name, then we specifically set the `pwszName` member to point to a valid server name. If there is no server name, we must null out the second member of `COSERVERINFO` or else the activation call will fail. Recall that when the server name member is `NULL`, COM will look up the server destination in the registry under the `RemoteServerName` named value. Notice that we use a *_bstr_t* object to encapsulate the resource management of the `BSTR` that holds the server name. We take advantage of *_bstr_t* so that we don't have to remember to call *SysFreeString* for `BSTR` deallocation.

```
//*****************************************************************
//*****************************************************************
//**  The Manual Technique
//*****************************************************************
```

```
//*********************************************************************
#include "..\OCRServer\OCRServer.h"
#include "..\OCRServer\OCRServer_i.c"
#include <atlbase.h>
void COCRClientDlg::OnManual()
{
    CWaitCursor wait ;
    // Update the member variables
    UpdateData(TRUE) ;

    // Creating the safe array to transfer the binary data.
    BinaryData binaryImageArray(m_strImageFileLocation) ;

    // Fill in the server info structure.
    _bstr_t bstrServerName;
    COSERVERINFO csi = { 0, NULL, NULL, 0 };
    // m_strServerName is a COCRClientDlg member variable that
    // is bounded to the ServerName edit control and it holds
    // the server name.
    if (!m_strServerName.IsEmpty()) {
        bstrServerName = m_strServerName;
        // Fill in the server name.
        csi.pwszName = bstrServerName;
    }
```

After we've filled in the COSERVERINFO structure, we then fill in the MULTI_QI structure to specify the interface or interfaces that we want to initially request upon activation. Since we can ask for multiple interfaces, let's query for both the *IOcrProcessor* and *ISpell* interfaces during activation. To do this, we fill these requests into the MULTI_QI array. After filling in these structures, we can ask COM to create an instance of our class on the local or remote machine, by calling *CoCreateInstanceEx*, as displayed here:

```
try {
    // Fill in the multi_qi structure.
    MULTI_QI mqi[] = {
        {&IID_IOcrProcessor, NULL, S_OK},
        {&IID_ISpell, NULL, S_OK}
    };

    HRESULT hr = CoCreateInstanceEx(CLSID_OcrProcessor, NULL,
        CLSCTX_SERVER, &csi, sizeof(mqi)/sizeof(mqi[0]), mqi);
    // Check for activation errors
    if (FAILED(hr)) _com_issue_error(hr);
```

Notice that we check for errors after calling the activation API function. In the earlier code, we use the FAILED macro to check for the failure of an invocation. If the activation call returns a bad HRESULT, then we call the special *_com_issue_ error* native compiler support function to generated an exception using an HRESULT. In the event that an exception is thrown, we immediately fall into the nearest exception handler (catch block).

However, if the call to *CoCreateInstanceEx* is a success, we may proceed to possibly using the requested interface pointers. The *IOcrProcessor* interface pointer is returned in the first element of the MULTI_QI array, and the *ISpell* interface pointer is returned in the second element of the MULTI_QI array. Before we can actually use these interface pointers, we must explicitly check each of their returned HRESULTs.

The next code snippet deals with the *IOcrProcessor* interface. Notice that we use the same error handling technique as in the activation invocation, because we throw a *_com_error* exception by calling *_com_issue_error* when an error occurs. If there's no error, we must cast the returned interface pointers in the MULTI_QI array into the appropriate interface pointer types before calling their supported methods.

It is important to note, in this code snippet, that we use a smart pointer to automatically manage the release of the *IOcrProcessor* interface pointer. When you initialize a *CComPtr* smart pointer using an interface pointer, as in the first bolded statement shown, the smart pointer automatically does an *AddRef* in an effort to abide by the rules of COM. This means that we must manually release the interface pointer returned within the first element of the MULTI_QI array, as shown in the second bolded statement shown. If we fail to do this, we'll have a dangling interface pointer that will never be released.

```
// Check IOcrProcessor
if (FAILED(mqi[0].hr)) _com_issue_error(mqi[0].hr);
CComPtr<IOcrProcessor> pOcr =
    reinterpret_cast<IOcrProcessor*>(mqi[0].pItf);
reinterpret_cast<IOcrProcessor*>(mqi[0].pItf)->Release();

BSTR bstrOcrText ;
hr = pOcr->OcrWholeImage(binaryImageArray.SafeArrayVariant(),
    &bstrOcrText) ;
if (FAILED(hr)) _com_issue_error(hr);
m_strOCRResults = bstrOcrText ;
::SysFreeString(bstrOcrText) ;
```

Similar to the previous code snippet, the following code snippet deals with the *ISpell* interface and it follows the same pattern as the previous code.

```
// Check ISpell
if (FAILED(mqi[1].hr)) _com_issue_error(mqi[1].hr);
CComPtr<ISpell> pSpell = reinterpret_cast<ISpell*>(mqi[1].pItf);
reinterpret_cast<ISpell*>(mqi[1].pItf)->Release();

PossibleWords pw;
hr = pSpell->Check(L"Test", &pw);
if (FAILED(hr)) _com_issue_error(hr);
m_strOCRResults += CString(CString("\r\nChoice1:")+CString(pw.wszOne));
m_strOCRResults += CString(CString("\r\nChoice2:")+CString(pw.wszTwo));
```

Although there are top-level conditional statements in all of the code for this handler shown thus far, there are no embedded conditional statements (i.e., nested `if-else` statements) to check and verify the returned status code of each method invocation—thanks to exception handling. This minimizes the need for code to release interface pointers in multiple places. If we receive a bad `HRESULT`, we turn it into a *_com_error* exception by calling *_com_issue_error.* If a *_com_error* exception is thrown anywhere within this `try` block, it will be handled by the `catch` block, as shown below. We simply use the *ErrorMessage* member function of *_com_error* to display the exact error condition in human-readable format.

```
    } catch (_com_error & error) {
       m_strOCRResults.Format(TEXT("%s[%x]"), error.ErrorMessage(),
       error. Error());
    }

    // Update the GUI
    UpdateData(FALSE) ;
}
```

As shown by the code in the *OnManual* handler, using the C++ exception handling feature is great because it makes the code much cleaner. Again, if we don't use this feature, we would definitely need a few embedded conditional statements, making the code more nebulous. The good thing is that we can capture the exception and construct a message using the *ErrorMessage* function of *_com_error,* allowing us to know the cause of error immediately. Client-side COM error handling is made simpler by *_com_error* and the *_com_issue_error* and *_com_issue_errorex* functions. Without them, using the `try`/`catch` clause would not be as nearly this simple.

That wraps up the manual method, so you should build and test this version.* Notice that the client contacts `OCRServer` using the host name specified in the `ServerName` edit control. This is exactly what you need—the ability to dynamically select a destination server. The drawback of this method is that you need to statically obtain the *OCRServer.h* header file and possibly the *OCRServer_i.c* file (if you don't know the CLSIDs and IIDs). This is different from the two previous techniques, which can dynamically generate wrapper classes for you. Another drawback of this technique is that you have to write a bit more code. You get more control with this technique, but it's definitely more complicated than the two previous methods.

## *The Reusable echnique*

The manual technique for using distributed components is pretty cool, as it allows you to write code to dynamically connect to remote components. Let's combine

---

* Remember to register the *OCRServerps.dll* proxy/stub DLL, because you're using the ISpell custom interface.

our knowledge from the three techniques discussed earlier to see if we can do any better. If you look at the code in the *OnManual* handler (in the previous section), you would realize that the code can be generalized. With this observation, let's wrap it up into a template class so that it will be easier to use in the future. With this mentality, we will write a smart pointer template class that allows us to use a specified interface pointer on a specific remote machine. This smart pointer class will be similar to the ones we've seen earlier in this chapter. It differs from all the smart pointers discussed thus far, because it allows us to specify the target server destination programmatically.

## The RemotePtr Class

Let's call this smart pointer class *RemotePtr*, which will allow a client to simply do the following:

- Instantiate the class, setting an interface type, its class identifier, and its interface identifiers as template parameters. During instantiation, a remote server name can be passed along.

- Call interface methods directly using the overloaded arrow operator (i.e., `operator->`).

The *RemotePtr* class is a template class that takes an actual interface type and references to its class and interface identifiers. Below is the implementation of the *RemotePtr* class separated in digestible chunks.

```
//-------------------------------------------------------------------------
//  Remote Interface Smart Pointer Template Class
//-------------------------------------------------------------------------
#ifndef _ _REMOTE_INTERFACE_PTR_H_ _
#define _ _ REMOTE_INTERFACE_PTR_H_ _

#ifndef _INC_COMDEF
    #include <comdef.h>
#endif _INC_COMDEF

template <class TInterface, const CLSID *pClassID, const IID* pInterfaceID>
class RemotePtr {
public:
```

To make this class easy to use, we provide three constructors of which one is the default. To support both ANSI and Unicode builds, the second overloaded constructor takes an ANSI character string and the third takes a Unicode character string; each of these character strings represents the target server name. Besides initializing member variables, the overloaded constructors call *Connect*, passing along the server name to connect to the target, remote COM object whose class is indicated by the template parameter `pClassID`.

```
    RemotePtr()
        : m_bConnected(false), m_pInterface(NULL) { }
```

```
RemotePtr(char *pServerName)
    : m_bConnected(false), m_pInterface(NULL) { Connect(pServerName); }
RemotePtr(wchar_t *pServerName)
    : m_bConnected(false), m_pInterface(NULL) { Connect(pServerName); }
```

The beauty of a smart pointer is that no clean up is necessary, since the destructor of this class will automatically release the interface. We will provide a method to *Disconnect*, but a client needs not call this function to release the interface, as the destructor will call this function automatically. Notice that we release the interface pointer we're holding in the *Disconnect* method shown here.

```
~RemotePtr() { Disconnect(); }

void Disconnect()
{
    if (m_pInterface) {
        m_pInterface->Release() ;
        m_pInterface = NULL ;
        m_bConnected = false ;
    }
}
```

Most of the functionality of this smart pointer class is embedded within the *Connect* member functions. The code in these functions is almost a replica of the implementation from the *OnManual* handler, discussed in the previous section. To support both ANSI and Unicode builds, we provide one *Connect* method taking an ANSI character string and another one taking a Unicode character string.

```
void Connect(char *pServerName)
{
    if (m_bConnected) { return; }

    _bstr_t bstrServerName;
    COSERVERINFO csi = { 0, NULL, NULL, 0 };
    if (strlen(pServerName)>0) {
        bstrServerName = pServerName; csi.pwszName = bstrServerName;
    }
    Connect(csi);
}

void Connect(wchar_t *pServerName)
{
    if (m_bConnected) { return; }

    _bstr_t bstrServerName;
    COSERVERINFO csi = { 0, NULL, NULL, 0 };
    if (wcslen(pServerName)>0) {
        bstrServerName = pServerName; csi.pwszName = bstrServerName;
    }
    Connect(csi);
}
```

Both of these functions set the server name for the COSERVERINFO structure and end up calling a third *Connect* method that takes a COSERVERINFO structure, as shown later. We are also being nice in that we support pass by make reference, preventing unnecessary object copying to save a few CPU cycles. The sole purpose of this third *Connect* function (shown later) is to activate a remote object that lives on a specific machine whose network address is stored within `csi.pwszName`. Specifically, we want to activate the COM class indicated by the CLSID passed in via the second template parameter (`pClassID`). Also, we want to query for the interface pointer indicated by the third template parameter (`pInterfaceID`) during the activation invocation. If activation fails, we throw a *_com_error* exception object, created by calling the *_com_issue_error* function and passing in a bad HRESULT. We also make sure that the HRESULT for the requested interface is a success before we set our member variable (`m_pInterface`) that caches the interface held to point to the returned interface pointer. If the HRESULT for the requested interface indicates failure, we throw an appropriate *_com_error* exception object.

```
void Connect(const COSERVERINFO & csi)
{
    MULTI_QI mqi[] = { {pInterfaceID, NULL, S_OK} };
    HRESULT hr = CoCreateInstanceEx(*pClassID, NULL,
        CLSCTX_SERVER, const_cast<COSERVERINFO*>(&csi),
        sizeof(mqi)/sizeof(mqi[0]), mqi);
    if (FAILED(hr)) _com_issue_error(hr);
    if (FAILED(mqi[0].hr)) {
        m_pInterface = NULL;
        m_bConnected = false ;
        _com_issue_error(mqi[0].hr);
    }
    m_pInterface = reinterpret_cast<TInterface*>(mqi[0].pItf);
    m_bConnected = true ;
}
```

We also overload the arrow operator (i.e., `operator->`) to make this object behave like a pointer, since *RemotePtr* is after all a smart pointer. If the interface pointer we're holding has not yet been initialized, we create our own *_com_error* exception object using the standard, predefined E_POINTER status code. See Chapter 3 for other commonly used status codes. If the pointer is valid, we simply return it.

```
TInterface *operator->()
{
    if (!m_pInterface) { _com_issue_error(E_POINTER); }
    return m_pInterface;
}
```

To keep it simple, we will prevent the copying and assignment of this object by hiding the copy constructor and the assignment operator.

```
private:
    // No copy and assignment allowed
    RemotePtr(const RemotePtr &rhs);
    RemotePtr &operator=(const RemotePtr &rhs);
```

A *RemotePtr* instance is a smart pointer that keeps two states: a **bool** noting whether this object instance is connected to a server and a pointer to the target interface held by this object instance. For now, the **m_bConnected** member variable simply indicates whether this object is connected to the target COM interface, but it can serve a better purpose in future enhancements to this class. The second member variable (**m_pInterface**) caches the interface pointer that this object is encapsulating. Notice that its type is **TInterface**, which is a placeholder for the interface type passed in as the first template parameter during smart pointer instantiation.

```
private:
    bool        m_bConnected ;
    TInterface *m_pInterface ;
} ;


#endif // _ _ REMOTE_INTERFACE_PTR_H_ _
```

Like the previously examined techniques, there are drawbacks with this class. For example, you can work with only one interface at a time using this object. However, the intention of this template class is to make the connection to a specific server simple and not to create a class that includes support for everything. You may want to enhance this template class to add support for multiple interfaces for your own use. The nice thing about this class is that it takes exception handling into account, making the lives of its users much simpler.

## Using the RemotePtr Class

Let's use the smart pointer class we have just developed to support the **Reuse** button. First, add a handler for the **Reuse** button and name this handler *OnReuseManual*. In this function, instantiate a *RemotePtr* object passing in *IOcrProcessor*, and references to **CLSID_OcrProcessor** and **IID_OcrProcessor**. Start calling interface methods using this smart pointer. And that's it. The following code for the *OnReuseManual* handler is straightforward and quite simple:

```
//********************************************************************
//********************************************************************
//**   The Reusable Technique
//********************************************************************
//********************************************************************
#include "..\include\remptr.h"
void COCRClientDlg::OnReuseManual()
{
    CWaitCursor wait ;
    UpdateData(TRUE) ;

    // Creating the safe array to transfer the binary data
    BinaryData binaryImageArray(m_strImageFileLocation) ;

    char *pszServerName = m_strServerName.GetBuffer(m_strServerName.
      GetLength());
```

```
try {
   RemotePtr<IOcrProcessor, &CLSID_OcrProcessor,
            &IID_IOcrProcessor> pOcr(pszServerName) ;
   BSTR pOcrText ;
   HRESULT hr = pOcr->OcrWholeImage(binaryImageArray.SafeArrayVariant(),
                                    &pOcrText);
   if (FAILED(hr)) _com_issue_error(hr);
   m_strOCRResults = pOcrText ;
   ::SysFreeString(pOcrText) ;
} catch (_com_error & error) {
   m_strOCRResults.Format("%s[%x]", error.ErrorMessage(), error.Error());
}
m_strServerName.ReleaseBuffer();
UpdateData(FALSE) ;
}
```

If you compare this handler with the *OnManual* handler seen in "The Manual Technique" section, you'll realize that this code removes many lines of boilerplate code, all of which are now pushed inside the *Connect* methods of the *RemotePtr* class. This technique also takes advantage of the native C++ compiler support for COM exceptions, making error handling much cleaner. In addition, notice that you don't have to call *Release* on the held interface pointer, since this is already done by the destructor of the *RemotePtr* object. Perhaps the greatest advantage is that it's easy to use: instantiate a *RemotePtr* object and start calling interface methods via this pointer.

At this point, you can build and test this technique. You will see that, similar to the manual technique, this technique also connects to the server specified in the ServerName edit control.

# *Review*

In this chapter, we have examined four different C++ techniques for using the services exposed by distribute components. In particular, these techniques, for lack of better names, include: 1) The *COleDispatchDriver* technique; 2) The #import technique; 3) The manual technique; and 4) The reusable technique. Which of these techniques to use depends on the situation. If you want to be simple, then use the *COleDispatchDriver* or #import techniques. If you want to be simple but need to dynamically connect to a particular server, then the reusable technique would be suitable. However, if you require more power and flexibility, then use either the manual technique or beef up the *RemotePtr* template class to support this requirement.

In any case, you can appropriately apply these techniques to use the services exposed by any COM server. As summarized earlier in Table 7-1, if there are type libraries lying around (in DLL, OCX, EXE, TLB, and OLB files), you may use their services by taking advantage of the *COleDispatchDriver* or #import techniques to simply reverse engineer their type information. Remember that the

*COleDispatchDriver* technique only works with *IDispatch*-based interface, whereas the `#import` technique works with all COM interfaces. If you have access to a header file that defines a particular interface, its IID, and associated CLSID, you may use such an interface by taking advantage of the manual or reusable techniques.

In the previous chapter, you've learned how to build components using ATL. In this chapter, you've learned how to use components in general. In the next chapter, you'll learn how to distribute our components widely.

# 8

# *COM in Cyberspace*

Almost everything on the Windows platform is built on top of COM. The technology is ubiquitous. In this chapter, we will take ourselves into the realm of COM and its coexistence with the Web. In order to successfully build and run the examples in this chapter, you should have the following software and environment:

- The `OCRServer` component, developed in Chapter 6, *Building Components with ATL*, must be installed and registered on a server machine.

- Microsoft Peer Web Server 3.0, or greater, must be installed, and the WWW service must be running. You can verify this using the Microsoft Internet Service Manager (*inetmgr.exe*) utility.

- You must have Microsoft Internet Explorer (IE) 3.0.2, or greater.

- You must have the `Wang Image Edit` ActiveX[*] Control, which is shipped with Windows NT 4.0 or greater.

Assuming that we have the preliminary requirements in place, we will develop a few *ActiveX controls* in this chapter. An ActiveX control is simply a COM object, because the only requirement for an object to be called an ActiveX control is that it implements the *IUnknown* interface. ActiveX controls live inside an in-process component (DLL or OCX) that can be dynamically loaded by an out-of-process component. This out-of-process server, which can be any EXE that implements the necessary interfaces, is specifically called an ActiveX container or simply a container. A perfect example of a container is IE, which can dynamically load and embed many ActiveX controls that run inside it. Even though a simple COM object

---

[*] Technology terms can be really confusing. The term ActiveX is a marketing flash that simply refers to a COM object that implements at least the *IUnknown* interface. There's really nothing special about an ActiveX control—it's just a COM object that often implements many interfaces.

can be called an ActiveX control, ActiveX controls typically expose many COM inter-faces to provide the rich functionality that they support (such as in-place activation). Almost all of these interfaces are implemented by the ATL and MFC frameworks, making developing ActiveX controls in these environments easy and seamless.

The goal of this chapter is to show you simple and practical examples that give you future insights in building web-enabled applications that mesh with cyberspace. You will build ActiveX controls using ATL and MFC, so that you can see the advantages and disadvantages of each framework. Once you have built the ActiveX controls, you will learn how to integrate them into web pages that can be accessed by dis-tant clients. This allows clients within an intranet or across the intergalactic inter-net to download and run your ActiveX controls. The ActiveX controls that you build will be visual elements on the web pages, and they talk to the back-end OCRServer component using Distributed COM.

# ATL ActiveX Controls

In this section, we will use ATL to build an in-process server that supports a sim-ple ActiveX control. We will call the in-process server ATLCyberServer and our ActiveX control ATLCyberOcr. ATLCyberOcr allows people across the globe to perform OCR processing. It allows a user to select an image from disk storage and requests OCR processing on the selected image. When asked to perform OCR pro-cessing, the ATLCyberOcr ActiveX control will delegate the task to the back-end OCRServer component that was built in Chapter 6.

In addition to this functionality, we will also learn how to attach proxy/stub code into the ATLCyberServer component that we're building to mitigate the setup and registration pain during component download.

## Creating the Project

Let's start off by creating the project as directed in the following steps:

1. Use the ATL COM AppWizard to create a new project. Name this project ATLCyberServer and click OK to proceed.

2. In Step 1 of the ATL COM AppWizard, select DLL as the Server Type.

3. Check the Allow merging of proxy/stub code check-box, so that the proxy/stub code will be merged into the resulting DLL. This is important for an ActiveX control that is downloaded across cyberspace. Recall that if the threading models of the in-process server and the hosting out-of-process server differ, marshaling will result. In order to successfully standard marshal a custom interface, you must provide and register its proxy/stub code. Selecting this option will automatically merge the code into the ATLCyberServer

component, so that no proxy/stub code needs to be registered on the client machine's registry.

4. Once these steps are done, click `Finish` to proceed.

5. A dialog box will appear to notify you that the `ATL COM AppWizard` will generate a number of files. Click `OK` and wait for the wizard to generate these files for your newly created project.

Performing the steps above permits the `ATL COM AppWizard` to generate the boilerplate code for the `ATLCyberServer` in-process component

## Adding an ActiveX Control

Now that we have a brand new project, let's add an ActiveX control into it. Select `New ATL Object` from the `Insert` menu to launch the `ATL Object Wizard`. In the `ATL Object Wizard` dialog box, select `Controls` in the list-box to the left and select `Lite Control` in the list-view on the right, as shown in Figure 8-1.

Selecting a `Full Control` creates an ActiveX control that can be inserted into any container because it implements all the interfaces that supports a full ActiveX control. Selecting a `Lite Control` creates a thin control that is made especially to interact with IE and is thus optimized for IE. Selecting a `Property Page` adds an object that supports a property page.[*]

We select `Lite Control` because we want IE to use this ActiveX control exclusively. If you want to support all types of containers, you will have to create a `Full Control`.

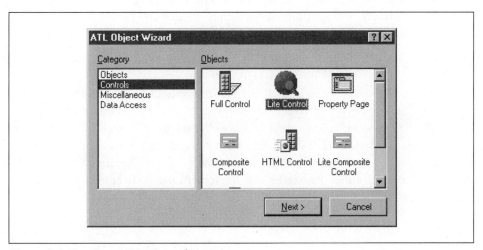

*Figure 8-1. Creating a "Lite Control"*

---

[*] Depending on the ATL version that you have installed, your `ATL Object Wizard` may look slightly different from the one shown in Figure 8-1.

After selecting Lite Control, click Next to launch the ATL Object Wizard Properties dialog box. In the Names tab, enter ATLCyberOcr as the Short Name. This is the textual name of your ActiveX control. Notice that the rest of the other edit boxes fill themselves automatically as you type the word ATLCyberOcr (you can leave these values as generated). The resulting Names tab should show the same information as displayed in Figure 8-2.

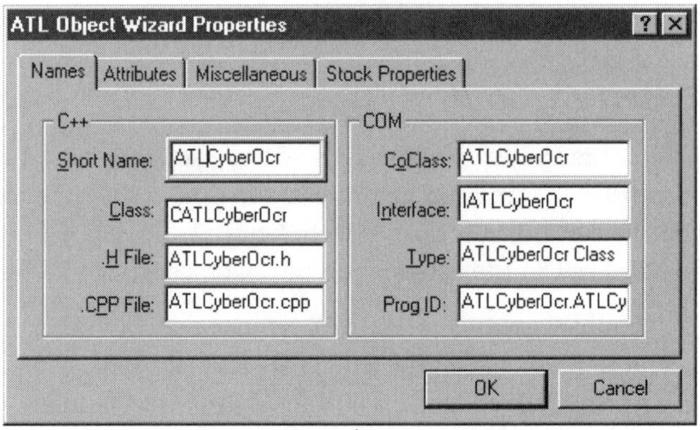

*Figure 8-2. Naming the newly created ActiveX control*

After you have entered the short name, switch to the Miscellaneous tab and select Static in the drop-down list-box labeled Add control based on. We do this because we want our ActiveX control to inherit the functionality of the standard Static control whose purpose is simply to display read-only text. Other than this modification, accept everything else on this dialog box as defaults and click OK to let the ATL Object Wizard generate preliminary code for the ATLCyberOcr ActiveX control.

If you look in ClassView now, you'll see that the ATL Object Wizard has generated the *IATLCyberOcr* interface along with the *CATLCyberOcr* class. The *CATLCyberOcr* class implements the *IATLCyberOcr* interface as well as many other interfaces that support an IE-specific ActiveX control. Take a look at the following generated code for the *CATLCyberOcr* class (shown for quick reference) and you'll see that it derives from six interfaces that implement the code specifically to support an IE-capable ActiveX control.*

---

* For brevity, this book doesn't discuss the interfaces that support Lite or Full ActiveX controls. Refer to SDK documentation for information regarding the detailed descriptions of these interfaces and the purpose of their exposed methods. At this level, we don't need to know these interfaces, since they are fully implemented by ATL. It is quite tedious to create an ActiveX control from scratch using pure C++, but it is very simple to do this using a class library such as ATL or MFC. These class libraries implement all the necessary interfaces for ActiveX controls, leaving us with only the custom business logic that we need to support.

```
class ATL_NO_VTABLE CATLCyberOcr :
 public CComObjectRootEx<CComSingleThreadModel>,
 public CComCoClass<CATLCyberOcr,&CLSID_ATLCyberOcr>,
 public CComControl<CATLCyberOcr>,
 public IDispatchImpl<IATLCyberOcr, &IID_IATLCyberOcr,&LIBID_ ATLCYBERSERVERLib>,
 public IPersistStreamInitImpl<CATLCyberOcr>,
 public IOleControlImpl<CATLCyberOcr>,
 public IOleObjectImpl<CATLCyberOcr>,
 public IOleInPlaceActiveObjectImpl<CATLCyberOcr>,
 public IViewObjectExImpl<CATLCyberOcr>,
 public IOleInPlaceObjectWindowlessImpl<CATLCyberOcr>
{ . . . };
```

Notice that *CATLCyberOcr* is derived from *CComControl*, which provides the support for an IE-compatible ActiveX control. Recall from Chapter 6 that *CComObjectRootEx* and *CComCoClass* form the foundation of reference counting and factory management for an ATL COM object. Since your interface is by default a dual interface, *IDispatchImpl* implements the default *IDispatch* behaviors for the *IATLCyberOcr* interface.

Look in the directory of this project and you'll find the file *ATLCyberOcr.htm*, which is a web page that embeds this ActiveX control. This web page is generated by the **ATL Object Wizard** each time you add a new COM object using the **ATL Object Wizard**. You can use this web page to test the ActiveX control. Additionally, you may enhance this web page and put it on your web server so that web surfers can download and use your ActiveX control.

## *Merging the Proxy/Stub Code*

During project creation, we mentioned that merging the proxy/stub code into our component makes the setup and administration efforts less painful on the client side. When you merge the proxy/stub code into your component, you save the client-side users from the pain of having to register the proxy/stub DLL against the local registry. There are users who think that having to register the component alone is bad enough; making them register another in-process server (proxy/stub DLL) is a turn-off. Besides, almost every COM programmer forgets to register the proxy/stub DLL at some point, so you cannot expect a non-programmer user to remember. Therefore, to help client-side setup and administration, merge the proxy/stub code into the component you're shipping. This simplifies setup and administration because only the deployed component needs to be registered—no proxy/stub DLL is needed because its code is built along with the shipped component.

Recall that you need the proxy/stub DLL for marshaling custom interfaces that you develop. You are building an in-process component, so theoretically everything happens within the address space of the container application that loads this in-process component. Chapter 5, *Infrastructure*, states that marshaling will not occur if the container and the loaded in-process server's COM object both support the same apartment type. This means that you don't need to provide the code to marshal your custom interfaces, as every interface pointer access is a direct access. However, if the in-process server's COM object is used by a container apartment that has a different apartment model, the sky will fall down if you don't provide the interface marshaling code to marshal your custom interfaces.* Simply put, provide the code to marshal your custom interfaces when you deploy (distribute) any component, whether it be an EXE or a DLL. You can do this by shipping the proxy/ stub DLL or linking the proxy/stub code inside your deployed component, but our immediate goal is to learn how to link the proxy/stub code into our component.

Remember that you've checked the `Allow merging of proxy/stub code` check-box when you created the project. This is not enough to merge the proxy/ stub code into your component though. You would have to follow these directions in order to actually take advantage of this feature:

1. You must define the `_MERGE_PROXYSTUB` preprocessor symbol, by using the `Project Settings` dialog box, which you can launch by pressing `ALT-F7`. Select the C/C++ tab and choose `Preprocessor` in the `Category` drop-down list-box. Append a comma and then the symbol `_MERGE_PROXYSTUB` to the edit control labeled `Preprocessor definitions`.

2. In the `Project Settings` dialog box, select the *dlldatax.c* file. Uncheck the `Exclude file from build` check-box for this file in the `General` tab. This will include this file in the current build, because by default, this file is not included in the build.

3. You need to prevent the use of a precompiled header for the *dlldatax.c* file. To do this, select `Precompiled Headers` in the `Category` drop-down list-box in the C/C++ tab. Click the `Not using precompiled headers` radio button.

4. Click `OK` to save the new project settings and to dismiss the `Project Settings` dialog.

Now, build the project to generate the necessary files to support the merging of proxy/stub code. These files include *dlldata.c* and *ATLCyberServer_p.c*. Remember that the former contains code for the necessary COM entry points, such as *DllGetClassObject* and friends. The latter contains the code to marshal all interfaces defined in the *ATLCyberServer.idl* file. Once you have followed the above steps and rebuilt the project, you have successfully merged the proxy/stub code into the `ATLCyberServer` component.

---

* Since our interface, *IATLCyberOcr*, is a [`dual`] interface, we technically don't need to merge the proxy/ stub code, because the Automation (type library) marshaler knows how to marshal Automation compatible interfaces. However, because the `Allow merging of proxy/stub code` feature is deviously subtle, we will march through this exercise.

# Adding Properties

Now that we have an ActiveX control that supports the *IATLCyberOcr* interface, let's examine how we can add a property to this interface. Recall that adding a property essentially creates two accessor interface methods: a getter and a setter. The property you'll add to the *IATLCyberOcr* interface holds the server name (hostname) of the back-end OCRServer component. A client, a web page for example, can obtain this property from your ActiveX control to verify the name of the OCRServer component currently in use. It can also set this server name property to indicate that it wants to use a specific OCRServer component.

Internally within your ActiveX control, you'll use this property to connect to the target OCRServer component. After connecting to the target OCRServer component, you can then use the *IOcrProcessor* interface exposed by the OcrProcessor COM object hosted by the OCRServer component to perform OCR processing on behalf of your client. This means that a web page is a client to your ActiveX control, and your ActiveX control is a client to the OCRServer component.

To add this server name property, follow these directions:

1. In ClassView, right-click on the appropriate interface, *IATLCyberOcr* in this case, to launch the context menu for adding a property.

2. Select Add Property on the context menu to launch the Add Property to Interface dialog box, as shown in Figure 8-3.

3. In the Property Type drop-down list control, choose BSTR as the type for your property. This is a basic string that will hold the target server name of the OCRServer component.

4. In the Property Name edit control, enter the name for this property. Type in *OCRServerName.*

5. Leave everything else as defaults and click OK to add the property to the selected interface.

Although we won't do it here, you can add parameters to each property. This is possible because a property is made up of two methods—and it is possible to add parameters to all methods. You can selectively specify whether you want a getter or a setter. For a put (setter) function, you can further specify whether the input parameter is passed by value ([propput] attribute) or by reference ([propputref] attribute), and the difference between these two attributes is that pass by reference is better for structures and arrays. Besides these attributes, you can attach other MIDL attributes to your property by clicking the Attributes button in the Add Property to Interface dialog box.

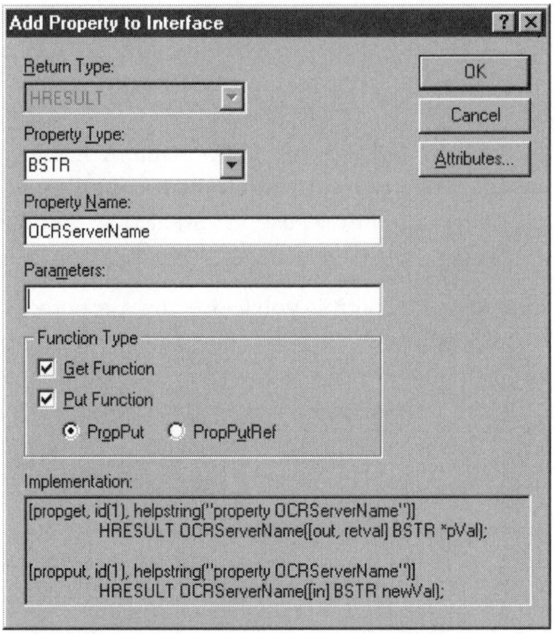

*Figure 8-3. Adding a property to an interface*

After adding the *OCRServerName* property, check out the generated code and you'll see that the getter and setter methods have been added to the selected interface, as shown here:

```
interface IATLCyberOcr : IDispatch {
    [propget, id(1), helpstring("property OCRServerName")]
            HRESULT OCRServerName([out, retval] BSTR *pVal);
    [propput, id(1), helpstring("property OCRServerName")]
            HRESULT OCRServerName([in] BSTR newVal);
};
```

You will also see that declarations and empty method implementations are generated for you. As shown later, the generated methods to support your added property are prefixed by the word get_ and put_. There are two differently named functions because you cannot overload functions in MIDL as you can in C++. For example, in C++, a single function name could be a getter (with no argument) and a setter (with one argument). In some sense, not being able to overload in MIDL is probably a good thing because you can easily tell which function you're dealing with by its prefix.

```
// In the header file
class ATL_NO_VTABLE CATLCyberOcr : public . . . {
public:
    STDMETHOD(get_OCRServerName)(/*[out, retval]*/ BSTR *pVal);
```

```
        STDMETHOD(put_OCRServerName)(/*[in]*/ BSTR newVal);
};


// In the implementation file
STDMETHODIMP CATLCyberOcr::get_OCRServerName(BSTR * pVal)
{return S_OK;}
STDMETHODIMP CATLCyberOcr::put_OCRServerName(BSTR newVal)
{return S_OK;}
```

Everything is generated with a few clicks. All you have to do is implement these methods, but before you can do that, you need to add a member variable to the *CATLCyberOcr* C++ class to keep track of the server name. ATL supports a *CComBSTR* that encapsulates a BSTR and manages the resource allocation and deallocation for you. So let's take advantage of this class. Add a private member variable named **m_OCRServerName** of type *CComBSTR* to the *CATLCyberOcr* class. You can add this either by hand or visually (right-click on the *CATLCyberOcr* icon and select **Add Member Variable**). Your resulting class definition should contain the following member variable:

```
class ATL_NO_VTABLE CATLCyberOcr : public . . .
{
private:
    CComBSTR m_OCRServerName;
};
```

Now, let's implement our getter and setter methods. The implementation for the getter method returns the server name to the caller. As shown in the following code, use the *Copy* function of *CComBSTR* to allocate a copy of a BSTR, which will be returned to the caller. A BSTR has to be managed by special allocators, which are used internally by the *Copy* function of *CComBSTR*.

```
STDMETHODIMP CATLCyberOcr::get_OCRServerName(BSTR * pVal)
{
    *pVal = m_OCRServerName.Copy();
    return S_OK;
}
```

The implementation for the put function simply sets the new server name, as shown:

```
STDMETHODIMP CATLCyberOcr::put_OCRServerName(BSTR newVal)
{
    m_OCRServerName = newVal;
    return S_OK;
}
```

That's it for adding and implementing a property of an ActiveX control.

## Adding Methods

We will now add a method, *OcrImage*, to the *IATLCyberOcr* interface to allow a client to request OCR processing. This method will take an image file name and return the OCR text after OCR processing. Internally, this method delegates the OCR processing to *IOcrProcessor::OcrWholeImage*, which is implemented by the `OcrProcessor` COM object inside the `OCRServer` component. This method delegation is shown by the pointed arrow in Figure 8-4.

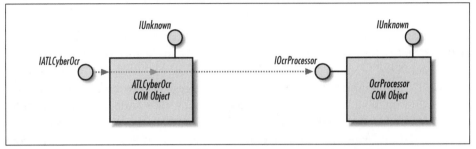

*Figure 8-4. IATLCyberOcr::OcrImage delegates to IOcrProcessor::OcrWholeImage*

Follow these directions to add the *OcrImage* method to the *IATLCyberOcr* interface:

1. In `ClassView`, right-click on the appropriate interface, *IATLCyberOcr* in this case, to launch the context menu for adding a method.

2. Select `Add Method` on the context menu to launch the `Add Method to Interface` dialog box, as shown in Figure 8-5.

3. In the `Method Name` edit control, type *OcrImage* as the name of the method. A client calls this method to request for OCR processing.

4. In the `Parameters` edit control, enter `[in] BSTR Image, [out, retval] BSTR *pText`. The first parameter is an input representing the name of an image file (including its path) that is to be OCR processed. The second parameter is an output that returns the OCR text for the indicated image. Notice that we specify the `[retval]` attribute to make the lives of VBScript and VB programmers easier.

5. Once everything is entered, click `OK` to dismiss the dialog box.

By following the previous steps, you will get a generated MIDL definition for the *OcrImage* method. In addition, the declaration of this method is inserted automatically into the appropriate header file and an empty implementation of this method is automatically inserted into the appropriate implementation file. You'll need to implement this method to actually support OCR processing.

As alluded to earlier, this method will communicate with the remote `OCRServer` component via the *IOcrProcessor* interface. In particular, it will internally call the *OcrWholeImage* method of the *IOcrProcessor* interface to perform OCR processing on behalf of the caller. In this sense, it doesn't do anything special except for delegating the OCR processing work to the `OCRServer` component. Here are the general steps that you'll take to implement this method:

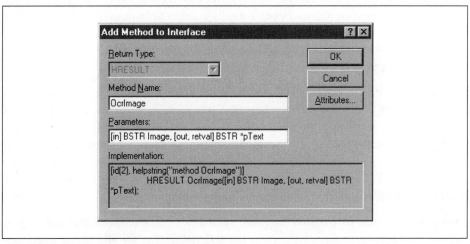

*Figure 8-5. Adding a method to an interface*

1. Merge the proxy/stub code for the *IOcrProcessor* interface into the **ATLCyberServer** component so that the **ATLCyberServer** component can marshal this interface without the need for a separate proxy/stub DLL. The *IOcrProcessor* interface must be marshaled between the **ATLCyberServer** and the **OCRServer** components, because **ATLCyberServer** uses *IOcrProcessor* and *IOcrProcessor* is implemented by **OCRServer**.

2. Use the *RemotePtr* template class developed in Chapter 7, *Using COM Objects*, to communicate with the selected **OCRServer** component. This means that we must include the *RemPtr.h* file that defines and implements the *RemotePtr* template class.

3. Add the code for *OcrImage* to delegate the OCR processing request to the *IOcrProcessor* interface exposed by the **OcrProcessor** COM object that lives inside the **OCRServer** component.

These steps are covered in more detail in the subsections below.

### Step 1: Merging the proxy/stub code for external (remote) interfaces

Because this chapter deals with distribution throughout cyberspace, you need to minimize the client-side setup and administration burden. When you download an ActiveX control, it must be registered on the local machine before you can use the control. Internet Explorer does this automatically for you upon ActiveX control download. However, if the downloaded ActiveX control uses Distributed COM to communicate with another distributed object's exposed custom interfaces, you must also register the remote object's proxy/stub code on the client machine to marshal the custom interface.

This situation applies to the **ATLCyberOcr** ActiveX control, since this control uses the services exposed by **OCRServer**, a totally different distributed component. To be precise, the **ATLCyberOcr** ActiveX control uses the *IOcrProcessor* interface exposed by COM objects instantiated from the **OcrProcessor** COM class (which is identified by the **CLSID_OcrProcessor** CLSID).

You've learned that in order to use a custom interface, you must register its proxy/ stub code. Since the *IOcrProcessor* interface is a custom interface, the proxy/stub code for the *IOcrProcessor* interface must be registered on the machine where the **ATLCyberOcr** ActiveX control runs. However, registering too many things on the client machine can be cumbersome and error-prone. The simplest way to relieve this burden on the client side is to bundle the proxy/stub code for the *IOcrProcessor* interface into the **ATLCyberServer** component.

To merge the code to marshal external interfaces (i.e., interfaces that are implemented by a remote component), copy the IDL definitions for all remote interfaces that the current ActiveX control uses. In your case, you need only *IOcrProcessor*, because that's the only remote interface that our **ATLCyberOcr** ActiveX control will use. Thus, simply copy the following interface definition from *OCRServer.idl* (which belongs to the **OCRServer** component) into *ATLCyberServer.idl*:

```
[
    object, uuid(00000001-AAAA-11D1-8753-006008CDD9AE),
    dual, helpstring("IOcrProcessor Interface"), pointer_default(unique)
]
interface IOcrProcessor : IDispatch
{
    [id(1), helpstring("method OcrWholeImage")]
    HRESULT OcrWholeImage([in] VARIANT binaryImageArray,
                          [out, retval] BSTR *pOcrText);
};
```

There is no magic here. We have already merged the proxy/stub code for all interfaces that the **ATLCyberServer** component supports. This implies that MIDL will generate proxy/stub code for all interfaces defined within *ATLCyberServer.idl*. All you're doing now is taking further advantage of this feature. You do this by adding the *IOcrProcessor* interface into the *ATLCyberServer.idl* file so that the MIDL compiler will generate the proxy/stub code to marshal the *IOcrProcessor* interface. Since all these interface marshalers are merged into one DLL (*ATLCyberServer.dll*) using the **Allow merging of proxy/stub code** feature, the client who downloads this DLL needs to register no interface marshalers on the client side.

To allow the MIDL compiler to add the marshaling code for the *IOcrProcessor* interface, you must now build the project. To verify that the proxy/stub code for the *IOcrProcessor* interface is indeed generated, search for *IOcrProcessor* in the *ATLCyberServer_p.c* or *ATLCyberServer.h* file.

For simplicity, we simply copy and paste external interfaces into our IDL file for the exercises illustrated throughout this book. However, a better way of doing this is to save these external interfaces you know clients will need into a separate IDL file, which you can deploy along with your binaries to allow C++ programmers easy access to your public interface definitions. For example, during the development of the **OCRServer** component in Chapter 6, the *IOcrProcessor* interface definition could have been saved in a separate file called *OcrPublic.idl*, instead of clumping it inside the normal *OCRServer.idl*. The latter can pull in the definitions from the former by using the **#include** MIDL directive, which is semantically and syntactically equivalent to a **#include** in C/C++. If this had been done, *ATLCyberServer.idl* could **#include "OcrPublic.idl"** to pull in the interface definition for *IOcrProcessor* so that no copying and pasting will be needed. This technique is superior to copying and pasting, since a change to the *OcrPublic.idl* file will be automatically propagated to all IDL files that include *OcrPublic.idl*.

Let's make it clear that this is different from merging the proxy/stub code, as discussed previously in the "Merging the Proxy/Stub Code" section. In that section, merging the proxy/stub code links in the proxy/stub for the *IATLCyberOcr* interface (or any interfaces specified and implemented in the **ATLCyberServer** component), whereas in the current discussion, we're pulling in an interface that is defined by some third-party server, namely the **OCRServer**.

However, both techniques are similar in that they achieve the same goal: minimizing client-side setup and administration burden. For example, we merged the proxy/stub code for the *IATLCyberOcr* interface into the **ATLCyberServer** in-process server, because we wanted to save the client from the pain and suffering of manually registering proxy/stub code for marshaling the *IATLCyberOcr* interface. Recall that COM dynamically loads the proxy/stub code when the apartment models of both the container and the ActiveX control differ, and thus the proxy/stub code must exist for marshaling to work. Instead of manually registering these proxy/stub DLLs, linking the proxy/stub code right inside the client code is a valuable technique, because it minimizes the setup and administration effort, which can be error prone and time consuming.

A minor drawback is that if you have ten different clients using the same proxy/stub code, you end up wasting a little bit of RAM because they all contain the same exact copy of the code needed to marshal the custom interface. Another drawback is that your client components get a little bit bulkier, because you're linking in more code. However, if you want to play devil's advocate, you can say that merging the code is an advantage because there's no need for COM to dynamically load a proxy/stub DLL to marshal custom interfaces—and dynamic loading is a minor performance hit.

### *Step 2: Reusing the RemotePtr class*

Earlier in Chapter 7, you saved the *RemotePtr* class in the file named *RemPtr.h*. Find this file and copy it into this project's directory if you like. To use this template class, you need to include this file, so let's make it easy and include this file in the *ATLCyberOcr.h* file, as follows (make sure your path is valid):

```
#include "..\..\include\RemPtr.h "
```

Now, you are ready to add a member variable to the *CATLCyberOcr* class to hold an interface pointer to the *IOcrProcessor* interface. You need this interface pointer before you can request OCR processing on behalf of your client. Use the *RemotePtr* smart pointer class developed in Chapter 7 to hold this interface pointer. This means that you'll add a member variable of type *RemotePtr* to the *CATLCyberOcr* class. Name this variable m_pRemoteOcr. By now, part of the class definition of *CATLCyberOcr* should look similar to the following:

```
class ATL_NO_VTABLE CATLCyberOcr : public . . . {
 . . .
private:
    CComBSTR m_OCRServerName;
    RemotePtr<IOcrProcessor, &CLSID_OcrProcessor,
             &IID_IOcrProcessor> m_pRemoteOcr;
};
```

Recall that the templatized *RemotePtr* class takes an interface, an address of a CLSID, and an address of an IID. Notice that m_pRemoteOcr is constructed without a server name, which means that you must call the *Connect* method of the *RemotePtr* class to connect to the target server before making method invocations to *IOcrProcessor*.

*IOcrProcessor* and IID_IOcrProcessor are defined in *ATLCyberServer.h*, which is generated by the MIDL compiler. CLSID_OcrProcessor is not yet defined so you should add an external forward declaration to make the compiler happy. For example, add the following line after the *RemPtr.h* inclusion:

```
EXTERN_C const CLSID CLSID_OcrProcessor;
```

Before proceeding, switch to the implementation file (*ATLCyberOcr.cpp*) and define CLSID_OcrProcessor as follows:

```
const CLSID CLSID_OcrProcessor =
{0x00000001,0xBBBB,0x11D1,{0x87,0x53,0x00,0x60,0x08,0xCD,0xD9,0xAE}};
```

You can copy this definition directly from *OCRServer_i.c* where it is defined. Once you have done this, you are ready to implement the *OcrImage* method of the *IATLCyberOcr* interface.

## Step 3: Coding the OcrImage method

In this method, you'll delegate the OCR processing request to the *OcrWholeImage* method of the *IOcrProcessor* interface, which is implemented by the OCRServer component. This is shown in the bolded statement in the later code snippet. Use the smart pointer that is a member variable of *CATLCyberOcr* to invoke the *OcrWholeImage* method. This smart pointer encapsulates the *IOcrProcessor* interface, which indeed implements the *OcrWholeImage* method in the OCRServer component. Here's the code for your *OcrImage* member function:

```
STDMETHODIMP CATLCyberOcr::OcrImage(BSTR Image, BSTR * pText)
{
    try {
        CComVariant vtImage; CComBSTR pOcrText;
        HRESULT hr = m_pRemoteOcr->OcrWholeImage(vtImage, &pOcrText);
        if (FAILED(hr)) throw _com_error(hr);
        *pText = pOcrText ;
        m_ctlStatic.SetWindowText(TEXT("Successfully processed..."));
    } catch (_com_error & error) {
        m_ctlStatic.SetWindowText(error.ErrorMessage());
    }
    return S_OK;
}
```

In the effort to keep the code simple, don't load the image from disk storage prior to OCR processing; instead, pass a dummy variant (vtImage) to the first parameter of *OcrWholeImage*. This is sufficient for this example, since you've already learned how to deal with a VARIANT containing a SAFEARRAY in previous examples.

To invoke the *OcrWholeImage* method of the *IOcrProcessor* interface, use the smart pointer, m_pRemoteOcr, which we keep as a member variable of the *CATLCyberOcr* class. You'll also return to the caller what *OcrWholeImage* returns (the second argument of *OcrImage* and *OcrWholeImage*). If an exception occurs, simply record the error message indicating the problem.

The earlier *OcrImage* function is straightforward, but you have not connected to the remote OCRServer component. If this function is invoked prior to connecting to the remote OCRServer, an exception will occur. To prevent this, a client must set the *OCRServerName* property. Therefore, you need to modify the put function of the *OCRServerName* property, which is exposed by your ActiveX control. When a user sets a new server name, you must first call *Disconnect* using the m_pRemoteOcr smart pointer, making sure that the current interface reference held by the smart pointer is released prior to connecting to a new server. Since the *Connect* method throws a *_com_error* exception (as we have implemented in Chapter 7), we wrap this call within a try-catch clause for easy error handling. Once connection is established, a client can freely call the *OcrImage* method.

```
STDMETHODIMP CATLCyberOcr::put_OCRServerName(BSTR newVal)
{
    if (m_OCRServerName==newVal) return S_OK;
```

```
    m_pRemoteOcr.Disconnect();
    m_OCRServerName = newVal;
    try {
        m_pRemoteOcr.Connect(m_OCRServerName);
    } catch (_com_error & error) {
        MessageBox(error.ErrorMessage());
    }

    return S_OK;
}
```

At this point, we have completed our **ATLCyberOcr** ActiveX control, but before building the project, you should turn on exception handling support since we're using it. You can do this using the **Project Settings** dialog (**ALT-F7**). After changing this setting, build the project to complete this exercise.

Congratulate yourself, because you've just created an ActiveX control that can be embedded into web pages and can be widely distributed throughout cyberspace. This control lives in an in-process server called **ATLCyberServer** (*ATLCyberServer.dll*). This in-process server serves as a middle man between the thin-client web page and the back-end **OCRServer** component. We have already developed **OCRServer**, so let's develop a web page to house this control.

# *Web-Enabled Clients*

If you look into the project directory for the **ATLCyberServer** component, you will see an HTML file (*ATLCyberOcr.htm*) that embeds the **ATLCyberOcr** ActiveX control. The **ATL Object Wizard** is so sure that you will distribute your ActiveX control across the web that it generates this file for you. You will update this web page and turn it into a thin, web-enabled client. At the end of this section, you will have built a web page as shown in Figure 8-6. Just like any other web page, this one can be downloaded from a web server and displayed within Internet Explorer (IE 3.0 or greater). Since IE is an ActiveX container, it can house ActiveX controls.

Let's briefly describe this web page. It contains a simple table with seven rows, as described below:

1. The first row is trivial, as it simply displays some text.

2. The second row is composed of six pushbuttons that allow a user to specify the preferred choice.

3. The third row is split into two columns. The right column allows a user to enter the remote server address for the target **OCRServer** component, which was developed in Chapter 6.

4. The fourth row allows a user to enter the full path and image file of the image to be OCR processed.

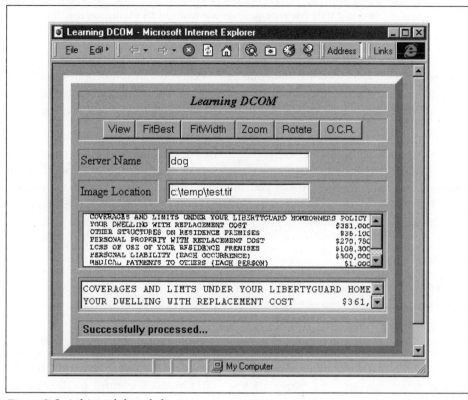

*Figure 8-6. A thin web-based client*

5. The fifth row contains the `Wang Image Edit` ActiveX control, which is a fully capable image viewer developed by Wang and is shipped freely with Windows NT (4.0 and above). We don't have its source code, but we can easily take advantage of it by integrating it into our simple web-based client. Now you really see the beauty of components and binary reuse. We don't have to suffer through developing an image viewer, because Wang has already taken the burden of developing this ActiveX control for us. The cool thing is that anyone can use this free `Wang Image Edit` ActiveX control without much effort. You will appreciate it soon when you realize the code involved in controlling this control (or for that matter, any ActiveX control) is very simple.

6. The sixth row contains a simple edit control that displays informational messages or the returned, processed text.

7. The seventh row contains the `ATLCyberOcr` ActiveX control that we have just developed in the last section. Recall that this control lives in the `ATLCyberServer` component. When a user clicks on the `OCR` pushbutton to ask the control to process the image, the control will delegate the work to the `OCRServer` component using Distributed COM. Recall that we merged the

proxy/stub code for the *IOcrProcessor* interface into the `ATLCyberServer` component. We did that earlier because we wanted to eliminate the client-side registration of proxy/stub code.

As you can see, this web page uses two ActiveX controls: one is developed by you and the other is developed by someone else. Yet, you can reuse both controls at the binary level, needing little or no source code. Users can simply download this web page and have a fully capable, distributed, and web-enabled OCR client.

To make all the visual elements on this web page interact with one another, we will use Visual Basic scripting (VBScript). You have now seen what we're going to build, so let's start writing HTML and VBScript code to make things happen. (I am assuming that you know HTML, so you should start off creating a table with seven rows. The first row can have whatever text you prefer. I will explain what you will need in each of the other rows below.)

## *Control Buttons*

As seen earlier in Figure 8-6, the second row of the table contains six pushbuttons. Each of these buttons serves a different purpose, as described:

`View`

> When pushed, a special VBScript subroutine will be called. This is the *ViewImageFile* subroutine, which we will write shortly using VBScript. Briefly, this subroutine tells the `Wang Image Edit` ActiveX control to display the image file indicated in the `Image Location` edit field (the right column of the fourth row).

`FitBest`

> This button allows a user to fit the currently loaded image as best possible within the `Wang Image Edit` ActiveX control. We simply call the *FitTo* method exposed by the `Wang Image Edit` ActiveX control, passing in a zero to obtain this functionality.

`FitWidth`

> This button allows a user to fit the width of the currently loaded image as best possible in the `Wang Image Edit` ActiveX control. We simply call the *FitTo* method exposed by the `Wang Image Edit` ActiveX control, passing in a one to get this functionality.

`Zoom`

> This button allows a user to zoom into a selected rectangular area drawn using the mouse prior to pressing this button. In other words, a user draws a rubber-band around the area to be magnified and then presses this button to see a magnified image portion. When this button is pressed, we simply call the *Zoom* VBScript subroutine, which we will write shortly.

Rotate

This button allows a user to rotate the currently loaded image clockwise. When this button is pressed, we simply call the *RotateRight* method exposed by the `Wang Image Edit` ActiveX control.

OCR

This button allows a user to perform optical character recognition on the currently displayed image. When this button is pressed, we will call a special VBScript subroutine called *ProcessImage*, which we will write shortly. *ProcessImage* will use the `ATLCyberOcr` ActiveX control to carry out this functionality. Since we've just developed the `ATLCyberOcr` ActiveX control, we know that it will end up delegating the request to the `OCRServer` component. The destination of this component is specified in the `Server Name` edit field, found in the third row (the right column) of the table shown earlier in Figure 8-6.

Having described the functionality of these buttons, let's see the HTML source code that makes this happen. Below is the code snippet that supports the second row of the table shown in Figure 8-6:

```
<input type="button" name="ViewImage" value="View"
    language="VBScript" onclick="Call ViewImageFile()">
<input type="button" name="Fit" value="FitBest"
    language="VBScript" onclick="WangImage.FitTo(0)">
<input type="button" name="Width" value="FitWidth"
    language="VBScript" onclick="WangImage.FitTo(1)">
<input type="button" name="ZoomRectangle" value="Zoom"
    language="VBScript" onclick="Zoom()">
<input type="button" name="RotateRight" value="Rotate"
    language="VBScript" onclick="WangImage.RotateRight">
<input type="button" name="OCRImage" value="O.C.R."
    language="VBScript" onclick="ProcessImage()">
```

As previously shown, on a click event, the button labeled `View` calls a VBScript subroutine *ViewImageFile*. This subroutine sets the `Image` property exposed by the `Wang Image Edit` ActiveX control, which we call `WangImage` in the HTML source code shown later. For the *Image* property, we pass the full path and file name of the image to be processed. A user can enter this image in the `Image Location` edit field, which we call `TIFFLocation` in the HTML source code below. Once we have set the image file, we tell the `Wang Image Edit` ActiveX control to display the image, by simply invoking its *Display* method. After the image is displayed, we call the *FitTo* method, passing in a zero, to tell the `Wang Image Edit` ActiveX control to fit the image to the width of the control for initial viewing. The snippet for the *ViewImageFile* subroutine looks as follows:

```
Sub ViewImageFile()
   WangImage.Image = TIFFLocation.value
   WangImage.Display()
```

```
WangImage.FitTo(0)
OcrText.value = "Image has not been OCRed"
end sub
```

Upon receiving a click event, the button labeled `FitBest` will invoke the *FitTo* method of the `Wang Image Edit` control, passing in 0 to signify that we want the whole image to fit inside the control. When the `FitWidth` button is clicked, we invoke the *FitTo* method of the `Wang Image Edit` control, passing in 1 to indicate that we want the width of the image to fit perfectly inside the control. When `RotateRight` is clicked, we invoke the *RotateRight* method of the `Wang Image Edit` control. If you need more information on the `Wang Image Edit` ActiveX control, see its online help.

When a user clicks on the `Zoom` button, we call the *Zoom* subroutine, which checks whether an image is currently displayed. If so, we call the *ZoomToSelection* method exposed by the `Wang Image Edit` control to zoom into the selected portion. Here's code for the *ZoomToSelection* subroutine:

```
Sub Zoom()
    if WangImage.ImageDisplayed then
        WangImage.ZoomToSelection()
    end if
end sub
```

Finally, when the `OCR` button is clicked, we will call the *ProcessImage* subroutine, which simply calls the *OcrImage* method exposed by the `ATLCyberOcr` ActiveX control. Recall that the `ATLCyberOcr` ActiveX control exposes a property called *OCRServerName* to allow a user to set the server destination of the back-end `OCRServer` component. Obviously, this control talks to the back-end `OCRServer` using Distributed COM. We obtain the server destination from the `Server Name` edit field, found on the third row of the table shown earlier in Figure 8-6.

```
Sub ProcessImage()
    ATLCyberOcr.OCRServerName = ServerName.value
    OcrText.value = ATLCyberOcr.OcrImage(TIFFLocation.value)
end sub
```

After setting the server destination, we simply call the *OcrImage* method exposed by the `ATLCyberOcr` ActiveX control, passing in the image file name, to request for OCR processing. When *OcrImage* returns, we place the resulting OCR text into the edit field found in the sixth row of the table shown in Figure 8-6. We name this edit field `OcrText` in our HTML script.

Remember that when we originally created the *OcrImage* method for the `ATLCyberOcr` ActiveX control, we specified it as follows:

```
HRESULT OcrImage([in] BSTR Image, [out, retval] BSTR *pText);
```

There can be only one `[out, retval]` parameter in a method specification, and it must describe the rightmost parameter in a method signature. The `[out,` retval] attribute combination allows an environment like VBScript to easily use the method. Specifically, it allows the return value to be captured on the left hand side of the method invocation, as evident in the bolded statement of the *ProcessImage* subroutine shown previously. However, this doesn't help C++ clients, as for these clients, we have to call *OcrImage* with two parameters.

## Server Name and Image Location

The third row of the table on our web page exists to capture the user-specified destination of the **OCRServer**. This row is split into two columns, with the left column displaying **Server Name** and the right column holding a text edit control. The *ProcessImage* VBScript subroutine pulls the server name from this edit control and sets the *OCRServerName* property of the **ATLCyberOcr** ActiveX control using this value. The HTML source code for the third row is as follows:

```
<td>Server Name</td>
<td><input type="text" size="25" name="ServerName" value="dog"></td>
```

The fourth row of the table on our web page exists to capture the location of the image to be processed. This row also has two columns with the left displaying the **Image Location** and right one holding a text edit control. The *ProcessImage* VBScript subroutine pulls the server name from this edit control and passes it as an argument to the *OcrImage* method exposed by the **ATLCyberOcr** ActiveX control. The HTML source code for the fourth row is as follows:

```
<td>Image Location</td>
<td>
   <input type="text" size="25" name="TIFFLocation" value="c:\temp\test.tif">
</td>
```

So, row three and four both exist to obtain required inputs from the user. Of course, since this is a simple example, we do no validation on the data that is entered into these text edit controls.

## Wang Image Edit ActiveX Control

In the fifth row of the table on our web page, we will embed the **Wang Image Edit** ActiveX control. We do this by using the <object></object> tag. Within this tag, we will specify the CLSID of the **Wang Image Edit** ActiveX control. Using *regedit.exe* to search for this ActiveX control's CLSID, we will see that it is [6D940280-9F11-11CE-83FD-02608C3EC08A].* So, the fifth row of the table contains code as shown below, which assumes that you have the **Wang Image Edit** ActiveX control installed and registered on the machine where this web page is

---

\* You can easily find out the CLSID of any COM server using the Window's Registry Editor (*regedit.exe*) or the OLE/COM Object Viewer (*oleview.exe*).

executed. The `Wang Image Edit` control comes for free with Windows NT 4.0, so there's no need to download this control from a particular web site.

```
<object id="WangImage"
    classid="CLSID:6D940280-9F11-11CE-83FD-02608C3EC08A"
    width="400" height="70">
</object>
```

In our web page, we refer to this control as `WangImage`, but we could have named it anything we like. Notice that we set the correct CLSID, which must be prefixed with `CLSID:`. In addition, we set the preferred width and height of the ActiveX control.

## OCR Results

In the sixth row, we need to add a text area (a multiline edit control) to display notification or error messages, including the returned result after OCR processing.

```
<textarea name="OcrText" rows="2"
    cols="47">Return message will be inserted here...</textarea>
```

Even though the initially displayed text is a simple message, this text area will be filled with the text that is returned from calling the *OcrImage* method of the `ATLCyberOcr` ActiveX control. Recall that the *ProcessImage* VBScript subroutine calls *OcrImage* when the `OCR` pushbutton is pressed.

## ATLCyberOcr ActiveX Control

The last row of our table contains an embedded `ATLCyberOcr` ActiveX control, which we've developed previously in this chapter. Similar to the `Wang Image Edit` ActiveX control, we need to know its CLSID. Since we're the developers of this control, we can obtain this CLSID from the interface definition file (*ATLCyberServer.idl*).

If you are doing local development and don't have Internet Information Server or Peer Web Server installed on your NT machine, this row should contain the code shown below:

```
<object id="ATLCyberOcr"
    classid="CLSID:C459B3C4-F08F-11D1-8754-006008CDD9AE"
    width="400" height="16"></object>
```

The code above assumes that you have the `ATLCyberOcr` ActiveX control installed and registered on the machine where this web page is executed. However, unlike the `Wang Image Edit` control, which lives on every Windows NT 4.0 machine that has it installed, no machine will have the `ATLCyberOcr` ActiveX control installed by default. Thus, in a real distributed environment, ActiveX controls should be dynamically downloaded as needed. To support this, we specify the URL for downloading the ActiveX control as needed. This is done with the codebase attribute of the `<object></object>` tag. Here's the snippet for allowing the dynamic downloading of the `ATLCyberOcr` ActiveX control:

```
<object id="ATLCyberOcr"
    classid="CLSID:C459B3C4-F08F-11D1-8754-006008CDD9AE"
    width="400" height="16"
    codebase="http://www.dcom.com/ATLCyberServer.dll"></object>
```

The above HTML snippet will download the *ATLCyberServer.dll* from the *www. dcom.com*\* web site to the client machine. In addition, IE will also automatically register the downloaded DLL against the local registry.

Notice that in our example, this is the only DLL that needs to be downloaded. No proxy/stub code for the `ATLCyberServer` or for the `OCRServer` components needs to be downloaded, because each is merged into the `ATLCyberServer` component. If we didn't merge the proxy/stub code for both of these components, the user would have to also download and register their proxy/stub DLLs. Again, you need the proxy/stub code for the `ATLCyberServer` when the container thread that creates the `ATLCyberOcr` ActiveX control has a different threading model than the control. You will always need the proxy/stub code for the `OCRServer` component, because the `OCRServer` component is a separate process, implying that marshaling will always happen. In addition, marshaling a custom interface requires the appropriate proxy/stub code.

## Complete HTML and VBScript Source Code

At this point, we have gone over all elements of the web-based user interface that allow a user to do distributed OCR processing. For easy reference, here's a complete listing of the HTML and VBScript code for this thin client:

```
<html>
<head><title>Learning DCOM</title></head>
<body bgcolor="#0CC0CC">

<center>
<table width=400 border="8" cellpadding="2" cellspacing="8"
bgcolor="#B0BCEC">
    <tr>
        <td colspan="2" align="center">
            <font size="3"><em><strong>Learning DCOM</strong></em></font>
        </td>
    </tr>
    <tr>
        <td align="center" colspan="2">
            <input type="button" name="ViewImage" value="View"
                language="VBScript" onclick="Call ViewImageFile()">
            <input type="button" name="Fit" value="FitBest"
```

---

\* At the time of this writing, no one has claimed the *dcom.com* domain name. For your own applications, of course, codebase will contain the real location of your DLL.

```
            language="VBScript" onclick="WangImage.FitTo(0)">
          <input type="button" name="Width" value="FitWidth"
            language="VBScript" onclick="WangImage.FitTo(1)">
          <input type="button" name="ZoomRectangle" value="Zoom"
            language="VBScript" onclick="ZoomToSelection()">
          <input type="button" name="RotateRight" value="Rotate"
            language="VBScript" onclick="WangImage.RotateRight">
          <input type="button" name="OCRImage" value="O.C.R."
            language="VBScript" onclick="OcrWholeImage()">
        </td>
    </tr>
    <tr>
        <td>Server Name</td>
        <td><input type="text" size="25" name="ServerName" value="dog"></td>
    </tr>
    <tr>
        <td>Image Location</td>
        <td>
            <input type="text" size="25" name="TIFFLocation"
            value="c:\temp\test.tif">
        </td>
    </tr>
    <tr>
        <td colspan="2" align="center">
          <object id="WangImage"
          classid="CLSID:6D940280-9F11-11CE-83FD-02608C3EC08A"
          width="400" height="70"></object>
        </td>
    </tr>
    <tr>
        <td colspan="2" align="center">
          <textarea name="OcrText" rows="2"
          cols="47">Return message will be inserted here...</textarea>
        </td>
    </tr>
    <tr>
        <td colspan="2" align="center">
          <object id="ATLCyberOcr"
          classid="CLSID:C459B3C4-F08F-11D1-8754-006008CDD9AE"
          width="400" height="16"></object>
        </td>
    </tr>
</table></center>

</body>
</html>

<script language="VBScript"><!--
Sub ViewImageFile()
        WangImage.Image = TIFFLocation.value
        WangImage.Display()
        WangImage.FitTo(0)
        OcrText.value = "Image has not been OCRed"
end sub
```

```
Sub OcrWholeImage()
        ATLCyberOcr.OCRServerName = ServerName.value
        strFileName = TIFFLocation.value
        OcrText.value = ATLCyberOcr.OcrImage(strFileName)
end sub

Sub ZoomToSelection()
        if WangImage.ImageDisplayed then
            WangImage.ZoomToSelection()
        end if
end sub
--></script>
```

You should now test this web page locally by opening it using Internet Explorer 3.0 or above. For dynamic downloading and distributed testing, you should copy the web page just created (*ATLCyberOcr.htm*) and the **ATLCyberServer** component (*ATLCyberServer.dll*), which hosts the **ATLCyberOcr** ActiveX control, to a downloadable URL that you specify in your web page.

On a different Windows NT machine, you can navigate to the target URL and download the *ATLCyberOcr.htm* web page. This action will also cause the downloading of the *ATLCyberServer.dll*. IE will then automatically register this DLL against the local registry.* Once the downloading is done, you have a thin, web-based OCR client. Check it out. When you are done testing and playing around, I hope you agree that Distributed COM is ubiquitous, as anyone in cyberspace can quickly download a completely functional component. The beauty is that the downloaded component can internally talk to other distributed components by taking advantage of Distributed COM, barring a few constraints that will be discussed next.

## Problems with COM over the Internet

So far in this chapter, we have a thin, web-enabled client that uses an in-process **ATLCyberServer** component, which in turn uses the **OCRServer** component that can potentially reside on a machine across the Internet. Before these two components can cooperate peacefully over the Internet, they must manage or deal with two problems: security and firewalls.

### Problems with security

Detailed security samples will be shown in both Chapters 9, *Applying Security*, and 10, *Connecting Objects*, but in this chapter I'll discuss particular security aspects that affect COM in cyberspace. When your thin, web-enabled client is sent across the Internet to a client workstation, the contained **ATLCyberServer** component

---

* Remember to configure the options in IE to allow downloading of ActiveX controls and execution of scripts.

will eventually communicate with a remote OCRServer component to carry out OCR processing requests. Clients over the Internet are traditionally anonymous and if you were to follow this model, you must make sure that the ATLCyberServer component sets the authentication level to RPC_C_AUTHN_NONE each time it invokes a method in the OCRServer component. The ATLCyberServer component can do this by using the *CoQueryClientBlanket* and *CoSetProxyBlanket* API functions, discussed in Chapter 5. If the client uses RPC_C_AUTHN_NONE, the server must also be configured or programmed to accept anonymous access. Since your server is out-of-process, you can use *CoInitializeSecurity* to set the process-wide security settings to include RPC_C_AUTHN_NONE. But of course, anonymous access can be a potential security problem, because you must allow launch and access permissions to all users of your server application.

An arguably better way of solving this problem is to hard-code a well-known user account into the ATLCyberServer component that will later use the account to communicate with the server. This will tighten security greatly, because ATLCyberServer can use the COAUTHINFO and COAUTHIDENTITY structures to dynamically activate distributed objects and invoke remote methods. On the server side, OCRServer can limit access to only the well-known account, thus closing many holes that can be possibly penetrated by intruders. This technique also allows the client and the server to use any authentication level, including the highest one that allows for full data encryption.

So far, we've dealt only with method calls going from the client to the server, but what about calls going from the server back to the client (such a call is called a *callback*, which reverses the role of the client and server)? This is an important question because in-process servers don't get the chance to call *CoInitializeSecurity*, as this is done by the container application, namely Internet Explorer. Because of this, in order for the client to capture callbacks from the server, you would have to use *dcomcnfg.exe* to configure the client machine to use RPC_C_AUTHN_NONE, allowing anonymous access to the whole client machine, which is much worse than anonymous access to a single application. (I don't recommend callbacks in components running freely over the Internet.)

### Problems with firewalls or proxy servers

As you push components into cyberspace, you have to deal with the existence of firewalls and the complexities that these agents bring into the COM equation. In the effort to protect intellectual property and prevent security attacks, companies defend their internal network with firewalls, which typically intercept all outer network traffic and reroute it to the correct internal destination. Likewise, all outgoing traffic must first cross a firewall before it goes out into cyberspace. To achieve this middleman effect, firewalls translate all actual internal IP addresses into the IP address of the firewall itself, so that external clients see only the firewall's IP address. However, address translation inhibits the operation of Distributed COM because the actual destination IP address is kept inside the marshal interface reference. So using COM to pass through firewalls that do address translation is out of the question; but for firewalls that don't translate IP addresses, COM is possible through some registry settings.

When two components need to communicate across a network boundary, COM tells the server component to load a specific network protocol that is compatible with the client and automatically assigns the server component a port or an endpoint. Because of this initialization, a server component can use a particular port at one time and a totally different one at a later time, which is great from an administrative standpoint since no server port must be configured. However, this unpredictable and sporadic assignment of ports is unacceptable in any environment with a firewall; imagine how your firewall administrator would react if you request 5000 ports to be opened for a particular IP address. If you can control and limit a port range that COM can use to dynamically assign components, your firewall administrator will be more likely to swallow your request.

Luckily, there is a way to pick a range of ports that can be assigned to server-side components that service remote clients. The DCOM configuration tool that comes with Windows NT 4.0 Service Pack 4 allows you easily configure machine-wide port usage through the `Default Protocols` property dialog box and application-level port usage through the `Endpoints` property dialog box. The `Default Protocols` property dialog box allows you to set the protocol usage order, and you need to set `Connection-oriented TCP/IP` as the first protocol on the client machine if you intend to allow servers to make callbacks to the client. Refer to Appendix C for more details on endpoint configuration.

# MFC Composites

The previous section showed you how to distribute your objects across intergalactic cyberspace, but you had to write VBScript code to tie everything on the web page together. The `ATLCyberOcr` ActiveX control in the last section was also pretty simple, since it had no real user interface, as it simply displayed a message. The user interface included all the controls defined in the HTML script.

That doesn't mean you can't build ActiveX controls with real user interfaces; in other words, a control that is composed of other controls. In this section, I will show you a quick way to develop a composite ActiveX control with a user interface. By the end of this section, you will have developed an ActiveX control similar to the one shown in Figure 8-7.

The web page that you are looking at in Figure 8-7 contains only some text and a single `<object></object>` tag, because the web page is dealing with only one ActiveX control. This ActiveX control has a toolbar, an image viewer, and a multi-line edit control. If you have experience with the Microsoft Foundation Classes (MFC), you may think that this ActiveX control looks much like an MFC dialog, and if that's your guess, you are right.

MFC is a set of C++ classes that makes developing Windows applications simple. The MFC wizards in Visual C++ use portions of the MFC classes to generate frameworks for a variety of applications, including ActiveX controls. Unlike ATL, MFC supports COM using the nested classes approach, since most of this framework code is developed prior to Visual C++'s support for multiple inheritance. Like ATL, MFC supports interface maps to make implementing interfaces easier. Actually, ATL borrows the idea of maps from MFC. As you've seen earlier, these maps are nothing more than macros that expand into a large code block, thus shielding all the boilerplate code from the developer.

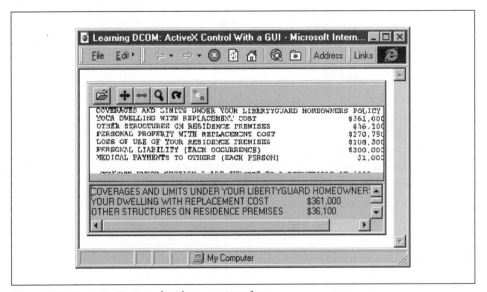

*Figure 8-7. An ActiveX control with a user interface*

You're going to piggyback on the MFC dialog template support to easily embed controls within a dialog. Collectively, a client will see our ActiveX control as a single entity, but within this ActiveX control, you can do anything you want. For example, the ActiveX control that you'll be developing uses the `Wang Image Edit` ActiveX control as the image view.

Before we start, I want to say that this section assumes that you know how to create a toolbar, create a dialog resource, add controls to a dialog, and assign resource identifiers to user interface elements using Visual C++. It also assumes that you have basic knowledge of MFC. There is a reason for this: I have no desire to write fifty pages for this section. If you don't have this preliminary knowledge, study the "Visual C++ Tutorials" in Visual C++'s online help before attempting to proceed with this section. With that said, let's buckle up and get started.

## Creating an MFC ActiveX Control Project

We will be creating an MFC ActiveX control using the `MFC ActiveX ControlWizard`, instead of using the `ATL COM AppWizard` as we did in the last few sections. The reason we are doing this is that user interface ActiveX controls are easier to build using MFC. This is partly due to the maturity of the MFC framework and its wizard support, which makes developing user interface oriented ActiveX controls very simple. Since the goal is simplicity, we will use MFC in order to piggyback on the MFC dialog template facility.

To get started, create a new project and name it `MFCCyberServer`. You would want to create this project using the `MFC ActiveX ControlWizard`, so make sure that you select the `MFC ActiveX ControlWizard` prior to clicking the `OK` button in the `New` dialog box. After you click `OK` to proceed, the `MFC ActiveX ControlWizard - Step 1 of 2` dialog will be shown. We will take the default options in these two wizard steps, so you can now click `Finish` to complete the project options.

### Understanding the generated code

The `MFC ActiveX ControlWizard` will generate a number of files, one of which is the object definition language (ODL) file, which serves the same purpose as an IDL file. It supports the same syntax as IDL, but is used only in MFC COM projects. Our generated ODL file is named *MFCCyberServer.odl* and it contains all the information regarding our ActiveX control's events, properties, and methods. The generated file looks, in a nutshell, like the following:

```
[uuid(E87E4EE5-FDCD-11D1-8761-006008CDD9AE), control]
library MFCCYBERSERVERLib
{
    [uuid(E87E4EE7-FDCD-11D1-8761-006008CDD9AE]
    dispinterface _DMFCCyberServer {
      properties:
      methods:
    };


     [uuid(E87E4EE8-FDCD-11D1-8761-006008CDD9AE)]
     dispinterface _DMFCCyberServerEvents {
       properties:
       methods:
    };


     [uuid(E87E4EE9-FDCD-11D1-8761-006008CDD9AE)]
     coclass MFCCyberServer {
       [default] dispinterface _DMFCCyberServer;
```

```
        [default, source] dispinterface _DMFCCyberServerEvents;
    };
};
```

Note that the [control] attribute describes the library MFCCYBERSERVERLib, telling the world that this library contains one or more ActiveX controls. Some tools or utilities look at this attribute to quickly determine whether the component contains ActiveX controls.

The generated *_DMFCCyberServer* interface is a dispatch interface, and it is the main interface that supports the functionality of the ActiveX control we're about to develop. As we add methods and properties, they will be inserted into the appropriate sections within this interface definition. Containers, like IE for example, will call methods or properties of this interface to use our ActiveX control.

Our control can also call back out to the hosting container. To do this, we can define events that our ActiveX control will fire (or throw) off to the hosting container. Events allow an ActiveX control to inform its hosting container of special notifications, such as a left mouse click inside the control. A container that wants to be conscious of this event must trap it. So the generated ODL file defines an event (callback) interface called *_DMFCCyberServerEvents*. This interface must be implemented by the container, as the ActiveX control will call the methods of this event interface in the container upon an occurrence of a specific event. Since the control fires off events, it is called a source. Since the container implements this interface and thus receives the notification, it is called a sink. Sources and sinks will be discussed in more detail in Chapter 10, *Connecting Objects*.

Look at the definition of the MFCCyberServer coclass in the ODL code shown earlier and you'll see that this coclass supports a dispatch interface called *_DMFCCyberServer*. In addition, it also defines a dispatch interface (*_DMFCCyberServerEvents*) that serves as a source from which a sink will receive wanted notifications. Really, the generated definition in this ODL file is no different from the IDL files that we have seen throughout this book.*

Besides the ODL file, the MFC ActiveX ControlWizard also generates a number of C++ classes needed to support an MFC ActiveX control. These include:

*CMFCCyberServerApp*
> Derived from *COleControlModule*. *COleControlModule* provides the initialization and termination hooks for your component. Other than this, it has no special purpose. You should note that the .*cpp* file associated with this class implements the *DllRegisterServer* and *DllUnregisterServer* entry points for in-process server registration and unregistration.

---

* MFC uses ODL for interface definitions, but ATL uses IDL for this purpose. ODL exists for historical reasons, so in the future, you will see less ODL and more IDL.

### CMFCCyberServerPropPage

Derived from *COlePropertyPage*. *COlePropertyPage* allows a user to edit the properties of the supported ActiveX control. The **MFC ActiveX ControlWizard** generates the framework for this class, including its associated dialog resource to allow you to add visual elements for editing the properties of your ActiveX control.

### CMFCCyberServerCtrl

Derived from *COleControl*. This class is the key to the implementation of an MFC ActiveX control. It implements nearly a score of different interfaces to support the management of ActiveX controls and the complex interconnections with its hosting container. With the **MFC ActiveX ControlWizard**, all this default implementation is provided to you for free—you write no code to get this support.

It would take a book to fully describe the how MFC implements COM.* However, the basic concepts are similar to ATL, as MFC also hides most of the boilerplate stuff under macros and within base classes. For example, as shown in the generated class definition below, **DECLARE_OLECREATE_EX** is enough to declare a class factory for this ActiveX control. The **DECLARE_DISPATCH_MAP** macro declares that this control supports a dispatch interface. As you add new properties or methods to this interface, the declarations of those properties or methods will be recorded between the **//{{AFX_DISPATCH** comments.

Likewise, the **DECLARE_EVENT_MAP** macro signifies that this control fires events. Any event that you add will be recorded between the **//{{AFX_EVENT** comments. To be specific, when you add an event, an inline function will be generated between the **//{{AFX_EVENT** comment blocks. You can call this special generated function at any time and anywhere within the code of this ActiveX control to fire off an event represented by the generated inline function to the hosting container.

```
class CMFCCyberServerCtrl : public COleControl {
public:
        CMFCCyberServerCtrl();

protected:
        ~CMFCCyberServerCtrl();

        DECLARE_OLECREATE_EX(CMFCCyberServerCtrl)

// Dispatch maps
        //{{AFX_DISPATCH(CMFCCyberServerCtrl)
        //}}AFX_DISPATCH
```

* To get a good discussion of how MFC implements COM, see MFC Technical Note 38, "TN038: MFC/ OLE IUnknown implementation." The *IUnknown* interface is implemented in a base class call *CCmdTarget* from which our *CMFCCyberServerCtrl* indirectly inherits.

```
        DECLARE_DISPATCH_MAP()

        afx_msg void AboutBox();

// Event maps
        //{{AFX_EVENT(CMFCCyberServerCtrl)
        //}}AFX_EVENT
        DECLARE_EVENT_MAP()
};
```

In the implementation file of *CMFCCyberServerCtrl*, the wizard inserts implementations for the preceding declarations; these implementations are also simplified by a few magic macros. The `IMPLEMENT_OLECREATE_EX` macro provides the default implementation of a standard class factory for this ActiveX control, as shown in the following generated code snippet.

The `BEGIN_DISPATCH_MAP` starts a map of implementations for properties or methods added to the supported dispatch interface and the `END_DISPATCH_MAP` ends this map. As each property or method is added, it gets inserted into the dispatch map and a stubbed (or empty) function will be generated. Your job is to simply fill in the functionality for this generated function.

The `BEGIN_EVENT_MAP` starts an event map for the events that can be fired off by this ActiveX control and the `END_EVENT_MAP` macro ends this map. As an event is added, an inline function will be generated to fire the associated event to the container. In this sense, you have to provide no custom implementation for events, except to call the appropriate generated event function to fire off the correct event to the container.

```
// Initialize class factory and GUID
IMPLEMENT_OLECREATE_EX(CMFCCyberServerCtrl,
    "MFCCYBERSERVER.MFCCyberServerCtrl.1",
    0xe87e4ee9, 0xfdcd, 0x11d1, 0x87, 0x61, 0, 0x60, 0x8, 0xcd, 0xd9, 0xae)

// Dispatch map
BEGIN_DISPATCH_MAP(CMFCCyberServerCtrl, COleControl)
        //{{AFX_DISPATCH_MAP(CMFCCyberServerCtrl)
        //}}AFX_DISPATCH_MAP
        DISP_FUNCTION_ID(CMFCCyberServerCtrl, "AboutBox",
                DISPID_ABOUTBOX, AboutBox, VT_EMPTY, VTS_NONE)
END_DISPATCH_MAP()

// Event map
BEGIN_EVENT_MAP(CMFCCyberServerCtrl, COleControl)
        //{{AFX_EVENT_MAP(CMFCCyberServerCtrl)
        //}}AFX_EVENT_MAP
END_EVENT_MAP()
```

Since *COleControl* is really the mastermind of an MFC ActiveX control and since *CMFCCyberServerCtrl* derives from *COleControl*, the *CMFCCyberServerCtrl* class represents the ActiveX control we're building. We will make modifications to this class to create an ActiveX control with a nice user interface.

Because we want to deal only with creating a user interface in this section, we will not add any methods, properties, or events to our ActiveX control. However, this is simple to do, as all you'd have to do is right-click the appropriate interface and select Add Method, Add Property, or Add Event from the popup context menu. Another way to this is by using the MFC ClassWizard, which you can launch by pressing CTRL-W. The Automation tab of the MFC ClassWizard allows you add methods or properties to the dispatch interface exposed by this ActiveX control. The ActiveX Events tab of the MFC ClassWizard allows you to add events that this control will fire to its hosting container.

If you build the control at this moment and test it out, you will see that the generated ActiveX control draws an ellipse. You can test this using a web page with the appropriate <object></object> tag to include the CLSID of this ActiveX control, which the MFC ActiveX ControlWizard automatically names MFCCyberServer by default. For example, the following HTML code will allow you to test this ActiveX control. Make sure you fill in the correct CLSID, because your CLSID will be different from the CLSID shown in this HTML snippet:

```
<html>
<head><title>Learning DCOM:  ActiveX Control With a GUI</title></head>
<body>
    <object id="MFCCyberServer"
        classid="CLSID:E87E4F05-FDCD-11D1-8761-006008CDD9AE"
        width="400" height="200"></object>
</body>
</html>
```

Alternatively, you can insert the control into the ActiveX Control Test Container for testing. You can launch the ActiveX Control Test Container by selecting it under Visual Studio's Tools menu or by executing *tstcon32.exe*, a utility that comes with Visual Studio.

### Creating the user interface

Now that we have created the project and understood the generated files, let's create the user interface elements for our ActiveX control. Before we can paint the user interface, we need to create a dialog resource using Visual Studio's Resource Editor. To do this, press CTRL-R to launch the Insert Resource dialog box. From this window, select a dialog resource and click the New button to create a new dialog resource. Once the dialog template is created, delete the OK and Cancel buttons on the dialog box because you will not use them.

Display the properties (ATL-ENTER) of this dialog resource and change the identifier of the dialog resource to IDD_DIALOG_IMAGING. In addition, as seen in Figure 8-8, you must set this dialog's Style property to Child. The reason you're doing this is that you want the dialog to be a child window of the ActiveX control. You should uncheck the Title bar check-box because you don't want it to show. You also need to make sure that the `Visible` style is checked in the `More Styles` tab; this will make the dialog visible at runtime.

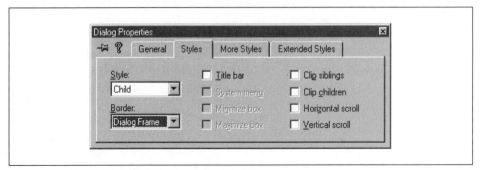

*Figure 8-8. The style of the dialog must be "Child"*

A dialog resource lets you place common and ActiveX controls on it. In addition, MFC's dialog template facility will manage these controls at runtime and this is the main reason we commit to piggyback on this facility to easily build the user interface for our `MFCCyberServer` ActiveX control. As you will soon see, we can easily trap command messages to handle toolbar button selections. Additionally, we will not have to write a single line of code to create, render, and manage the controls placed in the dialog box, since MFC's dialog template facility provides these for free.

Another interesting thing is that you can take advantage of `Dialog Data Exchange` (DDX) and `Dialog Data Validation` (DDV). DDX is an MFC feature that allows the exchange of data between controls and member variables, and DDV is an MFC feature that allows data validation of user data input. To use DDX and DDV to transfer data from the controls to their associated member variables, you can call `UpdateData(TRUE)`; to transfer data from the member variables to the associated controls, you call `UpdateData(FALSE)`.

Once you have given the dialog resource an identifier and changed its style to `Child`, you can proceed to generate a C++ class to represent this dialog. With the focus on the dialog resource, launch the `MFC ClassWizard` by pressing CTRL-W. The `MFC ClassWizard` will ask you to let it create a new C++ class. Allow it to do this and name this class *CImagingWindow*. Make sure that the new C++ class derives from *CDialog*, because the *CDialog* class supports the dialog template facility, which manages all child window creation, data exchange, and data validation.

Once the `MFC ClassWizard` has generated the C++ *CImagingWindow* class, you can add a multiline edit control to the dialog resource. Do this simply by dragging the edit control into the dialog resource. View its properties and change its identifier to `IDC_EDIT_TEXT`. Also, change its style to multiline to display more than one line of text. Check the `Horizontal scroll`, `Vertical scroll`, and

Read-only options, as these options will add scroll bars to the edit control and make the edit control read-only.

Now that you've added an edit control, you need to bind it to a member variable so that you can manipulate (e.g., resize it and set its text) it at runtime. To bind the edit control to a member variable of the *CImagingWindow* class, use the Member Variables tab of the MFC ClassWizard. Select the *CImagingWindow* class in the Member Variables tab of the MFC ClassWizard and select IDC_EDIT_TEXT. Click on the Add Variable pushbutton and bind this edit control to a member variable of type *CEdit*. Name this variable m_EditOcrText.

If you look back to Figure 8-7, you will see that the user interface contains a toolbar. Similar to creating a dialog resource, we can use the Resource Editor to create a toolbar resource. Assign the IDR_TOOLBAR_IMAGING identifier to the newly created toolbar resource. We'll add six buttons to it and give these buttons the following self-explanatory identifiers:

ID_BUTTON_BROWSE

> This button allows a user to browse a local or network directory for an image, which needs to be OCR processed.

ID_BUTTON_FIT_BEST

> This button allows a user to fit the image as best possible within the Wang Image Edit ActiveX control. We will add this control shortly.

ID_BUTTON_FIT_WIDTH

> This button allows a user to fit the width of the image as best possible within the Wang Image Edit ActiveX control.

ID_BUTTON_ZOOM

> This button allows a user to zoom into a selected rectangular region.

ID_BUTTON_ROTATE

> This button allows a user to rotate the image clockwise.

ID_BUTTON_OCR

> This button allows a user to OCR the selected image.

So far, we have all user interface elements except the Wang Image Edit ActiveX Control. We'll do this next.

### Using an ActiveX control within an ActiveX control

We are going to put an ActiveX control, developed by Wang, inside our own developed ActiveX control. We use the Wang Image Edit ActiveX control because it provides all the image rendering for us. Before we can use this control, we must first generate a C++ wrapper class for it. You can generate a wrapper class using the `Components and Controls Gallery`, which you can launch by selecting the `Project` menu, `Add To Project`, and `Components and Controls`. The `Wang Image Edit` control is found in the `Registered ActiveX Controls` folder. Find and select the `Wang Image Edit` control. After selecting the `Wang Image Edit` control, you will be asked which classes to generate. Choose the *CImgEdit* class and leave the filenames the same. *CImgEdit* is the C++ wrapper class that represents the `Wang Image Edit` ActiveX control, and you will use this class to manipulate this control in your code.

Once you have generated a wrapper class for this control, you should add a member variable called `m_Image` of type *CImgEdit* to the *CImagingWindow* class.* We will use this member variable to manipulate the `Wang Image Edit` ActiveX control, which serves as the image viewer inside our ActiveX control. Once you have added this member variable, a portion of the *CImagingWindow* class definition should look as follows:

```
class CImagingWindow : public CDialog
{
    . . .
    //{{AFX_DATA(CImagingWindow)
    enum { IDD = IDD_DIALOG_IMAGING };
    CEdit m_EditOcrText;
    //}}AFX_DATA
    CImgEdit m_Image;
    . . .
};
```

Before you implement the *CImagingWindow* class, you must do one important thing. Since you're using an ActiveX control (`Wang Image Edit` control) within the ActiveX control you're developing (*MFCCyberServerCtrl*), you need to tell the MFC framework that you want to enable containment of ActiveX controls. In other words, you want your ActiveX control to be a container of another ActiveX control, such as the `Wang Image Edit` control. You can do this by simply calling *AfxEnableControlContainer* anywhere before creating an instance of the `Wang Image Edit` control. The common place to call this function is in an application's *InitInstance* function, which is called once during component startup. Thus, you should add the following bolded code to the *InitInstance* function of *CMFCCyberServerApp*:

```
BOOL CMFCCyberServerApp::InitInstance()
{
    BOOL bInit = COleControlModule::InitInstance();
    if (bInit) {
        AfxEnableControlContainer() ;
    }
```

---

* Ideally, you should be able to drag and drop an ActiveX control onto your dialog just as an edit control; however, the `Wang Image Edit` ActiveX control does not behave well at runtime when this is done. As a work-around, we resort to creating and manipulating this control manually.

```
        return bInit;
    }
```

Again, doing this allows your ActiveX control to be a container to other ActiveX controls; or in other words, to be a composite. If you fail to do this, you will encounter an access violation when you run the ActiveX control that you're developing.

### Implementing the ActiveX Control: CMFCCyberServerCtrl

Remember that our original goal was to create an ActiveX control with user interface elements. We have thus far created the *CImagingWindow* dialog template and stuffed it with common and ActiveX controls. To fulfill our goal, we need to show this dialog in the bounding area reserved for our ActiveX control. In other words, what we need to do now is show an instance of *CImagingWindow* in the area that our ActiveX control occupies.

Currently, our ActiveX control draws an ellipse in the *OnDraw* function, which is called by the MFC framework automatically every time that our ActiveX control needs to be redrawn. We don't want to show this ellipse; instead, we want to show our dialog, so you should delete the two lines of generated code from the *OnDraw* function.

To display our own dialog in the bounding area occupied by the ActiveX control, we need to do a few things. We need to add a member variable of type *CImagingWindow* to the *CMFCCyberServerCtrl* class. When you do this, name this variable m_ImagingWindow. We also need to write two special functions as discussed below.

### CMFCCyberServerCtrl::OnCreate

We need to create an instance of *CImagingWindow* as a child window of the ActiveX control. To do this, we handle the WM_CREATE window message. We can create a handler for the WM_CREATE message using the MFC ClassWizard. In the MFC ClassWizard's Message Maps tab, select *CMFCCyberServerCtrl* in the Class name drop-down combo control, select *CMFCCyberServerCtrl* in the Object IDs list control, and double-click on WM_CREATE in the Messages list control, and this will generate the *OnCreate* handler in the *CMFCCyberServerCtrl* class. When the ActiveX control is being created, this function will be called by the framework to allow us to create any other child window we want. In our case, we want to create the *CImagingWindow* as the child window of our ActiveX control, so the code for this handler should look something like the following:

```
int CMFCCyberServerCtrl::OnCreate(LPCREATESTRUCT lpCreateStruct)
{
    if (COleControl::OnCreate(lpCreateStruct) == -1)
        return -1;
    m_ImagingWindow.Create(IDD_DIALOG_IMAGING, this);
    return 0;
}
```

We invoke the *Create* function of the *CDialog* class to create a dialog using the dialog template (identified by `IDD_DIALOG_IMAGING`) that we have painted in the beginning of this section. The second parameter to *Create* says that we want the ActiveX control we're developing to be the parent of `m_ImagingWindow`. This parenting is implied because the `this` pointer points the ActiveX control instance.

### CMFCCyberServerCtrl::OnDraw

Having created the *CImagingWindow*, we can now add code to the overridden *OnDraw* function. Remember that the user must see the dialog, because it contains all the user interface elements. Therefore, in this function, we'll resize m_ ImagingWindow to be as large as the visible rectangle taken up by the ActiveX control, as shown in the code below. Notice that we move the window to fit the bounding rectangle occupied by the ActiveX control by calling the *MoveWindow* function.

```
void CImagingControlCtrl::OnDraw(CDC* pdc,
                                 const CRect& rcBounds,
                                 const CRect& rcInvalid)
{
    if (IsWindow(m_hWnd))
        m_ImagingWindow.MoveWindow(rcBounds);
}
```

At this point, you can build the project. Test it by using either your web page developed earlier or the `ActiveX Control Test Container` utility that comes with Visual Studio. You should see the dialog but no toolbar or `Wang Image Edit` control. To add these elements, you need to add a few lines of code to the *CImagingWindow* class.

## Implementing CImagingWindow

To implement *CImagingWindow*, we need to add the member variables associated with the user interface elements of this dialog. We have already added two member variables; these are `m_EditOcrText` (of type *CEdit*) and `m_Image` (of type *CImgEdit*). The third member that we need to add is `m_Toolbar`, which will be an instance of *CToolBar* and will represent our toolbar on the dialog. You should now add this member to the *CImagingWindow* class definition, as shown here:

```
class CImagingWindow : public CDialog
{
    . . .
    //{{AFX_DATA(CImagingWindow)
    enum { IDD = IDD_DIALOG_IMAGING };
    CEdit m_EditOcrText;
    //}}AFX_DATA
    CImgEdit m_Image;
    CToolBar m_Toolbar;
    . . .
};
```

The next thing that we will do is to write the code to arrange the toolbar, edit control, and `Wang Image Edit` control nicely on the *CImagingWindow* dialog. We will also add the code to handle the toolbar selections. In other words, we'll write the code to handle each button shown in the toolbar.

### CImagingWindow::OnCreate

Before we can arrange the controls on our dialog, they need to be created first. The edit control is created and managed by the MFC's dialog template facility, because we've dragged and dropped the control onto the dialog template earlier.* We have not done that for the toolbar and the `Wang Image Edit` control, so we will have to manually create these user interface elements ourselves.

To do this, we need to handle the `WM_CREATE` message in the *CImagingWindow* class. Recall that we can easily do this using the `MFC ClassWizard`. In this handler, we need to create a toolbar and the `Wang Image Edit` control using the *Create* member function.

```
int CImagingWindow::OnCreate(LPCREATESTRUCT lpCreateStruct)
{
    if (CDialog::OnCreate(lpCreateStruct) == -1)  return -1;

    m_Toolbar.Create(this);
    m_Toolbar.LoadToolBar(IDR_TOOLBAR_IMAGING);
    m_Image.Create(0, 0, WS_VISIBLE|WS_CHILD, CRect(), this, IDC_CTRL_IMAGE);

    return 0;
}
```

There are two steps to creating a toolbar. First, we create the toolbar by using the *Create* function of *CToolBar*. In this call, we pass along the `this` pointer to indicate that the *CImagingWindow* dialog is the parent of the toolbar. Second, after creating the toolbar, we load the toolbar using the toolbar resource created earlier in this section.

To create the `Wang Image Edit` ActiveX control, we call the *Create* function supported by *CImgEdit*, which is a C++ generated class that wraps the `Wang Image Edit` control. Again, we pass the `this` pointer to indicate that this control is a child of the *CImagingWindow* dialog. We also pass the identifier `IDC_CTRL_IMAGE`; this is the identifier that can be used to refer to this control in its parent dialog. You should create or define this identifier using the `Resource Symbols Editor`. You can get to this editor by selecting `Resource Symbols` from the `View` menu.

---

* Specifically, this control is created during the call to *DDX_Control* in the *DoDataExchange* method of *CImagingWindow*.

### CImagingWindow::OnSize

After the child controls are all created, we can arrange them on the dialog. This means that we need to size the child controls relative to the size of the dialog, so we must handle the `WM_SIZE` window message. Again, we can easily add a message handler using the `MFC ClassWizard`. In this handler, we will move the toolbar to the top portion of the dialog. We will move `Wang Image Edit` control to the middle portion and the edit control to the bottom portion.

```
void CImagingWindow::OnSize(UINT nType, int cx, int cy)
{
    CDialog::OnSize(nType, cx, cy);

    if (IsWindowVisible()) {
        int dy=(int)(cy*.5), bar=30, pad=3;
        m_Toolbar.MoveWindow(0,0,cx,bar);
        m_Image.MoveWindow(0,bar,cx,dy);
        m_EditOcrText.MoveWindow(0,dy+bar+pad,cx,cy-dy-bar-pad);
    }
}
```

The previous code will arrange the child controls nicely within the dialog area. As indicated by the code, we arrange these child controls only when the *CImagingWindow* dialog is visible. We make this verification by calling the *IsWindowVisible* function. To move each of the user interface elements, we use the *MoveWindow* function. The algorithm for arranging the user interface elements is very simple. We assume that the toolbar's height is 30 pixels, the `Wang Image Edit` control occupies 50 percent of the height of our dialog, and the edit control gets the remaining height, less a 3-pixel padding.

After coding this `WM_SIZE` message handler, you should test this ActiveX control using either the web page that we wrote previously or the `ActiveX Control Test Container`. When you do this, you will see that all the child user interface elements are nicely arranged on the dialog.

### Handling command messages

We now have an attractive user interface; however, we haven't supported any functionality. For example, if you clicked any of the toolbar buttons, you would realize that the button is depressed but nothing happens. Nothing happens because we haven't added any code to handle those commands. In Windows programming, a menu, a toolbar, or an accelerator key is associated with a command. As a toolbar is selected, a command message is generated and to handle that command message, you must provide a *command handler*, which is just a member function that is mapped to an associated symbolic command identifier. We will write command handlers for the following commands, each of which is associated with a button on the toolbar created earlier in this section (thanks to our work with the `Resource Editor`).

ID_BUTTON_BROWSE

ID_BUTTON_FIT_BEST

ID_BUTTON_FIT_WIDTH

ID_BUTTON_ZOOM

ID_BUTTON_ROTATE

ID_BUTTON_OCR

Creating a command handler is similar to creating a *message handler*, such as WM_SIZE; you use the MFC ClassWizard to do it. You first have to let the MFC ClassWizard know that our toolbar is associated with the *CImagingWindow* class. To do this, you open the toolbar resource and launch the MFC ClassWizard. The MFC Class Wizard will require you to associate the toolbar with a C++ class, so choose the *CImagingWindow* class. Once you have associated the toolbar with the *CImagingWindow* class, here are the steps to add a command handler for the ID_BUTTON_BROWSE command message.

1. In the MFC ClassWizard, choose the **Message Maps** tab.
2. Select *CImagingWindow* in the **Class name** combo-box.
3. Select the command (e.g., ID_BUTTON_BROWSE) that you want to handle in the **Object IDs** list-box.
4. Double-click on **COMMAND** in the **Messages** list-box to create the handler.

Assuming that you have followed the above procedure, the MFC ClassWizard will generate the code for the selected command handler. You should repeat these four steps to create handlers for all the other commands.

Once you have done this, add the implementation for each command, which is associated with a generated handler function. For instance, in *OnButtonBrowse*, a command handler for ID_BUTTON_BROWSE, simply display the common Windows file selection dialog, which will allow the user to browse the local or network drive and pick an image for OCR processing. Once an image file is selected, tell the Wang Image Edit ActiveX control to display the image.

```
void CImagingWindow::OnButtonBrowse()
{
   CFileDialog adtDlg(TRUE,0,0,0, _T("TIFF Images(*.tif)|*.tif"));
   if (adtDlg.DoModal()==IDOK) {
      m_Image.SetImage(adtDlg.GetPathName()) ;
      m_Image.Display() ;
   }
   m_Image.RedrawWindow();
}
```

The *OnButtonFitBest*, *OnButtonFitWidth*, *OnButtonZoom*, and *OnButtonRotate* handlers are straightforward and, thus, self-explanatory. These are listed here for convenience.

```
void CImagingWindow::OnButtonFitBest()
{
   if (m_Image.GetImageDisplayed()) {
      VARIANT v; v.vt = VT_BOOL; v.boolVal = TRUE;
      m_Image.FitTo(0, v);
      m_Image.RedrawWindow();
   }
}

void CImagingWindow::OnButtonFitWidth()
{
   if (m_Image.GetImageDisplayed()) {
      VARIANT v; v.vt = VT_BOOL; v.boolVal = TRUE;
      m_Image.FitTo(1, v);
      m_Image.RedrawWindow();
   }
}

void CImagingWindow::OnButtonZoom()
{
   if (m_Image.GetImageDisplayed()) {
      m_Image.ZoomToSelection() ;
      m_Image.RedrawWindow();
   }
}

void CImagingWindow::OnButtonRotate()
{
   if (m_Image.GetImageDisplayed()) {
      m_Image.RotateRight() ;
      m_Image.RedrawWindow();
   }
}
```

The *OnButtonOcr* handler simply returns some hard-coded text, saved in the global variable g_szFakeOcrText. Since the focus of this exercise is to create an ActiveX control with a user interface, we omit talking to the OCRServer component via Distributed COM.

```
void CImagingWindow::OnButtonOcr()
{
   m_EditOcrText.SetWindowText(g_szFakeOcrText) ;
}
```

At this point, we achieved our goal. You should test this ActiveX control using the web page that you've developed earlier, and you will see that the buttons now respond to your request.

## ATL Composites

In the previous exercise, you used MFC to create an ActiveX control with a user interface. You can also do this using ATL. If you have an older version of ATL (prior to ATL 3.0), refer to the Microsoft Knowledge Base Article Q175503, entitled "HOWTO: Write a Dialog-based ActiveX Control Using ATL." However, if you have ATL 3.0* or greater, you can use the ATL Object Wizard to generate the necessary code for an ActiveX control with user interface elements. Formally, ATL uses the term *composite control* to refer to this type of ActiveX control.

Even though the ATL Object Wizard supports composite controls, it takes some work to get the composite control to host other ActiveX controls. In this section, you'll learn how to take advantage of ATL to create a composite control that looks like the web-enabled client developed previously.

## Creating the Project

Using the ATL COM AppWizard, create a new project and name it ATLCyberComposite. In Step 1 of the ATL COM AppWizard, select DLL as the Server Type and click Finish to allow the ATL COM AppWizard to generate the code for your project.

## Adding a Composite Control

Creating a composite control is similar to creating a Lite Control or a Full ActiveX Control. You simply choose Composite Control, and let the ATL Object Wizard handle the rest. Here are the steps for adding a composite control into an ATL COM AppWizard generated project:

1. Select New ATL Object from the Insert menu to launch the ATL Object Wizard.

2. In the ATL Object Wizard dialog box, select Controls in the list-box to the left and select Composite Control in the list-view on the right. Note that Composite Control is nonexistent in versions prior to ATL 3.0, so if you don't see this item, proceed to the "ActiveX Control Properties" section of this chapter, because you will not be able to complete this particular exercise.

3. Once you have selected Composite Control, click Next to proceed. This will launch the ATL Object Wizard Properties dialog box.

4. In the Short Name edit-box, type ATLCyberGUI and click OK to proceed.

At this point, the ATL Object Wizard has generated the necessary code for the newly added ActiveX control, which happens to be a composite control (per our request). As we have seen earlier in this chapter, the ATL Object Wizard generates an initial COM interface for our COM object and a C++ class that implements our COM object. The main difference between an ATL ActiveX control and a ATL ActiveX composite control is that the latter is derived from *CComCompositeControl*, as shown in the code snippet here:

---

* Version 3.0 of ATL is shipped with Visual C++ 6.0.

```
class CATLCyberGUI : . . ., public CComCompositeControl<CATLCyberGUI>,. . . {
. . .
public:
        enum { IDD = IDD_ATLCYBERGUI };
};
```

The *CComCompositeControl* class implements the functionality for a composite
control by taking advantage of the Win32 dialog template facility. In order to associate a composite control with its dialog template, the ATL Object Wizard generates an anonymous enum that holds this association, as shown by the second
emphasized statement in the earlier code snippet.

## Creating the User Interface

Immediately after you've added a composite control, you are presented with a dialog template into which you can embed common or ActiveX controls. Using this dialog template, create a user interface similar to the one shown back in Figure 8-6.

### Putting common controls onto the composite

First, add six buttons to the top of the dialog template to create a toolbar. These
buttons should have the following resource identifiers:

IDC_BUTTON_VIEW_IMAGE

> This button allows a user to view an image noted in the Image Location
> edit-box.

IDC_BUTTON_FIT_BEST

> This button allows a user to fit the image as best possible within the Wang
> Image Edit ActiveX control.

IDC_BUTTON_FIT_WIDTH

> This button allows a user to fit the width of the image as best possible within
> the Wang Image Edit ActiveX control.

IDC_BUTTON_ZOOM

> This button allows a user to zoom into a selected rectangular region.

IDC_BUTTON_ROTATE

> This button allows a user to rotate the image clockwise.

IDC_BUTTON_OCR

> This button allows a user to OCR the selected image.

After you have added these six buttons, you should add two static text controls
and their associated edit controls to hold the Server Name and the Image
Location. Assign the following identifiers to the edit controls:

`IDC_EDIT_SERVER_NAME`

This edit control is associated with the **Server Name** label (static text control).

`IDC_EDIT_IMAGE_LOCATION`

This edit control is associated with the **Image Location** label.

The last common control that you should add is a multiline edit control, which is used to hold the return OCR processed text. Give this control the identifier `IDC_EDIT_TEXT`.

### Putting ActiveX controls onto the composite

To add an ActiveX control into the dialog template, do the following:

1. Right-click on the dialog template and select **Insert ActiveX Control** on the popup menu.

2. When the **Insert ActiveX Control** dialog appears, find and select the **Wang Image Edit** ActiveX control.

3. Assign the following identifier to the **Wang Image Edit** control: `IDC_IMAGE_EDIT`.

### Testing the user interface

Build the component and test it using the following HTML script, which is generated by the **ATL Object Wizard**:

```
<HTML>
<BODY bgcolor="#0CC0CC">
   <OBJECT ID="ATLCyberGUI"
           CLASSID="CLSID:77C07844-2739-11D2-883E-006008CDD9AE">
   </OBJECT>
</BODY>
</HTML>
```

The user interface should appear on the web browser, but none of the buttons work. We'll have to write code to make them function.

## Implementation

In this section, we'll write the code to manipulate the **Wang Image Edit** control. In addition, we'll learn how to add message and command handlers to our COM object so that relevant messages and commands can be handled appropriately.

### Importing the embedded ActiveX control

Since we are using the **Wang Image Edit** control, we should use the `#import` compiler directive to generate an interface wrapper class that we can use to easily manipulate the **Wang Image Edit** control. As we have learned in Chapter 7, we can import an ActiveX control as follows:

```
// Make sure the path is correct.
#import "c:\winnt\system32\imgedit.ocx" \
   raw_native_types, no_namespace, \
   rename("_DImgEdit", "WangImageEdit"), \
   high_property_prefixes("Get","Set","PutRef_")
```

Remember that the **#import** statement generates a *.tli* and a *.tlh* file for you. To acquire the prototype for each method invocation, look into the *.tlh* file.

Once you have the *.tli* and *.tlh* files, you are ready to add a member variable to hold the interface pointer for the **Wang Image Edit** control. To do this, insert the following line into the class definition of *CATLCyberGUI*:

```
CComPtr<WangImageEdit> m_pWang;
```

To correctly initialize this smart pointer, you need to handle the **WM_INITDIALOG** window message. Windows sends this message to allow you to perform a one-time initialization for our dialog. To handle this message, add the bolded statement to the message map as follows:

```
BEGIN_MSG_MAP(CATLCyberGUI)
   MESSAGE_HANDLER(WM_INITDIALOG, OnInitDialog)
END_MSG_MAP()
```

The following code snippet is the handler for the **WM_INITDIALOG** window message. You handle this message to cache the interface pointer for the **Wang Image Edit** control, and you cache the pointer because many command handlers (to be written in a moment) will need to use this interface pointer.

```
LRESULT OnInitDialog(UINT uMsg, WPARAM wParam, LPARAM lParam, BOOL& bHandled)
{
    SetDlgItemText(IDC_EDIT_SERVER_NAME, "dog") ;
    SetDlgItemText(IDC_EDIT_IMAGE_LOCATION, "c:\\temp\\test.tif") ;
    HWND h = GetDlgItem(IDC_IMAGE_EDIT);
    try {
       if (h!=NULL) {
          CComPtr<IUnknown> pUnk;
          AtlAxGetControl(h, &pUnk);
          if (pUnk!=NULL) {
             HRESULT hr = pUnk->QueryInterface(IID_IDispatch,
                           reinterpret_cast<void**>(&m_pWang));
             if (FAILED(hr)) _com_issue_error(hr);
          }
       }
    } catch (_com_error & er) {
       if (er.Description().length()>0) {
          MessageBox(er.Description(), "Description");
       } else {
          MessageBox(er.ErrorMessage(), "Error");
       }
    }

    return 0;
}
```

As you can see, there are a number of steps that must be taken before you can get this interface pointer. These steps are described in the following list, and they are the key to successfully embedding an ActiveX control inside an ATL composite control:

1. You need to get the native window handle using the control's identifier. Use the *GetDlgItem* method to do this.

2. You need to get the *IUnknown* pointer associated with the native window handle, by calling the global ATL function named *AtlAxGetControl*.

3. Once you've obtained this *IUnknown* pointer, you can use it to query for the Wang Image Edit control's *IDispatch* interface pointer.

4. Upon successfully obtaining an interface pointer to the Wang Image Edit control, save it to a member variable called m_pWang for later usage.

Essentially, what you're doing is caching the interface pointer to the Wang Image Edit control so that it can be easily accessed. For example, the command handlers for the pushbuttons on our dialog template will use this cached interface pointer to manipulate the Wang Image Edit control, as discussed next.

### Adding command handlers in ATL

Adding a command handler in ATL is similar to adding a message handler. To handle a command message, you must add an entry to the message map. For example, if you were to handle the IDC_BUTTON_VIEW_IMAGE command message, you would add the following emphasized entry into the message map:

```
BEGIN_MSG_MAP(CATLCyberGUI)
    MESSAGE_HANDLER(WM_INITDIALOG, OnInitDialog)
    COMMAND_HANDLER(IDC_BUTTON_VIEW_IMAGE, BN_CLICKED, OnViewImage)
END_MSG_MAP()
```

The first parameter is the identifier for the control that generates notifications, the second parameter is the notification that you want to handle, and the third parameter is the name of the handler function that you will write. To implement this handler function, you simply create a function with the following generic command handler prototype. This function prototype is the same for all command handlers written in ATL.

```
LRESULT OnViewImage(WORD wNotifyCode, WORD wID, HWND hWndCtl,
                    BOOL& bHandled);
```

In your *OnViewImage* handler, you display the image indicated by the content of the Image Location edit control. To get the text within the Image Location edit control, use the *GetDlgItemText* function, passing in the identifier of the associated edit control.

```
LRESULT OnViewImage(WORD wNotifyCode, WORD wID, HWND hWndCtl, BOOL& bHandled)
{
```

```
try {
   TCHAR szImageFile[MAX_PATH];
   GetDlgItemText(IDC_EDIT_IMAGE_LOCATION, szImageFile, MAX_PATH);
   CComBSTR tif(szImageFile);
   // Set the image to be displayed.
   m_pWang->SetImage(tif);
   // Display the image inside the Wang image edit control.
   m_pWang->Display();
} catch(_com_error & er) {
   if (er.Description().length()>0) {
      MessageBox(er.Description(), "Description");
   } else {
      MessageBox(er.ErrorMessage(), "Error");
   }  }
   return 0;
}
```

As you can see from the code snippet, you use **m_pWang** to call *SetImage* and
*Display*, which map to methods exposed by the **Wang Image Edit** control. Methods such as *SetImage* and *Display* are generated by the **#import** directive based
on the type information stored in the type library. These generated methods call
special compiler-supported functions that throw a *_com_error* exception when an
error is encountered, thus allowing us to use C++ exception handling.

The command handlers for the other five buttons are similar and their implementations are shown here. Since they're fairly straightforward, I'll show them without
further discussion:

```
BEGIN_MSG_MAP(CATLCyberGUI)
   MESSAGE_HANDLER(WM_INITDIALOG, OnInitDialog)
   COMMAND_HANDLER(IDC_BUTTON_VIEW_IMAGE, BN_CLICKED, OnViewImage)
   COMMAND_HANDLER(IDC_BUTTON_FIT_BEST, BN_CLICKED, OnFitBest)
   COMMAND_HANDLER(IDC_BUTTON_FIT_WIDTH, BN_CLICKED, OnFitWidth)
   COMMAND_HANDLER(IDC_BUTTON_ZOOM, BN_CLICKED, OnZoom)
   COMMAND_HANDLER(IDC_BUTTON_ROTATE, BN_CLICKED, OnRotate)
   COMMAND_HANDLER(IDC_BUTTON_OCR, BN_CLICKED, OnOcr)
END_MSG_MAP()

LRESULT OnFitBest(WORD wNotifyCode, WORD wID, HWND hWndCtl, BOOL& bHandled)
{
   try {
      VARIANT v; v.vt = VT_BOOL; v.boolVal = TRUE;
      m_pWang->FitTo(0, v);
   } catch(_com_error & er) {
      if (er.Description().length()>0) {
         MessageBox(er.Description(), "Description");
      } else {
         MessageBox(er.ErrorMessage(), "Error");
      }  }
      return 0;
}

LRESULT OnFitWidth(WORD wNotifyCode, WORD wID, HWND hWndCtl, BOOL& bHandled)
{
```

```
        try {
          VARIANT v; v.vt = VT_BOOL; v.boolVal = TRUE;
          m_pWang->FitTo(1, v);
        } catch(_com_error & er) {
          if (er.Description().length()>0) {
            MessageBox(er.Description(), "Description");
          } else {
            MessageBox(er.ErrorMessage(), "Error");
          }
        }
        return 0;
    }


    LRESULT OnZoom(WORD wNotifyCode, WORD wID, HWND hWndCtl, BOOL& bHandled)
    {
        try {
          m_pWang->ZoomToSelection() ;
        } catch(_com_error & er) {
          if (er.Description().length()>0) {
            MessageBox(er.Description(), "Description");
          } else {
            MessageBox(er.ErrorMessage(), "Error");
          }    }
        return 0;
    }


    LRESULT OnRotate(WORD wNotifyCode, WORD wID, HWND hWndCtl, BOOL& bHandled)
    {
        try {
          m_pWang->RotateRight() ;
        } catch(_com_error & er) {
          if (er.Description().length()>0) {
            MessageBox(er.Description(), "Description");
          } else {
            MessageBox(er.ErrorMessage(), "Error");
          }    }
        return 0;
    }

    LRESULT OnOcr(WORD wNotifyCode, WORD wID, HWND hWndCtl, BOOL& bHandled)
    {
        SetDlgItemText(IDC_EDIT_TEXT, g_szFakeOcrText) ;
        return 0;
    }
```

### Testing the final product

At this moment, if you build and test the composite control using the HTML script discussed earlier, you will see that all buttons respond to your request.

# ActiveX Control Properties

So far in this chapter, we've been concentrating on ActiveX controls, which can be considered little client applets that are widely distributed throughout cyberspace.

Almost all of these ActiveX controls' exposed properties can be manipulated at runtime by users. To allow users the most convenience in manipulating these properties at runtime, ActiveX controls expose property pages. An example of a property page is shown in Figure 8-9.

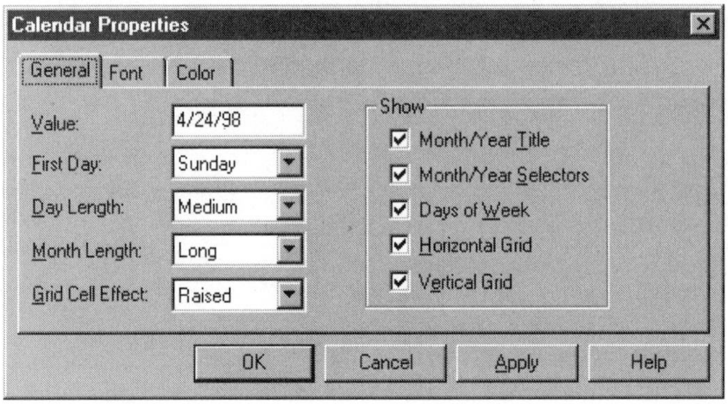

*Figure 8-9. Property pages supported by the Microsoft Calendar control*

These property pages pictorially show properties of the corresponding ActiveX control. To modify a property, a user simply selects a check-box or chooses an item from a list control shown within the property page. Once the user clicks the **Apply** button, the properties of the ActiveX control will be updated accordingly.

In this section, you will learn how to launch these property pages within your applications, be they normal applications or ActiveX controls that are embedded inside arbitrary containers. Once launched, a user can change the properties of the associated ActiveX controls by merely playing with the property pages.

## Playing with Property Pages

We will start off by creating an application that contains and uses two ActiveX controls. The first is the `MFCCyberServer` ActiveX control, the one developed earlier in this chapter, and the other is the Microsoft `Calendar` ActiveX control that's freely available. Even though you have probably never seen the `Calendar` control before, you will be able to use it in your applications at the binary level. You need no source code nor any header file for this control, as all the type information is maintain in this control's type library.

Once we have inserted these two ActiveX controls into our application, we will write some code to display the property pages of these two controls to the user upon request. Through these property pages, the user can modify the properties of these ActiveX controls.

To give you a heads up, the application that we're building looks similar to the one shown in Figure 8-10. This application has a splitter window that has two panes. The left pane holds a view that displays the MFCCyberServer ActiveX control and the right pane holds a different view that displays the Microsoft Calendar ActiveX control. Under the Help menu of our application, we will override the About menu item to display the property pages of the two ActiveX controls. This means that when a user selects the About menu item under the Help menu, the property pages for the embedded ActiveX controls will appear. At this point, the user can modify these properties.

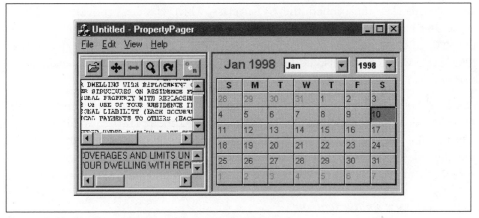

*Figure 8-10. Simple application with two ActiveX controls*

When a user changes the properties of these controls, the visual elements of the controls will update appropriately as requested by the user. For example, a user can choose to show or hide the toolbar that belongs to the MFCCyberServer ActiveX control. Similarly, a user can choose to display long day names, such as Monday, instead of short day names, such as M, in the Calendar ActiveX control.

To play with property pages exposed by these ActiveX controls, follow the steps outlined here.

### Step 1: Creating the application

The first thing you need to do is create a new project for this application. You want to create an MFC Single Document Interface (SDI) Application, which you will name PropertyPager. To do this, you need to use the MFC AppWizard(exe). When the MFC AppWizard appears, select the SDI option and click Finish to generate this application. After the MFC AppWizard has generated all the files for the shell of an SDI application, you should test it to make sure everything is okay.

## Step 2: Adding the two views

The next thing that you need to do is add two views to this project. As you can see back in Figure 8-10, there is a view on the left that holds an ActiveX control and a view on the right that holds another ActiveX control. You can create these two views using the `MFC ClassWizard`.

Let's create the first view that will eventually hold the `MFCCyberServer` ActiveX control. Launch the `MFC ClassWizard` using the `CTRL-W` hotkey and click the `Add Class` button to add a new class. You should call this class *CCyberServerView* to intuitively signify that this class is a view that holds an `MFCCyberServer` ActiveX control. This class must inherit the *CView* class, which is a class provided by MFC. Once you have entered all this information, you can click the `OK` button to allow the `MFC ClassWizard` to generate the newly added class, *CCyberServerView*. The `MFC ClassWizard` will also add this class to your project, so check to make sure that you can see it in `ClassView`.

Creating the second view to hold the `Calendar` ActiveX control is similar to the previous directions. This time name the class `CCalendarView` to intuitively signify that this class is a view that holds a `Calendar` ActiveX control. Similar to the previous view class, this class must inherit the *CView* class. Again, check to make sure that you can see this newly created class, *CCalendarView*, in `ClassView`.

## Step 3: Adding a splitter window

Having the two views is not enough to get the user interface shown in Figure 8-10. To display the two views, you need the help of a splitter window. A splitter window, technically referred to as a *CSplitterWnd* class, is a special window provided by MFC. It is a special window that can be subdivided into a number of panes, each of which can hold a view. Since you have two views, you will create a splitter window with two panes, with the left pane holding the *CCyberServerView* view and the right pane holding the *CCalendarView* view.

First, you need to attach this splitter window to the generated *CMainFrame* class, which is essentially the main window of your application. To get started in this direction, add a member variable (`m_Splitter`) of type *CSplitterWnd* to the *CMainFrame* class. After you've done this, override a virtual function called *OnCreateClient*. This function, shown later, is automatically called by the MFC application framework when the main window's client area is created. Within this override, create your splitter window and attach the appropriate views to the panes of the splitter window.

To create the splitter window, use the *CreateStatic* member function of the *CSplitterWnd* class. The first parameter is a pointer to the parent window. The parent window of the splitter window is the current *CMainFrame* instance, so the first parameter to the *CreateStatic* function should be the `this` pointer. When you create a splitter window using the *CreateStatic* function, you need to specify the number of rows and columns that the splitter window will have. In this case, you want a splitter window with one row by two columns, so your second and third arguments will be 1 and 2, respectively. The first C++ statement in the following code shows how you should create the splitter window.

After you've created the splitter with the correct dimension, you need to place the appropriate view into the panes of your splitter window. In row one, column one, you will store the *CCyberServerView* view, and in row one, column two, you will store the *CCalendarView* view. The second and third C++ statements in the following code snippet store these views into their appropriate splitter panes:

```
BOOL CMainFrame::OnCreateClient(LPCREATESTRUCT lpcs,
                               CCreateContext* pContext)
{
    // Create a splitter with 1 row x 2 col.
    m_Splitter.CreateStatic(this, 1, 2);

    // Create the CCyberServerView view in column 1.
    m_Splitter.CreateView(0, 0, RUNTIME_CLASS(CCyberServerView),
                          CSize(300,0), pContext);

    // Create the CCalendarView view column 2.
    m_Splitter.CreateView(0, 1, RUNTIME_CLASS(CCalendarView),
                          CSize(0,0), pContext);
    return TRUE ;
}
```

This code creates a one-row by two-column splitter window. The left pane hosts the *CCyberServerView* view and the right pane hosts the *CCalendarView* view. To verify this, you should build and run the application at this moment. You will see that your application has been modified: there will be a vertical splitter bar somewhere in the main window of the application.

### Step 4: Putting the two ActiveX controls on their appropriate views

If you tested the previous application in Step 3, you discovered that there weren't any ActiveX controls on the two splitter panes. That's because they weren't added and shown in their appropriate views.

First, you need to add the two ActiveX controls into your application. In doing so, the appropriate wrapper classes for the ActiveX controls will be generated and added to your project. You use these wrapper classes to programmatically manipulate their associated ActiveX controls. To get these wrapper classes, use the Components and Controls Gallery. To refresh your memory, you can launch the Components and Controls Gallery dialog box by following the Project, Add To Project, and Components and Controls menu links. When this dialog box appears, you want to drill down to the Registered ActiveX Controls folder, where you should find and insert the MFCCyberServer ActiveX control.

This will generate the wrapper class, which is named *CMFCCyberServer*, for this ActiveX control, and insert the class into your application. Once you've done this, you should find and insert the `Calendar Control 8.0` ActiveX control. This will generate the corresponding wrapper class, which is named *CCalendar*, for this control.

Now that you've added the required ActiveX controls into your application and generated the corresponding wrapper classes, you need to place these ActiveX controls into their appropriate views.

Let's first take care of *CCyberServerView*. You need to add a member variable of type *CMFCCyberServer* to this class and name this variable **m_Cyber**. This object, which is type of *CMFCCyberServer*, represents the **MFCCyberServer** ActiveX control and it will be a child of *CCyberServerView*.

You need to do the same thing to *CCalendarView*, so add a member variable of type *CCalendar* to the *CCalendarView* class and name this variable **m_Calendar**. This object, which is of type *CCalendar*, represents the **Calendar** ActiveX control and it will be a child of *CCalendarView*.

After you've added these two member variables, you need to create the instances of these controls within the appropriate views. You'll make the **MFCCyberServer** ActiveX control a child window of the *CCyberServerView* and the **Calendar** ActiveX control a child window of the *CCalendarView*.

To create the **MFCCyberServer** ActiveX control within *CCyberServerView*, you need to handle the **WM_CREATE** window message in the *CCyberServerView* class. We have done this before, so here's the code for it, without any further ado.

```
int CCyberServerView::OnCreate(LPCREATESTRUCT lpCreateStruct)
{
    if (CView::OnCreate(lpCreateStruct) == -1)
        return -1;
    m_Cyber.Create(0, 0, WS_VISIBLE|WS_CHILD, CRect(), this, ID_CYBER);
    return 0;
}
```

Similarly, you need to create the **Calendar** ActiveX control within *CCalendarView*. Again, to do this, you would handle the **WM_CREATE** message in the *CCalendarView* class, as shown here:

```
int CCalendarView::OnCreate(LPCREATESTRUCT lpCreateStruct)
{
    if (CView::OnCreate(lpCreateStruct) == -1)
        return -1;
    m_Calendar.Create(0, 0, WS_VISIBLE|WS_CHILD, CRect(), this, ID_CALENDAR);
    return 0;
}
```

After creating the controls in their appropriate containers, resize the controls to be the size of their parent views. You do this because you want the controls to cover the whole client area of their parent views. As you have seen earlier, to do this, you need to handle the `WM_SIZE` message in the appropriate view classes.

For example, in the *CCyberServerView* class, you would handle this message as follows:

```
void CCyberServerView::OnSize(UINT nType, int cx, int cy)
{
    CView::OnSize(nType, cx, cy);
    m_Cyber.MoveWindow(0,0,cx,cy);
}
```

And in the *CCalendarView* class, you would handle this message as follows:

```
void CCalendarView::OnSize(UINT nType, int cx, int cy)
{
    CView::OnSize(nType, cx, cy);
    m_Calendar.MoveWindow(0,0,cx,cy);
}
```

In both cases, simply resize the controls to be the size their corresponding parent views. Once you have done all this, you should build and run the application. After launching the application, you should see both the `MFCCyberServer` and `Calendar` ActiveX controls in your application.

### Step 5: Showing the property pages

So far, you have created a application that holds two ActiveX controls. Now, you'll learn how to display the property pages of these ActiveX controls upon user request. When these property pages are shown, the user will be able to edit the properties of these ActiveX controls. For example, a user will be able to do something such as changing the current date in the `Calendar` control.

In the interest of brevity, we will simply delete the code generated in the *CPropertyPagerApp::OnAppAbout* function, which is the handler for the `ID_ABOUT` menu item. By default, this function displays the `About` dialog box, but we will delete this code and add the code to display the property pages exposed by the two ActiveX controls that live within our application.

Keep in mind that your goal for this handler is to display the property pages of the two ActiveX controls hosted by your simple application. To do this, COM provides a function called *OleCreatePropertyFrame*, which creates a property sheet dialog that holds all the property pages that are passed along during the call to this function.

```
HRESULT OleCreatePropertyFrame(
    HWND hwndOwner,          // Parent window of the property sheet
    UINT x,                  // x position
    UINT y,                  // y position
    LPCOLESTR lpszCaption,   // Title of the property sheet dialog
    ULONG cObjects,          // Number of IUnknown pointers in lplpUnk
    LPUNKNOWN FAR* lplpUnk,  // Array of IUnknown pointers
```

```
   ULONG cPages,          // Number of property pages in lpPageClsID
   LPCLSID lpPageClsID,   // Array of CLSIDs for each property page
   LCID lcid,             // Locale identifier
   DWORD dwReserved,      // Reserved
   LPVOID lpvReserved     // Reserved
);
```

The important parameters of this function are shown in bold. The fifth parameter indicates the size of the array of *IUnknown* pointers passed in as the sixth parameter. This array must contain the *IUnknown* pointers of all ActiveX controls that have property pages passed into the *OleCreatePropertyFrame* function call. COM will use these *IUnknown* interface pointers to get back to the appropriate ActiveX controls and tell them to update themselves when their properties are modified. The seventh parameter indicates the number of property pages that will be displayed to the user. These property pages are represented by their associated CLSIDs, which is a simple array shown in the eight parameter. Each CLSID in this array may be a property page that belongs to a unique ActiveX control. Again, these ActiveX controls are represented by their associated *IUnknown*, which is an array passed as the sixth parameter.

Now that you know that the magic of displaying property pages of ActiveX controls happens under the *OleCreatePropertyFrame* function call, you can begin to implement the *CPropertyPagerApp::OnAppAbout* handler. The code of this handler is fairly lengthy, so let's break it up into digestible chunks.

The first thing that we need to do is obtain the *IUnknown* interface pointers of the Calendar and the MFCCyberServer ActiveX controls. *IUnknown* is our first handle into a COM object, as every COM object implements the *IUnknown* interface. To get the *IUnknown* interface pointer for the Calendar ActiveX control, we first need to get a pointer to the *CCalendarView*. This view is attached to the right hand pane of our splitter window, which is a child window of the main window (*CMainFrame*). The *CCalendarView* holds the Calendar ActiveX control as a member variable. We can use this member variable to get the *IUnknown* interface, by calling the *GetControlUnknown* function.

```
void CPropertyPagerApp::OnAppAbout()
{
    // Get the IUnknown for the Calendar control
    CCalendarView *pCalView = (CCalendarView *)
        ((CMainFrame*)AfxGetMainWnd())->m_Splitter.GetPane(0,1);
    IUnknown *pUnkCal = pCalView->m_Calendar.GetControlUnknown();
```

*GetControlUnknown* is provided by the *CWnd* class of MFC and it simply returns the *IUnknown* interface pointer of the ActiveX control. We will use this *IUnknown* pointer to query for other interfaces from the Calendar control in a short moment.

While we're at it, let's also obtain the *IUnknown* interface pointer for the MFCCyberServer ActiveX control. The process is the same as earlier, but this time, we are interested in the left pane of the splitter window. Also, we are deal-ing with a *CCyberServerView*, not a *CCalendarView*.

```
// Get the IUnknown for the MFCCyberServer control
CCyberServerView *pCyberView = (CCyberServerView *)
    ((CMainFrame*)AfxGetMainWnd())->m_Splitter.GetPane(0,0);
IUnknown *pUnkCyber = pCyberView->m_Cyber.GetControlUnknown();
```

After getting the *IUnknown* pointers, we create three temporary variables. These temporary variables will be holding the CLSIDs of the property pages exposed by the two ActiveX controls, and they will be clear when we use them.

```
// Variables to hold CLSIDs of ActiveX controls' property pages
CAUUID caCalGUID, caCyberGUID;
GUID *pArrayClsid = 0;
```

Next, we use the *IUnknown* pointer of the `Calendar` ActiveX control to query for the *ISpecifyPropertyPages* interface. Every control that supports property pages must implement the *ISpecifyPropertyPages* interface. This interface offers the *GetPages* method that allows us to get the GUIDs of all property pages supported by the ActiveX control. In calling *GetPages*, we pass along a pointer to a `CAUUID` structure, indicated in the later code snippet as `caCalGUID`. When the call to *GetPages* returns, this structure is filled in with a list of GUIDs, each of which rep-resents a CLSID of a property page supported by the ActiveX control. We need these CLSIDs in order to actually display their associated property pages.

There are two minor points to note in the following code snippet. The *Chk* function that you see is an inline function that simply throws an exception using *_com_issue_error* when it encounters a bad `HRESULT`. So, in the event of an error, control will be transferred to the exception handler (`catch` clause). Besides this, notice that we use *CComPtr* to avoid manually calling *Release* on the interface pointer.

```
try {
    CComPtr<ISpecifyPropertyPages> pCalISPP;
    // Get ISpecifyPropertyPages of the Calendar control
    HRESULT hr = pUnkCal->QueryInterface(IID_ISpecifyPropertyPages,
        (void **)&pCalISPP); Chk(hr);
    // Get the GUIDs for all property pages of the Calendar control
    hr=pCalISPP->GetPages(&caCalGUID);  Chk(hr);
```

Now, we have to do the same thing for the `MFCCyberServer` ActiveX control. As you can see in the code snippet below, we query for the *ISpecifyPropertyPages* interface of the `MFCCyberServer` ActiveX control. From this interface, we obtain a list of GUIDs for all property pages exposed by the `MFCCyberServer` ActiveX control by calling the *GetPages* method of the *ISpecifyPropertyPages* interface.

```
CComPtr<ISpecifyPropertyPages> pCyberISPP;
// Get ISpecifyPropertyPages of the MFCCyberServer control
hr = pUnkCyber->QueryInterface(IID_ISpecifyPropertyPages,
    (void**)&pCyberISPP); Chk(hr);
// Get the GUIDs for all property pages of the MFCCyberServer control
hr=pCyberISPP->GetPages(&caCyberGUID); Chk(hr);
```

At this point, we have obtained the CLSIDs of all the property pages of both the `Calendar` and `MFCCyberServer` ActiveX controls. The next thing that we will do is create an array of two CLSIDs, each of which represents the first property page exposed by one of the two ActiveX controls. For example, in the first *memcpy* statement below, we copy the CLSID of the first property page exposed by the `Calendar` control into the first cell of the array of CLSIDs (`pArrayClsid`). In the second *memcpy* statement, we copy the CLSID of the first property page exposed by the `MFCCyberServer` ActiveX control into the second cell of the array of CLSIDs. We create this array of property page CLSIDs in preparation for calling the *OleCreatePropertyFrame* function, which will display all the property pages.

```
// Create an array of GUIDs to pass to OleCreatePropertyFrame
int elems = 2;
pArrayClsid = new GUID[elems];
ZeroMemory(pArrayClsid, elems*sizeof(GUID));
memcpy(&pArrayClsid[0], caCalGUID.pElems, sizeof(GUID));
memcpy(&pArrayClsid[1], caCyberGUID.pElems, sizeof(GUID));
```

Passing an array of property page CLSIDs is not enough. We also need to pass an array of *IUnknown* interface pointers so that COM can get back to the appropriate ActiveX control and tell it to update its properties as modified in the property pages. To meet this requirement, we simply create an array that is composed of the two *IUnknown* interface pointers.

```
// Array of IUnknown pointers for our ActiveX controls
IUnknown *ArrayUnk[2] = { pUnkCal, pUnkCyber };
```

Once we have the array of *IUnknown* interface pointers and the array of property page CLSIDs, we can call the *OleCreatePropertyFrame* function to display the two property pages, each belonging to its corresponding ActiveX control. This call is simple, as shown in the code snippet that follows. Notice the bolded arguments because they are the key to making the property pages appear in the property sheet and making ActiveX control properties modifiable.

```
// Call OleCreatePropertyFrame to display the property pages
hr = OleCreatePropertyFrame(
        AfxGetMainWnd()->m_hWnd,
        0,
        0,
        OLESTR("Calendar and MFCCyberServer Properties"),
        sizeof(ArrayUnk)/sizeof(ArrayUnk[0]),
        ArrayUnk,
        elems,
        pArrayClsid,
        0L,
        0L,
        NULL); Chk(hr);
} catch (_com_error & error) {
    AfxMessageBox(error.ErrorMessage());
}
```

```
    // Clean up after ourselves
    if (pArrayClsid) delete [] pArrayClsid ;
    if (caCalGUID.pElems) CoTaskMemFree((void *)caCalGUID.pElems);
    if (caCyberGUID.pElems) CoTaskMemFree((void *)caCyberGUID.pElems);
}
```

Having written this handler function, you're now ready to build and execute the application. After the application is launched, you can display the property pages simply by selecting the **About** menu item under the **Help** menu. When you do this, you should see the two property pages. The first property page shows all the editable properties for the **Calendar** ActiveX control, and the second property page shows all the editable properties for the **MFCCyberServer** ActiveX control.

Now you can modify the properties of the **Calendar** ActiveX control. To actually see the changes, you need to click the **Apply** button or the **OK** button. Notice, however, that there are no properties on the property page associated with the **MFCCyberServer** ActiveX control. We will deal with this next.

## Adding a Property to CMFCCyberServerCtrl

When testing your application, you see no properties for your **MFCCyberServer** ActiveX control. This is to be expected, because although you have developed the **MFCCyberServer** ActiveX control, you have not yet added any property to it. We know so because we developed it. This exercise would fall short without a demonstration of how to add and manipulate properties within an MFC ActiveX control. Therefore, we will add a simple property to ours. This property will allow a user to dynamically show or hide the toolbar that belongs to our **MFCCyberServer** ActiveX control. Here are the steps for adding this property:

1. To begin, open the **MFCCyberServer** project.

2. In **ClassView**, place the mouse cursor over the icon for the *_DMFCCyberServer* COM interface.

3. Right-click to launch the context menu and choose **Add Property**. This menu command launches the **Add Property** dialog box, which allows you to add a property to the selected interface.

4. In the **Add Property** dialog box, type *ShowToolbar* in the **External name** combo-box. This is the name that clients of your control will use to refer to this specific property. Notice that when you type the word *ShowToolbar*, the **Variable name** edit-box is automatically filled with **m_showToolbar**. Internally within your control, you can refer to the *ShowToolbar* property programmatically using the **m_showToolbar** member variable. Notice that the **Notification function** edit-box is also automatically filled with *OnShowToolbarChanged*. This is the function that will be automatically called by the MFC framework when the *ShowToolbar* property is modified.

5. Select BOOL as the type in the **Type** combo-box. The *ShowToolbar* property can either be TRUE, meaning that the toolbar will be shown, or FALSE, meaning that the toolbar will be hidden.

Once you have done the preceding steps, the wizard will generate some code in the *CMFCCyberServerCtrl* class. In particular, it generates a member variable m_showToolbar of type BOOL in the class definition of *CMFCCyberServerCtrl*. It also generates a member function called *OnShowToolbarChanged* that is automatically called by the MFC framework when the *ShowToolbar* property is modified. To complete adding the *ShowToolbar* property to our ActiveX control, you need to implement the *OnShowToolbarChanged* method as follows:

```
void CMFCCyberServerCtrl::OnShowToolbarChanged()
{
    m_ImagingWindow.m_Toolbar.ShowWindow(m_showToolbar);
    SetModifiedFlag();
}
```

By the time this generated function is called by the MFC framework, the member variable m_showToolbar associated with the *ShowToolbar* property has already been updated. All that you need to do is use this flag to show or hide the toolbar. Notice from the bolded code earlier that you use the *ShowWindow* method to show or hide the toolbar, which belongs to the dialog that lives within your MFCCyberServer ActiveX control.

Now that you have everything in place for the *ShowToolbar* property, you need to update the generated property page resource to hold the visual elements for manipulating the properties of your ActiveX control. This property page is generated during project creation. Specifically, you need to add a check-box to this property page and bind it to the *ShowToolbar* property. Then at runtime, when a user checks this control, you will display the toolbar. Should a user uncheck this control, you will hide the toolbar. Here are the simple steps to update the generated property page:

1. In ResourceView, find and edit the IDD_PROPPAGE_MFCCYBERSERVER dialog template. This is the dialog template for the default property page of our ActiveX control. At this point, there are no visual elements on this dialog template except the default generated text, which reads something like TODO: Place controls to manipulate properties.

2. Delete the TODO: status text area control.

3. Add a check button onto the dialog box, giving it the identifier, IDC_CHECK_ SHOWTOOLBAR, and label it Show Toolbar.

4. Launch the MFC ClassWizard and select the Member Variables tab.

5. Find IDC_CHECK_SHOWTOOLBAR and click the Add Variable button. The Add Member Variable dialog box will be shown.

6. In the `Member variable name` edit-box, enter `m_bShowToolbar`. This member variable will be added to the *CMFCCyberServerPropPage* class.

7. In the `Optional property name` combo-box, type the external property name of the property to which you want to bind this visual control (check-box). In your case, the external property name is *ShowToolbar*. So type *ShowToolbar* in this combo-box. You do this to associate a visual control, such as a check-box, with an ActiveX property, such as *ShowToolbar*.

8. Click `OK` to generate the necessary code that binds this visual control (check-box) to the ActiveX property (*ShowToolbar*).

Once you have this in place, build the `MFCCyberServer` component and test the `PropertyPage` application. When you launch the property pages this time, you will see the `Show Toolbar` check-box on the second property page. If you alternate the check mark and press the `Apply` button, you will see that the toolbar in the `MFCCyberServer` ActiveX control shows and hides itself accordingly.

In summary, this chapter explains the necessary elements for widely distributing components. The examples illustrated in this chapter should give you a starting point for inventing and incorporating other distributed functionality into your own components. In the next chapter, we will jump into security.

# 9

*In this chapter:*
- *Server-Side COM Security*
- *Access Token*
- *Audit Trail*
- *Administrative Alert*
- *Client-Side Security*

# Applying Security

You learned COM security fairly thoroughly in Chapter 5, *Infrastructure*. However, Chapter 5 discussed COM security in general, without practical hands-on examples. In this chapter, you'll create a server and a client component that take security into consideration. You'll develop a typical server application that accounts for the following:

1. Server-Side COM Security—This section covers the use of COM security on the server side. We will make use of the *CoGetCallContext* API function and the *IServerSecurity* interface to learn about the calling client.

2. Access Token—If you want to inquire about the detailed information of the calling client, you must use platform-specific security support. In Windows NT 4.0, COM uses the NTLM security provider. We will take advantage of NT security to obtain the access token of the caller. Given this access token and permissions to impersonate, we can find pretty much everything about the caller. In our exercise, we will obtain the user's unique security identifier (SID) and the groups to which the user belongs.

3. Audit Trail—An audit trail allows application servers to log important messages (e.g., security violations) that can be traced and audited. In typical applications, these audit messages are written to text files. However, since the NT event log allows a common facility to log audit or application messages, we will use this facility to log security violations.

4. Administrative Alert—When there is a severe problem (e.g., a severe security violation) that needs immediate attention, special personnel must be notified immediately. NT has an `Alerter` service that allows this type of notifications to be immediate propagated to any configured user accounts or machines. We will learn how to use this feature in this section.

Once you've learned these four important server-side, security-related features, you'll write a client component that uses the server component. Unlike earlier client applications, this one customizes COM security through programming. By the time you finish this chapter, you should feel comfortable using COM and Windows NT security in real applications. Coupled together, COM and Windows NT security will allow you to build great server and client components.

This chapter assumes you have an understanding of COM security, as discussed in Chapter 5. At a minimum, you should know how to configure COM security using *dcomcnfg.exe*. (I'll tell you to configure specific settings using *dcomcnfg.exe*, but I won't show you how to do it, because we're dealing only with the programmatic aspects of security in this chapter.)

# Server-Side COM Security

In this section, you'll learn how to deal with COM security on the server side. You'll start by creating an application to which you'll add additional security features throughout this chapter.

## Creating the Project and a COM Object

Let's begin by developing a brand new server component:

1. Use the `ATL COM AppWizard` to create an `Executable (EXE)` component and name it `SecureOcrServer`.

2. Add a `Simple Object` to this new component using the `ATL Object Wizard`.

3. Name this COM object `SecureOcrProcessor`.

4. In the `Attributes` page of the `ATL Object Wizard Properties` dialog, check `Support ISupportErrorInfo`. You do this so that you can later return customized error descriptions to the client. We'll illustrate a way to return your own messages back to the client to describe the problem that exists on the server. Not only is this valuable in deployed systems, but it's very valuable for debugging purposes.

5. Add a method called *SecureOcrImage* to the *ISecureOcrProcessor* interface. To make it simple, we will not add any parameter to this method, since all we're interested in is security handling.

## Implementing the SecureOcrImage Method

Now that you have a component and a simple COM object, here's the plan. A client application will invoke the *SecureOcrImage* function that you've just added. Within this method, the server component will obtain the security context of the invocation and will validate the call. If you can validate the call, you will impersonate the client and perform work in place of the client; otherwise, you return an error to the caller.

As shown in the following code snippet, you can obtain the *IServerSecurity* interface on the server side using the *CoGetCallContext* API function. Recall from Chapter 5 that the *IServerSecurity* interface supports four important methods: *QueryBlanket*, *ImpersonateClient*, *RevertToSelf*, and *IsImpersonating*. The first three methods have corresponding shorthand wrappers, such as *CoQueryClientBlanket*, *CoImpersonateClient*, and *CoRevertToSelf*, respectively. However, in your exercise, you won't use these shorthand API functions for performance reasons. You simply get a pointer to the *IServerSecurity* interface once and use it until you no longer need it, as shown in the method below:

```
STDMETHODIMP CSecureOcrProcessor::SecureOcrImage()
{
    HRESULT hr = S_OK;
    try {
        CComPtr<IServerSecurity> pSecure;
        hr = CoGetCallContext(IID_IServerSecurity,
            reinterpret_cast<void**>(&pSecure)); Chk(hr);

        if ( (hr=ValidateCall(pSecure)) == S_OK ) {
            hr = pSecure->ImpersonateClient(); Chk(hr);
            //*********************************************
            //* Here's where you would do work for the client
            //* using the client's credentials.
            //*********************************************
            hr = pSecure->RevertToSelf(); Chk(hr);
        }

    } catch (_com_error & er) {
        MessageBox(NULL, er.ErrorMessage(), TEXT("ErrorMessage"),
            MB_OK|MB_ICONINFORMATION|MB_SERVICE_NOTIFICATION);
        hr = er.Error();
    }
    return hr;
}
```

As you can see, once you have obtained the *IServerSecurity* interface pointer, you use it to validate the call. This validation is application specific. You'll write the code to perform it in a moment, but for now, if the call is successfully validated, you will try to impersonate the client by calling *ImpersonateClient*. Remember that you can impersonate only if the client has given permission to do so, implying that the client must specify at least the RPC_C_IMP_LEVEL_IMPERSONATE impersonation level. Once the thread that invokes this method is put in impersonating mode, it can do anything on the server machine in place of the client, except access remote resources or hop to other machines. This is the where you would do the necessary work for the *SecureOcrImage* method. Once this thread has done the work for the client, in place of the client, it can revert to the security context of the server process.

However, if we cannot validate the client who called this method, we return the HRESULT obtained from calling *ValidateCall*. We will learn how to pass along a detailed description associated with this return code in a moment.

Notice from the method above that if any other method call returns a bad HRESULT, we throw a *_com_error* exception, which forces us into the catch clause. Recall from the last chapter that *Chk* was an inline function that threw this exception object. One important thing that you should notice in the catch clause is that we're using the MB_SERVICE_NOTIFICATION flag, which is important because this component may not be running under the identity of the interactive user (this can be configured using *dcomcnfg.exe*). If the component is not running under the identity of the interactive user and you have not specified this special flag, the actual user won't see the message box. Thus, the thread that throws up the message box will be blocked forever, since the OK button on the message box will never be pushed.

## *Validating the Invocation*

Now that you know what the *SecureOcrImage* method does, let's examine the code for the *ValidateCall* function. The steps of this function are straightforward:

1. Get simple information about the remote caller so that we can display it for observation and learning purposes.

2. Get the caller's access token. With this access token, we can obtained detailed security information regarding the caller.

3. Check whether the call is encrypted at the highest level (RPC_C_AUTHN_LEVEL_PKT_PRIVACY). If this is not the case, we'll record this call in an audit trail. This implies that the caller must specify this authentication level.

4. Assuming that the call is successful up to this point, check whether the user is listed under our hit list.* If so, immediately alert an administrator or an appropriate security personnel.

Notice that these four tasks are application specific. In your own application, you may choose to handle custom security management and checking any way you like. The four validation tasks shown earlier should give you some ideas for the kinds of custom security features to consider when you develop server-side components. These four tasks are handled in the *ValidateCall* function.

---

* For lack of better terminology, this is the list of illegal users who are threats to our server.

Since this function is fairly long, let's break it apart into smaller pieces for discussion. In the following code, we're using the important *IServerSecurity* interface pointer passed into this function to invoke the *QueryBlanket* method. In doing this, we want to retrieve two things. One of the two pieces of information that we need is the authentication level specified by caller, because we need this to verify whether the call is encrypted. We also obtain the client identity, information whose format depends upon the security package being used. If the NTLM package is used, we get this information in the form of **DomainName\UserName**. For the parameters that are of no interest to us, we simply pass zeros in to the call to *QueryBlanket*. For learning purposes, we simply display the client identity so that we know that everything works as expected:

```
HRESULT ValidateCall(IServerSecurity *pSecure)
{
    HRESULT hr = S_OK;

    DWORD dwAuthnLevel = 0; void *pClientIdentity = 0;
    // Grab the AuthLevel and ClientIdentity.  We can get the
    // same information using the Access Token (shown shortly).
    hr = pSecure->QueryBlanket(0, 0, 0, &dwAuthnLevel, 0,
        &pClientIdentity, 0); Chk(hr);
    // Show the client identity so that a user can view it.
    // You should use the MB_SERVICE_NOTIFICATION, in
    // case you haven't configured
    // RunAs interactive user using dcomcnfg.exe.
    MessageBoxW(NULL, (wchar_t *)pClientIdentity,
        L"ClientIdentity - Authentication",
        MB_OK|MB_ICONINFORMATION|MB_SERVICE_NOTIFICATION);
```

The *QueryBlanket* method itself it not powerful enough for what we want to do. In order to go further with security, we need to be more platform specific. In other words, the code from this point onwards is specific to a security package. Specifically, we're dealing with NTLM, since this is the only security package supported by Windows NT at the time of this writing. To intimately work with security in Windows NT, we need to obtain the remote user's access token, which gives us practically every piece of security related information about the remote user except the user's password. We will learn how to do all this by writing a reusable class called *CImpersonatedUser* in the next section. For now, note that we create an instance of *CImpersonatedUser* and retrieve the remote user's access token using the appropriate *IServerSecurity* interface pointer, as shown by the two statements below:

```
//-------------------------------------------------
// Get the client Access Token from the call context.
//-------------------------------------------------
CImpersonatedUser user;
user.ObtainAccessToken(pSecure);
```

Next, we check to see if the call is totally encrypted. Let's assume that the caller is sending confidential information to the server. In our system, this implies that an unencrypted call means a security violation; in this case, we must record this invocation and the caller into our audit trail (so that we can later hunt down the violators). We record this problem by calling the *LogSecurityViolation* function, which we will write in the "Audit Trail" section.

```
#define E_UNENCRYPTED_CALL 0x201
#define E_IN_HIT_LIST      0x202
//----------------------------------------------------
// Audit Trail: Call must be made using RPC_C_AUTHN_LEVEL_PKT_PRIVACY
// or we will record this violation in the audit trail.
//----------------------------------------------------
if (dwAuthnLevel!=RPC_C_AUTHN_LEVEL_PKT_PRIVACY) {
    LogSecurityViolation(user);
    hr = AtlReportError(CLSID_SecureOcrProcessor,
        TEXT("[Security Violation] Secret has been leaked ")
        TEXT("because a remote invocation was NOT encrypted."),
        IID_ISecureOcrProcessor,
        MAKE_HRESULT(SEVERITY_ERROR, FACILITY_ITF, E_UNENCRYPTED_CALL));
    return hr;
}
```

Notice that we use the *AtlReportError* function to attach a detailed message that will be returned to the client. This function simply sets up the *IErrorInfo* interface that the caller can use to get a detailed description of the method failure. We simply pass the CLSID of our object, the description, the IID, and a predefined or custom HRESULT into the *AtlReportError* function. Notice that we create a custom HRESULT using the MAKE_HRESULT macro, and remember that a custom error code must be greater that 0x200, as specified by the COM Specification.

The *AtlReportError* function will create an error information (exception) object and return the error back to the remote caller. Internally, this function creates an exception object by calling the *CreateErrorInfo* COM API function. After it sets up the exception with relevant information, it calls the *SetErrorInfo* COM API function to raise the exception.[*]

Moving on to the next point, even if the call is encrypted as required, the caller may be a security threat to our server. If we know these individuals, we can record them in a hit list. When these individuals make this method call, we immediately sound the burglar alarm—or in our terms, generate an administrative alert by calling *GenerateAdminAlert*, which we will write in the "Administrative Alert" section.

```
//----------------------------------------------------
// Administrative Alert
//----------------------------------------------------
if (IsUserInHitList(user)) {
    GenerateAdminAlert(user);
    TCHAR szMsg[MAX_PATH];
```

---

[*] If you're interested in seeing how this is done, see the implementation of *AtlSetErrorInfo* in the ATL library. The *AtlReportError* function calls *AtlSetErrorInfo*, which can be found in *atlimpl.cpp*.

```
        wsprintf(szMsg,
            TEXT("[Security Violation] Be careful.")
            TEXT("You [%s/%s] are in our hit list."),
            user.ObtainDomainName().data(),
            user.ObtainUserName().data());
        hr = AtlReportError(CLSID_SecureOcrProcessor, szMsg,
        IID_ISecureOcrProcessor,
        MAKE_HRESULT(SEVERITY_ERROR, FACILITY_ITF, E_IN_HIT_LIST));
        return hr;
    }
    return hr;
}
```

This code snippet returns a custom HRESULT to the caller. The error code of this
HRESULT is E_IN_HIT_LIST, which is greater than 0x200. Again, *AtlReportError*
will turn the information that it receives into an exception object that a client can
use to discover detailed information regarding a method invocation. You'll learn
how to capture these detailed descriptions on the client side when you develop
the client component later in this chapter.

Before we move on to the next section (and since we'll refer back to
*ValidateCall*), let's remind ourselves that the *ValidateCall* function uses the following helper functions:

1. *LogSecurityViolation*, written in the "Audit Trail" section.

2. *IsUserInHitList*, written in the "Administrative Alert" section.

3. *GenerateAdminAlert*, written in the "Administrative Alert" section.

In addition, the *ValidateCall* function also uses a helper object called
*CImpersonatedUser*, a C++ class that we will create from scratch. This is the object
that encapsulates the handling of Windows NT security for your application, and
it's the focus of the next discussion.*

## *Access Token*

In Windows NT, an *access token* is an important security element that identifies
not only a specific user, but much more information. A few important elements of
an access token include a user's access privileges, security identifier (SID), and
group SIDs, which represent the groups in which the user belongs. If you have a
specific user's access token and the appropriate access rights, you can know pretty
much everything about the user.

In the previous section, the *ValidateCall* function instantiated a *CImpersonatedUser*
C++ class and invoked the *ObtainAccessToken* method to obtain the remote user's
access token. Because the *CImpersonatedUser* class encapsulates an access token,

---

* You may want to reuse (and even extend) this object in the COM server applications that you develop.

we will be able to inquire for the following client security information. Due to the way NTLM works, we can obtain all this information on the server side without knowing the client's password.

- Security identifier (SID)—Unique identifier that identifies a specific user. Each user account is automatically assigned a SID on Windows NT when the account is created. Even if you delete and create a brand new account with the same name as the previous account, you will not get the same SID; instead, NT assigns a new and unique SID each time.

- User name.

- Domain name.

- SIDs of the groups in which the user belongs.

- Names of the groups in which the user belongs.

As shown in the following code, the *CImpersonatedUser* class is straightforward, so let's briefly introduce the bolded member functions of this class, as we'll implement them soon. The *ObtainAccessToken* member function obtains the access token of the thread executing the code that creates an instance of *CImpersonatedUser.*

The *ObtainUserSID* member function returns a pointer to a SID which can be passed to other Win32 API functions that takes a SID pointer as a parameter. The Win32 *ReportEvent* function is one such function that takes a SID pointer as a parameter. Passing a SID into the *ReportEvent* function allows Windows NT to extract the domain and user name and log them into the event log.

The *UserGroupBySID* member function returns a group name of the NT group indicated by the SID pointer passed as an argument.

```
class CImpersonatedUser {
public:
    CImpersonatedUser() ;
    ~CImpersonatedUser() ;

    // Obtains the access token of the executing thread
    void ObtainAccessToken(IServerSecurity *pSecure);

    // Returns a user SID
    PSID ObtainUserSID();
    // Returns a user name
    const string & ObtainUserName() ;
    // Returns the name of the domain in which the user belongs
    const string & ObtainDomainName() ;

    // Returns a list of SIDs indicating the groups in which the user belongs
    deque<PSID> * ObtainUserGroupSIDs() ;
    // Returns a list of group names for the groups in which the user belongs
    deque<string> * ObtainUserGroupNames() ;
```

```
        // Given a group SID pointer, return the name of the group
        string UserGroupBySID(PSID pSid) ;

    private:
        // Private method to obtain and cache the domain and user name
        bool RetrieveDomainAndUserName() ;

    private:
        // No copy and assignment allowed
        CImpersonatedUser(const CImpersonatedUser & rhs) ;
        CImpersonatedUser & operator=(const CImpersonatedUser & rhs) ;

    private:
        HANDLE m_hAccessToken ;      // Access token
        string m_strUserName ;       // Cached user name
        string m_strDomainName ;     // Cached domain name
        deque<PSID> m_dequeGroupPSID ;    // List of group SIDs
        unsigned char *m_pByteGroupsUserBelongsTo ;   // Raw data for NT groups
        deque<string> m_dequeUserGroups ; // List of group names
        unsigned char *m_pUserTokenInfo ; // Raw data for user
    } ;
```

This simple class keeps a number of important member variables:

- Access token of the current executing thread, which is valid for the duration of this method invocation

- User name

- Domain name

- Deque* of SIDs representing NT groups

- Pointer to a stream of bytes that contain group information for the groups of which the user is a member

- Deque of group names

- Pointer to a stream of bytes that contain the user's security information

Now that we have a general idea of the goals of this C++ class, let's dive in and implement its methods.

## *Constructor and Destructor*

The constructor simply initializes all the member variables on the initializor list.

```
CImpersonatedUser::CImpersonatedUser()
    : m_hAccessToken(NULL),
      m_strUserName(""),
      m_strDomainName(""),
      m_dequeGroupPSID(),
      m_pByteGroupsUserBelongsTo(0),
```

---

* Pronounced "deck," as in "a deck of cards." Think of a deque as a fancy term for a list in STL.

```
                m_dequeUserGroups(),
                m_pUserTokenInfo(0)
    {
    }
```

The destructor closes the handle to the access token that you're caching, and also frees the buffers allocated to hold the token information for the user and groups associated with the access token.

```
CImpersonatedUser::~CImpersonatedUser()
{
    if (m_hAccessToken) { ::CloseHandle(m_hAccessToken) ; }
    if (m_pByteGroupsUserBelongsTo) { free(m_pByteGroupsUserBelongsTo) ; }
    if (m_pUserTokenInfo) { free(m_pUserTokenInfo) ; }
}
```

## Getting the Access Token

The interesting method of this class is the *ObtainAccessToken* method, whose goal is to get the access token of the current running thread. Once you've obtained the access token, you can perform quite a few things; for instance, you can obtain the user's SID, and thus the user's name, domain name, and groups. To successfully get the access token, you first obtain the handle of the current thread by calling the Win32 API function, *GetCurrentThread*, and then impersonate the client. It should be obvious that impersonation would fail if the client component didn't specify at least the RPC_C_IMP_LEVEL_IMPERSONATE impersonation level. During impersonation, query for the current thread's access token, which is really the remote user's access token (since you are impersonating).

To actually obtain the access token, you must call a Win32 API function called *OpenThreadToken*, as shown below. The first parameter to this function is a handle of the thread whose access token is the one you want to retrieve. The second parameter identifies the desired access; in your case, you just want to query for the access token of the thread identified by hThread, so you simply pass in TOKEN_QUERY.* The third parameter can be either TRUE, which means that Windows NT will perform access checks using the security context of the process, or FALSE, which means that Windows NT will perform access checks using the security context of the thread, which may be under impersonation.

```
    void CImpersonatedUser::ObtainAccessToken(IServerSecurity *pSecure)
    {
        // Get the access token of the current thread first.
        HANDLE hThread = ::GetCurrentThread() ;
        if (hThread==NULL) return ;

        // You have to impersonate the caller before you can get
        // the access token of the caller.
```

---

* See SDK documentation for numerous other types of desired access.

```
        // This also requires that the caller has granted the server
        // impersonating rights.
        HRESULT hr = pSecure->ImpersonateClient();   Chk(hr);
        if (!::OpenThreadToken(hThread, TOKEN_QUERY, TRUE, &m_hAccessToken)) {
            _com_issue_error(GetLastError());
        }
        hr = pSecure->RevertToSelf(); Chk(hr);
    }
```

After you have obtained the access token, you revert to the thread's original security context. Typically, this is the security context of the account (or identity) that activated the server process. Remember that you can configure this under the identify tab of *dcomcnfg.exe*.

## Getting User Information

By using the access token you just obtained, you have the power to know almost everything about the remote user. To briefly demonstrate this, you'll get the user's domain and user name using this access token. Remember that you can get both of these things by calling *IServerSecurity::QueryBlanket*, which is the platform independent technique. The technique currently discussed is platform dependent and it requires two important Win32 API functions: *GetTokenInformation* and *LookupAccountSid*[*].

Since you have the remote user's access token, you can use the *GetTokenInformation* API function to get the SID of the remote user. The user's SID is stored inside a raw buffer, which contains all user-related security information. You can query for this binary buffer by passing TokenUser into the second parameter of *GetTokenInformation*, and as you can see from later code, you typically call this function twice. In the first call, you get the size of the buffer, so that you can dynamically allocate enough memory for holding the buffer. In the second call, you get the raw binary data that represents the part of the access token that contains user-related security information. Then, you save this buffer into a member variable of the *CImpersonatedUser* object so that you can later refer to it.

As we've just mentioned, the user SID lives inside this raw buffer, so to pull it out, you must cast this buffer into a PTOKEN_USER type and retrieve the User.Sid member. Once you have the user's SID, you can call the *LookupAccountSid* API function to get the domain and user name.

```
    // Look up token information and get the domain and user name
    bool CImpersonatedUser::RetrieveDomainAndUserName()
    {
        BOOL bRc = FALSE ;
        if (m_hAccessToken) {
```

---

[*] The *LookupAccountSid* API function works only when a caller's SID is a local account or an account in the primary or trusted domain.

```
        DWORD dwTokenInfoBufferSize = 0;
        // Inquire on the size of the buffer
        ::GetTokenInformation(m_hAccessToken, TokenUser,
                0, 0, &dwTokenInfoBufferSize) ;

        // Allocate memory to hold token buffer
        m_pUserTokenInfo = (unsigned char*) malloc (dwTokenInfoBufferSize) ;

        // Now get the token buffer.
        bRc = ::GetTokenInformation(m_hAccessToken, TokenUser,
                m_pUserTokenInfo,
                dwTokenInfoBufferSize, &dwTokenInfoBufferSize) ;
        if (!bRc) return false ;

        DWORD dwUserNameSize = UNLEN, dwDomainNameSize = DNLEN ;
        TCHAR szUserName[UNLEN+1], szDomainName[DNLEN+1];
        SID_NAME_USE snu ;

        bRc = ::LookupAccountSid(0, ((PTOKEN_USER) m_pUserTokenInfo)->User.Sid,
                szUserName, &dwUserNameSize, szDomainName,
                &dwDomainNameSize, &snu) ;
        if (!bRc) return false ;

#ifdef UNICODE
        USES_CONVERSION;
        m_strUserName = W2A(szUserName) ;
        m_strDomainName = W2A(szDomainName) ;
#else
        m_strUserName = szUserName ;
        m_strDomainName = szDomainName ;
#endif

        bRc = TRUE ;
    }
    return (bRc?true:false) ;
}
```

In this code, we use the convenient W2A macro to convert a wide-character string into an ANSI-character string. Converting between ANSI and Unicode can be a pain in the neck. To alleviate this discomfort, the SDK headers support a number of shorthand macros to convert from ANSI to Unicode and backwards. To use these shorthand macros, you must add the USES_CONVERSION macro, as shown above. These macros use the _alloca routine to dynamically allocate variable buffers on the stack (as opposed to the heap) relieving you from having to deallocate the buffers.

The *ObtainUserSID*, *ObtainUserName*, and *ObtainDomainName* methods, shown below, rely on the previous method to get the necessary information. These methods are straightforward and require no further discussion.

```
// Get the user SID.
PSID CImpersonatedUser::ObtainUserSID()
{
```

```
        if (m_pUserTokenInfo==NULL) {
            RetrieveDomainAndUserName() ;
        }
        return (((PTOKEN_USER) m_pUserTokenInfo)->User.Sid) ;
}


// Get the user name.
const string & CImpersonatedUser::ObtainUserName()
{
    if (m_strUserName.empty()) {
        RetrieveDomainAndUserName() ;
    }
    return m_strUserName ;
}


// Get the domain name of user.
const string & CImpersonatedUser::ObtainDomainName()
{
    if (m_strDomainName.empty()) {
        RetrieveDomainAndUserName() ;
    }
    return m_strDomainName ;
}
```

## Getting Group Information

The *GetTokenInformation* API function is very versatile because it allows you to query for more than just a user's SID. Instead of passing `TokenUser`, you can pass `TokenPrivileges` to obtain the token's privileges, and pass `TokenOwner` to obtain the default owner for newly created objects. In our exercise, we will pass `TokenGroups` to obtain the groups associated with the token—in other words, the groups that have this user as a member.

Like user accounts, NT groups themselves have SIDs. You'll obtain a list of these SIDs by passing `TokenGroups` into the second parameter of the *GetTokenInformation* API function. Again, you'll call this function twice. The second call will retrieve a buffer that contains the information for all groups associated with the access token (**m_hAccessToken**) passed into the first parameter of *GetTokenInformation*.

```
    // Get the SIDs for all the groups that the user belongs to
    deque<PSID> *CImpersonatedUser::ObtainUserGroupSIDs()
    {
        if (m_dequeGroupPSID.empty() && m_hAccessToken) {
            // Inquire on the size of the buffer
            DWORD dwTokenInfoBufferSize = 0 ;
            ::GetTokenInformation( m_hAccessToken, TokenGroups,
                0, 0, &dwTokenInfoBufferSize ) ;

            // Allocate memory to hold the buffer
            unsigned char *m_pByteGroupsUserBelongsTo =
                (unsigned char*) malloc(dwTokenInfoBufferSize) ;
```

```
        // Now get the buffer
        BOOL bRc = ::GetTokenInformation( m_hAccessToken, TokenGroups,
                m_pByteGroupsUserBelongsTo, dwTokenInfoBufferSize,
                &dwTokenInfoBufferSize ) ;
        if (!bRc) { return NULL ; }

        DWORD dwGroupCount =
            ((TOKEN_GROUPS*)m_pByteGroupsUserBelongsTo)->GroupCount ;

        for (int i=0; i< dwGroupCount; i++) {
            PSID pSid = ((TOKEN_GROUPS*)m_pByteGroupsUserBelongsTo)->Groups[i].
                Sid ;
            if (IsValidSid(pSid)) {
                // Creating deque (list) of group SIDs
                m_dequeGroupPSID.push_back( pSid ) ;
                string strUserGroup = UserGroupBySID(pSid) ;
                if (strUserGroup!="") {
                    // Creating deque of group names
                    m_dequeUserGroups.push_back(strUserGroup) ;
                }
            }
        } // for
    }

    return ( &m_dequeGroupPSID ) ;
}
```

After you obtain the buffer that holds the security information for all the groups associated with the access token, you create two lists. The first is a list of SIDs (m_dequeGroupPSID) for all groups associated with the access token. You keep the group SIDs around in a list so that if you wish you can use them later to get additional information. Before you add a SID to this list, you need to check that it's indeed a valid SID by calling the *IsValidSid* API function.

The second list (m_dequeUserGroups) that you're creating holds the names of all NT groups associated with the access token. As you add a SID to the first list (m_dequeGroupPSID), you also get the group name associated with the SID by calling a member function of the *CImpersonatedUser* class called *UserGroupBySID*, which you will write next. Each time you get a group name, you add it to the list of user groups (m_dequeUserGroups).

Following is the code for getting a group name given a group SID. There's nothing special in the *UserGroupBySID* method shown; you simply use the *LookupAccountSid* API function to obtain the group name and the domain associated with the group. Of course, this time the SID pointer (pSid) that you're passing into the second parameter is a group SID, not a user SID as in the earlier case.

```
    //-------------------------------------------------------------------
    // returns a group name given a group SID
    //-------------------------------------------------------------------
    string
```

```
CImpersonatedUser::UserGroupBySID( PSID pSid )
{
    DWORD dwGroupNameSize = GNLEN ;
    DWORD dwDomainNameSize = DNLEN ;
    TCHAR szGroupName[GNLEN+1];
    TCHAR szDomainName[DNLEN+1];
    SID_NAME_USE snu ;

    if (!::LookupAccountSid(0, pSid, szGroupName, &dwGroupNameSize,
            szDomainName, &dwDomainNameSize, &snu)) {
        return "" ;
    } else {
        string strGroupName ;
#ifdef UNICODE
        USES_CONVERSION;
        strGroupName = string(W2A(szGroupName)) + string("[") +
            string(W2A(szDomainName)) + string("]");
#else
        strGroupName = string(szGroupName) + string("[") +
            string(szDomainName) + string("]");
#endif
        return strGroupName ;
    }
}
```

Having written *ObtainUserGroupSIDs* earlier, the next method is simple. As shown in the following code, the *ObtainUserGroupNames* method returns a pointer to a list of group names created in the *ObtainUserGroupSIDs* method:

```
deque<string> *
CImpersonatedUser::ObtainUserGroupNames()
{
    if (m_dequeUserGroups.size()==0) {
        ObtainUserGroupSIDs() ;
    }

    return &m_dequeUserGroups;
}
```

It is obvious that you can get lots of information regarding a remote user if you can get a hold of the user's access token. Of course, you can do this only if the client has allowed you impersonation rights.

# *Audit Trail*

It is important to leave an audit trail for security or application problems. Traditionally, you record this kind of audit information into a persistent file so that an auditor or administrator can review it to detect and track down system problems.

On Windows NT, a common and secure place to record messages is the Windows NT event log. In this section, you'll learn how to take advantage of this facility.*

While in the *ValidateCall* function (discussed earlier), we verify whether the method invocation is fully encrypted by looking at the authentication level that the client had set. This must match RPC_C_AUTHN_LEVEL_PKT_PRIVACY or you'll record this violation in the audit trail. To refresh your memory, here's the relevant code from *ValidateCall* that performs the check:

```
if (dwAuthnLevel!=RPC_C_AUTHN_LEVEL_PKT_PRIVACY) {
    LogSecurityViolation(user);
    . . .
}
```

Notice that you call the *LogSecurityViolation* function to log a violation message and the user who issued the call into the Windows NT event log. You'll write this function, but before you can to that, you must consider the following:

- Create a message file—Windows NT requires that event log messages be stored in a binary message file that it can read. If you don't provide this message file, your messages will not be correctly formatted and will look strange in the Windows NT event viewer (*eventvwr.exe*). To get this binary message file, you must first create a source message file and then compile the message source file using the message compiler (*mc.exe*). You'll learn how to do this.

- Update the registry with event source information—You need to add the appropriate configuration entries for your event source to the registry so that your messages will be recorded appropriately in the event log.

- Log message—You'll finally learn how to log messages to the event log.

We will develop a simple C++ class that supports message logging to the Windows NT event log; we'll call this class *CEventLog*. The constructor will get an event source handle (m_hEventSource), which will be used by the *LogError* method to log messages and by the destructor to close the handle. The static *UpdateRegistry* function can be called with a **true** to register the entries necessary for event logging support. A **false** will remove these entries from the registry.

```
class CEventLog {
public:
    CEventLog();
    ~CEventLog();
    void LogError(TCHAR *pMessage, PSID pSid);
    static bool UpdateRegistry(bool bUpdate);
private:
    HANDLE m_hEventSource;
};
```

---

* You should record only crucial problems in the Windows NT event log—don't overflow or abuse the event log with unnecessary messages. For example, writing ten messages to the event log per method invocation is probably too excessive.

Before we implement this class, we'll first create the message file, as described in the next section.

## Creating Message Files

In order to pleasantly see the messages in the Windows NT event viewer, you need to create template messages. These template messages are created in a simple text file, much like a source code file. This file needs to be compiled using the message compiler to create a corresponding header file (*.h*) and a message resource file (*.rc*). You'll create and compile a simple message file for your component's messages.

### Creating a message file for your component

A message file includes the messages that you want to log. The syntax for a message file is straightforward, as shown in the following. Each message has a message identifier; for instance, the first bolded line starts a definition for the message with identifier 0x0. Your message has a `SymbolicName` called `OCR_SECURITY_` `VIOLATION`, which is an alias that you can use to refer to this message in your source code. You can specify a number of strings, each for a specific language. In this example, your message is in English as indicated by the `Language=English` line.

```
;//-------------------------------------------------------------------
;// Event Messages for SecureOcrServer
;//-------------------------------------------------------------------
MessageID=0x0
SymbolicName=OCR_SECURITY_VIOLATION
Language=English
[Security Violation] %1
.
```

The last bolded line is the actual text for this message. As you can see, `%1` is a placeholder for additional text that will be inserted at runtime. For example, when this message is reported, you won't see `%1`, but you will see something like the following:

[Security Violation] Secret has been leaked because a remote invocation was NOT encrypted.

One last thing to note is that each message definition ends with a single period on a line by itself. If you have more than one message, they must be separated by a line with a single period.

Having seen the basic syntax of a message file, create a file as shown earlier and save it as *EvMsgOcr.mc*.

### Compiling a message file

After creating the message file, you need to compile it to get a header and a message resource file. At the command prompt, move to the correct directory (which stores *EvMsgOcr.mc*) and type the following command:

*mc EvMsgOcr.mc*

This will create two files: *EvMsgOcr.h* and *EvMsgOcr.rc*. In the header file (*EvMsgOcr.h*), you will see a `#define` for your message, and of course, if you have defined more than one message, you'll see a number of these `#define`s. In the message resource file (*EvMsgOcr.rc*), you will see that it references the binary file *MSG00001.bin*, which contains your template messages in binary format. You need to add this resource file to the `SecureOcrServer` project, since you want to link this resource into this component. One easy way to do this is to append the text in *EvMsgOcr.rc* to the end of *SecureOcrServer.rc*, but you can also do this in the IDE by adding *EvMsgOcr.rc* into the project.

## Updating the Registry with Event Source Information

You now need to provide a way to register the information regarding the messages that you support in the registry. In essence, you are advertising to Windows NT that your component indeed has event messages. Since out-of-process servers use the `-RegServer` and `-UnRegServer` command-line options to register and unregister themselves, you'll take advantage of these options to register and unregister the registry information necessary for our event messages.

To support registration and unregistration, you'll write a static function that has a single parameter. When a `true` is passed into this function, you'll register the message information into the registry; when a `false` is passed, you'll unregister this information from the registry to clean up after yourselves. As shown in a number of following fragments, the code for the static *UpdateRegistry* function is fairly straightforward.

```
// Static function
static bool CEventLog::UpdateRegistry(bool bUpdate)
{
    // Get the full path name of the module
    TCHAR szModuleFileName[MAX_PATH] ;
    ::GetModuleFileName(_Module.GetModuleInstance(),
                    szModuleFileName, MAX_PATH);
    // Get the name of the binary executable from the full name
    TCHAR szExeName[MAX_PATH];
    _tsplitpath(szModuleFileName, NULL, NULL, szExeName, NULL) ;
```

The important thing is to create a subkey under the following registry key:

```
[HKLM\SYSTEM\CurrentControlSet\Services\EventLog\Application]
```

The subkey should be the name of your module, which you can obtain by calling the *GetModuleFileName* Win32 API function, as shown in the earlier code snippet.

Since you're using ATL, take advantage of the *CRegKey* class, which is an ATL class that makes managing the registry easier.

```
// Add registry information to support event logging for this server.
CRegKey EventLogKey ;
TCHAR ServerEventKey[MAX_PATH] ;
lstrcpy(ServerEventKey, TEXT("SYSTEM\\CurrentControlSet\\")
        TEXT("Services\\EventLog\\Application\\"));
lstrcat(ServerEventKey, szExeName) ;

long lRc = 0;
if (bUpdate) {
    // Creating the key for our server.
    lRc = EventLogKey.Create(HKEY_LOCAL_MACHINE, ServerEventKey) ;
    if (lRc != ERROR_SUCCESS) return false ;
```

Once you've created this subkey, you need to add a named value called `EventMessageFile`. This named value should point to the full path and filename of the binary file that contains the event messages. In your case, this is the path and the name of the EXE file of your component; something like `c:\SecureOcrServer.exe`. This is important, because it's the place where the event logging service will search for message resources needed to correctly log event messages for your application.

```
// Add the EventMessageFile to let the OS know where your messages are.
lRc = EventLogKey.SetValue(szModuleFileName, TEXT("EventMessageFile")) ;
if (lRc!=ERROR_SUCCESS) return false;
```

Another named value to add is `TypesSupported`, which tells Windows NT that the event source indicated by `EventMessageFile` supports the types of messages indicated in the `TypesSupported` named value. As shown in the following code snippet, we support five different message types: error, warning, informational, success audit, and failure audit:

```
// Set the types of events supported.
lRc = EventLogKey.SetValue( EVENTLOG_ERROR_TYPE |
        EVENTLOG_WARNING_TYPE |
        EVENTLOG_INFORMATION_TYPE |
        EVENTLOG_AUDIT_SUCCESS |
        EVENTLOG_AUDIT_FAILURE,
        TEXT("TypesSupported") ) ;
    if (lRc!=ERROR_SUCCESS) return false ;
} else {
    lRc=RegDeleteKey(HKEY_LOCAL_MACHINE, ServerEventKey);
    if (lRc!=ERROR_SUCCESS) return false ;
}
return true ;
}
```

The last bolded statement shows that we delete our subkey if the user requested to unregister our component.*

## Logging Messages

Once you've done the preliminaries for event logging as described in the last section, logging event messages is easy. Let's first examine the *LogSecurityViolation* function, which is called by *ValidateCall* when a remote invocation is unencrypted. As you can see later, you simply instantiate *CEventLog* and invoke the *LogError* method, passing in our message and a user SID, which can be obtained from the *CImpersonatedUser* instance by calling *ObtainUserSID*.

```
void LogSecurityViolation(CImpersonatedUser & user)
{
    CEventLog EventLog;
    // Because the method call was made without encryption,
    // we must record this violation in the Event Log so that
    // auditors can review it.
    EventLog.LogError(TEXT("Secret has been leaked ")
        TEXT("because a remote invocation was NOT encrypted."),
        user.ObtainUserSID());
}
```

Given that we know *LogSecurityViolation* uses the *CEventLog* object, we can write the code to support event logging. To log an event to the Windows NT event log, just follow these directions.

1. Call the *RegisterEventSource* Win32 API function to get a handle to the event source. This handle will allow you to write messages to the event log.

2. Call the *ReportEvent* Win32 API function as many times as you like to report events to the Windows NT event log. Calling this function requires the event source handle opened in step 1.

3. Call the *DeregisterEventSource* Win32 API function to close the handle returned by *RegisterEventSource*.

You'll write the code for step 1 in the constructor of *CEventLog*. The first parameter of *RegisterEventSource* allows you to specify the machine on which you want to log messages. Pass a NULL to indicate that you want to log messages to the local machine, as opposed to a remote machine indicated by a non-NULL server name. The second parameter indicates which event source you want to open; in your case, it's SecureOcrServer.

```
class CEventLog {
public:
```

---

* As an alternative to writing code to register and unregister message resource information, you may want to do all this by entering these named values and subkey into the ATL COM AppWizard generated registry script file, *SecureOcrServer.rgs*.

```
CEventLog() : m_hEventSource(0)
{
    TCHAR szExeName[MAX_PATH];
    S_GetExeName(szExeName);
    m_hEventSource = RegisterEventSource(NULL, szExeName);
}
```

The destructor simply closes the handle to the open event source by calling *DeregisterEventSource*.

```
~CEventLog()
{
    DeregisterEventSource(m_hEventSource);
}
```

The *LogError* method is where we actually report the event to the event log by using the *ReportEvent* Win32 API function. There are nine arguments passed into this function, so we'll only concentrate on the ones that are related to our message. The first argument is a handle (m_hEventSource) to the opened event source and it's always required. The second argument (EVENTLOG_ERROR_TYPE) indicates the type of event that is being logged. The fourth argument indicates the message to be logged, using the symbolic name OCR_SECURITY_VIOLATION. The fifth argument (pSid) indicates the SID of the user who made the remote method invocation. The event logging service will extract the information from this SID and nicely display it in the event viewer, so you don't have to suffer from doing this.

```
void LogError(TCHAR *pMessage, PSID pSid)
    {
        if (m_hEventSource != NULL) {
            // Write to event log
            ReportEvent(m_hEventSource,
                        EVENTLOG_ERROR_TYPE,
                        0,
                        OCR_SECURITY_VIOLATION,
                        pSid,
                        1, 0,
                        (const TCHAR **) &pMessage,
                        NULL);
        }
    }

private:
    HANDLE    m_hEventSource;
};
```

The sixth argument specifies the number of insert strings that exists in the pMessage buffer, the eight argument. Each insert string must be NULL-terminated within this buffer, but since we have only one insert string, we don't need to do anything special.

# Administrative Alert

There are times when your application must notify the administrator or authorized personnel immediately. For example, you would want to do this when you detect that the local hard-disk has reached a low watermark of available space. Or as in the exercise that we're about to embark upon, we want to immediately raise a red flag when we detect illegal users.

Windows NT comes with two services that handle this kind of notifications. These are the `Messenger` and `Alerter` services; in Windows NT 4.0, you can see these if you launch the `Services` applet in the `Control Panel`.* In this section, you'll learn how to take advantage of this operating system level of support. You need to learn an administrative task and a programming task:

1. We need to configure the workstation to generate administrative alerts, because if this is not done, your alert messages won't be generated.

2. We'll learn how to generate an administrative alert by using the *NetAlertRaiseEx* API function.

## Administrative Alert Setup

Before you start coding, you need to learn how to configure the workstation so that administrative alerts will be generated. First, you need to start the `Messenger` and `Alerter` services. The machine that *receives* administrative alerts must run the `Messenger` service, and the machine that *sends* administrative alerts must run the `Alerter` service. To start these services, use the `net start` command or the `Services` applet found in the `Control Panel`. After you have done this, use the following procedure to configure the local system to generate administrative alerts:

1. Launch the `Server Manager` utility. One way to do this is to execute the `Server` applet (not to be confused with the `Services` applet), which can be found in the `Control Panel`.

2. Click the `Alerts` button to launch the `Alerts` dialog box.

3. In the `New Computer or Username` edit-box, type in the computer or user name that you want to receive administrative alerts that are generated by applications running on this workstation.

4. After you've typed a computer or user name, click the `Add` button to insert it into the `Send Administrative Alerts To` list-box.

You must do this on all workstations with applications that send administrative alerts; otherwise, no alerts will be generated.

---

* On Windows 2000, launch the Microsoft Management Console (MMC).

# *Generating an Administrative Alert*

Now that you know how to set up the workstation to support administrative alerts, let's learn how generate them. Remember that after *ValidateCall* verifies that the method invocation is indeed encrypted, it proceeds to check whether the user belongs in an NT group called `HitList`. It does so by calling the helper function *IsUserInHitList*. Notice in the later code snippet that this function takes a single parameter—a *CImpersonatedUser* object. Without this parameter, you won't be able to figure out whether the user belongs in the `HitList`.

The first bolded statement of the following code creates a temporary string that identifies the `HitList`; this is a concatenation of the word `HitList` and the domain name (e.g., `HitList[DOG]`). The second bolded statement calls the *CImpersonatedUser::ObtainUserGroupNames* method to get a list of groups in which the user has membership. Now loop through this list and make the comparison. If the third bolded condition evaluates to `true`, the user is a member of `HitList`, in which case, you return `true` to the caller (*ValidateCall*), indicating that the user belongs in the `HitList`.

```
#define HIT_LIST_NT_GROUP "HitList"  // Ideally, should be a registry entry
bool IsUserInHitList(CImpersonatedUser & user)
{
    // You must add the "HitList" group using "User Manager".
    // Add a user to this group and then test out this functionality.
    string HitListGroup = string(HIT_LIST_NT_GROUP) + string("[") +
        string(user.ObtainDomainName()) + string("]");

    // Get the group names of all groups that the user belongs to.
    deque<string> *pGroupNames = user.ObtainUserGroupNames() ;
    deque<string>::iterator i ;
    // Loop through the list.
    for (i=pGroupNames->begin(); i!=pGroupNames->end(); i++) {
        string Group = (*i).data();
        if (HitListGroup==Group) {
            // If we get here, the user is in the hit list.
            return true;
        }
    }
    return false;
}
```

Given the code shown, you need to add a `Local Group` called `HitList`; you can do this by using the `User Manager` utility. Once you have created this group, add one or more users into this group to successfully test the functionality discussed in this subsection.

Remember that if *IsUserInHitList* returns `true` to *ValidateCall*, *ValidateCall* will generate an administrative alert by calling the *GenerateAdminAlert* helper function, which you are about to write. The key to generating an administrative alert is the call to the *NetAlertRaiseEx* API function.

```
#include <lmalert.h>  // needed for NetAlertRaiseEx
#include <lmerrlog.h>
void GenerateAdminAlert(CImpersonatedUser & user)
{
    TCHAR szExeName[MAX_PATH];
    S_GetExeName(szExeName);

    USES_CONVERSION;
#ifdef UNICODE
    wchar_t *pSvc = szExeName ;
#else
    wchar_t *pSvc = A2W(szExeName) ;
#endif
```

First, you create a message that includes the domain and user name, as shown here:

```
wchar_t wszMsg[MAX_PATH];
wsprintfW(wszMsg, L"THE SYSTEM IS UNDER ATTACK - Hacker: [%s/%s]",
    A2W(user.ObtainDomainName().data()),
    A2W(user.ObtainUserName().data()));
```

Next, you need to correctly format the alert message. Use the generic error code and message format defined by Microsoft for OEM use. This is the NELOG_OEM_Code error code, which has nine insert strings. Fill these two pieces of data in the ADMIN_OTHER_INFO structure, as shown here:

```
// All OEMs must use NELOG_OEM_Code
ADMIN_OTHER_INFO ai = {NELOG_OEM_Code, 9};
```

Each insert string is Unicode and must be concatenated into a single buffer, delimited by Unicode NULLs (i.e., two byte NULLs). Since you have only one insert string (wszMsg), you have to add eight Unicode NULLs for the first eight insert strings. Call this your NUL_PADDING, as shown in the following:

```
int iMsgLen = ByteLen(wszMsg);  // Length of the alert message.
int NUL_PADDING = 16;    // 8 wide-character are 16 bytes.
```

The total length of your message is composed of the size of ADMIN_OTHER_INFO, the length in bytes of wszMsg, and the NULL padding (NUL_PADDING). Given this total length, you can correctly allocate enough memory to hold all the necessary information prior to passing this memory buffer into the *NetAlertRaiseEx* API function.

```
// Total buffer length.
int iBufLen = sizeof(ai) + iMsgLen + NUL_PADDING;
BYTE *pAlertBuf = new BYTE[iBufLen];
memset(pAlertBuf, 0, iBufLen);
// Copy the header.
memcpy(pAlertBuf, &ai, sizeof(ai));
// Skip the place holders for 8 wide-characters.
BYTE *pMsgOffset = pAlertBuf + sizeof(ai) + NUL_PADDING;
// Copy the message into the buffer at the appropriate location.
memcpy(pMsgOffset, wszMsg, iMsgLen);
```

When calling the *NetAlertRaiseEx* API function, pass `ALERT_ADMIN_EVENT` as the first argument, indicating that you want to generate an administrative alert. The second argument is a pointer to the formatted buffer, which includes the `ADMIN_OTHER_INFO` header and the message with insert strings delimited by Unicode NULLs. The length of this buffer is passed as the third argument. And the last argument is the name of the service or application that generates this administrative alert.

```
    // Raise the alert.
    NetAlertRaiseEx(ALERT_ADMIN_EVENT, pAlertBuf, iBufLen, pSvc);
    delete [] pAlertBuf;
}
```

Since you're using the *NetAlertRaiseEx* API function, you must link in *netapi32.lib*.

At this point, we've completed the security support for the server side. To test out the functionality discussed so far, we need a client-side component.

## Client-Side Security

In this section, you'll build a simple client component that will use the `SecureOcrServer` component to test out the security features discussed previously. You'll learn how to set the default security for all proxies instantiated within this client process. This default can be altered prior to making an activation or a normal function call; for example, you can use any user identity to activate an object or invoke a method. Furthermore, you can specify the authentication and impersonation levels for each activation or method call. Here's a brief summary for the topics that you'll learn in this section:

1. Setting the authentication identity using the `SEC_WINNT_AUTH_IDENTITY_W` structure. This includes the user's domain, name, password.

2. Setting the process-wide security for all proxies using *CoInitializeSecurity*.

3. Merging the proxy/stub code. You've done this before in Chapter 8, *COM in Cyberspace*, but you'll learn another technique—manually using the *CoRegisterPSClsid* API function. This subsection has nothing to do with security, but it shows you how to internally register interface marshalers for an out-of-process EXE component.

4. Using activation security. This is security that is applied to activation API functions such as *CoGetClassObject* or *CoCreateInstance(Ex)*.

5. Using call security. This is security that can be set for each method invocation using the *IClientSecurity::SetBlanket* method or its shorthand, the *CoSetProxyBlanket* API function.

6. Handling errors. You'll also learn how to obtain error descriptions that the server component has set by calling the *SetErrorInfo* API function. This

subsection has nothing to do with security, but it shows you how to handle COM exceptions on the client side.

Before we start, we should first mention that the security options that we set in this section will apply only when the client and server components are running on separate machines. When the client and server components run on the same machine, all security options will act as if they are maximized. For example, even if you set the authentication level to RPC_C_AUTHN_LEVEL_DEFAULT, it will be bumped up to RPC_C_AUTHN_LEVEL_PKT_PRIVACY automatically.

I'll let you decide how you want to write your client application. You can write a simple console application with a *main* that takes the following command-line options:

*Target server*

> This is the name of the machine on which the **SecureOcrServer** component executes.

*Authentication identity (user security information)*

> This includes information of the account being used for authentication, including the user's domain, name, and password. This information is ignored when the client and server are running on the same machine.

*Authentication levels*

> This allows you to set different authentication levels and see their effect. Whe the client and server run on the same machine, RPC_C_AUTHN_LEVEL_PKT_ PRIVACY will be used, regardless of the authentication level you set. Recall from Chapter 5 that COM defines the following authentication levels: RPC_C_ AUTHN_LEVEL_DEFAULT, RPC_C_AUTHN_LEVEL_NONE, RPC_C_AUTHN_ LEVEL_CONNECT, RPC_C_AUTHN_LEVEL_CALL, RPC_C_AUTHN_LEVEL_PKT, RPC_C_AUTHN_LEVEL_PKT_INTEGRITY, and RPC_C_AUTHN_LEVEL_PKT_ PRIVACY. See Chapter 5 for a detailed discussion of each of these authentication levels.

Alternatively, you can write a dialog application with a user interface that allows you to set these options, so that you can test and see the effect of changing them.*
Whatever you decide to do, you need to write the code discussed later, which is broken up in digestible chunks, to test out the **SecureOcrServer** component. Note that the code assumes a dialog application implementation. In addition, all code fragments belong to one code block (same function) and are shown in order. Thus, all code fragments are dependent upon the ones previously shown.

---

* The code that accompanies this book is a dialog-based application.

## *Setting the Authentication Identity*

Setting the authentication identity is optional, but if you don't do this, COM will use the credentials of the user who starts the client component. If you set the authentication identity, you can selectively and finely control the identity that will be used for activation and method invocations. For example, you can manipulate user **Edie** to activate a distributed object, user **Rob** to invoke **OcrImage**, and user **Maureen** to invoke **CheckSpelling**. Despite the identity differences, all these invocations can take place in a single thread of execution, allowing you a lot of freedom in designing custom security management for the component-based systems that you will build. However, as we have alluded to earlier, setting the authentication identity will apply only when the client and server components run on different machines.

There are three elements that make up an authentication identity: the user's name, the user's domain, and the user's password. The following code shows that you'll get these values from the command-line options or via a user interface. Specifically, **m_strUserID**, **m_strDomain**, **m_strPassword** are string *CString* objects (or simply character arrays), set prior to executing this code fragments. In your program, you convert each of these *CString* objects into a corresponding *_bstr_t* object, as shown here:

```
HRESULT hr = S_OK;

// Get the security information entered by the user
_bstr_t bstrUser(m_strUserID);
_bstr_t bstrDomain(m_strDomain);
_bstr_t bstrPassword(m_strPassword);

// Set AuthIdentity
SEC_WINNT_AUTH_IDENTITY_W AuthIdentity = {
   bstrUser,
   bstrUser.length(),
   bstrDomain,
   bstrDomain.length(),
   bstrPassword,
   bstrPassword.length(),
   SEC_WINNT_AUTH_IDENTITY_UNICODE
};
```

Under the NTLM security provider, the authentication identity structure (**COAUTHIDENTITY**) is **SEC_WINNT_AUTH_IDENTITY_W**. As you can see from the earlier code, this structure allows you to set the user's name, domain, and password, including their associated lengths. The string values that represent these three elements must be in Unicode, and the last member of this structure must be **SEC_WINNT_AUTH_IDENTITY_UNICODE**.

We'll apply the authentication identity to activation and method invocations in a moment.

## Setting the Process-Wide Security

For client components, COM provides a way for you to programmatically set up security once for the whole process using the *CoInitializeSecurity* API function. You call this function during the startup of the client component to set the default process-wide authentication and impersonation levels that will be used by all proxies. This means that when a remote method invocation is made, COM uses the authentication and impersonation levels specified in this function call. See also the discussion of *CoInitializeSecurity* in Chapter 5, as this API function applies to server-side, process-wide security.

```
CoInitialize(0);
try {
    // process wide security - for all proxies not specifically refined
    hr = CoInitializeSecurity(
            NULL,
            -1,
            NULL,
            NULL,
            RPC_C_AUTHN_LEVEL_DEFAULT,     // UDP promotes to RPC_AUTHN_LEVEL_PKT
            RPC_C_IMP_LEVEL_IMPERSONATE,   // Allow the server to impersonation
            NULL,
            EOAC_NONE,
            NULL);   Chk(hr);
```

Even though we have specified the default authentication level (which resolves to RPC_C_AUTHN_LEVEL_CONNECT in NTLM), this is automatically promoted to RPC_ AUTHN_LEVEL_PKT if a datagram transport (e.g., UDP) is used. By default, COM uses UDP on Windows NT 4.0, so it is easy to verify this statement. In the SecureOcrServer component, simply display the incoming authentication level in the *ValidateCall* method. Test this client application using different authentication levels and you'll see that all authentication levels lower than RPC_AUTHN_ LEVEL_PKT will automatically be promoted to RPC_C_AUTHN_LEVEL_PKT.*

You must set the impersonation level to RPC_C_IMP_LEVEL_IMPERSONATE to allow the server component to impersonate the security context of each call made from this client. Remember that the SecureOcrServer component impersonates the client to get detailed security information in order to perform the specific validations that it requires. Without this setting, the server component will not be able to impersonate the caller.

Security settings specified using the *CoInitializeSecurity* API function are defaults used by the whole process. In this case, RPC_C_AUTHN_LEVEL_DEFAULT and RPC_C_IMP_LEVEL_IMPERSONATE are the defaults for all proxies in this

---

* The client and server components must be on separate machines. If they're on the same machine, you'll always see RPC_C_AUTHN_LEVEL_PRIVACY.

client component. However, these settings can be overridden at the method call level, as you'll see shortly.

## *Merging Proxy/Stub Code into a Client EXE Component*

You've learned how to merge proxy/stub code into a DLL written using the `ATL COM AppWizard` in Chapter 8. You didn't have to do much, because you simply clicked a few buttons, including the `Allow Merging of Proxy/Stub Code` check-box, and the proxy/stub code (for all interfaces defined in the *.idl* file) was be merged into the DLL. That was pretty much magic.

 This subsection has nothing to with security, but it shows you how to internally register interface marshalers for an out-of-process EXE component. This technique will enlarge the size of the final component, but it relieves the component user from having to separately register the proxy/stub DLL (using *regsvr32.exe*).

To do this manually, we need to use a special API function called *CoRegisterPSClsid*. It is important to learn how to do this, because the `ATL COM AppWizard` disables the `Allow Merging of Proxy/Stub Code` check-box when you're building an EXE file. There are two reasons for doing this:

1. To show a manual way of merging proxy/stub code into an EXE component.

2. To ignore having to register a proxy/stub DLL on the client side. The test that we will perform will be only valid when the client and server run on separate machines. Therefore, we must either register a proxy/stub DLL on the client side to support all custom interfaces or merge the proxy/stub code directly into the client EXE. We'll choose the latter for the topic of this discussion.

Having said that, here are the steps to manually merge proxy/stub code into an executable:

1. Obtain the server-side source files for the proxy/stub code that is generated by the MIDL compiler. Since you're using the `SecureOcrServer` component, the files you need include *dlldata.c*, *SecureOcrServer_p.c*, and *SecureOcrServer_i.c*.

2. If you're building an MFC dialog application client, use the `Settings` dialog to inhibit the use of `precompiled headers` for these files.

3. Add the `_WIN32_DCOM` preprocessor definition to the project.

4. Internally register the proxy/stub code, which will be discussed immediately after these enumerated steps.

5. Link in *rpcrt4.lib*.

6. Compile and link the above source files with your project.

Merging the proxy/stub code into your application is not enough for successful remote method invocation because you still need to register it. However, this registration is not done externally using *regsvr32.exe* on the proxy/stub DLL (as we've witnessed in the previous chapters), but dynamically and internally during the startup of the client application. This means that no interface-related registry entry is needed, as this information is registered dynamically during component execution. Let's learn how to dynamically and internally register interface marshalers.

Since *dlldata.c* implements the *DllGetClassObject* entry point, we will call *DllGetClassObject* to get the class object that knows how to instantiate interface proxies for marshaling the *ISecureOcrProcessor* interface. We must register this class object with COM so that COM can instantiate interface proxies when needed. The CLSID for this class object is assigned the same GUID as the interface we're marshaling, `IID_ISecureOcrProcessor`. This is why you see `IID_ISecureOcrProcessor` as the first argument to *DllGetClassObject* in the first emphasized statement below.

Once we have the *IUnknown* pointer to the class object that can instantiate interface proxies for the *ISecureOcrProcessor* interface, we use the *CoRegisterClassObject* API function to register the class object with COM.

```
// Internally register the proxy/stub
// Got to get all the source for the proxy/stub generated by MIDL.
// Turn of pre-compiled header and added rpcrt4.lib into the link
   settings.
CComPtr<IUnknown> pUnk;
hr = DllGetClassObject(IID_ISecureOcrProcessor, IID_IUnknown,
                       (void **)&pUnk);
Chk(hr);
DWORD dwCookie=0;
hr = CoRegisterClassObject(IID_ISecureOcrProcessor, pUnk,
    CLSCTX_INPROC_SERVER, REGCLS_MULTIPLEUSE, &dwCookie);
Chk(hr);
hr = CoRegisterPSClsid(IID_ISecureOcrProcessor, IID_ISecureOcrProcessor);
Chk(hr);
```

Finally, we need to let COM know that we're intending to internally use a proxy or stub, so we do this by calling the *CoRegisterPSClsid* API function. The first parameter to this API function is an IID and the second is a CLSID. The *CoRegisterPSClsid* call that we're making in the previous code lets COM know that interface proxies or stubs for the *ISecureOcrProcessor* interface (first argument) can be instantiated by the class object with CLSID `IID_ISecureOcrProcessor` (second argument). Because this class object has been registered using the *CoRegisterClassObject* API function in the previous statement, COM has no problems in finding it.

## Using Activation Security

When you activate a distributed object, you can dynamically choose the appropriate security settings. So if a client lacks the security or identity characteristics required by the server, activation never even gets off the ground. Recall that you typically use activation API functions such as *CoCreateInstanceEx* or *CoGetClassObject* to instantiate distributed objects. These activation API functions take a parameter of type COSERVERINFO, which is a structure that contains a COAUTHINFO structure as a member. Within the COAUTHINFO structure, you can specify in detail the authentication information that you want to use for remote object activation.

As shown later in the code snippet, you set the authentication level to the current combo-box selection chosen by the user (or if you were developing a console application, this would come from the command line). Also, you set the impersonation level to RPC_C_IMP_LEVEL_IMPERSONATE, allowing the server impersonation rights. The authentication and impersonation levels specified in COAUTHINFO will affect only object activation—never method invocations. Remote method invocations use the authentication and impersonation levels specified in the call to *CoInitializeSecurity*.

The sixth member of the COAUTHINFO structure is interesting; as you can see, we point it to the authentication identity that we've just filled out a moment ago. Recall that the authentication identity includes the user's domain, name, and password. The ability to do this allows us fine control over the appropriate security settings for activating remote objects. For example, a client component may be executing under the security context of user Katherine, but we can activate a specific object using the security context of user Christie.

```
COAUTHINFO AuthInfo = {
    RPC_C_AUTHN_WINNT,
    RPC_C_AUTHZ_NONE,
    NULL,
    m_ctrlAuthLevel.GetCurSel(),   // The authentication level used
    RPC_C_IMP_LEVEL_IMPERSONATE,
    (COAUTHIDENTITY*)&AuthIdentity,
    EOAC_NONE
};

_bstr_t bstrServer(m_strServer);

// Using activation security; i.e., using the indicated
// userid and password
COSERVERINFO csi = {0, bstrServer, &AuthInfo, 0};
MULTI_QI mqi[] = {&IID_ISecureOcrProcessor, NULL, S_OK};
hr = CoCreateInstanceEx(CLSID_SecureOcrProcessor, NULL,
                        CLSCTX_SERVER, &csi, 1, mqi);
Chk(hr); Chk(mqi[0].hr);
CComPtr <ISecureOcrProcessor> pSecureOcr((ISecureOcrProcessor*)mqi[0].
  pItf);
```

Notice that we put the authentication information into the third member of the
COSERVERINFO structure prior to calling *CoCreateInstanceEx* to remotely create an
instance of SecureOcrProcessor and retrieve its *ISecureOcrProcessor* interface
pointer.

## Using Call Security

The use of an authentication identity does not stop at activation security, because
you can also use the authentication identity to finely control each method invocation. This implies that even though the client component starts executing using a
specific user identity, you can use ten different user identities to call ten different
remote methods. This is just another illustration that client-side COM security can
be finely controlled.

In the following code, you call the *SecureOcrImage* method with the default security for proxies and stubs, configured by using the *CoInitializeSecurity* API function. This means that you're using the default access token and authentication
identity; in other words, you use the security context of the user that started this
client application. Furthermore, you're using the authentication and impersonation
levels specified in the call to *CoInitializeSecurity*. Of course, if you hadn't called
*CoInitializeSecurity*, these security settings are obtained from the local registry.

Since the SecureOcrServer component expects invocations to be encrypted, the
call to *SecureOcrImage*, as shown in the following code, will return a custom
return code, E_UNENCRYPTED_CALL. This custom error code is returned because
this specific call to *SecureOcrImage* uses the default authentication level for all
proxies within this process. The default authentication level is specified in the call
to *CoInitializeSecurity*.

```
try {
    // This call should fail because no encryption is used.
    // Our server expects the call to be totally encrypted.
    hr = pSecureOcr->SecureOcrImage();
    Chk(hr, pSecureOcr, IID_ISecureOcrProcessor);
} catch(_com_error & er) {
    if (er.Description().length()>0) {
        ::MessageBox(NULL, er.Description(), TEXT("Description"), MB_OK);
    } else {
        ::MessageBox(NULL, er.ErrorMessage(), TEXT("ErrorMessage"), MB_OK);
    }
}
```

Remember that when an invocation is made without encryption, the
SecureOcrServer component uses the *AtlReportError* function to return a
detailed description back to the client. We will discuss the internals of the overloaded *Chk* helper function, which takes three arguments, in a moment. For now,
simply notice that we display the description; that is, we're calling *Description*

instead of *ErrorMessage*. If there isn't a description, this method call has failed for reasons other than E_UNENCRYPTED_CALL.

Now, let's crank up to full encryption and invoke this method again. We dynamically refine the security of the *ISecureOcrProcessor* proxy using a specific user's domain, name, and password. We can refine security settings by using either the *IClientSecurity::SetBlanket* method or the shorthand *CoSetProxyBlanket* API function. For convenience, we've chosen the latter, as shown below. Notice from the emphasized code that we dynamically configure the authentication level, impersonation level, and authentication identity (filled out in the beginning of this section).

```
hr = CoSetProxyBlanket(pSecureOcr, // Apply the security on this proxy
    RPC_C_AUTHN_WINNT, RPC_C_AUTHZ_NONE, NULL,
    m_ctrlAuthLevel.GetCurSel(),  // Use the authentication level selected
    RPC_C_IMP_LEVEL_IMPERSONATE,  // Allow impersonation
    &AuthIdentity,  // Using a specific AuthIdentity.
    EOAC_NONE);
Chk(hr);
```

The *CoSetProxyBlanket* call will permanently change the security settings for the proxy pointed to by pSecureOcr. Therefore, if you want to preserve the original security settings on this proxy, you must first call *CoCopyProxy* to make a new copy of this proxy. In this exercise, we purposely don't do this because we don't care about preserving this proxy's original security settings.

Once you've changed the security settings, method invocations made using this proxy will use the updated security settings. For example, if you execute this component using the RPC_C_AUTHN_LEVEL_PKT_PRIVACY authentication level, the *SecureOcrImage* remote method invocation will pass the check for full data encryption.

```
try {
    hr = pSecureOcr->SecureOcrImage();
    Chk(hr, pSecureOcr, IID_ISecureOcrProcessor);
} catch(_com_error & er) {
    if (er.Description().length()>0) {
        ::MessageBox(NULL, er.Description(), TEXT("Description"), MB_OK);
    } else {
        ::MessageBox(NULL, er.ErrorMessage(), TEXT("ErrorMessage"), MB_OK);
    }
}
} catch(_com_error & er) {
    ::MessageBox(NULL, er.ErrorMessage(), TEXT("ErrorMessage"), MB_OK);
}
CoUninitialize();
```

Again, this call to *SecureOcrImage* can succeed or fail, and this all depends on the authentication level that you set via the command line or the user interface of your client application. In addition, even if the authentication level is set to RPC_C_ AUTHN_LEVEL_PKT_PRIVACY, the call may fail for other reasons. For example, the client that makes the call may be a member of the `HitList` NT group, meaning that this call will fail.

## Handling Errors

Previously, when developing the `SecureOcrServer` component, you used the *AtlReportError* function to return a detailed description when an error occurs. On the client side, the easiest way to obtain this description is by using a compiler-supported function called *_com_issue_errorex*. Unlike *_com_issue_error*, seen in Chapter 7, *Using COM Objects*, this function takes an `HRESULT`, a pointer to the interface that generated the error, and its IID. It uses this information to create and throw a *_com_error* exception object. Given this information, you write an inline function that uses *_com_issue_errorex* to throw a COM exception when the `HRESULT` is bad, as shown here:

```
inline void Chk(HRESULT hr, IUnknown *pUnk, REFIID riid)
{
    if (FAILED(hr)) _com_issue_errorex(hr, pUnk, riid);
}
```

 This subsection has nothing to with security, but it shows you how to deal with COM exceptions on the client side—an important consideration for developing user-friendly and easy-to-debug client components. If you find this discussion a distraction, you may move on to the next section.

There's no magic to the *_com_issue_errorex* function. You can observe the internals of this compiler-supported function by rewriting the *Chk* function as shown later. This code fragment requires that the server object implements the *ISupportErrorInfo* interface. In your `SecureOcrServer` component, this is automatically done for you because you clicked on the `Support ISupportErrorInfo` check-box when you created the COM object during the development of `SecureOcrServer`.

```
inline void Chk(HRESULT hr, IUnknown *pUnk, REFIID riid)
{
    if (FAILED(hr)) {
        CComQIPtr<ISupportErrorInfo, &IID_ISupportErrorInfo>
                                     pSupportError(pUnk);
        HRESULT hrTest = pSupportError->InterfaceSupportsErrorInfo(riid);
        if (FAILED(hrTest)) throw _com_error(hrTest);
        CComPtr<IErrorInfo> pErrorInfo;
        hrTest = ::GetErrorInfo(0, &pErrorInfo);
        if (FAILED(hrTest)) throw _com_error(hrTest);
        throw _com_error(hr, pErrorInfo);
    }
}
```

As shown in the first emphasized statement, you use the interface pointer (pUnk) associated with the error to query for the *ISupportErrorInfo* interface, making sure that the target object supports standard error handling. You then use the retrieved pointer (pSupportError) to invoke the *InterfaceSupportsErrorInfo* method, passing in the IID of the interface that returned the bad HRESULT. This process verifies that the methods of the interface indicated by riid handle errors using the *AtlReportError* function, which internally uses the *CreateErrorInfo* and *SetErrorInfo* API functions.

To get the error information, call the *GetErrorInfo* COM API function to retrieve the *IErrorInfo* interface pointer set by the last call to *SetErrorInfo* on the server side for this logical thread. Once you've obtained the *IErrorInfo* interface, you can call its methods to obtain detailed error information, such as a description of the error. However, instead of doing this manually, you can create and throw a *_com_ error* exception object, which has an overloaded constructor that takes an *IErrorInfo* interface pointer, including the bad HRESULT. The code that uses this *Chk* function to verify the success of a method invocation can obtain the error's detailed description by simply calling *_com_error::Description*.

## *Testing and Understanding COM Security*

Now that you've gone over the code for the client component, let's test the client and server components to see the behaviors of COM security. Try out different options for your tests. Add more message boxes to display the information that are of interest to you for better understanding.

Remember that security is pretty much maximized if you leave the client and server components running on the same workstation. No matter what authentication level you specify, RPC_C_AUTHN_LEVEL_PKT_PRIVACY will be used. In addition, authentication identity information (i.e., COAUTHIDENTITY) will be ignored and the default access token of the client process will be used.

Therefore, to see different combinations of security, you must execute the client and server components on different machines. Because the test scenarios discussed later require two different physical machines, it is recommended that you set two machines next to one another so that you don't have to run back and forth. If you don't have two machines, you should still read the test scenarios discussed, because they tell you not only the results of each test but the reasoning behind it.

You don't have to register a proxy/stub DLL on the client side because you have merged the proxy/stub code for the *ISecureOcrProcessor* interface into the client component. Simply take the client component to a different machine and execute it. Make sure that the target server points back to the machine with the SecureOcrServer component registered and ready to run.

You can test these two components however you like. Change different security settings in *dcomcnfg.exe* to see the effect, but you should at least observe the following scenarios.

### Test Scenario I—Observing call-level security and logged events

To observe the effect of call-level security, security violations, and logged events, perform the following steps:

1. Make a note of the currently logged-on account on the client machine. The client component is running under this user account's security context.

2. Set (either via the command line or through a user interface) a different but valid account, including domain, user, and password. Obviously, this account is different from the account that starts the client component.*

3. Set the authentication level to RPC_C_AUTHN_LEVEL_PKT_PRIVACY.

4. Execute the code discussed above, and you should see a message on the server workstation showing the user that invoked the method, in the format of DOMAIN\exec_user. This is the first method invocation, which uses the default security settings, so this message should display the user account that executed the client application.

5. Dismiss this message on the server workstation, and you will see the following message on the client workstation: [Security Violation] Secret has been leaked because a remote invocation was NOT encrypted. This should be intuitive, because the first method call that you make uses the default security settings for proxies, which happens to be RPC_C_AUTHN_LEVEL_DEFAULT (because you earlier called *CoInitializeSecurity* using this authentication level).

6. Recall that when a call is unencrypted, you log it into the event log. So launch the event viewer (*eventvwr.exe*) on the server machine and look into the Application log. You'll see the same message, including full details of the user that has caused the problem.

7. Now for the second method call. Remember that in this call, you programmatically (via *CoSetProxyBlanket*) use the authentication identity and authentication level specified on the command line or via a user interface. If you dismiss the message on the client workstation, you'll see another message on the server workstation showing the user that invoked the method. This is the second user

---

\* Make sure that these two accounts have access and launch permissions on the server machine. You can configure this using *dcomcnfg.exe*; if you don't know how to do this, refer to the "Security" section in Chapter 5. In addition, if you're using different domains, the easiest thing to do is set up accounts with the same user IDs and passwords on both machines to use Windows NT's fallback authentication. If two local (not domain) accounts on different machines have the same user IDs and passwords, Windows NT assumes that these accounts belong to the same user.

account; the one you use to fill out the `SEC_WINNT_AUTH_IDENTITY_W` structure, as discussed in the "Setting the Authentication Identity" section. Seeing this message verifies that the second method invocation indeed uses call-level security through the *CoSetProxyBlanket* API function.

8. Dismiss this message on the server workstation. This time, you don't see a message on the client workstation because the second call is encrypted.

### *Test Scenario II—Observing administrative alerts*

To observe administrative alerts being scatter to configured users and machines, perform the following:

1. Follow the same procedure described in the "Test Scenario I," except for step 2.

2. For step 2 of "Test Scenario I," set a different, but valid account, including domain, user, and password. In addition, this user has to be a member of an NT group called `HitList` on the server machine.

3. Run the test as described in "Test Scenario I." You should see similar results to the previous test. However, things change in step 8 of "Test Scenario I."

4. On the client machine, you should see the following message: `[Security Violation]  Be careful.  You [DOMAIN\HitList_User] are in our hit list.`

5. At about the same moment, administrative alerts will be sent out to all configured users and workstations on the network. The alert message should read: `THE SYSTEM IS UNDER ATTACK—Hacker: [DOMAIN\HitList_User].`*

### *Test Scenario III—Observing activation security*

One thing that you can't observe by virtue of displaying messages is activation security. You can't do this because the server component is not yet running until it is activated by COM. However, you can observe the effect of activation security by performing the following steps:

1. On the server machine, allow access and launch permissions to the account that is currently used as the logged-in account on the client machine. Use *dcomcnfg.exe* to do this.

2. On the server machine, pick a different account. Using *dcomcnfg.exe*, allow access permissions but deny launch permissions to this account.

3. Launch the client component on the client workstation. Set the account configured in step 2 as the authentication identity used for activation and run the test.

---

* In order to see administrative alert messages, the machine that receives administrative alerts must run the `Messenger` service and the machine (where the `SecureOcrServer` component executes) that sends alerts must run the `Alerter` service. Also, use the `Server Manager` utility to configure the alert message destinations.

4. You will immediately see the **Access Denied** message on the client workstation, because launch permissions are denied to this user. This is true even though the logged-in account has launch permissions, since customized activation security is used.

Describing these scenarios to you doesn't mean much. You've got to run the tests to get the real gist of COM security.

# 10

## Connecting Objects

In this chapter:
- *Object Reference*
- *Referrers*
- *Connection Points*
- *Event Sources*
- *Event Sinks*
- *Performance Impact of Connection Points*
- *Security Impact of the OBJREF*

Thus far, you've written only uncomplicated interfaces with methods that take and return simple data types. In this chapter, you will develop a simple distributed architecture that involves passing interface pointers from one object to another—and from this second object to yet a third object. Interface pointers can be passed around in this fashion to maintain connections among peers.

You'll exploit the sharing of interface pointers by building a simple distributed system that includes a referrer (also called a middleman or a broker), a server, and a client. Figure 10-1 shows the architectural view of this system, which names these three distributed components ChatBroker, ChatServer, and ChatClient, respectively. Briefly, this system works as follows:

1. A ChatServer registers itself with a ChatBroker.

2. A ChatClient connects to the ChatBroker and requests to join a chat discussion, which is managed by a ChatServer.

3. Once a ChatClient has joined a discussion, it can directly send chat messages to the ChatServer that manages the discussion, without any further collaboration with the ChatBroker. In other words, once a client has connected to the server, the broker is virtually out of the picture.

4. Upon receiving a chat message, the ChatServer broadcasts the message to all connected ChatClients.

The ChatBroker's job is to keep track of the ChatServers that have registered themselves, and it exposes the *IRegisterChatServer* interface for this purpose. In addition, it supports the *IDiscussions* interface for ChatClients to query for the discussions that a user can join.

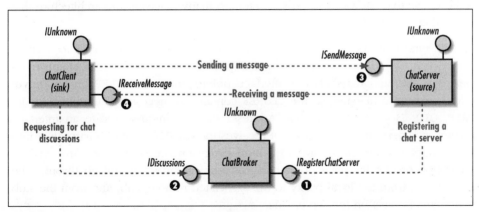

*Figure 10-1. The chat architecture*

Each **ChatServer** represents a chat discussion, and it supports an *ISendMessage* interface to allow **ChatClients** to send chat messages. Many **ChatClients** can connect to a given **ChatServer**. In the event that a **ChatServer** receives a chat message, it propagates the same message to all connected **ChatClients** so that every chatter will see all the messages relevant to a given discussion. When a **ChatServer** starts up, it registers itself with the **ChatBroker** by passing an *ISendMessage* interface pointer to the **ChatBroker**, via the *IRegisterChatServer* interface. When it goes down, it unregisters itself from the **ChatBroker**.

A **ChatClient** can connect to a **ChatBroker** and ask for the available discussions or chat topics, via the **ChatBroker**'s *IDiscussions* interface. Given this list of discussions, a **ChatClient** can choose a discussion and request the **ChatBroker** to return the registered *ISendMessage* interface pointer associated with the chat discussion (or **ChatServer**). The **ChatClient** then uses this interface to send chat messages to the **ChatServer**. Since the **ChatClient** is interested in chat messages targeting the discussion that it has joined, it must pass an interface (*IReceiveMessage*) to the **ChatServer**. This is a callback interface that the **ChatServer** will use to return the chat messages that it receives.

This whole architecture revolves around two important notions that are key to maintaining connections among objects in Distributed COM. These are the *object reference* and *connection points*. An object reference is the key element of Distributed COM because it allows an interface pointer to be passed from one machine to any other machine (or machines) in cyberspace. Connection points is a standard technique for implementing bidirectional communications in COM.

## *Object Reference*

We have already talked about the object reference (OBJREF) in Chapter 5, *Infrastructure*, but we must review it to stress its importance here. Besides, the OBJREF is the magic that allows us to pass pointers to many places in the architecture that we're about to build.

Let's assume that you need to get an interface pointer from a server to a client component. When an interface pointer is passed from a server to a client, COM creates a stub and marshals the interface pointer into an OBJREF on the server side. In standard marshaling, the OBJREF contains all necessary information (e.g., OXID, OID, IPID, OXID Resolver Address, etc.) to uniquely locate an interface pointer in cyberspace. When a client receives the OBJREF, COM unmarshals it into an interface pointer that points to a local proxy on the client side. Any method invocation on the interface pointer in the client component will go through the local proxy, from the local proxy to the associated remote stub, and from the stub to the target object on the server side.

In our simple distributed chat system, a method call from the ChatClient should go back to the ChatServer that has registered its interface pointer against the ChatBroker. This is obvious—or is it?

As a developer, you don't have to worry about this because it should just work as expected. The Distributed COM infrastructure should worry about this, which it does through a process known as OXID resolution. Specifically, an OXID Resolver is the agent that resolves OXIDs into string bindings that represent target apartment destinations. Since there's an OXID Resolver on every machine that runs Distributed COM, OXID resolution is coordinated among cooperating machines to guarantee resolution. And since an IPID is unique within an OXID, COM can find the interface pointer, even in the titanic cyberspace.* Remember, the IPID, OXID, and OXID Resolver's address are recorded inside the OBJREF.†

Given the behavior of the OBJREF, if a ChatServer passes an interface pointer to the ChatBroker and the ChatBroker in turn passes the same interface pointer to a ChatClient, the client will be able to directly invoke methods on the ChatServer. Even if the ChatBroker went down, the ChatClient would still be able to invoke methods on the ChatServer. This is because each time an interface pointer is marshaled from one apartment to another, an OBJREF is sent across. Since the OBJREF contains all the information needed to get back to the original apartment (OXID and, if needed, OXID Resolver), this should be of no surprise.

OXID resolution calls for a little more explanation in relation to how it works for our chat architecture. When a ChatServer registers itself against the ChatBroker, it passes an *ISendMessage* interface pointer, thus requiring COM to marshal the *ISendMessage* pointer into an OBJREF and create an interface stub on the

---

* This discussion assumes knowledge of the "Transparency" section in Chapter 5.

† Just in case you've forgotten, the OID is used internally by Distributed COM to perform distributed garbage collection via the use of delta pings.

`ChatServer`. COM sends the `OBJREF` to the `ChatBroker`, whose COM marshaling layer will unmarshal the `OBJREF` to create an interface proxy. Through OXID resolution, this interface proxy connects back to the correct, remote interface stub, because the `OBJREF` contains the information to get back to the `ChatServer`.

This is straightforward, but what happens when the `ChatBroker` passes *ISendMessage*, which really belongs to the `ChatServer`, to a `ChatClient`? Things change a bit in this case, because the `ChatBroker` holds a reference to the *ISendMessage* interface pointer but doesn't own the pointer. When the `ChatBroker` passes the *ISendMessage* to the `ChatClient`, COM simply sends the original `OBJREF` to the `ChatClient`, without having to create an unnecessary, intermediary interface stub on the `ChatBroker`. Once the `ChatClient` receives the original `OBJREF`, COM unmarshals it into an interface proxy on the `ChatClient`. Through OXID resolution, this interface proxy connects back to the `ChatServer`, not the `ChatBroker`, because the `OBJREF` contains the destination information for the `ChatServer`. Clearly from this discussion, once OXID resolution has taken place, the middleman (`ChatBroker`) is no longer an important agent for the link between the `ChatServer` and `ChatClient`.

Now that we have made our points regarding an `OBJREF`, let's develop the `ChatBroker` to gain practical hands-on experience.

# Referrers

Referrers or brokers are so named because they are responsible for referring clients to a particular object. In some systems, clients usually don't know where the target servers run, but they know one important agent, the broker, who can refer them to the appropriate servers. Typically, servers register themselves with a broker when they start up. When a client asks the broker for a particular service, the broker will return the registered server that supports the requested service. Brokers can do much more than this; for example, load balancing is something that can be done by the broker to equally distribute server loads. However, referrals are enough to illustrate the importance of the `OBJREF`.

Therefore, in our exercise, we'll create a `ChatBroker` to refer a `ChatClient` to an appropriate `ChatServer`. As alluded to earlier, a `ChatServer` uses the *IRegisterChatServer* interface to register itself by passing its *ISendMessage* interface pointer to the `ChatBroker`. The `ChatBroker` keeps a list of *ISendMessage* interface pointers exposed by `ChatServer`s, each representing a particular discussion topic. From this discussion list, a `ChatClient` may choose to join one of these discussions. Once the choice is made, the `ChatBroker` passes the *ISendMessage* interface pointer to the `ChatClient`. The `ChatClient` uses the *ISendMessage* to send chat messages to the `ChatServer`, even though it has no idea where in cyberspace the `ChatServer` runs.

## Creating the ChatBroker Component

Let's start off by creating a new project called `ChatBroker`. Use the `ATL COM AppWizard` to create an `executable(EXE)` component. Once the project is created, use the `Settings` dialog box and turn on exception handling, because you'll use this C++ feature.

In addition, make the main apartment a multithreaded apartment (MTA). To do this, simply go to the generated *_tWinMain* function and make sure that the *CoInitializeEx* API function is used to initialize the COM library, as shown below:

```
//  This means that calls come in on a random RPC thread.
HRESULT hRes = CoInitializeEx(NULL, COINIT_MULTITHREADED);
```

Doing this will allow calls to arrive on random RPC threads, which means that multiple calls can be simultaneously handled by an object living in the MTA. Such concurrency may slightly improve the performance of your `ChatBroker`, but this means that your code and COM objects running in this MTA had better be thread-safe.

## Adding a Broker COM Object

Now that you have the `ChatBroker` component, you need to add the broker COM object. Here are the steps for creating this object:

1. Use the `ATL Object Wizard` to add a simple COM object to the `ChatBroker` component.

2. In the `Names` tab of the `ATL Object Wizard Properties` dialog box, name this object `ChatBrokerObj` to generate a *CChatBrokerObj* C++ class.

3. Also, name the first interface *IRegisterChatServer*. Specifically, change *IChatBrokerObj* to *IRegisterChatServer* in the `Interface` edit-box. Do this because you don't want to use the default, generated name, *IChatBrokerObj*; you want this interface to be named *IRegisterChatServer* to match the architecture shown in Figure 10-1.

4. In the `Attributes` tab, select the `Free` threading model to indicate that you want the object to be used by multiple threads simultaneously.

5. Select `Custom` because you want *IRegisterChatServer* to be a custom interface.

6. Select the *ISupportErrorInfo* option because you'll send custom error messages to clients.

To improve performance somewhat, you'll allow this object to be a singleton object so that the object will be created only once. This means that there is only one instance of *CChatBrokerObj* running per `ChatBroker`, thus saving memory and instantiation time. This singleton instance will service multiple and simultaneous `ChatClients` and `ChatServers`.* To make this object a singleton, all you would have to do is add the boldface line, shown in the following, to the class definition of *CChatBrokerObj*:

```
class CChatBrokerObj :
    public CComObjectRootEx<CComMultiThreadModel>,
    public CComCoClass<CChatBrokerObj, &CLSID_ChatBrokerObj>,
    public ISupportErrorInfo ,
    public IRegisterChatServer,
{
public:
    DECLARE_CLASSFACTORY_SINGLETON(CChatBrokerObj)
    CChatBrokerObj() { }
    . . .
};
```

This COM object supports two interfaces: *IRegisterChatServer* is used by the `ChatServers` and *IDiscussions* is used by `ChatClients`. Both of these interfaces will be described below.

### The IRegisterChatServer interface

The *IRegisterChatServer::Register* method allows a `ChatServer` to register an *ISendMessage* interface with the `ChatBroker`. At this point, you don't know the definition of the *ISendMessage* interface yet, as you'll define this interface when we develop the `ChatServer` component. But, since all interfaces are directly or indirectly derived from *IUnknown*, you may use *IUnknown* in place of *ISendMessage*. This is fine; however, to get an *ISendMessage* pointer from this *IUnknown* pointer, a client must call *QueryInterface*. This is an extra round-trip that could be saved if we had used *ISendMessage* instead of *IUnknown*. But since you haven't developed the `ChatServer`, you'll live with this extra round trip (for the clarity of this exercise).

Associated with this *IUnknown* pointer is a string that represents the name of the discussion topic. When a `ChatServer` closes down, it must call *IRegisterChatServer::Unregister* to allow the `ChatBroker` to release a reference to the interface that it's been keeping in its discussion list.

Use the `Add Method to Interface` dialog box to add the following methods into the *IRegisterChatServer* interface. Recall that if you use this dialog to add the interface methods, it will generate the empty method implementations for you.

```
HRESULT Register([in] IUnknown *pChatServer,
                 [in, string] wchar_t *pwszDiscussion);
HRESULT Unregister([in, string] wchar_t *pwszDiscussion);
```

---

* Alternatively, you don't have to make this object a singleton (which is more correct according to the description of *IClassFactory::CreateInstance*). However, if you take this route, a brand new object will be created for each connected client, which means there is a slight performance and resource hit.

### The IDiscussions interface

The previous interface is generated by the `ATL Object Wizard`, but to add the *IDiscussions* interface (or to add more interfaces to an ATL-generated COM object), you need to do it by hand. Therefore, manually add the following interface definition to the *ChatBroker.idl* file. Remember that you can get a GUID by using the *guidgen.exe* utility.

```
[
    object,
    uuid(573F3BE4-A81A-11d1-87A6-006008CDD9AE),
    helpstring("IDiscussions Interface"), pointer_default(unique)
]
interface IDiscussions : IUnknown
{
    HRESULT GetDiscussionList([out, string] wchar_t **ppwszDiscussionList);
    HRESULT GetChatServer([in, string] wchar_t *pwszDiscussion,
                          [out] IUnknown **ppUnk);
};
```

A `ChatClient` will call *IDiscussions::GetDiscussionList* to obtain a list of discussions registered to the `ChatBroker`. To make things simple, this list is an array of Unicode characters. This array can represent a number of discussions, each delimited by a return character ('\n'). Obviously, the delimiter helps parse out each discussion. A `ChatClient` must obtain this list before it can choose which discussion (`ChatServer`) it wants to join. To join a particular discussion, a `ChatClient` would invoke *IDiscussions::GetChatServer* passing in a Unicode string indicating the discussion name and get back an *IUnknown* pointer, which really belongs to the `ChatServer`. Because `ppUnk` is an `[out]` parameter, COM will pass an `OBJREF` associated with this interface pointer to the `ChatClient` which will unmarshal it. The `ChatClient` will get all the information that exists in the `OBJREF` for `OXID` resolution.

Other than adding the *IDiscussions* interface definition, add the *IDiscussions* interface to the `coclass` definition as shown by the following bolded code:

```
[
    uuid(573F3BE6-A81A-11d1-87A6-006008CDD9AE),
    helpstring("ChatBrokerObj Class")
]
coclass ChatBrokerObj
{
    [default] interface IRegisterChatServer;
    interface IDiscussions;
};
```

In order to support the *IDiscussions* interface, you must do the following:

1. Derive *CChatBrokerObj* from the *IDiscussions* interface.

2. Add a `COM_INTERFACE_ENTRY` entry for the *IDiscussions* interface.

3. Add the declarations for the *IDiscussions* interface methods to the class definition of *CChatBrokerObj*.

The relevant code for all this is shown in the following code in boldface:

```
class CChatBrokerObj :
    public CComObjectRootEx<CComMultiThreadModel>,
    public CComCoClass<CChatBrokerObj, &CLSID_ChatBrokerObj>,
    public ISupportErrorInfo,
    public IRegisterChatServer,
    public IDiscussions  // Add this manually
{
public:
DECLARE_CLASSFACTORY_SINGLETON(CChatBrokerObj)
        CChatBrokerObj(){}

DECLARE_REGISTRY_RESOURCEID(IDR_ChatBROKEROBJ)

BEGIN_COM_MAP(CChatBrokerObj)
    COM_INTERFACE_ENTRY(IRegisterChatServer)
    COM_INTERFACE_ENTRY(IDiscussions)  // Add this manually
    COM_INTERFACE_ENTRY(ISupportErrorInfo)
END_COM_MAP()

// ISupportsErrorInfo
    STDMETHOD(InterfaceSupportsErrorInfo)(REFIID riid);

// IRegisterChatServer
public:
    STDMETHOD(Unregister)(/*[in,string]*/ wchar_t *pwszDiscussion);
    STDMETHOD(Register)(/*[in]*/ IUnknown *pChatServer,
                        /*[in,string]*/ wchar_t *pwszDiscussion);

// IDiscussions  --  Add these manually
public:
    STDMETHOD(GetDiscussionList)(/*[out, string]*/ wchar_t
                                 **ppwszDiscussionList);
    STDMETHOD(GetChatServer)(/*[in,string]*/ wchar_t *pwszDiscussion,
                             /*[out]*/ IUnknown **ppUnk);
};
```

In addition, add this interface into *CChatBrokerObj::InterfaceSupportsErrorInfo* to
indicate that *IDiscussions* supports error handling. This is shown in the following
boldfaced line:

```
STDMETHODIMP CChatBrokerObj::InterfaceSupportsErrorInfo(REFIID riid)
{
    static const IID* arr[] =
    {
        &IID_IRegisterChatServer,
        &IID_IDiscussions
    };
    . . .
}
```

# Caching a List of Discussions

Because the ChatBroker needs to keep a list of all registered ChatServers (discussions), you'll create a special class that models a list called *CChatDiscussionList*. You'll do this for two reasons. First, this class will provide a simple interface for adding a discussion, removing a discussion, getting the list of discussions, and getting a reference to the target ChatServer for a particular discussion. Second, whatever list you use must be thread-safe because the *CChatBrokerObj* object is a singleton that lives inside an MTA. This implies that the object (and therefore the *CChatDiscussionList*) may be simultaneously accessed by many threads. It is easy to create a thread-safe list by using a critical section object, as shown in the following code snippet:

```
// We're using STL's map and string classes
#pragma warning(disable:4786)
#include <map>
#include <string>
using namespace std;

// Typedef for easier code reading
typedef map<string, IUnknown*> DiscussionMap;

// Thread-safe discussion list encapsulates a map object for fast lookups
class CChatDiscussionList {
public:
    CChatDiscussionList();
    ~CChatDiscussionList();

    bool AddDiscussion(wchar_t *pswDiscussion, IUnknown *pUnk);
    void RemoveDiscussion(wchar_t *pswDiscussion);
    wchar_t *GetDiscussionList();
    IUnknown *GetChatServer(wchar_t *pwszDiscussion);
    long GetSize();

private:
    DiscussionMap m_map;       // The list of discussions
    CComCriticalSection m_cs;  // Critical section object
};
```

As you can see from the previous class definition, this class simply encapsulates a *map* object for fast lookups. A *map* has a key-value pair; for example, a discussion called DiscussDCOM may be a key and the interface pointer that supports this discussion is its corresponding value. Thus, given a discussion name, the ChatBroker can look in this *map* to get the target interface pointer. However, a *map* is not enough, as you must make it thread-safe, so you wrap the *map* object inside *CChatDiscussionList* and provide a critical section object to control multi-threaded accesses to the *map*. The *CComCriticalSection* object is a simple ATL object that encapsulates a Win32 critical section object, making it easier to use.

For simplicity, add the *CChatDiscussionList* class definition to the *StdAfx.h* file. Also, you'll keep only one discussion list in the whole ChatBroker process, so you'll add a member variable of type *CChatDiscussionList* to the *CExeModule* class definition, as shown in the code snippet here:

```
class CExeModule : public CComModule
{
public:
    LONG Unlock();
    DWORD dwThreadID;
    CChatDiscussionList m_list;
    . . .
};

extern CExeModule _Module;
```

Given this addition, you can get to this discussion list from anywhere within this process by using _Module, which is a global instance within the ChatBroker process (and representing the ChatBroker process). For example, you would do the following to refer to the discussion list:

```
_Module.m_list
```

Now that we know in general what this class does, let's peer into the details of its member functions.

### CChatDiscussionList::AddDiscussion

The *AddDiscussion* member function allows a caller to add a discussion into the discussion list using a key-value pair, which includes the discussion name and the target interface pointer. As shown here, this member function is protected by your critical section object. To enter the critical section, call *CComCriticalSection::Lock*, and to exit, call *CComCriticalSection::Unlock*. The critical section object (m_cs) is initialized in the constructor of this list through the call to *CComCriticalSection::Init*, and it is destroyed in the destructor of this list through the call to *CComCriticalSection::Term*.

```
bool
CChatDiscussionList::AddDiscussion(wchar_t *pwszDiscussion, IUnknown *pUnk)
{
    bool bRc = false ;

    m_cs.Lock();

    USES_CONVERSION;
    string strKey = W2A(pwszDiscussion);
    DiscussionMap::iterator index = m_map.find(strKey);
    if (index==m_map.end()) {
        pUnk->AddRef();
        // Discussion server has not been added.
        // Add the Discussion into the map.
        m_map.insert(DiscussionMap::value_type(strKey, pUnk));
```

```
        bRc = true ;
    }

    m_cs.Unlock();

    return bRc ;
}
```

Within the critical section, first check whether this discussion (based on the name of the discussion) has already been added by calling *map::find*. If so, you return **false** to indicate that duplicate discussions are not allowed. Otherwise, you immediately call *AddRef* on the received pointer to indicate to the **ChatServer** that you're keeping an outstanding reference to it. You then insert the discussion and the associated interface pointer into the *map* that you're managing and return **true** to indicate successful addition.

### CChatDiscussionList::RemoveDiscussion

The *RemoveDiscussion* member function allows a caller to remove a particular discussion from the discussion list and release the associated interface held. Like the previous function, this function is protected by your critical section object.

```
void CChatDiscussionList::RemoveDiscussion(wchar_t *pwszDiscussion)
{
    m_cs.Lock();

    DiscussionMap::iterator index;
    USES_CONVERSION;
    string strKey = W2A(pwszDiscussion);
    index = m_map.find(strKey);
    if (index!=m_map.end()) {
        // Discussion found.  Release the interface pointer.
        IUnknown *pUnk = (*index).second;
        pUnk->Release();
        // Remove the Discussion from the map.
        m_map.erase(index);
    }

    m_cs.Unlock();
}
```

As exhibited here, when you find the indicated discussion in the map, you retrieve the associated interface pointer and invoke *Release* upon it to release a reference to the **ChatServer**. You do this so that the **ChatServer** can appropriately shut down. To remove the key-value pair from the *map*, you call *map::erase*.

### CChatDiscussionList::GetDiscussionList

The *GetDiscussionList* member function allows a caller to get a list of discussions. To make things simple and to minimize network round-trips, this function creates a string that is composed of all discussions, each delimited by a return character.

To return this string buffer to the `ChatClient`, this function must use *CoTaskMemAlloc* to dynamically allocate the returned buffer.

```
wchar_t *CChatDiscussionList::GetDiscussionList()
{
   m_cs.Lock();

   // Create the list of discussions in a string buffer
   DiscussionMap::iterator index;
   string strDiscussionList;
   for (index = m_map.begin(); index != m_map.end(); index++) {
      strDiscussionList += (*index).first;
      strDiscussionList += string("\n");
   }

   wchar_t *pRetList = (wchar_t*)CoTaskMemAlloc((strDiscussionList.
      size()+1)*2);
   if (pRetList) {
      USES_CONVERSION;
      wcscpy(pRetList, A2W(strDiscussionList.data()));
   } else {
      pRetList = NULL;
   }

   m_cs.Unlock();

   return pRetList;
}
```

### CChatDiscussionList::GetChatServer

The *GetChatServer* member function returns an interface pointer associated with a particular discussion. To support this, the *GetChatServer* function tries to find the discussion in the *map*. If the discussion exists, it invokes *AddRef* to bump up the reference count prior to returning the interface pointer to the `ChatClient`.

```
IUnknown *CChatDiscussionList::GetChatServer(wchar_t *pwszDiscussion)
{
   IUnknown *pUnk=NULL; // Assume discussion doesn't exist

   m_cs.Lock();

   DiscussionMap::iterator index;
   USES_CONVERSION;
   string strKey = W2A(pwszDiscussion);
   // Find the IUnknown pointer.
   index = m_map.find(strKey);
   if (index!=m_map.end()) {
      // Found the discussion
      pUnk = (*index).second;
      pUnk->AddRef(); // AddRef for the client
   }

   m_cs.Unlock();
```

```
        return pUnk;
    }
```

### CChatDiscussionList::GetSize

The *GetSize* function simply returns the size of the *map*, as shown here:

```
long CChatDiscussionList::GetSize()
{
    return m_map.size();
}
```

### ChatBroker's special condition for component lifetime management

If you're wondering why we wrote *CChatDiscussionList::GetSize*, here's the answer. Recall from Chapter 4, *Components*, that server lifetime management typically includes external reference counts and number of living objects. However, the **ChatBroker** has a special condition for server shutdown. Besides the typical shutdown conditions mentioned, you should shut down only when the discussion list is empty. To support this, you must modify the *CExeModule::Unlock* method, generated by ATL for component lifetime management. As shown by the following boldfaced line, this is straightforward:

```
LONG CExeModule::Unlock()
{
    LONG l = CComModule::Unlock();
    if ( (l == 0) &&
         (m_list.GetSize()==0) )   // Add this condition for server shutdown.
    { . . . }
    return l;
}
```

This special condition applies only to the **ChatBroker** component that you're building. Indeed, different types of components may have different conditions for managing component lifetime, so remember to think about this issue when you develop your own components.

## Implementing the Interface Methods

Given the implementation for your discussion list, implementing the methods of your two interfaces is easy. For example, consider the implementation of *IRegisterChatServer::Register*. Remember that this function will be called by a **ChatServer** component to register itself to the **ChatBroker**. A single **ChatServer** supports one and only one discussion topic, so if a second **ChatServer** registers a duplicate discussion, the function will return a custom error using the *AtlReportError* function.

```
STDMETHODIMP
CChatBrokerObj::Register(IUnknown *pChatServer, wchar_t *pwszDiscussion)
{
    HRESULT hr = S_OK;
```

```
    if (_Module.m_list.AddDiscussion(pwszDiscussion, pChatServer)==false) {
        hr = AtlReportError(CLSID_ChatBrokerObj,
            TEXT("[Duplicate Discussion] Broker refused to
                "register ChatServer."),
            IID_IRegisterChatServer,
            MAKE_HRESULT(SEVERITY_ERROR, FACILITY_ITF, 0x201));
    }
    return hr;
}
```

As shown here, you delegate the functionality of adding a discussion to the discussion list object, which you can obtain by referring to _Module.m_list.

The *IRegisterChatServer::Unregister* method is called by ChatServer to notify the ChatBroker that it wants to shut down. Thus, it calls this method to remove itself from the ChatBroker's discussion list. Like the previous method implementation, this one uses _Module.m_list to refer to the thread-safe discussion list.

```
STDMETHODIMP
CChatBrokerObj::Unregister(wchar_t *pwszDiscussion)
{
    _Module.m_list.RemoveDiscussion(pwszDiscussion);
    return S_OK;
}
```

Let's shift gears and examine the *IDiscussions* methods. The implementation for *IDiscussions::GetDiscussionList* is called by ChatClients to obtain a list of discussions that they can join. This method returns a Unicode character string that represents a list of discussions. Again, we're doing this for simplicity and to allow the client to get a list of discussions in one network round-trip.

```
STDMETHODIMP
CChatBrokerObj::GetDiscussionList(wchar_t **ppwszDiscussionList)
{
    *ppwszDiscussionList = _Module.m_list.GetDiscussionList();
    return S_OK;
}
```

Recall that this buffer is allocated using the *CoTaskMemAlloc* by the discussion list object. This is necessary because you're returning this buffer to the ChatClient and dealing with a secondary pointer.

A ChatClient calls *IDiscussions::GetChatServer* to get an interface pointer for the ChatServer object that manages the discussion identified by pwszDiscussion.

```
STDMETHODIMP
CChatBrokerObj::GetChatServer(wchar_t *pwszDiscussion, IUnknown **ppUnk)
{
    *ppUnk = _Module.m_list.GetChatServer(pwszDiscussion);
    if (*ppUnk==NULL) {
        return AtlReportError(CLSID_ChatBrokerObj,
            TEXT("[Invalid Discussion] Where did you say to get this"
                "discussion?"),
            IID_IDiscussions,
```

```
            MAKE_HRESULT(SEVERITY_ERROR, FACILITY_ITF, 0x202));
    }

    return S_OK;
}
```

If a **NULL** is returned from calling *CChatDiscussionList::GetChatServer*, you return a custom error to the **ChatClient** to notify that such a discussion doesn't exist in your discussion list.

## *Merging Proxy/Stub Code into a Server EXE Component*

You learned how to merge proxy/stub code into an *out-of-process client component* in Chapter 9, *Applying Security*. However, since you haven't done this for an *out-of-process server component*, we will briefly go through this exercise. Again, you do this so that you don't have to manually register the interface marshalers. Here are the general steps:

1. Add the *ChatBroker_p.c* (the file that contains the marshaling code for all interfaces used within this component) and *dlldata.c* files to your project. Remember that these files are generated by the MIDL compiler. To obtain these files, simply compile your IDL file (*ChatBroker.idl*).

2. Turn off precompiled headers for these files.

3. Add the **_WIN32_DCOM** preprocessor definition to the project.

4. Link your project with *rpcrt4.lib*.

Since you have two interfaces to marshal, you'll have to register both of them internally. You can perform the internal registration and unregistration in the *_tWinMain* function of your component.

```
extern "C" int WINAPI _tWinMain(. . .)
{
    . . .
    if (bRun)
    {
        // Register interface marshalers.
        DWORD dwIRegisterChatServer =
            RegisterInterfaceMarshaler(IID_IRegisterChatServer);
        DWORD dwIDiscussions = RegisterInterfaceMarshaler(IID_IDiscussions);

        hRes = _Module.RegisterClassObjects(CLSCTX_LOCAL_SERVER,
                                            REGCLS_MULTIPLEUSE);
        MSG msg;
        while (GetMessage(&msg, 0, 0, 0)) DispatchMessage(&msg);
        _Module.RevokeClassObjects();

        // Unregister interface marshalers.
        UnregisterInterfaceMarshaler(dwIRegisterChatServer);
        UnregisterInterfaceMarshaler(dwIDiscussions);
```

```
        }
        . . .
    }
```

The *RegisterInterfaceMarshaler* and *UnregisterInterfaceMarshaler* functions are helper functions that internally register and unregister interface marshalers. These functions are shown below. Since you've seen this code earlier, there is no need for further discussion.

```
DWORD RegisterInterfaceMarshaler(REFIID riid)
{
    DWORD dwCookie=0;
    try {
        IUnknown *pUnk=0;
        HRESULT hr = ::DllGetClassObject(riid, IID_IUnknown, (void**)&pUnk);
        if (FAILED(hr)) throw _com_error(hr);
        hr = ::CoRegisterClassObject(riid, pUnk,
                   CLSCTX_INPROC_SERVER,
                   REGCLS_MULTIPLEUSE, &dwCookie);
        if (FAILED(hr)) throw _com_error(hr);
        hr = ::CoRegisterPSClsid(riid, riid);
        if (FAILED(hr)) throw _com_error(hr);
    } catch (_com_error & er) {
        ::MessageBox(0, er.ErrorMessage(), 0, MB_OK);
    }

    return dwCookie;
}

void UnregisterInterfaceMarshaler(DWORD dwCookie)
{
    ::CoRevokeClassObject(dwCookie);
}
```

At this point, we have completed the development of our ChatBroker component, so build it and you're ready to service both ChatServers and ChatClients. You don't have to manually register interface marshalers, because you have internally done this. However, if you take ChatBroker to another machine, you should register it using the -RegServer command-line option.

The important point to keep in mind about this exercise is the OBJREF. The ChatBroker takes a pointer from a ChatServer and gives it to any requesting ChatClient. After this referral is made, the ChatBroker can leave the picture, as the ChatClient talks directly with the ChatServer, even though the ChatClient has no idea where the ChatServer lives. That's the job of the Distributed COM's OXID resolution infrastructure, which requires the information from the OBJREF. Since the OBJREF is the marshaled representation of an interface pointer and contains an IPID, OXID, and OXID Resolver, the target component can be found.

# *Connection Points*

This chapter asks you to think of an **OBJREF** every time an interface pointer is marshaled, but besides this, this chapter also focuses on bidirectional communications. It is obvious that a client can talk to a server by calling an interface method. However, there are times when you want the server to call back to the clients to notify them of events that are of interest.

Given the knowledge gained in this book so far, you can simply implement a COM object on the client side that exposes a callback interface for the server's use. When special events occur, the server will call back to the client using the callback interface. This is a completely legal and straightforward technique for implementing bidirectional communications, but since bidirectional communications is a general need, Microsoft has developed a number of standard interfaces that support it. In COM terminology, bidirectional communications is supported by a mechanism called connection points.

This mechanism includes an event source* and an event sink. A COM object, such as an object within a **ChatServer**, that sends out event notifications is called an *event source*. For example, when a **ChatServer** object receives a chat message, it sends the same message out to all connected **ChatClients**. In other words, it propagates the same message to all chatters. On the other hand a COM object, such as an object within a **ChatClient**, that receives these broadcast messages or event notifications is a called an *event sink*.

There are two important interfaces for implementing connection points: *IConnectionPointContainer* and *IConnectionPoint*. The *IConnectionPointContainer* interface is shown below. A connection point container (*IConnectionPointContainer*) knows about all connection points (*IConnectionPoint*) that the event source supports. This allows a client to use the *IConnectionPointContainer* interface to ask the object whether it supports a particular connection point. In addition, a caller can use this interface to enumerate (via *IEnumConnectionPoints*) all the connection points supported by the source object.

```
[object, uuid(B196B284-BAB4-101A-B69C-00AA00341D07), pointer_default(unique)]
interface IConnectionPointContainer : IUnknown
{
    // Get IEnumConnectionPoints for enumerating the connection points
    // supported by the source object.
    HRESULT EnumConnectionPoints([out]IEnumConnectionPoints **ppEnum);
    // Find a connection point (identified by riid) in the object's
    // connection point container.
    HRESULT FindConnectionPoint([in] REFIID riid,
                                [out] IConnectionPoint **ppCP);
}
```

---

* Event sources are also called *connectable objects*.

Each outgoing interface (i.e., an interface that is called by the source but implemented by the sink) must be associated with a connection point object, which implements the *IConnectionPoint* interface shown later. This interface allows a sink to call *Advise* to signal that it is interested in receiving callbacks (and of course, *Unadvise* to notify that it's no longer interested). The connection point object is not the same object as the server COM object that implements the *IConnectionPointContainer* interface (shown previously).

```
[object, uuid(B196B286-BAB4-101A-B69C-00AA00341D07), pointer_default(unique)]
interface IConnectionPoint : IUnknown
{
    // Gets the IID of the interface associated with this connection point.
    HRESULT GetConnectionInterface([out] IID * piid);
    // Gets the connection point container that owns this connection point.
    HRESULT GetConnectionPointContainer([out]IConnectionPointContainer
        **ppCPC);
    // Notifies a source that a sink is interested in events associated
    // with pUnkSink.  A cookie is returned for calling Unadvise.
    HRESULT Advise([in] IUnknown *pUnkSink, [out]  DWORD *pdwCookie);
    // Notifies disinterest.
    HRESULT Unadvise([in] DWORD dwCookie);
    // Enumerates the connections associated with the connection point.
    // There can be many clients connected to this single connection point.
    HRESULT EnumConnections([out]   IEnumConnections **ppEnum);
}
```

Given these two standard interfaces, an event source is responsible for the following:

1. Implementing the standard *IConnectionPointContainer* interface. This interface allows the sinks to enumerate or find connection points supported by the event source.

2. Implementing the standard *IConnectionPoint* interface for each outgoing interface. This is done to allow the event sink to establish a connection with the source. During connection, the sink sends a callback interface pointer to the source, so that the source can later make callbacks.

3. Calling back to the registered event sinks.

On the opposite end, an event sink is responsible for the following:

1. Implementing the event sink object so that the event source can make callbacks.

2. Notifying the event source that it is interested in receiving events. A sink typically requests the *IConnectionPointContainer* interface from the event source and calls *FindConnectionPoint* to make sure that the event source supports the callback interface implemented by the event sink. This will return an *IConnectionPoint* interface pointer associated with the callback interface. A sink then uses the returned *IConnectionPoint* interface pointer to call *Advise*. In this method invocation, the sink sends a pointer to the its own callback

interface to the event source. When this invocation returns, the sink will receive a registration cookie.

3. When a sink object no longer wants to receive events associated with the call-back interface, it must notify the event source of this withdrawal by calling *Unadvise* using the registration cookie received from calling *Advise*.

Before we move on, an event source can be thought of as a container that holds a bunch of connection points. Imagine a bunch of little sockets on the event source object and you will logically see that an event source is simply a container for connection points. As a container, it implements the *IConnectionPointContainer* interface. Remember that clients query for this interface to find a particular connection point (socket or jack).

Enough with the talk. Let's develop a component (**ChatServer**) that supports an event source and one (**ChatClient**) that supports an event sink to get some practical experience.

## *Event Sources*

In this section, you will create the **ChatServer** component that exposes a COM object called an event source. This COM object, which you'll name **ChatServerObj**, supports the *ISendMessage* interface for **ChatClients** to post chat messages. It also supports a connection point associated with a callback interface called *IReceiveMessage* that is implemented by the **ChatClient** component (which will be developed in the "Event Sinks" section of this chapter). The **ChatServer** uses this callback interface to propagate chat messages to all chatters

Figure 10-2 shows the connections between a **ChatClient** and a **ChatServerObj** COM object. Notice that besides *ISendMessage*, **ChatServerObj** implements the *IConnectionPointContainer* interface to allow a client to find a particular supported connection point.

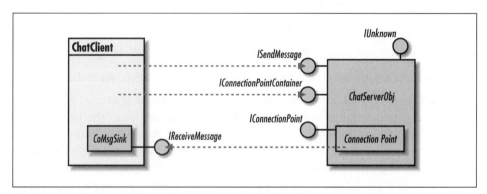

*Figure 10-2. ChatServerObj is a source object and CoMsgSink is a sink object*

As you can see from Figure 10-2, the server component supports a connection point object that is associated with the *IReceiveMessage* interface, implemented by a client-side sink object, *CoMsgSink*. The client simply finds a connection point using the *IConnectionPointContainer* interface and tells the connection point that it wants to receive notifications by calling *IConnectionPoint::Advise*. The event source will make callbacks to the sink object at appropriate times.

## Creating an Event Source Object

Our immediate goal is to create a server component that will be our **ChatServer**. Within this server component, we'll add the **ChatServerObj** object that will support callbacks.

To start off, create a new project called **ChatServer**. Use the **ATL COM AppWizard** to create an **Executable (EXE)** component, because this component will be a standalone process (out-of-process server). Remember to enable exception handling because you will use this C++ feature.

Once the code for your component is generated, add a simple COM object. Here are the steps for creating this COM object:

1. Use the **ATL Object Wizard** to add a simple COM object to the **ChatServer** component.

2. In the **Names** tab of the **ATL Object Wizard Properties** dialog box, name this object **ChatServerObj** to generate a *CChatServerObj* C++ class.

3. Also, name the first interface *ISendMessage*. Specifically, change *IChatServerObj* to *ISendMessage* in the **Interface** edit-box.

4. In the **Attributes** tab, select the **Free** threading model, indicating that you want the object to be used by multiple threads simultaneously.

5. Select **Custom** because you want *ISendMessage* to be a custom interface.

6. Make sure that you choose the **Support Connection Points** option. This will add a default implementation of *IConnectionPointContainer* into the generated COM object, making your object an event source.

If you have followed the directions given above, the generated class definition for this COM object will derive from a default implementation of *IConnectionPointContainer* that is provided by ATL, as shown in the first bolded line in the following code snippet. This line is all you need to obtain the default implementation of *IConnectionPointContainer*.

In addition to this line, the *IConnectionPointContainer* interface must be added to the COM map so that a *QueryInterface* for this interface will succeed. This is done by the second bolded line shown in the same code snippet. This line is generated by the `ATL Object Wizard` when you choose the `Support Connection Points` option.

```
class CChatServerObj :
    public CComObjectRootEx<CComMultiThreadModel>,
    public CComCoClass<CChatServerObj, &CLSID_ChatServerObj>,
    public IConnectionPointContainerImpl<CChatServerObj>,
    public ISendMessage
{
public:
    . . .
BEGIN_COM_MAP(CChatServerObj)
    COM_INTERFACE_ENTRY(ISendMessage)
    COM_INTERFACE_ENTRY_IMPL(IConnectionPointContainer)
END_COM_MAP()

BEGIN_CONNECTION_POINT_MAP(CChatServerObj)
    // List all connection points here
END_CONNECTION_POINT_MAP()
    . . .
};
```

This option also generates a connection point map. Remember that an event source may support many connection points, each one associated with a sink or callback interface. This map records all the connection points supported by *CChatServerObj*. You'll add a connection point associated with the *IReceiveMessage* interface (which is implemented by the `ChatClient`) within these two macros in a moment. For now, know that these are the lines of code that support connection points for event source objects generated by ATL.

## Adding a Connection Point

In this section, you'll implement a connection point that is associated with the *IReceiveMessage* callback interface implemented by the client. The `ChatServer` component will not implement this interface; it makes callbacks using this interface. This interface is implemented by the `ChatClient` component to receive chat messages fired off by a `ChatServer`. To implement a connection point, you need to take the following steps.

### Step 1: Define a callback interface using MIDL

The first thing that you must do is to define the callback interface, *IReceiveMessage*, that the `ChatClient` component must implement. You won't implement this interface in the `ChatServer` component, but will need its definition so that you know its binary layout and so that you can generate the correct marshaling code for marshaling this interface. As shown below, this interface is straightforward:

```
[object, uuid(3CA09BF1-A827-11d1-87A6-006008CDD9AE), pointer_default(unique)]
interface IReceiveMessage : IUnknown
```

```
    {
        HRESULT OnReply([in, string] wchar_t *pwszReply);
    };
```

If you want scripting environments, such as VBScript, to receive callbacks, you must make *IReceiveMessage* a `dispinterface`*, but you aren't doing this for the sake of simplicity. Specifically, if you make this interface a `dispinterface`, you'll have to implement the methods of *IDispatch*. Because you don't want to implement these *IDispatch* methods, you simply derive this interface from *IUnknown*.

Notice that this interface defines one method, *OnReply*, which the event sink must implement. As you will see in a moment, the `ChatServer` will invoke this method to pass a chat message back to a connected `ChatClient`.

You need to add this interface into the *ChatServer.idl* file by hand. Remember to use the *guidgen.exe* utility to get a unique GUID for this interface.

In addition to adding this interface definition, you should also add this interface as a `[source]` interface into the `coclass` definition of this COM object. This signifies that the interface is an outgoing interface and that it is not implemented in this COM object. However, this COM object can make callbacks to this interface, no matter who implements it.

```
    [uuid(573F3C13-A81A-11d1-87A6-006008CDD9AE)]
    coclass ChatServerObj
    {
        [default] interface ISendMessage;
        [source] interface IReceiveMessage;
    };
```

### Step 2: Implement a connection point object

Once you know the specification of an *IReceiveMessage* interface, you can proceed with creating a connection point object that is associated with *IReceiveMessage*. A connection point object must implement the *IConnectionPoint* interface as discussed earlier. Since you're using ATL, you'll take advantage of ATL's default implementation for this interface, so that you won't have to implement the *IConnectionPoint* methods yourself. The ATL class that provides this default implementation is called *IConnectionPointImpl*.

Given this free implementation, here's how you can implement your connection point object to support the *IReceiveMessage* interface. As shown in the following code, you create a class, *CReceiveMessageCP*, for this connection point. Further, it is a template class so that any event source object can support this connection point by simply deriving from *CReceiveMessageCP*. This point will be clear in a

---

* ATL 3.0 automatically generates a source `dispinterface` when you check the `Support Connection Points` option. However, we won't use this `dispinterface`, because we are providing our own interface, `IReceiveMessage`.

moment (in the "Step 3: Add a connection point to the event source object" subsection).

For now, notice that T, in the code below, is a placeholder for a C++ class that is an event source. In your case, T will stand for *CChatServerObj*. Notice also that you associate the *IReceiveMessage* interface (using IID_IReceiveMessage) with the default implementation of *IConnectionPoint*, as shown in the first boldfaced line:

```
// Connection point object for IID_IReceiveMessage

template <class T>
class CReceiveMessageCP :
    public IConnectionPointImpl<T, &IID_IReceiveMessage>
{
public:
    void Fire_OnReply(wchar_t * pMessage)
    {
        T* pT = (T*)this;
        pT->Lock();  // Enter critical section.

        IUnknown** pp = m_vec.begin();  // First element of the array
        IUnknown** ppEnd = m_vec.end(); // Last element of the array
        for ( ; pp < ppEnd ; pp++ ) {
            if (*pp!=NULL) {
                IReceiveMessage* pReply = reinterpret_cast<IReceiveMessage*>
                    (*pp);
                // Send the message back to all sinks
                pReply->OnReply(pMessage);
            }
        }

        pT->Unlock();  // Exit critical section.
    }
};
```

In addition to creating a class, you write a wrapper member function, *Fire_OnReply*, that is responsible for sending chat messages back to all registered event sinks. This wrapper method simply encapsulates the code to fire off chat messages, so that the ChatServer component can simply call *Fire_OnReply* (instead of writing a dozen lines of code). This code block is protected with a critical section to prevent concurrent access. The *IConnectionPointImpl* class keeps a member variable called m_vec, which you are using from the earlier code snippet. This member variable is an array of *IUnknown* pointers, which are callback (sink) interface pointers registered against this connection point by ChatClients via *IConnectionPoint::Advise.** As you can see in the for loop, you simply march down this array and make the callback by invoking *OnReply* on each *IReceiveMessage* interface pointer.

---

* We'll see how clients can register their callback interface pointers with a particular connection point in the section entitled "Event Sinks" later in this chapter.

Notice that we write only one wrapper member function because the *IReceiveMessage* interface exposes only one method. Had the *IReceiveMessage* interface supported ten different methods, we would have written ten different wrapper methods.

### Step 3: Add a connection point to the event source object

Now that you have a connection point object that is specifically associated with the *IReceiveMessage* interface, you can make the *CChatServerObj* support this particular connection point. You do so by deriving *CChatServerObj* from *CReceiveMessageCP*, as shown in the first boldfaced line of the following code:

```
class CChatServerObj :
    public CComObjectRootEx<CComMultiThreadModel>,
    public CComCoClass<CChatServerObj, &CLSID_ChatServerObj>,
    public IConnectionPointContainerImpl<CChatServerObj>,
    public ISendMessage,
    public CReceiveMessageCP<CChatServerObj>
{
public:
    . . .
BEGIN_CONNECTION_POINT_MAP(CChatServerObj)
    CONNECTION_POINT_ENTRY(IID_IReceiveMessage)
END_CONNECTION_POINT_MAP()
    . . .
};
```

As we have said earlier, the connection point map allows you to add the connection points that your event source object supports. You can add as many connection points as you want to this map, but since we have only one connection point, we'll demonstrate adding a single connection point into this map. This connection point will be associated with the *IReceiveMessage* that is implemented by the client. This is shown in the second boldfaced line in the previous code.

Having done this for one connection point, the procedure for adding an additional connection point is similar. Simply repeat the process discussed in this subsection; this process can be summed up as follows:

1. Define a callback interface using MIDL. If this interface is already defined elsewhere, you can simply copy it.

2. Implement a connection point object for each callback interface. This basically means creating an object that implements the *IConnectionPoint* interface for a particular IID.

3. Add a connection point to the event source object. Remember that an event source can have zero, one, or many connection points. Clients can find a particular connection point by using the *IConnectionPointContainer* interface implemented by the event source object.

## Receiving and Disseminating a Chat Message

To allow a client to send a chat message to the ChatServer, you need to supply a method that a client can call. For this, you'll add a simple method to the *ISendMessage* interface. You can use the Add Method to Interface dialog box to add this method so that Visual Studio will generate an empty implementation function for you. The method that you're adding has the following signature:

```
HRESULT Talk([in, string] wchar_t *pMessage);
```

Given this method, here's how you would implement it to disseminate the received chat message to all chatters connected to our ChatServer component:

```
STDMETHODIMP CChatServerObj::Talk(wchar_t * pMessage)
{
    // Format the message
    Lock();
    TCHAR tbuffer [9]; _strtime( tbuffer );
    TCHAR szBuf[1024] ; sprintf(szBuf, "[%s] ", tbuffer) ;
    CComBSTR msg(szBuf) ;
    msg.Append(pMessage) ;
    Unlock();

    // Send the message back to all sinks
    Fire_OnReply(msg);

    return S_OK;
}
```

As you can see, you attach the current time to the received message and then call the *Fire_OnReply* function to disseminate the same chat message back to all chatters. That's all there is to creating an event source object.

## The Responsibility of the ChatServer Application

To complete this exercise, you have to decide how the ChatServer component is to operate. Here are the issues that you must consider at the component (not object) level in order to complete the development of this component.

* Making the main apartment an MTA. You've done this before in the last exercise. In _tWinMain, simply call CoInitializeEx(NULL, COINIT_ MULTITHREADED). This will allow multiple threads to invoke your singleton ChatServerObj COM object, which will be instantiated only once in the ChatServer component but can support multiple, concurrent threads.

* Handling of command-line options.

* Registering interface marshalers.

* Opening and closing the discussion.

A detailed discussion of these issues will follow (except for the first issue, which is self-explanatory).

### Handling of command-line options

When the ChatServer component runs, we would like to associate it with a discussion topic. In addition, we need to somehow specify the broker to which this ChatServer is going to register itself. A simple way to take care of both of these issues is to provide command-line options for them. For example, we can specify that a particular ChatServer supports a discussion called DiscussCOM and that it registers itself against the ChatBroker on a machine named dog by the using the following command:

*ChatServer.exe #DiscussCOM #dog*

As you may have guessed, the # signs are used for simple parsing. Giving this command-line specification, we can write the following code to parse the command line. This code should be placed in the following block of the generated *_tWinMain* function:

```
if (bRun)
{
    // Command-line handling
    TCHAR szDiscussion[MAX_PATH];
    TCHAR szBroker[MAX_PATH];
    TCHAR szTokens[] = _T("#");

    // Find the discussion name.
    LPCTSTR lpszDiscuss = FindOneOf(lpCmdLine, szTokens);
    if (lpszDiscuss==NULL) {

        // No # signs means that the command line is invalid - i.e., no
        // discussion name and no broker name.
        MessageBox(0, "Command Line:\n\nChatServer    #DiscussCOM"
          "#ChatBroker",
          "Usage", MB_OK|MB_SERVICE_NOTIFICATION|MB_ICONINFORMATION);

        // Bail out. . .
        return nRet;
    }

    // We've got the discussion name at this point.

    // Find the broker name.
    LPCTSTR lpszBroker = FindOneOf(lpszDiscuss, szTokens);
    if (lpszBroker==NULL) {

        // No broker name, so assume the broker exists on the local machine.
        char szComputerName[MAX_COMPUTERNAME_LENGTH+1];
        DWORD dwSize = MAX_COMPUTERNAME_LENGTH+1;
        ::GetComputerName(szComputerName, &dwSize);
        strcpy(szBroker, szComputerName);
        strcpy(szDiscussion, lpszDiscuss);
```

```
    } else {

        // Got the broker name.
        strcpy(szBroker, lpszBroker);
        strncpy(szDiscussion, lpszDiscuss, lpszBroker-lpszDiscuss-2);
        szDiscussion[lpszBroker-lpszDiscuss-2] = '\0';
    }

        . . . // Code to be discussed next. Omitted for clarity.

    }
```

Notice that you use the ATL-generated *FindOneOf* helper function to find the next occurrence of the # sign. The command line must have at least one string prefixed with a # sign, or you'll bail out. One # sign means that a broker destination is not specified. In this case, we take the local machine to be the broker destination. The first string prefixed with a # sign means that it's the name of a discussion associated with this **ChatServer** instance. Of course, with two # signs, the first string represents the discussion name and the second represents the broker destination.

### Registering interface marshalers

After parsing the command line, you need to internally register the proxy/stub code for the interfaces that this component will marshal across apartments. These interfaces include the *ISendMessage*, *IReceiveMessage*, and *IRegisterChatServer*. The *ChatServer.idl* file already contains the first two interfaces, but since it doesn't have the *IRegisterChatServer* interface, you need to add it. You can copy this interface definition from the *ChatBroker.idl* file.*

```
[object, uuid(573F3BE3-A81A-11d1-87A6-006008CDD9AE), pointer_default(unique)]
interface IRegisterChatServer : IUnknown {
    HRESULT Register([in] IUnknown *pChatServer,
                     [in, string] wchar_t *pwszDiscussion);
    HRESULT Unregister([in, string] wchar_t *pwszDiscussion);
};
```

Remember also that you need to add the *ChatServer_p.c* and *dlldata.c* files to your project, turn off precompiled header for these two files, define **_WIN32_DCOM**, and add *rpcrt4.lib* to your link options.

Having done this, you can now register these interfaces as follows:

```
if (bRun)
{
    // Command-line handling. . . shown above.
    . . .
    // Register interface marshalers
```

---

\* Remember, we are copying and pasting to make the exercise simple, but in your own systems, think about the public interfaces that clients will use and place them in a separate, public IDL file. Your clients can use #include to pull in your interface definitions without resorting to copying and pasting.

```
DWORD dwBroker = RegisterInterfaceMarshaler(IID_IRegisterChatServer);
DWORD dwServer = RegisterInterfaceMarshaler(IID_ISendMessage);
DWORD dwClient = RegisterInterfaceMarshaler(IID_IReceiveMessage);

. . .  // Code to be discussed next.  Omitted for clarity.
}
```

We've talked about the *RegisterInterfaceMarshaler* helper function in the last exercise, so we won't spend any more time on this. See the "Merging Proxy/Stub Code into a Server EXE Component" section discussed earlier in this chapter.

### Opening and closing the discussion

At this point, we can create a single instance of *CChatServerObj* and then pass an interface pointer of this object to the **ChatBroker** component to register a discussion. The following code creates this single instance of *CChatServerObj* using the *CoCreateInstance* API function:

```
if (bRun)  // Existing code
{
   // Command-line handling
   . . .
   // Register interface marshalers
   . . .
   // Existing code to register class objects
   hRes = _Module.RegisterClassObjects(CLSCTX_LOCAL_SERVER, REGCLS_
      MULTIPLEUSE);
   _ASSERTE(SUCCEEDED(hRes));

   // Registering a discussion with the ChatBroker
   HRESULT hr=S_OK;
   try {
      CComPtr<ISendMessage> pSend;
      hr = CoCreateInstance(CLSID_ChatServerObj, 0, CLSCTX_SERVER,
         IID_ISendMessage, (void**)&pSend);
      Chk(hr);
```

To obtain the *IRegisterChatServer* interface pointer, you must call *CoCreateInstanceEx* because the broker may be running on a different machine that is specifically indicated by **szBroker**.

```
      // Register the interface pointer with the ChatBroker
      MULTI_QI mqi[] = { {&IID_IRegisterChatServer, 0, S_OK} };
      COSERVERINFO csi = {0, CComBSTR(szBroker), 0, 0};
      // CLSID for the broker object, copied from ChatBroker_i.c
      const CLSID CLSID_ChatBrokerObj =
```

{0x573F3BE6,0xA81A,0x11d1,{0x87,0xA6,0x00,0x60,0x08,0xCD,0xD9,0xAE}};
```
      hr = CoCreateInstanceEx(CLSID_ChatBrokerObj, 0, CLSCTX_SERVER,
                              &csi, sizeof(mqi)/sizeof(mqi[0]), mqi);
      Chk(hr); Chk(mqi[0].hr);
```

As shown later, once you have the *IRegisterChatServer* interface pointer, use it to invoke its *Register* method to register this server as the **ChatServer** that manages the discussion indicated by `bstrDiscussion`. Thus, the call to *IRegisterChatServer::Register* includes the interface pointer (`pSend`) to the *CChatServerObj* object and the name of the discussion that this object manages. Note that you use the *_com_issue_errorex* compiler-level support function as seen later, because you know that the **ChatBroker** component will return a custom error message when this server registers a duplicate discussion name.

```
// Register the ChatServer with the ChatBroker.
// This server will support the bstrDiscussion topic.
CComPtr<IRegisterChatServer> pBroker((IRegisterChatServer*)mqi[0].
                                pItf);
CComBSTR bstrDiscussion(szDiscussion);
hr = pBroker->Register(pSend, bstrDiscussion);
if (FAILED(hr))
_com_issue_errorex(hr, pBroker, IID_IRegisterChatServer);
```

To keep things simple, you'll put up a message box to identify the discussion that this particular server manages. When a user clicks the OK button on this message box, you'll close down the **ChatServer** component. Remember that this apartment is a MTA, which means that it can support many threads concurrently.

```
// For simplicity, run the server until a user hits the OK button.
// Note that we don't use the MB_SERVICE_NOTIFICATION flag.
::MessageBox(0, "Chat Server Currently Running...\n\n"
                "Press OK to end server.", szDiscussion,
                MB_OK|MB_ICONINFORMATION);
```

When you're told to shut down (by the user of course), you invoke *IRegisterChatServer::Unregister* to unregister yourself from the broker and to notify the broker that you're closing down this discussion topic.

```
    // Unregister the server from the ChatBroker
    pBroker->Unregister(bstrDiscussion);
} catch (_com_error & er) {
  if (er.Description().length()>0) {
     ::MessageBox(NULL, er.Description(),
              TEXT("Error Description"),
              MB_OK|MB_SERVICE_NOTIFICATION|MB_ICONERROR);
  } else {
     ::MessageBox(0, er.ErrorMessage(),
              "ChatServer",
              MB_OK|MB_SERVICE_NOTIFICATION|MB_ICONERROR);
  }
}
```

The following three lines of wizard-generated code are removed because you don't support STA objects. The lifetime of your server is completely decided by the user who clicks the OK button on the popup dialog.

```
//    MSG msg;
//    while (GetMessage(&msg, 0, 0, 0))
//      DispatchMessage(&msg);
```

As shown in the following code, before the server completely shuts down, you revoke all class objects and unregister all interface marshalers.

```
_Module.RevokeClassObjects();

// Unregister interface marshalers
UnregisterInterfaceMarshaler(dwBroker);
UnregisterInterfaceMarshaler(dwServer);
UnregisterInterfaceMarshaler(dwClient);
}
```

## Running the ChatServer

At this point, you have completed the ChatServer exercise. You can now execute a number of these ChatServers and allow them to manage chat discussions. Since you have merged the proxy/stub code into this component, you don't need to register the proxy/stub DLL yourself. Simply take this server to any machine and run it, but remember to point to the correct ChatBroker destination. For example, to start a ChatServer for managing the DiscussCOM discussion, you would enter the following on the command-line:

*ChatServer.exe #DiscussCOM #dog*

This assumes that the broker is registered and is ready to run on the machine named dog. Executing this command will launch a message box that tells you the name of the discussion that the current ChatServer supports. This ChatServer instance will run until you press the OK button on this message box to shut it down. Since the main apartment of the ChatServer component is an MTA and the event source object is thread-safe, concurrent access is permitted. You can launch as many of these ChatServers as you wish.

# Event Sinks

Now that you have the ChatServer component in place, you'll build the ChatClient component. As shown earlier in Figure 10-2, this component implements a COM object that is an event sink that will receive all messages fired off by the event source object in the ChatServer component. Specifically, as soon as the ChatServer component receives a chat message, it sends the same message back to all connected ChatClients through the client's event sink object, shown in Figure 10-2 as *CoMsgSink*. The *CoMsgSink* object supports a callback interface called *IReceiveMessage* that the ChatServer component can utilize to make callbacks. Recall that you've defined this interface earlier in the last section, but you haven't implemented it. You'll do that in this section.

Besides implementing an event sink in this section, you'll see the special contribution of this chapter in the subsection on "Joining and Leaving a Chat Discussion" where you contact the ChatBroker to find a ChatServer. You get a handle to the `ChatServer` via an interface pointer. Remember that this interface pointer is passed from the `ChatServer` to the `ChatBroker` to the `ChatClient` in the form of an `OBJREF`, and an `OBJREF` is the key that opens up distributed computing.

## Creating the ChatClient Project

Our goal in this section is to develop a client application that looks similar to the one shown in Figure 10-3. So let's use the `MFC AppWizard EXE` to create a `Dialog base` application and name this project `ChatClient`.

### Creating the user interface and adding command handlers

Once the project is generated, modify the generated dialog resource for the dialog application so that it looks like the one shown in Figure 10-3. As you drag and drop controls onto this dialog resource, you should assign appropriate resource identifiers to the edit-boxes, combo-boxes, and pushbuttons. In addition, you should bind these controls to appropriate member variables of the generated dialog class so that you can later manipulate them at runtime. Here are the resource identifiers for the controls on this dialog box:

IDC_EDIT_BROKER

> This is the resource identifier for the edit-box that allows a user to enter the destination of the `ChatBroker`. Remember that a `ChatClient` has to connect to the `ChatBroker` prior to retrieving available chat discussions that the `ChatClient` can join. After adding this edit-box and assigning it this identifier, bind this edit-box to a *CEdit* member variable called m_Broker. Remember that you can bind controls to member variables by using the `Member Variables` tab of the `MFC ClassWizard`.

IDC_EDIT_ALIAS

> This is the resource identifier for the alias edit-box. This is the edit-box shown on the top-right corner of Figure 10-3. A chatter would simply fill in his/her alias in this edit-box prior to connecting to the `ChatBroker`. As this user sends messages to the discussion server, the user's alias is passed along so that others can see who has actually sent the message. After adding this control and assigning it this identifier, bind this control to a *CEdit* member variable called m_Alias.

IDC_COMBO_DISCUSSION

> This is the resource identifier for the combo-box that shows the names of all discussions that a chatter can join. As a user connects to a `ChatBroker`, you'll retrieve the list of available discussions by calling *IDiscussions::GetDiscussionList*, which is implemented by the `ChatBroker` component. You insert the discussions from this list into this combo-box. A user chooses a discussion from this combo-box before joining the discussion.

After adding this control and assigning it this identifier, bind this control to a *CComboBox* member variable called m_Discussion.

### IDC_LIST_CONVERSATION

This is the resource identifier for the list-box that will store all received messages that are fired off by the discussion server. You use a list-box to easily add chat messages. After adding this control and assigning it this identifier, bind this control to a *CListBox* member variable called m_Conversation.

### IDC_EDIT_MESSAGE

This is the resource identifier for the edit-box shown at the bottom of the user interface. This is where a chatter would enter a message prior to pushing the Send button to send the message to the discussion server. After adding this control and assigning it this identifier, bind this control to a *CEdit* member variable called m_Message.

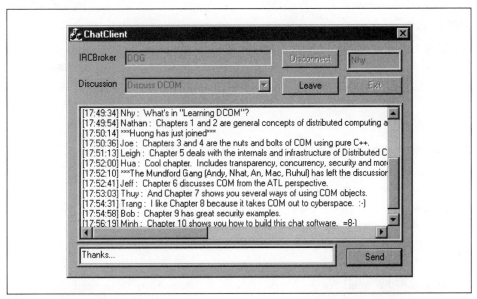

*Figure 10-3. ChatClient's user interface*

Besides these controls, you need to add the following buttons and message handlers for them. You'll write the code for these handler functions later in this section.

### IDC_BUTTON_CONNECT

This is the resource identifier for the Connect/Disconnect button. This button is initially shown as Connect, but will toggle to Disconnect when the ChatClient is connected to a ChatBroker. After adding this button and assigning it this identifier, bind it to a *CButton* member variable called m_Connect. In addition, use the Message Maps tab of the MFC

`ClassWizard` to add a message handler for this button. You'll write the code in this handler function to connect to the `ChatBroker` in a moment.

### IDC_BUTTON_JOIN

This is the resource identifier for the `Join/Leave` button. This button is initially shown as `Join`, but will toggle to `Leave` when a chatter joins a selected discussion group. After adding this button and assigning it this identifier, bind it to a *CButton* member variable called m_Join. In addition, use the **Message Maps** tab of the **MFC ClassWizard** to add a message handler for this button.

### IDC_BUTTON_EXIT

This is the resource identifier for the `Exit` button, which allows a chatter to exit the `ChatClient` application. After adding this button and assigning it this identifier, bind it to a *CButton* member variable called m_Exit. In addition, use the **Message Maps** tab of the **MFC ClassWizard** to add a message handler for this button.

### IDC_BUTTON_SEND

This is the resource identifier for the `Send` button, which allows a chatter to send a chat message to the `ChatServer`. After adding this button and assigning it this identifier, bind it to a *CButton* member variable called m_Send. In addition, use the **Message Maps** tab of the **MFC ClassWizard** to add a message handler for this button.

### *Merging proxy/stub code into a project without an IDL File*

Remember that the `ChatClient` component uses the *IDiscussions* interface exposed by the `ChatBroker` to get a list of available discussions. In addition, the `ChatClient` component uses the *ISendMessage* interface exposed by the `ChatServer` to send chat messages to all chatters. The `ChatClient` component must implement the *IReceiveMessage* interface to receive messages sent off by the discussion server.

To eliminate the need for registering separate proxy/stub DLLs manually, you'll add proxy/stub code for all of these interfaces to your `ChatClient` application. Here are the steps for merging the proxy/stub code into a project without a generated IDL file:

1. Create a new IDL file and name it appropriately; for example, *ChatServerBroker. idl*. Be sure to import the *oaidl.idl* and *ocidl.idl* files, because these contain the base interface definitions.

2. Define the interfaces that require marshaling code in this application. For example, you need to use the *IDiscussions* interface, so copy the *IDiscussions* interface definition from *ChatBroker.idl* and paste it into *ChatServerBroker.idl*.

3. You also need marshaling code for the *ISendMessage* and *IReceiveMessage* interfaces, so copy the definitions for these two interfaces from *ChatServer.idl* and paste them into *ChatServerBroker.idl*.

4. Add a custom build step for the *ChatServerBroker.idl* file using the `Settings` dialog box. This build step should use the MIDL compiler to compile and generate marshaling code for all interfaces defined in the IDL file. For example, the custom build step for this file should be: `midl.exe ChatServerBroker.idl`. The reason you're doing this is to obtain the MIDL generated *dlldata.c*, *ChatServerBroker_p.c*, and *ChatServerBroker_i.c* files, which include the marshaling code for all interfaces defined in the *ChatServerBroker.idl* file. Remember to compile *ChatServerBroker.idl* in order to obtain these files. Alternatively, instead of adding a custom build step, remember that you can execute this command (`midl.exe ChatServerBroker.idl`) on the command line to get the same generated files.

5. You need to add the files generated in Step 4 to the `ChatClient` project and make sure that they are included in the build.

6. Using the `Settings` dialog box, turn off pre-compiled headers for these marshaling-related source files, and add the `_WIN32_DCOM` preprocessor definition for the project.

7. Link the `ChatClient` project with *rpcrt4.lib*.

All that is left for merging proxy/stub code is to internally registered the interface marshalers. You'll do this prior to connecting to the `ChatBroker`.

## Connecting to and Disconnecting from a ChatBroker

You've just finished setting up the preliminaries for our `ChatClient` application. Let's now implement the handler for the `Connect/Disconnect` button. If you had taken the default handler function name when you generated the handler for this button, you would have gotten an empty *OnButtonConnect* member function.

This function is called when the `Connect/Disconnect` button is pressed, so within this function, you need to connect to the `ChatBroker` component specified in the `ChatBroker` edit-box. You do this when the button's label reads `Connect`; of course, you would disconnect from the `ChatBroker` component if the button's label reads `Disconnect`. In addition, you need to toggle this button's label appropriately. This function is shown in many (but continuous) code snippets:

```
void CChatClientDlg::OnButtonConnect()
{
    // Cookies for interface marshaler registration
    static DWORD dwBroker, dwServer, dwClient;
```

```
CString strButtonLabel;
m_Connect.GetWindowText(strButtonLabel);
if (strButtonLabel==CString("Connect")) {
   // If the buttons reads "Connect," connect to the ChatBroker...
```

Prior to connecting to the **ChatBroker** component, you need to initialize COM. In addition, you need to internally register the interface marshalers for the *IDiscussions, ISendMessage*, and *IReceiveMessage* interfaces. Notice that you save the cookies associated with these interface marshalers in three static variables.

```
// Initialize COM
CoInitialize(0);
// Register interface marshalers internally
dwBroker = RegisterInterfaceMarshaler(IID_IDiscussions);
dwServer = RegisterInterfaceMarshaler(IID_ISendMessage);
dwClient = RegisterInterfaceMarshaler(IID_IReceiveMessage);
```

You need to update the user interface appropriately during connection to the ChatBroker component. For example, you need to at least toggle the label of this button to **Disconnect**.

```
// Change the label of this button to "Disconnect".
m_Connect.SetWindowText("Disconnect");
// Disable the exit button.
m_Exit.EnableWindow(FALSE);
// Enable the join button to allow joining.
m_Join.EnableWindow(TRUE);
// Disable the broker edit-box.
m_Broker.EnableWindow(FALSE);
```

Having done the preliminaries, you now can connect to the **ChatBroker** to retrieve the *IDiscussions* interface pointer, as shown in the following code. Notice that you get the broker destination from the **ChatBroker** edit-box (**m_Broker**). Furthermore, you save the *IDiscussions* pointer into a member variable called **m_pBroker**, so remember to add this member variable (which is of type *IDiscussions \**) to the *CChatClientDlg* class.

```
// Connect to the broker.
CString strBroker;
m_Broker.GetWindowText(strBroker);
_bstr_t bstrBroker(strBroker);
COSERVERINFO csi = { 0, bstrBroker, NULL, 0 };
MULTI_QI mqi[] = { {&IID_IDiscussions, NULL, S_OK} };
try {
   HRESULT hr = CoCreateInstanceEx(CLSID_ChatBrokerObj, NULL,
      CLSCTX_SERVER, &csi, sizeof(mqi)/sizeof(mqi[0]), mqi);
   Chk(hr); Chk(mqi[0].hr);
   m_pBroker = reinterpret_cast<IDiscussions*>(mqi[0].pItf);
```

The successful call to the *CoCreateInstanceEx* API function will return the *IDiscussions* interface pointer, which you can use to invoke the *GetDiscussionList* method. This method call will return a string that represents a list of discussions that the broker currently supports. Remember that each of the discussions within this string buffer is delimited by a return character.

```
// Get back a list of discussion from the broker.
wchar_t *pList;
m_pBroker->GetDiscussionList(&pList);
CString strList = (char*)_bstr_t(pList);
if (pList) CoTaskMemFree(pList);
```

If the returned string buffer is empty, it means that there are no discussions available. Otherwise, you parse through the string buffer and add each discussion to the discussion combo-box on the ChatClient's user interface. After adding all discussions to this combo-box, you select the first discussion by default. A chatter may select a different discussion to join later on.

```
// Add the discussions into the combo-box.
m_Discussion.ResetContent();
if (strList.IsEmpty()) {
   m_Join.EnableWindow(FALSE);
   MessageBox("No Chat Servers available");
} else {
   while (!strList.IsEmpty()) {
      int i = strList.Find('\n');
      if (i==-1) {
         // The last discussion in the string buffer returned.
         // Add it.
         m_Discussion.AddString(strList);
         break;
      }
      CString strDiscuss = strList.Left(i);
      // Add it.  There are more discussions in the buffer.
      m_Discussion.AddString(strDiscuss);
      strList = strList.Mid(i+1, strList.GetLength());
   }
   // By default: select the first discussion.
   m_Discussion.SetCurSel(0);
}
} catch (_com_error & error) {
   MessageBox(error.ErrorMessage());
   return ;
}
} else {
```

If this Connect/Disconnect button doesn't read Connect, you disconnect from the ChatBroker component. You simply do this by invoking *Release* upon the *IDiscussions* interface, which you have saved in the m_pBroker member variable. After releasing, you unregister all internally used interface marshalers, uninitialize COM, and reset the controls on the dialog as appropriate.

```
if (m_pBroker)
   m_pBroker->Release();
m_pBroker = NULL ;

// Unregister interface marshalers
```

```
            UnregisterInterfaceMarshaler(dwBroker);
            UnregisterInterfaceMarshaler(dwServer);
            UnregisterInterfaceMarshaler(dwClient);

            // Uninitialize COM
            CoUninitialize();

            // Change the label of this button to Connect and
            // disable/enable other controls as appropriate.
            m_Connect.SetWindowText("Connect");
            m_Exit.EnableWindow(TRUE);
            m_Join.EnableWindow(FALSE);
            m_Broker.EnableWindow(TRUE);
        }
    }
```

## *Joining and Leaving a Chat Discussion*

After you connect to the **ChatBroker** component and retrieve a list of discussions from it, a chatter can join a selected discussion. To join, a chatter simply clicks the **Join** button, which can be toggled between two different states: **Join** and **Leave**. When a chatter clicks this button, the following handler will be called. This handler is shown in the many (but contiguous) following code snippets:

```
    void CChatClientDlg::OnButtonJoin()
    {
        CString strButtonLabel;
        m_Join.GetWindowText(strButtonLabel);
        if (strButtonLabel==CString("Join")) {
```

If the button's label reads **Join**, you'll join the selected discussion. In this case, you update the user interface to set the label of this button to **Leave**. Also, you'll enable the **Send** button for a chatter to send chat messages, and disable both the **Connect/Disconnect** button and discussion combo-box.

```
            // Update the GUI.
            m_Join.SetWindowText("Leave");
            m_Connect.EnableWindow(FALSE);
            m_Send.EnableWindow(TRUE);
            m_Discussion.EnableWindow(FALSE);
```

You then get the selected discussion from the discussion combo-box. Use this discussion to call *IDiscussions::GetChatServer*. A successful call to this method will return an *IUnknown* pointer for the target object that supports the given discussion. Remember that this object is implemented by the **ChatServer** component, but its *IUnknown* pointer is passed to the **ChatBroker** during **ChatServer** registration. Since the **ChatBroker** holds onto this *IUnknown* pointer, it can return the pointer to the **ChatClient** that calls *IDiscussions::GetChatServer*.

Let's reiterate—this is the beauty of a distributed technology. The three processes can live on three different machines regardless of locality, but connections to one another can be seamlessly maintained by virtue of an interface pointer. From the point of view of Distributed COM, the wire format of an interface pointer is an OBJREF. The ChatClient that obtains this interface pointer doesn't care where the ChatServer is located. The Distributed COM infrastructure will resolve the OXID, which is a part of the OBJREF, to make sure that calls on this interface pointer will arrive at the correct ChatServer.

Once you've obtained the *IUnknown* interface pointer from the object that supports the requested discussion, you specifically query for the *ISendMessage* interface, because that's the interface that supports chatting.* Upon successful retrieval of this interface pointer, we save it to a member variable called **m_pSendMessage**, which is of type *ISendMessage* pointer.

```
// Get the selected discussion.
CString strServer;
m_Discussion.GetLBText(m_Discussion.GetCurSel(), strServer);

try {
    // Get the IUnknown pointer for the selected discussion.
    IUnknown *pUnk=0;
    HRESULT hr = m_pBroker->GetChatServer(_bstr_t(strServer), &pUnk);
    Chk(hr);
    // Get ISendMessage pointer from the IUnknown pointer.
    // Save it into the m_pSendMessage member variable.
    hr = pUnk->QueryInterface(IID_ISendMessage, (void**)&m_pSendMessage);
    Chk(hr);
    ASSERT(m_pSendMessage);
```

Once you have the *ISendMessage* pointer, you can query for the *IConnectionPointContainer* interface. Recall that the *CChatServerObj* COM object is an event source and all event source objects implement this interface. In general, if you can query for this interface from any COM object, it means that the target object is an event source. Otherwise, the target object is not an event source and thus does not support events.

```
// Get the IConnectionPointContainer interface pointer.
CComPtr<IConnectionPointContainer> pConn;
hr = m_pSendMessage->QueryInterface(IID_IConnectionPointContainer,
                                    (void**)&pConn);
        Chk(hr);
```

You should successfully query for this interface since you've implemented it in the ChatServer component. Once you have this interface pointer, you can invoke the *FindConnectionPoint* method to retrieve an interface pointer to a particular

---

* As alluded to earlier, this extra round-trip can be removed if we had known the definition of the *ISendMessage* interface when we developed the ChatBroker. However, as we have clearly mentioned in that section, we didn't want to define the *ISendMessage* interface at that moment because we didn't want to obscure the focus of the exercise. You need to think about round-trips in your own distributed systems, though, because round-trips are very expensive.

connection point. If this call returns a success, it means that the server can make
callbacks to clients that implement the `IID_IReceiveMessage` interface. Otherwise, the requested connection point indicated by this IID is not supported by
the server.

```
CComPtr<IConnectionPoint> pConnPoint;
hr = pConn->FindConnectionPoint(IID_IReceiveMessage,
                                (IConnectionPoint**)&pConnPoint);
Chk(hr);
```

With the *IConnectionPoint* pointer for the *IReceiveMessage* interface, you can now
invoke the *Advise* method to let the server object know that you're interested in
receiving events; that is, you want to receive all chat messages relating to a particular discussion. As you'll see later in the "Receiving Chat Messages" section,
**g_MsgSink** is an event sink object that we implement on the client side to receive
chat messages. This sink object keeps a pointer to the conversation list-box, so
that it can add chat messages received from the **ChatServer** component to this
list-box.

```
// The sink object keeps a pointer to the conversation list-box.
g_MsgSink.m_pConversation = &m_Conversation;
// Let the server know that you want to receive chat messages.
hr = pConnPoint->Advise(&g_MsgSink, &m_dwCookie);
Chk(hr);
```

When you call *IConnectionPoint::Advise*, you pass a pointer to the event sink
(**g_MsgSink**) object to the first parameter of *Advise*. It is important to note that this
is the place where you actually associate a connection point on the server to a
event sink object on the client. A successful call to *Advise* returns a cookie that
you must later use to signify to the connection point that you're no longer interested in receiving chat messages. Notice that you save this cookie in a DWORD
member variable called **m_dwCookie** for later use.

Having successfully registered your interest in receiving chat messages, you send
the first message to the **ChatServer**. Using the *ISendMessage* pointer that you've
earlier saved, you invoke the *Talk* method (as shown in the following code) to
send a message to notify everyone in the discussion group that a chatter, with a
particular alias identified by **m_Alias**, has just joined the discussion. This message
will get to the **ChatServer**. The **ChatServer** will then send the same message
out to all connected **ChatClients**, so that all chatters can see the message. This is
the beauty of connection points. The event source multiplexes the same message
out to many different event sinks regardless of their locality and distance.

```
CString strAlias; m_Alias.GetWindowText(strAlias);
CString strMessage;
strMessage.Format("***%s has just joined***", strAlias);
hr = m_pSendMessage->Talk(_bstr_t(strMessage));
Chk(hr);
} catch (_com_error & error) {
```

```
            m_pSendMessage = NULL;
            MessageBox(error.ErrorMessage());
    }
} else {
```

If the button's label is **Leave**, then you'll leave the discussion. First, you send a message to notify everyone that you're leaving the discussion. Second, you query for the *IConnectionPointContainer* interface, so that you can find the connection point for IID_IReceiveMessage.[*] Third, you then invoke *IConnectionPoint::Unadvise* by using the cookie that you've earlier saved to terminate the interest of receiving chat messages. Finally, you must invoke *Release* on the saved *ISendMessage* interface pointer (m_pSendMessage) to notify the **ChatServer** component that you're no longer holding a reference to it.

```
    if (m_pSendMessage) {
        try {
            CString strAlias; m_Alias.GetWindowText(strAlias);
            CString strMessage;
            strMessage.Format("***%s has left the discussion***", strAlias);
            HRESULT hr = m_pSendMessage->Talk(_bstr_t(strMessage));
            Chk(hr);

            CComPtr<IConnectionPointContainer> pConn;
            hr = m_pSendMessage->QueryInterface(IID_
                IConnectionPointContainer,
                                          (void**)&pConn);
            Chk(hr);
            CComPtr<IConnectionPoint> pConnPoint;
            hr = pConn->FindConnectionPoint(IID_IReceiveMessage,
                                      (IConnectionPoint**)&pConnPoint);
            Chk(hr);
            hr = pConnPoint->Unadvise(m_dwCookie);
            Chk(hr);
            m_pSendMessage->Release();
            m_pSendMessage = NULL ;
        } catch (_com_error & error) {
            MessageBox(error.ErrorMessage());
        }
    }
```

After leaving a discussion, you update the controls on the dialog as appropriate.

```
        m_Join.SetWindowText("Join");
        m_Connect.EnableWindow(TRUE);
        m_Send.EnableWindow(FALSE);
        m_Discussion.EnableWindow(TRUE);
    }
}
```

---

[*] Instead of doing this, we could have saved the *IConnectionPoint* interface pointer as a member variable and reused that pointer here. The above technique is shown for clarity, but it involves round-trips that could be shaved off.

## Sending a Chat Message

Having seen the code for joining and leaving a discussion, sending a chat message should be obvious (since you've sent a message upon joining and leaving a discussion). To send a chat message, a chatter enters a chat message in the message edit-box and then click the **Send** button. This will cause the following handler to be called. Notice that you first prefix the chat message with the chatter's alias. You then send the formatted message to the **ChatServer** component by calling *ISendMessage::Talk*. After the message is sent, you clear out the message edit-box so that the chatter can enter a new chat message.

```
void CChatClientDlg::OnButtonSend()
{
   ASSERT(m_pSendMessage);
   CString strAlias; m_Alias.GetWindowText(strAlias);
   CString strMsg; m_Message.GetWindowText(strMsg);
   CString strMessage;
   strMessage.Format("%s :  %s", strAlias, strMsg);

   try {
      HRESULT hr = m_pSendMessage->Talk(_bstr_t(strMessage));
      Chk(hr);
   } catch (_com_error & error) {
      MessageBox(error.ErrorMessage());
   }
   // Clear the message edit-box, so that the chatter can enter a new
   //message.
   m_Message.SetWindowText("");
}
```

## Receiving Chat Messages

Now let's create the event sink object that will receive all chat messages from a particular **ChatServer** component. This sink object is just another COM object, and you'll call it *CoMsgSink*, which will implement the *IReceiveMessage* interface.

You could use ATL or MFC to implement this object, but since it's so simple, you'll use pure C++ (also, you don't want to forget what you learned in Chapter 3, *Objects*). As you can see in the following class definition, *CoMsgSink* implements *QueryInterface*, *AddRef*, and *Release* from *IUnknown*. Notice that this class doesn't keep a reference count, because it is instantiated only once globally and dies when the client application exits.

```
//**********************************************************
// The following code shows you how to implement the sink
// object using pure C++.
//**********************************************************
class CoMsgSink : public IReceiveMessage {
public:
   CoMsgSink() : m_pConversation(NULL) {}
   STDMETHODIMP QueryInterface(REFIID riid, void **ppv)
```

```
    {
        if (ppv==NULL) { return E_INVALIDARG; }
        if (riid==IID_IUnknown || riid==IID_IReceiveMessage) {
            *ppv= static_cast<IReceiveMessage*>(this);
        } else {
            *ppv=NULL; return E_NOINTERFACE ;
        }

        reinterpret_cast<IUnknown *>(*ppv)->AddRef();
        return S_OK;
    }


    STDMETHODIMP_(ULONG) AddRef(void)
    { return 1; }       // Don't care because object is global.

    STDMETHODIMP_(ULONG) Release(void)
    { return 1; }       // Don't care because object is global.

    // IReceiveMessage Methods
    STDMETHODIMP OnReply(wchar_t *pwszReply)
    {
        if (m_pConversation) {
            // Insert the chat message into the conversation list-box.
            m_pConversation->InsertString(-1, (char*)_bstr_t(pwszReply));
            // Set the caret so that we scroll to the bottom of the list-box.
            int iCount = m_pConversation->GetCount();
            m_pConversation->SetCaretIndex(iCount);
            // If list-box has too many messages, delete the oldest one.
            if (iCount>20) m_pConversation->DeleteString(0);
        }
        return S_OK;
    }


    CListBox *m_pConversation;  // The conversation list-box in the GUI.
} g_MsgSink;   // A global instance
```

*CoMsgSink* also implements the *OnReply* method from the *IReceiveMessage* interface. As already mentioned, this is the method that the ChatServer component will call to propagate chat messages. Within this method, you simply insert the message that you receive from the ChatServer component into the conversation list-box on the ChatClient's user interface. Notice that you keep a pointer to the conversation list-box; recall that you set this relationship when a chatter joins a discussion. In addition, remember that a pointer to this object is passed to the ChatServer component during the call to *IConnectionPoint::Advise*, so that the ChatServer component can make callbacks to the correct event sink.

Also, you should notice that there isn't a class object (factory) associated with this sink object, because this sink object doesn't need to be dynamically activated. In other words, no one is calling *CoCreateInstance*, *CoCreateInstanceEx*, or *CoGetClassObject* to instantiate this COM object, as it's a private object known only to the ChatClient application. The application instantiates a single, global instance of this object, which lives for the lifetime of this application.

# Performance Impact of Connection Points

Generally, you want to minimize network round-trips because round-trips are very expensive. We discussed the connection points technique in this chapter because it is a standard way to support events in COM. In fact, if you want VBScript clients to trap events, you must use connection points. In addition, as we have mentioned earlier, the callback interface must also be a `dispinterface`.

It is generally a good practice to conform to a standard, but connection points are extremely expensive if you take round-trips into account. For example, it takes four round-trips to set up a connection: (1) Client queries for the *IConnectionPointContainer* interface; (2) Client finds the connection point; (3) Client registers interest by calling *IConnectionPoint::Advise*; and (4) Server makes a *QueryInterface* back to the client to verify that the client indeed supports the interface associated with the connection point. This must be done because *IConnectionPoint::Advise* takes an *IUnknown* pointer, instead of a specific pointer type (such as an *IReceiveMessage* pointer).

If you were to implement callbacks yourself without using connection points, you could reduce connection setup to a single round-trip. For instance, simply provide a method in the server component to accept an interface pointer of a specific type (i.e., not *IUnknown* but the callback interface's type). To set up a connection, a client calls this method to pass the callback interface to the server component, resulting in just one round-trip.

In this regard, you would definitely have to weigh performance against a standard, but I'll leave this decision up to your discretion.

# Security Impact of the OBJREF

We have concentrated on the `OBJREF` and connection points in this chapter. Both of these discussions involve the passing of an interface pointer from one object to another. This is very powerful, but even if a client receives an interface pointer, it doesn't mean that the client can successfully invoke methods using the received interface pointer. The reason for this is security. The receiver can invoke methods on the received interface pointer, barring security constraints.

For example, a `ChatClient` component successfully obtains a `ChatServer` object's *IUnknown* interface pointer from the `ChatBroker` component. Nevertheless, this doesn't mean that the `ChatClient` component can send chat messages to the `ChatServer` component. This depends upon the `ChatServer` component's access security, which can be configured programmatically using *CoInitializeSecurity* or manually using *dcomcnfg.exe*. Even if these are correctly configured, the authentication levels and impersonation levels may also be a factor in successful invocations. You'll have to correctly configure security in order for successful method invocations among different components.

As a different but related example, consider that a `ChatClient` component successfully sends a chat message to a server, because it has access. However, it may be possible that the `ChatServer` component cannot make callbacks to the client, because the client cannot authenticate the server. For instance, if you've configured the `ChatServer` component to run under a specific user identity (using *dcomcnfg.exe*) but that user cannot be authenticated by the machine running the `ChatClient` component, the callback will fail.

A simple solution for this callback problem is to allow everyone in the universe access permissions to the client component. You can do this by calling the *CoInitializeSecurity* API function in the client process, as follows:

```
// In the ChatClient process. . .
CoInitializeSecurity(0, -1, 0, 0,
    RPC_C_AUTHN_LEVEL_NONE,       // No authentication
    RPC_C_IMP_LEVEL_IDENTITY,     // Identify only
    0, EOAC_NONE, 0);
```

The above is simple, but it turns off all security on the client side, which can be a security compromise. To maintain security and still make callbacks, set the appropriate authentication level and allow access to an account on the client machine for the authentication identity used on the server machine to make the callbacks.

This is a bit tedious, but security is supposed to be tedious—at least for intruders. If activation fails, you simply need to give launch permissions to the client. However, there are many permutations in which a method invocation can fail because of security. You'll have to think about security when you design your distributed systems.

# *Debugging Techniques*

The integrated debugging environment provided by Visual C++ is very powerful. You can use the debugger to start and debug an application by simply stepping through each instruction. During a debug session, you can inspect your variables, memory, registers, call stack, etc. With the new `Edit and Continue` feature provided by Visual C++ 6.0, you can even change the code on-the-fly while debugging. The Visual C++ debugger is great for debugging local applications, but debugging distributed components requires a little more work.

This appendix shows three simple, but very powerful, techniques for debugging distributed components. The first two are a poor-man's techniques for detecting what went wrong. The third technique is an easy way to break into an executing component on the server side.

## *Using the FormatMessage Function*

Recall that you must check the returned `HRESULT` for all COM API function and method invocations, because the `HRESULT` is an important element in determining what has gone wrong in the most recent COM-related call. In the following code snippet, if the returned `HRESULT` is bad, we call a special helper function, *DisplayError*, to display the error message associated with the `HRESULT`:

```
HRESULT hr = pOcr->OcrImage(. . .);
if (FAILED(hr)) DisplayError(hr);
```

To obtain the textual representation of a system-defined `HRESULT`, you can use the *FormatMessage* Win32 API function. Here's the *DisplayError* helper function that uses *FormatMessage* to obtain the error string associated with a particular status code.

```
void DisplayError(HRESULT hr)
{
    if (hr == S_OK) return;

    if (HRESULT_FACILITY(hr) == FACILITY_WINDOWS)
        hr = HRESULT_CODE(hr);

    wchar_t *pwszStatus;
    // FormatMessageW is the Unicode version of FormatMessage.
    FormatMessageW(
        FORMAT_MESSAGE_ALLOCATE_BUFFER |
        FORMAT_MESSAGE_FROM_SYSTEM,
        NULL,
        hr,
        MAKELANGID(LANG_NEUTRAL, SUBLANG_DEFAULT),
        (LPWSTR)&pwszStatus,
        0,
        NULL
    );

    // MessageBoxW is the Unicode version MessageBox.
    MessageBoxW(NULL, pwszStatus, L"DisplayError", MB_OK);

    LocalFree(pwszStatus);
}
```

The previous code snippet displays the error string associated with an **HRESULT**. This information helps tremendously in debugging your code, since it presents to you the exact problem that has occurred in the last COM-related invocation. For example, if a piece of client code calls *CoCreateInstanceEx* to activate a COM class but the class is not registered, you'll receive a message saying that "The class is not registered." Knowing the exact error helps you take the appropriate actions.

Note that a helper function like *DisplayError* can be used on both the client and server side. Whenever you receive a bad **HRESULT**, call this function to find out exactly what went wrong.

## Using the _com_error Class

The Visual C++ compiler-level support for COM includes a class called *_com_error*. In order to use this class, you must include *comdef.h*. Like the *FormatMessage* technique, this class allows you to display the error string of an associated **HRESULT**. Moreover, this class allows you to deal with COM exceptions via the *IErrorInfo* interface. An abbreviated class definition of *_com_error* follows:

```
class _com_error {
public:
    // Constructors
    _com_error(HRESULT hr, IErrorInfo* perrinfo = NULL) throw();

    // Accessors
    HRESULT Error() const throw();
```

```
    // IErrorInfo method accessors
    _bstr_t Description() const throw(_com_error);

    // FormatMessage accessors
    const TCHAR * ErrorMessage() const throw();

    . . .

};
```

Using this class, you can simply display the error message associated with the bad HRESULT by calling the *_com_error::ErrorMessage* method, as shown here:

```
HRESULT hr = pOcr->OcrImage(. . .);
if (FAILED(hr)) {
    _com_error error(hr);
    MessageBox(NULL, error.ErrorMessage(), L"Error", MB_OK);
}
```

The *_com_error* class is better than the *FormatMessage* technique because it can deal with COM exceptions via *IErrorInfo*. For example, the following code snippet is similar to the previous code. However, it is expanded to check for COM exception support that is provided by the object. Notice that if the object doesn't support COM exceptions, you pass only the HRESULT into the constructor of *_com_error*, but if the object supports COM exceptions, you pass both the HRESULT and the *IErrorInfo* interface pointer into the constructor of *_com_error*.

```
HRESULT hr = pOcr->OcrImage(. . .);
if (FAILED(hr)) {
    // Check to see of object support COM exception handling.
    CComQIPtr<ISupportErrorInfo, &IID_ISupportErrorInfo> pSupportError(pOcr);
    HRESULT hrTest = pSupportError->InterfaceSupportsErrorInfo(riid);
    if (FAILED(hrTest)) {
        // Object doesn't support COM exception handling.
        _com_error error(hrTest);
        MessageBox(NULL, error.ErrorMessage(), L"Error", MB_OK);
    } else {
        // Object supports COM exception handling.
        CComPtr<IErrorInfo> pErrorInfo;
        hrTest = ::GetErrorInfo(0, &pErrorInfo);
        if (FAILED(hrTest)) throw _com_error(hrTest);

        // Instantiate a _com_error object
        // using the obtained IErrorInfo pointer.
        _com_error error(hr, pErrorInfo);
        if (error.Description().length()>0) {
            MessageBox(NULL, error.Description(), TEXT("Description"), MB_OK);
        } else {
            MessageBox(NULL, error.ErrorMessage(), TEXT("Error"), MB_OK);
        }
    }
}
```

Similar to *FormatMessage*, this technique can be used by both the client and server side. It also tells you what went wrong with the most recent COM call, helping you debug your components.

# *Breaking into the Server*

On the client side, it is very easy to set a breakpoint because you are in full control of the client component. You can set a breakpoint and debug the client component as a normal application. The execution will stop at the breakpoint because your client component is being interactively debugged.

However, it is much more difficult to set a breakpoint for server components. Recall from Chapter 4, *Components,* that a class object that is registered (via the *CoRegisterClassObject* API function) to be REGCLS_SINGLEUSE can be used only by one client. This is because REGCLS_SIGNLEUSE tells COM to remove the class object from public view once a client has connected to it. A second client needing this class object will cause another component (i.e., a totally different process) to be activated.

For example, let's assume that you start this kind of server component using Visual C++'s debugger and set a breakpoint at a specific location in the server code. Let's further assume that the class object has been removed from the public view by the mere fact that its hosting component is executing (because it is being debugged).* In this case, if a client requests to activate this class object, a separate process will be spawned to host the newly activated object. Therefore, you will never reach the breakpoint that you've set for the first activated component, which is still patiently sitting in the debugger waiting for a breakpoint that will never occur.

Assuming there's no security problem, one way to reach a particular server-side breakpoint is to use the *DebugBreak* Win32 API function, which causes a breakpoint exception to be thrown. If you don't catch this exception (and you shouldn't), a message similar to the one shown in Figure A-1 will be launched.

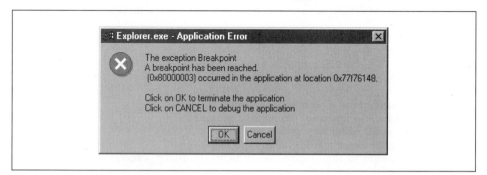

*Figure A-1. DebugBreak launches this dialog*

---

* For the curious, this phenomenon is possessed by an MFC SDI application with a *CDocument* object that supports Automation.

If you click OK on this dialog box, the server component will shut down, but if you click Cancel, a registered debugger will launch itself. Once launched, the debugger will break within the *DebugBreak* function. Press F10 (step over) twice to move out of this function, and you can then step through each line of code in your component as if you were debugging a normal application.

Here's is an example that shows the usage of this API function:

```
STDMETHODIMP CoOcrEngine::OcrImage(. . .)
{
    // Debugger will break within the DebugBreak API function.
    // Press F10 twice to get out of DebugBreak...

    DebugBreak();

    // ...so that you can start debugging your own code.

    ProcessTheImage(); .
}
```

The *DebugBreak* function simply wraps the _asm int 3 instruction, which means that the earlier code is functionally equivalent to the following:

```
STDMETHODIMP CoOcrEngine::OcrImage(. . .)
{
    _asm int 3;    // Debugger will break here.

    ProcessTheImage();
}
```

I prefer to use this instruction over *DebugBreak*, because I don't want to press F10 twice to get to my own code. This instruction and *DebugBreak* usually work fine for in-process components with objects that have a matching apartment model as the container. However, these techniques fall short when ORPC is involved, meaning that we need to do some more work if we want to dynamically attach a debugger to an out-of-process component.

Remember that *DebugBreak* causes a breakpoint exception to occur. When ORPC is involved (i.e., when you are debugging an out-of-process component), the COM infrastructure (including marshaling code, RPC, and COM) will eat all unhandled exceptions. This is good for robustness reasons from the COM infrastructure standpoint, but it prevents you from seeing the Application Error dialog box, which means that you won't be able to launch the debugger.

To understand what is meant by the phrase "eat all unhandled exceptions," consider the following code snippet:

```
try {
    asm int 3;
} catch(...) {}
```

Given this code, you will never see the `Application Error` dialog box, because the breakpoint exception is eaten by the `catch` clause, which catches all exceptions. The COM runtime services catch exceptions as shown here. Therefore, you will not be able to debug the application.

To guarantee that you will see the `Application Error` dialog box, you must prevent the COM infrastructure from eating the breakpoint exception. In other words, you must somehow route this exception to the operating system so that the `Application Error` dialog box will appear. You can use the *UnhandledExceptionFilter* Win32 API function to do this. This function requires that you use structured exception handling (SEH)—a low-level technique that doesn't mix with C++ exception handling or C++ object construction and destruction. Therefore, you need to write a separate function to simulate the functionality of *DebugBreak*, as shown here:

```
// Use this helper function in out-of-process servers
// to dynamically launch a debugger.
void DebugBreakDuringORPC()
{
    __try {
        _asm int 3;
    } __except (UnhandledExceptionFilter(GetExceptionInformation())) {}
}
```

Again, the *UnhandledExceptionFilter* API function passes the unhandled breakpoint exception to the operating system to cause the `Application Error` dialog to appear. Don't forget to configure the server component to run as the *interactive user* when debugging a remote out-of-process component, or you'll never see the dialog.

Given the above *DebugBreakDuringORPC* helper function, you can use it in place of *DebugBreak* to break into an running out-of-process component. For example, here's a rewritten version of the previously shown *CoOcrEngine::OcrImage* method:

```
STDMETHODIMP CoOcrEngine::OcrImage(. . .)
{
    DebugBreakDuringORPC();

    ProcessTheImage();
}
```

This version will launch the debugger on the machine where the *CoOcrEngine::OcrImage* method executes. The first call to *CoOcrEngine::OcrImage* will launch the debugger and return the error "The server threw an exception" to the client. However, subsequent calls will break at the `_asm int 3` instruction, allowing you to step through and debug your code.

# B

# *Performance*

This appendix captures the results obtained from running the `DetailsClient` component that comes with this book. This executable (EXE) can be built from the accompanying source code, which can be downloaded from the O'Reilly FTP site. To obtain the results shown in this appendix, do the following:

1. Build the `DetailsEXE` and `DetailsDLL` components.

2. Register `DetailsEXE` using the `-RegServer` command-line option.

3. Register the `DetailsDLL` component using the *regsvr32.exe* utility.

4. Build the proxy/stub code, *DetailsPS.dll*.

5. Register this proxy/stub DLL using the *regsvr32.exe* utility.

6. Build the `DetailsClient` client component.

7. Install `DetailsEXE` on a remote machine and register it. Don't forget to install and register the proxy/stub code.

8. Use *dcomcnfg.exe* to set the `RemoteServerName` entry (on the machine where the `DetailsClient` component executes) to point to the remote machine (where the remote `DetailsEXE` component will run).

9. Use *regedit.exe* to change the `ThreadingModel` of the CLSID_Details COM class to empty (i.e., `ThreadingModel=""`) and execute `DetailsClient`. The performance output will be saved in a file called *perform.log*. Observe the performance output.

10. Repeat step 9 for the models `ThreadingModel="Apartment"`, `ThreadingModel="Free"`, and `ThreadingModel="Both"`.

The following are performance results that I have obtained using the above procedure. Your performance results may be different but they should be relative to the ones shown in this appendix.

# *Performance Results for ThreadingModel=""*

This section captures the performance results when the `ThreadingModel` of `CLSID_Details` is `ThreadingModel=""`. Remember that a COM class within an in-process server must specify its threading semantics using the `ThreadingModel` registry named value. If this named value is missing for a given in-process COM class, `ThreadingModel=""` is assumed. This means that an instance of this COM class will always be activated inside the main STA.

To make the discussion easier, concentrate on the `VoidCall` column in each table shown below. Note the following:

- In all rows shown in Table B-1 through Table B-3, the client apartment is different from the server apartment. This implies that marshaling will result.

- For all in-process method invocations (the rows labeled "In-process"), the client apartment marshals interface pointers between itself and a different apartment, the main STA.

- In-process and local out-of-process method invocations are essentially equivalent when the client and server exist in different apartments.

- A remote method invocation is about 16 to 18 times more expensive than an in-process or a local out-of-process method invocation.

- The results for `MTAThread1` and `MTAThread2` should be very similar, because both of these threads live in the one and only MTA within the client process.

*Table B-1. Client Apartment: STA (Secondary STA Thread)*

|            | FirstCall | VoidCall | ArrayCall | LongCall |
|------------|-----------|----------|-----------|----------|
| In-process | 0.000134  | 0.000126 | 0.000131  | 0.001157 |
| Local      | 0.000780  | 0.000173 | 0.000182  | 0.001608 |
| Remote     | 0.037674  | 0.001804 | 0.001955  | 0.017856 |

*Table B-2. Client Apartment: MTA (MTAThread1)*

|            | FirstCall | VoidCall | ArrayCall | LongCall |
|------------|-----------|----------|-----------|----------|
| In-process | 0.000104  | 0.000095 | 0.000106  | 0.000864 |
| Local      | 0.000620  | 0.000091 | 0.000100  | 0.000814 |
| Remote     | 0.037725  | 0.001683 | 0.001912  | 0.016920 |

*Table B-3. Client Apartment: MTA (MTAThread2)*

|            | FirstCall | VoidCall | ArrayCall | LongCall |
|------------|-----------|----------|-----------|----------|
| In-process | 0.000105  | 0.000097 | 0.000105  | 0.000861 |

*Table B-3. Client Apartment: MTA (MTAThread2) (continued)*

|  | FirstCall | VoidCall | ArrayCall | LongCall |
|---|---|---|---|---|
| Local | 0.000629 | 0.000091 | 0.000100 | 0.000779 |
| Remote | 0.039485 | 0.001691 | 0.001881 | 0.016646 |

# Performance Results for ThreadingModel="Apartment"

This section captures the performance results when the `ThreadingModel` of `CLSID_Details` is `ThreadingModel="Apartment"`. To make the discussion easier, concentrate on the `VoidCall` column in each table. In Table B-4, note the following:

- For in-process method invocations, the client and the server share the same apartment. This implies that method calls are made directly, without marshaling.

- From the data shown in Table B-4, a direct method call is about 170 times more efficient than a local out-of-process method invocation. It is about 1800 times more efficient than a remote out-of-process method invocation.

For Table B-5 and Table B-6, note the following:

- The client apartment is different from the server apartment. This implies that marshaling will result.

- For all in-process method invocations, the client apartment marshals interface pointers between itself and a different apartment, a different STA.

- In-process and local out-of-process method invocations are essentially equivalent, when the client and server exist in different apartments.

*Table B-4. Client Apartment: STA (Secondary STA Thread)*

|  | FirstCall | VoidCall | ArrayCall | LongCall |
|---|---|---|---|---|
| In-process | 0.000005 | 0.000006 | 0.000005 | 0.000007 |
| Local | 0.000812 | 0.000172 | 0.000183 | 0.001776 |
| Remote | 0.039747 | 0.001798 | 0.002399 | 0.017383 |

*Table B-5. Client Apartment: MTA (MTAThread1)*

|  | FirstCall | VoidCall | ArrayCall | LongCall |
|---|---|---|---|---|
| In-process | 0.000103 | 0.000094 | 0.000103 | 0.000808 |
| Local | 0.000612 | 0.000091 | 0.000099 | 0.000795 |
| Remote | 0.037605 | 0.001695 | 0.001885 | 0.016981 |

*Table B-6. Client Apartment: MTA (MTAThread2)*

|  | FirstCall | VoidCall | ArrayCall | LongCall |
|---|---|---|---|---|
| In-process | 0.000102 | 0.000096 | 0.000103 | 0.000836 |
| Local | 0.000627 | 0.000105 | 0.000099 | 0.000781 |
| Remote | 0.038961 | 0.001700 | 0.001891 | 0.016747 |

# Performance Results for ThreadingModel="Free"

This section captures the performance results when the `ThreadingModel` of `CLSID_Details` is `ThreadingModel="Free"`. To make the discussion easier, concentrate on the `VoidCall` column in each table.

A key point to note for Table B-7: for in-process method invocations, the client and the server exist in different apartments. This implies that marshaling will take place.

Here is a key point to note for Table B-8 and Table B-9: for in-process method invocations, the client and the server share the same apartment, implying that method invocations will be direct method calls.

*Table B-7. Client Apartment: STA (Secondary STA Thread)*

|  | FirstCall | VoidCall | ArrayCall | LongCall |
|---|---|---|---|---|
| In-process | 0.000119 | 0.000108 | 0.000113 | 0.000924 |
| Local | 0.000866 | 0.000463 | 0.000268 | 0.001908 |
| Remote | 0.039941 | 0.001799 | 0.001965 | 0.017295 |

*Table B-8. Client Apartment: MTA (MTAThread1)*

|  | FirstCall | VoidCall | ArrayCall | LongCall |
|---|---|---|---|---|
| In-process | 0.000005 | 0.000005 | 0.000005 | 0.000006 |
| Local | 0.000609 | 0.000090 | 0.000097 | 0.000742 |
| Remote | 0.037247 | 0.001719 | 0.001882 | 0.016600 |

*Table B-9. Client Apartment: MTA (MTAThread2)*

|  | FirstCall | VoidCall | ArrayCall | LongCall |
|---|---|---|---|---|
| In-process | 0.000005 | 0.000004 | 0.000005 | 0.000006 |
| Local | 0.000841 | 0.000094 | 0.000100 | 0.000748 |
| Remote | 0.037925 | 0.001698 | 0.001895 | 0.016808 |

# Performance Results for ThreadingModel="Both"

This section captures the performance results when the `ThreadingModel` of `CLSID_Details` is `ThreadingModel="Both"`. To make the discussion easier, concentrate on the `VoidCall` column in each table.

Note that for all in-process method invocations, the client and the server share the same apartment, because in-process COM classes that support `ThreadingModel="Both"` can be loaded into any client apartment (STA or MTA). Method invocations are direct. Thus, if you were to put a COM object within in-process servers, try to support `TheadingModel="Both"`. If you don't do this, you might as well build an out-of-process server instead, because an out-of-process server is much more fault-tolerant than an in-process one.

*Table B-10. Client Apartment: STA (Secondary STA Thread)*

|            | FirstCall | VoidCall  | ArrayCall | LongCall  |
|------------|-----------|-----------|-----------|-----------|
| In-process | 0.000005  | 0.000005  | 0.000005  | 0.000007  |
| Local      | 0.000909  | 0.000430  | 0.000410  | 0.001978  |
| Remote     | 0.844881  | 0.001794  | 0.001960  | 0.017808  |

*Table B-11. Client Apartment: MTA (MTAThread1)*

|            | FirstCall | VoidCall  | ArrayCall | LongCall  |
|------------|-----------|-----------|-----------|-----------|
| In-process | 0.000005  | 0.000005  | 0.000005  | 0.000006  |
| Local      | 0.000617  | 0.000090  | 0.000098  | 0.000722  |
| Remote     | 0.045469  | 0.001706  | 0.001882  | 0.016604  |

*Table B-12. Client Apartment: MTA (MTAThread2)*

|            | FirstCall | VoidCall  | ArrayCall | LongCall  |
|------------|-----------|-----------|-----------|-----------|
| In-process | 0.000005  | 0.000005  | 0.000005  | 0.000006  |
| Local      | 0.000761  | 0.000094  | 0.000100  | 0.000750  |
| Remote     | 0.038146  | 0.001692  | 0.001906  | 0.016598  |

# C

# *New COM Features and COM+*

This appendix captures some of the new COM features that will likely be bundled with the up-and-coming release of Windows NT 4.0 Service Pack 4 and Windows 2000. In addition, we will briefly discuss COM+. At the time of this writing, the details of these features are fairly unstable. Because the information contained herein may be inaccurate by the time these features are released, you should verify these features for yourself if you ever intend to use them.

Throughout the book, we have talked about a number of new COM features, including:

- The Global Interface Table, which can store interface pointers that can be used by multiple apartments in the same process. This feature has been around since Windows NT 4.0 Service Pack 3.

- Delegation, which allows the server component to impersonate the client and access remote resources using the client access token. When delegation is coupled with the cloaking capability, a client token can be passed from one component to another across multiple machine hops, allowing possibly endless chaining of impersonation.

- The active directory, which supports distributed setup and administration.

- The support for **structs** in dispatch and dual interface definitions. This means that interface methods can contain parameters that are **structs**. User-defined structures have not been allowed in dispatch and dual interfaces up to now, but Windows NT 4.0 Service Pack 4 will make this feature real.

Besides these features, a couple of other features that are interesting are endpoint configuration and nonblocking calls.

# *Endpoint Configuration*

In traditional client/server systems that use TCP/IP for client/server communications, the server listens for client requests on a specific endpoint, which is more often referred to as a port. A client has to know the server IP address and the server port for successful communications with the server.

Unlike traditional client/server systems, COM dynamically activates components. Upon activation, COM dynamically assigns the launched component a connection endpoint, so a given component can use a different endpoint every time it is activated. For example, a connection endpoint for a given component may be 4000 at one time but be 5000 at another time.

Because component endpoints are dynamically assigned, it is painful to configure a component object for use through a firewall. You know that port 135 must be opened, because the Distributed COM infrastructure uses this port (See Figure 5-10 in Chapter 5, *Infrastructure*). One port is understandable, but imagine going through the correct firewall/network/security people to open up a wide range of ports for a particular IP address. To ameliorate this problem, Windows NT 4.0 Service Pack 4 allows you to statically configure an endpoint for each `AppID`. Once configured, the component associated with this `AppID` will be activated using the specified endpoint every time.

The *dcomcnfg.exe* utility that comes with Windows NT 4.0 Service Pack 4 has a newly added property page called `Endpoints`, as shown in Figure C-1.

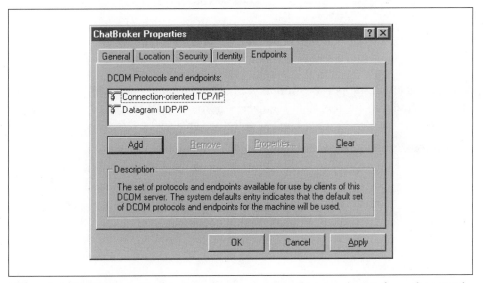

*Figure C-1. The "Endpoints" property page allows you configure endpoints for each protocol*

This property page allows you to configure the endpoints that COM will use for a particular component (COM application). The Add button allows you to add a number of protocols that you want the component to support, and the Properties button allows to you configure the endpoints for a selected protocol. Once configured, the endpoint information for all added protocols will be stored under the Endpoints named value of the appropriate AppID key, as shown in the following registry entries:

```
[HKEY_CLASSES_ROOT\AppID\{80477681-35F6-11D2-91C0-006008052F2D}]
@="ChatBroker"
"Endpoints"=hex...
```

Since endpoint information is stored in hexadecimal, you need to use the Endpoints property page in *dcomcnfg.exe* for easy configuration.[*]

## *Nonblocking Calls*

Asynchronous communication is supported in Windows 2000 by a feature that is called *nonblocking calls*, which allows a client to request a lengthy operation without being blocked. In other words, the client can proceed with further processing after requesting the operation. The server component will notify the client when the lengthy operation is completed. Windows 2000 supports asynchronous invocation via a new MIDL interface attribute called async_uuid. An example of an asynchronous interface is shown here:

```
[ object, uuid(D9F23D61-A647-11d1-ABCD-00207810D5FE),
  async_uuid(AAAAAAAA-AAAA-AAAA-AAAA-AAAAAAAAAAAA) ]
interface IOcr : IUnknown {
    HRESULT OcrImage([in] long lImageSize,
                     [in, size_is(lImageSize)] byte * pbImage,
                     [out, string] wchar_t **pwszOcrText);
}
```

Because this MIDL snippet uses the async_uuid attribute, MIDL will generate two interface definitions for the *IOcr* interface: a normal (synchronous) version and an asynchronous version. You are familiar with the synchronous version:

```
interface IOcr : public IUnknown {
public:
    virtual HRESULT OcrImage(
        /* [in] */ long lImageSize,
        /* [size_is][in] */ byte *pbImage,
        /* [string][out] */ wchar_t **pwszOcrText) = 0;
};
```

---

[*] Actually, since endpoints is really a named value of type REG_MULTI_SZ, you can edit the endpoints using the Multi-String Editor in *regedt32.exe*, which is not the same as *regedit.exe*. But why bother using this antiquated utility when it's much easier to use *dcomcnfg.exe* to achieve the same goal.

But you've never seen the asynchronous version:

```
interface AsyncIOcr : public IUnknown {
public:
    virtual HRESULT begin_OcrImage(
        /* [in] */ long lImageSize,
        /* [size_is][in] */ byte *pbImage) = 0;
    virtual HRESULT finish_OcrImage(
        /* [string][out] */ wchar_t **pwszOcrText) = 0;
};
```

The asynchronous version supplies two methods for each method specified in the interface definition. The *begin_* method contains all the [in] parameters, and the *finish_* method contains all the [out] parameters.

The component object that implements the *IOcr* interface is a normal component object. However, to support nonblocking calls, this object must implement the *ICallFactory* interface, which has one method named *CreateCall*. The implementation of this method is responsible for creating a *call object*, which implements the generated, asynchronous interface: *AsyncIOcr*. This means that you must develop two objects in order to support asynchronous communications. These two objects are illustrated in Figure C-2.

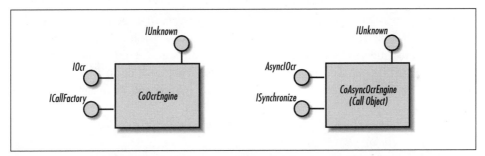

*Figure C-2. CoOcrEngine's call object supports asynchronous methods calls*

Any component object that supports the *ICallFactory* interface signifies that it supports asynchronous method invocations. However, the asynchronous management lies in the hands of the call object, which implements the asynchronous interface, such as *AsyncIOcr*.

On the client side, you can query for the *ICallFactory* interface to determine whether the target object supports asynchronous method invocations, as shown later. Remember from Chapter 7, *Using COM Objects*, that *CComQIPtr* is a smart pointer that automatically calls *QueryInterface* to retrieve an interface pointer identified by the template parameters.

```
extern IOcr *pOcr;
// Does CoOcrEngine support async method invocations?
CComQIPtr<ICallFactory, &IID_ICallFactory> pFactory(pOcr);
```

```
// Create a call object for async method invocations.
CComPtr<AsyncIOcr> pAsyncIOcr;
pFactory->CreateCall(IID_AsyncIOcr, 0, IID_AsyncIOcr, (void**)&pAsyncIOcr);

// Begin the async method call. This is a nonblocking call,
// so the client can immediately proceed to doing other work.
pAsyncIOcr->begin_OcrImage(/*inputs*/);

// The lengthy-processing request is submitted, we'll check for its
// completion later. For now, since we're not blocked, we will
// do as much client-side processing here as we want.

// Maybe two hours later, we want to check whether the
// lengthy-processing request has been completed.
CComQIPtr<ISynchronize, &IID_ISynchronize> pSynchronize(pAsyncIOcr);

// Check for completion
if (pSynchronize->Wait(0, 0)==RPC_S_CALLPENDING) {
    // Call is still in progress, so do some more client-side work.
}

// Wait until the async call completes.
pSynchronize->Wait(0, INFINITE);

// Async method call is completed, so retrieve return values.
pAsyncIOcr->finish_OcrImage(/*outputs*/);
```

In this pseudocode snippet, you use the *begin_OcrImage* method to make the asynchronous call. This is a nonblocking call (meaning it returns immediately), so you can do as much client-side processing as you want at this point. To check whether the call is completed, call *ISynchronize::Wait*, passing in 0 as the second argument. If this call returns RPC_S_PENDING, the call is still in progress. To wait infinitely until the call completes, pass INFINITE as the second argument to *ISynchronize::Wait*. Once the call has completed, you call retrieve the return values by calling *finish_OcrImage*.

On the server side, component objects that support asynchronous communications must implement the asynchronous interface (in this case, *AsyncIOcr*) and at least the *ISynchronize* interface, which is shown here:

```
[object, uuid(00000030-0000-0000-C000-000000000046)]
interface ISynchronize : IUnknown {
    // Allows client to inquire for async method completion or
    // wait for the async call to be completed.
    HRESULT Wait([in] DWORD dwFlags, [in] DWORD dwMilliseconds);
    // Allows server to signal that the async call has been completed.
    HRESULT Signal();
    // Allows the server to reset the call object.
    HRESULT Reset();
}
```

As previously noted, a client uses the *begin_* method to start the asynchronous method invocation. The implementation of this method must make sure that only one asynchronous method invocation is being handled at a time, prior to starting the processing. When the processing is completed, the server must notify the client of the completion by calling *ISynchronize::Signal*, as shown in the following pseudocode fragment:

```
STDMETHODIMP CoAsyncOcrEngine::begin_OcrImage(/*inputs*/)
{
    // Only handle one call at a time.

    // Do processing for the async method call.

    // When processing is completed, signal the client.
    CComQIPtr<ISynchornize, &IID_ISynchronize> pSynchronize((IUnknown*)this);
    pSynchronize->Signal();

        return S_OK;
}
```

When a client calls the *finish_* method, the server will make sure that the asynchronous processing is completed by calling *ISynchronize::Wait*. Once the processing is completed, this method resets the call object by calling *ISynchronize::Reset*. This method also collects outputs and returns them to the client.

```
STDMETHODIMP CoAsyncOcrEngine::finish_OcrImage(/*outputs*/)
{
    // Make sure that the async operation is indeed completed.
    CComQIPtr<ISynchornize> pSynchronize((IUnknown*)this);
    pSynchronize->Wait(INFINITE);

    // Reset the call object.
    pSynchronize->Reset();

    // Return the outputsreturn S_OK;

    return S_OK;
}
```

# *COM+*

COM is a successful and mature technology, but it has been criticized for lacking large-scale distributed computing support and for being too difficult to use. To remedy these problems, Microsoft has enhanced COM to provide a rich runtime layer that simplifies COM programming and supports a powerful mechanism called *interception*, which allows for runtime extensibility. The former hides grungy stuff like class registration, dynamic invocation, versioning, reference counting, threading, etc., but the latter allows anyone to extend the runtime layer. These enhancements are important enough give COM a new name, COM+. COM is by no means obsolete; it is simply being enhanced. In fact, even with the existence of COM+, developers may still want to use COM to obtain full control in developing and using components.

Figure C-3 shows the architecture of COM+, which, as you can see, is composed of the runtime and services layers. The services layer can have one or more services that can be plugged directly into the runtime via interception. The boxes marked `Registration`, `Object Management`, and `Metadata` are built-in, runtime-level services that simplify COM usage and development. The boxes marked as `COM+ Services` and `Third-Party Services` are flexible extensions to the COM+ runtime and thus layer on top of the runtime. COM+ 1.0 will not support third-party services because it doesn't expose activation and interception mechanisms, but future COM+ releases will likely add this support. In COM+ 1.0, Microsoft provides a number of services that plug right into the COM+ runtime via interception; these are the services that support large-scale enterprise needs.

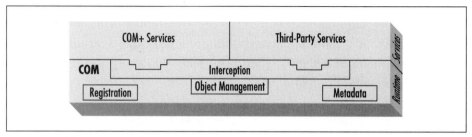

*Figure C-3. The COM+ architecture*

Before we proceed further, remember that the information given in this section (as well as the whole appendix) may not be completely accurate, because COM+ has not been released. In addition, most of the features that we discuss won't even be supported in COM+ 1.0; however they are important to read about in order to recognize the potential benefits that future versions of COM+ will possibly bring. Having said that, you should take this information with a grain of salt.

## *Runtime that Simplifies Component Development and Usage*

COM+ 1.0 doesn't support the features discussed in this subsection, but they show where COM+ will take us in the future. One of the purposes of the runtime is to simplify component development and usage. To support this goal, the runtime must hide as much nonbusiness logic complexities as possible, so that developing a component requires no code that doesn't support the business logic exposed by the component. Likewise, using a component requires no more code than simply creating an object and calling its methods.

### Hide nonbusiness logic complexities

Recall from Chapter 3, *Objects*, and Chapter 4, *Components*, that it takes a lot of work to create a component. For instance, you need to take into account interface negotiation, reference counting, registration, threading, security, activation, and component lifetime support. This stuff has nothing to do with the business logic (such as performing optical character recognition or calculating an invoice) of your component; yet you have take it into account to be in accordance with the laws of COM.

COM+ removes these nonbusiness logic complexities from the component developer and user. Its hides them within the COM+ runtime, shown in Figure C-3. With COM+, you won't have to provide your own code to obtain the following necessary COM features, because they are provided by the runtime.

- *IUnknown* implementation
- Class factory implementation
- Component registration
- Component startup and shutdown
- Metadata (type information)
- Dynamic invocation

If you wanted to use these features in COM, you would need to implement them by yourself. However, by the simple virtue of using COM+, you will automatically get all these features under the cover.

### Simplify component development and usage

Chapter 3, and 4 taught you component development and usage using pure C++. In those chapters, you had to write a bunch of boilerplate code, which had nothing to do with the business logic of your component. Recall that the boilerplate code included the following:

- *IUnknown* implementation
- Class factory implementation
- Component registration
- Component startup and shutdown

In Chapter 6, *Building Components with ATL*, you learned how ATL macros and template classes hide away this boilerplate code. You no longer had to write the boilerplate code in Chapter 6, but you had to add the correct macros and derive from the correct base classes to obtain the boilerplate code.

COM+ provides enhanced metadata support in the form of something called the COM+ catalog, which keeps track of detailed information (e.g., transaction, state, threading, and data source attributes, including definitions for classes, interfaces, methods, arguments, fields, etc.) for all components on the system. By using the COM+ catalog, a future version of Visual C++ can provide support for attribute-based programming to alleviate component development and usage. With attribute-based programming, you no longer have to worry about the fore-mentioned boilerplate code at all. You simply worry about your application's business logic. Nonbusiness logic and infrastructure features can be specified using *attributes* similar to MIDL attributes. For example, the following pseudocode illustrates the simplicity of component development in using attribute-based programming, which relies on the information recorded in the COM+ catalog:

```
[threading="apartment"]
coclass CoOcrEngine : implements IOcr {
    // Write the code to support our business logic;
    // for example, we can OCR and image.
    HRESULT OcrImage(. . .);
};
```

Looking at the previous pseudocode snippet, you should note the following:

- The pseudocode above indicates that the `CoOcrEngine` class supports the apartment model by using an attribute.

- The class doesn't implement the *IUnknown* interface. This means that this class doesn't have to worry about object lifetime management and interface negotiation, as COM+ will manage both of these features in its runtime. If the object requires a transaction, all you would have to do is add an attribute (`transaction="required"`) and COM+ would make sure that the object executes as part of a transaction.

- There's no class factory, as this is supported by the COM+ runtime.

- There's no registration code, as this is supported by the COM+ runtime.

- You simply worry about the business logic of your COM object. Specifically, performing OCR on an image (*OcrImage*) is the business logic that the above COM object supports.

You can write normal COM code to use the `CoOcrEngine` component object shown above. However, COM+ makes using a COM object much simpler, as shown in the following pseudocode:

```
// Activate an object.
CoOcrEngine *pOcr = new CoOcrEngine;

// Call its method.
pOcr->OcrImage(. . .);
```

As this pseudocode illustrates, you need not worry about calling *CoCreateInstanceEx* to activate the object, because `operator new` will signal the COM+ runtime to do so. In addition, you need not worry about calling *AddRef* or

*Release*, because memory management is handled automatically by the COM+ runtime.

## Services that Support Large-Scale Enterprise Needs

COM+ not only makes COM programming easier, but supports a set of enterprise-wide services that enable development and deployment of large-scale distributed software. These services are represented by the COM+ `Services` box in Figure C-3. COM+ provides the following services for free. Most of these are existing functionality or services supported by Microsoft Transaction Server (MTS), so in a sense, you can think of COM+ as the merging of COM and MTS:

*Transactions*

> In large systems, a single object doesn't work alone. It interacts with many other objects to carry out a particular transaction, which can make updates to one or more databases. Transactions support scalability, fault tolerance, and database integrity, because they must comply with the ACID properties, as described in the following items:

*Atomicity*

> All work performed by a transaction is either committed or rolled back completely.

*Consistency*

> There's no confusion about the state of a transaction at any point in time. In other words, all the work that a transaction does to get from state A to state B must be successfully carried out before the transaction can be shifted to state B; otherwise, the transaction will remain at state A, never anywhere between A and B.

*Isolation*

> A transaction is processed in isolation, so that no external entity can know its internal, intermediate state (i.e., somewhere between state A and B).

*Durability*

> Once the transaction has been committed, the updated data will be persistently stored and can be later retrieved, even if system failures occur in the interim.

*Load balancing*

> Load balancing is a technique that is used to help make a system scalable. In order to support load balancing, there is a load balancing broker/router that distributes the workload equally among a cluster of applications that can support a client's request. The client first makes a request to the broker, and the broker routes the client request to an appropriate server. From then on, the

client communicates directly with the server, without any further interaction from the broker.

*In memory database*

Besides scalability, performance is a big issue in large systems. As the name implies, this feature is, simply put, a database in memory. It is valuable for developing applications that perform constant access to a particular database table. Because the table is cached in memory, accessing this table is much quicker than accessing a table in a persistent database.

*Object pooling*

Like the previous feature, this one exists to improve the performance of a distributed system. Object pooling allows objects that are not currently in use to be put in a pool. When the object is needed, it is activated using a feature called just-in-time activation. Just-in-time activation pulls the object from the pool to service the request. This means that the object doesn't have to be created and destroyed every time, as it is cached in a pool.

*Queued components*

COM+ allows you to specify that your method invocations can be queued. This feature allows you to develop asynchronous and loosely coupled systems based on a message queue. An application can enqueue a method invocation, which can later be dequeued by a different application anytime it wishes. In other words, the second application doesn't even have to exist at the time the request is enqueued. In addition, once the first application has enqueued the request, it can immediately perform other processing. Besides this asynchronous aspect, queued components receive transactional support for free.

*Role-based security*

COM+ supports a new security feature called *role-based security*. A role is an alias that stands for a set of users and/or groups. By default, authorization (access checking) is performed only at the application level. Role-based security goes beyond this to support authorization at the process, object, interface, and method level. A big advantage of role-based security is that it is easy to use. You simply create and attach a role to. a process, object, interface, or method, and access checks will be performed at the correct level for you.

*Concurrency*

Since multithreading in COM is fairly complex, COM+ goes further to make your lives better. COM+ introduces a new concurrency model called the thread-neutral apartment (TNA) model. It is similar to an MTA in that there's only one TNA per process and that many threads can enter and concurrently execute inside it. This allows a client thread to call an object living in the TNA without the overhead of inter-apartment marshaling. To make it easy for developers and users, COM+ can also synchronize calls to your component objects. The ability to demand this allows you to put thread-ignorant objects into the NTA. Even though these objects are thread ignorant, many threads can concurrently use them because COM+ synchronizes these thread-ignorant objects for you.

*Event management*

Connection points is a technique that allows bidirectional communications, but the event source and sink must intimately know about one another. In this regard, connection points inherently introduces too much coupling. COM+ reduces this coupling by introducing an event management service (think of it as a broker). Publishers (servers that fire events) can publish themselves through the event management service. Subscribers (clients that receive events) subscribe to a particular publisher through the event service.

In short, COM+ bundles together COM and Microsoft Transaction Server (MTS). COM+ also internally uses Microsoft Message Queue (MSMQ) to provide support for asynchronous systems, without requiring the programmer to write MSMQ code. MTS supports transactions and role-based security, and MSMQ supports asynchronous and loosely-coupled systems based on the concept of a message queue. Messages are guaranteed to be handled by the appropriate server once they are enqueued onto the correct queue.

Besides these services, which are provided by COM+ by default, COM+ allows you to extend its runtime through the concept of *interception*. As shown by the `Third-Party Services` box in Figure C-3, you can hook your own custom services into the COM+ runtime. This permits you to extend the COM+ runtime to do whatever you want. For example, using interception, you can build a service to perform custom security management or custom handling of instance creation and method call/return.

# D

## *Hello, Universe!*

This appendix captures the basic code that makes up a simple distributed system using COM, for people who like to see all essential components of a technology in one place. Some programmers learn best with all the code at hand, and if you belong to this group, this appendix may be helpful because it's a short summary, mostly mirroring Chapter 3, *Objects*, and Chapter 4, *Components*. The source code from this appendix is in the *Hello* directory of the files on the O'Reilly FTP site. You can take this appendix as an abbreviated summary for building simple distributed components, but you must read the whole book in order to obtain the necessary knowledge you need to build real distributed systems using COM. Having said that, let's say "Hello, Universe!"

To uphold the Kernighan and Ritchie tradition, we'll create a distributed system to print a message similar to the classic "Hello, World!" program. Unlike the original Kernighan and Ritchie example, which operates within a single process, our example will break not only the process barrier but also the machine barrier. In our application, a client program can print the "Hello, Universe!" message in a remote console on a totally different machine. In other words, a client simply calls a method that is implemented by a remote server, and the server prints the message "Hello, Universe!" on the server machine's console.

 Throughout this simple example, C++ comments that start with the symbol [Chapter] indicate that the immediate and following implementation is discussed in depth at the suggested chapter's section. The code shown in this appendix is stripped down so that it is easy to follow. For brevity, the code doesn't show error handling and resource reclamation. However, these are important considerations for building robust distributed applications, so you should definitely read the whole book.

The source code that we will write in this short appendix will be bare-bones code, with only high-level explanations. The details are explained in Chapters 3, 4, and 5, so the code exhibited in this appendix lacks error handling, component management, marshaler registration, component registration, security, and more. However, the advantage of this appendix is that all code for this simple distributed system is shown in one consolidated location, so that you can really get the basic gist of distributed component development using Distributed COM.

Again, you can find the code to this simple distributed system in the *Hello* directory of the source code that accompanies this book. To test it out, you should run the server first and then execute the client. The server will stay alive until you press CTRL-C, but the client can be executed as many times as you like. Each time that you execute the client, the server will write the message "Hello, Universe!" to the console.

In general, the development of a distributed system that uses Distributed COM includes the following responsibilities:

1. Define COM interfaces, which are really application level client/server specifications. See the "Interfaces"section of Chapter 3.

2. Develop the server component and objects that implement the specified interfaces. See the "Objects" section of Chapter 3 and the "Servers" section of Chapter 4.

3. Develop the client component that uses the interface implemented by the server component. See the "Clients" section of Chapter 4.

We will follow these steps to develop our simple "Hello, Universe!" distributed system below.

# *Client/Server Protocol = COM Interface*

In the world of distributed computing, the first rule that you must follow is to define an application-level client/server communications protocol. This communications protocol provides a way for the client and server to communicate with one another, and in COM, we call this communications protocol a COM interface.

A protocol may have many verbs, each of which corresponds exactly to an interface method. In this example, the one and only verb that you want to support is *SayHello*, and thus you'll make this verb a method of your interface, as shown in the following interface definition. This verb or method allows a client to tell a remote server to print the message "Hello, Universe!" to the console on the remote machine. The client component will use this COM interface to send a hello message to the server component, and the server component will implement and support this interface.

```
// Include the specification of the IUnknown interface
import "unknwn.idl";

// [Chapter 3: Interfaces]
//   Interface for IHello
[ object, uuid(11111111-1111-1111-1111-111111111111) ]
interface IHello : IUnknown
{
    HRESULT SayHello();
}
```

Given an interface definition, marshaling code must be generated to convert the verbs or methods into network streams that can be sent across to a remote machine. The MIDL compiler, which is discussed in Chapter 3, can take this interface definition and automatically generate the corresponding marshaling code that the client and server components can use for remote communications. You can register this marshaling code against the registry of every machine with components that use the code, and Chapters 3, 4, 5, and 6 show you how to perform this registration. If you don't want to register this marshaling code, you can directly bundle it into both the client and server components; Chapters 8, 9, and 10 show several techniques for merging interface marshaling code into your components.

# Client Component

You haven't develop the server component yet, so let's assume for the moment that you have such a component and it supports an object that implements the *IHello* interface, shown previously in the last section. In order to use the *IHello* interface, you need to know both the GUID of the *IHello* interface and the GUID associated with the class factory that can generate objects that implement the *IHello* interface. At this moment, just think of a class factory as something that can instantiate objects that a client needs, but don't worry yet why it's required. Once you have these two unique identifiers, we can do the following to cause the server component to dump the message "Hello, Universe!" to the remote console:

1. Initialize COM. Chapters 4 and 5 discuss the details of initialization, which is very important in terms of concurrency management.

2. Register the interface marshaler (marshaling code) for *IHello*, an optional step that you need not perform if the interface marshaler is registered against the system's registry. Techniques for registering interface marshalers against the registry are discussed in Chapters 3, 4, 5, and 6, while techniques for bundling interface marshalers into a component are discussed in Chapters 8, 9, and 10.

3. Create the object on a remote machine. For this you must know the machine name and the GUID associated with the class factory that can create objects that implement the *IHello* interface. You would also need to know the GUID

of the *IHello* interface if you were using the *CoCreateInstanceEx* method for object creation. See the "Creating an Object" section in Chapter 4 for more information regarding object activation.

4. Once the object is created, you may use the *IHello* interface to call the *IHello::SayHello* method, which will tell the server component to spit out your famous message. See the "Using an Object" section in Chapter 4 for more information on calling interface methods.

These four steps are annotated in the following code:

```
//******************************************************************
//* GUID for Hello class object.
//******************************************************************
const CLSID CLSID_Hello = {
    0xCCCCCCCC,0xCCCC,0xCCCC,{0xCC,0xCC,0xCC,0xCC,0xCC,0xCC,0xCC,0xCC}
};

//******************************************************************
//* GUID for IHello interface.
//******************************************************************
const IID IID_IHello = {
    0x11111111,0x1111,0x1111,{0x11,0x11,0x11,0x11,0x11,0x11,0x11,0x11}
};

//******************************************************************
//*  Client component's main() routine.
//******************************************************************
void main(int argc, char **argv)
{
    // Step 1.
    // [Chapter 4:  Initialization and Termination]
    CoInitializeEx(NULL, COINIT_MULTITHREADED);

    // Step 2.
    // [Chapter 9][Chapter 10] Register the marshaling code for IHello.
    RegisterInterfaceMarshaler();

    // Step 3.
    // [Chapter 4:  Creating an Object]
    // Request for the IHello interface.
    MULTI_QI mqi[] = { {&IID_IHello, NULL, S_OK} };
    // Target hostname is "dog"; change it to your hostname.
    COSERVERINFO csi = {0, L"dog", NULL, 0};
    // Create an instance of the Hello distributed COM object.
    CoCreateInstanceEx(CLSID_Hello,
                    NULL,
                    CLSCTX_SERVER,
                    &csi,
                    sizeof(mqi)/sizeof(mqi[0]),
                    mqi);

    // Step 4.
    // [Chapter 4:  Using an Object]
    IHello *pHello = (IHello *)(mqi[0].pItf);
```

```
    pHello->SayHello();
}
```

# Server Component

Now that you know how to write a simple client component, let's write a simple server component that will support the client component's request. When developing a server component, you must do three things, aside from defining the supported interface using MIDL:

1. Develop a server that exposes the supported class factories to the outside world. There are several types of server components, discussed in the "Servers" section of Chapter 4.

2. Develop a C++ class for each class factory that can instantiate supported objects. The "Class Factories" section in Chapter 3 shows you how to develop custom and standard factories.

3. Develop a C++ class for each object that implements supported COM interfaces. The "Objects" section in Chapter 3 shows you how to develop a COM object that meets the laws of COM.

You'll follow these steps in the following subsection to create your server component that can display the phrase "Hello, Universe!"

## The main ( ) routine

The *main* routine for your server component simply exposes a class factory that can instantiate objects that implement the *IHello* interface. In brief, this routine does the following:

1. Instantiate a global instance of your class factory whose implementation will be discussed in a moment.

2. Initialize COM.

3. Register the interface marshaler for the *IHello* interface.

4. Make your class factory public by calling the *CoRegisterClassObject* COM API function. See the "Dynamic Activation Support" section in Chapter 4 for more information.

5. Once executed, the server will wait until a user presses CTRL+C. Meanwhile, each time a client component calls *IHello::SayHello*, the server component will display the famous message to the console. We will show this functionality in the implementation of *IHello::SayHello* shortly.

These five steps are annotated in the following code:

```
//********************************************************************
//* [Chapter 3: Interfaces]
```

```
//*  GUID for IHello interface.
//******************************************************************
const IID IID_IHello = {
    0x11111111,0x1111,0x1111,{0x11,0x11,0x11,0x11,0x11,0x11,0x11,0x11}
};


//******************************************************************
//* [Chapter 3: Interfaces]
//*  GUID for Hello class object.
//******************************************************************
const CLSID CLSID_Hello = {
    0xCCCCCCCC,0xCCCC,0xCCCC,{0xCC,0xCC,0xCC,0xCC,0xCC,0xCC,0xCC,0xCC}
};


//******************************************************************
//* The factory that can create Hello objects is a globally defined.
//******************************************************************
// Step 1.
CoHelloFactory g_HelloClassFactory;


//******************************************************************
//* The server component's main() routine.
//******************************************************************
void main(int argc, char **argv)
{
    // Step 2.
    // [Chapter 4:  Initialization and Termination] Initialize COM
    CoInitializeEx(NULL, COINIT_MULTITHREADED);

    // Step 3.
    // [Chapter 9][Chapter 10] Register the marshaling code for IHello.
    RegisterInterfaceMarshaler();

    DWORD dwCookie=0;
    // Step 4.
    // [Chapter 4:  Dynamic Activation Support]
    //              Make the Hello class factory public.
    CoRegisterClassObject(CLSID_Hello,
                    &g_HelloClassFactory,
                    CLSCTX_SERVER,
                    REGCLS_MULTIPLEUSE,
                    &dwCookie);

    printf("Press CTRL-C to stop this server.\n");

    // Step 5.
    // For demonstration, this component will live forever.
    Sleep(INFINITE);
}
```

## *The Class Factory*

A class factory is a special COM object that can create another COM object. You may wonder, "Why in the world would you need a class factory?" The quick answer is "a class factory allows a standard protocol for any client component to create needed COM objects." If you don't like this short answer, refer to the "Class Factories" section in Chapter 3 for a full explanation.

 At this point, the code may be overwhelming for some readers, but if you experience this feeling, don't panic, because Chapter 3, 4, and 5 explain all the mysteries.

For now, you need to create an object that represents the class factory that you've just globally instantiated in the last section. The purpose of this class factory is to instantiate objects that implement the *IHello* interface. Here's what you need to do to create a simple, standard class factory:

1. Create a C++ class and derive it from the standard *IClassFactory* interface, which is already defined by Microsoft. See the "Class Factories" section of Chapter 3 for more on this interface.

2. Since all COM interfaces derive from *IUnknown* (and *IClassFactory* is no exception), you need to implement the methods for *IUnknown*, which include *QueryInterface*, *AddRef*, and *Release*. See the "Objects" section of Chapter 3 for the rules that you must obey when implementing these methods.

3. We also need to implement the methods of the *IClassFactory* interface, which include *CreateInstance* and *LockServer*. See the "Class Factories" section of Chapter 3 for more information. In the following code, notice that you dynamically create an instance of *CoHello* in the *CreateInstance* method.

These three steps are annotated in the following class definition:

```
//*****************************************************************
//* [Chapter 3: ClassFactories]
//*   Class Factory that manufactures CoHello objects.
//*****************************************************************
// Step 1.
class CoHelloFactory : public IClassFactory
{
public:
    // Step 2.
    // IUnknown Methods
    STDMETHODIMP QueryInterface (REFIID riid, void** ppv)
    {
        // If client requests for IUnknown or IClassFactory,
        // return the pointer; else, return NULL.
        if (riid==IID_IUnknown||riid==IID_IClassFactory) {
```

```
         *ppv= (IClassFactory *) (this);
      } else {
         *ppv=NULL; return E_NOINTERFACE ;
      }

      return S_OK;
   }

   STDMETHODIMP_(ULONG) AddRef(void)
   {
      return 1;
   }

   STDMETHODIMP_(ULONG) Release(void)
   {
      return 1;
   }

   // Step 3.
   // IClassFactory Methods
   STDMETHODIMP CreateInstance(LPUNKNOWN pUnkOuter, REFIID riid, void **ppv)
   {
      // [Chapter 3: ClassFactories]
      // Dynamically create an instance of CoHello, an object
      // developed in the next section.
      CoHello * pHello = new CoHello;
      return pHello->QueryInterface(riid, ppv);
   }

   STDMETHODIMP LockServer(BOOL fLock)
   {
      // [Chapter 3: ClassFactories][Chapter 4: Servers]
      return S_OK;
   }
};
```

## The COM Object

Since the *CoHelloFactory::CreateInstance* dynamically creates a *CoHello* object, you need to provide the implementation for *CoHello*. Derived from the *IHello* interface, *CoHello* implements *IHello::SayHello*, which simply outputs the famous message to the console. Since *IHello* derives from *IUnknown*, *CoHello* must also implement the methods of the *IUnknown* interface. The "Objects" section of Chapter 3 shows you how to implement an object in great details.

```
//******************************************************************
//* [Chapter 3: Objects]
//*  CoHello COM object implementation.
//******************************************************************
class CoHello : public IHello {
public:
   // constructors/destructors
   CoHello() : m_lRefCount(0)
   {
```

```
            // [Chapter 3: Objects][Chapter 4: Servers]
        }

        ~CoHello()
        {
            // [Chapter 3: Objects][Chapter 4: Servers]
        }

    public:
        // IUnknown Methods
        STDMETHODIMP QueryInterface(REFIID riid, void **ppv)
        {
            // [Chapter 3: Objects]
            // If client requests for IUnknown or IHello,
            // return the pointer; else return NULL.
            if (riid==IID_IUnknown||riid==IID_IHello) {
                *ppv= (IHello *)(this);
            } else {
                *ppv=NULL; return E_NOINTERFACE ;
            }

            AddRef();
            return S_OK;
        }

        STDMETHODIMP_(ULONG) AddRef(void)
        {
            // [Chapter 3: Objects]
            return ++m_lRefCount;
        }

        STDMETHODIMP_(ULONG) Release(void)
        {
            // [Chapter 3: Objects]
            long lCount = m_lRefCount-1;
            if (lCount == 0) {
                delete this;
            }
            return lCount;
        }

        // IHello Methods
        STDMETHODIMP SayHello()
        {
            printf("Hello, Universe!\n");
            return S_OK;
        }

    private:
        // [Chapter 3: Objects]
        LONG m_lRefCount;
    };
```

You now have all the code for the client and server components that make up a simple distributed system. What we have omitted is server component registration, a topic discussed in the "Servers" section of Chapter 4. As a result, this server component cannot be activated automatically, so you must start the server component prior to executing the client component when testing these two applications.

# Comforting Words

If you have read the book prior to reading this appendix, you should:

- Realize that this appendix is a summary of mostly Chapters 3 and 4, with references to important areas throughout the whole book.

- Understand the code shown throughout this appendix.

- Be able to pinpoint the spots where error handling and resource reclamation must be performed.

- Be able to pinpoint a few flaws in the code. Review Chapters 3, 4, 5, 9, and 10 for some hints.

However, if you haven't read the book, don't expect to fully absorb all the code shown here. It is more important that you get the gist of what's needed to develop distributed components using Distributed COM. You should study the `Hello` example that comes with the book, compile it, and run it to experience first hand client/server interaction for this simple distributed system. Be aware that this sample system is very general; you need the knowledge and insights of Chapters 3, 4, and 5 in order to build real distributed applications. Don't expect to jump up and develop distributed applications using Distributed COM at this point, because you need much more information than a short appendix like this can supply.

And yes! What's shown in the last few sections for creating this simply distributed system is definitely a lot of code, especially when you are comparing it with the original Kernighan and Ritchie example, which goes something like this:

```
void main()
{
    printf("Hello, World!\n");
}
```

However, the original version operates only within a confined process, whereas our "Hello, Universe!" example breaks not only the process, but also the machine boundary. There are reasons for this amount of code and Chapters 3, 4, and 5 expose these reasons to you. But don't be discouraged, because you don't really have to write all this code, as it is repeatable and boilerplate. Class libraries like MFC (Chapter 8) and ATL (Chapter 6) generate enough boilerplate code for you so that, for the most part, all you really have to write is the code for the *SayHello* method.

# *Index*

## About the Author

Thuan L. Thai started computer programming 15 years ago but has never been tired of this hobby—one that he truly considers an art. He is currently a Senior Systems Engineer at SAIC where he has led the architecture and development of several successful distributed and COM-based imaging systems. He also teaches Win32, MFC, and COM programming courses for Learning Tree International. Prior to all this, Thuan worked for AMS where he developed multi-tiered object frameworks using C++ and RPC. He received his Bachelor of Science in Computer Science from the University of Virginia.

When not developing software, Thuan enjoys strumming his six strings and writing songs every now and then. He often plays 9-ball with the same buddies with whom he has played the game for over eight years. Thuan hopes to play more tennis, the only sport that he has ever played for more than eight hours in a single day.

## Colophon

Our look is the result of reader comments, our own experimentation, and feedback from distribution channels. Distinctive covers complement our distinctive approach to technical topics, breathing personality and life into potentially dry subjects.

The animals on the cover of *Learning DCOM* are dachshunds. Dachshunds are easily identified by their long bodies, short legs, and long, hanging ears. Dachshund coats can be shorthaired, longhaired, or wirehaired. The American Kennel Club recognizes two sizes of dachshund: miniature (those weighing less than 10 pounds) and standard (those weighing 11 to 25 pounds). In Europe three sizes of dachshund, determined by chest circumference when the dogs are 15 months old, are recognized. The sizes are: standard (chest circumference of more than 35 cm), dwarf (30-35 cm), and miniature (less than 30 cm).

The word "dachshund" means "badger dog" in German, and this peculiarly shaped dog was first bred in Germany to hunt badgers and other burrowing animals. They are fearless and independent dogs who can follow a badger into its burrow, put up a fierce fight, and retrieve the badger. Their independence is an important trait for badger hunting, as dachshunds need to be able to decide what to do without guidance from their masters when they are deep inside a badger hole. This same independence, however, can make them difficult dogs to train. Despite this, they are extremely loyal to their owners, and as of 1996 the AKC listed them as the sixth most popular dog.

Jeffrey Liggett was the production editor for *Learning DCOM*. Sheryl Avruch was the production manager. Robert Romano and Rhon Porter created the illustrations using Adobe Photoshop 5.0 and Macromedia Freehand 8.0. Mike Sierra provided FrameMaker technical support. Editorial and production services were provided by Rashelle Perez and David Leiser at *Electro-Publishing*. Becky Peveler was the copyeditor.

Edie Freedman designed the cover of this book, using a 19th-century engraving from the Dover Pictorial Archive. The cover layout was produced with Quark XPress 3.32 using the ITC Garamond font. Whenever possible, our books use RepKover™, a durable and flexible lay-flat binding. If the page count exceeds RepKover's limit, perfect binding is used.

The inside layout was designed by Nancy Priest and implemented in FrameMaker 5.5 by Mike Sierra. The text and heading fonts are ITC Garamond Light and Garamond Book. This colophon was written by Clairemarie Fisher O'Leary.

# How to stay in touch with O'Reilly

## 1. Visit Our Award-Winning Web Site

### http://www.oreilly.com/

★ "Top 100 Sites on the Web" —*PC Magazine*
★ "Top 5% Web sites" —*Point Communications*
★ "3-Star site" —*The McKinley Group*

Our web site contains a library of comprehensive product information (including book excerpts and tables of contents), downloadable software, background articles, interviews with technology leaders, links to relevant sites, book cover art, and more. File us in your Bookmarks or Hotlist!

## 2. Join Our Email Mailing Lists

### New Product Releases

To receive automatic email with brief descriptions of all new O'Reilly products as they are released, send email to:
**listproc@online.oreilly.com**
Put the following information in the first line of your message (*not* in the Subject field):
**subscribe oreilly-news**

### O'Reilly Events

If you'd also like us to send information about trade show events, special promotions, and other O'Reilly events, send email to:
**listproc@online.oreilly.com**
Put the following information in the first line of your message (*not* in the Subject field):
**subscribe oreilly-events**

## 3. Get Examples from Our Books via FTP

There are two ways to access an archive of example files from our books:

### Regular FTP

- ftp to:
  **ftp.oreilly.com**
  (login: anonymous
  password: your email address)
- Point your web browser to:
  **ftp://ftp.oreilly.com/**

### FTPMAIL

- Send an email message to:
  **ftpmail@online.oreilly.com**
  (Write "help" in the message body)

## 4. Contact Us via Email

**order@oreilly.com**
To place a book or software order online. Good for North American and international customers.

**subscriptions@oreilly.com**
To place an order for any of our newsletters or periodicals.

**books@oreilly.com**
General questions about any of our books.

**software@oreilly.com**
For general questions and product information about our software. Check out O'Reilly Software Online at **http://software.oreilly.com/** for software and technical support information. Registered O'Reilly software users send your questions to: **website-support@oreilly.com**

**cs@oreilly.com**
For answers to problems regarding your order or our products.

**booktech@oreilly.com**
For book content technical questions or corrections.

**proposals@oreilly.com**
To submit new book or software proposals to our editors and product managers.

**international@oreilly.com**
For information about our international distributors or translation queries. For a list of our distributors outside of North America check out:
**http://www.oreilly.com/www/order/country.html**

O'Reilly & Associates, Inc.
101 Morris Street, Sebastopol, CA 95472 USA
TEL    707-829-0515 or 800-998-9938
         (6am to 5pm PST)
FAX    707-829-0104

# International Distributors

## UK, EUROPE, MIDDLE EAST AND AFRICA (EXCEPT FRANCE, GERMANY, AUSTRIA, SWITZERLAND, LUXEMBOURG, LIECHTENSTEIN, AND EASTERN EUROPE)

**INQUIRIES**
O'Reilly UK Limited
4 Castle Street
Farnham
Surrey, GU9 7HS
United Kingdom
Telephone: 44-1252-711776
Fax: 44-1252-734211
Email: josette@oreilly.com

**ORDERS**
Wiley Distribution Services Ltd.
1 Oldlands Way
Bognor Regis
West Sussex PO22 9SA
United Kingdom
Telephone: 44-1243-779777
Fax: 44-1243-820250
Email: cs-books@wiley.co.uk

## FRANCE

**ORDERS**
GEODIF
61, Bd Saint-Germain
75240 Paris Cedex 05, France
Tel: 33-1-44-41-46-16 (French books)
Tel: 33-1-44-41-11-87 (English books)
Fax: 33-1-44-41-11-44
Email: distribution@eyrolles.com

**INQUIRIES**
Éditions O'Reilly
18 rue Séguier
75006 Paris, France
Tel: 33-1-40-51-52-30
Fax: 33-1-40-51-52-31
Email: france@editions-oreilly.fr

## GERMANY, SWITZERLAND, AUSTRIA, EASTERN EUROPE, LUXEMBOURG, AND LIECHTENSTEIN

**INQUIRIES & ORDERS**
O'Reilly Verlag
Balthasarstr. 81
D-50670 Köln
Germany
Telephone: 49-221-973160-91
Fax: 49-221-973160-8
Email: anfragen@oreilly.de (inquiries)
Email: order@oreilly.de (orders)

## CANADA (FRENCH LANGUAGE BOOKS)
Les Éditions Flammarion ltée
375, Avenue Laurier Ouest
Montréal (Québec) H2V 2K3
Tel: 00-1-514-277-8807
Fax: 00-1-514-278-2085
Email: info@flammarion.qc.ca

## HONG KONG
City Discount Subscription Service, Ltd.
Unit D, 3rd Floor, Yan's Tower
27 Wong Chuk Hang Road
Aberdeen, Hong Kong
Tel: 852-2580-3539
Fax: 852-2580-6463
Email: citydis@ppn.com.hk

## KOREA
Hanbit Media, Inc.
Sonyoung Bldg. 202
Yeksam-dong 736-36
Kangnam-ku
Seoul, Korea
Tel: 822-554-9610
Fax: 822-556-0363
Email: hant93@chollian.dacom.co.kr

## PHILIPPINES
Mutual Books, Inc.
429-D Shaw Boulevard
Mandaluyong City, Metro
Manila, Philippines
Tel: 632-725-7538
Fax: 632-721-3056
Email: mbikikog@mnl.sequel.net

## TAIWAN
O'Reilly Taiwan
No. 3, Lane 131
Hang-Chow South Road
Section 1, Taipei, Taiwan
Tel: 886-2-23968990
Fax: 886-2-23968916
Email: benh@oreilly.com

## CHINA
O'Reilly Beijing
Room 2410
160, FuXingMenNeiDaJie
XiCheng District
Beijing, China PR 100031
Tel: 86-10-86631006
Fax: 86-10-86631007
Email: frederic@oreilly.com

## INDIA
Computer Bookshop (India) Pvt. Ltd.
190 Dr. D.N. Road, Fort
Bombay 400 001 India
Tel: 91-22-207-0989
Fax: 91-22-262-3551
Email: cbsbom@giasbm01.vsnl.net.in

## JAPAN
O'Reilly Japan, Inc.
Kiyoshige Building 2F
12-Bancho, Sanei-cho
Shinjuku-ku
Tokyo 160-0008 Japan
Tel: 81-3-3356-5227
Fax: 81-3-3356-5261
Email: japan@oreilly.com

## ALL OTHER ASIAN COUNTRIES
O'Reilly & Associates, Inc.
101 Morris Street
Sebastopol, CA 95472 USA
Tel: 707-829-0515
Fax: 707-829-0104
Email: order@oreilly.com

## AUSTRALIA
WoodsLane Pty., Ltd.
7/5 Vuko Place
Warriewood NSW 2102
Australia
Tel: 61-2-9970-5111
Fax: 61-2-9970-5002
Email: info@woodslane.com.au

## NEW ZEALAND
Woodslane New Zealand, Ltd.
21 Cooks Street (P.O. Box 575)
Waganui, New Zealand
Tel: 64-6-347-6543
Fax: 64-6-345-4840
Email: info@woodslane.com.au

## LATIN AMERICA
McGraw-Hill Interamericana
Editores, S.A. de C.V.
Cedro No. 512
Col. Atlampa
06450, Mexico, D.F.
Tel: 52-5-547-6777
Fax: 52-5-547-3336
Email: mcgraw-hill@infosel.net.mx

## O'REILLY®

O'Reilly & Associates, Inc.
101 Morris Street
Sebastopol, CA 95472-9902
1-800-998-9938

*Visit us online at:*
**http://www.ora.com/**
**orders@ora.com**

## O'REILLY WOULD LIKE TO HEAR FROM YOU

Which book did this card come from?

_____

Where did you buy this book?
- ❏ Bookstore
- ❏ Direct from O'Reilly
- ❏ Bundled with hardware/software
- ❏ Computer Store
- ❏ Class/seminar
- ❏ Other _____

What operating system do you use?
- ❏ UNIX
- ❏ Windows NT
- ❏ Other _____
- ❏ Macintosh
- ❏ PC(Windows/DOS)

What is your job description?
- ❏ System Administrator
- ❏ Network Administrator
- ❏ Web Developer
- ❏ Programmer
- ❏ Educator/Teacher
- ❏ Other _____

❏ Please send me O'Reilly's catalog, containing a complete listing of O'Reilly books and software.

Name _____    Company/Organization _____

Address _____

City _____    State _____    Zip/Postal Code _____    Country _____

Telephone _____    Internet or other email address (specify network) _____

Nineteenth century wood engraving
of a bear from the O'Reilly &
Associates Nutshell Handbook®
*Using & Managing UUCP.*

POST CARD

# BUSINESS REPLY MAIL

FIRST CLASS MAIL   PERMIT NO. 80   SEBASTOPOL, CA

*Postage will be paid by addressee*

**O'Reilly & Associates, Inc.**
101 Morris Street
Sebastopol, CA  95472-9902